W9-DAY-477

ENCYCLOPEDIA OF THE MIDDLE PASSAGE

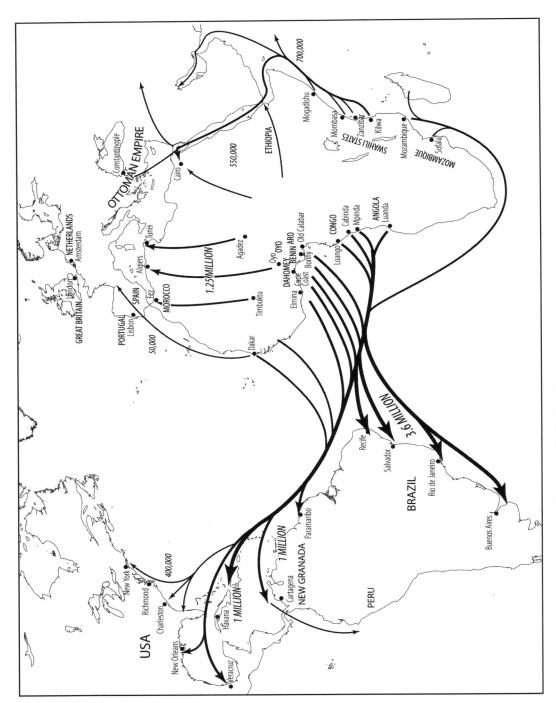

African slave trade routes. Courtesy of Saverance Publishing Services.

ENCYCLOPEDIA OF THE MIDDLE PASSAGE

Edited by
Toyin Falola and
Amanda Warnock

Greenwood Milestones in African American History

GREENWOOD PRESS
Westport, Connecticut • London

Library of Congress Cataloging-in-Publication Data

Encyclopedia of the middle passage : Greenwood milestones in African
American history / edited by Toyin Falola and Amanda Warnock.
  p. cm.
  Includes bibliographical references and index.
  ISBN-13: 978–0–313–33480–1 (alk. paper)
  1. Slave trade—Africa—History—Encyclopedias. 2. Slave trade—
United States—History—Encyclopedias. 3. Slave trade—Atlantic
Ocean—History—Encyclopedias. 4. African Americans—History—
Encyclopedias. I. Falola, Toyin. II. Warnock, Amanda.
  HT1322.E63 2007
  306.3'6209603—dc22   2007016156

British Library Cataloguing in Publication Data is available.

Library of Congress Catalog Card Number: 2007016156
ISBN-13: 978–0–313–33480–1
ISBN-10: 0–313–33480–3

First published in 2007

Greenwood Press, 88 Post Road West, Westport, CT 06881
An imprint of Greenwood Publishing Group, Inc.
www.greenwood.com

Printed in the United States of America

The paper used in this book complies with the
Permanent Paper Standard issued by the National
Information Standards Organization (Z39.48–1984).

10 9 8 7 6 5 4 3 2 1

To Eric Williams and Joseph Inikori,
for their contributions to the study of the Atlantic slave trade

CONTENTS

LIST OF ENTRIES

GUIDE TO RELATED TOPICS

Abolition

Abolitionism
Abolition of the Slave Trade,
 Brazil
Abolition of the Slave Trade,
 France
Abolition of the Slave Trade,
 Great Britain
Abolition of the Slave Trade,
 Spain
Abolition of the Slave Trade,
 United States
African Institution
African Squadrons, The
British Navy
Closure of the Slave Trade
Haitian Revolution, The
Humanitarianism
Legitimate Commerce
Regulations

Art, Literature, and Film

Adanggaman (2000)
Amistad (1997)
Benito Cereno (1855)
Middle Passage, The (2000)
"Middle Passage" (1966)
"Slavers Throwing Overboard
 the Dead and Dying—
 Typhon Coming On" (1840)

Concepts

Asiento
Christianity
Decentralized Societies

Destinations
Entrepôts
Ethnicity
Gender and Slave Exports
Islam and Muslims
Life Expectancy
Monopoly
Ounce Trade
Plantations
Ports
Price
Religion
Reparations
Slavery in Africa
Triangular Trade
Volume
Wars, African

Documenting and Memorializing the Slave Trade

Archeology
Door of No Return
Eric Williams Thesis
 (1944)
Folklore
Handbooks for Slave
 Traders
Historical Memory
Historiography
Key West African
 Cemetery
Museums
Narratives by Slave
 Traders
Oral History

Plans and Diagrams
Slave Narratives and Slave
 Autobiography
Tourism
*Trans-Atlantic Slave Trade
 Database*

Execution of the Slave Trade

Arrivals
British Slave Trade
Cowry Shells (Cowries)
Credit and Finance
Danish Slave Trade
Dutch Slave Trade
Enslavement and Procurement
Escapes and Runaways
 (Maroonage)
Free Trade
French Slave Trade
Illegal Slave Trade,
 Brazil
Illegal Slave Trade, Spanish
 Caribbean
Insurance
Internal Slave Trade, Brazil
Internal Slave Trade,
 United States
Licensing
Minor European Nations
Portuguese Slave Trade
Profits and Investors
Re-Export
Royal Africa Company
"Seasoning"
Supply and Demand

INTRODUCTION

From the fifteenth through the nineteenth centuries, Europe's imperial powers transported between 9 and 15 million Africans to the Americas. This process, known as the trans-Atlantic slave trade, formed part of the larger process of European expansion during the same period. European imperialism and the slave labor that propelled it have left an indelible mark on Western and, indeed, world history.

The term Middle Passage constituted one leg of what has been called the "triangular trade," a phrase most often associated with the British. This trade pattern consisted of three voyages: one from Europe (or later, the Americas) to Africa with manufactured goods and alcohol, the second from Africa to the Americas with slaves, and the third from the Americas to Europe, with bills of exchange and trade commodities. The Middle Passage refers to the second part of the journey, undertaken by slaves, captains, and crews, that brought slaves from the coast of Africa to the Americas.

Throughout the history of the African slave trade, participants and observers published memoirs and exposés recounting the details of the trans-Atlantic crossing. Yet the Middle Passage has been a subject of interest to the general population only since late-eighteenth-century abolitionist campaigns called attention to the horrors associated with the trade. Although interest in the Middle Passage waned in the mid-nineteenth century with abolition, in the last thirty years, scholars have produced a sizeable body of work on the subject. Their contributions to this field of inquiry are reflected in this volume.

Slavery in Africa

The tradition of slavery had existed in Africa in the centuries before contact with Europe, but the nature of the relationship between master and slave differed drastically from that which would come to characterize American slavery. Within Africa, slaves were not held for the primary purpose of producing export commodities. A slave in Africa might labor as a skilled artisan or marry into the family of his or her master. Various forms of African slavery included clientage, pawnship, debt bondage, and apprenticeship.

Slavery in Africa was in fact a varied, diverse institution. Rather than speak of the "African slave trade," we might well refer to the "trades" that transported African slaves from one locale to another. Existing before the era of trans-Atlantic slavery, the Indian Ocean trade in southeast Africa and the trans-Saharan trade were responsible for the enslavement and removal of what scholars believe to be millions of slaves over the course of many centuries.

This tradition of slavery helped to shape the involvement of African states and leaders in the trans-Atlantic slave trade. Wars, raids, kidnappings, and the collection of tribute payments led to the enslavement and sale of millions of men, women, and children. African leaders, in turn, saw their power increase as they gained access to imported goods such as guns, allowing them to wage war against neighboring states. Some scholars have referred to this phenomenon as the "gun-slave" cycle. Political upheaval, exacerbated by the introduction of firearms, aided the trade as wars between African states resulted in the capture and exportation of increasing numbers of slaves.

For many captured or sold into bondage, the long passage to the Americas began in the interior of the African continent. Just as the slave trade did not end once captive Africans arrived on American shores, the slave trade did not begin with embarkation but rather with a forced march to the coast. African merchants would purchase a group of slaves, chain them together in a coffle, and supervise their trek to a holding cell or *barracoon* located by the sea. In this manner, millions are thought to have perished as the journey, often hundreds of miles, proved too arduous, particularly for children and the infirm. Upon arrival, slaves were frequently baptized or branded then stowed in the *barracoon* to await their transfer to vessels bound for the Americas.

From 1441 until 1867, European powers (and later the United States) shipped approximately 12 million Africans to Europe and the Americas. Determining the ethnic or regional origin of those transported presents considerable difficulty for scholars because slaves exported from one of the major points of embarkation might have originated deep in the interior. Therefore, even the best efforts at record-keeping do not provide adequate information on ethnicity. We do know, however, that Africans belonging to dozens of ethnic groups were transported to the Americas and that the ethnic composition of cargoes differed based on African supply and American demand. Protracted military campaigns in West African states resulted in an increase in the supply of slaves available for sale. Such was the case in the seventeenth and eighteenth centuries when Oyo, Dahomey, and Asante waged wars of expansion, generating large numbers of prisoners of war. Demand in the Americas varied based on many factors. Although virtually all slaves in good health would find a buyer, planters frequently expressed preferences for particular ethnic groups because of skills they possessed or the qualities they were thought to exhibit. South Carolina plantation owners, for example, sought to procure field slaves from the Gold Coast because of their experience in rice cultivation. They also sought Igbos, believed to be particularly docile, for their service as domestic slaves.

With the increase in slave raiding and exportation, African societies experienced significant transformations in modes of production and gender roles. As slavery expanded, Africans began to rely more heavily on the labor of slaves and, in particular, on women because the majority of captives exported were men. In parts of West Africa, particularly Yorubaland, the trans-Saharan trade, which took more women than men, contributed heavily to the increase in prices paid for female captives. High prices combined with American planters' preferences for male slaves resulted in fewer women than men being sent across the Atlantic. One consequence of this process was a shift in gender roles as women assumed more responsibility for productive activities. Despite the effects of the slave trade on West Africa, historian John Thornton has argued that indigenous forms of slavery helped to protect African societies from the extreme demographic impact and social dislocations associated with the trans-Atlantic trade.[1]

The institution of slavery was transformed radically upon its removal to the Americas. Instead of the kinship ties that bound master to slave, slave owners in the Americas held slaves as chattel. In European colonies and settlements, laws upheld the rights of masters to buy, sell, and hold African slaves. Although most colonial powers would eventually create guidelines or, in some cases, regulations for the treatment of slaves, masters continued to exercise control over virtually every aspect of their slaves' lives.

The Trans-Atlantic Slave Trade

The first recorded instance of sub-Saharan Africans shipped as slaves by Europeans dates from 1441 when Prince Henry the Navigator of Portugal received ten African slaves as part of the cargo of a voyage of trade and exploration to West Africa. Over the course of the following decades, merchants would frequently bring slaves to Lisbon for re-export to other parts of Europe, particularly Portugal and Spain. By the late fifteenth century, scholars estimate that 35,000 Africans lived in Portugal alone. Because the European mainland lacked a substantial agricultural export economy, slaves in Europe worked in a variety of occupations, including fishing, public works, and agricultural cultivation for local markets, and worked as vendors and domestic servants.

Although the transportation of slaves to Europe constituted a significant episode in the history of the slave trade, the majority of Africans taken from the continent were destined for the Americas. Slaves in the Americas, as in Europe, would engage in a diverse range of productive activities, but the trans-Atlantic slave trade grew out of the need for an inexpensive source of labor for sugar plantations. In the mid-fifteenth century, Spain and Portugal had begun to cultivate sugar in the Canaries, Madeira, and São Tomé and Principe. Following Christopher Columbus's 1492 voyage, the Spanish crown sought to develop plantation agriculture in the Americas as well. Spanish *conquistadores* initially relied on the labor of the native population to work in mining and agriculture on the islands of Hispaniola and Cuba. The decimation of the Taino and Ciboney in the late fifteenth and early sixteenth centuries and the subsequent ban on the enslavement of the indigenous, however, prompted the importation of slaves directly from Africa after 1518.

In the sixteenth century, when sugar production began in earnest, the American continent was the shared domain of Spain and Portugal. The Treaty of Tordesillas, ratified by the two kingdoms in 1494, divided the known world into Eastern and Western spheres—Spain, based on Columbus's explorations of the Caribbean, controlled the west, and Portugal, based on late-fifteenth-century African explorations, controlled the east. The treaty not only secured Portugal's African possessions, but also awarded the easternmost portion of American territory to Portugal, thus establishing the Portuguese as one of the major colonizers of the Americas. By mid-century, the plantations established in Brazil far outstripped the production of their Spanish Caribbean counterparts. Like the Spanish, the Portuguese did not initially employ Africans as the primary labor force on Brazilian plantations. It was only following the failure of their efforts to use indigenous workers that they turned to Africa for slaves, and the forts, factories, and settlements on the West and Central African coast provided an ample supply.

The importation patterns varied, but the greatest numbers of slaves landed in Brazil are thought to have originated in Angola and Guinea, with the former supplying the majority of slaves for the first 150 years of the trade and the latter ascending in importance in the late seventeenth century. With the expansion of slave commerce, merchants began to specialize, often linking a Brazilian port to an African region. For example, Bahia imported more West Africans (referred to as "Sudanese") than Bantu. In contrast, Bantu slaves predominated in Pernambuco. The slave trade to Brazil, carried out over the course of more than three centuries, would result in the forced removal of approximately 4,800,000 Africans. Indeed, the Portuguese transported slightly more than 40 percent of the total number of slaves traded during the epoch of the trans-Atlantic slave trade.

The seventeenth century constituted a radical shift in the dynamics of the trans-Atlantic trade. Great Britain's stake in the slave trade dates from 1562 with John Hawkins's capture and transport of 300 Africans from the Guinea Coast to the Caribbean island of Santo Domingo. In the late sixteenth century, British privateers began to prey on Spanish shipping and, by the mid-seventeenth century, British maritime ascendancy had resulted in the usurpation of several of Spain's Caribbean colonies. Lacking experience in the trans-Atlantic trade, the Portuguese and Dutch initially supplied slaves to the British sugar islands. Great Britain did not begin to trade slaves in significant numbers until the establishment of the Royal Africa Company (RAC, originally named the Company of Royal Adventurers Trading to Africa) in 1660. Propelled by the monopoly privileges enjoyed by the RAC, the late seventeenth century saw the continuing expansion of the British share of the slave trade. Merchants extended their presence on the West African coast by establishing new trade forts or conquering existing Dutch and Portuguese settlements. When the crown revoked the RAC's monopoly privileges in 1698, traders from Bristol and Liverpool, often interlopers with a background in slave commerce, eagerly commenced participation. With the rapid expansion of sugar cultivation in the British Caribbean, particularly on the islands of Jamaica and Barbados, slave imports increased throughout the eighteenth century. Over the course of approximately 150 years, the British slave trade resulted in the importation of 1.9 million slaves to Great Britain's Caribbean colonies and planted the seeds of the abolitionist movement that would intensify in the late eighteenth and early nineteenth centuries.

The eighteenth century also witnessed the steady growth of the sugar-producing colony of Saint Domingue (later Haiti) and the concurrent rising importance of the French slave trade. French vessels had participated in the trans-Atlantic trade since the sixteenth century, but it was only in the late seventeenth and eighteenth centuries with the establishment of Caribbean colonies that French slavers established regular trading routes. The French slave trade followed a similar pattern to the triangular trade most often associated with the British. French vessels departed from Nantes or Bordeaux for the coast of Africa, normally trading in an area that ranged from Senegal in the north to Angola in the south. From there, they carried slaves to the French Caribbean where they loaded staple commodities, most often sugar, for transport to France. Following the loss of Saint Domingue in 1804 and the legal prohibition of the slave trade in 1815, the French slave trade declined, although merchants in Nantes and Bordeaux continued to outfit slaving vessels regularly until the late 1820s. Throughout their long involvement in the slave trade, scholars estimate that French vessels transported almost 1.5 million slaves to the Americas.

The late eighteenth century revolution in the French colony of Saint Domingue coincided with and in many ways assisted the radical transformation of Cuba from the backwater of the Spanish Empire to an important sugar-producing colony. From 1762 through 1763, the British occupied Havana, opening the port to free trade and importing 10,000 slaves to labor on Cuban plantations. Although this experiment ended with the departure of the British in 1789, Spain—hoping to stimulate sugar cultivation—declared free trade in slaves to the port of Havana. Under the *asiento*, a system in which Spain contracted with foreign nationals to ship slaves to the American colonies during the sixteenth through the eighteenth centuries, Spanish merchants had relied on the assistance of outsiders rather than investing the time and money in developing the trade. Because Spanish-Cuban merchants lacked a slaving infrastructure on the West African coast and had little familiarity with the process of executing a successful voyage, Great Britain, the United States, and Denmark dominated the Cuban slave trade from 1789 through 1803.[2] After 1803, however, Spanish-Cuban merchants began regularly outfitting vessels for the Guinea Coast. Within several years, they would take over the bulk of the slave trade to the island. In spite of legal restrictions and the establishment of the Court of the Mixed Commission at Havana, merchants continued to engage in trans-Atlantic slaving voyages long after the traffic had been extinguished in other regions. From the late eighteenth century through 1867, between 600,000 and 1 million African slaves arrived in Cuba.

Historians have long debated the reasons behind the decline in the trans-Atlantic slave trade in the early nineteenth century. Today, most accept that a combination of factors led to abolition, first of the slave trade and later of slavery in the Americas. First, slave resistance during the Middle Passage and throughout the American colonies served as a constant reminder of the lengths to which Africans were willing to go to secure their freedom. The constant threat of shipboard uprisings prompted captains and crew to exercise repressive measures during the trans-Atlantic crossing. In the late eighteenth century, abolitionists would publicize these and other offenses in an effort to sway the British public to support a ban on the slave trade. However, it was the violent revolution in Saint Domingue, begun in 1791, that significantly compromised the institution of slavery in the Americas. The island-wide uprising of slaves inspired similar rebellions in other colonies and instilled terror in the white planter class in the Caribbean.

Second, humanitarian objectives informed the debate over the slave trade and slavery. Although religious groups, particularly Quakers, spoke out against the slave trade from at least the late seventeenth century, the growth of the British abolitionist movement is commonly acknowledged to stem from the late-eighteenth-century attempts by small groups of Britons to publicize the horrors of the slave trade. Influenced by the new ideologies of individual rights, equality, and justice, abolitionists disseminated tracts and pamphlets exposing the conditions aboard slave ships and decrying the inhumanity of the traffic. Olaudah Equiano, a former slave and influential abolitionist, published his personal account, *The Interesting Narrative of the Life of Olaudah Equiano or Gustavus Vassa, The African, Written by Himself*, in an effort to familiarize the public with his experience of enslavement and the Middle Passage. The movement increased in numbers and influence throughout the late eighteenth and early nineteenth centuries. Yet, despite the efforts of religious leaders and politicians, such as Thomas Clarkson and William Wilberforce, the West Indian planter lobby prevented the passage of legislation barring the traffic until 1807.

Finally, historians have debated to what extent economics played a role in the abolition of the slave trade. In 1944, Eric Williams, author of the seminal text *Capitalism and Slavery*, advanced the argument that economics rather than humanitarianism led to the abolition of the slave trade and American slavery. He suggested that, following the U.S. War for Independence, slavery had declined in profitability for West Indian planters. Thus, they shifted their positions such that they no longer opposed the abolition of the slave trade.[3] Other historians contend that slavery actually increased in profitability during the early nineteenth century as the disruption in sugar imports from Saint Domingue benefited British West Indian planters. Most recently, Joseph Inikori focused on the idea that abolition relied less on profits from the slave trade than on the role of the "slavery-induced" commerce that aided the Industrial Revolution. Industrialists as well as planters helped to shape debates over abolition, promoting the position that the end of the slave trade would result in the loss of competitive advantage for British goods, causing prices to rise.

Under heavy pressure from the abolitionist movement in 1807, British Parliament passed the Abolition Act, which outlawed slave trading by British subjects, and in 1808 the United States followed suit. Motivated by a combination of humanitarian motives and economic self-interest, from 1807 until 1870, Great Britain invested considerable resources in attempting to coerce other nations to abolish the trans-Atlantic slave trade. In an effort to advance the cause of abolition, the British frequently applied economic and diplomatic pressure in their negotiations with other nations. In 1817, these measures resulted in a treaty, signed by the Spanish and Portuguese, designed to curb the trade. Modified over the years but largely ignored, the Portuguese continued to transport slaves from their African colonies and outposts to Brazil until the 1850s, while the Spanish continued to carry out slaving voyages to Cuba, the last of which occurred in 1867.

British efforts to intercept slaving vessels departing from Africa or arriving in the Americas met with mixed results. Naval patrols, dispatched to the west coast of Africa from 1815 to 1870, captured slave ships and brought them before tribunals, condemning the vessel and freeing and resettling the captives. In response to Great Britain's attempts to enforce the ban on the slave trade, Portuguese and Spanish traders either moved their activities to areas in which the British did not maintain an active presence or endeavored to outwit the African Squadrons.

By the 1860s, the turning tide of public opinion, combined with the increased enforcement of antislaving laws, lead to the cessation of the trans-Atlantic slave trade. Concurrent with the nineteenth century decline of the slave trade, colonial powers and American nations began the process of abolishing slavery on the continent. Many of the new states of Latin America freed slaves as a reward for participation in the independence struggles. In contrast, following the War for Independence from Great Britain, the United States opted to retain the institution of slavery, only abolishing it as the result of a civil war. In other nations, the mounting pressures of abolitionist movements resulted in emancipation. Because of intense lobbying by antislavery organizations in Great Britain, the abolition of slavery in the British West Indies occurred in 1833, although the apprenticeship program established for former slaves continued until 1838. Other nations, too, in an effort to avoid the economic dislocations that came with the end of slavery, enacted programs of gradual emancipation. Both Cuba (1886) and Brazil (1888) abolished slavery after periods of gradual emancipation. In addition to transitioning former slaves to free labor, planters, always concerned about their supply of workers, collaborated with national governments to promote immigration, both of white Europeans and of indentured Chinese, to toil on American plantations.

The Experience of the Middle Passage

The experience of the Middle Passage varied greatly, but in most cases it was characterized by cramped, unsanitary conditions, with little food and water, few opportunities for exercise, frequent sexual assaults, suicides, and occasional shipboard rebellions. Captains of slave ships thought more of maintaining security and preventing loss of life than of the comfort of the slaves, thus subjecting their captives to constant supervision and discipline while offering only the most rudimentary level of care during the long, arduous trans-Atlantic crossing.

Of the millions of Africans who endured the Middle Passage, many did not live to reach American shores. Disease, dehydration, abuse, and suicide contributed significantly to what scholars believe to be high mortality rates aboard slave ships. Other factors, such as overcrowding, length of the voyage, season of the year, provisions, sanitation, and medical care could affect the success of a voyage as well. During the late eighteenth century, legislation designed to improve conditions on slave ships and prevent excessive mortality, such as Dolben's Act of 1788, attempted to reduce overcrowding and provide adequate provisions and medical care. The eighteenth century also saw the development of the technological innovation of copper sheathing, which reduced dampness in the ship and the duration of voyages and which may have had the secondary effect of lowering the rate of shipboard mortality.

Merchants, captains, and crew, in efforts to reduce disease and mortality—and thus protect their economic investment in a slaving voyage—generally preferred to provide the slaves with enough food, water, and exercise to sustain life. Although the food given to the slaves normally prevented starvation, the lack of variety, small portions, and overall poor quality of the rations frequently left slaves hungry and unfulfilled. On the majority of slave ships, captives received two meals and one pint of water per day, taken on the deck of the ship. Food varied based on the point of embarkation and might include maize, manioc flour, yams, millet, beans, and rice. The meager rations of water given to the slaves did not replace the water lost as the result of perspiration, seasickness, and diarrhea, and most slaves suffered from significant dehydration during the Middle Passage.

Similarly, the exercise afforded to slaves did little to alleviate the effects of the immobility that resulted from being confined below deck for the majority of the voyage. Once a day, typically after breakfast, the slaves, often shackled together, were forced to dance on the deck. The practice of "dancing the slaves" existed both for the entertainment of captain and crew and for the prevention of illness and mortality that could result from lack of circulation and loss of muscle tone. Forced to simulate joy and exuberance, slaves could be flogged for exhibiting reluctance to participate and lack of enthusiasm.

During meal times and exercise, slaves were shackled in pairs to prevent mass suicide or violent retribution against their captors. Control of mobility on a slave ship was paramount. Inspired by the awful shipboard conditions, the fear of white cannibalism or the belief that once dead they would return to their homeland, slaves frequently committed or sought to commit suicide during the trans-Atlantic voyage. To avoid the possibility of slaves throwing themselves overboard, they remained in the hold of the ship, where they were often chained, and were allowed on deck only once or twice a day.

Captains and crew maintained a high level of vigilance over all slaves, but the shipboard experience differed considerably based on gender. In many cases, crews separated women, of whom there were fewer, from men, stowing male slaves below deck and women and children above, allowing them to roam freely. Sexual assault and rape are thought to have been common experiences for female slaves during the Middle Passage. Because of the abuse suffered at the hands of captain and crew and the greater freedom of mobility, some scholars also believe that suicide rates were higher for women than men.

Thus, captive Africans endured the Middle Passage. The crossing typically lasted from five weeks to three months, depending on the points of embarkation and arrival, seasonal conditions, weather, size and condition of the vessel, and skill of the captain and crew. Vessels departing from West Africa would normally complete the voyage in less time and with less difficulty than those departing from Southeast Africa. Likewise, voyages begun during the rainy season, from February through May, were more likely to meet with such problems as severe storms and disease. Despite problems associated with the length of the voyage and the conditions encountered, an experienced captain and crew could more easily navigate the exigencies of the hazardous journey than relative newcomers to the slave trade. Still, no matter the preparations made or the care taken to ensure the success of the voyage, slaves continued to resist their enslavement both aboard the ship and upon arrival in the Americas.

A Research Agenda for the Middle Passage

In the past several decades, scholars have devoted a great deal of attention to the subject of the trans-Atlantic slave trade. From W.E.B. Du Bois's monumental text, first published in 1897, to Philip Curtin's pioneering study of the demographic contours of the slave trade published in 1969, to the completion of the Trans-Atlantic Slave Trade Database in 1999, our understanding of the dynamics and demographics of the slave trade has grown by leaps and bounds.

Interest in the Middle Passage developed as the abolitionist campaigns of the late eighteenth and nineteenth centuries called attention to the abuses of the slave trade in an effort to put an end to it. As the result of a concerted effort on the part of abolitionists, beginning in the late eighteenth century, the British held Parliamentary hearings on the subject of the slave trade. Evidence introduced by individuals and agencies both associated with the trade and charged with its extirpation revealed the horrors of the Middle Passage. Although subsequent studies of the Parliamentary hearings have treated some of the evidence as dubious, it served the function of mobilizing the British citizenry to demand an end to the slave trade. Following the final abolition of the slave trade in the mid-nineteenth century, interest in the Middle Passage waned.

Although few works treating the Middle Passage appeared during the mid- to late-nineteenth century, the 1897 publication of W.E.B Du Bois's doctoral dissertation, *The Suppression of the African Slave Trade to the United States, 1638–1870*, stirred debate over the trans-Atlantic slave trade and initiated the modern, academic study of what we refer to today as African American history. Du Bois argued that the economic benefits of continuing the slave trade to the United States thwarted political and legislative attempts to abolish it. Other works by Du Bois stressed the contributions of African Americans to U.S. history. Although these arguments might seem obvious today, at the time of publication, they constituted a radical departure from the overwhelmingly racist scholarship of the nineteenth century.

As a pioneer in the field of African American history, Du Bois inspired countless studies on the trans-Atlantic slave trade and, more broadly, on the history of African-descendant peoples in the Americas. In the early to mid-twentieth century, scholarship on the slave trade and the history of slavery continued, generating new publications despite the climate of extreme hostility toward African Americans. Published from 1930 to 1934, Elizabeth Donnan's impressive four-volume collection of primary sources, *Documents Illustrative of the Slave Trade to America,* became widely used by historians conducting research on the slave trade and remains referenced to this day.

The field of anthropology as well felt the weight of Du Bois's influence. The 1941 publication of anthropologist Melville Herskovits, *The Myth of the Negro Past,* built on the insights of early-twentieth-century scholarship on the slave trade and the legacies of slavery by challenging the notion, expressed by E. Franklin Frazier and others, that the dislocations of the Middle Passage combined with the effects of slavery had, in effect, erased most African cultural traditions. Herskovits countered that, in fact, the legacies of Africa in the Americas were evident in religion, food, dance, music, family and community structure, speech and syntax, and folklore and, furthermore, that elements of African culture had been adopted by the white population. Herskovits's work represented an early effort to understand how African cultural traditions had survived the Middle Passage and contributed to American societies.

While anthropologists were beginning to understand the legacies of slavery on African populations of the Americas, Caribbean historians conducted perhaps the most significant historical studies of this period treating the slave trade, abolitionism, and the postabolition era. In the British West Indies, the 1930s saw an increase in militancy of heretofore unorganized workers and the proliferation of nationalist ideologies: the result of decades of anticolonial struggle combined with the economic deprivation caused by the worldwide depression. Following World War II, West Indian leaders pushed for and gradually won the right to self-government. Scholars such as C.L.R. James and Eric Williams emerged from this political climate. Both James and Williams furthered scholarly understanding of the relationship between Caribbean slavery and European political and economic development, with Williams's seminal text, *Capitalism and Slavery* (1944), instigating debate for decades to come. Williams argued that slavery and the slave trade generated the capital that fueled Great Britain's Industrial Revolution. With the rise of industrial capital, the slave trade and plantation slavery declined in importance. Thus, economic rather than humanitarian motives propelled abolitionism. Although the Eric Williams Thesis, as it has come to be known, has been debated and revised in the years since its first publication, Williams's advances in challenging Eurocentric historiography cannot be underestimated.[4]

In the United States, the influence of the civil rights struggle of the 1960s and the concurrent growth of the field of African American history, rekindled interest in the subject of the slave trade. Within this environment, the publication of Philip Curtin's 1969 text, *The Atlantic Slave Trade: A Census,* sparked the debate that invigorated scholarship on the demography of the trans-Atlantic slave trade. Using available published sources, Curtin estimated the number of Africans brought to the Americas during the era of the trans-Atlantic trade at between 9 and 13 million.[5] Although his figure is, with some modification, still accepted today, at the time of publication, it sparked a firestorm of rebuttals, mostly by scholars who estimated the volume of the slave trade much higher than Curtin had.

Using Curtin's estimates, in 1978 Herbert Klein published a text that specifically addressed the trans-Atlantic crossing. In *The Middle Passage*, Klein not only detailed the demographic profile of the slave trade but also provided a comprehensive review of the financing, timing, routes, and mortality rates associated with the Middle Passage. With the publication of the book, Klein stirred controversy of his own, outlining mortality rates associated with the Middle Passage that were much lower than had been previously believed. In spite of the criticism generated by *The Middle Passage,* his work is seen by many as a classic text on the slave trade and remains widely read and referenced by scholars in the field.[6]

In the last several decades, historians have built up an impressive body of work that treats both the economic and social aspects of slavery and the slave trade. Seymour Dresher's *Econocide* (1977) revised the work of Eric Williams, arguing that the slave trade and slavery remained profitable to the British after the U.S. War for Independence. Works by Stanley Engerman, Robin Law, Colin Palmer, Jay Coughtry, David Northrup, Leslie Bethell, Robin Blackburn, Boubacar Barry, Paul Lovejoy, John Thornton, Barbara Solow, Patrick Manning, G. Ugo Nwokeji, and Joseph Dorsey have elaborated the dynamics of the slave trade and slave societies on both sides of the Atlantic. In recent contributions to the field of what is increasingly referred to as Atlantic history, Joseph Inikori's *Africans and the Industrial Revolution in England* (2002) argues for the centrality of trade to the Industrial Revolution in England and the importance of Africans, both on the continent and in the Americans, as producers of export commodities and consumers of manufactured goods, while Toyin Falola and Akinwuni Ogundiran's *The Archaeology of Atlantic Africa and the African Diaspora* (2007) uses material culture to update the scholarship on slavery in general and trans-Atlantic connections in particular.

Perhaps the most significant advancement that has taken place in recent years within the scholarship on the slave trade has been the 1999 publication of *The Trans-Atlantic Slave Trade: A Database on CD-ROM* by David Eltis, Stephen Behrendt, David Richardson, and Herbert Klein. This work brings together and analyzes data from more than 27,000 slaving ventures. Using this material, a new generation of scholars has embarked on research dealing with the movement of people from Africa to the Americas, including specific information of African region and ethnicity. Toyin Falola and Matt Childs's volume, *The Yoruba Diaspora in the Atlantic World* (2004), builds on decades of scholarship, from the pioneering work of Herskovits, to the demographic studies of Curtin and Eltis, to understand how the traditions and contributions of one African group, the Yoruba, have been pivotal in shaping societies throughout the Atlantic World.

About This Encyclopedia

Within this volume, we have provided a broad range of material related to the Middle Passage. To give our reader the widest coverage possible, we have included 228 entries that treat topics as varied as ports of departure and arrival, financing, mortality, demographic characteristics of slaves, African culture, and representations of the Middle Passage. Although entries may vary with regard to numerical estimates of volume or mortality, for example, this merely reflects the state of scholarship and the diversity of interpretations of the contributors.

Readers can locate their subject of interest quickly by using the alphabetical and topical lists of entries in the front of the book or can consult the index. For those seeking more information on a topic, cross-references can be found in boldface in the entries and following "*See also*" at the end of each entry. "Further Readings" will guide the reader to both traditional and electronic sources. To assist readers with their research, we have included a comprehensive bibliography on the Middle Passage as well as a timeline extending from the fifteenth through the late twentieth century.

Notes

1. John Thornton, *Africa and Africans in the Making of the Atlantic World: 1400–1800* (Cambridge: Cambridge University Press, 1998).

2. Recent research has challenged the view of Spanish "backwardness" that has long dominated discussions of this aspect of the slave trade. See José G. Ortega, *Money, Power, and Control: The Cuban Slave Regime, 1789-1844* (Ph.D. Dissertation, UCLA, 2007).

3. Eric Eustace Williams, *Capitalism and Slavery; with a new introduction by Colin A. Palmer* (Chapel Hill: University of North Carolina Press, 1994 [1944]).

4. Williams, *Capitalism and Slavery,* 1994.

5. Phillip Curtin, *The Atlantic Slave Trade: A Census* (Madison: University of Wisconsin Press, 1969).

6. Herbert S. Klein, *The Middle Passage: Comparative Studies in the Atlantic Slave Trade* (Princeton, NJ: Princeton University Press, 1978).

References

Barry, Boubacar. *Senegambia and the Atlantic Slave Trade.* African Studies Series No. 92, ed. J. M. Lonsdale. Cambridge: Cambridge University Press, 1997.

Blackburn, Robin. *The Making of New World Slavery: From the Baroque to the Modern, 1492–1800.* New York: Verso Press, 1997.

Conrad, Robert Edgar. *World of Sorrow: The African Slave Trade to Brazil.* Baton Rouge: Louisiana State University Press, 1986.

Costanzo, Angelo, ed. *The Interesting Narrative of the Life of Olaudah Equiano or Gustavus Vassa, the African, Written by Himself.* Peterborough, Canada: Broadview Press, 2001.

Curtin, Phillip D. *The Atlantic Slave Trade: A Census.* Madison: University of Wisconsin Press, 1969.

Donnan, Elizabeth, ed. *Documents Illustrative of the History of the Slave Trade to America.* 4 vols., 1930–1935.

Dubois, Laurent. *Avengers of the New World: The Story of the Haitian Revolution.* Cambridge, MA: Harvard University Press, 2004.

Du Bois, W.E.B. *The Suppression of the African Slave Trade to the United States of America, 1638–1870.* New York: Longmans, Green and Company, 1904.

Eltis, David, Stephen D. Behrendt, David Richardson, Herber S. Klein, eds. *The Trans-Atlantic Slave Trade: A Database on CD-ROM.* Cambridge: Cambridge University Press, 1999.

Falola, Toyin, and Matt D. Childs, eds. *The Yoruba Diaspora in the Atlantic World.* Bloomington: Indiana University Press, 2004.

Geggus, David, ed. *The Impact of the Haitian Slave Revolt in the Atlantic World.* Columbia: University of South Carolina Press, 2001.

Inikori, Joseph E. *Africans and Industrial Revolution in England: A Study of International Trade and Economic Development.* Cambridge: Cambridge University Press, 2002.

Klein, Herbert. S. *The Middle Passage: Comparative Studies in the Atlantic Slave Trade.* Princeton, NJ: Princeton University Press, 1978.

———. *The Atlantic Slave Trade.* Cambridge: Cambridge University Press, 1999.

Lovejoy, Paul E. *Transformations in Slavery: A History of Slavery in Africa.* Cambridge: Cambridge University Press, 1993.

Miller, Joseph C. *Way of Death: Merchant Capitalism and the Angolan Slave Trade.* Madison: University of Wisconsin Press, 1988.

Schwartz, Stuart B. *Sugar Plantations in the Formation of Brazilian Society, Bahia, 1550–1835.* Cambridge: Cambridge University Press, 1985.

Solow, Barbara, ed. *Slavery and the Rise of the Atlantic System.* New York: Cambridge University Press, 1991.

Thomas, Hugh. *The Slave Trade: The History of the Atlantic Slave Trade, 1440–1870.* London: Macmillan, 1998.

Thornton, John K. *Africa and Africans in the Making of the Atlantic World, 1400–1800.* 2nd ed. Cambridge: Cambridge University Press, 1998.

Williams, Eric Eustace. *Capitalism and Slavery; with a new introduction by Colin A. Palmer.* Chapel Hill: University of North Carolina Press, 1994 (1944).

CHRONOLOGY

1415   Prince Henry the Navigator of Portugal initiates the first expedition to the West African coast.

1441   First cargoes of African slaves are brought to Lisbon, Portugal.

1444   Portuguese land on Gorée Island off the coast of Senegal.

1455   Pope Nicholas V issues Papal Bull entitled "Romanus Pontifex," justifying enslavement of non-Christians.

1456   Cape Verde islands discovered by the Portuguese.

1471   Portuguese sailors sight Fernando Po in the Gulf of Guinea.

1472   Portuguese make contact with the Kingdom of Benin.
Portuguese navigators claim the uninhabited island of Annobon.

1482   Portuguese navigator, Diogo Cao, visits Congo River.
Portuguese build trading fort at Elmina in the Gold Coast of Africa.

1485–1486   Portuguese establish factory at Gwato, Benin.

1490 c.   Leo Africanus, author of *Description of Africa,* is born.

1492   Christopher Columbus's voyage to the Caribbean initiates American contact.

1494   Treaty of Tordesillas divides the known world into eastern and western spheres belonging to the Portuguese and Spanish, respectively.

1499   Spaniards arrive in Curaçao in the Caribbean.

1501   Governor of Santo Domingo, Nicolás de Ovando, orders the first shipment of slaves to the island.

1503   *Casa de Contratación,* the Spanish government agency in charge of trade, is established in Seville.

1512	Afonso I of the Kongo accepts Catholicism as the state religion.
1518	Carlos I of Spain grants the first *asiento* (agreement) contract, authorizing the shipment of African slaves to Spain's American colonies by monopoly traders.
1526	King Afonso I of Kongo attempts to ban trade with Europeans and expel all foreign merchants.
1530s	Portuguese establish a slave-trading station at Luanda.
1532	Slave trader John Hawkins is born in England.
1534	Slaves are permitted entrance to the Rio de la Plata region of South America.
1545	City of Potosí, in modern-day Bolivia, is founded.
1550	Leo Africanus's *Description of Africa* is published.
1562	John Atkins undertakes England's first slave-trading voyage.
1576	City of Luanda, in modern-day Angola, is founded.
1580	Portuguese arrive in Ouidah, on the Slave Coast.
1580	San Pedro Claver, a missionary who worked with slaves in Cartagena, is born.
1588	Dutch capture Gorée Island from Portuguese.
1602	Dutch East India Company is formed.
1619	First shipment of slaves sent to British North America (Jamestown).
1620–1640s	Portuguese slave trade from Congo increases steadily.
1621	Dutch West India Company is formed.
1626	France establishes its first West Indian colonies.
1627	Barbados settled by the British, who begin introducing large numbers of slaves.
1634	Dutch capture Curaçao.
1635	French colonize Martinique.
1637	First slaving expedition from British North America departs for the Caribbean.
1638	Dutch settle Mauritius.
1641–1661	Garcia II rules the Kingdom of Kongo.
1641–1648	Dutch occupy territories in Brazil and Angola.
1642	Dutch capture the Portuguese slave-trading post Elmina.
1644	First slaving expedition from a British North American colony departs for Africa from Boston.

1649	First Danish slave ship arrives on the West African coast.
1650	Fort Carolusburg (later renamed Cape Coast Castle) is built by Polish architect Henry Caerlof.
1655	John (Jean) Barbot, slave trader and author, is born in France.
1655	British take over Jamaica.
1658	First Danish fort established on the West African coast.
1661	First permanent British colony in Africa is established at James Island in Gambia River.
1664	French West Indian Company is established.
1664	British capture Gorée Island from the Dutch.
1665	Battle of Mbwila leads to unraveling of the Kingdom of Kongo.
1672	Royal Africa Company (RAC) replaces the failed Company of Royal Adventurers.
1677	French capture Gorée Island from the British and establish it as an important center of the French slave trade.
1678	São Salvador, the capital of Kongo, is sacked, leading to a strengthening of Portuguese control of the region.
1685	*Code Noir* establishes conditions for slaves in the French West Indies.
1688	Mennonites in Germantown, Pennsylvania, protest against the slave trade in the British North American colonies.
1696	Pennsylvania Quakers make an official declaration for abolitionism.
1697	Spain cedes the western third of Hispaniola to France. Saint Domingue is established.
1698	King William III of England revokes the RAC monopoly.
1701	The first Asantehene, Osei Tutu, becomes the ruler of all the Asante people.
1713	Treaty of Utrecht grants a British monopoly (or *asiento*) to supply slaves to the Spanish colonies.
1713	Anthony Benzenet, a Quaker antislavery activist, is born in France.
1720s	Dahomean invasion of Allada.
1725	John Newton, slave trader turned abolitionist, is born in England.
1731	RAC ceases its participation in the slave trade.
1732	John Barbot's *A Description of the Coasts of North and South-Guinea* is published in English.

1735	John Atkins's work, *A Voyage to Guinea, Brasil, and the West-Indies; in His Majesty's Ships, the Swallow and the Weymouth*, is published.
1739	The Stono Rebellion, one of the earliest North American slave uprisings, takes place in South Carolina.
1740s	New England rum is produced for 5 pence a gallon.
1745	Writer and abolitionist Olaudah Equiano is born in present-day Nigeria.
1753	Poet Phillis Wheatley is born in the Senegambia region of West Africa.
1757	Abolitionist Quobna Ottobah Cugoano is born in present-day Ghana.
1759	British abolitionist William Wilberforce is born in England.
1760	Anthony Benzenet's pamphlet, "Observations on the [Enslaving,] Importing and Purchasing of Negroes," is published.
1761	Phillis Wheatley arrives in Boston from Senegal.
1762	British occupation of Havana temporarily opens Cuba to free trade in slaves.
1768	Danish slave ship, the *Fredensborg,* wrecks off the coast of Norway.
1774	The First Continental Congress declares a temporary embargo on the importation of new slaves into America.
1775	British governor of Virginia issues a proclamation granting freedom to indentured servants and slaves if they join British forces.
1786 c.	The slave house, *Maison des Esclaves,* is built on Gorée Island.
1778	Spanish take possession of Annobon, Fernando Po.
1783	The *Zong* affair, in which diseased slaves were thrown overboard to prevent contamination of an entire cargo, comes to the attention of the British public, causing an uproar and fueling the abolitionist cause.
1786	Swedish West India Company is established.
1787	Cugoano's *Thoughts and Sentiments on the Evil of Slavery and Commerce of the Human Species* is published in London.
1788	Dolben's Act establishes guidelines for the British slave trade.
1788	*Société des Amis des Noirs* (Society for the Friends of Negroes) is founded in France.
1789	Spain declares free trade in African slaves.
1789	Olaudah Equiano's *The Interesting Narrative of the Life of Olaudah Equiano or Gustavus Vassa, the African, Written by Himself* is published in London.

1791	The Haitian Revolution begins.
1792	Denmark becomes the first state to outlaw the slave trade.
1793	Rebellion occurs on board the Rhode Island slave ship, the *Nancy*.
1794	U.S. Congress bans building or outfitting slave ships.
1794	French abolish slavery.
1802	Napoleon reinstates slavery in French colonies.
1804	Haiti is declared an independent republic.
1807	British declare the abolition of the African slave trade.
1808	United States mandates the closing of the Atlantic slave trade.
1811	Great Britain makes slave-trading a felony.
1812	Aponte rebellion attempts to end slavery in Cuba.
1814	Netherlands outlaws the slave trade.
1814	France prohibits the slave trade.
1815	Portugal outlaws slave-trading north of the equator.
1816	The American Colonization Society is established.
1817	Anglo-Portuguese treaty enforces limits on slave-trading.
1817	On September 23, Great Britain and Spain sign a treaty banning the slave trade.
1819	Britain's official Royal Navy West African Squadron begins patrolling the West African coast. Court of Mixed Commission established in Sierra Leone.
1819	The United States makes participation in the slave trade a felony.
1820	Anglo-Spanish treaty outlawing the slave trade becomes effective.
1821	Liberia is established.
1823	The umbrella organization the Anti-Slavery Society is created for the coordination of abolitionist efforts.
1827	Spanish slave ship the *Guerrero* wrecks off of Key Largo, Florida, drowning 41 of the more than 550 slaves on board.
1831	Emperor of Brazil, Pedro I, agrees to begin phasing out the slave trade. Britain establishes Gorée Island as the center of the West African Squadron.

1834	Abolition of slavery takes effect in Britain's American colonies.
1835	On June 28, the Anglo-Spanish treaty is renewed. "Equipment articles" are established.
1835	Inspired by Islamic teachings, slaves rise up in Bahia, Brazil. This rebellion becomes known as the Malé Revolt.
1839–1841	The *Amistad* affair in which Cuban slaves mutiny, killing the white crew and piloting the ship (the *Amistad*) to the United States, is litigated in U.S. courts.
1840	J.M.W. Turner's "Slavers Throwing Overboard the Dead and Dying—Typhon Coming On" painting is exhibited in London.
1841	Quintuple Treaty between Great Britain, France, Russia, Prussia, and Austria includes "equipment clause," banning equipment used to conduct the slave trade.
1841	Calabar, West Africa, fully transitions to palm oil exports.
1841	Madison Washington leads revolt on board the *Creole,* which is bound for Louisiana.
1842	Webster-Ashburton Treaty between the United States and Great Britain establishes joint cruising on the West African coast.
1843	Slave trader Pedro de Zulueta is tried and acquitted in the British courts.
1844	Conspiracy of La Escalera attempts the abolition of slavery in Cuba.
1847	Liberia gains independence from the United States.
1848	Slavery is abolished in French Caribbean colonies.
1849	Last known French slave ship leaves La Havre.
1860	*Clotilda* transports slaves to the United States from Ouidah, Bight of Benin, in violation of U.S. legal prohibitions.
1862	Washington Treaty allows British to search and seize suspected U.S. slavers.
1863	Dutch abolish slavery in all of their colonies.
1865	United States abolishes slavery.
1868	AfricaTown, Alabama, located just north of Mobile, is established by slaves freed from the *Clotilda* slave ship.
1870	British Royal Navy West African Squadrons cease patrolling the coast.
1886	Cuba abolishes slavery.
1888	Brazil abolishes slavery, making it the last nation in the Americas to end the practice.
1896	End of the Asante Empire of West Africa.
1930	Writer Kamau Brathwaite is born in Barbados.

1944   *Capitalism and Slavery,* by Eric Williams, is published in the United States.

1945   Robert Hayden writes the poem "Middle Passage."

1962   John Newton's logbooks are published as the *Journal of a Slave Trader.*

1978   The United Nations Educational, Scientific, and Cultural Organization (UNESCO) declares *Maison des Esclaves* a world heritage monument.

1985   AfricaTown, Alabama, is designated a historic landmark by the Alabama State legislature.

1989   UNESCO declares Gorée Island a world heritage site.

1999   *The Trans-Atlantic Slave Trade: A Database on CD-ROM* is published.

2000   The film, *Adanggaman,* premieres at the Venice Film Festival.
The film, *The Middle Passage*, premieres in North America at the Toronto Film Festival.

A

Abolitionism

Abolitionism is a political movement that sought to abolish slavery and the worldwide trade in slaves, especially the **enslavement** of Africans and people of African descent in Europe, the Americas, and continental Africa. The movement began during the eighteenth century, grew to large proportions in several nations during the nineteenth century, and largely succeeded in attaining its goals.

Abolitionism began as blacks' resistance to slavery during the fifteenth century, as enslaved Africans sought to kill their captors or themselves. It was later championed in the late 1700s by the **Christians** whose doctrines on morality, liberty, human rights, and economic changes frowned on human enslavement and, therefore, led to efforts to end it.

The trans-Atlantic slave trade, which began in Africa in mid-1400s and lasted into the nineteenth century, was "pioneered" by Portuguese traders who purchased small numbers of Africans from the West African coast and transported them to Portugal and Spain. The trade in slaves became a huge enterprise as European nations colonized the Americas in 1500s. By the 1600s, European countries had begun fighting fiercely with one another. The Dutch, British, and French contested the control of the trade with the Portuguese, and by 1713, Britain had emerged as the dominant slave-trading nation in the world.

The total number of enslaved Africans has been a subject of serious dispute. The W.E.B. Du Bois Institute for Afro-American Research put the number at between 15 and 20 million, with about 2 million dead during slave raids and 1 million more dead during the Middle Passage. More than 15 million finally reached the Americas.

During the Middle Passage, slaves were **chained**, **branded**, crowded into disease-infested ships, **raped**, and sexually abused by crewmembers and, in the New World, by slaveholders and supervisors. Deprived of basic human rights and disrobed of all vestiges of human dignity, African slaves were made to endure dreadful conditions and forced to perform horrendous tasks in disease-infested **plantations**. This inhuman treatment played

Granville Sharp, who helped to free slaves through the courts, was a founding member of the 1787 committee formed to campaign against the slave trade. Courtesy of Anti-Slavery International.

decisive roles in the origin of abolitionism. Resistance peaked by the eighteenth century when slaves in the West Indies, **Brazil**, Mexico, Venezuela, and the British colonies in North America revolted and formed maroon communities, which were located in inaccessible areas where recapture was difficult, if not impossible. The inherent cruelty associated with slavery was underscored by the risks, severe punishments, and death that slaves endured to **escape** from slavery. Antislavery sentiment was therefore kindled by the combination of revolts, escape to inaccessible areas, inability of recapture, and periodic violent raids by slaves from these communities.

Despite these factors, opposition to slavery developed slowly for two important reasons. First, socio-political and economic lives revolved around possession of huge plantations, which required enormous labor forces that only slavery could satisfy. Second, the general perspective current in Europe was that blacks were considered mentally, culturally, and morally inferior to whites. From the late eighteenth century, revolutionary ideas, such as equal rights and equality before the law, began to challenge and replace the old beliefs. This development, the activities of the Quakers, and black resistance inspired radical changes in Europe and the Americas.

The Quakers, the first whites to denounce and challenge slavery, believed that all people, regardless of race, had a divine spark inside of them and were equal before God. The movement achieved successes in legal battles, protection for slaves, and the eventual abolition of slavery in Europe and the Americas. Despite this fact, the movement failed to end racism and to establish equal political and social rights for freed slaves and their descendants. It also failed to end practices like contract labor, sharecropping, child labor, and sweatshops. *See also* Abolition of the Slave Trade, Brazil; Abolition of the Slave Trade, France; Abolition of the Slave Trade, Great Britain; Abolition of the Slave Trade, Spain; Abolition of the Slave Trade, United States; Closure of the Slave Trade; Haitian Revolution, The; Havana; Hispaniola; Illegal Slave Trade, Brazil; Illegal Slave Trade, Spanish Caribbean; Jamaica; Portuguese Slave Trade; Sierra Leone; Spanish Caribbean.

Further Readings: Brown, Christopher Leslie. *Moral Capital: Foundations of British Abolitionism.* Chapel Hill: University of North Carolina Press, 2006; Davis, David Brion. *Inhuman Bondage: The Rise and Fall of Slavery in the New World.* Cambridge, MA: Harvard University Press, 2006; Davis, David Brion. *The Problem of Slavery in the Age of Revolution, 1770–1823.* New York: Oxford University Press, 1999; Eltis, David, Behrendt, Stephen D., Richardson, David, and Klein, Herbert S., eds.

The Trans-Atlantic Slave Trade: A Database on CD-ROM. Cambridge: Cambridge University Press, 1999; Gould, Philip. *Barbaric Traffic: Commerce and Antislavery in the Eighteenth-Century Atlantic World.* Cambridge, MA: Harvard University Press, 2003; Hellie, Richard. *Slavery in Russia, 1450–1725.* Chicago: University of Chicago Press, 1982; Kolchin, Peter. *Unfree Labor: American Slavery and Russian Serfdom.* Cambridge, MA: Belknap Press, 1987; Wise, Steven M. *Though the Heavens May Fall: The Landmark Trial That Led to the End of Human Slavery.* Cambridge, MA: Da Capo Press, 2005.

Oyeniyi Bukola Adeyemi

Abolition of the Slave Trade, Brazil

Brazil was one of the last countries in the Americas (after the Spanish colonies) to abolish the Atlantic slave trade and the last to abolish slavery itself. Slaves in Brazil worked, for the most part, on **sugar plantations**; the slave trade and slavery survived for as long as it did because of the power of sugar planters and their political representatives. It was largely as a result of foreign pressure that the slave trade was abolished, because the British government viewed the expansive and successful Brazilian plantation economy as a major impediment to their mission against human trafficking.

At first, Brazil's Portuguese colonizers enslaved her indigenous population, and this practice persisted in some areas until 1755. From the seventeenth century, African slavery gradually replaced native bondage and continued to grow with the rapid rise of Brazilian sugar; particular success followed the setbacks in French sugar production that resulted from the **Saint Domingue** revolution. The demands of sugar cultivation engendered an appalling **mortality** rate on the plantations, making planters ineluctably dependent on the slave trade to replenish their depleted enslaved labor forces. So many people were imported that, by 1800, half of the Brazilian population was enslaved. Although sugar was the country's leading export for much of the first half of the century, it would come under increasing competition from coffee, imported from Arabia via Indonesia.

Throughout much of the nineteenth century, real political power in Brazil remained with the large sugar planters. Without economic equals since the decline of gold mining in the province of Minas Gerais, they shied away from political initiatives that would entail a diminution of their control over the Brazilian economy. As such, they isolated themselves from contemporary abolitionist sentiment, propounded most notably by Great Britain. Having resolved in 1807 to ban the trade, and from a position of strength as the Napoleonic Wars began to turn in her favor, Britain exhorted her dependent allies to work toward prohibition.

The Congress of Vienna was held in 1815 to configure a post-Napoleon world order. Great Britain viewed the meeting as an opportunity to promote abolition among the delegate countries. British representatives granted Portugal a grace period of a few years to replenish labor supplies in expectation of imminent abolition; Britain paid Portugal, as they would later pay Brazil, large sums as an encouragement. In spite of these concessions, Portugal found little reason to abandon the commerce in humans. Brazil, following independence in 1822, took the same tack.

Brazilian sugar revenues, planter commitment to the aristocratic lifestyle and hierarchical ethos that slaveholding sustained, and a lack of European immigrant labor kept the Brazilian slave trade alive. Brazilian slavery also aided the wider Atlantic trade. Profiteering slavers from other countries ferried slaves to Brazil. Many hailed from the United States, despite its 1808 abolition law. Naturally, **African wars** of **enslavement** also continued as long as a market for slaves existed. Largely as a consequence of Brazil's attachment to slavery, between 1821 and 1843 (the period immediately following the first abolition treaties with Great Britain) about 1,153,000 slaves crossed the Atlantic; between 1801 and 1820, the figure was 1,486,000. This influx of enslaved laborers caused further rapid expansion in the Brazilian plantation economy.

Pedro I, the first emperor of an independent Brazil, agreed in 1831 to phase out the slave trade. Made under pressure from Great Britain, this covenant was never kept; traffic to Brazil continued unabated. His son Pedro II, the first emperor to be native born, was personally convinced of the iniquity of slavery: He freed his own slaves in 1840 and advocated coffee production as a less pernicious alternative to sugar. Despite his misgivings, Pedro remained less than enamored of high-handed British attempts to enforce the ban (in 1845 the Royal Navy received government sanction to regard all slavers as pirates; worse still, malefactors were to be tried in British Admiralty courts rather than by joint British-Brazilian bodies). Between 1846 and 1847, 150,000 West African slaves arrived in Brazil.

Matters came to a head in 1850 when Britain warned that a squadron would enter Brazilian territorial waters to seize vessels carrying slaves. The threats provoked a storm of protest in Brazil, particularly because Brazilian pressures in favor of abolition were just then beginning to mount. Brazilian coastal forts even exchanged sporadic fire with British cruisers. With diplomatic relations reaching a breaking point, the Brazilian Parliament promulgated the Eusébio de Queiroz Law. Under its conditions, the slave trade was made piracy, masters and **captains** trading on the Atlantic coast were required to give their bond that they would not transport slaves, and **crews** were rewarded with the proceeds of captured slavers.

Yet, because public sentiment was not initially strongly in favor of the statute, its implementation proved difficult. Violations were so flagrant that the order to allow British cruisers to seize suspects in Brazilian waters (briefly suspended after the Queiroz settlement) was restored early in 1851. But shortly after the middle of the century a change in Brazilian attitudes, especially notable among public officials, made enforcement possible. Enslaved people made up 33 percent of the entire population in 1850; following the end of slave imports and an increase in free immigration, this figure would later drop to 15 percent. *See also* Abolitionism; Abolition of the Slave Trade, France; Abolition of the Slave Trade, Great Britain; Abolition of the

Slave Trade, Spain; Abolition of the Slave Trade, United States; Internal Slave Trade, Brazil.

Further Readings: Bethell, Leslie. *The Abolition of the Brazilian Slave Trade: Britain, Brazil and the Slavery Question, 1807–1869.* Cambridge: Cambridge University Press, 1970; Conrad, Robert Edgar. *World of Sorrow: The African Slave Trade to Brazil.* Baton Rouge: Louisiana State University Press, 1986; Tavares, Luís Henrique Dias. *Comércio proibido de escravos.* São Paulo: Ática, 1988.

Tristan Stubbs

Abolition of the Slave Trade, France

French merchants had shipped slaves across the Atlantic since the sixteenth century, when they sold them to Spanish and Portuguese settlers in the New World. The establishment of French **plantation** colonies in the Caribbean in the seventeenth century increased French participation in the slave trade. During the eighteenth century, about one slave ship out of five crossing the Atlantic was French. Although French involvement in the slave trade was ancient, it was not until the middle of the eighteenth century that an enlightened minority of Frenchmen began to criticize the practice. Concrete political projects, which emerged in the late 1780s, aimed to put an end to the slave trade as soon as possible, whereas slavery was to be abolished progressively, over two or three generations. The French Revolution gave a decisive impulse to the abolitionist cause, which led to the first and immediate abolition of slavery in 1794. Napoleon Bonaparte reestablished slavery in 1802, a decision which led to the independence of Haiti. Other French colonies had to wait until 1848 for slavery to be abolished.

Criticism of slavery became apparent in the 1740s, when French philosophers like Charles-Louis de Secondat, Baron de la Brède et de Montesquieu; Jean-Jacques Rousseau; and Jacques-Henri Bernardin de Saint-Pierre began to point out the criminal and immoral character of the slave trade and slavery. Despite some ambivalence and contradictions, notably by Voltaire, their writings were fundamental in informing contemporaries—or at least, the minority of Frenchmen who were able to read—about the horrors of the Middle Passage and the inhuman living conditions of black slaves in the French colonies: a remote reality of which most Frenchmen had but a vague idea. Consistent with the notion of the common humanity of mankind, they critiqued slavery as based on racial prejudice and inequality. If they condemned slavery, however, they did not develop a program aiming for its abolition.

In the 1770s, Louis-Sébastien Mercier and Guillaume Thomas François Raynal, among others, introduced a new element into the debate. In their writings, they vividly depicted the horrors of a general slave uprising leading to the independence of the colonies, which they considered as the inevitable consequence of slavery. The antislavery discourse—it was still not a political movement—urged henceforth for some kind of reforms of the existing system. The development of this literature contributed to the birth of the first French antislavery movement seeking a political response to the questions of the inhumanity of the slave trade and slavery.

The Société des Amis des Noirs (Society of the Friends of Negroes) was founded in Paris on February 19, 1788, and it continued its activities for four years, at a crucial moment in French history. The Société was not a philanthropic institution devoted to the improvement of the slaves' living conditions, but rather pursued political goals. Its members promoted a better knowledge of colonial realities by translating and publishing relevant texts, and they tried to exert some influence on the king and on the minister of the Navy, who was in charge of the colonies and of French shipping and trade. They wanted the abolition of the slave trade, which they considered necessary to improve the slaves' fate in the French colonies, and which they viewed as the starting point to change the economy of colonial production, leading ultimately, within two or three generations, to the final abolition of slavery and its replacement with waged work. If the Société was strongly influenced by its **London** equivalent, with which it corresponded, its methods were adequate to the French political system and the absence of a Parliament under the *ancien régime*. But the Société, which ceased its meetings in the winter of 1791–92, was unable to obtain any concrete results, despite the major political upheavals in France and the proclamation of equality and liberty of mankind in the declaration of human rights (1789). Such principles were unable to lead to the immediate abolition of slavery, because of the powerful colonial lobby (Club Massiac), the priority given to internal political problems, and faction fights.

It was the French Revolutionary Convention led by Maximilien François Marie Isidore de Robespierre who abolished slavery on February 4, 1794. Historians tend to interpret the decision to abolish slavery as the logical outcome of the ideal of the equality of the human kind and as the consequences of the slave uprising in **Saint Domingue**. Léger-Félicité Sonthonax, the French commissioner, had freed the slaves of the island in August 1793, after they had helped him to fight against counter-revolutionary planters.

This decision concerned, in theory, 700,000 slaves. The law effectively put an end to slavery in Guadeloupe and French Guyana, and confirmed the situation in Saint Domingue. It had no consequences, however, in Martinique, which the British occupied in March 1794, or in the French colonies in the **Indian Ocean**, where planters successfully prevented its enforcement.

The first abolition of slavery in the French colonies lasted until the first consul Bonaparte, who was influenced by his Martinique-born wife Josephine and the planters' lobby, reintroduced slavery on May 20, 1802, a decision that met no major reactions. Troops were sent to the **French Caribbean** to implement the law. They were successful in Guadeloupe, where slavery was reinforced after a bloody military campaign (10,000 casualties) and massive deportations. But they failed to reintroduce slavery in Saint Domingue, where the 23,000 soldiers sent under General Charles Victor Emmanuel Leclerc met a fierce resistance and yellow fever. Bonaparte's decision to reintroduce slavery ultimately led to the independence of Haiti in 1804.

France officially forbade slave trade in 1814, but it took thirty years before slavery was abolished in the French colonies—that is, Martinique,

Guadeloupe, French Guyana, and the Bourbon Island in the Indian Ocean (today's Reunion Island). On April 27, 1848, the provisional government born out of the liberal February Revolution decided to abolish slavery immediately. The initiative came from Victor Schoelcher (1804–1893), parliamentary state undersecretary to the ministry of the Navy and the Colonies, who had joined the abolitionist movement after a trip to **Cuba** in 1830, which induced him to devote his life to the abolitionist cause.

This second and lasting abolition crowned the efforts of different abolitionist groups created in the 1820s and 1830s, such as the Société de la Morale Chrétienne or Society for Christian Morality (1822), or the French Society for the Abolition of Slavery (1834), which published *L'Abolitioniste français* in 1844. The word *abolitionnisme* first appeared in the Dictionary of the French Academia in 1836. But the 1848 abolition was also a direct consequence of the British abolition in 1833, which contributed to increase the number of slave revolts in the French colonies. Some 190,000 slaves became French citizens. Their former owners were to receive compensation. *See also* Abolitionism; Abolition of the Slave Trade, Brazil; Abolition of the Slave Trade, Great Britain; Abolition of the Slave Trade, Spain; Abolition of the Slave Trade, United States; French Slave Trade; Haitian Revolution, The.

Further Readings: Bénot, Yves, and Dorigny, Marcel, eds. *Rétablissement de l'esclavage dans les colonies françaises, 1802. Aux origines d'Haïti*. Paris: Maisonneuve et Larose, 2003; Blackburn, Robin. *The Overthrow of Colonial Slavery 1776–1848*. New York: Verso, 1988; Dorigny, Marcel, ed. *Les abolitions de l'esclavage de L. F. Sonthonax à V. Schoelcher, 1793-1794-1848*. Saint-Denis: Presses universitaires de Vincennes; Paris: UNESCO, 1995; Dorigny, Marcel, and Bernard Gainot, eds. *La Société des Amis des Noirs, 1788–1799. Contribution à l'histoire d el'abolition de lesclavage*. Paris: Editions de l'UNESCO, 1998; Schmidt, Nelly. *Abolitionnistes de l'esclavage et réformateurs des colonies, 1820–1851*. Paris: Karthala, 2000.

Silvia Marzagalli

Abolition of the Slave Trade, Great Britain

Great Britain was not the first European country to end its involvement in the slave trade—Denmark abolished the trade in 1792. But Britain's ascendant position at the end of the Napoleonic Wars gave it the military and economic might to enforce abolition on other European powers. In many of the countries where the slave trade was abolished, however, its profitability militated against its complete abandonment. The Royal Navy played a key role in ensuring that the provisions of abolition treaties were met.

Many eighteenth-century British abolitionists derived their opposition from a deeply held Protestant faith. **Christian** exhortations about the unity of mankind were crucial to the success of the movement. Yet abolition was achieved only after several decades and stages of pressure. An early fillip was Somerset's Case in 1772, in which the Earl of Mansfield ruled that slaveholders were unable to remove slaves from England under duress, rendering slavery unenforceable there. Petitioning by the Committee for the Relief of the Black Poor prompted in 1787 the establishment of **Sierra**

Leone as a colony for free Africans, freed slaves, and those bondspeople who had fled their American owners to fight for the Loyalist side in the American Revolution.

Seeking to widen their popular base, abolitionists also exploited print culture: Gruesome images of the horrors of slavery illustrated their pamphlets and novels. Although abolitionists did succeed in getting Dolben's Act of 1788, which provided for the more humane treatment of slaves, through Parliament, early attempts at a legislative ban were unsuccessful.

But there was a populist tone to opposition, too. Cartoons claimed that abolition would cause **prices** to rise and portrayed newly freed people enslaving their former captors in retaliation for years of bondage. Nationalism was often important: Britons feared they would be disadvantaged in commercial competition with those who maintained the slave trade. Furthermore, many associated reform of any sort with the French Revolution of 1789, an upheaval anathema to instinctively conservative British sentiment.

British Caribbean plantation economies benefited from the disruption to French **sugar** exports caused by the successful slave rebellion in the colony of **Saint Domingue** (later Haiti) between 1791 and 1804. The early nineteenth century witnessed the abandonment of American protectionism following the Revolution (North America had been the Caribbean's chief market). For the time being, West Indian plantations would remain the British Empire's principal source of **sugar**—merchants would later shift to cheaper sources in the East. And mercantilist trade policies were still largely resistant to the laissez-faire principles that would doom imperial preference by mid-century. These economic factors motivated slaveholders to oppose abolition; most important, however, was that much of their capital was tied up in land and slaves. It was for this reason that planters demanded, and received, large payouts when plantation slavery itself was outlawed in British colonies in 1834.

Planters therefore had little incentive voluntarily to abandon the slave trade. This is at variance with some **historiography**, which has argued that the slave trade was banned because slavery itself was no longer profitable to Caribbean planters. But if economic pressures cannot adequately explain **abolitionism**, neither can a narrow focus on religiously inspired **humanitarianism**. Broader cultural pressures were also at play. Early-nineteenth-century Britain, a more liberal, middle-class society than before, looked to marginalize reactionary West Indian landholders. Imbued with the spirit of progress, many Britons now viewed the slave trade and slavery as abhorrent, anachronistic, and deplorable.

Prime Minister William Pitt the Younger sought to appeal to this constituency, and in 1805 prohibited the importation of slaves to newly captured territories from 1807; in the interim, he limited the introduction of slaves to 30 percent of the number already there. Pitt died the following year, ushering in the reformist "Ministry of All Talents," which took the abolitionist program still further. Their Foreign Slave Trade Act of 1806 forbade the supply of slaves to conquered territories and foreign colonies. This legislation was presented as a necessary expedient to limit the territories' economic strength at a time of war. The zenith of the abolition process came in 1807, however: The Abolition Act banned slave-trading by British subjects and the import of slaves into British colonies not covered by the 1806 act. By 1811, participation in the slave trade was made a felony.

The Napoleonic Wars saw Britain seize many Dutch and **French Caribbean** colonies; as the tide of the wars turned in Britain's favor, her Navy's global power was confirmed. The next stage of the abolition process saw Britain employ her international strength to pressure other states into abolishing or limiting slaving. Although certainly influenced by moral concerns, the British position was again partly driven by a desire to prevent rival plantation economies from gaining economic advantage over their non-slaving British competitors. Pressure was first exerted on Britain's dependent allies, and in 1814 the Netherlands abolished the trade with effect from 1818. In 1815, Britain persuaded the restored Bourbon monarchy to end French slaving; at the Congress of Vienna, which was convened to discuss the postwar geopolitical order, British pressure forced a declaration against the slave trade.

Next Britain urged Portugal, assisted during the Peninsular War by British troops, to restrict the trade in preparation for abolition. Because Portuguese **Angola** was the origin, and Portuguese **Brazil** the destination, of many African slaves, her acquiescence was vital. In 1817, an Anglo-Portuguese treaty limited the slave trade in Brazil to south of the Equator; a contemporary Anglo-Spanish treaty contained similar provisions.

With pressure against slaving mounting, the United States, a new nation conscious of its international reputation and convinced of the sustainability of its naturally reproducing enslaved population, had in 1807 abolished the trade with effect from January 1, 1808. From then on, the British determined to seize American slavers contravening the ban, although American federal ships enforced prohibition with similar alacrity right up to the Civil War. Great Britain's dominant naval power and trans-Atlantic reach permitted an effective abolitionist policy in the years following the Napoleonic Wars. In the first half of the century, their most successful force, based in West Africa, patrolled the region's coastlines and transported freed slaves into Sierra Leone. Cape Town would become an important post for British intervention south of the Equator after the treaty with Brazil was amended in 1826.

Force was not the only weapon in the British arsenal, however. Diplomatic approaches, although often supported by the threat of reprisals, also proved fruitful. **African rulers** were pressed into agreeing to end the trade and to conduct **legitimate commerce** in its stead. Moreover, British recognition of the independence of Spain's former American colonies was dependent on their commitment to abolition, while her relationship with the short-lived Republic of Texas involved the same condition.

Distinct from enslaved populations in the United States, bondspeople in other American regions were largely unable to increase their numbers through natural reproduction. As long as the institution of slavery existed in the British Caribbean, therefore, a market for clandestine slave imports prevailed. Sugar **profits**, the seductive, aristocratic planter lifestyle, and a lack of alternative labor ensured the viability of **smuggling**. Moreover, the postponement of abolition by other colonial powers encouraged unscrupulous

Britons to sell people to—and thereby sustain—foreign slave economies. Once direct trade with Africa was restricted, internal Caribbean slaving became particularly important to colonies such as Puerto Rico.

British policy elsewhere was even less successful. French ships made at least 193 slaving voyages between 1814 and 1820, although there were few after 1831. In 1839, the British took unilateral action against recalcitrant Portuguese slavers after negotiations failed. Abolition became a particularly thorny issue in relations between Great Britain and Brazil. Their 1826 treaty (ratified in 1827) exacted a Brazilian commitment to end the slave trade within three years; Brazil's General Assembly passed a law to that effect in 1831. Brazilian enforcement, however, was never more than lackluster. Increasing European demand for coffee encouraged an annual inflow of 50,000 slaves toward the end of the 1840s. By 1850, 2 million people were in bondage in Brazil.

Great Britain's 1845 Slave Trade Act sanctioned the Royal Navy to treat slavers as pirates. Much to the anger of Brazil, the Navy began to pursue ships into Brazilian waters. Yet continued British raids, and the threat of further reprisals if inaction continued, forced the Brazilian Parliament to pass in 1850 the Eusébio de Queiroz Law, formally abolishing the slave trade. At the time of the law, enslaved people made up 33 percent of the entire Brazilian population; following the end of slave imports, this figure fell to 15 percent.

British abolition of the slave trade and that of slavery itself occurred at different times but were undertaken for similar reasons. Acknowledging the futility of abandoning slave trafficking without also ending the institution of slavery, and buoyed by the electoral popularity and relative success of slave trade abolitionism, Earl Grey's reformist Whig ministry passed in 1833 the Emancipation Act, which freed slaves in British colonies from August of the following year. But the legal prohibition of slavery did not end the tight control of labor in British plantation economies. Trinidad and British Guiana imported a large population of Indian **indentured servants**; on the Caribbean islands, many former slaves were pressed to continue working in the sugar fields. *See also* Abolition of the Slave Trade, Brazil; Abolition of the Slave Trade, France; Abolition of the Slave Trade, Spain; Abolition of the Slave Trade, United States; African Squadrons, The; British Navy; British Slave Trade; Closure of the Slave Trade; "Slavers Throwing Overboard the Dead and Dying—Typhon Coming On"; Wilberforce, William; Zulueta, Pedro de.

Further Readings: Anstey, Roger. *The Atlantic Slave Trade and British Abolition, 1760–1810.* London: Macmillan, 1976; Drescher, Seymour. *Capitalism and Anti-slavery: British Mobilization in a Comparative Perspective.* New York: Oxford University Press, 1987; Engerman, Stanley L., and Solow, Barbara Lewis, eds. *British Capitalism and Caribbean Slavery: The Legacy of Eric Williams.* Cambridge: Cambridge University Press, 2004; Jennings, Judith. *The Business of Abolishing the British Slave Trade, 1783–1807.* London: Frank Cass, 1997; Oldfield, J. R. *Popular Politics and British Anti-slavery: The Mobilisation of Public Opinion Against the Slave Trade, 1787–1807.* London: Frank Cass, 1998; Williams, Eric Eustace. *Capitalism and Slavery; with a new introduction by Colin A. Palmer.* Chapel Hill: University of North Carolina Press, 1994 (1944).

Tristan Stubbs

Abolition of the Slave Trade, Spain

Spain outlawed the slave trade—that is, prohibited its subjects from participating in any aspect of the trade anywhere in the world—in an 1817 treaty with the United Kingdom, which became effective worldwide in 1820. Between 1817 and 1867, when the outlawed trade actually ceased, the 1817 treaty's terms were implemented, clarified, and modified in three subsequent royal *cedulas* (decrees), three more agreements with the United Kingdom, and two statutes enacted by Spain's *Cortes*.

In contrast to the United Kingdom and the United States, where international slaving was banned in response to internal political agitation often expressed in moral terms, Spain's reasons for abolishing the trade were as much practical as philanthropic. Spain's abolition was likewise announced as being for **humanitarian** reasons, but it resulted from both practical and ideological factors internal to Spain and its colonies, as well as external pressure, largely from the United Kingdom.

Spain's first step toward outlawing slave-trading by its subjects—Spanish and colonial citizens, residents, business entities, and ships—was taken in 1804, as the involvement of Spanish-flagged ships in the trade and the total number of slaves imported each year into Spain's colonies was increasing. For the 272 years between 1517 until 1789, Spain's role in the African slave trade primarily had been that of a licensor, authorizing ships—almost always under non-Spanish colors—to import slaves to its New World colonies under *asiento* contracts. Only after 1789, when abolition efforts in the United States and United Kingdom suggested a likely end to their ships' involvement, had the role of Spanish-flagged slavers become more significant. By 1804, Carlos IV's 1789 *cedula* opening up slave-trading with Spain's colonies to everyone interested had been followed by ten more royal decrees designed to increase it and by a substantial increase in the **volume** of African slaves brought into its colony of **Cuba**. Cuba's Spanish **plantation** owners were buying large numbers of newly imported slaves, in the hopes of increasing their **sugar** production to take advantage of reduced sugar exports to Europe from Saint Domingue (Haiti), the result of slave revolts there in the 1790s. After Congress banned slave-trading by U.S. subjects beginning in 1808, the role of Spanish ships in the trade further expanded, as many U.S.-flagged slavers were reregistered under the Spanish flag.

At the same time, by 1804 and 1817, although the volume of the Spanish colonial slave trade was increasing, the number of Spanish colonial slaving ports was contracting. There was little demand for new African slaves in Spain's continental American colonies, and Spain's hold on those colonies was slipping. By the mid-1820s, Cuba and Puerto Rico were Spain's only remaining American colonies. The practical effect of the 1817 treaty's outlawing of Spanish and colonial slave imports, therefore, was limited to prohibiting slaves from being brought into Cuba, Puerto Rico, and peninsular Spain itself—nowhere else. The added effect of the treaty's also prohibiting Spanish ships from slave-trading was likewise limited. In practice, it banned Spanish ships only from bringing new African slaves into the few

non-Spanish ports in the Americas where they were still marketable—
primarily to **Brazil**, where the demand was greatest, and to a much lesser
extent the Southern United States—in addition to Cuba and Puerto Rico.

Although one Spanish figure apparently urged total abolition of the Spanish slave trade in 1802, Spain's first step toward abolition in 1804 was a
comparatively small one. The Saint Domingue slave revolts had raised concerns over the potentially disruptive effect of importing large numbers of
African slaves into Cuba. In response to that concern, while extending the
right of anyone who wished to import African slaves into Spain's colonies
for additional years, Carlos IV's slave trade *cedulas* of 1804 outlawed inter-
American slave-trading. Lawful imports into Spain's colonies were thereafter
limited to slaves coming directly from Africa through the Middle Passage,
who would hopefully be unexposed to revolutionary thinking.

Spain's next step toward abolition of its subjects' participation in the
slave trade was taken during the later years of the Napoleonic Wars, when
it agreed to the United Kingdom's request that the Royal Navy be allowed
to search Spanish-flagged merchant ships, to see whether they were carrying slaves and whether their Spanish papers were genuine, and to seize
them if there were grounds for doing so. The U.K. Parliament had sent
George III an 1806 request asking him to work with other governments to
abolish the slave trade worldwide, but at the time the United Kingdom was
amidst its sixteen years of war with Napoleon, the Spanish government was
its ally, and it was unwilling to condition aid to the Spanish government
upon abolition.

During this same period, the Spanish *Cortes* gave its first consideration to
total abolition of the slave trade, but rejected it as a threat to Spain's colonial system, and to the legitimacy of the Spanish government itself. Legitimacy was an especially important issue from 1808 to 1813, for both the
United Kingdom and the Spanish, when Napoleon's brother Josef Bonaparte
was sitting on its throne and most of Spain was occupied by French troops.
Most members of the Spanish government had fled, an extraordinary *Cortes*
had eventually been organized on the Island of Leon, and the old Spanish
government had been reformed in Cadiz.

The first *Cortes* debate took place in 1811, after a resolution for the slave
trade's immediate abolition was introduced, and the debate alone resulted
in Cuba's *Cabildo* considering secession from Spain. An 1812 slave revolt in
Cuba was attributed to resultant tensions. Possible abolition was again
raised in the *Cortes* in 1813, but it was promptly dropped because of colonial pressure.

Once European peace was seemingly restored in mid-1814, the United
Kingdom and Spain began the extensive talks that resulted in their 1817
treaty abolishing the Spanish slave trade. The United Kingdom wanted not
only to quickly abolish the slave, but also to retain Spain's friendship and
Cuban stability, and thereby to maintain the position of the United Kingdom
and its empire, including **Jamaica** and other Caribbean islands, by way of
the United States and the Caribbean's revolutionaries. Spain was concerned
that the slave trade was essential to Cuba's economy, and it did not want to
risk a Cuban declaration of independence. Its interests in Argentina and

Chile were under attack by South American revolutionaries, and its interests in the Floridas were questioned by the United States, and it did not want to risk losing the United Kingdom's friendship either—or risk the closing of the U.K. markets to Cuban and Spanish goods.

Finally, on September 23, 1817, after more than three years of back and forth negotiations, Spain and the United Kingdom signed a treaty under which (1) the U.K. paid Spain £400,000 for the declared purpose of compensating it for purported wrongful interference with Spanish-flagged merchant ships over the previous eight years, (2) Spain immediately outlawed Spanish slave-trading north of the equator, and (3) the Spanish slave trade was abolished *in toto* effective May 30, 1820.

The ultimate impetus to reach agreement apparently was a secret clause in a treaty signed by Spain and Russia on August 11, 1817, under which Spain had already agreed to use the £400,000 it was anticipating to receive from the United Kingdom for the purchase of eight warships. Spain hoped to use them to retain and recover its South American colonies.

Other provisions of the 1817 treaty, ratified in early 1818, allowed the Spanish and U.K. navies to search each other's merchant ships if suspected of slaving, and seize them if slaves were found on board. The seizure provision was clarified in a later treaty, signed in 1822, allowing ships to be seized if slaves had previously been on board them during a voyage, to discourage the tossing of slaves into the ocean as patrolling ships approached. Mixed U.K.-Spanish commissions at **Sierra Leone** and **Havana** were to adjudicate ship captures. Captured ships engaged in illegal trading were to be confiscated and sold. Captured slaves were to be emancipated and delivered to the Spanish or U.K. governments to become free laborers or free servants. Convicted individual participants were to be punished with imprisonment for ten years in the Philippines. The latter provision quickly became internal Spanish law under a *cedula* issued in December 1817.

The Spanish slave trade became illegal, worldwide, on October 30, 1820—an extended date agreed on by Spain and the United Kingdom—but that did not mean that it ceased. An illegal Spanish trade continued, and often flourished despite higher per slave sale **prices**, raised to cover the risks and costs of evading the law or bribery. The illegal trade lasted for nearly fifty more years, until the late 1860s, when there was no longer any demand for new African slaves in Puerto Rico, Brazil, the Southern United States, or Cuba. By then, Chinese laborers were being recruited to meet the demand for new labor in Cuba's sugar fields.

Between 1826 and 1867, there were a number of additional agreements and enactments, modifying and supplementing the 1817 treaty for the declared purpose of stopping the illegal trade. A royal *cedula* of 1826 required that logbooks of ships arriving in Cuba from Africa be examined by naval authorities for evidence of slaving, and it offered freedom to any slave who reported a slave landing.

In 1835, a new Spanish government, operating under a new constitution of 1832, agreed to a new treaty allowing ships equipped for slave-trading to be seized, too, thus enabling the interdiction of eastbound Spanish ships en route to Africa, as well as westbound ships returning with slaves. The 1835 treaty further provided for the destruction of captured ships instead of their sale, a term that prompted insurers to stop underwriting Spanish-flagged slave ships, and most Spanish ships to change to Portuguese registration. It added that slaves seized from Spanish slavers were no longer to be turned over to Cuba's colonial government, which had been effectively re-enslaving them, but rather moved to a U.K. ship posted in Havana harbor, the *Romney*, and later distributed to islands in the British West Indies.

In 1845, Spain's *Cortes* enacted its first internal legislation forbidding slave-trading. That legislation provided for the destruction of slave ships and included imprisonment, fines, and internal exile as punishments for convicted slave ship owners, officers, and **crews**. It included, however, provisions added at the behest of Cuban planters that limited prosecutions to cases of slave ships coming directly to Cuba from Africa without stopping elsewhere—stops that could be added—and that denied Cuban law enforcement authorities the right to enter plantations to investigate where their slaves had come from. The latter provision was effectively repealed in 1854, but only briefly, in a quickly withdrawn royal decree providing for the registration of all slaves in Cuba.

In May 1867, when Spanish slave-trading was already at its end, the *Cortes* enacted a second antislave-trading law, criminalizing all direct and indirect actions having anything to do with slave-trading, allowing the prosecution of Spanish subjects found on unregistered slave ships, increasing potential criminal sentences and fines, allowing ordinary criminal courts to hear slave-trading cases, and providing for all slaves in Cuba to be registered. *See also* Abolitionism; Abolition of the Slave Trade, Brazil; Abolition of the Slave Trade, France; Abolition of the Slave Trade, Great Britain; Abolition of the Slave Trade, United States; British Caribbean; British Navy; Closure of the Slave Trade; Drownings; French Caribbean; Haitian Revolution, The; Hispaniola; Illegal Slave Trade, Brazil; Illegal Slave Trade, Spanish Caribbean; Portuguese Slave Trade; Spanish Caribbean.

Further Readings: Bergad, Laird W., Garcia, Fe Iglesias, and del Carmen Barcia, Maria. *The Cuban Slave Market, 1790–1880.* Cambridge: Cambridge University Press, 1995; Corwin, Arthur F. *Spain and the Abolition of Slavery in Cuba, 1817–1886.* Austin: University of Texas Press, 1967; Dorsey, Joseph C. *Slave Traffic in the Age of Abolition: Puerto Rico, West Africa, and the Non-Hispanic Caribbean, 1815–1859.* Gainesville: University Press of Florida, 2003; Du Bois, W.E.B. *The Suppression of the Slave Trade to the United States of America, 1638–1870.* New York: Russell & Russell, 1965; Eltis, David. *Economic Growth and the Ending of the Trans-Atlantic Slave Trade.* New York: Oxford, 1987; Fladeland, Betty. *Men and Brothers: Anglo-American Antislavery Cooperation.* Urbana: University of Illinois Press, 1972; Howard, Warren S. *American Slavers and the Federal Law, 1837–1862.* Berkeley: University of California Press, 1963; Klein, Herbert S. *The Middle Passage: Comparative Studies in the Atlantic Slave Trade.* Princeton, NJ: Princeton University Press, 1978; Marx, Karl, and Engels, Friedrich. *Revolution in Spain.* Honolulu: University Press of the Pacific, 2001; Mathieson, William L. *Great Britain and the Slave Trade, 1839–1865.* London: Longmans, Green and Company, 1929; Mannix, Daniel Pratt, with Cowley, Malcolm. *Black Cargoes: A History of the Atlantic Slave Trade, 1518–1865.* New York: Viking, 1962; Miers, Suzanne. *Britain and the Ending of the Slave Trade.* New York: Africana, 1975; Murray, David. *Odious Commerce: Britain, Spain, and the Abolition of the Cuban Slave Trade.* Cambridge: Cambridge University Press, 1980; Rawley, James A., with Behrendt, Stephen D. *The*

TransAtlantic Slave Trade, A History. Rev. ed. Lincoln: University of Nebraska Press, 2005; Thomas, Hugh. *The Slave Trade: The Story of the Atlantic Slave Trade, 1440–1870.* New York: Simon & Schuster, 1997; Ward, W.E.F. *The Royal Navy and the Slavers: The Suppression of the Atlantic Slave Trade.* New York: Pantheon, 1969.

Steven B. Jacobson

Abolition of the Slave Trade, United States

The idea of abolishing the Atlantic slave trade by the United States was nothing new when it was passed in 1808. Even before a group of Mennonites protested against the traffic of human chattel in 1688, a number of colonists were uncomfortable with the trans-Atlantic slave trade.

There were a number of antislavery ideas in place before 1808 that led to the end of the slave trade. These included religious ideals, including the Quakers, revolutionary antislavery ideas and the rhetoric of the Revolution, private manumission, gradual emancipation, and a number of Congressional and court decrees and ordinances. Furthermore, debates over the status of slavery were going on across the new nation, and its future was very much in question. This debate was especially heated during the Constitutional Convention.

Before the eighteenth century, few people questioned the morality of slavery; however, the Quakers did. The Quaker **religion** holds that all people are equal before God and that all people were created by the same God. Therefore, to the Quakers, enslaving any person is an abhorrence in God's eyes. They became early leaders in what would become the United States antislavery movement. In 1696, they made an official declaration for **abolitionism** in Pennsylvania. By 1775, they founded the first American antislavery group, and throughout the 1700s, they led a movement toward the prohibition of slavery.

George Fox, who founded the Quaker group "Society of Friends," preached against slavery in the late seventeenth century. Some Quakers, however, did own slaves. Eventually, that group became extremely small in number, and the group united behind the opposition to slavery. In 1780, Quakers in Pennsylvania passed "An Act for the Gradual Abolishment of Slavery." Quaker writers such as **Anthony Benezet** wrote pamphlets that urged the government to outlaw slavery, and his work was noticed by the likes of Benjamin Franklin and Benjamin Rush. In 1787, Franklin and Rush led the Pennsylvania Society for Promoting the Abolition of Slavery. Other states abolished slave importations as well, including South Carolina.

By far the largest obstacle in ending the Atlantic slave trade was the debate over the Constitution for the new United States of America. The delegates to the Constitutional Convention knew that any provision ending slavery or the slave trade would be a nail in the coffin for those trying to get the Constitution ratified. After much debate, it was decided to table the issue until 1808, which was decided as the earliest possible date to abolish the trade. The Constitution did not foresee a ban on interstate slave-trading and left that decision up to the states. Nor did the Constitution consider the eventual termination of domestic slavery, because this would have sent half of the delegates to the convention home. The federal government did prohibit the slave trade in the District of Columbia and set **regulations** regarding the size of ships used in coastal trading.

The trans-Atlantic slave trade was something the delegates to the Constitutional Convention were willing to discuss. The majority of delegates wished to ban the traffic either immediately or after a few years. Some states, such as Georgia, however, were inflexible. The southernmost states of the union threatened that they would reject the Constitution if it ended the slave trade. The twenty-year prohibition on federal action was the best that could be achieved while keeping most states happy.

Most northern states voluntarily abolished slavery by 1804. Some states abolished slavery immediately following the Revolutionary War, but others, like New York and New Jersey, passed gradual emancipation laws, which freed slaves after a certain period of time or when slaves reached a given age (usually in their twenties). The British had outlawed the slave trade in 1807. Even after the federal prohibition of the Atlantic slave trade on January 1, 1808, slave importation continued as **smugglers** continued their operations illegally. *See also* Abolition of the Slave Trade, Brazil; Abolition of the Slave Trade, France; Abolition of the Slave Trade, Great Britain; Abolition of the Slave Trade, Spain; Closure of the Slave Trade; Humanitarianism; Internal Slave Trade, United States; Liberia.

Further Readings: Jordan, Winthrop. *White over Black: American Attitudes toward the Negro, 1550–1812.* Chapel Hill: University of North Carolina Press, 1968; Kolchin, Peter. *American Slavery, 1619–1877.* New York: Hill and Wang, 2003; Thornton, John. *Africa and Africans in the Making of the Atlantic World, 1400–1800.* 2nd ed. Cambridge: Cambridge University Press, 1998.

James E. Seelye, Jr.

Accidents and Explosions

The trans-Atlantic slave trade like all other types of maritime trade was exposed to series of accidents during the period from 1500 to 1800. Accidents were occasionally caused by the unfavorable weather that caused **shipwrecks**. In some cases, accidents were the result of attacks between one European vessel and another. Accidents and explosions also occurred as a result of slave mutinies during the Middle Passage.

Occasionally, shipwrecks occurred along the **Slave Coast** before and during the trans-Atlantic voyage. Sometimes, ships wrecked because of unfavorable **storms** and weather. Shipwrecks also occurred after slave ships had been attacked by pirates. A wrecked ship lost all of its slaves and supplies. The activities of pirates were traditionally connected with national rivalries in which one European nation blamed another for employing pirates to attack its ship. In a bid to guard against pirates, slave ships were fortified with guns and muskets.

Slave revolts or mutinies were common during the Atlantic voyage. Although equipped with guns and other ammunition, in some cases, the **crew** of a slave ship could not prevent a slave mutiny during the Middle

Passage. During a slave mutiny, a ferocious confrontation led to the seizure of the ship by the slaves. Slaves who survived the confrontation with the crew automatically became free. One interesting and provocative story is worth narrating. On June 1, 1730, Captain George Scott of the sloop *Little George* sailed from the Guinea Coast with a **cargo** of ninety slaves, thirty of whom were men. Six days into the voyage, the slaves slipped out of the shackles. Breaking through the bulkhead, they gained the deck, where they were confronted by the crew. Frightened, the captain, three men, and a boy sought refuge in the cabin below and were promptly imprisoned by the slaves. One of the sailors tried to fire a bomb by filling two bottles with **gunpowder**. The sailor's plan was uncovered by a slave who dropped an axe on the bottle just as the sailor lit the fuse. The explosion set a fire to a keg of gunpowder, blew and opened the door, raised the deck, discharged all except one musket, and seriously injured both the captain and the bombmaker. This episode is just one of the numerous such events that took place throughout the period from about 1500 to the mid-1800s.

Bombing of forts and vessels were common features of the European slave trade in Africa. Europeans sometimes transferred their continental aggression to Africa. During the Seven Years' War (1756–1763), European nations notably France and Britain were involved in series of attack on each other's ships along the West Africa coastal waters. The mid-nineteenth century might be regarded as the period that experienced the highest degree of coastal bombing. Britain, in her bid to force Africans and her European counterparts to stop the slave trade, frequently attacked slave ships and set the captives free. Cannon were positioned along the West African coast to force African merchants and governments to stop the slave trade. The breakdown of negotiations to stop the slave trade and some complex politically and economically driven motives led to the British bombardment of **Lagos** in 1851 and to the attack on several coastal communities in the Delta region. *See also Guerrero,* The; *Henrietta Marie,* The; Key West African Cemetery.

Further Readings: Greene, Lorenzo. "Mutiny on the Slave Ship." *Phyton* 5, 4 (1944): 346–354; Inikori, J. E., ed. *Forced Migration: The Impact of the Export Slave Trade on African Societies.* London: Hutchinson University Library for Africa, 1982; Palmie, Stephan, ed. *Slave Cultures and the Cultures of Slavery.* Knoxville: University of Tennessee Press, 1995.

Saheed Aderinto

Accra

During the Atlantic slave trade, Accra was a town on the eastern **Gold Coast** (present-day Ghana) where the Dutch, English, and Danish trading companies maintained permanent **trade forts**. Accra was the headquarters of Denmark's slave trade in Africa. The main Danish fort at Accra, now known as Christiansborg Castle, was initially built in the 1660s to protect Danish interests in purchasing West African gold in nearby coastal markets. During the eighteenth century, that early fort was expanded to include slave dungeons, coinciding with Denmark's growing interest in buying enslaved

Africans to ship to its colony in the Caribbean, St. Thomas. Three smaller Danish forts were also used for Denmark's slave trade at Accra.

The greater Accra area is home to the Ga ethnic group who formed the Ga kingdom in the late seventeenth century. The traditional economy of the Ga was lagoon fishing and salt-making. Both fish and salt were traded with neighboring communities to the north. **Textiles** and other goods imported by European traders expanded the scale of Ga trade from the seventeenth century. The Ga were conquered and lived under the foreign rule of the more militarily powerful African states of Akyem, Akwamu, and **Asante** between the 1680s and 1820s.

Between 1744 and the 1820s, Accra was a subject territory of the Asante Empire. During this time, the road from the Asante capital to Accra was the main artery of trade between Asante and Europeans on the coast. Accra became the principal market for Asante to import guns, ammunition, and other goods that were essential to the maintenance and expansion of Asante rule in the interior. The Asante invasion initially destroyed parts of Accra, but eventually it improved the city's commercial potential. Many Ga merchants functioned as intermediaries in the trade between Asante and European merchants. The increased trans-Atlantic commerce at Accra in the second half of the eighteenth century enriched the lives of many Accra families.

After colonizing the Gold Coast, Great Britain established its colonial capital at Accra. Since Ghana's independence in 1957, Accra has been that nation's capital city. Accra now has a population of more than two million people. It is the center of business, commerce, and higher education in Ghana. Christiansborg Castle, the former Danish trade fort, is currently used as the seat of government in Ghana. *See also* Asante; Danish Slave Trade.

Further Readings: Fynn, John Kofi. *Asante and Its Neighbors.* Evanston: Northwestern University Press, 1971; Ghana Castle Web site: www.ghanacastle.gov.gh; Hernæs, Per O. *Slaves, Danes and African Coast Society: The Danish Slave Trade from West Africa and Afro-Danish Relations on the Eighteenth-Century Gold Coast.* Trondheim: Norwegian University of Science and Technology, 1995; Van Dantzig, Albert. *Forts and Castles of Ghana.* Accra: Sedco Publishing, 1980.

Rebecca Shumway

Adanggaman (2000)

Directed by Roger Gnoan M'bala, *Adanggaman*, which premiered at the 2000 Venice Film Festival and later in North America at the 2000 Toronto Film Festival, resulted from the international collaboration of the Ivory Coast filmmaker with screenwriters Jean-Marie Adlaffi and Bertin Akaffou. It is a significant irony that the internationally produced film generated no small amount of controversy as a result of its unrelenting depiction of an aspect seldom shown in the contemporary consideration: the history of slavery within Africa's borders. Taking as its subject the **enslavement** and exploitation of Africans by other Africans, *Adanggaman* also marked a return to the subject of slavery, which, as scholarly critics such as Françoise Pfaff point out, has typically been an infrequent subject of consideration in

African cinema. The film is often credited as the first in African cinema to treat this particular historical dimension.

The events of *Adanggaman* take place during the late seventeenth century in West Africa and center on intertribal conflicts instigated and exploited by the titular king, Rasmane Ouedraogo, a powerful despot whose collaborations with European traders—personages who film critic Ken Fox astutely notes are conspicuously never seen—fulfill his selfish appetites as well as increase his dominance over rival groups. Aided by an elite troop of fierce female warriors, Adanggaman conquers nearby populations, capturing and enslaving his neighbors and killing those deemed less useful to him. The village of the film's protagonist, the prodigal Ossei (Ziable Honore Goore Bi), is attacked and, of his loved ones, only his mother Mo Akassi (Albertine N'Guessan) remains alive, although enslaved. In his efforts to rescue her he, too, is captured. Throughout his struggle to free himself and his mother, the film depicts various configurations of inhumane bondage and **violence** inflicted on Africans by other Africans.

The scenes portraying these events are harrowing; critic and scholar Mbye Cham, in his analysis of the film, isolates the persistent use of extended shots during scenes of Africans brutalizing and exploiting other Africans as one of the film's most affecting visual strategies, refusing the viewer any easy opportunity to look away. Although some critics argued that *Adanggaman*'s depiction of Africans enslaving Africans might diffuse critical attention to the role of Europeans in the trafficking of slaves, the film is perhaps better understood as a work of historical fiction that emphasizes the capriciousness of slavery in all its forms. By presenting haunting images in which the oppressor and oppressed cannot be easily distinguished through racial dichotomies, *Adanggaman* provides a painful, unique glimpse of a past that many would long to forget at a time when such arbitrary violence continues in many corners of the world. *See also* African Rulers and the Slave Trade; Historical Memory; Slavery in Africa.

Further Readings: Cham, Mbye. "Film and History in Africa." In Pfaff, Françoise, ed. *Focus on African Films.* Bloomington: Indiana University Press, 2004; Fox, Ken. "Cry Freedom." [Online, February 14, 2006]. TV Guide Web site: http://online.tvguide.com/movies/database/showmovie.asp?MI=43049; Guglar, Josef. *African Film: Re-Imagining a Continent.* Bloomington: Indiana University Press, 2003; M'bala, Roger Gnoan, dir. *Adanggaman.* Produced internationally in Ivory Coast, France, Burkina Faso, and Switzerland and distributed in the United States by New Yorker Films, 2000; Mitchell, Elvis. "Africans Making Slaves of Africans." *New York Times,* July 11, 2001. [Online, February 7, 2006]. *New York Times* Web site: http://query.nytimes.com/gst/fullpage.html?res=9C02EED-C1E38F932A25754C 0A9679C8B63; Pfaff, Françoise. "Introduction." In Pfaff, Françoise, ed. *Focus on African Films.* Bloomington: Indiana University Press, 2004.

Ilya T. Wick

African Fears of Cannibalism

The fear of cannibalism was an important element of the slave experience on both sides of the Atlantic and during the terrifying journey of the Middle Passage. Especially in the later years of the slave trade, rumors of the cannibalistic urges of the white colonial intruders were widespread throughout the coastal regions of Africa. The slave ship itself, into which African bodies disappeared, came to be a potent symbol of death and consumption. Travel **narratives** and ship logs suggest that **slave traders** were well aware of the terror that their alleged cannibal tendencies produced in the imaginations of their **cargo**, and consequently they did little to discourage the rumors. For example, the eighteenth-century narrative of freedman **Olaudah Equiano** suggests that, in some cases, whites played on African fears for their own amusement and as part of a larger discourse of control.

Upon arrival in the New World, Africans were presented with a new group of alleged cannibals, the indigenous peoples of the Americas. Colonial actors purposely disseminated tales of the fierce, flesh-eating Indian to discourage African slaves from fleeing the **plantations**. Cannibalistic practices were reported among the Tupi peoples of **Brazil**, but it was in the Caribbean that the practice received the most attention. The Carib, from whom the term cannibal is etymologically derived, were accused of engaging in anthropophagy dating from the time of Columbus's first voyage. This led to a decree by the Spanish crown that allowed for the **enslavement** of all of the indigenous groups thought to be cannibals. The degree to which these speculations and accusations were believed by Africans is unclear, but what is certain is that the theme of cannibalism, real or imagined, had emerged as a master trope in the ongoing dialogue over control and domination in the colonial world. It became one of the most widespread and effective ways of dehumanizing non-European peoples and it discouraged potentially subversive alliances between Indians and Africans. Cannibalism became strongly linked to savagery and therefore was used to justify the violent exploitation of African and indigenous peoples by Europeans.

The question of whether or not African fears of cannibalism were well-founded remains a highly contested one. Scholarship today is somewhat conflicted over the extent to which cannibalism actually occurred, because it certainly served as an ideological tool. Most scholars accept that the extent and nature of cannibalism were distorted and exaggerated by the colonial powers to justify the abusive treatment of enslaved populations.

Further Readings: Baker, Francis, Hulme, Peter, and Iverson, Margaret, eds. *Cannibalism and the Colonial World.* Cambridge: Cambridge University Press, 1998; Rice, Alan. *Radical Narratives of the Black Atlantic.* New York: Continuum, 2003.

Erika M. Robb

African Institution

In 1807, Britain abolished the slave trade in its colonies. Hailed by abolitionists as a great feat, this event nonetheless raised further questions, such as how the antislavery movement should now progress. There were many possibilities, such as introducing bills for emancipation into Parliament, pushing for more direct intervention into Africa to cut off the slave trade at its roots, or perhaps establishing a naval blockade in West Africa to stop slave ships. British abolitionists could exert moral pressure, with or without their government's approval, on countries still slaving, hoping to convince them to stop the trade. In this environment, discussions began about a new antislavery organization that would pick up the crusade from now-defunct groups, such as the Abolition Committee. The result of these discussions was the African Institution.

The first organizational meeting of the African Institution was held in July 1807. The leadership of the new group included virtually all of the important antislavery figures, such as **William Wilberforce**, Thomas Clarkson, Zachary Macaulay, Granville Sharp, William Allen, and others. Most of the group's purpose and plans were laid out at this meeting and were presented thereafter at the first public meeting of the group. The members present at this first meeting resolved to do what they could to promote Africa's well-being, determined to spread practical information throughout Africa and to circulate throughout Britain information about Africa's agricultural and commercial prospects. Thus, the idea of so-called **legitimate commerce** was already an issue for abolitionists.

It was naive to expect, as most abolitionists did, that the abolition of Britain's slave trade would naturally be followed by a period of "development" and "civilization" in Africa, but the process of examining a potential trade relationship between Africa and Britain was reasonable. Before legitimate commerce (as non-slave-based trade was called) could flourish, Britons needed to know "what was there." As long as slaving was a legal enterprise, there would be little economic incentive for European and American businessmen to foster any economic development within Africa.

Over the next few years, the group's focus began to change and expand. Exploiting their personal connections with Britain's top politicians, members of the African Institution managed to keep antislavery issues on (or close to) the front burner. From the beginning, however, the group was handicapped by a lack of financial resources. Although many wealthy people contributed to the organization, it simply never commanded the kind of fiscal power necessary to carry out its most ambitious plans. The African Institution wished to promote Western education in Africa, but it could barely afford to send books and could not afford to support its few teachers for long. To encourage British interest in African products, the African Institution hoped to facilitate the cultivation of certain cash crops (such as hemp for rope, cotton, rice, and so on) that would demonstrate Africa's potential. The group offered incentives to those who imported African products, but the quantities imported were insignificant. In addition, few people even took the group up on its offer.

Early on, the organization realized that key to the success of its goals was enforcement of Britain's antislavery laws, as well as those passed by foreign countries. The African Institution exerted considerable influence on its own government on African-related issues, but it was obviously infinitely trickier for the group to pressure foreign governments. Nonetheless, foreign slave-trading became a major issue for the organization and for Britain. At the Congresses of Vienna, Aix-la-Chapelle, and Verona, the group kept British diplomats "on task" in pursuing the issue with other countries and kept their diplomats well supplied with relevant antislavery literature. Some minor successes can in fact be traced to the group's diligence, as other European powers slowly abandoned their slave trades and set up joint admiralty courts to try those accused of illegal slaving.

The efforts of the African Institution in terms of African development were most noticeable in **Sierra Leone**. In a real sense, Sierra Leone provided a true testing ground for development schemes and programs. Slaves freed from seized slave ships usually landed in Sierra Leone, providing a regular influx of new settlers, and the African Institution virtually selected the first several governors of the colony after it came under crown control in 1807. The group corresponded regularly with these governors, sending school supplies and books when possible. As with other matters, the attention given Sierra Leone by the African Institution meant that the British government would follow developments there carefully. The colony was fairly stable and economically viable by the late 1820s, but how much credit the African Institution deserves is debatable (although their lack of effort is not).

The abolitionists envisioned a Sierra Leone that was based on the individual farmer, working independently on small farms. These free farmers would form the basis of a successful agricultural economy. Key to the success of this idea was the regular arrival of new settlers. Were the government to sponsor a mass transportation of free blacks from the Western Hemisphere, the hopes of the reformers might become reality. This would have surely helped the colony, but there were no such plans. A free black American named Paul Cuffe, however, was willing to lead such expeditions and had lined up prospective colonists. The African Institution supported Cuffe as much as they possibly could, continually trying to intervene on his behalf to make his efforts more fruitful and easier to complete. Ultimately, Cuffe did bring thirty-four immigrants, but the War of 1812 and Cuffe's death in 1817 prevented any further similar projects.

After Cuffe's failure to settle more than a handful of new residents in Sierra Leone, the African Institution turned increasingly from a group that attempted practical activities, such as colonization and agricultural projects, into a body that fought mainly political battles against the injustices of slavery and later against the institution of slavery itself. Along these lines, group members began closely monitoring slave conditions in the West Indies, advocating the creation of slave registries in all of the West Indian colonies. Abolitionists believed that these registries would help not only improve the condition of slaves indirectly, but also stop illegal slave importing. The African Institution began gathering information on slave-trading in East Africa and the **Indian Ocean**. Antislavery supporters had never paid much attention to these areas, and the group was the first to tackle the problem. The group continued a detailed correspondence with Henri Christophe, Haiti's first and only black king. Political realities prevented the British government from recognizing Christophe as a legitimate ruler, but the African Institution provided moral support and even arranged for several teachers to go to Haiti. Christophe's success would have been a sizable boost to the abolitionist agenda—a successful, independent black king ruling his own territory in an "enlightened" fashion—but Christophe was overthrown and murdered in 1820.

What emerges from any reasonable analysis of the African Institution is a picture of a group whose primary goals were left, at best, only partly fulfilled. The group's personal connections with the government did not ensure that all of its plans would be carried out, but they did allow the group to make its agenda part of national planning and international concern. The African Institution was the premier national British antislavery group from 1807 to 1823, when its role was increasingly played by the new Antislavery Society. The African Institution came to an end in 1827, after carrying (alone) the antislavery banner for nearly two decades and spawning a new generation of antislavery agitators. *See also* Abolitionism; Abolition of the Slave Trade, Great Britain; African Squadrons, The; British Navy; British Slave Trade; Closure of the Slave Trade; Humanitarianism.

Further Readings: Ackerson, Wayne. *The African Institution (1807–1827) and the Antislavery Movement in Great Britain.* Ceredigion, United Kingdom: Mellen Press, 2005; Davis, David Brion. *The Problem of Slavery in the Age of Revolution, 1770–1823.* New York: Oxford University Press, 1999; Temperley, Howard. *British Antislavery, 1833–1870.* Columbia: University of South Carolina Press, 1972.

Wayne Ackerson

African Rulers and the Slave Trade

When the Portuguese began exploring the coast of Africa in the fifteenth century, African rulers already participated in the internal African slave trade. Long before the arrival of Portuguese explorers and traders, African pastoralists living in Central and Western Sudan engaged slaves to increase the cultivation of crops and to provide domestic service. In West Africa, slaves represented a large section of the population and slaves could attain positions of importance in the royal household or could serve as advisors to African rulers. Overall, European **slave traders** rarely traveled into Africa's interior for the purpose of capturing their human **cargo**. Slavers depended on African rulers to provide captives to feed the slave trade. From the beginning of the external slave trade, African rulers attempted to control the trade by limiting slave markets to commercial centers. A captive of war or kidnapping might be ransomed, but more often than not, captives were sold to merchants or soldiers handed their captives over to their king. Because local African governments obtained slaves through wars, raids, kidnapping, and tribute collection, these same African rulers would also supply slaves to the coast for sale to the European slavers.

Long before the arrival of Europeans along the West African coast, slavery had become fully integrated into African society, and Western society accepted the practice of slavery. The early slave trade in Africa lacks detailed descriptions because of an absence of detailed studies and a lack of evidence; however, Africans engaged in slavery and a slave trade before the development of the Atlantic slave-trading system. The Portuguese first sailed down the coast of Africa searching for gold, but they soon learned they could also offer shipping services for which they would be paid in gold. Portuguese sailors and merchants exchanged cloth and horses from Morocco along with metals (copper and brass) from Europe for beads, pepper, and slaves. The pepper could be sold in Europe, but the Portuguese sold the beads and slaves on the **Gold Coast** in exchange for gold. The first slaves purchased by Portuguese traders were sold to other Africans. Once the demand for labor increased on the **plantations** in the Caribbean and the Americas, Portuguese slavers no longer sold slaves to Africans.

The definition of slavery varied across the multiple societies that kept human beings in bondage. The West considered slaves property to be bought and sold similar to livestock or other property, but African society demonstrated a more complex definition of slavery. African society contained a number of social and economic disparities that could be considered slavery. African rulers held war captives in bondage who were expected to work in agriculture, mining, and other arduous tasks. For various other reasons, individuals could be bonded to a particular ruler or society. People agreed to become slaves to pay a debt or for protection. In time of famine, parents would sell children for **food**, thus ensuring that their children would be fed. Some slaves were criminals, kidnapping victims, concubines, or slave soldiers. Whatever their method, the slave-owning society considered these slaves as outsiders, almost as nonpeople. Over time, outsiders could become absorbed into the local community through marriage or service. By the 1400s, slavery had become quite common, but slaves were divided into hierarchical groups with clear distinctions between domestic slaves who could not be sold and slaves who had been captured in war or purchased. Although most slaves were female, free women often used and owned slaves.

In some instances, African rulers amassed vast amounts of slaves and depended on the use of slaves to expand agricultural production. In the Central Sudan region, Kutumbi, the leader of the Kano in the first half of the seventeenth century, developed his well-known reputation as a slaver by capturing thousands of slaves. Kutumbi settled several hundred of his own slaves near Kano. Relying on captives, one of Kutumbi's generals built his headquarters and sent another 2,000 slaves to Kano. In some cases, slaves were used by African rulers as militia for defensive purposes. Further east, captives were settled around the capital of the Sultanate of Sennar by Badi II as farmers; these slaves also provided military support in case of foreign invasion. These slave-farmers provided little military opposition to the well-armed and well-trained armies of the other states in the Sudan. Although not much use militarily, Badi II valued the slaves for their agricultural production that would feed his armies. During the eighteenth century, the Sultans of Dar Fur employed slaves on agricultural settlements adjacent to their capital. In addition to producing food, slaves could be employed to produce other manufactured goods. Some Dar Fur aristocrats could have as many as 600 slaves working within their domain.

In addition to West Africa and Central Africa, East Africa developed an extensive trade in ivory and slaves. Because East African ivory was less brittle and held its color longer than Indian ivory, **Muslim** merchants became interested in obtaining ivory for shipment to India. Along with the ivory, slaves were purchased and sent to India, Arabia, and the Persian Gulf. Muslim merchants joined with African leaders—for example, Mirambo of

Nyamwezi—in opening trade routes, establishing states, and returning large quantities of ivory and slaves. Mirambo began by hiring Ngoni mercenaries and later adding war captives, escaped slaves, and deserters, forming them into an armed militia. Mirambo and his army successfully operated during the age of the slave trade, and his mercenary armies were linked with other chiefs to form a single state in southern Tanzania, eastern Zambia, and Malawi.

With the arrival of Europeans, particularly the Portuguese, the **internal slave trade** changed as the external slave trade developed. Local African laws required the payment of a fine for legal transgressions, but as the external demand for slaves increased, African rulers imprisoned convicted criminals who would later be sold as slaves to Europeans. Although the sources of slaves varied, many of the slaves sold on the coast were prisoners, the result of local wars fought to establish new African states or to expand states in the African interior.

The Muslim Fulbe of Futa Jalon created a new state by waging war against their neighbors, creating an abundant supply of war captives who could be sold into slavery. The rulers of Oyo, **Dahomey**, and **Asante** engaged in political wars of expansion, becoming powerful African states. As a rule, African leaders infrequently sold their own subjects into slavery, but they also knew the handsome **price** that European slavers offered could make them quite wealthy. Local territorial conflicts produced a steady and abundant supply of human commodities.

Located west of where the Niger River empties into the Atlantic Ocean, the Bight of Benin became one of the major slave-exporting regions of West Africa. Beginning slowly, the export of slaves grew to enormous heights surpassing the Portuguese-controlled region around **Luanda**, earning the Bight of Benin the moniker the **Slave Coast**. The export slave trade became the first state **monopoly** controlled by the Oyo. Increased hostile conflict, which led to many new war captives, accounts for the major upsurge in the **enslavement** of numerous people from the interior of Africa. Several wars instigated by the Yoruba kingdom of Oyo against the coastal towns of Ardrah, Whydah, Porto Novo, and **Lagos** resulted in increased numbers of people indentured for the slave trade. Also located inland, the Dahomey raided further north, obtaining captives for sale in the coastal trade, and challenged Oyo and the coastal towns for dominance of the trade with the Europeans. Oyo eventually forced Dahomey to pay tribute, but hostilities between Oyo, Dahomey, and the coastal towns continued producing combat prisoners who served as human commodities fueling the slave export business. Examining various regions of Africa suggests that African rulers conducted trade based on local conditions. The Slave Coast experienced little European contact depending on the closeness of European ships to the coastal towns and the activities of Muslim traders. African leaders dealt with Muslim traders who brought slaves and other trade goods from the interior to the coast through an interregional trading system. Developments within the Slave Coast trading system hinged on political centralization. The rulers of the Oyo and Dahomey kingdoms created stronger centralized governments because of their dealings with other nations to the north and the necessity to maintain control over their own territory. African rulers understood that maintaining the military readiness necessary to acquire new captives and to defend itself required an organization and a bureaucracy to regulate European trade. Traveling west from the Slave Coast, seventeenth- and eighteenth-century traders would land in the towns of **Accra**, Winneba, Cape Coast, or **Elmina** along an area that Europeans called the "Gold Coast." In terms of the slave trade, the Gold Coast never reached the significance of the Slave Coast, but Europeans still landed there because of the area's reputation as a source of gold. Although not a major source of slaves, political strife among the Akan resulted in a supply of captives. The Asante rulers and their armies successfully subdued several smaller states and took control of the Gold Coast. In the second half of the eighteenth century, the Akan wars resulted in approximately 150,000 slaves. Taken as a whole, the Gold Coast mirrored the Slave Coast. Few European traders traveled inland, and African leaders and the newly formed centralized African states restricted European trade to a few coastal towns. To the east of the Niger Delta, in the Bight of Biafra, another area emerged where African leaders participated in the slave trade. Because of its mangrove swamps, the coast along the Bight of Biafra developed later than the Gold Coast or Slave Coast as a source of slaves. By the late 1670s, the towns of Aboh, **Bonny**, and Elem Kalabari were noted depots of the slave trade, but the major economic expansion in the Bight of Biafra occurred later in the eighteenth century. The coastline proved to be inhospitable even to the heartiest slavers, leading to a sparse presence of Europeans. The minimal Muslim influence demonstrates the difficulty in conducting trade on the swampy coast. Because of the harsh terrain, the strong centralized governments that emerged within the areas around the Slave Coast and Gold Coast rarely materialized along the Bight of Biafra. As a result, the slave trade developed a different character. Instead of prolonged warfare, including punitive reprisals, raids, and tribute payments, local village leaders organized and conducted slave raids and kidnapping expeditions against neighboring villages bringing captives to the coast in canoes down the winding delta tributaries. Although the Bight of Biafra never reached the same level of slave exports in the eighteenth century as the Slave Coast, it has the distinction of surpassing all other West African regions.

The Fulbe of Futa Jalon and along the coast in the Gulf of Guinea, the centralized monarchies of the Asante, Dahomey, and Oyo accumulated large amounts of state-owned slaves through repeated, extended wars. Because these confrontations between kingdoms vying for control of the slave trade often decided the economic and political stability of the region, African leaders often chose to execute their enemies and turncoats as part of their victory. Although African leaders transported large amounts of captives to the coast, African rulers curtailed the removal of people within their own kingdoms. The Asante on the Gold Coast ended the mass removal of local people to the coast, and once the Oyo became dominant along the Bight of Benin, they prevented the export of slaves from within their own boarders. Once the Oyo Empire lost its strong grip, exports of Yoruba slaves increased.

Slavery and the slave trade needed the support and protection of the centralized government to survive, expand, and produce immediate short-term wealth. The political authorities ensured property rights for slave owners and traders. Governments protected the transportation of slaves and the slave markets, making **escape** or rescue difficult. Government **regulation** and involvement in the trade, however, did not translate into ownership of all slaves. For example, the kings of Asante and Dahomey exercised rights over all slaves within their kingdoms, but they did not own all slaves. Government interest in the capture, transportation, and sale of slaves resulted in the establishment of laws and regulations governing the trade. Regulations required the payment of a variety of fees, duties, and other charges. African states imposed monetary charges on traders for anchorage, wood, and water. Depending on the level of control African rulers exercised over commercial activities, traders may have been required to pay for brokers, interpreters, and other services. Beginning with the Portuguese, traders built several forts along the coast of Africa, with Elmina on the Gold Coast being the most notable. These forts served as trading depots during the slave trade while others doubled as protection against **interlopers**. None of these forts would have lasted without the permission of the local African ruler or community. The occupier of the fort paid **taxes** and obtained provisions from the surrounding villages. These forts were useful in making available the interior trading routes and contact with slavers and merchants.

Moving from codifying slavery and the slave trade into law, it was a short step to making slavery a social institution that could be passed to future generations as part of African social tradition. Many African states grew and prospered from their capability to control the slave trade. With government involvement, the law, a new social tradition, and the increased external demand for slaves, African rulers appeared more than willing to exchange their greatest asset, young men and **women**, for money. *See also* Decentralized Societies; Ethnicity; Garcia II of Kongo; Slavery in Africa; Trans-Saharan Slave Trade.

Further Readings: July, Robert W. *A History of the African People.* 5th ed. Prospect Heights, IL: Waveland Press, 1998; Curtin, Philip, Feierman, Steven, Thompson, Leonard, and Vansina, Jan. *African History.* Boston: Little, Brown, 1978; Davidson, Basil. *The African Slave Trade.* Rev. ed. Boston: Little, Brown, 1980; Klein, Herbert S. *The Atlantic Slave Trade.* New York and Cambridge: Cambridge University Press, 1999; Lovejoy, Paul E. *Transformations in Slavery: A History of Slavery in Africa.* New York and Cambridge: Cambridge University Press, 1993; Manning, Patrick. *Slavery and African Life: Occidental, Oriental, and African Slave Trades.* African Studies Series, ed. J. M. Lonsdale. Cambridge: Cambridge University Press, 2000; Shillington, Kevin. *History of Africa.* 2nd ed. New York: Palgrave Macmillan, 2005.

Michael Bonislawski

African Squadrons, The

Four independently operating African Squadrons of the United Kingdom, United States, French, and Portuguese navies patrolled the West African coast at various times between 1819 and 1870. The African Squadrons, and smaller naval units before them, were part of efforts by those nations to enforce—or create the appearance of enforcing—their own antislave-trading laws, as well as any international antislave-trading treaties to which they were parties.

The United Kingdom was the world's leading naval power after the Battle of Trafalgar in 1805, and its Royal Navy retained its leading position throughout the nineteenth century. The Royal Navy's African Squadron was the first to be sent to the West African coast, and it was the largest, most significant, and last to be brought back. The U.S., French, and Portuguese African Squadrons came later, were smaller, captured fewer ships and slaves, and were withdrawn earlier.

A combination of measures enacted by Parliament in 1806 and 1807 had prohibited U.K. subjects—individuals, business entities, and ships flying its flag—from participating in the slave trade after April 30, 1807. In 1808, to set the stage for that prohibition's active enforcement, the United Kingdom sent two Royal Navy ships on an exploratory cruise of the West African coast, even as the United Kingdom's ongoing wars with Napoleon continued. Five other Royal Navy ships were sent to the West African coast in 1811, after the United Kingdom had begun to acquire treaty rights to board other nations' ships to halt slaving. The ships sent in 1811 succeeded in capturing a number of slave ships and their slave **cargoes** between 1811 and 1813.

Other Royal Navy ships were sent to patrol the West African coast beginning in late 1815, once they were no longer needed for the Napoleonic Wars and the War of 1812. An official Royal Navy West African Squadron was established in 1819 and remained on duty until 1870, when it was clear that the trans-Atlantic slave trade had ended. The Royal Navy had three ships assigned to West Africa by 1816, seven by 1819, ten by 1827, and nineteen by 1839. Its West African Squadron ranged from thirteen to thirty-six ships between 1840 and 1860, the numbers being reduced when the United Kingdom was involved in conflicts elsewhere (for example, China, the Crimea, and India), and averaged twenty ships in the 1860s before being withdrawn.

The Royal Navy's patrols, which eventually expanded to officially include the African coast from **Cape Verde** (latitude 14°40' north) to Cape Frio (latitude 18° south), were at first concentrated on the 2,000 miles of coastline from the Isles de Los (latitude 9° north) to the Gabon estuary (at the equator). The slave trade further north was largely French, the slave trade further south was largely Portuguese, and neither trades were initially covered by antislave-trading treaties. The United Kingdom's patrols were later expanded southward, after Brazilian independence created grounds to assert that earlier understandings allowing the southern Portuguese trade to continue no longer applied.

At first the Royal Navy's tasks were to sail along the West African coast, capture slave ships and people enslaved in violation of laws or treaties, and bring the captured ships and slaves before an appropriate tribunal, usually at Freetown in **Sierra Leone**. Those tasks were quickly expanded to include searches up West Africa's coastal creeks, where slave-selling factors and slave-buying traders moved in to conceal their trafficking. The Royal

Navy later negotiated with African kings and chiefs to obtain treaties—sometimes negotiated at gunpoint and often ignored after being executed—promising that they would stop trading slaves. To aid disputants willing to sign such treaties, it interjected itself into African political and succession contests.

The Royal Navy's West African duty was generally regarded as unpleasant and unhealthy, so unhealthy that, although the effects of malaria-carrying mosquitoes were then unknown, it issued orders that **crew** members not be allowed to stay onshore overnight. It was difficult duty and sometimes dangerous. Onshore slavers could be heavily armed, and some **slave traders** soon began using fast and heavily armed vessels capable of outrunning and outgunning the Royal Navy's ships.

The much smaller U.S. Navy was the next to begin antislave-trading African patrols. It sent five vessels out in 1820 and 1821, which interdicted at least eleven slave ships before returning home, and it occasionally sent out others over the next twenty-two years. The United States created its permanent African Squadron in 1843 to implement the provisions of the Webster-Ashburton Treaty (1842). Under this treaty, the United Kingdom and United States not only agreed on the boundary between the United States and Canada, but also promised to maintain independent naval squadrons along the African coast to enforce their own laws and treaty obligations for the slave trade's suppression.

The U.S. Navy's African Squadron was small. Between 1843 and 1859, it consisted of between two and seven ships. The entire U.S. Navy had only twenty-five to thirty ships. Because of health and supply concerns, the U.S. squadron was based in the Cape Verde islands, nearly 1,000 miles from West Africa's principal slave-trading area.

The U.S. squadron was created largely in the hopes of stopping Royal Navy interference with U.S. merchant ships. Its first commander's orders were to stop abuse of the American flag and assert American rights. In fact, the Royal Navy's practice of boarding American merchant ships during the Napoleonic Wars was one of the causes of the War of 1812.

The U.S. Navy's African Squadron was most productive in 1860 and 1861, when it grew as part of an increase in the overall size of the Navy under 1858 legislation. The squadron returned to the states once the Civil War began in 1861, so that its ships could be used to blockade Confederate ports. In 1862, while the Civil War raged, the United States agreed for the first time that the Royal Navy's African Squadron could board suspicious-looking American ships to search for slaves.

The first French West African Squadron was in place by 1825 and operated through 1831. There were comparatively few antislave-trading tasks for the French Navy after that, because there were few French-flagged slavers after France's 1830 revolution. France had not negotiated treaties with other countries (other than the United Kingdom) authorizing the French Navy to search their ships for slaves.

Another, small French squadron (two to six ships) was sent to patrol West Africa's coast after France signed an 1833 convention with the United Kingdom. The new French squadron's size was increased to fourteen ships in 1842, largely to counter the Royal Navy's allegedly improper interference with French merchants, under the guise of exercising mutual search rights France and the United Kingdom had granted each other in 1831.

An Anglo-French convention of 1845 followed. Instead of allowing a continued right of search, France promised to have twenty-six of its own naval ships patrol the West African coast for the next ten years. That promise was briefly kept, but the size of the French squadron was reduced in the late 1840s and early 1850s. The 1845 convention was not renewed when it expired in 1855.

Portugal's Angolan Squadron came last and left first. It resulted from an 1842 treaty between Portugal and the United Kingdom, entered into after Parliament enacted 1839 legislation asserting a right to interdict Portuguese slave ships even without a treaty. It, too, was thus seen as a means of reducing assertedly improper U.K. interference with another nation's merchant shipping. Portugal's Angolan Squadron consisted of four to nine ships, operated only from 1843 to 1848, and was similarly limited to policing slave ships flying Portuguese colors.

An estimated one-sixth of the ships engaging in the Middle Passage slave trade between 1808 and 1870 were eventually lost to their owners, after being interdicted by naval patrols along the West African coast. The vast majority of the ships forfeited, around 85 percent, were stopped by the Royal Navy. An estimated 160,000 (one-sixteenth) of the slaves being shipped through the Middle Passage during those years were captured and freed. *See also* Abolition of the Slave Trade, Brazil; Abolition of the Slave Trade, France; Abolition of the Slave Trade, Great Britain; Abolition of the Slave Trade, Spain; Abolition of the Slave Trade, United States; African Rulers and the Slave Trade; Angola; British Navy; British Slave Trade; Closure of the Slave Trade; Enslavement and Procurement; Free Trade; French Slave Trade; Portuguese Slave Trade; Slave Coast; Slavery in Africa; Trade Forts; Wars, African; Zulueta, Pedro de.

Further Readings: Bethell, Leslie. *The Abolition of the Brazilian Slave Trade: Britain, Brazil and the Slave Trade Question, 1807–1869.* Cambridge: Cambridge University Press, 1970; Catterall, Helen Tunnicliff. *Judicial Cases Concerning American Slavery and the Negro.* vol. 1. Washington, DC: Carnegie Institution, 1926; Drescher, Seymour. *The Mighty Experiment: Free Labor versus Slavery in British Emancipation.* New York: Oxford University Press, 2002; Du Bois, W.E.B. *The Suppression of the Slave Trade to the United States of America, 1638–1870.* New York: Russell & Russell, 1965; Eltis, David. *Economic Growth and the Ending of the Transatlantic Slave Trade.* New York: Oxford University Press, 1987; Fladeland, Betty. *Men and Brothers: Anglo-American Antislavery Cooperation.* Urbana: University of Illinois Press, 1972; Howard, Warren S. *American Slavers and the Federal Law, 1837–1862.* Berkeley: University of California Press, 1963; Klein, Herbert S. *The Atlantic Slave Trade.* Cambridge: Cambridge University Press, 1999; Lloyd, Christopher. *The Navy and the Slave Trade.* London: Longmans, Green and Company, 1949; Matheson, William L. *Great Britain and the Slave Trade, 1839–1865.* London: Longmans, Green and Company, 1929; Miers, Suzanne. *Britain and the Ending of the Slave Trade.* New York: Africana, 1975; Mannix, Daniel Pratt, with Cowley, Malcolm. *Black Cargoes: A History of the Atlantic Slave Trade, 1518–1865.* New York: Viking, 1962; Murray, David. *Odious Commerce: Britain, Spain and the Abolition of the Cuban Slave Trade.* Cambridge: Cambridge University. Press, 1980; Porter, Dale H. *The Abolition of the Slave Trade in England, 1784–1807.* Hamden, CT: Archon

Books, 1970; Thomas, Hugh. *The Slave Trade: The Story of the Atlantic Slave Trade, 1440–1870.* New York: Simon & Schuster, 1997; Ward, W.E.F. *The Royal Navy and the Slavers: The Suppression of the Atlantic Slave Trade.* New York: Pantheon, 1969.

Steven B. Jacobson

Africanus, Leo (c. 1490–c. 1530)

Leo Africanus was a diplomat, traveler, and author who was famous for his book *Description of Africa.* The book represented the first major work written by someone from Africa for Europeans, and it provided prospective European explorers with information about African peoples and geography. Africanus was one of the only Africans in the early sixteenth century captured by Europeans who left behind an account of his travels.

Africanus was born around 1490 in Granada of Islamic parents and was given the name Al Hazzan Ibn Muhammad Al Wazzan, also known as Al Hazzan Al Wazzan. During his early childhood, his family moved to Fez, a city located in North Africa south of the strait of Gibraltar. While living in Fez, Al Hazzan Al Wazzan served the sultan of Fez as a diplomat and traveled to several regions, including Egypt and Constantinople.

In 1518, Al Hazzan Al Wazzan was captured and given to Pope Leo X in Rome as a gift. After a few years in captivity, Al Hazzan Al Wazzan converted to **Christianity**, which resulted in Pope Leo X giving him the Christian name, Leo Africanus. Following his conversion, Africanus was released from captivity but remained in Rome where he wrote *Description of Africa.* It is generally agreed that Africanus remained in Rome for about ten years, possibly longer. Rome was sacked in 1527 and it is uncertain whether he escaped to Africa, died in Rome, or became a captive of the invaders. He probably returned to Africa, possibly to Tunisia, where he died around 1532. Spirited debate regarding his conversion to Christianity questions his religious affiliations and whether his return to Africa was contingent on his conversion back to **Islam**.

Africanus's lasting influence was *Description of Africa.* Published posthumously in 1550, the book described different peoples, wars, trade, and geography within Africa. The book became a best seller and was published in Latin, English, French, and later, German. One of the book's most important descriptions provided information about the famed city of Timbuktu along with other geographic details. Historians have debated the accuracy of *Description of Africa,* leading to instances in which some details are refuted while others verify specific information. Regardless of the work's overall accuracy, it shaped European views of Africa, such as Timbuktu using nuggets of gold for money, and gave Europeans information about Africa at a time when exploration was continuing and the European slave trade was not yet an established institution in Africa. *See also* Slave Narratives.

Further Readings: Davis, Natalie Zemon. *Trickster Travels: A Sixteenth-Century Muslim Between Worlds.* New York: Hill and Wang, 2006; "Leo Affricanus: Description of Timbuktu." Fordham University Web site: www.fordham.edu/halsall/med/leo_afri.html.

Adam Paddock

AfricaTown, Alabama

Established by West Africans in 1868, and located three miles north of Mobile, Alabama, AfricaTown was developed in connection with **the *Clotilda* smuggling** episode. Despite the tragic context out of which it emerged, AfricaTown became a productive, viable community characterized by social order, self-reliance, and communalism.

AfricaTown's founding mothers and fathers entered the United States as captives aboard the slave ship *Clotilda,* during the second half of the nineteenth century. Trapped in Alabama, they pooled their resources to acquire land on which they established the community known currently as AfricaTown. Its name reflects the fact that the community is shaped by, and rooted in, the indigenous West African traditions and values that its founders transferred to Alabama. AfricaTown's governance, for example, modeled the age-grade system of rule that exists in many West African communities. Under this model, junior members of the community show deference to their elders whose collective experience, knowledge, and wisdom are highly respected. AfricaTown's elders delineated its codes of moral and social conduct, imposing sanctions against residents who violated them.

The exigencies of American slavery, and the perpetration of domestic terrorism against blacks during the Reconstruction period forced Africans and their descendants to be self-sufficient. Intradependence was facilitated by the ingenuity of African peoples who were endowed with agricultural, metallurgical, carving, sculpting, tanning, weaving, and other indigenous knowledge and skills that not only ensured their survival, but also contributed to the success of **plantation**, industrial, and household economies in the Americas. Rice and indigo plantations would not have succeeded without Senegambian, Ibo, and Yoruba Africans who retained and shared their expertise for cultivating those crops that are indigenous to West Africa, especially because European plantation owners did not possess such knowledge. Arguably, the world's premier cultivators are located in West Africa, explaining, in part, American planters' preferences for West African laborers over European ones.

Hailing from West African agricultural societies, AfricaTown's founders applied their agricultural expertise in Alabama where they cultivated gardens from which they harvested bountiful crops. In the spirit of communalism, they shared **food**, herbal medicines, and other important resources, thereby improving the quality of their lives while contributing to the sustainability of their community. Some of the descendants of AfricaTown's founders continue to reside in AfricaTown where they continue to cultivate gardens in the tradition of their West African ancestors who did not allow their indigenous practices and values to disintegrate under the treachery of American slavery.

The descendants preserve aspects of their West African heritages and architectural sites that document AfricaTown's history, including Union Baptist Church. Located in proximity to the church is Plateau Cemetery where AfricaTown's founders, and some of their descendants, are interred. In

1985, the Alabama State legislature designated AfricaTown a historic land-mark. Today, AfricaTown stands as a microcosm of African America that was forged by intelligent, industrious, talented, and resilient Africans, and their descendants, who, on several important levels, rose above their victim-ization as enslaved peoples in the United States. *See also* Lewis, Cudjo.

Further Readings: Hurston, Zora Neale. "Cudjo's Own Story of the Last African Slaver." *Journal of Negro History* 12 (October 1927): 648–663; Pettaway, Addie E. "Afri-caTown, USA: Some Aspects of Folklife and Material Culture of an Historic Landscape." Madison: Wisconsin Department of Public Instruction, 1985; Robertson, Natalie S. "The African Ancestry of the Founders of AfricaTown, Alabama." Ph.D. dissertation, University of Iowa, 1996; Roche, Emma Langdon. *Historic Sketches of the South*. New York: Knick-erbocker Press, 1914; Williams, Henry C. *AfricaTown, U.S.A.: A Pictoral History of Pla-teau and Magazine Point, Alabama*. N.p.: American Ethnic Science Society, 1981.

Natalie Suzette Robertson

Allada

Allada is one of the numerous Aja kingdoms of West Africa. Before the nineteenth century, the Aja occupied the western portion of the Yoruba country. Other important Aja kingdoms included Whydah, Popo, **Daho-mey**, and Jakin. The history of the slave trade in Allada is a history of seri-ous power struggle between the empire and its neighbors and private merchants as well as between the empire and the Europeans. This power struggle was inevitable if understood within the significance of the geo-graphic location of Allada's two major ports: Offra and Jakin. These two ports offered beautiful navigation and posed no threat to European vessels. In addition, the densely populated nature of the **Slave Coast** and unpalat-able relations among the Aja-speaking people resulted in the capture of slaves as booty of war. In 1681, thirty-three out of thirty-five English vessels identified as embarking or intending to embark on the Slave Coast went to Offra.

Whydah and Allada's rivalry originated from the need to attract European **slave merchants**. Europeans preferred to trade with Whydah for a number of reasons. The slaves from Allada cost them much more than the slaves from Whydah. The cost of poterage was higher at Allada than at Whydah, presumably because the Allada capital, where the trade was centered, was farther inland than the European forts at Whydah. At Allada, slaves were bought in lots and Europeans were forced to take the good and the bad slaves. In Whydah, the slaves were bought singly and the Europeans could choose the good ones and reject the bad ones. Although Allada traders insisted in being paid in **cowries** for slaves, their Whydah counterpart (who also preferred cowries) did not mind being paid in cheap goods if the European traders told them that cowries were not available.

In the mid-eighteenth century, the Allada monarchy was traditionally rigid in providing concession to European traders. Allada refused to reverse inimical policies in spite of consistent European threats to aban-don its ports. It was difficult, however, for European merchants to aban-doned Allada because moving to another port meant building forts and other slave-trading facilities. On Allada's part, the best means of avoiding crises between the monarchy and the intermediaries was to control the trade in a centralized and bureaucratic form. Excessive state control of trade presented the monarchy and the intermediaries with conflicts of interest. Royal attempts to control the trade by forcing inland merchants to deal with officials were a major factor in the Dahomean invasion of Allada in the 1720s. *See also* African Rulers and the Slave Trade; Decentralized Societies.

Further Readings: Akinjogbin, Adeagbo. *Dahomey and Its Neigbours, 1708–1818.* Cambridge: Cambridge University Press, 1967; Burton, Richard. *A Mission to Gelele, King of Dahome.* London: Tinsley Brothers, 1864; Priestley, Margaret. *West African Trade and Coast Society.* London: Oxford University Press, 1969.

Saheed Aderinto

Amistad (1997)

Amistad is a film depicting a dramatized account of the slave mutiny and subsequent trial known as the *Amistad* affair. Starring Matthew McConaughey, Morgan Freeman, Anthony Hopkins as John Quincy Adams, and Djimon Hounsou as Cinque (the leader of the slave revolt on board the Amistad), it is a historical film directed and produced by Steven Spielberg. It is also Spielberg's second film on the African American experience, after his adaptation of Alice Walker's *The Color Purple* (1985). The film chronicles the events of the mutiny and court cases from the point of view of McConaughey's character, Roger Sherman Baldwin.

Amistad received critical acclaim and was nominated for four Academy awards, including Morgan Freeman for Best Supporting Actor. The film garnered four Golden Globe nominations and won two Image Awards, the NAACP's highest honor for film.

Although the film received acclaim from both critics and African and African American groups, it was also criticized for its lack of historical accuracy. Unlike Spielberg's *Schindler's List* (1993), the director here exercised certain artistic liberties regarding the historical accuracy of the events. First, Freeman's character, Theodore Joadson, was not an actual person but rather a composite character of the various black abolitionists who rallied around the *Amistad* case.

Another plot device was Cinque's meeting with President Quincy Adams in his home. Adams was an avid botanist and in the film he shows Cinque an African violet. The sight of the flower reminds Cinque of his lost home. In reality, the U.S. Circuit Court judge in Hartford kept the Africans in custody throughout their trials and appeals. Second, the African violet is a flower native to modern Tanzania and Kenya in East Africa. Cinque and his fellow Africans were Mende speakers from West Africa. It is highly unlikely that he would have ever seen an African violet in the wild.

The Jamaican board of film censors removed the opening scenes depicting the violent slave mutiny from all copies of the film released in Jamaican theatres. *See also* Abolition of the Slave Trade, Spain; Abolition of the Slave Trade, United States; *Amistad*, The; Cuba.

Further Readings: Owens, William. *Slave Mutiny: Revolt on the Schooner Amistad.* New York: J. Day Company, 1953; Spielberg, Steven, dir. *Amistad.* Released by Dreamworks Pictures in association with HBO Pictures, 1999.

Roy Doron

Amistad, The

The *Amistad* affair (also called the *Amistad* case and the *Amistad* mutiny) is the name commonly given to a mutiny of enslaved Africans on board the slave transport ship, *Amistad*, its capture off the coast of Long Island, New York, and the subsequent court cases reaching the U.S. Supreme Court regarding the status of the slaves who mutinied.

Discovery of the Mutiny

On August 25, 1839, word came that a mysterious "negro pirate ship" had landed on the coast of Long Island. For several months, rumors of the existence of this ship had circulated throughout the United States. The schooner USS *Washington* seized the ship the following day and transported the ship's passengers to New London, Connecticut (where slavery was still legal until 1848). Aside from the slaves, two Spaniards, Jose "Pepe" Ruiz and Pedro Montez, remained on board and told the story of the mutiny. The *Amistad* was en route from **Havana** to Puerto Principe when one of the slaves, Joseph Cinque, used an old rusty nail to free himself from his shackles, free the other slaves, and murder the entire **crew**. Ruiz and Montez were spared only because they had navigation skills and were ordered to take the ship to Africa.

Ruiz stated that instead of taking the ship to Africa, he steered the *Amistad* on a generally northern direction for two months until the ship ran out of supplies and was forced to land in New York. Although Ruiz furnished passports for all the slaves showing that they were all born as slaves in **Cuba**, not a single one of them could speak Spanish, and they all could speak only native African tongues, later to be discovered to be Mende, from the general area of **Sierra Leone**.

The Trials

After being taken to New London and placed in jail to await trial for piracy and murder, news of the arraignment reached Lewis Tappan, one of the leaders of the abolitionist movement in New York City. Immediately recognizing the potential of this case to publicize the abolitionist movement, he began to collect funds and build a

Cinque, leader of *Amistad* rebellion. Courtesy of Anti-Slavery International.

defense team to try the case in the Connecticut district courts beginning September 17, 1839. Not knowing where in Africa the slaves had come from, Tappan arrived in New London with three "natives of Africa." One of them spoke "Geshee," which some of the prisoners could understand but none could speak.

Tappan sought to cultivate a romantic air around the prisoners, and especially about Cinque whom he described as being "about five feet eight inches high, of fine proportions, with a noble air" (*New York Journal of Commerce*, September 8, 1839). For Tappan, this trial was as much about saving the lives of these Africans as it was about bringing attention to the inhumanity of slavery everywhere, especially in the United States.

The initial trial was a convoluted case involving several claims from the abolitionists who sought the freedom of the slaves, the surviving Spanish crew who wanted the mutineer slaves returned to Cuba, and the lawyers of both the captain of the USS *Washington* and a Captain Green, who was the first man on Long Island to meet with the Africans. Both lawyers demanded salvage rights to the *Amistad* and a percentage of its crew or proper compensation. Because these slaves were of Spanish origin, the federal government petitioned that they were subject to Pinckney's Treaty of 1795 and should thus be placed under the direct control of President Martin Van Buren.

The court's verdict was a mixed one. First, because the mutiny occurred in Spanish territory on board a Spanish ship and to Spanish citizens, the United States had no jurisdiction in the matter. As to the prisoners, however, the court ruled that they were to remain in custody until the property case was settled, and a new date was set for that trial (October 31, 1839). To keep the case fresh in the minds of the American Public, on October 17 Tappan arranged for the arrest of Montez and Ruiz on counts of kidnapping and false imprisonment in New York.

This new trial would determine the fate of the Africans and the Spanish traders and the salvage rights brought forward by both men on the USS *Washington* and Captain Green of Long Island. It would be the testimony of Cinque and another African, Grabeau, however, that would make this trial a hallmark of the abolition movement.

For President Martin Van Buren, the case was one of problematic publicity. Because 1840 was an election year, he wanted to end the case as quickly as possible so that it did not harm his reelection prospects. If the Africans were to be returned to Cuba as freedmen according to the treaty between Spain and Britain, they were entitled to work for seven years as **indentured servants** and then regain full free rights. In reality, however, most of these people did not survive the seven years of servitude. To this end, Van Buren summoned the schooner USS *Grampus* from its antislavery patrols in the Atlantic to the harbor at New Haven to transport the Africans to Havana with the British superintendent of **liberated Africans** in Cuba, Richard Robert Madden. Madden, who knew what the fate of the *Amistad* men would be in Cuba, volunteered to help Tappan keep the men in the United States. Moreover, Madden had spoken to the owners of the **barracoon** in Havana and he was convinced that the Africans would be executed upon their return to Cuba as a deterrent against any future mutinies and insurrections.

President Van Buren's plan was to wait for a verdict stating that the men were slaves and should be returned to Cuba. Then, the president could expedite the delivery of the men to Cuba, thus subverting due process and not allowing Tappan any time to mount an appeal before the slaves were returned to Cuba. The verdict, which was delivered on January 13, 1840, was to render the plans moot.

Connecticut Circuit Court Judge Andrew T. Judson read his verdict to a largely pro-African courtroom. Tappan, who was weary of Judson's inclinations regarding the abolition movement, could not have hoped for a better verdict. Judson stated that the men were indeed Africans who "were born free and ever since have been and still of right are free and not slaves." Furthermore, he declared that their actions on board the *Amistad* came from a "desire of winning their liberty and returning to their families" and thus could not be punished as they were the direct result of an unlawful **enslavement**. Judson ordered that the Africans be placed under the control of the executive branch of the government and be returned to Africa.

The U.S. government appealed the case to the Connecticut Supreme Court, which upheld Judson's decision and eventually to the Federal Supreme Court, which convened to hear the case in January 1841. For the arguments in the Supreme Court, Tappan secured the help of former President John Quincy Adams to aid defense lawyer Roger Baldwin (the main character portrayed in Steven Spielberg's film *Amistad*) who was to argue most eloquently for the emancipation of the Africans. Justice Joseph Story later called Adams' argument "extraordinary for its power, for its bitter sarcasm, and for its dealing with topics far beyond the record and points of discussion."

On March 9, the Supreme Court issued its decision, largely upholding the lower courts. Justice Story would say that the actions of the Africans on the *Amistad* were not criminal but rather that the "ultimate right of human beings in extreme cases is . . . to apply force against ruinous injustice." The Africans were thus finally free to stay or to return to Africa.

After several months in New York working for Tappan and the abolitionist movement, Tappan decided that the time had come to return the men to Africa. On December 4, 1841, the Mendians (as they were now called, after their language) boarded the barque *Gentleman*, with several missionaries and teachers and, after a final meeting with Adams, during which they presented him with an elegant bible, Cinque and his compatriots returned to Sierra Leone.

In November 1840, Van Buren lost his reelection bid to William Henry Harrison.

The *Amistad* affair's significance is that it was the first trial of enslaved Africans to receive national publicity and was widely and hotly debated in the press. Tappan and his fellow abolitionists used the case not only to publicize the plight of the *Amistad* men, but also to showcase slavery as a whole. For Tappan, ending the slave trade would not be possible while slavery existed because it was the institution of slavery that fueled the demand for slaves and thus for the trade itself. *See also* Abolition of the Slave Trade, Spain; Abolition of the Slave Trade, United States; *Amistad* (1997).

Further Reading: Jones, Howard. *Mutiny on the* Amistad: *The Saga of a Slave Revolt and Its Impact on American Abolition, Law, and Diplomacy.* Oxford: Oxford University Press; 1987.

Roy Doron

Angola

Angola is in southwest Africa. It may be referred to as the region between the Rivers Dande and Longa. The hinterland stretches several hundred miles inland. Originally, the name of the land was Ndongo. The Portuguese named it Angola, derived from the name or title of its ruler (Ngola), after their first contact. It has a diverse landscape including beaches, forests, savanna, and desert.

The African slave trade played an important role in its history. The trade was conducted between the fifteenth and nineteenth centuries. Originally, the bulk of the slave supply was from Guinea. By the sixteenth century, however, the regions of Congo and Angola had become major suppliers of African slaves. Apart from Congo, Angola was the only other slave-supplying area that was accessible by sea that the Portuguese could turn to. The human reservoir for slaves in the Angola hinterland was inhabited by the Bantu. Thousands of slaves were purchased by European **slave traders** on the coast of the Angola Kingdom.

The Portuguese tried to conquer Angola, but stiff resistance from the Mbundu and tropical **diseases** decimated their troops. They, thereafter, resigned themselves to being regular slave traders. From the 1530s, the Portuguese had established a slaving station at **Luanda**. From there, they bought slaves from the Ngola who was the southern rival of the king of Congo. The power of the Ngola was greatly strengthened by the trade in captives during the sixteenth century. He produced many captives by conquest. These military invasions on weaker peoples, in turn. expanded his kingdom.

Slaves from Angola, called Angolares, were carried to the Portuguese island of **São Tomé**, along with other captives from **Benin** and places along the coast from between Benin and Cape St. Catherine. From there, they were shipped to Portugal or to the Americas. Of particular importance was Pernambuco in **Brazil**. During this period, the fortunes of Angola depended largely on the Portuguese colony of Brazil because of the human trade between them. At the same time, some Angola slaves were sold illegally into **Buenos Aires** directly from Luanda or via Brazilian **ports**. These captives were intended for sale in **Potosí** or High Peru. These kinds of slaves were sold usually for a few squares of palm cloth in Angola, but they fetched 400 to 600 pesos in Peru. The **price** depended on the age and physical wellness of the slaves.

Angola's waterways (known as *libambos*) are important in the country's slave-trading history. They were used to carry African slaves from the interior to the Atlantic Ocean. During the eighteenth century, sources of slave supply became wider in West Central Africa and shifted beyond Matamba and Kasanje to the Lunda Empire on the Kasai. Estimates of slaves exported in the seventeenth century from the regions of Congo and Angola was an average of 15,000 per year. By the mid-eighteenth century, Luanda alone was exporting more than 10,000 captives a year. *See also* African Rulers and the Slave Trade; Garcia II of Kongo; Loango; Portuguese Slave Trade; Vili.

Further Readings: "Breaking the Silence, Learning about the Slave Trade, Slave Routes." Anti-Slavery International Web site: www.antislavery.org; Davidson, Basil. *A History of East and Central Africa to the Late Nineteenth Century.* Garden City, NY: Doubleday, 1969; Kaplan, Irving, and Roth, H. Mark, eds. *Angola: A Country Study.* Washington, DC: American University, 1979; Miller, Joseph. *Way of Death: Merchant Capitalism and the Angolan Slave Trade.* Madison: University of Wisconsin Press, 1988; McEwan, P.J.M., ed. *Africa from Early Times to 1800.* London: Oxford University Press, 1976; Minter, W. M., and Wiley, D. S. "Angola." Blacknet UK Web site: www.blacknet.co.uk.

Oyekemi Olajope Oyelakin

Annobon

The small island of Annobon (meaning New Year), located southwest of **São Tomé**, Príncipe, and **Fernando Po** in the Gulf of Guinea, served as a European base for cultivating foodstuffs, manufacturing trade goods, and provisioning ships during the trans-Atlantic slave trade from the sixteenth to nineteenth centuries. Portuguese navigators on New Year's Day 1472 were the first to claim the uninhabited volcanic island, which spans only seven square miles (eighteen square kilometers). Until the Spanish took possession of Annobon in 1778, the island's social, political, and commercial life was inextricably tied to that of its larger Portuguese neighbor, São Tomé, whose residents maintained control over trade and government for much of the sixteenth and seventeenth centuries. Throughout the eighteenth century, slave ships sailing from West Africa stopped in Annobon for supplies before making the uncertain journey across the Atlantic. In the nineteenth century, Britain operated a portion of its **African Squadron** from the island, attempting to quash the **illegal slave trade** still thriving along the Angolan coast and in the **Congo River** region. Today, Annobon belongs to Equatorial Guinea. Many of its roughly 3,000 inhabitants are descendents of Angolan slaves brought by the Portuguese from São Tomé to cultivate the island.

Patterning its development of Annobon after a form of **plantation** production previously tested on various Atlantic islands, Portugal established a system of royal land grants on the island to stimulate cultivation of **sugar** in the sixteenth century. Despite the success of similar arrangements on the islands of Madeira, the Azores, and São Tomé, Annobon never became an important source of the prized staple. Instead, several hundred slaves worked the island's volcanic soil to produce a range of agricultural goods, such as oranges, lemons, coconuts, and bananas. Although never achieving the wealth of other Atlantic "sugar islands," Annobon's agricultural production, as well as its strategic position off the African mainland just below the equator, sparked a brisk trade with slave ships and merchant vessels eager to replenish their supplies. The island also produced a limited amount of high-quality cotton, which merchants exchanged with Dutch, Spanish, and São Toméan traders.

Throughout the seventeenth and eighteenth centuries, Annobon furnished agricultural goods, wood, water, and other supplies to ships plying the African coast, including European vessels sailing for the East Indies, as well as slave ships making the two-week journey from West Africa on their way to the Caribbean. Annobon provided an essential, intermediate pit stop for slave ships destined for the Americas. Although some vessels sailed directly to Annobon from such **ports** as **Calabar**, Whydah, Cape Mount, and **Cape Coast Castle**, others stopped first in São Tomé or Príncipe. From Annobon, slave ships began the Middle Passage by sailing southwest, catching the southeast trade winds that would push them across the Atlantic to various ports in Martinique, **Saint Domingue**, Dominica, and **Jamaica**. *See also* Entrepôts.

Further Readings: Raimundo, José da Cunha Matos. *Corografia Hisorica das Ilhas de S. Tomé e Principe, Ano Bom e Fernando Pó.* São Tomé: Imprenza Nacional, 1916; Serafim, Cristina Maria Seuanes. *As Ilhas de São Tomé no Século XVII.* Braga, Portugal: Centro de História de Além-Mar, 2000; Abelardo de Unzueta y Yuste. *Islas del Golfo de Guinea.* Madrid: Instituto de Estudios Políticos, 1945.

Edward D. Maris-Wolf

Archeology

Archaeological research has significantly contributed to understandings of Africans and their **enslavement**. Archaeology can be defined as the scientific study of the human past that focuses on artifacts and historic places. Because it is a subfield of anthropology (the study of human beings), archaeology is particularly concerned with culture and a holistic view of people's behavior and experiences. African diaspora archaeology is the product of scholarship that extends back at least to the 1930s, when **plantations** slowly became the target of research among North American scholars in the United States. It was only in the 1960s, however, that archaeologists became concerned with the Africans who were engulfed in the Middle Passage and its aftermath. It was no coincidence that archaeologists began taking Africans and their descendants in the Americas seriously at this time, as Civil Rights, the historic preservation movement, and African independence struggles transformed academia and institutions on both sides of the Atlantic.

Chronologically speaking, archaeologists have studied Africans living in sites in the Americas from the 1500s until the end of slavery. Plantations, slave castles, slave forts, urban residences, kitchen buildings, cellars, rural homesteads, cemeteries, and maroon communities are included in the main types of archaeological sites. Most sites that have been excavated relate to the eighteenth and nineteenth centuries, although earlier periods are slowly receiving more attention. U.S. and Caribbean sites have been studied more than Latin American ones. The range of themes that has emerged from these studies include foodways, health, pottery production, architecture, Africanisms, status, resistance, **ethnicity**, cultural identity, **religion**, and landscape.

African sites provide evidence of slave depots on the African coast. Castle São Jorge da Mina was founded in 1482 by Portuguese traders. By 1637, it was captured by the Dutch, who held it until the nineteenth century. British soldiers occupied the castle in the late 1800s, until it was destroyed by **Asante** forces. Chris Decorse's research teams have excavated more than thirty buildings and nearly 100,000 artifacts from El Mina. European and local pottery, imported glasswares, metal hardware, and trade beads are among the most notable remains recovered to date. The process of culture contact has resulted in the creation of syncretic items such as ritual vessels constructed from European metals. According to Decorse, European-made clothing accessories (buckles), writing implements (slates, pencils), and stone wall architecture were all introduced because of the European presence. Plants and animals were also introduced, such as tobacco and geese. Wild and domesticated animals were consumed there, based on the faunal remains from the site. Much work remains to be done on inland sites of the African slave trade. Burial sites found in the floors of some of El Mina's homes demonstrate the African influence that has been found in the Americas.

A slave ship is a fruitful area of marine archaeology. **The *Henrietta Marie*** was a ship that wrecked about thirty miles off the coast of Florida, in 1700. A caste bronze bell with the ship's name confirmed its identity. The large number of shackles provided another clue about its function and identity. Jamaican shipping records also assisted in the identification of the vessel. An enormous cache of artifacts was recovered, including glass beads of various colors, shapes, and sizes; stoneware; ceramics; and pewter utensils. Remains of the ship have been on display in a traveling exhibit.

A field of research called "bioarchaeology," the archaeological study of skeletal biology and human health, has expanded our understanding of the physical evidence for people of African descent in the Americas. From the 1890s until the 1930s, bioarchaeologists and anatomists from universities such as Oxford, Northwestern, and Columbia identified a few African burials in the Caribbean. On islands such as **Jamaica** and Barbados, Africans were unexpected discoveries in areas that also contained Colonial-period Taino (Native Americans) burial remains. Dental features and filing or modification were diagnostic indicators of African origins. These characteristics have been found in studies of skeletal populations in other places such as **Cuba**, that were associated with maroons ("runaway slaves") and religious enclaves.

By the 1970s, North American physical anthropologists were examining large samples of colonial and modern people of African descent. One interesting case, an African whose remains dated to the 1800s, was buried in a 3,000-year-old Native American mound. Bioarchaeological studies have discovered evidence for the traumas caused by enslavement. For instance, a study of a plantation near **Charleston**, South Carolina, identified malnutrition among individuals who died between 1840 and 1870. Both city (**New Orleans** and Philadelphia) and rural cemeteries have been studied to learn about the lives of Africans in the Americas. Waterloo plantation (Surinam) illustrated the terrible effects of syphilis, which was evident from lesions on the skeletons. The rich documentary evidence examined for Waterloo suggests that **rape** on slave ships and concubinage of African house servants spread the **disease**. Caribbean burials such as those of Newton Plantation, Barbados, have illustrated the adverse affects of lead contamination and alcohol consumption, and more positive aspects such as the ability of enslaved people to manifest their own aesthetics through the adornment of brass bracelets.

During the 1990s, studies began on nearly 400 burials in the well-known New York City African Burial Ground (1600s to the 1790s). These studies have expanded our views of violent injuries (spiral fractures), strenuous work (robust muscle attachment and arthritic bone degeneration), and disease. A flattened musketball embedded in one skeleton speaks to a crime of lethal force or an execution. One mother was buried with her child en utero. Shroud pins illustrate the personal nature of belongings interred with bodies. A heart-shaped arrangement of tacks on one coffin from the African Burial Ground resembles a heart symbol found in Adinkra symbols from Ghana, West Africa, which is called Nya Akoma ("patience; endurance"). Elements of Ghanaian culture, such as "day-names," are well documented in cases of African influence, survival, and transformation in the Americas. Cranial and DNA (deoxyribonucleic acid) research has linked the burials to Asante, Yoruba, Senegambian, and Ibo populations, among others. The New York burial ground study became a highly politicized project, as people of African descent struggled for representation on the project and for the right to provide what they felt were proper ceremonies of commemoration.

Plantations have been the most intensively examined type of African diaspora archaeological site. Kingsley (Florida), El Padre (Cuba), Drax Hall (Jamaica), and Monticello (Virginia), the estate of President Thomas Jefferson, are some of the more well-known plantations that have been excavated in the past. Middleburg Plantation (1600s–1800s) in South Carolina, studied by Leland Ferguson, provides good examples of the types of material evidence that have been derived from plantation archaeology. Ferguson discovered that the labor invested in the clearing and maintenance of lowcountry rice fields and banks was about the same as that required to build some of the largest mounds and pyramids in the world. Middleburg's rice banks stretched for two miles along the Cooper River. A range of artifacts illustrates the everyday life of enslaved laborers. Pottery, bone, glass, shackles, locks, buttons, pipes, and hoes are among the artifacts found at plantations such as Middleburg. A handmade type of pottery called "Colonoware" was also found at Middleburg. This type of pottery has been discovered at sites mainly in North America and the Caribbean. Colonoware is important because it was a "creolized" expression of African and Native American potting. Africans were encouraged and forced to practice their skills and use their knowledge in artisanry, healing, blacksmithing, and other areas.

Postholes are important features because they are the only remaining evidence for an African architectural process that resulted in the construction of mud, thatch, and timber homes. Postholes at Middleburg were visible to archaeologists only through the circular stains they left in the soil. The postholes were arranged in rectangles that illustrated the type of structural support as well as the size of the houses. Pavements of ceramics, brick, or glass have been found in the freed African homestead at Parting Ways in Plymouth, Massachusetts, as well as the Sylvestor Manor site in Shelter Island, New York. These two places are important because they are examples of how slavery was as important in the U.S. North as it was the U.S. South, the Caribbean, and Latin America.

Many items used by enslaved Africans never survived long enough to be found by archaeologists. A fragment of woven grass basketry that was excavated from a South Carolina privy compares well with modern sweetgrass baskets, such as "fanners," that were once used for rice processing. Present-day descendants such as the Gullah still manufacture these baskets. African baskets have been compared with these South Carolina examples. Other artifacts that are rarely found at slavery sites—more for the fact that they were highly valued and more carefully kept—include marbles, gaming pieces (ground pottery), coins, and even weapons.

Africans in the Americas continue to be one of the most prolific areas of archaeological research. Archaeologists and bioarchaeologists have explored the past using material culture, **oral history**, ethnography, and documents. They strive to provide a holistic view of a complex and traumatic period of human history. Archaeology has uncovered the suffering, cultural resiliency, and everyday life of enslaved Africans. Inferences can be made about possessions, behaviors, and meanings from material culture and historic places. Archaeology is important to understanding the history of enslaved Africans because of the relative lack, destruction, or deterioration of detailed documents concerning enslaved people of African descent. A variety of issues, locations, and scholars have generated a growing body of research that provides one of the most tangible records of the costs and consequences of slavery and African life in the Americas. *See also* Elmina; Escapes and Runaways; Shipwrecks; Trade Forts.

Further Readings: Blakey, Michael L. "Bioarchaeology of the African Diaspora in the Americas: Its Origins and Scope." *Annual Review of Anthropology* 30 (2001): 387–422; Decorse, Christopher R. *An Archaeology of Elmina: Africans and Europeans on the Gold Coast, 1400–1900.* Washington, DC: Smithsonian Institution Press, 2001; Ferguson, Leland G. *Uncommon Ground: Archaeology and Early African America, 1650–1800.* Washington, DC: Smithsonian Institution Press, 1992; Orser, Charles. "The Archeology of the African Diaspora." *Annual Review of Anthropology* 27 (1998): 63–82; Singleton, T. A., and Bograd, M. D. *The Archaeology of the African Diaspora in the Americas.* Guide to the Archaeological Literature of the Immigrant Experience in America, No. 2. Tucson, AZ: Society for Historical Archaeology, 1995.

Terrance Weik

Aro

Aro refers to the people, settlements, and cultural forms of the town of **Arochukwu** and of the Aro diaspora dispersed in the southeast and parts of the Middle Belt of Nigeria. The Aro are descended both from the original settlers of Arochukwu and from the many immigrants whom the Aro have incorporated since the seventeenth century when the Aro began their expansion. Apart from the Arochukwu homeland, the largest Aro towns are Arondizuogu and the Ndieni cluster in central Igboland and Inokun in Ibibioland.

The Aro were predominantly traders. They thrived on the Atlantic slave trade, playing a major role in its expansion in the Bight of Biafra. Their control of the trade and of the feared Ibiniukpabi oracle, which the British called "Long Juju," gave the Aro enormous influence in the region. The oracle served as the de facto supreme court of the region. As agents of the oracle, the Aro diaspora took the non-Aro to the oracle for the adjudication of the cases they brought. By the nineteenth century, Aro expansion had seen the group inhabit more than 150 settlements, overwhelmingly among the **Igbo**, with whom the vast majority of the Aro identify. The Aro settlements were linked to Arochukwu and to one another by a network of institutions. Aro control of the Ibiniukpabi oracle, massive incorporation of the non-Aro into their group, and alliance with Arochukwu's warrior neighbors gave the Aro advantages over other hinterland groups in the control of trade.

There has not been a uniform Aro culture since the Aro began to establish permanent settlements outside Arochukwu. Like Aro dialects, localized variants of Aro cultural forms developed in the various settlements, which invariably acquired elements of non-Aro immigrant and neighboring cultures. Yet, the Aro everywhere maintain distinct pan-Aro institutions, such as the Ekpe confraternity, the Ihu homage system, and the annual Ikeji festival. The Aro diaspora have the right to settle in Arochukwu whenever the need arises, as happened following the Nigerian civil war (1967–1970) when the Aro in several non-Igbo regions were persecuted as Igbo. Some maintain dual residences in their respective settlements and in Arochukwu, although growing scarcity of land has limited this possibility in recent times.

Aro cohesiveness has weakened considerably since British conquest in 1902. Although the Igboland-based Aro identify themselves as Igbo, the identity of their counterparts in non-Igbo regions—among the Ibibio, Igala, and Idoma—is complicated. The Aro outside Igboland share Aro identity with their Aro counterparts in Igboland. They combine this identity with local non-Igbo identities in their non-Igbo locations. Most of these Aro are as non-Igbo as the Aro-Igbo are non-Ibibio or Igala. Apart from shared institutions, the Aro today are under the nominal leadership of Eze Aro (the Aro king) and they maintain a semblance of a common formal front in a sociocultural organization called the Aro-Okeigbo. *See also* African Rulers and the Slave Trade; Arochukwu; Slavery in Africa.

Further Readings: Dike, K. O. *The Aro of South-Eastern Nigeria, 1650–1980: A Study of Socio-Economic Formation and Transformation in Nigeria.* Ibadan: University Press Ltd., 1990; Ijoma, J. Okoro, ed. *Arochukwu: History and Culture.* Enugu: Fourth Dimension Publishers, 1986; Nwokeji, G. Ugo. "The Biafran Frontier: Trade, Slaves and Aro Society, c. 1750–1905." Ph.D. dissertation, University of Toronto, 1999.

G. Ugo Nwokeji

Arochukwu

Located by the Enyong creek in southeastern Nigeria, at the **Igbo**-Ibibio-Efik borderland, west of the Cross River, the historic town of Arochukwu is the homeland of the **Aro** people who are dispersed in settlements in the southeast and eastern middle belt of the country. The town headquartered the major pan-Aro institutions, including the Ibiniukpabi oracle ("Long Juju"), which today is the principal historical monument in this tourist town. Arochukwu's estimated population of 150,000 is distributed in nineteen quarters ("villages"), grouped into nine lineage groups, which in turn form three lineage-group clusters. Although today the population is solidly Igbo, the town has multiethnic origins in the sixteenth century, which were established by Igbo, Ibibio, Efik, Annang, and Ekoi elements, as well as a later-arriving relatively small group of Akpa migrants from the eastern Nigerian middle belt. Arochukwu's control of the Ibiniukpabi oracle, which served as the highest appeal court in the region, and its ubiquitous diaspora settlements, facilitated Aro control of the Atlantic slave trade era in the hinterland of the Bight of Biafra. The Aro diaspora were linked to Arochukwu through a variety of pan-Aro institutions and through the respective Arochukwu quarters of the founders of the settlements.

Aro dominance ended in 1901–1902, when the British Aro Expedition's "Aro Field Force" conquered Arochukwu, destroyed their oracle, and killed or imprisoned their leaders. The average Arochukwu person who once commanded multiple **languages** of the Cross River region now can speak only Igbo fluently. *See also* African Rulers and the Slave Trade; Slavery in Africa.

Further Readings: Dike, K. O. *The Aro of South-Eastern Nigeria, 1650–1980: A Study of Socio-Economic Formation and Transformation in Nigeria.* Ibadan: University Press Ltd., 1990; Ijoma, J. Okoro, ed. *Arochukwu: History and Culture.* Enugu: Fourth Dimension Publishers, 1986; Kanu, P. Okoro. *Pre-British Aro of Arochukwu: Notes and Reflections on an African Civilization.* New York: USAfrica Books, 2001.

G. Ugo Nwokeji

Arrivals

The notion of Africans arriving to the Americas as slaves often invokes images of the treacherous voyages through the Middle Passage from one holding cell to another, slaves herded into to prisons along the **Slave Coast** in present-day Ghana, **Sierra Leone**, Senegambia, Nigeria, **Liberia**, and other places. Slaves were often captives of war or individuals kidnapped from their homes and sold for European goods, including guns, horses, and cloth. Once captured, slaves were held in slave prisons, such as **Elmina** and James Fort, until loaded onto slaving vessels and shipped to various **ports** around the Atlantic Ocean and throughout the Caribbean. These ports include Veracruz, **Liverpool**, **Nantes**, **Cartagena**, Boston, Salem, Savannah, and others. Slaves were packed into the belly of ships, **chained** together. Once they arrived at their **destinations**, slaves were then cleaned

Recently arrived Africans exposed for sale as chattel slaves. Courtesy of Anti-Slavery International.

up; that is, they were covered in oils to make them look healthier and more appealing to potential buyers.

This process of acquiring and selling slaves among the European nations began in the fifteenth century with the Portuguese. The Portuguese were among the first European nations to begin trade in slaves from West Africa; slavery had existed throughout the Saharan region of Africa for centuries. Slavery was legitimated by the idea of **Christian** conversion; the purpose of slavery soon became to redeem the souls of Africans considered sinners by the tenets of Roman Catholicism. In the fifteenth and sixteenth centuries, African slaves were shipped from **Kongo**, **Benin**, and ports in West Africa, such as Elmina, to Portugal and its neighboring islands, Spain, and other early colonial settlements in the Mediterranean and Atlantic, such as **São Tomé** and Príncipe. Their work consisted of agrarian labor (both skilled and unskilled in sugarcane fields), gold and silver mining, and artisan trades.

African slaves appeared in the Americas with the first Spanish ships. The Spanish, because of their trade with the Portuguese, were familiar with the usage of African slave labor. There were only a small number of slaves aboard these ships in the earliest days of colonization and conquest. Nevertheless, the successful conquest of territory in the New World introduced the Spanish economy to new markets and new resources and the demand for African slaves increased substantially. The earliest explorers, such as Christopher Columbus, immediately began to establish **sugar plantations** that needed adequate labor to produce the revenue that the Spanish monarchy demanded. The need emerged for a labor force willing to work and able to survive the rough living conditions. Indigenous populations were often unwilling to work as the Spanish demanded or were able to lead successful rebellions. They had the advantage of knowing the landscape and more often fled rather than work as demanded. Consequently, the Spanish turned to Africans. The large numbers of Africans came to the Americas forcibly working as **indentured servants** and then later as slaves. The earliest African slaves arrived in the Americas from the Canary Islands with the first European travelers to the New World.

The Portuguese and the Spanish were among the first European nations to establish colonial settlements in the Caribbean and Central America. As their colonies developed and the need for laborers increased, so did their reliance on Africans as a labor resource. With the help of the Pope, Spain and Portugal negotiated the boundaries of their geopolitical power and their control of the slave trade. The ***asiento***, as it was called, was given initially to the Spanish. For many years, the Spanish controlled the sale and acquisition of African bodies from Western Africa to the Caribbean, North America, and Europe. They established ports in their colonial settlements, including Veracruz, **Havana**, **Hispaniola**, Florida, and Cartagena. Veracruz helped supply New Spain or Mexico; Cartegena supplied the upper regions of South America, such as Peru, Colombia, and Venezuela. This ensured a steady supply of African labor throughout the sixteenth century; Mexico and Hispaniola had large populations of slaves; slave imports often exceeded Spanish immigration to their colonies. Slaves worked to build the infrastructure of Spanish American settlements and partook in the growth of agricultural products, such as sugar and indigo.

The Spanish and Portuguese lost their influence in the Atlantic Slave trade during the seventeenth century. The Dutch, French, and the English had waited to enter the geopolitical market for new land, new resources, and new labor. Competition increased as the Dutch West India Company and the English colonial companies, such as the Virginia Company and the **Royal Africa Company**, gained significant ground in both the acquisition of slaves and colonial settlements. The English had successfully established colonies in Virginia and **New England**, and the need for slave labor increased with the realization that tobacco could be grown and sold along with sugar. By the mid-seventeenth century, the Royal Africa Company had established a number of ports along the West African coast. The English monopolized the Atlantic trade in slaves.

Both the English and the French developed slave codes, the legislative **regulation** of slave activities on Caribbean plantations and colonial settlements in North America. These codes sought to control slaves and prevent both the reality and the threat of revolution. The codes were a part of the "**seasoning**" process. Newly arrived Africans were broken into **enslavement** with harsh and cruel treatment. Rebellious slaves were held in **coffles** and punished with whips and other brutal instruments of terror. *See* *also* African Fears of Cannibalism; *Bozal*; British Slave Trade; French Slave Trade; Internal Slave Trade, Brazil; Internal Slave Trade, United States; Ports; Portuguese Slave Trade; "Saltwater Negroes"; Violence.

Further Readings: Blackburn, Robin. *The Makings of New World Slavery: From the Baroque to the Modern, 1492–1800.* New York: Verso Press, 1997; Franklin, John Hope. *From Slavery to Freedom: A History of Negro Americans.* 3rd ed. New York: Vintage Books, 1969.

Tara Bynum

Asante

Asante was a powerful West African empire during the era of the slave trade. The name Asante (sometimes spelled "Ashanti" or "Ashantee") also refers to the language and **ethnicity** of the people of the Asante Region of present-day Ghana. The Asante Empire was ruled by a king, known as the *Asantehene*, who ruled from the capital city, Kumase. The king was assisted by a large number of chiefs and priests and a large professional army. Asante participated heavily in trade with European **slave traders** on the **Gold Coast** and was recognized by Europeans on the coast as being the main source of the enslaved people who were sold at coastal markets. In exchange for captives, Asante received imported goods, including cotton and wool **textiles**, guns, alcohol, and tobacco.

The wealth of the Asante Empire was based on vast amounts of gold that the Asante people and their ancestors mined for personal use and for trade. Beginning around 1400 C.E., gold from the Asante area was traded to merchants who traversed the vast commercial networks spanning the Sahara desert. From the fifteenth to eighteenth centuries, this north-bound gold trade was gradually depleted by the growth of Asante's gold trade with European traders on the Atlantic coast, to the south. During the eighteenth century, the trade in enslaved Africans became a greater component of Asante's coastal trade than the gold trade. The main trading partner of the Asante Empire was the Dutch West India Company, which was based at **Elmina** on the Gold Coast. Throughout the eighteenth century, the Asantehene kept an ambassador at Elmina and maintained regular correspondence with the Dutch director-general there.

The power of the Asantehene was founded on his spiritual authority. The first Asantehene, Osei Tutu, became ruler of all the Asante people in 1701 when, according to tradition, a golden stool descended from the heavens and landed on his lap, signifying his divine right to be king. Subsequent Asantehenes expanded the kingdom through wars of conquest that continued into the nineteenth century. Prisoners of war taken during these battles to expand the empire were usually sold as slaves to European and American slavers on the Gold Coast. At its height, the Asante Empire encompassed an area slightly larger than present-day Ghana.

The golden stool has remained the symbol of Asante power since Osei Tutu's time. It was seized temporarily by British troops in 1901 as part of the colonial conquest of Asante. This golden stool is still an important possession of the Asantehene who resides in a palace in Kumase to this day. *See also* African Rulers and the Slave Trade; Dutch Slave Trade.

Further Readings: Fynn, John Kofi. *Asante and Its Neighbors.* Legon History Series. Evanston: Northwestern University Press, 1971; Perbi, Akosua Adoma. *A History of Indigenous Slavery in Ghana: From the 15th to the 19th Centuries.* Accra: Sub-Saharan Publishers, 2004; Yarak, Larry W. *Asante and the Dutch 1744–1873.* New York: Oxford University Press, 1990.

Rebecca Shumway

Asiento

An *asiento* was a transferable contract with the Spanish crown allowing its holder to sell African slaves in Spanish colonies in the Americas.

Asientos arose from a proposal for assisted migration to Spanish colonies, presented to King Carlos I of Aragon and Castile, later Holy Roman Emperor Charles V, by Bartolome de Las Casas in 1517. Las Casas's proposal allowed each immigrant to Spanish colonies to import twelve African slaves, in order to replace Indian slaves.

By 1518, Carlos I had granted the first *asiento*, for shipping 4,000 African slaves to the Spanish West Indies for purchase by colonists there, to a courtier, Lorens de Gomenot of Savoy, who promptly sold the right to a Genoese merchant group for 25,000 ducats. The Genoese then bought **cargoes** of African people, one cargo on the Guinea coast but the others in **Lisbon**, and transported them across the Atlantic to be resold. Initially, most *asiento* slaves were purchased from Portuguese traders, because a Papal Bull of 1493 and the Treaty of Tordesillas of 1494 had given Portugal exclusive control of European trade with Africa.

By 1789, Spanish, Portuguese, Genoese, Flemish, Dutch, and British merchants all held *asiento* contracts, obtained either directly from the Spanish crown or indirectly by purchasing *asientos* or shares of *asientos* from other merchants. *Asiento* merchants sometimes suffered huge losses from their authorized slave-trading, but *asientos* could have other values because they presented opportunities to **smuggle** in other goods or larger numbers of slaves than authorized.

Between 1580 when the Spanish and Portuguese crowns were unified under Felipe II and 1701 when Spain's newly crowned Felipe V (grandson of France's reigning Louis XIV) awarded a French company an *asiento*, most *asientos* were sold to Portuguese merchants. Felipe II needed revenues, especially after the Spanish Armada was defeated in 1588, and he viewed *asientos* as one means of obtaining them. **Seville** merchants held an *asiento* from 1651 to 1662, and Seville's Casa de Contratacion briefly controlled the *asiento* trade after 1676, but they both failed to deliver the numbers of slaves required, and their *asientos* reverted to the Portuguese.

After France lost the War of the Spanish Succession, and in breach of a promise to share the trade with its Dutch ally, Great Britain received an exclusive *asiento* under the Treaty of Utrecht (1713) to supply 4,800 slaves per year to Spain's colonies in the Americas for thirty years. Britain's rights were then sold to the South Sea Company, which was owned by **London** venturers and soon famous for a 1720 bubble in the price of its stock. The British *asiento* trade was not as regular or profitable as expected. Spain was owed £68,000, and was threatening to terminate Britain's *asiento*, when the War of Jenkins' Ear between Britain and Spain was declared in 1739. The Treaty of Aix-la-Chapelle (1748) ended that war and extended Britain's *asiento* rights, but Spain bought them back for £100,000 under the Treaty of Madrid (1750).

Spain had created the Royal Company of **Havana** to assume the importing of slaves into its colonies, but the company failed in 1760. *Asientos* were again sold in 1765, 1773, 1780, and 1783, with **Liverpool**'s Baker and Dawson shipping 5,306 slaves to Spanish America under the last *asiento*. Carlos IV abolished the *asiento* system by decree in 1789, opening up slave-trading in Spain's colonies to everyone interested. *See also* Abolition of the Slave Trade, Spain; Buenos Aires; Dutch Slave Trade; Enslavement and Procurement; French Slave Trade; Illegal Slave Trade; Spanish Caribbean; Import Records; Jamaica; Portuguese Slave Trade; Slave Merchants (Slave Traders).

Further Readings: Corwin, Arthur F. *Spain and the Abolition of Slavery in Cuba, 1817–1886.* Austin: University of Texas Press, 1967; Du Bois, W.E.B. *The Suppression of the Slave Trade to the United States of America, 1638–1870.* New York: Russell & Russell, 1965; Du Bois, W.E.B. *The Negro.* Philadelphia: University of Pennsylvania Press, 2001; Eltis, David. *Economic Growth and the Ending of the Transatlantic Slave Trade.* New York: Oxford University Press, 1987; Mannix, Daniel Pratt, with Cowley, Malcolm. *Black Cargoes: A History of the Atlantic Slave Trade, 1518–1865.* New York: Viking, 1962; Murray, David. *Odious Commerce.* Cambridge: Cambridge University Press, 1980; Rawley, James A., with Behrendt, Stephen D. *The TransAtlantic Slave Trade, a History.* Rev. ed. Lincoln: University of Nebraska Press, 2005; Thomas, Hugh. *The Slave Trade: The Story of the Atlantic Slave Trade, 1440–1870.* New York: Simon & Schuster, 1997; Trevelyan, G. M. *England under Queen Anne: The Peace and the Protestant Succession.* London: Longmans, Green and Company, 1934.

Steven B. Jacobson

Atkins, John (1685–1757)

Born in 1685, John Atkins was a **surgeon** in the Royal Navy who spoke out against the slave trade. He did so most publicly in his 1735 work, *A voyage to Guinea, Brasil, and the West-Indies; in his Majesty's ships, the Swallow and the Weymouth*.

The voyage in Atkins' book was a two-year trek lasting from February 1721 until February 1723, the aim of which was pirate suppression. His work contains observations of the natives and inhabitants encountered during his journeys through Africa and the Americas, including annotations on their colors, **languages**, habitats, diets, **religions**, customs, and manners. Additionally, it includes notes regarding the slave, gold, and ivory trade markets, as well as information on the winds, currents, and tides of several coasts. The narrative addresses the undesirable nature of a sea-dependant livelihood. The sections of perhaps the most historical interest involve Atkins's commentary on the slave trade.

Therein, he stated the following:

We who buy Slaves, say we confer a Good, removing them to a better state both of Temporals and Spirituals; the latter, few have the Hypocrisy (among us) to ... own, and therefore I shall only touch on the former ...; To remove Negroes then from their Homes and Friends, where they are at ease, to a strange Country, People, and Language, must be highly offending against the Laws of natural Justice and Humanity; and especially when this change is to hard Labour, corporal Punishment. (Atkins, pp. 177–178)

Atkins was opposed to the trans-Atlantic slave trade on not just an ethical level, but also on a practical one. Slaves frequently battled to **escape** the ships of their captors. Such rebellions typically happened while the shore was still in sight, but there are many reports of these mutinies occurring far out at sea as well. Such inevitabilities jeopardized the well-being of all on board.

Atkins wrote of his belief that slaves thought—

themselves bought to eat, and more, that Death will send them into their own Country, there has not been wanting Examples of rising and killing a Ship's Company, distant from land, tho' not so often as on the coast; but once or twice is enough to show a Master's Care and Diligence should never be over till the Delivery of them. (*Resistance to Slavery*, p. 4)

Also drawing Atkins's ire was the intracontinental slave-trafficking in Africa. As African groups such as the Ashantes and Dahomeans grew more reliant on trades with European merchants, they began seizing fellow Africans and selling them into slavery in exchange for guns and other commodities. In 1727, Atkins spoke out against such tactics, commenting on the irony that the negro who sold his fellow Africans as slaves on one day might be sold himself a few days later.

Atkins later published a medical textbook, *The Navy Surgeon*. A copy of that text can be found in the Foyle Special Collections Library. He died in 1757. *See also* British Navy; Narratives by Slave Traders.

Further Readings: Davis, David Brion. *The Problem of Slavery in Western Culture.* New York: Oxford University Press, 1966; New Acquisitions Archive, September 2003. [Online, October 8, 2006]. King's College London Web site: 2003. http://www.kcl.ac.uk/depsta/iss/library/speccoll/acqarch/acqarch03.html; "Resistance to Slavery, the Anti-Slavery Movement, and Abolition." University of Calgary, 2001. [Online, October 8, 2006]. University of Calgary Web site: http://www.ucalgary.ca/applied_history/tutor/migrations/four4.html.

Michael Lombardo

B

Baquaqua, Mahommah Gardo (1824/31–?)

Mahommah Gardo Baquaqua was enslaved as a **Muslim** and a young adult in the northern region of what is now known as Republic of **Benin** while serving as a bodyguard in the palace of one of the local rulers of the region. After several changes of ownership he was, in 1845, taken to **Ouidah**, the notorious slave-trading port of **Dahomey**, from where he was shipped to the Pernambuco region of **Brazil**. On his arrival there, Baquaqua was sold to a baker who lived in a town outside Recife. According to his own testimony, Baquaqua worked under harsh conditions in the baker's custody. This prompted him to **escape** on one occasion and to attempt **suicide** on another. Eventually, from the region of Recife, Baquaqua was sold to a ship captain, identified as Clemente Jose da Costa, at Rio de Janeiro, Brazil. Under his new master, he served on board a slave ship (partly owned by his master) as a cabin steward, making two voyages south along the coast of Brazil to Rio Grande do Sul and the island of Santa Catarina.

In 1847, Baquaqua sailed on his master's ship to New York where a local (and predominantly black-based) abolitionist group known as the New York Vigilance Society supported him in his fight for freedom. In particular, they assisted Baquaqua and two other slaves, namely Jose da Rocha and Maria da Costa, to file a writ of *habeas corpus* requiring that Captain da Costa deliver the three slaves in question to the Court of Common Pleas of New York. At the first hearing in this court, the female slave, Maria da Costa, indicated that she was not interested in the suit, and thereafter the case involved only the two male slaves. However, in the end the court's ruling was not favorable for Baquaqua and Rocha as the presiding judge, Charles P. Daly, ruled that the two male slaves should be returned to the ship, on the grounds that that they were crewmembers, and their return was therefore required under the terms of the treaty of reciprocity between Brazil and the United States governing the desertion of crewmembers. Following this court decision, Baquaqua escaped from a New York jail to Boston where he became a free man. Thereafter, he moved to Haiti, and between 1847 and 1849 associated himself with the American Baptist Free Mission there. In

1849, following his conversion to **Christianity** in Haiti, Baquaqua moved back to North America, and in due course attended the New York Central College in MacCrawville. Eventually, he recorded his memoir in 1854 while he resided at Chatham, Canada West (Ontario), which at the time was one of the main termini of the Underground Railroad from the United States. This memoir is a valuable source for the history of the African diaspora partly because it contains Baquaqua's experiences, especially as a slave and an activist in abolitionist networks, which throw light on the situation of enslaved and free blacks during the nineteenth century. *See also* Abolition of the Slave Trade, Brazil; Brazil; Illegal Slave Trade, Brazil; Slave Narratives.

Further Reading: Law, Robin, and Lovejoy, Paul E. *The Biography of Mahommah Gardo Baquaqua: His Passage from Slavery to Freedom in Africa and America.* Princeton, NJ: Markus Wiener, 2001.

Mohammed Bashir Salau

Barbot, John (Jean) (1655–1712)

John (Jean) Barbot was a **slave trader** and author. Born on May 25, 1655, in Saint Martin on the Ile de Ré (opposite the port of La Rochelle, on France's Atlantic coast), Barbot grew up in a Protestant (Huguenot) family. In 1678–1679 he served as a commercial agent (*commis*) on a slave ship sent to West Africa and the Caribbean by La Rochelle merchants. A second voyage followed in 1681–82, by which time the merchants' businesses had been absorbed into the **monopoly** of a state company, the Compagnie du Sénégal. The revocation of the Edict of **Nantes** in 1685 obliged Barbot and his brother to flee to **London**, where he continued his mercantile career, probably participating in slaving as well as other ventures. In 1690, he married a woman from La Rochelle and became an English subject (hence John rather than Jean). A decade later he retired from mercantile life in London and in 1703 or 1704 moved to Southampton, where he appears to have worked for the English secret service, gathering information from French prisoners-of-war. He died on December 27, 1712.

Barbot's main importance is as the author of three lengthy documents: a journal of his 1678–1679 voyage (about 50,000 words, in French), a French manuscript account of West Africa in letter form (about 250,000 words, completed in 1688), and an enormous English account (about 500,000 words, partly based on the French account, published posthumously in 1732). In addition to his own observations, the last two documents contain a considerable amount of material derived from seventeenth-century publications, such as those of Dapper, Villault, de Marees, and Bosman. Nevertheless, Barbot's writings constitute one of the most important sources for the history of the West African coast in the late seventeenth century. They deal particularly with the coast from **Senegal** to what is now Benin, as well as with **Calabar** (Nigeria) and the island of Príncipe.

Much of what Barbot wrote about the slave trade was copied from earlier sources or derived from colleagues, and his views on the subject were largely conventional. But he provides some firsthand information on how slaves were purchased and treated, as well as on how they were perceived. *See also* French Slave Trade; Narratives by Slave Traders.

Further Readings: Debien, Gabriel, Marcel Delafosse, and Guy Thilmans, eds. "Journal d'un voyage de traite en Guinée, à Cayenne et aux Antilles fait par Jean Barbot en 1678–1679." *Bulletin de l'I.F.A.N.* 40B (1978): 235–395; Barbot, John. *A Description of the Coasts of North and South-Guinea.* London: n.p., 1732; Hair, P.E.H., Jones, Adam, and Law, Robin, eds. *Barbot on Guinea: The Writings of Jean Barbot on West Africa 1678–1712.* 2 vols. London: Hakluyt Society, 1992.

Adam Jones

Barracoons

A slave barracoon (a barrack-like hut) served as a temporary prison or holding pen used to confine enslaved persons under armed guard. The barracoon represented just one stopping place along the road from freedom to **enslavement**. Free people in the interior of Africa became slaves for a variety of reasons. Captives acquired because of warfare were the most common reason for enslavement. Not as prevalent as warfare, slave raids produced an abundant supply of slaves. Next came kidnapping, which created fewer slaves and was usually aimed at particular individuals. Enslavement could also result from judicial proceedings in which slavery would be meted out as a form of punishment. Slaves could also be paid as a form of tribute. The stronger, larger kingdoms often forced smaller, weaker kingdoms to pay tribute in slaves.

The next step toward enslavement usually involved a forced march to the coast. Some of the weaker or injured captives would expire before their arrival at the slave depot on the coast. European slave transport ships would be waiting at the coast where its captain or merchant would deal with their African agents for the purchase of slaves. African agents coordinated bringing the captives to the coast to coincide with the arrival of the slave ship, which often proved a difficult task. Coming close to shore could prove too

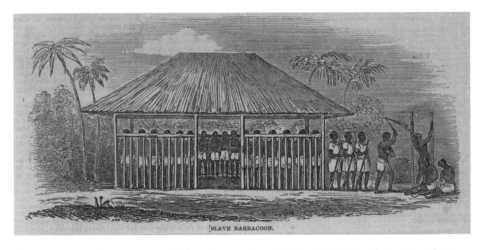

Slave barracoon, Sierra Leone, 1840s. Special Collections, University of Virginia Library.

dangerous for the slave ships. Ship **captains** would risk their ships if they could purchase a full or near full shipload of slaves. Slave dealers **chained** the captives together and then locked them in wooden cages called barracoons. Slave agents purchased captives from the slave raiders in small amounts until they accumulated enough captives to entice one of the slave ships to come close to shore. The captain of the ship and a **slave merchant** would come ashore and barter with the local slave agent until they agreed on a **price** for the slaves.

The whole process from reaching the coast to boarding the slave ship may only last a few days or could last months. Captives remained in the barracoon the entire time. The barracoon provided little protection against the elements, captives received little or no medical care, and local slave dealers provided little **food**, making the barracoon a dangerous place. The slave dealer's only goal was to sell the captives as soon as possible. The open bars surrounding the barracoon provided ample opportunity for buyers and sellers to examine and barter over their new human property. *See also* Branding; Cape Coast Castle; Coffle; Elmina; Entrepôts; Gorée Island; Trade Forts; Ventilation and Suffocation.

Further Readings: Manning, Patrick. *Slavery and African Life: Occidental, Oriental, and African Slave Trades.* In J. M. Lonsdale, ed. African Studies Series. Cambridge: Cambridge University Press, 2000; Shillington, Kevin. *History of Africa.* 2nd ed. New York: Palgrave Macmillan, 2005.

Michael Bonislawski

Benezet, Anthony (1713–1784)

Quaker philanthropist, teacher, writer, and antislavery activist Anthony Benezet was known for his progressive views and for the influence his writings wielded on the foremost figures in the abolition movement. Benezet was born on January 31, 1713, in St. Quentin, France, to a Huguenot merchant family. The Benezets, besieged by widespread Protestant persecution, moved to **London**. Benezet received a liberal education befitting his social standing and was apprenticed to a mercantile house at fourteen. In 1731, his family emigrated to Philadelphia. There, he joined the Quakers. At eighteen, Benezet entered the trade business. In 1736, he married Joyce Marriott. Finding little success in trade, he relocated to Delaware to try manufacturing. That career proved unsatisfying as well.

Following these setbacks, Benezet became an educator. Upon returning from Delaware, he taught at Germantown Academy in 1739. Three years later, Benezet transferred to the Friends' English Public School in Philadelphia. He excelled at teaching, expressing disdain for severe discipline. Believing that kindness generated beneficial personal relationships, Benezet made that idea the cornerstone of his pedagogical style. In 1750, he set up a night school at his home for slave children. Dismayed by the inferior education offered to women, Benezet left the Friends' English Public School in 1754 to establish the first female public school in America.

By the 1760s, Benezet was a passionate abolitionist. Through travelers' reports and interaction with the Quaker minister John Woolman, he became concerned about slavery. Together with Woolman, he convinced the attendees of the Philadelphia Quaker Yearly Meeting to officially recognize that slavery was inconsistent with **Christian** doctrine. Benezet wrote abolitionist pieces for newspapers and almanacs and, at his expense, published free antislavery pamphlets.

As a writer, Benezet specialized in rhetorical appeals and stereotype reversal. In his 1760 pamphlet "Observations on the [Enslaving,] Importing and Purchasing of Negroes," Benezet argued that buyers were complicit in slavery because their demands kept the trade alive. As a justification for ending slavery, he emphasized the Biblical dictum "Do unto others as you would have them do unto you." In 1772, he composed the pamphlet "Some Historical Account of Guinea," extensively citing travelers' accounts in his positive and realistic portrayals of life on the African continent. These portrayals contradicted the nightmarish depictions of slavery proponents. Benezet's writings were instrumental in galvanizing abolitionists like John Wesley and Thomas Clarkson. His correspondence with both Wesley and the British abolitionist Granville Sharp, who reprinted and circulated Benezet's writings across England, helped sustain an informal campaign against slavery in the British Isles. His letters to Benjamin Franklin persuaded the latter to join the abolitionist cause in 1769.

In 1770, with the support of the Quakers, Benezet founded the Negro School at Philadelphia for free and enslaved black children. Five years later, he established the Pennsylvania Abolition Society. He helped defeat a 1780 amendment to the gradual emancipation act that would re-enslave unregistered blacks. Benezet donated his estate to the Negro School after his wife's death. He died on May 3, 1784, in Philadelphia. *See also* Abolitionism.

Further Readings: "Abolition, Anti-Slavery Movements, and the Rise of the Sectional Controversy." African American Odyssey Web site: http://www.brycchancarey.com/abolition/benezet.htm; Brookes, George S. *Friend Anthony Benezet*. Philadelphia: University of Pennsylvania Press, 1937; "Founding of Pennsylvania Abolition Society." Africans in America. PBS Online Web site: http://www.pbs.org/wgbh/aia/part3/3p249.html; Sassi, Jonathan D. *Anthony Benezet's African Library: African Travel Narratives and Revolutionary-Era Antislavery*. College of Staten Island and the Graduate Center, City University of New York, n.d.

Cassandra Newman

Benin

The kingdom of Benin (not to be confused with the modern-day Republic of Benin) was among the earliest, longest-lasting, and most active participants in the European trade on the **Slave Coast**, including the trade in slaves. From pre-European times, Benin was one of the mightiest powers on the eastern Slave Coast. The Portuguese probably reached Benin in 1472, but it established strong relations with the kingdom only in 1485–1486, when they founded a trade "factory" at the port of Gwato. Europeans demanded slaves from the beginning of trade with Benin, and it was there that the Portuguese purchased their first large slave **cargoes**. Portugal (until the mid-sixteenth century), the Netherlands (late sixteenth to the early eighteenth centuries), and

Great Britain (mid-eighteenth to the nineteenth centuries, culminating in the occupation of the country in 1897) successively became the dominant European powers in the Benin region, although the French, Germans, and others intermittently established presences there. Before the mid-seventeenth century, Benin exported slaves not only to the New World, but also to Europe and the **Gold Coast**. In 1506, a slave typically cost between 12 and 15 *manillas* (brass bracelets); by 1517, the **price** had risen to 57 manillas. After the 1520s, **cowry shells** replaced manillas as the most popular "money" in the slave trade (in 1522, 50 manillas were equal to 6,370 cowries). Goods such as hats, beads, and so on were also bartered for slaves. From the late sixteenth to the late seventeenth century, Benin never sold its own citizens, but only female captives captured in war or purchased from neighboring peoples (including **Igbo**, Sobo, Ijaw, and others). From the mid-seventeenth to eighteenth centuries, however, slaves became the principal trade "goods" acquired by Europeans, and foreign male prisoners and eventually citizens of Benin itself were also sold abroad. In the heyday of the slave trade, Benin supplied 3,000 slaves a year. A contemporary related that "The West India planters prefer the slaves of Benin . . . to those of any other part of Guinea."

The overseas slave trade's influence on Benin should not be overestimated, however, and Benin-European trade relations cannot be reduced to the history of the slave trade. Slavery and the slave trade in Benin preexisted the arrival of the Europeans. Slaves were never the only—and until the mid-seventeenth century were not the principal—article purchased by the Europeans (others included pepper, ivory, cloth, and so on). The slave trade from Benin continued until the late nineteenth century, long after the official abolition of the overseas slave trade, and slavery existed within Biniland until the 1920s. Most significant, the course of Benin's socio-cultural development was firmly established before the Europeans arrived. Unlike some West African societies, such as **Ouidah** and **Calabar**, Benin's rise and decline were not determined primarily by the slave trade, although the European presence in general and the slave trade in particular did accelerate or hinder specific social, economic, political, and cultural processes. In particular, the rise of Benin, accompanied by intensive military expansion and the growth of inland trade—both preconditions for obtaining growing numbers of slaves—began several decades before the Europeans' arrival and ended in the early seventeenth century, long before the slave trade's end. Conversely, Europeans supplied Benin with **firearms**—sometimes in exchange for slaves—and served as mercenaries in the kingdom's armies, allowing Benin to expand more rapidly and successfully. Benin acquired captives mainly through slave raids on its neighbors, but European demand also stimulated trade with inland peoples. At the same time, the kingdom's growing demand for slaves undermined the loyalty of its dependencies. In the seventeenth century, the European presence encouraged the coastal Itsekiri, who played the role of intermediaries in the overseas trade, to acquire their independence from Benin. Although the overseas slave trade was declared a royal **monopoly**, it enriched and enhanced the political power of the courtiers who traded in the king's name, contributing to the effective transfer of power to court officials at the expense of the king.

In the cultural sphere, the association of the Bini deity of wealth, Olokun, with the sea may be due to trade with Europeans; some **folklore** motifs and royal ceremonies were introduced in the same connection. The flowering of Benin's celebrated royal art owes a considerable debt to the inflow of metals received from Europeans as payment for local goods, including slaves; new themes such as depictions of Europeans and even new art media such as the so-called Afro-Portuguese plastics and bronze plaques appeared.

Although the slave trade formed part of the Benin-European trade in general, its influence proved particularly strong in the two areas of demography and morality. The slave trade led to the depopulation of the inland areas from which people were taken away for sale. It led to a depreciation in the value attached to human life and freedom in Benin, as demonstrated by the **enslavement** and sale of free-born Bini and by an increase in human sacrifices—phenomena that continued until the end of the nineteenth century, despite the decline of the overseas slave trade. *See also* African Rulers and the Slave Trade; Dutch Slave Trade; Portuguese Slave Trade.

Further Readings: Graham, James D. "The Slave Trade, Depopulation, and Human Sacrifice in Benin History." *Cahiers d'Études Africaines* 5, 2 (1965): 317–334; Roese, Peter M., and Bondarenko, Dmitri M. *A Popular History of Benin: The Rise and Fall of a Mighty Forest Kingdom.* Frankfurt am Main: Peter Lang, 2003; Ryder, Alan F. C. *Benin and the Europeans. 1485–1897.* London: Longmans, Green and Company, 1969.

Dmitri M. Bondarenko

Benito Cereno (1855)

Benito Cereno is best known as the Spanish sea **captain** portrayed in Herman Melville's novella *Benito Cereno* (1855), a fictional recounting of an actual shipboard rebellion by African slaves, previously imported into South America, who were being transported on Cereno's ship from Valparaiso to Lima. In his play "Benito Cereno," which is part of his *The Old Glory* trilogy (1964), Robert Lowell loosely adapted Melville's story and moved it to the Middle Passage, setting it in an island harbor on the Trinidad coast.

The real Captain Benito Cereno's ship, the *Tryal*, was seized in a December 1804 revolt by slaves who hoped to sail it to **Senegal**. They killed their owner, Don Alexandro Aranda of Mendoza, in present-day Argentina, along with most of the ship's **crew**. Cereno escaped the *Tryal* two months later, after the slave leaders had him sail it to the uninhabited island of Santa Maria for fresh **water** and **food**, only to find the U.S. merchant ship *Perseverance* there already. The *Perseverance*'s Duxbury captain Amasa Delano, an indirect ancestor of Franklin Delano Roosevelt, boarded the *Tryal* and provided water, cider, and food to those on board, but did not realize the slaves were in control until his whaleboat was shoving off to return him to his ship, when Cereno desperately leaped to join him. The real Cereno was an ingrate. He later attempted, unsuccessfully, to avoid compensating Delano for recapturing the *Tryal* and its remaining **cargo** by submitting false depositions from three escaped Botany Bay convicts who had been *Perseverance* crewmembers to the Viceroy at Lima.

Melville's tale is an adaptation and expansion of Delano's 1817 narrative of his experience. Melville was a master of painterly description and symbolism, with great interest in ambiguity. He created an atmosphere of gray to reflect his *Benito Cereno*'s ambiguity, plus white and black to reflect Delano's perceptions, and it is rife with symbols that have tantalized generations of readers, scholars, and critics.

Melville changed several facts in his book. He changed the name of the *Tryal* to the *San Dominick*, a variation of the Spanish name for the French colony of **Saint Domingue** (Haiti); the day it left Valparaiso to May 20, Toussaint L'Ouverture's birthday; and the tale's year to 1799, when L'Ouverture's supporters obtained control over all of Saint Domingue. Delano's ship became the *Bachelor's Delight*, merging the names of the *Bachelor* and the *Delight* from Melville's *Moby Dick* (1851). The slave revolt leader's name remained Babo, which means an emphatic "no" in Hausa, a language with which Melville appears to have been familiar.

Most of Melville's tale is a narrative of what Delano fictionally perceived on the day Cereno escaped. What Delano thinks he sees after boarding the decrepit *San Dominick* is largely inaccurate. He views the relationship of Cereno and Babo, who Cereno introduces as his faithful body-servant, as one of "beautiful" confidence and fidelity, although he finds Cereno's allowing Babo to be overly familiar annoying, and Babo's and Cereno's whisperings together inappropriate. He has forebodings, but his concerns are with Cereno's deviations from a ship captain's expected behavior, not with Babo. Delano is apparently incapable of perceiving Babo as anything other than a dutiful slave, until Babo jumps into Delano's whaleboat after the escaping Cereno and attempts to stab him—an event Melville created for his tale. Because of Delano's blindness to Babo and Cereno's other captors, *Benito Cereno* has been seen as a predecessor of Ralph Ellison's *Invisible Man*.

As the *San Dominick* attempts to sail away, a canvas shroud wrapping its figurehead comes open to reveal the skeleton of slain slave owner Aranda, under which were scrawled the words "Follow Your Leader"—additional inventions by Melville. The skeleton had replaced the ship's original figurehead of Columbus. Melville's Babo remains silent after being overpowered in the whaleboat, throughout his trial before Spanish authorities in Lima, and at his execution. His head is then mounted on a pole, looking across the Plaza toward the church where Aranda's skeleton is buried and across the Rimac River toward a monastery. Melville's Cereno profusely thanks Delano but is haunted by "memory." When Delano asks, "What has cast such a shadow upon you?" Cereno's ambiguous reply is "the Negro." Cereno faints when pressed to testify against Babo. Then, "three months after being dismissed by the court," Cereno, "borne on the bier, did, indeed, follow his leader," dying in the monastery Babo's head is facing, on a hill aptly named Mount Agonia—just as Carlos I, who first authorized the Spanish slave trade, had died, in one scholar's words, "a symbolic ghost" in a monastery.

Interpretations of Melville's novella have radically differed. Melville has been seen as fiercely condemning slavery, or as not even commenting upon its morality. Babo has been viewed as a socialist-communist revolutionary, Christ, or a representation of evil itself. Cereno has been seen as destroyed by Babo, guilt, fear, or "blackness." The "leader" Cereno followed into death has been viewed as Babo, Aranda, Carlos I, or the founder of the Dominican Order.

Many now regard Melville's *Benito Cereno* as one of America's best stories. Lowell's play has a smaller circle of partisans. In addition to moving Melville's tale to Trinidad, Lowell's *Benito Cereno*—in Lowell's own words—hardened and politicized it, changing Captain Delano from a poignant innocent into an imperial know-it-all state department autocrat who himself shoots and kills Babo. Although three reviewers were enthusiastic, including the later dean of Yale's Drama School and Randall Jarrell, the play's New York reviews were generally mixed and it received uniformly poor reviews after it crossed the North Atlantic to **London** in 1967. *See also* Amistad, The; *Asiento*; Buenos Aires; Haitian Revolution, The.

Further Readings: Adler, Joyce Sparer. "Babo's Creative Genius." *Melville Society Extracts* 114 (September 1998); Adler, Joyce Sparer. *Dramatization of Three Melville Novels*. Lewiston, NY: Edward Mellen, 1992; Colatrella, Carol. *Literature and Moral Reform: Melville and the Discipline of Reading*. Gainesville: University Press of Florida, 2002; Delbanco, Andrew. *Melville: His World and Work*. New York: Knopf, 2005; Sanborn, Geoffrey. *The Sign of the Cannibal: Melville and the Making of a Postcolonial Reader*. Durham, NC: Duke University Press, 1998; Wallace, Robert K. *Douglass and Melville: Anchored Together in Neighborly Style*. New Bedford: Spinner, 2005; Wallace, Robert K. *Melville and Turner: Spheres of Love and Fright*. Athens: University of Georgia Press, 1992.

Steven B. Jacobson

Bissagos

The Bissagos (also Bijagos and Bujagos) occupy the Bissagos Islands off the coast of present-day Guinea-Bissau. From the sixteenth through the nineteenth centuries, they organized themselves through relatively decentralized political institutions yet still managed to produce significant numbers of slaves for sale to Atlantic merchants. Sixteenth-century observers made clear that on each of the islands strong warriors occasionally emerged as powerful local leaders, but there were no noticeable differences between how they and others lived. There was, then, no Bissago monarchy or state, and none had emerged by the nineteenth century.

Well before the sixteenth century, Bissago developed boat-building and navigation skills so that they could tap rich fisheries around their islands. As Atlantic merchants increasingly visited the area, Bissago redirected their skills toward producing tradable captives. From enormous boats containing dozens of rowers, Bissago warriors staged hit-and-run raids on the coastal villages of Balanta, Papel, Biafada, Floup, and other groups living on and between the Cacheu and Grande Rivers. Bissago often reached the mainland in the early morning and set fire to houses. As inhabitants fled the flames, Bissago warriors killed males who resisted and quickly seized **women** and children, dragging them to their boats and retreating before victims' families could organize a response.

By the seventeenth century, Bissago had transformed their islands into major slave-trading centers visited by Portuguese, Dutch, French, British, and Spanish merchants. The British, in particular, frequented the Bissagos, making the short journey there from the **Gambia River**. This raised the ire of Portuguese officials who were stationed nearby at Bissau and Cacheu, but militarily they were too weak to respond. The Portuguese saw the Bissagos as theirs, but could never enforce a **monopoly** on trade with the islands. In the late eighteenth century, British abolitionist Philip Beaver attempted to colonize an island near the Bissagos. However, his settlers were harassed, kidnapped, and killed by Bissago warriors, forcing Beaver to abandon his colonization scheme.

Bissago raids had several consequences. First, they forced coastal societies to change the architecture of their settlements by fortifying villages with palisades and constructing houses with many exits. Second, to counter the Bissago, coastal groups increasingly militarized, organizing young men into cohesive units that could defend against attacks. In some cases, these military units were used for offensive purposes, coastal societies preying on one another to harvest captives for trade. Third, although many societies successfully combated Bissago raids, some did not. This was particularly true of Biafada, the most frequent victims of Bissago attacks. In the seventeenth century, Biafada kings Emchabole, Mangali, and Bamala wrote letters to the Portuguese monarch seeking protection. Although missionaries saw Biafada as promising converts to **Christianity**, Portuguese military assistance was not forthcoming. Finally, because females were most often the target of Bissago raids, Bissago warriors frequently retained some of them, marrying them and relying on them to do much of their fieldwork. Bissago agricultural practices, then, became feminized as females, both slave and non-slave, were forced to carry out almost all society's food production and processing work. *See also* Decentralized Societies.

Further Reading: Thomas, Hugh. *The Slave Trade: The Story of the Atlantic Slave Trade, 1440–1870.* New York: Simon & Schuster, 1997.

Walter Hawthorne

Black Sailors

Black sailors played a crucial role in the commercial revolution that the slave **plantation** brought to the New World. Armed with skills that some acquired in Africa, learned when pressed into service during the Middle Passage, or served as stewards and servants on ships during **enslavement**, the black sailor became an important worker of the Atlantic slave trade. At the height of slavery, they ferried goods from place to place in the Chesapeake and Mississippi regions and between the Caribbean Islands. During the American Revolution (1776), the American Civil War (1864), and until the World Wars, the black sailor was a ubiquitous presence in the American military, especially the navy. Finally, some served as part of the Underground Railroad network to freedom.

Before European (Portuguese) arrival off the African coast in the fifteenth century, African canoe mariners sailed the Atlantic sea, albeit often remaining close to the coastline. As well, a complex and extensive commercial network of waterways served large parts of West Africa from the Niger-**Senegal**-Gambia region to the Hausa States and Yorubaland region. The West Central Africa and Congo regions were also connected by coastal commerce by boat. African canoes, capable of carrying from 5 to more than 100 people, were used for both fishing and riverine commerce. The **Gold Coast** canoemen and the Kru of **Liberia** impressed European merchants with their boat-handling skills. In fact, they were largely responsible for ferrying goods as well as slaves between European ships on the high seas and European forts and castles on the West African coast. European-chartered companies sometimes used "castle slaves" as boatmen. African mariners also served as linguists, pilots, and surfmen for Euro-African commercial interests. Some Africans carried this maritime experience into Atlantic slavery. Not surprisingly, about 22 percent of eighteenth-century black mariners were African born.

From the early European voyages of exploration (fifteenth century) black sailors (free and unfree) journeyed with Christopher Columbus, Balboa, Cortez, and others to different parts of the world. With the establishment of the plantation complex in the New World, black sailors (free and unfree) constituted part of the workers of the Atlantic trade—working on ships, fishing, and handling other maritime activities. With the high rate of **mortality** among European sailors during the slave trade, ships were sometimes left shorthanded. In these instances, slaves were taught to handle aspects of seafaring work. Aboard slave ships, such "sailors" performed whatever jobs they were taught to perform. European eyewitness accounts indicate that ship **captains** sometimes trained some of their slaves "to use the oar" in the Caribbean.

Furthermore, black sailors were pressed into service on British ships during the turbulent eighteenth century, especially during the wars of Spanish succession, Austrian succession, the Seven Years' War, the American Revolution, and the French Revolution, all between 1700 and 1815. Thus, black sailors covered every corner of the Atlantic bringing tangible skills that they had learned in Africa or during the Middle Passage to the Americas or as free men in the New World. Sea travel bestowed freedom on slaves, and unceasing demands for maritime labor resulted in numerous blacks working on coasters and ships. They served as coxswains of rowing craft, captains of sloops and schooners, and in the Chesapeake, as pilots of oceangoing vessels. During the American revolutionary wars, some black sailors (maritime slaves) piloted British invasionary forces in the hopes of attaining their freedom in the event of a British victory.

The plantation complex benefited from the services of black sailors in many ways. Boats and canoes moved rice, timber, tobacco, and other items along the labyrinth of southern waterways of the Chesapeake Bay. Similarly, ship-to-shore lighterage, especially from the Caribbean to the Chesapeake was undertaken by boats manned by black sailors. Dugouts and hybridized boats with European-style sailing rigs (similar to Senegambian canoes) served the slaves' transportation needs in the Chesapeake. Black sailors helped in constructing and handling the ubiquitous small craft that became common on the early American waterfront. Enslaved black sailors, using small boats and canoes, facilitated their masters' business in the Atlantic basin.

In the Caribbean, slave boatmen looped from place to place along and between islands, fishing as well as transporting goods. Ships with black and white sailors, and even **runaway** slaves, crammed the shipping lanes between the Caribbean Islands. From the Caribbean to Africa, the Americas, and Europe, black sailors became an integral part of the workers of the new commercial capitalist maritime revolution.

Black sailors were important in the struggle against the slave trade, especially in the Underground Railroad network, especially from 1812. In the coastal waters of the Carolina lowcountry and the Chesapeake Bay, black sailors were important in transporting runaway slaves. They used their freedom on the water to spread information about abolition in many parts of the United States and the Atlantic Basin. They guided people to freedom and played the "role of newspapers and royal mail service across the Atlantic," passing news and messages complete with regional and local differences.

A majority of black sailors during the U.S. Civil War, especially 1863–1864, were "contrabands" or "boys." They served on many vessels and provided labor at shore installations. They occupied the lowest rungs of the hierarchy of authority and had the lowest rating among sailors, besides being the lowest paid. Because of racial prejudice, many black sailors worked as laborers and servants rather than using their seafaring skills. Others worked as cooks and stewards who prepared meals. Naval officers, as part of the larger American society, generally regarded African Americans as inferior and subservient. Prejudice militated against black sailors being commissioned as officers.

By the 1840s and 1850s, many black sailors from Philadelphia, Baltimore, New York, and Boston had commercial maritime experience on steamships lines. Some in the Virginia region, especially near Norfolk, had experience on a warship. Others from **New England** had participated in two- to three-year whaling voyages. In Ohio, Missouri, and the upper Mississippi, many black sailors gained experience as deckhands, stewards, cooks, barbers, and cabin attendants. They stoked furnaces and tended boilers on steamboats. Some black sailors joined the navy, while others served on pirate ships.

Some black sailors ended up as seamen because of the masters' decisions. Others negotiated with their masters to allow them to go to sea, inspired by the love of travel, the prospect of "freedom on the sea," and the image of distant horizons. Black sailors served as sailors in both slavery and freedom. Circumstances of war often provided the opportunity for black men to enlist in the navy. More often than not, these men escaped from slavery, and the navy became one of the few establishments in which the federal government protected them and gave them the opportunity to serve. *See also* British Navy; Crew.

Further Readings: Bennett, Michael J. "Union Jacks: The Common Yankee Sailor of the American Civil War, 1861–1865." Ph.D. dissertation, St. Louis University, 2001; Bolster, W. Jeffrey. *African American Seamen in the Age of Sail.* Cambridge, MA: Harvard University Press, 1997; Langley, Harold D. "The Negro in the Navy and the Merchant Service, 1798–1860," *Journal of Negro History* 52 (October 1967): 273–286; Merrill,

James M. "Men, Monotony, and Mouldy Beans—Life on Board Civil War Blockaders." *American Neptune* 16 (January 1956): 49–59; Putney, Martha S. *Black Sailors: Afro-American Merchant Seamen and Whalemen Prior to the Civil War.* Westport, CT: Greenwood Press, 1987.

Edmund Abaka

Bonny

Bonny is one of the city states of the Niger Delta, a region now located in southern part of contemporary Nigeria. In 1846, a period that coincides with the abolition of the slave trade and introduction of **legitimate commerce** in palm oil, the geographic location of Bonny was noted as follows: "By its safe and extensive anchorage, its proximity to the sea, and connection with the great rivers of Central Africa, Bonny is now the principal seat of the palm oil trade as it was formerly of the slave trade in West Africa" (Dike, 1956).

Bonny and **Calabar** in the mouth of the Niger has been identified as one of the four major slave trade centers in West Africa. The remaining three areas include the Guinea Coast, **Senegal**, and Congo. Figures are readily available to demonstrate the significance of Bonny as a major slave port of West Africa. One of the most readily cited figures is the one produced by Captain John Adams in 1822. The captain observed that 20,000 slaves left the port of Bonny on a yearly basis. In terms of ethnic composition, 16,000 of the slaves came from the hinterland country of Ibo. This country alone, according to the captain, sold about 320,000 slaves in twenty years.

One unique and amazing aspect of the slave trade in Bonny and other city states of the Niger Delta is the ways slaves were acquired for the trans-Atlantic slave trade. Although a good percentage of slaves from other parts of the **Slave Coast**—most important, **Lagos, Gold Coast, Congo River**, and **Dahomey**—came largely through wars and raids in the hinterlands, Bonny had the opportunity of being supplied with slaves acquired through oracular devices. The **Igbo** country of the hinterland sent slaves to the coast after they had been banished by the **Aro** oracle for committing crimes or other antisocial offenses. The theories of the origin of the Aro oracle are complex. Some historians believe that the founders of the oracle were formerly residents of Bonny and other parts of the Niger Delta, but migrated into the hinterland and founded the Ibo towns of **Arochukwu** for the sole purpose of sending slaves to the coast. The overwhelming influence of the oracle limited the acquisition of slaves through other means. The Aro oracle was not the only slave-producing oracle in the Ibo country. Other less prominent ones include the Agballa at Awka, Igwe at Umunora, and Onyili-ora near Nri. *See also* Enslavement and Procurement; Entrepôts; Legitimate Commerce; Ports; Slavery in Africa.

Further Readings: Dike, Onwuka. *Trade and Politics in the Niger Delta, 1830–1885.* Oxford: Clarendon Press, 1956; Jones, G. I. *The Trading States of the Oil Rivers: A Study of Political Development in Eastern Nigeria.* London: Oxford University Press, 1963; Priestley, Margaret. *West African Trade and Coast Society.* London: Oxford University Press, 1969.

Saheed Aderinto

Bordeaux

The city of Bordeaux, France, founded by the Romans during the third century B.C., was one of the most active **ports** in France during the days of slavery (along with La Rochelle, Le Havre, and **Nantes**). Indeed, from 1672 to 1792, what is usually referred to as *la traite des noirs* (the trade in negroes) in French consisted mostly of importing slaves from Africa and sending them to French territories overseas (the West Indies) by way of Bordeaux. In spite of a first attempt to abolish slavery after the French Revolution (in 1794), it was later revived by Napoleon until he put an end to it definitively in 1848. The prosperity of the French colonies depended largely on the continuous import of slaves from Africa (particularly Guinea). To keep the production stable, some 1.25 million slaves were sent from France to the Caribbean. Between 1717 and 1789, French exports were multiplied by ten, with Bordeaux being responsible for 40 percent of the trade between France and the West Indies. The city's main traders managed to export most of the goods coming from the **French Caribbean** to other European ports, for example, Amsterdam, Hamburg, or **London**. Some of these traders named their slave ships with sometimes ironic names such as *Amitié* (Friendship), *La Fortune* (*The Fortune*), or *Liberté* (Liberty). The last belonged to Isaac Couturier in Bordeaux and was the first ship to be sent to the Caribbean in 1762. In the next couple of years, only a few vessels were to leave Bordeaux, because the traders were still unsure about the success of this type of trade. One of the main concerns was to keep the slaves alive because of the poor conditions on board (the slaves were often malnourished, carried **diseases**, and so on). If the amount of surviving slaves was superior to 20 percent, the trip was regarded as successful. That was the case for the *Lys*, owned by Teillard and Gachet, two famous traders, which carried 492 slaves on board and arrived in the Caribbean with 464 still living. In 1717, Bordeaux foreign trade was already starting to reach incredible heights compared with other cities of the same sizes (13 million *livres*, which represented about 10 percent of the nation's foreign trade). By the time of the French Revolution, Bordeaux was one of the wealthiest French cities, bringing in some 238 million *livres* (25 percent of France's foreign trade). Although Nantes was considered to be the leading city in terms of slave trade, the reason for its economic success was mostly that Bordeaux had a late start organizing its own trade; however, by the mid-1730s, Nantes was no longer the first leading port between France and its colonies.

Slavery had a huge impact on the culture of Bordeaux: many streets were named after famous slave owners, and some of the most popular buildings were built with the money gained from the slave trade under the reign of Louis XV. One of the most famous **museums** for instance is the "Musée Colbert," which was named after Louis XV's infamous minister, who wrote the Code Noir. There are, however, no official monuments in memorial of the black people who unwillingly contributed to the wealth of the city. Although Bordeaux's past as a city importing slaves has been kept secret for a long time and is still a taboo in many respects, some historians have recently begun to research Bordeaux's past as a slave port. In 2001, the

French Parliament publicly denounced the evils of the slave trade and called it "a crime against humanity." A committee of writers, historians, and scholars gathered under the name "Diverscité" and are currently working to create greater awareness regarding Bordeaux as a colonial city. *See also* French Caribbean; French Slave Trade; Historical Memory; Nantes.

Further Readings: Crouzet, François. *Britain, France, and International Commerce: From Louis XIV to Victoria, Collected Studies Series*. Brookfield, VT: Variorum, 1996; Thomas, Hugh. *The Slave Trade: The Story of the Atlantic Slave Trade, 1440–1870*. New York: Simon & Schuster, 1997.

Steve Puig

Bozal

The term *bozal* is of Spanish origin and was frequently used in Iberia and in Spain's and Portugal's American colonies to describe people born in Africa. Iberian groups believed that a *bozal* was a culturally inferior person and a savage. In the Americas, the term was used to identify an enslaved African brought directly from Africa to the Americas and who did not speak an Iberian **language** (for example, Spanish or Portuguese). A *bozal* did not practice Catholicism and therefore was not religiously baptized. The term was commonly used in the Atlantic slave trade era from the sixteenth through nineteenth centuries to describe the large influx of enslaved Africans who were forced to cross the Atlantic Ocean from West Africa. Other European groups used comparable words to *bozal*, including the British, who used **"saltwater negroes."**

Bozales found themselves in the two-tier slave system developed throughout the Americas. *Bozales* performed backbreaking tasks and were assigned the hardest work on a **plantation** or a ranch and in the mines and forests. Consequently, many of the newly enslaved Africans were moved into the interior of Central and South America to extract or produce raw materials such as gold, silver, **sugar**, cocoa, and leather.

Despite a *bozal*'s initial inability to display or understand Iberian culture, Spain's residents and subjects believed that a *bozal* could be molded into a **Christian**, which was desired of all enslaved Africans living in the Spanish and Portuguese empires. Shortly after a suspected *bozal*'s arrival in Spain or in the American colonies, a *bozal* was baptized and forced to adopt and practice Catholicism. They had to learn to speak Spanish or Portuguese to communicate with their slave master, driver, and other enslaved Africans. Thus, the term *ladino* was introduced to differentiate between those who refused to give up their African heritage or who could not successfully speak Spanish and display a high level of Iberian acculturation and those who did. In some cases, *bozales* would **escape** the clutches of their new fate in the Americas and establish themselves in their own African community, called a *palenque*. Many enslaved Africans were deemed *bozal* throughout the colonial period in Latin America, revealing that African culture was not entirely destroyed in the Middle Passage as earlier scholars have suggested.

Further Readings: Landers, Jane. *Black Society in Spanish Florida*. Urbana: University of Illinois Press, 1999; Rout, Leslie. *The African Experience in Spanish America: 1502 to the Present Day*. Cambridge: Cambridge University Press, 1976.

Nadine Hunt

Branding

The trans-Atlantic slave trade encompassed a series of acts perpetrated by slavers that were meant to reduce the African to a slave, destroying his or her freedom and severing family and tribal ties. Part of the physical and psychological transitions Africans endured in the process of being enslaved was that of branding. Throughout the trans-Atlantic slave trade, participants branded Africans to illustrate their ownership of the captives and to signify slave status. Branding was also an act of disempowerment.

Branding was particularly necessary when the slaves belonged to several owners. Differentiating brands, typically fashioned from pieces of silver wire or small irons, were heated to a red-hot state and the branding iron was impressed onto the skin of slaves before they were transferred to the slave ship that would transport them to the New World and a life of slavery. Brands were often placed on the shoulder, arm, or breast of the slave. In the unsanitary conditions of the slave ships, the burns often became infected, inducing fevers and even gangrene.

Many of the European governments, **slave traders** and trading companies, and African monarchs branded the Africans to ensure that others were aware to whom the slaves belonged. Brands typically were used to indicate ownership, but additional brands might be imprinted on the slaves for various reasons. A brand, for example, could indicate that the appropriate

Branding slaves, nineteenth century. Special Collections, University of Virginia Library.

export duties had been paid. A royal insignia denoted permanent servitude to the crown, and a cross signified that the slave had been baptized. Individual masters sometimes distinguished their slaves from those of others by stamping their slaves with branding irons on specific parts of their bodies.

The scars produced by the branding were both physical and emotional and served as a permanent reminder of the trauma endured by those who passed through the Middle Passage. *See also* Enslavement and Procurement; Torture; Violence.

Further Readings: Clarkson, Thomas. *The History of the Rise, Progress, and Accomplishment of the Abolition of the African Slave-Trade by the British Parliament*. London: Cass, 1968 (1808); Falconbridge, Alexander. *An Account of the Slave Trade on the Coast of Africa*. New York: AMS Press, 1973 (1788); Thomas, Hugh. *The Slave Trade: The Story of the Atlantic Slave Trade, 1440–1870*. New York: Simon & Schuster, 1997.

Sharon A. Roger Hepburn

Brathwaite, Kamau (1930–)

The creative work of the Caribbean poet, critic, and historian Kamau Brathwaite is important to a study of the Middle Passage. The Barbadian's publications as a historian and his creative writing are built around an investigation of the lasting imprint of the trans-Atlantic crossing on the Caribbean and New World experience. His academic writing in cultural history discusses the impact of the encounters between Europeans and Africans on Caribbean and New World identities. His theorizing on creolization seeks to explain the ways in which the melting pot of cultures in the Caribbean has forged a new experience that synthesises the various racial and cultural inputs into Caribbean society. Arguably, Brathwaite's most significant contribution to Middle Passage discourse is located in his creative writing, for which he is more widely known and acclaimed.

His poetic work transcends the traditional label of poetry. His creative collections are poetry, and at the same time they are cultural critiques and philosophical documents. His seminal collection of poetry *The Arrivants: A New World Trilogy* (1973) explores the nature of African New World civilization, in which the Middle Passage is crisis, grave, and limbo moment. In this work, one of the protagonists, a descendent of Africa called Omowale, returns home by way of exploring the complex passageway between the old and new world. Significantly, Brathwaite's work is not chronological but cuts across time and space to reveal the connection between history, the present, and the future.

Brathwaite has contributed significantly to an understanding of the Middle Passage not only as a historical process, but also as a contemporary construct. His reading of the Caribbean creolization process is built around an examination of the centrifugal dissemination of cultural relations outward from the process of enduring the Middle Passage. In his poetry, the Middle Passage is holocaust; it is physical and psychological **rape**. But paradoxically, it is also a festering space for new creative cultural phenomena. His understanding of the impact of this process on the African's creative cultural sensibility is dramatized in his poetic treatment of the limbo dance. His poem "Caliban" represents the cramped and contorted position of the

African below deck in the contemporary ritual of the limbo dance. The creative ability to go under and to resurface again represents the resilient potential of the African.

His "tidalectics" (a play on the Western notion of dialectics) draws from the metaphor of the waves lashing and receding from the shore of the islands of the New World. But the waves are themselves also metaphors for the ocean, the limitless unceasing process of the passage of time. They are a trope of history. The sea is therefore ever present in his poetry. In poems like "New World A-Comin" and "Caliban" and in collections like *Mother Poem* (1977) the waves on the shore are in an instant transformed into the rhythms of the ocean. The sea is a grave, but it is also a gateway to possession and potential spiritual liberation. In "Caliban," the rhythmic beating of the African drum anticipates a process of unceasing ebb and flow, of cultural death and rebirth. This is also evident in later collections.

His Sycorax video style (in which he experiments with computer and digital fonts, point sizes, and Web phonetics) is born out of an understanding of capitalism, exploitation, and conquest, which is symbolized by the Middle Passage. In *X/Self* (1987), the evil trade is recast with the incarceration of the African within the system, matrix, and digital Middle Passage of our age. Hence, Brathwaite's writing style (in which he flouts the rules of standard English to privilege Nation language, the vernacular) reflects an artistic quest to find liberation and to bring about covert revolt by appropriating the vehicle of **language** that still threatens to carry the New World African into new virtual **enslavement**. *See also* Historical Memory.

Further Readings: Brathwaite, Kamau. *The Arrivants*. Oxford: Oxford University Press, 1973; Brathwaite, Kamau. *Roots*. Ann Arbor: University of Michigan Press, 1993; Rohlehr, Gordon. *Pathfinder*. Tunapuna: Gordon Rohlehr, 1981.

Curwen Best

Brazil

Brazil was the largest importer of slaves in the Atlantic slave trade. The Portuguese American prominence in the import of African slave labor grew up with the rise of the colony as the major tropical goods exporter, which turned it into the first American **plantation** model. Thus, if in the sixteenth century Brazil was a secondary destination of African arms exports, then in the following century it gradually took over the first place, as its **sugar** exports increasingly supplied the European market.

The use of African compulsory work was the cornerstone of colonial Brazilian society and economy. As a result of the Atlantic slave trade, the presence of African slaves spread throughout Portuguese American territories and encompassed every economic and social activity up to the late abolition of slavery in 1888.

In the first half of the seventeenth century, the sugar plantations of the Portuguese colony became closely tied to its main slave source: **Angola**. From the late sixteenth century, Indian labor was being replaced for African slaves in the cane fields and sugar mills of Bahia and Pernambuco, which were major sugar plantation captaincies.

Brazilian coal and vegetable vendors, 1816–1831. Special Collections, University of Virginia Library.

When the Dutch invaded and conquered the Pernambuco captaincy (1630–1654), they soon realized the necessity of controlling the source of slaves. For this reason, they seized **Luanda**, Benguela, and **São Tomé** (1641), from where they brought most of Brazil's slaves. The Dutch were expelled from Angola by troops from Brazil. Brazilian settlers at Rio de Janeiro and Pernambuco organized the African expedition. These events reveal the close relations between the Portuguese colonies on both sides of the South Atlantic.

In the first century and a half of Brazilian colonization, enslaved blacks came from two main regions: The Guinea Coast (West Africa) and Congo and Angola (West Central Africa). From the former region, the slaves came from the mainland (Senegambia) but almost all went through the **Cape Verde** Archipelago and, increasingly, thousands were channeled from Southern **ports**, chiefly from the Bight of Benin through São Tomé Island. For this reason, Portuguese settlers talked about Africa as "Guinea" and about Africans as "Guinea Negroes."

Between the years 1620 and 1640 the Portuguese slave trade became steady from Congo, turning West Central Africa into the major Atlantic slave exporting region. From Luanda, the Portuguese penetrated the backland and mixed with the native people, originating a Luso-African population. The Luso-Brazilian merchants' control over the Luanda and, later, Benguela slave trade owed partially to the formation of that mixed population, supporting the increasing demand for slaves in Brazil's sugar plantations.

On the opposite side of Atlantic, Brazilian sugar exports underwent a crisis in the late seventeenth century, while the gold-mining trade rose in the

Center South region of the colony, causing Brazilian slave imports to increase dramatically. From the early eighteenth century on, Rio de Janeiro was on par with Bahia and Pernambuco in the slave trade. Rio became the greatest slave importer, with the majority of its captives coming from Angola.

The new colonial exportation boom (1789–1815) forced Brazil to import Africans at unprecedented rates when compared with the previous two centuries. The prohibition of the slave trade above the equator (1815) and the proximity of total slave trade abolition (legally forbidden from 1831 on) hastened even more the importation of African slaves. Thus, in the last fifty years of the Brazilian slave trade, more than 1.5 million slaves landed in Brazilian ports, despite the legal prohibition of this trade in the two last decades (1831–1850).

In general, African slaves exported to Brazil came from two primary ethnic groups: Bantu and Sudanese. The former predominated in the first 150 years of the Portuguese slave trade, while the latter were imported in large **volume** from the late seventeenth century on. In the late eighteenth and early nineteenth centuries Brazil landed an impressive volume of slaves from the **Indian Ocean** region, including the Bantu people who were brought from **Mozambique**.

Bantu and Sudanese slaves were taken to various Brazilian regions, but a slave import pattern varied according to each port and captaincy. In Bahia, where the West African imports predominated, Sudanese were known as *Jejes* (Fon and Daomé) and *Nagôs* (Yoruba), among others. Rio de Janeiro, the Southern region (including the River Plate through **Buenos Aires**), and Pernambuco imported more Bantu than Sudanese slaves. Although they had received large numbers of West African slaves mainly in the first half of the eighteenth century, the majority of the slaves imported by Pernambuco and Bahia traders and some by Rio de Janeiro traders themselves.

Brazil's slave importation pattern throughout three centuries, nevertheless, gave rise in Brazil to the general distinction between "Mina" captives (exported from West Africa) and "Angola" slaves (brought from West Central Africa).

The fact that most of Luso-Brazilian slavery ventures came from Portuguese America in the eighteenth century, and that those **slave merchants** traded with colonial goods (tobacco and cane **rum**) along Africa's shore, could explain the relatively low cost of slaves in Brazil and the resulting widespread dissemination of slave labor in its several productive branches. Slaves were common on large plantations and in mining, but they also could be found in small groups or enslaved as personal property in towns. The owners of those small groups used their slaves in **food** crops such as manioc, which was important in colony purveyance or even in the small-scale tobacco farms for export, including the supplying of the Atlantic slave market. In towns, slaves worked on infrastructure, as craftsmen and street sellers ("profit slaves"), and as domestic servants.

Having been the main West African slave importer, Brazil showed a peculiar demographic pattern among American slave societies. From the mid-sixteenth to the mid-eighteenth century, Brazil imported about 4.8 million slaves or slightly more than 40 percent of all of the African slaves who landed in the New World. In the eighteenth century, Brazil alone imported almost 1.7 million slaves and, by the turn of the nineteenth century, the imports of African slaves had another major increase, reaching about 2 million captives between 1790 and 1850.

Close to 1798, however, slaves made up 40 percent of Brazil's population—nearly 3.25 million—including the *ladinos* (Brazil born) and *boçais* (African born). Their slave imports rose to unprecedented rates, but the slave share of Luso-Brazilian population decreased slightly to 38 percent in the years from 1800 to 1810 and reduced itself further in 1819 to 31 percent. On the eve of the abolition of slavery (issued in 1888), Brazil's slave population was only slightly bigger than it had been nearly one century earlier, reaching about 1.5 million people.

Several reasons led to this low share of the slave population in the Brazilian population when compared with the import of high numbers of Africans. The abundance of slaves and the low cost of the Luso-Brazilian slave commerce were the main factors. The possibility of replacing slaves led slaveholders to exploit the slaves' work and take little interest in their longevity.

The high percentage of males in the traffic to Brazil (like to all America) caused an unbalance between male and female slaves. Furthermore, the small share of children imported through the Middle Passage (as well as the high rate of childhood **mortality** among slave offspring and the low fertility of slave **women**) were conditions that lead to low rates of natural slave reproduction.

Mistreatment, harsh punishments, bad nutrition and housing, hard work in the field, and epidemic **disease**, which affected more captives than free people, contributed to low **life expectancy** among the slave population. For all these reasons, only the steady import of slaves was able to keep the Brazilian slave population at levels required to meet the slaveholders' demands.

Those features contradict the so-called mildness of slavery in Brazil (when compared with slavery in the Anglo-American colonies). Unlike the United States, which forbade importation of slaves in 1808 and saw the slave share of the North American population increase almost six times up to the eve of the abolition of slavery in 1865, Brazil kept the slave trade until 1850, during which time the slave population diminished. Miscegenation practices and the relative number of free colored people in the colonial and post-colonial society did little to improve slave life in Brazil.

It is not a matter of chance that the Atlantic slave trade and the omnipresence of slave work in Brazil have played an important role in Brazilian **historiography**. Since the 1930s, slavery in general and the slave trade in particular figured prominently into the historiographical models that provided explanations of the formation of Brazilian society and Brazil's place within the worldwide economy.

Currently, the most predominant model is the one that usually relates Brazil's process of social and economic formation with the expansion of the European market and the capital accumulation in the dynamic centers of the Western economy. The low cost of production—that is, land and labor—would have established highly profitable exporting activities in the Americas. Hence, slave commerce would be one mechanism of transferring the colonial economic surplus, consolidating the slavery system in peripheral regions and fostering primitive capital accumulation in the center. Thus, it would be the slave trade that permitted the formation of slave societies in the Americas and led to the Industrial Revolution in Northwest Europe.

This historiography presented at least one chief problem: its approach to the slave trade lacked original research. Only recently have some works presented thorough research on the slave trade. These works have tried to demonstrate that by drawing on locally grown commodities (mainly tobacco and a sugarcane brandy, *jeribita*) merchants from a few Brazilian ports (chiefly Bahia and Rio de Janeiro in the eighteenth century) could control the slave trade.

Recent historiography has renewed and corrected certain ideas that scholars debated in the 1960s and 1970s. Nonetheless colonial control over the Brazilian slave trade seems to be restricted only to the eighteenth century and to Luso-Brazilian South Atlantic ports. Furthermore, even in Bahia and Rio de Janeiro, metropolitan merchant capital had some importance in financing slave trade ventures to share risks and **profits** arising from this enterprise. *See also* Abolition of the Slave Trade, Brazil; Abolition of the Slave Trade, Great Britain; Angola; Credit and Finance; Illegal Slave Trade, Brazil; Internal Slave Trade, Brazil; Kongo; Lisbon; Portuguese Slave Trade.

Further Readings: Alden, Dauril. "Late Colonial Brazil, 1750–1808." In Leslie Bethell, ed. *Cambridge History of Latin America*. Cambridge: Cambridge University Press, 1986; Alencastro, Luiz Felipe. "The Apprenticeship of Colonization." In Barbara Solow, ed. *Slavery and the Rise of the Atlantic Economies*. Cambridge: Cambridge University Press, 1993; Blackburn, Robin. *The Making of New World Slavery*. New York: Verso, 1997; Inikori, Joseph E. *Africans and Industrial Revolution in England*. A Study of International Trade and Economic Development. Cambridge: Cambridge University Press, 2002; Prado Junior, Caio. *Colonial Background of Modern Brazil*. Berkeley, California: University of California Press, 1967; Schwartz, Stuart B. *Sugar Plantations in the Formation of Brazilian Society, Bahia, 1550–1835*. Cambridge: Cambridge University Press, 1985.

Gustavo Acioli Lopes and Maximiliano Mac Menz

Bristol

As a great British seaport town, Bristol, England, owes its notoriety to the development of the **triangular trade**, shipping, and shipbuilding. The slave and **sugar** trades in the Caribbean made Bristol the second city of England for the first three-quarters of the eighteenth century. An early English annalist from Bristol noted that "there is not a brick in the city but what is cemented with the blood of a slave. Sumptuous mansions, luxurious living, liveried menials, were the produce of the wealth made from the suffering and groans of the slaves bought and sold by the Bristol merchant" (Williams, 1994). In 1552, the merchants of Bristol obtained a Royal charter that established them as the Society of the Merchant Venturers of the City of Bristol, which sought exclusive control of overseas trade. The Bristol

Merchant Venturers date back to the fourteenth century. It was during this century of great trade that the Bristol Merchants also set up the Merchants Guild to share the burden of entertaining visitors who came to the port. The purpose of the Guild was to set up trading links and to share any risk attached in these links to set up new trade. The Merchant Venturers were a powerful lobby, responsible in the eighteenth century for ensuring that Bristol had its share of the trade in African slaves. The Society defended the trade on the grounds that the city's prosperity depended on it. By the late eighteenth century, an additional lobby, the West Indian Society, whose members included some Merchant Venturers, took up the cause of defending planter interests in the Caribbean. The West Indian trade was worth to Bristol twice as much as all of its other overseas commerce combined (Williams, 1994). With the decline of Bristol as a major port in the nineteenth century, the Society lost much of its influence. There are still many reminders today of the influence these powerful merchants once had on the development of Bristol as a major trading city.

The British trade in West Africa began with Sir John Hawkins's illegal shipment of human **cargo** to the Spanish West Indies in 1562. In its peak of success during the latter half of the eighteenth century, England accounted for half of all the slaves transported across the Atlantic Ocean. The bulk of the trade was to the West Indies, **Jamaica** in particular, amounting to more than 1.6 million people. Fewer Bristol ships sailed to West Africa; more sailed directly to the Caribbean. By the end of the eighteenth century, Britain had become the largest and most accomplished slaving nation in the world. The **profits** transformed the lives of people living in Britain; it changed their landscapes (money was poured into new buildings, houses, schools and universities, **museums**, libraries, and so on), their tastes (turned sugar from a luxury item to a commodity), and their local economies (banks grew rich from the profits made by some of Britain's most notorious **slave traders**). Eventually this process of transformation would leave Britain as the world's first industrial power, its slave economy indivisible from the whole.

The changing fortunes of the sugar industry and the abolitionist campaigns led to the abolition of the trade in 1807. Slavery itself continued to thrive, until resistance from slaves and abolitionists alike succeeded and emancipation was finally granted in 1833. Merchants, however, would continue to trade in slave-produced commodities like tobacco and cotton long after abolition of the trade, and, given their preeminence, goods manufactured in the industrial heartland still found their way to the African coast to be exchanged for human beings. *See also* Atkins, John; British Caribbean; British Slave Trade; Credit and Finance; Eric Williams Thesis; Liverpool; London; Ports.

Further Readings: Thomas, Hugh. *The Slave Trade: The Story of the Atlantic Slave Trade, 1440–1870*. New York: Simon & Schuster, 1997; Williams, Eric Eustace. *Capitalism and Slavery; with a new introduction by Colin A. Palmer*. Chapel Hill: University of North Carolina Press, 1994 (1944).

Nicholas Jones

British Caribbean

The Caribbean became the economic center of the **British slave trade** and one of the last bastions of slavery within the Empire. The British encountered existing slave systems as they acquired territory in the Caribbean. A slave-based economic system subsequently evolved throughout the region and led to the rise of a powerful planter class that exerted a significant influence on British politics in the nineteenth century. The end of the slave trade and the subsequent abolition of slavery marked the decline of the planter aristocracy and the marginalization of the Caribbean within the British Empire.

Colonization and Slavery

Spain was the Caribbean's first colonial power, but although they claimed the entire region, the Spaniards settled only a few of the major islands. By the late 1500s, British privateers and pirates began using the islands to attack Spanish treasure galleons en route from the mines in South America. The formal British presence in the Caribbean began in 1621, when the British settled St. Croix. In 1625, Barbados was claimed by the crown and two years later a settlement was established on the island. That same year, there was an unsuccessful attempt to settle Tobago. In 1628, Nevis was colonized by the British, and in 1632, settlements were established at Antigua and Montserrat.

The whip was frequently used to coerce the most out of the enslaved workforce; any unapproved rest could result in brutal punishment. Courtesy of Anti-Slavery International.

The first settlers on Barbados included eighty Britons and ten slaves. Following the model established by the North American colonies, the Barbadians established a legislative assembly in 1639, making it the third representative body created in the Western Hemisphere (after Virginia and Massachusetts). As other British colonies were founded in the Caribbean, they too created legislatures, also continuing the dichotomy of democracy and slavery created in the colonies to the north.

Sugar became the dominant crop on the island and planters began using **indentured servants** and convicts to secure enough labor to work the fields. The planters were unable to secure a large enough labor force through indenture, however, and there was a high **mortality** rate among the Britons. Other islands used indentured servitude with similar results. Many of the former servants eventually formed a small middle or merchant class on some islands. Others, including **runaways**, formed renegade bands that lived in the jungles. One group of Scots was transferred to Barbados for taking part in the Jacobite rebellion against the monarchy. A large number of the highlanders escaped into the jungles where they became known as the "Red Legs" because their legs became sunburned below their kilts.

In the 1640s, Barbadian planters began importing slaves from Dutch and Portuguese **slave traders**. Barbados became the most profitable of the Caribbean colonies and dominated the region's sugar production. The number of slaves imported grew steadily, but a number of natural disasters in the 1660s, including a major fire and a hurricane, devastated the economy.

One of the wealthiest British colonies in the area was established in 1655 when British forces under William Penn conquered **Jamaica**. In 1670, the island was officially ceded to the British. The population of Jamaica was about 3,000 when it was conquered by the British, including about 1,500 slaves. The British retained the slave system and new colonists to Jamaica also acquired new slaves, which were supplied by Dutch traders. By the early 1700s, Jamaica had supplanted Barbados as the area's major sugar producer, although both colonies were extraordinarily wealthy. Meanwhile, planters on the other British colonies increased their use of slave labor. Other colonies acquired by conquest included Trinidad, which was taken from Spain in 1797, and Tobago, which was ceded to the British in 1814.

To capture the revenues of the slave trade, the monarchy chartered the **Royal Africa Company** (RAC) in 1660. The company was granted a **monopoly** on the slave trade between Africa and Great Britain's colonies in the Western Hemisphere. The RAC subsequently established new slave posts along the African coast, or it conquered existing posts from colonial rivals such as the Dutch or Portuguese. By the 1680s, the RAC supplied the American and Caribbean colonies with some 5,000 slaves per year on average. The RAC's monopoly was revoked in 1698, and other firms began participating in the trade. **Bristol** soon became the hub of the slave trade, followed closely by **Liverpool**. In 1731, the RAC abandoned the slave trade to concentrate on other products and goods, and in 1752, the company was dissolved.

One of the byproducts of the manufacture of sugar is molasses. Planters and slaves began to distill the molasses to create an alcoholic drink, **rum**.

Distillers in **New England** soon became the major producers of rum, while the Caribbean colonies supplied the molasses. The result was the development of the **triangular trade**. One form of the system involved the shipment of molasses from the Caribbean **plantations** to the distilleries in New England. Rum and other trade goods were then shipped to Africa where they were traded for slaves. The slaves were then transported to the Caribbean and Southern colonies. Other versions of the trade included the shipment of sugar to Bristol or Liverpool, where slavers transported trade goods to Africa for slaves. The slaves were moved to the American or Caribbean colonies via the Middle Passage. By the mid-1700s, New Englanders dominated the slave trade and the importance of Bristol and Liverpool slowly diminished.

Slaves in the North American colonies had a high rate of natural increase, but conditions in the Caribbean caused a high mortality rate and necessitated the importation of more slaves. Only about one-quarter of children born to slave parents survived into adulthood. Malnutrition, overwork, and poor sanitation left slaves susceptible to **diseases** such as malaria and yellow fever and took their toll on the adult population. **Life expectancy** for field slaves in the British Caribbean was short, about 35 years. Recent slaves were the most at risk, some 15 to 20 percent died during their first year in the Caribbean. Most field slaves only endured about eight years of hard labor before their demise.

The population of the British colonies in the Caribbean grew to about 500,000 by 1750. The majority of the population, approximately 425,000 people, were slaves. In several of the colonies, slaves made up some 90 to 95 percent of the population. To maintain a sizable enough white population to deter or defeat slave revolts, several colonies enacted laws that mandated a proportion of whites to slaves. For instance, in Jamaica, plantations had to have one white male for every ten slaves, up to the first twenty slaves, thereafter, there had to be one settler for every twenty slaves.

The number of slaves continued to increase in the colonies until the slave trade was abolished. Despite their smaller geographic size, the Caribbean colonies took in about 40 percent of the total number of slaves brought into the British colonies in the Western Hemisphere. Between 1651 and 1807, the British brought approximately 1.9 million slaves to their Caribbean colonies in addition to a migration from the islands. For instance, on Barbados, large sugarcane plantations gradually bought out and absorbed small farms and midsize plantations. Many of the displaced planters resettled, and one group moved northward to form the colony of South Carolina in 1670.

Slave revolt was a constant fear among the white plantation owners in the Caribbean. One manifestation of this fear was the creation of restrictive slave codes. These codes were more severe than those in the North American colonies and included greater restrictions on manumission. The limitations on manumission reflected opposition by whites against a free black population on the islands. Planters were often allowed to employ especially harsh punishments. For example, a 1688 Barbadian law granted owners the right to kill or cripple slaves for a range of infractions, some relatively minor. There were three major revolts on Jamaica (1655, 1673, and 1760). And through the 1700s, the colonies averaged one slave revolt every five years. One of the most significant rebellions was the 1816 revolt in Barbados. The insurrection eventually involved more than 5,000 slaves who burned and looted more than forty estates on the island. Open fighting continued for four days until the main slave force of 400 was defeated by British regulars. Some 124 slaves were killed during the rebellion and 214 were executed afterward (some historians contend that as many as 1,000 slaves were killed in the subsequent reprisals). An additional 123 slaves were deported to other islands. Only one white settler died during the fighting. The rebellion enhanced abolitionist arguments in Parliament and led the government to grant Barbados greater autonomy.

The End of the Slave Trade and Abolition

The first major abolitionist group was formed by the Quakers in 1729. Abolitionists initially concentrated their energies on ending the slave trade. Many believed that if the supply of slaves was curtailed, slavery itself would end as planters would be forced to find alternative sources of labor. The first major victory in the abolitionist movement was the 1772 *Somerset Case* in which a court ruled that individuals could not be kept as slaves in Great Britain itself. This ruling created a dichotomy within the empire: slavery was illegal in Great Britain, but legal in the colonies. Planters mounted a series of unsuccessful legal challenges, but the abolitionist movement accelerated its drive. Through the 1770s, there were motions introduced in Parliament to abolish the slave trade or slavery.

The popular effort to end slavery continued to be led by the Quakers, while the political campaign was led by conservative politicians, including **William Wilberforce**, Thomas Clarkson, and the future Prime Minister William Pitt the Younger. The major support for slavery and the slave trade came from the West Indian planter lobby. The planters enjoyed the support of King George III, and his son, William, the Prince of Wales. William, the future William IV, led opposition to abolition in the House of Lords.

The American Revolution dramatically altered the British slave trade and patterns of slavery in the Caribbean. The British offered American slaves freedom if they ran away and enlisted in the British Army or Navy (several thousand did). The conflict also limited the triangular trade with New England, although, after the war, American slavers again dominated the slave trade with the Caribbean colonies. The conflict also led to new colonization. Some 8,000 loyalists were resettled in the Bahamas after the war, and thousands of former slaves who joined the British military in exchange for their freedom settled in **Sierra Leone**.

The onset of the Napoleonic Wars led to a decline in the demand for sugar as Napoleon ordered his allies and conquered nations to ban the import of British sugar. This led to a concurrent decline in the economic and political power of the West Indian planter lobby in Parliament. Nonetheless, the planters and their allies in the House of Lords were able to reject abolitionist bills that were approved by the House of Commons in 1799, 1801, and 1802.

In 1805, the House of Commons again passed a ban on the slave trade. Faced with widespread public and political support for the measure, the King relented and the bill was approved by the House of Lords and the crown. The ban on the slave trade went into effect in 1807.

The ban ended the widespread importation of slaves, although many planters purchased large numbers of slaves in anticipation of the end of the trade. In addition, **smuggling** slaves continued until the end of the Napoleonic Wars in 1815, which allowed the British to devote more resources to suppressing the trade. A naval squadron was stationed off the coast of Africa, and the government was able to negotiate agreements with more than thirty countries that allowed the Royal Navy to stop, search, and, if appropriate, seize suspected slave ships. The only major power to refuse such a treaty was the United States.

In 1823, Parliament passed laws designed to improve the lives of slaves. The new measures allowed slaves to purchase their freedom and gave them the right to own property. Punishment was limited and owners were required to keep a log of any punishment meted out. Finally, all colonies were required to appoint an ombudsman to oversee the health and safety of slaves. The Caribbean legislatures balked at many of the laws and only Barbados, the Bahamas, Grenada, St. Vincent, and Tobago appointed the requisite official. Legislatures from Antigua to Jamaica refused to comply. Nonetheless, the planter lobby defeated repeated attempts to ban slavery through the 1820s, but the group became increasingly tied to the Tories. When the Tories were defeated in the 1832 election, sixteen pro-planter members of Parliament lost their seats, leaving only thirty-five openly proslavery members in the legislature. More than 100 members formed a bloc to support any abolitionist bills. The West Indian colonies had seriously undercut any public support among the general population through their actions in opposition to Parliamentary initiatives. Antislavery groups presented Parliament with a succession of petitions in favor of abolition. In 1833, the House of Commons received 500 separate petitions in favor of abolition, while the House of Lords received 600. One petition contained 187,000 signatures. The following year, on August 29, Parliament finally approved a measure to ban slavery throughout the empire by 1834. To compensate planters for the loss of their slaves, Parliament authorized £20 million in grants.

Abolition was not immediate. Instead, the colonies were allowed to authorize five-year apprenticeship systems in which the slaves were supposed to be prepared and trained for freedom. Many planters took advantage of the system, but nevertheless, by 1838, slavery had ended in the British Caribbean. *See also* Abolitionism; Abolition of Slave Trade, Great Britain; African Rulers and the Slave Trade; African Squadrons, The; *Asiento*; British Navy; Closure of the Slave Trade; Haitian Revolution, The; Leeward Islands; Monopoly; Spanish Caribbean; Windward Islands.

Further Readings: Craton, Michael. *Empire, Enslavement and Freedom in the Caribbean*. Princeton, NJ: Markus Wiener, 1997; Goveia, Elsa. *Amelioration and Emancipation in the British Caribbean*. St. Augustine: University of the West Indies, 1977; Higman, Barry. *Slave Populations of the British Caribbean, 1807–1834*. Baltimore:

Johns Hopkins University Press, 1984; McDonald, Roderick, ed. *West Indian Accounts: Essays on the History of the British Caribbean and the Atlantic Economy in Honor of Richard Sheridan.* Kingston: University of the West Indies Press, 1996; Turley, D. *The Culture of English Anti-Slavery, 1780–1860.* London: Routledge, 1991.

Tom Lansford

British Navy

The British Navy initially helped expand slavery but later served as the main instrument to suppress the slave trade. The Royal Navy played a major role in the conquest of the Dutch and French colonies in the Caribbean in which slavery already existed. The Navy subsequently served to protect slave ships from pirates, privateers, and even enemy ships during times of war. The antipiracy campaigns of the Royal Navy in the early and mid-1700s were especially important in ending widescale pirate attacks on slave ships. For instance, the infamous pirate Bartholomew Roberts captured more than 100 vessels between 1720 and 1722 with a small fleet of pirate ships. Most of the captured vessels were slavers. In February 1722, a British squadron captured his ships and killed Robert during a battle. The Navy also undertook operations to end slave revolts in British colonies. For instance, the Navy helped defeat slave revolts in Belize in 1773 and 1820. Sailors and Royal Marines were used to recapture runway slaves during the rebellions.

The constant need for manpower in the Navy resulted in some former slaves serving as British sailors. Unlike the Royal Army, there were no racial prohibitions on service in the Royal Navy. During the American Revolution, the Royal Navy forcibly recruited some 185,000 sailors through the practice of impressment. Among those who joined the service were **runaway** slaves and freed slaves who were taken from captured American slave vessels. In addition, some slaves were pressed into service in the British Navy following attacks on the colonial possessions of Britain's enemies during the 1700s.

Parliament outlawed the slave trade in 1807, during the Napoleonic War. Because of the law, few resources were available to help suppress slavers. However, the government did station two ships along the West African coast to deter slavers. In addition, slave ships of the belligerent powers were routinely captured by the British. Freetown, the capital of the later colony of **Sierra Leone**, was established in 1787 as a refuge for former slaves who had joined the British during the American Revolution. During the Anglo-French conflict, the colony also served as an area where captured slaves of other countries could be granted freedom after 1807. The Napoleonic War lasted until 1815 and, during that period, Royal Navy ships would be given a bounty for captured enemy combatant slave ships and for each slave released. After the war, Parliament maintained this practice, thereby providing a monetary incentive for the capture of slavers.

In 1817, a British court ruled in the Le Louis case that Royal Navy ships could not stop vessels of other countries that were engaged in slavery without the consent of the home country. This led the British government to engage in a diplomatic offensive to secure treaties with other countries that

GROUP OF SLAVES ON THE PARADE, FORT AUGUSTA.

Africans liberated from a slave ship, Jamaica, 1857. Special Collections, University of Virginia Library.

would allow the Royal Navy to stop, search, and, if necessary, seize suspected slave ships of other countries. In 1815, Portugal had already granted the British the right to stop suspected Portuguese slave ships north of the equator and, eventually, the British were able to gain consent agreements from thirty nations. The United States was the only major power that refused to grant Great Britain the power to stop and search suspected slave vessels. As a result, many slavers of other nations began illegally traveling under the American flag to avoid arrest by the British.

The antislavery flotilla increased in size and scope after the end of the Napoleonic War and the subsequent agreements that allowed the search and seizure of foreign vessels. The force became known as the West **African Squadron** and was stationed at **Fernando Po**, off the coast of Nigeria with bases in Sierra Leone and Capetown. The squadron reached its full strength in 1819 and, for the remainder of its existence, the unit numbered approximately twenty-five ships and 2,000 sailors (with an additional 1,000 native sailors, commonly known as "Kroomen"). At its peak, the squadron consisted of one-sixth of the total number of ships in the Royal Navy and cost Great Britain about 2 percent of its annual gross national product. During the early years of the force, some twenty-five slavers per year were captured and, on average, 5,000 slaves were freed. Some 1,000 slave ships were eventually captured by the squadron, the majority (595) between 1843 and 1861. It is estimated that the Royal Navy freed some 160,000 slaves.

Service in the West African Squadron was not popular in the Navy. Although sailors were able to gain additional income from the bounties on captured slave ships and freed slaves, the squadron had a **mortality** rate that was ten times higher than the rest of the Navy. **Disease** and heat took their toll on many British sailors and officers; some 5,000 British sailors died during the history of the squadron. In addition, service in the squadron usually meant that sailors would not see Great Britain for years.

The force was supplemented by naval units from other countries. In 1820, a four-ship flotilla from the United States was dispatched to aid the British. However, the force was withdrawn in 1824 after capturing only two ships. A French naval squadron began joint operations with the British in 1837, and the combined force achieved a significant number of captures and prosecutions. In 1842, the Webster-Ashburton Treaty led the United States to dispatch another flotilla to the region to cooperate with the British. The new American forces captured twenty-four slavers by 1861. The Civil War resulted in more American support through the Union naval blockade of Southern **ports** and the 1862 Washington Treaty, which finally allowed the British to stop suspected American slavers.

In addition to interdicting slave vessels, the Royal Navy was ordered to begin disrupting the supply of slaves in the 1830s. Funds were allocated to provide local leaders with subsidies for local chiefs who agreed to end their participation in the slave trade. The British also purchased colonies or acquired territory to end slavery. The Navy was authorized to take direct military action against local slavers. Naval forces dethroned the king of **Lagos** in 1851 after he refused to end the slave trade. Further British expansion along the coast and the closure of slave markets in **Cuba** in 1886 and in **Brazil** in 1888 ended the need for the squadron. *See also* Abolitionism; Abolition of Slave Trade, Brazil; Abolition of the Slave Trade, France; Abolition of Slave Trade, Great Britain; Abolition of the Slave Trade, Spain; Abolition of Slave Trade, United States; African Rulers and the Slave Trade; British Caribbean; British Slave Trade; Closure of the Slave Trade; French Slave Trade.

Further Readings: Alpers, Edward. *Ivory and Slaves.* Berkeley: University of California Press, 1975; Lovejoy, Paul. *Transformations in Slavery: A History of Slavery in Africa.* New York: Cambridge University Press, 2000; Mannix, Daniel Pratt, with Cowley, Malcolm. *Black Cargoes: A History of the Atlantic Slave Trade, 1518–1865.* New York: Viking, 1962; Miers, Suzanne. *Britain and the Ending of the Slave Trade.* New York: Longmans, Green and Company 1972; Northrup, David, ed. *The Atlantic Slave Trade.* Boston: Houghton Mifflin, 2002; Ward, W.E.F. *The Royal Navy and the Slavers: The Suppression of the Atlantic Slave Trade.* New York: Pantheon, 1969.

Tom Lansford

British Slave Trade

Through the eighteenth century, the British colonies in the Western Hemisphere were the largest importers of slaves; however, during the nineteenth century, the British led the effort to abolish the slave trade and end slavery. To some extent, Great Britain entered the slave trade relatively late. The Spanish and Portuguese had longstanding and well-developed slave routes to the New World by the time the first British settlements were established in the Western Hemisphere. The first shipment of slaves to a British colony, Jamestown, in the Western Hemisphere occurred in 1619.

North American Colonies

Although the status of slaves was initially ambiguous in the Chesapeake colonies, after 1619, the number of slaves steadily grew in Virginia and Maryland. Between 1640 and 1666, colonial legislatures passed a series of legislation that institutionalized slavery and restricted the freedom of Africans. By 1700, the slave population of Virginia and Maryland was 13,000. As the British colonies expanded, so too did slavery. The Dutch brought slaves to their colonies in the Hudson River basin in 1626 and when the British took over these colonies, and renamed the territory New York, slaves accounted for approximately one-quarter of the population. South Carolina was founded by **plantation** owners from Barbados, and slavery was enshrined in the colony's charter.

To supply slaves to the growing colonies, the monarchy granted the **Royal Africa Company** (RAC) a **monopoly** on the slave trade with British colonies in 1660. The royal family was one of the main **investors** in the new company. Over the next few decades, the RAC established a number of slave posts and factories along the West African coast. In 1661, the first permanent British colony in Africa was established at James Island on the **Gambia River**. By the 1680s, the RAC transported about 5,000 slaves per year to the Western Hemisphere. Merchants complained about the monopoly and charged that the RAC alone could not supply enough slaves for the North American and Caribbean colonies. Other companies were allowed to bring slaves to the British colonies, but they had to pay a special 10 percent **tax** to the RAC. In 1698, King William revoked the RAC's monopoly, and other merchants and firms quickly entered the slave trade. **Bristol**, England, became the hub of the slave trade, supplanting **London**. In 1731, the RAC ceased participation in the slave trade and began to concentrate on other goods (the company was dissolved in 1752).

In 1644, the first effort to procure slaves by American settlers was undertaken by three merchant ships from Boston. One of the ships was able to trade a **cargo** load of goods for slaves in Africa and then transport them for sale in Barbados, where the ship took on a new cargo of goods for sale in **New England**. This trip marked the beginnings of the **triangular trade**, whereby manufactured goods such as **rum** were sold for slaves on the African coast. The slaves were then transported to the Caribbean or Southern colonies for raw goods such as molasses, tobacco, or rice. The RAC's monopoly and the danger posed by foreign warships and pirates constrained the participation of New Englanders through most of the seventeenth century. Many American vessels began sailing to Madagascar to bypass the RAC. The revocation of the RAC's monopoly and the terms of the Treaty of Utrecht (1713), which gave the British a monopoly, or *asiento*, to supply slaves to the Spanish colonies, led to a dramatic expansion of the American role in the slave trade. Under the terms of the treaty, the British were to supply the Spanish with 4,800 slaves per year. Soon merchants from Massachusetts and Rhode Island controlled between 60 and 90 percent (depending on the year) of the North American slave trade. In Newport, Rhode Island, about 150 vessels, or two-thirds of the colony's ships, were dedicated to the slave trade. The triangular trade also resulted in the dramatic expansion of distilling in New England. Molasses from the Caribbean colonies was brought to New England and turned into rum for export to Africa. By the mid-1700s, Rhode Island had thirty distilleries, while Massachusetts had sixty-three. New England distilleries reduced the cost of production so that, by the 1740s, they could produce a gallon of rum for 5 pence. A gallon of rum was sold in Africa for ten times that amount. Meanwhile, around 1700, the **price** for slaves in Africa was £4 to £5. The slaves were then sold in the Caribbean for £30 to £80. In addition to rum, the most common trade goods included iron products, **firearms**, blankets, and small goods such as mirrors and beads. Over time, the price of slaves in Africa increased dramatically. By the 1790s, a typical male slave was acquired for two muskets, shot, **gunpowder**, flints, iron pots, several yards of cloth and other clothing, and beads, as well as rum, knives, and cutlasses.

The colonial governments taxed the ships' cargoes to fund various expenditures, including road and port construction. In 1750, Spain revoked its *asiento* and the New England merchants concentrated their trade with the Southern and Caribbean colonies. By 1750, the slave population of the British North American colonies was 236,400, but that figure grew rapidly as more and larger ships began transporting slaves to the region.

The use of larger ships, which transported 100 or more slaves at a time, became common. At the height of the slave trade ships transported between 450 and 600 slaves per voyage. These larger vessels could transport larger trade cargoes of molasses and rum and were therefore more profitable. The leg of the voyage in which slaves were transported as part of the triangular trade was known as the Middle Passage. This voyage between Africa and the Caribbean or Southern colonies lasted between five and eight weeks. The Middle Passage typically had **mortality** rates of 10 percent and many ships lost higher numbers of slaves as a result of **disease** and **suicide**. Smallpox, tuberculosis, and dysentery were the most common diseases.

The American Revolution marked a transition away from British dominance of the slave trade to American domination. In 1774, the First Continental Congress declared a temporary embargo on the importation of new slaves into America (this was done in an effort to harm British **slave traders**). In 1775, the British governor of Virginia, Lord Dunmore, issued a proclamation granting freedom to **indentured servants** and slaves if they joined British forces. Several thousand slaves eventually joined the British. After the war, these freed slaves were resettled in Canada and eventually **Sierra Leone**.

During the period of British control of the North American colonies, more than 4 million slaves were imported into the settlements. The region that is now Nigeria supplied most of the slaves for the British trade. Between 1711 and 1810, approximately 39 percent of all slaves bound for the British colonies came from present-day Nigeria (Ghana supplied about

15 percent and the Ivory Coast about 12 percent). By the early 1700s, the British had a series of established slave **ports** along the African coast, including Sierra Leone, which later became a haven for freed slaves.

Caribbean Colonies

Many of the British colonies in the Caribbean had slave systems in place when they were acquired by Great Britain. For instance, **Jamaica** was seized from the Spanish in 1655 and already had a large slave population. Other colonies imported slavery. Barbados was settled in 1627 by the British and began to import slaves soon after the establishment of the colony. The wealth of the Caribbean colonies was tied to **sugar**. Jamaica quickly became the world's largest supplier of sugar, producing 77,000 tons of sugar each year by 1800. As the sugar industry came to be dominated by large plantations, many small farmers and planters were displaced. Most of these colonists migrated to North American settlements, such as South Carolina, which was founded by planters from Barbados.

Slaves were initially supplied to the Caribbean colonies by the RAC and later by New Englanders. Modern rum was first distilled in the colonies when it was discovered that molasses, a byproduct of refining sugarcane, could be distilled into a alcoholic drink. Rum was initially given to slaves as an incentive for work, but it later became popular among the colonists. The New Englanders perfected the distillery process and initiated the triangular trade, which supplied slaves to the Caribbean colonies in exchange for molasses and sugar. Slaves had a much higher mortality rate in the Caribbean than in the North American colonies. Tropical diseases such as malaria and yellow fever killed tens of thousands of slaves and caused higher importation rates than the North American settlements.

By the mid-1700s, the population of the **British Caribbean** colonies was about 500,000, including approximately 425,000 slaves. In several of the Caribbean colonies, the slave population accounted for 90 to 95 percent of the population. The high concentration of slaves resulted in more restrictive slave codes than in the North American colonies. There were restrictions on manumission and harsh punishments for infractions. For instance, the 1688 Barbadian slave law gave owners broad powers to kill or permanently maim slaves for relatively minor infractions. A Jamaican law required one white colonist for every ten slaves up to twenty, and then one white for every twenty slaves. The Caribbean colonies faced more significant slave revolts than the North American colonies. Jamaica had major revolts in 1655, 1673, and 1760; Barbados had a large-scale rebellion in 1816 and Guyana was controlled for almost a year by slaves in 1763. Fear of revolt led to some restrictions on slave imports. For instance, following the slave rebellion in Santo Domingo in 1791, several British colonies banned the importation of slaves from the former French colony. Until the abolition of the slave trade in 1807, the number of slaves imported into the colonies continued to expand. By 1807, the Caribbean settlements accounted for approximately 40 percent of the total number of slaves imported into the British colonies located in the Western Hemisphere (and about 17 percent of the total number of slaves imported into the Western Hemisphere).

Between 1651 and 1807, some 1.9 million slaves were imported into the British Caribbean colonies.

The American Revolution curtailed trade with the New Englanders, many of whom concentrated on the slave trade to the U.S. Southern colonies. However, the independence of the United States also led to new colonization by the British. Some 8,000 loyalists and their slaves were resettled in the Bahamas after the war. In addition, despite prohibitions against trade with the United States, much of the slave trade in the Caribbean continued to be dominated by American firms.

Ending the Slave Trade

The planter elite of the Caribbean colonies developed a powerful political bloc in the Parliament that was able to consistently prevent measures that would have limited slavery or the slave trade. Efforts to abolish the slave trade were focused, ironically, on the slave trade hub of Bristol. Local Quakers launched a series of initiatives to abolish the slave trade in the 1770s. Their drive was accelerated by the 1772 *Somerset Case* in which Lord Mansfield ruled that individuals could not be held as slaves in Great Britain. This created a two-tiered system in which slavery was illegal in Great Britain, but legal in the colonies. Caribbean plantation owners funded several legal challenges to the decision, but none were successful. Meanwhile, in 1776, the first motion to abolish slavery throughout the empire was introduced in Parliament. Various Quaker groups began to campaign to abolish the slave trade with the idea that ending the trade would cause the system of slavery to wither and eventually end. Leading politicians such as **William Wilberforce**, Thomas Clarkson, and the future Prime Minister William Pitt the Younger became active in the antislave-trade movement. Nonetheless, the powerful sugar lobby in Parliament was able to consistently defeat legislative measures to end the slave trade. The lobby enjoyed the support of King George III who opposed any restrictions on slavery or the slave trade. In Parliament, the king's son, William (the future William IV), led the opposition to restrictions on the slave trade. William was able to convince the House of Lords to reject abolitionist measures approved by the House of Commons in 1799, 1801, and 1802.

By the 1800s, the efforts of antislavery groups had turned the majority of Britons against slavery. In addition, colonial legislatures in the Caribbean undercut any support in Great Britain when they refused to enact legislation that would have made it a crime to kill a slave. Furthermore, the price of sugar had declined over the preceding decade, which eroded the economic clout of the planters. When the House of Commons enacted a ban on the slave trade in 1805, it was also passed by the House of Lords, despite the efforts of William. Faced with a measure that received widespread popular support, King George gave royal assent to the bill even though the planters and colonial legislatures petitioned the monarchy to reject the measure.

The ban on the slave trade went into effect in 1807. Although there was a dramatic decrease in the importation of slaves, non-British ships, including American, Dutch, and Spanish vessels, continued to **smuggle** slaves into the colonies. The end of the Napoleonic Wars in 1815 led to increased enforcement of the ban, both in the Caribbean and along the African coast. The **British Navy** also undertook a number of operations to suppress slave stations along the African coast. In addition, the government was able to negotiate treaties that allowed British ships to stop and search suspected slavers of thirty other countries (only the United States refused assent among the major powers of the day).

In 1823 a group known as the Society for Mitigating and Gradually Abolishing Slavery throughout the British Dominions (commonly known as the Anti-Slavery Society) was created as an umbrella organization to coordinate abolitionist efforts in Great Britain. The Anti-Slavery Society exerted pressure on the government, but abolitionists were unable to gain passage of a general abolition bill through the 1820s. In 1832, elections led sixteen pro-planter members of Parliament to lose their seats and antislavery groups presented Parliament with a petition signed by more than 187,000 people in favor of abolition. In 1833, Parliament finally enacted a general abolition bill that ended slavery within the empire by 1834. The bill did allow a five-year apprenticeship system to transition slaves into freedom, and it provided £20 million in grants to plantation owners to compensate for the loss of their slaves. By 1838, slavery was ended within the British Empire and along with it, the British slave trade. *See also* Abolitionism; Abolition of Slave Trade, Brazil; Abolition of the Slave Trade, France; Abolition of Slave Trade, Great Britain; Abolition of the Slave Trade, Spain; Abolition of Slave Trade, United States; African Institution; African Rulers and the Slave Trade; African Squadrons, The; *Asiento*; *Brookes*, The; Closure of the Slave Trade; Eric Williams Thesis; Fernando Po; French Slave Trade; Interlopers; Lagos; Leeward Islands; Liverpool; Newton, John; Ouidah; "Saltwater Negroes"; Trans-Atlantic Slave Trade Database; *Zong*, The.

Further Readings: Carton, Michael. *Empire, Enslavement and Freedom in the Caribbean*. Princeton, NJ: Markus Wiener, 1997; Hayward, Jack, ed. *Out of Slavery: Abolition and After*. London: Frank Cass, 1985; Higman, Barry. *Slave Populations of the British Caribbean, 1807–1834*. Baltimore: Johns Hopkins University Press, 1984; Miers, Suzanne. *Britain and the Ending of the Slave Trade*. New York: Longmans, Green and Company, 1975; Temperley, Howard. *British Antislavery, 1833–1870*. Columbia: University of South Carolina Press, 1972; Turley, D. *The Culture of English Anti-Slavery, 1780–1860*. London: Routledge, 1991; Ward, W.E.F. *The Royal Navy and the Slavers: The Suppression of the Atlantic Slave Trade*. New York: Pantheon, 1969.

Tom Lansford

Brookes, The

The *Brookes* was a ship used to transport slaves during the Middle Passage. Constructed in **Liverpool** in 1781, the ship was named after co-owner Joseph Brookes, Jr., a British merchant. It was a 297-ton vessel consisting of main, lower, half, and quarter decks. Also on board were gratings, slave compartments, a cabin, and a gunroom.

The stowage **plans** of the *Brookes* were meticulously documented and would provide argumentative fodder for abolitionists seeking to end the slave trade. Infamous for its **overcrowding**, the *Brookes* set sail with as

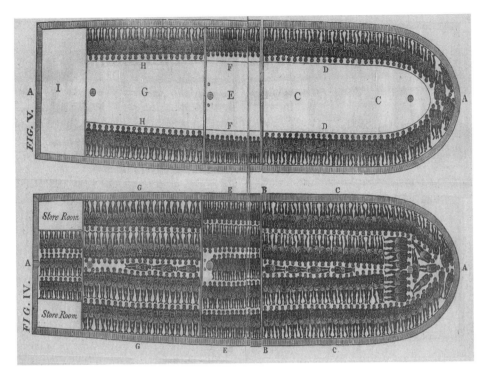

Cross-section of the slave ship the *Brookes*. In 1789, 700 posters were printed showing 482 enslaved Africans crammed on board. This picture shocked people at the time and remains one of the most enduring images associated with the trans-Atlantic slave trade. Courtesy of Anti-Slavery International.

many as 704 people crammed into its **hold**, a remarkable number given its less-than-remarkable size. The lower deck of the ship was but 100 feet long and just over 25 feet wide; the height between the lower and main decks was a mere 5 feet and 8 inches. Wooden platforms between the main and lower decks created an additional venue for placing even more slaves.

The *Brookes* made four voyages from Africa's **Gold Coast** to Kingston, **Jamaica**, between the years 1781 and 1786, carrying no less than 600 individuals on any given journey. This inhumane variety of travel solicited a great deal of social and governmental scrutiny. In 1788, an Act of Parliament was passed that limited the number of slaves eligible for transportation during any single passage. The *Brookes* was one of nine ships measured that year as a part of a Parliamentary enquiry into the procedural aspects of slave trade.

In 1789, the Society for Effecting the Abolition of the Slave Trade (a **London** Committee better known as SEAST) published the *Description of a Slave Ship*, a work which included illustrations of the *Brookes* based on measurements taken by Parliament while the ship was laid up in Liverpool.

The *Description of a Slave Ship* revealed that, even after the passing of the 1788 Act of Parliament, the ship was still transporting an illegally high number of slaves for a vessel of its size, carrying 292 on the lower deck, 130 on the wooden platforms, and 20 to 30 more on the poop deck. A more detailed version of the publication, titled *Description*, came out later that same year and referenced diagrammatic plans and overviews to further clarify the scope of the overcrowding epidemic on the *Brookes*.

The *Description* became the most widely disseminated and commonly cited slave ship documentation of the times. The egregious congestion of slaves on the *Brookes* incited a backlash among abolitionists on an international level. People in Britain, France, and America were appalled by the conditions on board the vessel. Leading abolitionists **William Wilberforce** and the Count of Mirabeau each had models of the *Brookes* assembled based on the measurements within the *Description*. They later used these models to exemplify the horrific manner in which slaves were being transported.

The *Brookes* continued functioning as a slave ship until 1804, when it was captured and held by authorities in **Buenos Aires**. *See also* Abolition of the Slave Trade, Great Britain; British Slave Trade; *Zong*, The.

Further Readings: "Brookes Slave Ship." *Port Cities Liverpool.* [Online, September 30, 2006]. E. Chambré Hardman Archive Web site: http://www.mersey-gateway.org/server.php?show=ConGallery.30; "Looking for the Material Culture of the Middle Passage." *Journal for Maritime Research*, December 2005. [Online, September 30, 2006]. Journal for Maritime Research Web site: http://www.jmr.nmm.ac.uk/server?show=ConJmr Article.209&setPaginate=No&outputFormat=print; "Stowage of the British Slave Ship Brookes." *Virtual Jamestown*, 1998. [Online, September 30, 2006]. Virtual Jamestown Web site: http://www.virtualjamestown.org/gallery.html.

Michael Lombardo

Buenos Aires

The city of Buenos Aires, its name meaning fair winds, is situated across the Rio de la Plata from Uruguay. Originally settled in 1536, Buenos Aries was abandoned a year later because of a shortage of fresh **water** and repeated attacks from Indians. Reestablished permanently in 1580 by Juan de Garay, the city is the modern capital of Argentina. The founders hoped Buenos Aires would become a major South American port, but they soon realized the bay floor was an extension of the flat pampa plains surrounding the city, making it an unfavorable harbor. Ships coming into port were forced to anchor a few miles away from the city and horse-drawn carts carried in their **cargo**. Buenos Aires was constrained by Spanish colonial policy, which allowed only four of their American **ports** to participate in European trade. Buenos Aires did not enjoy this status and was instead considered a remote region under control of the Viceroyalty of Peru. Despite these geographic and economic constraints, the city, like many other colonial cities, engaged in illicit trade, spurring on urban growth despite official colonial policy. Finally in 1778, to curb the loss of money from illegal trade, the crown granted all colonies **free trade** privileges to ships flying Spanish flags. This coincided with the creation of the Viceroyalty of la Plata in 1776, with Buenos Aires as the administrative capital. Napoleon's invasion of Spain in 1808 led to the end of Spanish rule in the region by 1810, when the Viceroy was deposed on May 25. Colonial rule, however, did not officially end until six years later in 1816.

In 1534, slaves were first permitted into the Rio de la Plata area, but by 1595, there were only 233 Africans in the city. Through a series of *asientos* granted first to a Portuguese merchant and later to a succession of merchants and trading companies, the crown encouraged and attempted to control the importation of slaves. The British South Sea Company held the *asiento* for the longest time, from 1715 on and off until 1750. Between the French and the British, 14,000 slaves entered Buenos Aires during the first half of the eighteenth century. Other traders, however, largely ignored the *asientos* and entered into the port illegally with the compliance of local officials. Some traders even came into port claiming their ship had been injured at sea and needed repair, meanwhile dropping off their human cargo. With this dual slave trade it is hard to estimate how many Africans arrived in Buenos Aires during the colonial period. For example, only 288 of the 12,778 slaves who came through the port between 1606 and 1625 were legal. In 1778, after another attempt at granting *asientos* to individual merchants, Spain abandoned the idea entirely and relented to limited free trade.

Most of the slaves entering in the port of Buenos Aires did not remain in the city, but instead were sent inland to northern Argentina, Paraguay, Chile, and Upper Peru (present-day Bolivia). By the late 1700s, African slaves constituted half of the inland population. Slaves remaining in port usually worked as domestic servants or agricultural laborers while those who went inland frequently ended up at silver mines.

Tracing the African origins of the slave population who came through Buenos Aires poses a challenge. Historians have commonly pointed to the Congo, **Mozambique**, and **Angola** as countries of origin for slaves in the Rio de le Plata region. Historian George Reid Andrews, however, finds the West African presence often underestimated in scholarship. Census information is further complicated by the fact that many *portenos* (natives of Buenos Aires) knew little about Africa and tended to equate Africa with Guinea, referring to Africans as *negros de guinea*. This misnomer implies both that *portenos* had substantial contact with West Africans and that the census data are probably unreliable.

Looking at the census, however, does reveal an interesting pattern: the 1778 census records that blacks constituted 30 percent of the population (7,256 out of 24,363), and the 1810 census reveals a similar percentage (around 9,615). Three years later, with the abolition of the slave trade and the passing of the law of the free womb (granting freedom to all slaves born after January 31, 1813), large-scale migration of Africans to the area ended. The population of blacks in Argentina began to drop proportionately and, by 1887, had dropped in total numbers as well to 8,005, or less than 2 percent. Theories of this drastic drop in population point to nineteenth-century wars, *mestizaje* or racial mixing, high **mortality** rates caused by **disease**, and, ultimately, the end of the slave trade. Also to blame is the intentional Europeanization of Argentina during the nineteenth century during which time the government led a concerted effort to attract European immigrants. *See also* British Slave Trade; French Slave Trade; Kongo; Potosí.

Further Readings: Andrews, George Reed. *The Afro-Argentines of Buenos Aires, 1800–1900*. Madison: University of Wisconsin Press, 1980; Rout, Leslie B., Jr. *The African Experience in Spanish America 1502 to Present Day*. Cambridge: Cambridge University Press, 1976.

Emily Brownell

C

Calabar

Tucked into a corner of southeastern Nigeria on the Bight of Biafra, the region of Calabar (variously known as Callabar, Calabari, Calbari, Kalabar, or Kalabari) figured prominently in the historic trans-Atlantic slave trade. The earliest maps on which the name Calabar appears are Dutch maps from the mid-seventeenth century, although the Portuguese and others certainly had been in the area previously. Two of the small towns of the Calabar region, Old Calabar (or Duke Town), situated at the mouth of the Calabar and Cross River estuary, and New Calabar (Creek Town), located approximately 15 miles upstream on the New Calabar River, were key players in trade. Large European vessels originally anchored near Old Calabar because of the difficult passage up the New Calabar River. Increasing familiarity with the river eventually permitted their large ships to sail to New Calabar. This, in turn, enabled New Calabar to become a significant slave-trading point.

The region of Calabar, including neighboring **Bonny**, was one of the most heavily trafficked slave-trading areas in Africa, but it did not become a major player in the slave trade until well into the eighteenth century. Although slavery existed in Calabar before Europeans arrived, their demand for slaves led to a significant increase in captured slaves. As the predominant tribe in Calabar, the Efik people controlled both the hinterland populations and trade with the Europeans on the coast. They never allowed a European nation to build a trading post and they controlled the **prices** of trade goods (primarily elephant "teeth") and slaves. No slave **barracoons** or holding areas were ever established. Rather, when a ship was sighted, traders would travel upriver in their canoes to procure slaves who were then sold to the Europeans (primarily the English). Ship **captains** paid a tribute or **tax** to the chief and then were allowed to trade. The notorious massacre of 1787 was purportedly in retaliation against the high tribute exacted by the king of Old Calabar. In it, seven English sea captains assisted people from New Calabar in massacring those of Old Calabar. Old Calabar was destroyed and did not regain trading prominence for many years.

Slaves from Calabar were notorious for being smaller and less healthy than other West African slaves, likely because of a nonnutritious, yam-intensive diet. In addition, they had a reputation for much more volatile tempers than slaves from other regions. Because slaves from Calabar were more troublesome, less hardy, more difficult to procure (it was a much longer trip to reach this part of the coast), they were not highly prized in the Caribbean and Americas. Even so, the sheer numbers of slaves in Calabar made the market profitable. As a result, they were often purchased by privateers and **interlopers** rather than by trading companies, and usually sold for a lower price than their African counterparts.

Slaves were traded from Calabar until 1841, when the regional economy fully transitioned to palm oil exports. To this day the Calabar and Cross Rivers are called the Oil Rivers of Nigeria. *See also* British Slave Trade; Entrepôts; Legitimate Commerce; Ports; Slavery in Africa.

Further Readings: Forde, Daryll, ed. *Efik Traders of Old Calabar.* London: Oxford University Press, 1956; Hair, Paul E., Jones, Adam, and Law, Robin, eds. *Barbot on Guinea: The Writings of Jean Barbot on West Africa 1678–1712.* London: The Hakluyt Society, 1992; Heuman, Gad, and Walvin, James, eds. *The Slavery Reader.* London: Routledge, 2003; Mayer, Brantz. *Captain Canot, an African Slaver.* New York: Arno Press and the *New York Times*, 1968; Sparks, Randy L. *The Two Princes of Calabar: An Eighteenth-Century Atlantic Odyssey.* Cambridge, MA: Harvard University Press, 2004.

Rachel Horlings

Cape Coast Castle

Cape Coast Castle was one of the largest European structures outside of Europe at the time of its construction. Strategically located in a sheltered beach where waves break against a rocky ridge to the east of the Castle, Cape Coast Castle was difficult to attack by land. It began life as Fort Carolusburg, built by Henry Caerlof at Cabo Corço (Portuguese for short cape and later corrupted to read Cape Coast) in 1650 for the Swedish African Company. This Polish architect also built other Swedish lodges.

Caerlof returned to Europe in 1665, leaving the Swede Krusenstjerna residing in the new fort. The fort was named Carolusburg after Charles X of Sweden (1655–1660). In 1665, the English captured Fort Carolusburg from the Swedes and re-built it into Cape Coast Castle. From the Restoration period (1660 onward), England revived trade on the Guinea coast and the Company of Royal Adventurers of England Trading to Africa was chartered for that purpose.

The 1660s was a period of intense Anglo-Dutch rivalry. In 1664, England seized New Amsterdam (renamed New York) and, along the West African coast, Admiral Holmes took the Dutch forts on the Island of Gorée (**Senegal**) and on the **Gold Coast**, at Takoradi, Shama, and Mouri, among others. Dutch Admiral De Ruyter replicated the same feat in 1665 and took Gorée, and later Fort Kormantin. Ruyter also seized, and later blew up, the English fort at Takoradi, but Carolusburg had been reinforced and withstood the siege. It was later rebuilt into Cape Coast Castle and became headquarters of the English. In 1672, the Company of Royal Adventurers was

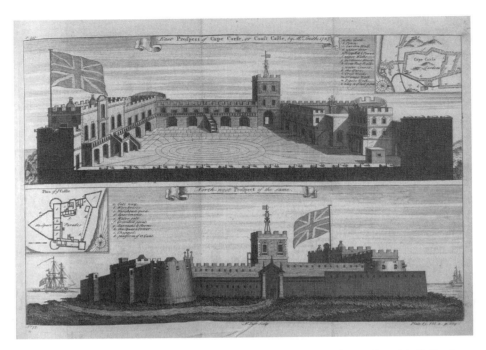

Cape Coast Castle, Gold Coast, 1727. Tracy W. McGregor Library, Special Collections, University of Virginia Library.

abolished and the **Royal Africa Company** was established. Based in Cape Coast Castle, the company shipped large quantities of gold to **London**. However, the slave trade superseded the gold trade as the major enterprise of the British traders in the Castle.

Cape Coast Castle was extended at this time (seventeenth century) and the Atlantic side of the castle was heavily fortified. A low platform that mounted several cannons was added, making the castle impregnable. The new addition enclosed large underground dungeons ventilated with grates and a few small holes along the sides of the structure. These underground dungeons became some of the most significant slave prisons in the history of the Atlantic slave trade. They could contain up to a thousand slaves at any particular time and these "underground bunkers" of the Cape Coast Castle were designed to forestall slave insurrection. Locked up in the bowels of the castle, there was no way the slaves could mount any effective insurrection. Additionally, there are peep holes through which the activities of the slaves could be monitored from the courtyard. From 1672, the Royal Africa Company exported about 70,000 slaves a year from Cape Coast Castle. Between 1766 and 1773, the Committee of Merchants made further modifications to the castle to give it its present look.

Early in the 1750s, Cape Coast Castle became the venue for introducing Western education to the Gold Coast. The Society for the Propagation of the Gospel sent Phillip Quacoe to England to train as a minister. After his ordination, Quacoe became chaplain and school master in the castle. In the 1870s, Cape Coast Castle became the headquarters of the West Indian

Regiment and the Hausa Constabulary, all of which were mobilized against **Asante**'s stranglehold on the Coastal states. *See also* Trade Forts.

Further Readings: Dantzig, Albert van. *Forts and Castles of Ghana*. Accra: Sedco Publishing, 1980; Lawrence, A. W. *Trade Castles and Forts of West Africa*. Stanford, CA: Stanford University Press, 1963.

Edmund Abaka

Cape Verde

Cape Verde, called Cabo Verde in Portuguese, is a republic located on an archipelago in the Macaronesia ecoregion of the North Atlantic Ocean, off the western coast of Africa. The group of islands is 385 miles (620 kilometers) west of **Senegal**, West Africa, in the Atlantic Ocean. Its official name is The Republic of Cape Verde, and it covers 4,030 square kilometers. Cape Verde is named for Cap-Vert, now in Senegal, the westernmost point of Africa.

Cape Verde is made up of two distinctly different types of islands. Six of the islands, which are located more to the west, are characterized by their mountainous landscapes. The remaining four are distinguished by their long sandy beaches. It has about eight islets, and the main islands are divided into two groups. Barlaventos is the northern island group consisting of Santo Antão, São Vicente, Santa Luzia, São Nicolau, Sal, and Boa Vista. Sotaventos is the southern island group consisting of Maio, Santiago, Fogo, and Brava. Out of all of them, only Santa Luzia is uninhabited, and presently it is a natural reserve. All the islands are volcanic, but an active volcano exists on only one of the islands, Fogo. The islets are Branco and Razo.

The previously uninhabited islands were discovered and colonized in 1456 by the Portuguese, who established **plantations** there. As these agricultural concerns developed massively, the Portuguese realized they needed external labor to work the plantations and mills. They subsequently turned to Africa for a supply. The captives brought to the islands were used to replenish slavers' ships when they stopped for their supply of slaves on the islands. The Portuguese then traded the produce from the plantations in the estuary of the Geba River for more slaves captured in local **African wars** and raids.

Soon after African slaves were brought in, these islands started to support a sizeable population of colonists and the larger number of Africans who were brought as slaves from the Guinea Coast. Cape Verde played a major role in the slave trade because of its unique position, which is midway between Europe, Africa, and America and facing the **Slave Coast**. From the sixteenth century onward, with the significant expansion in the black slave trade, Cape Verde became a transit point for slaves from several regions on the western coast of Africa because of this strategic location. The slaves were initially transported to be sold in Europe and later to the Americas. The islands were a prosperous center for the slave trade, but they suffered economic decline after abolition in 1876.

Most inhabitants of Cape Verde are descendants of the white Portuguese settlers and black African slaves. Most Cape Verdeans descend from both groups. There are also a significant number of Cape Verdeans in **São Tomé** and Príncipe, Senegal, France, and the Netherlands. *See also* Portuguese Slave Trade.

Further Reading: Duncan, T. B. *Atlantic Islands: Madeira, the Azores, and the Cape Verde in Seventeenth-Century Commerce and Navigation.* Chicago: University of Chicago Press, 1972.

Oyekemi Olajope Oyelakin

Captains

The selection of a skillful captain was of critical importance in the success of slaving ventures. Because managing partners could not personally oversee the purchase and sale of slaves on the African coast, captains became the de facto managers of ventures. Captains were not only mariners; they were businessmen. After a ship left port, her fate was in the hands of her master, and **slave merchants** had to depend on the ability of their captains to deal effectively with native African slave traders, manage a ship and **crew** under difficult circumstances, defend the ship against privateers, and navigate the complexities of commodity exchange in Africa and the Americas to negotiate the best possible deal for the owners. As the result of these responsibilities, captains were well rewarded for their expertise. Although a crewman's wages were customary, captains were able to negotiate for additional benefits in addition to their wages. These wages could be substantial, but the sale of "privilege" slaves, coast commissions, primage, and other bonuses formed the major part of a captain's compensation. Experienced captains were much in demand, and a market existed for captains in **Liverpool** and other centers of the British trade. Skilled captains were so important that slave traders often purchased ships for particularly skillful or experienced men. Slaving partnerships, such as Crosbie & Trafford of Liverpool, used the promise of larger ships in an attempt to recruit captains from rival traders. Although many captains were employees recruited by reputation alone, a significant number were connected to partnership groups by kinship bonds or associational ties arising from personal or professional relationships. Many captains were themselves partners in the ventures they managed, a practice designed to motivate captains to succeed. In the **British slave trade**, many opportunities existed for shrewd captains, both with and without advantageous connections, to enter the ranks of slave traders. In the Liverpool slave trade, for instance, 26 percent of the captains were involved in at least one venture as a partner between 1695 and 1775 (**Trans-Atlantic Slave Trade Database**). A significant number of slave traders began their careers as supercargoes or resident slave factors in the **plantations**, before becoming partners. For example, John Crosbie, William Boates, Ambrose Lace, and other Liverpool captains grew rich in the slave trade, eventually becoming prominent slave traders and important men in their communities. Between 1695 and 1775, the average sailing career for Liverpool captains who later became partners was a little over two years. In organizing ventures, this experience provided captains with expertise that gave them an advantage over **investors** who did not have direct slaving experience. The prominent Liverpool slave trader William Earle, for instance, captained two ships, the *Lucy* and the *Chesterfield*, during three voyages between 1748 and 1750, before joining his former employers as a partner. Earle's experiences suggest that a career pattern existed for at least some captains in the Liverpool slave trade. In the conduct of their trade, slave merchants did not so much send ships to Africa, as they sent captains. *See also* Ports.

Further Readings: Anderson, Bruce. "The Lancashire Bill System and Its Liverpool Practitioners: The Case of a Slave Merchant." In W. H. Chaloner and Barrie Ratcliffe, eds. *Trade and Transport: Essays in Economic in Honor of T. S. Willan.* Manchester, United Kingdom: Manchester University Press, 1977; Baines, Thomas. *History of the Commerce and Town of Liverpool, and of the Rise of Manufacturing Industry in the Adjoining Counties, 1852.* The Daybook of William Earle, January 23, 1760, through September 23, 1761, Earle MS, D/EARLE/2/2. Merseyside Maritime Museum, Liverpool; Power, Michael. "Councilors and Commerce in Liverpool, 1650–1750." *Urban History* 24 (1997): 301–323; Richardson, David. "Profits in the Liverpool Slave Trade: The Accounts of William Davenport." In Roger Anstey and P.E.H. Hair, eds. *Liverpool, the African Slave Trade, and Abolition.* Widnes, United Kingdom: Historical Society of Lancashire and Cheshire, 1976.

Brian W. Refford

Cargoes

Beginning from the late 1400s, the Europeans built forts that served as trading posts along the coast of West Africa. European sailors brought **rum**, cloth, guns, and other factory-made goods from Europe to these posts and traded them with Africans for human beings. Both the human beings and goods that served as a medium of exchange between the Europeans and the Africans formed what constituted the cargoes. These were carried as freight across the Atlantic, first from Europe to Africa, and later from Africa to Europe and the Americas. Understood in this way, cargoes therefore refer to the African slaves and the European goods used in exchange for them.

After obtaining the captives, often through unequal trade terms, war, diplomacy, and raids, the merchants forced African slaves to trek thousands of miles, sometimes shackled and underfed. Only half the people survived these death marches. The weary and the sick were often killed by the merchants themselves or left on the road to die. Fredrick Lord Lugard, perhaps the greatest British administrator in colonial Africa, and the person who amalgamated North and South Nigeria in 1914, noted that during the period bones of African slaves littered the roads; just as the vultures dominated the sky. Those who reached the coasts were put into underground dungeons, called **barracoons**, where they stayed for a long time, sometimes for as long as a year, until they boarded ships for the Atlantic crossing.

The Atlantic crossing was as horrifying as the death marches. On the first leg, **slave merchants** delivered made-in-Europe goods at West African **ports**, and, on the second leg, European ships transported enslaved Africans across the Atlantic Ocean for sale in the New World where **plantation** and mine owners utilized them as slaves.

Africans being forced below deck before transportation to the Americas. Courtesy of Anti-Slavery International.

A typical voyage took between sixty and ninety days, although some lasted for as long as four months. During this horrendous journey, Africans were treated no better than goods. Men were separated from **women**, shackled and confined below deck. **Chained** wrist to wrist, and ankle to ankle and in pairs, they were forced to lie naked on wooden planks in ships' **holds** that were not more than 1.8 meters (6 feet) long and not high enough to allow an individual to sit upright.

Crowded together in this way, they were forced to endure each other's feces, urine, and blood. **Diseases** such as smallpox, dysentery, and yellow fever spread like wildfire. Many died from these diseases, because medical facilities were either inadequate or reserved for the crewmembers and the European merchants. To lighten the burden and prevent wholesale epidemics, the diseased were thrown overboard. To enable control, cruel measures such as iron muzzles, whippings, and **rape** were adopted.

Olaudah Equiano, a former slave, turned abolitionist, agonized: "The closeness of the place, and the heat of the climate, added to the number in the ship, which was so crowded that each had scarcely room to turn himself, almost suffocated us. This produced copious perspirations, so that the air soon became unfit for respiration ... from a variety of loathsome smells ... many died" (Equiano, 1789). To amuse and satisfy their sexual pleasures, the crew sometimes allowed Africans to come on deck. This opened unlimited and unhindered opportunities for the slave merchants and the crew to rape the women and sexually abuse the children.

Faced with the nightmarish conditions of the voyage, the unknown future that awaited them at the other side of the Atlantic, and the general hopelessness of their situations, many Africans refused to eat or jumped into the sea at the slightest opportunity. From the captain's point of view, these human cargoes were extremely valuable and must be kept alive and uninjured at whatever cost. Therefore, any slave caught refusing **food** or attempting to jump into the Atlantic was severely tortured. Those who refused food were force-fed using the "speculum orum," a contraption that held their mouths open while food was forced down their throats.

Despite efforts to keep the enslaved alive and uninjured, **mortality** rates on the Middle Passage were high. Efforts at determining the number of deaths during the Atlantic crossing have yielded contestable figures. Undoubtedly, an estimated 10 and 20 percent (that is, between 2 and 4 million Africans) must have died.

Unlike the lifeless cargoes brought to the coast of Africa, the human cargoes taken to Europe and the Americas were, upon arriving at the New World, dressed up in preparation for sale at auction. Whether sold to the planters or miners, the Africans were neither treated nor employed as humans but as slaves. *See also* Daily Schedule; Dancing and Exercise; Duration of Voyages; Mortality, Slave; Overcrowding; Shipmate; Suicide; Torture; Trade Commodities; Trade Forts; Ventilation and Suffocation.

Further Readings: Ballagh, James Curtis. *White Servitude in the Colony of Virginia: A Study of the System of Indentured Labor in the American Colonies.* Baltimore: Johns Hopkins University Press, 1973; Breen, T. H., and Innes, Stephen. *Myne Owne Ground: Race and Freedom on Virginia's Eastern Shore, 1640–1676.* New York: Oxford University Press, 1980; Eltis, David, Behrendt, Stephen D., Richardson, David, and Klein, Herbert S., eds. *The Trans-Atlantic Slave Trade: A Database on CD-ROM.* Cambridge: Cambridge University Press, 1999; Equiano, Olaudah. *The Interesting Narrative of the Life of Olaudah Equiano, Written by Himself,* ed. Robert J. Allison. Boston: Bedford Books of St. Martin's Press, 1995; Franklin, John Hope, and Moss, Alfred A., Jr. *From Slavery to Freedom: A History of African Americans.* 7th ed. New York: McGraw-Hill, 1994; Howard, Thomas, ed. *Black Voyage: Eyewitness Accounts of the Atlantic Slave Trade, by Alexander Falconbridge.* Boston: Little, Brown, 1971.

Oyeniyi Bukola Adeyemi

Carpenters

The ships used to transport slaves for the Middle Passage were usually modified merchant and cargo ships. European royalty, nobility, and leading merchants saw the slave trade as a prosperous investment and commissioned to have the large ships built for use in their lucrative new industry.

Skilled carpenters and shipbuilders from England, France, the Netherlands, and Portugal were hired to build the merchant ships. In many instances, captured slaves who had previous carpentry and building skills were forced to modify the ships for the transport of slaves.

Because two of the legs of the triangular passage were to transport goods other than slaves, the modification of the ships for slave transport was slight. The goals of the ship modification were to fit as many slaves aboard as possible, to prevent the slaves from attacking the crew in rebellion, and to prevent the slaves from jumping overboard. Construction and modifications were made with these three goals in mind.

The ship carpenters, their apprentices, and sometimes their captured slaves were instructed to build a platform to divide the hull into two separate "between decks." This allowed the crew to fit as many slaves as possible into the cramped hull area. Strong fences were built along the decks of some of the merchant ships to prevent the slaves from jumping overboard. Many of the shipbuilders and carpenters erected strong fences to protect the ship's crew from being attacked by rebellious slaves. *See also* Hold; Shipyards; Triangular Trade.

Further Readings: "The Middle Passage." Africans in America. PBS Online Web site: http://www.pbs.org/wgbh/aia/part1/1p277.html; "The Middle Passage." University of Michigan Web site: http://www.umich.edu/ece/student_projects/slavery/middlepassage.html.

Kathryn Vercillo

Cartagena

Cartagena de las Indias, today Cartagena in Colombia, was one of the most important **ports** of the Iberian trans-Atlantic slave trade and the trade in general in the system of the *Carrera de Indias* since 1533. The villa de Cartagena, officially founded in the same year by Pedro de Heredia, in a place already known as a center of commerce of Indian slaves, developed because of its strategic situation as the main port of slave trade for the Spanish centers in Mesoamerica (including Portobello, Nombre de Díos, San Juan, and Panamá), as well as in South America (including Bogotá, Quito, and Perú). In a triple sense, Cartagena was the most important and best-fortified port of South America: first, as the economic and strategic center of the *Nuevo Reino de Granada* (since 1739 a viceroyalty) and the *tierra firme* (the coasts of today Colombia and Venezuela); second, as a point of entry of slaves, contraband (**Jamaica**), and European as well as African goods to Perú; and third, as a center of silver and other exports of South America (like gold from the mining centers between Antioquia, La Plata, and Timaná or the Chocó in New Granada).

Since 1610 a court of the inquisition was established in Cartagena, investigating heresy and new **Christians** suspected to be Jews. In many cases, these new Christians were organizing the slave trade and contraband from African slave ports (**Luanda**, Cacheu, **Cape Verde**, **Gold Coast**, and **Slave Coast**) to Cartagena, Portobello, Nombre de Díos, and Veracruz or **Havana**. During the long voyages from Africa along the Atlantic coast of South America, the **slave traders** organized **smuggling** and slave contraband with the ports of (later) **Brazil**, the places on the "Wild Coast" (later Guayanas) and Cumaná, Caracas, Maracaibo, and Santa Marta. In the seventeenth century Cartagena was a Jesuit center of religious conversion for the incoming slaves (**Saint Peter Claver**, Alonso de Sandoval). From 1750 onward, the slave trade declined. On various occasions, Cartagena was heavily destroyed by pirates or it was besieged, with the most heavy destructions occurring in 1816 with the *reconquista* of Cartagena by Spanish troops under General Morillo. In 1741, one of the greatest British and British-American fleets ever seen in colonial times in South America attacked Cartagena, but it could not conquer the fortifications.

Further Readings: Bushnell, David. *Colombia—A Nation in Spite of Itself.* Berkeley: University of California Press, 1993; Ferry, Robert J. *The Colonial Elite of Early Caracas: Formation and Crisis, 1567–1767.* Berkeley: University of California Press, 1989; McFarlane, Anthony. *Colombia before Independence: Economy, Society and Politics under Bourbon Rule.* Cambridge: Cambridge University Press, 1993; Olsen, Margaret M. *Slavery and Salvation in Colonial Cartagena de Indias.* Gainesville: University Press of Florida, 2004; Parsons, James J. *Antioquia's Corridor to the Sea: An Historical Geography of the Settlement of Urabá.* Berkeley: University of California Press, 1967; Thornton, John K. *Africa and the Africans in the Making of the Atlantic World, 1400–1880.* 2nd ed. Cambridge: Cambridge University Press, 1998; Wade, Peter. *Blackness and Race Mixture: The Dynamics of Racial Identity in Colombia.* Baltimore: Johns Hopkins University Press, 1993.

Michael Max P. Zeuske

Chains

Chains and shackles remain perhaps the most vivid material culture imagery from the Middle Passage. Slaves were shackled and chained together at all stages of their journey from Africa to the New World. From when they were first captured inland and marched to the coast to when they boarded the slave ships and often throughout the Middle Passage, slaves were shackled and chained together to prevent rebellion and insurrection. However, whether slaves remained chained together for the **duration of the voyage** varied from ship to ship. Some **captains** removed the shackles once the slaves were on board; others kept the slaves in shackles at all times. This decision was largely based the origin of the slave population on the ship

Shackles used on a slave ship, 1845. Special Collections, University of Virginia Library.

(certainly also based on the captain's temperament and how large the **crew** was). Some slaves, such as Angolans, were believed to be "very peaceable" and were therefore often unchained once land was no longer in sight, whereas **Bonny** slaves were considered vicious and violent (Rawley with Behrendt, 2005). Chaining slaves not only kept them from rebelling but also prevented slaves from committing **suicide** by jumping off the ship. When chained, slaves were shackled and chained in pairs, left leg to right leg, left wrist to right wrist. **Women** and children usually were not shackled, but remains from the wreck of **the *Henrietta Marie***, a slave ship that sank in 1701 near Key West, included several small-size leg irons.

Chains are significant to the history of the Middle Passage because they became a widely familiar symbol of the abolition movement in the eighteenth century. The English potter Josiah Wedgwood in 1787 began making medallions for the abolition movement with the relief of a supplicant African slave on his knee with his legs and arms in shackles and chains. Carved above the images was the question, "Am I not a man and a brother?" Wedgwood sent a consignment of these cameos to Benjamin Franklin in 1788, and they soon became fashion accessories in the United States, worn as bracelets and hair ornaments or used to decorate snuffboxes. The image and inscription were the official seal for the Society for Effecting the Abolition of the Slave Trade in England and became the most recognizable image associated with the abolition movement in the United States and England. The image was also used on antislavery broadsides, including one printed in 1837, which included John Greenleaf Whittier's poem, "Our Countrymen in Chains." Used both in the visual and written arts, chains became a universal symbol for the inhumanity of the Atlantic slave trade. Today, they are synonymous with human bondage. *See also* Coffle; Enslavement and Procurement.

Further Readings: Rawley, James A., with Behrendt, Stephen D. *The TransAtlantic Slave Trade: A History.* Rev. ed. Lincoln: University of Nebraska Press, 2005; "HarpWeek American Political Prints, 1766–1876." HarpWeek Web site: http://loc.harpweek.com/LCPoliticalCartoons/DisplayCartoonMedium.asp?MaxID=&UniqueID=27&Year=1837&YearMark=.

Emily Brownell

Charleston

Until 1740, most Africans bound for slavery in North America entered the colonies through the port of Charleston, South Carolina. Charleston's easily navigable waterways, natural harbor, substantial population, geographic proximity to the West Indies, and developing commercial system attracted traders, and the region's burgeoning rice and indigo industry stimulated demand among planters for slaves. The slave-trading **season** lasted from March through to October. Until 1703, the majority of slaves sold during these months came from the West Indies. Increased slave revolts in the Caribbean, however, translated into prohibitive **taxes** on imported West Indian slaves, thus encouraging planters and traders to deal in Africans. Planters from across the lower south deliberately purchased slaves in their prime, specifically male slaves between the ages of fifteen and twenty-five and female slaves between the ages of fourteen and twenty. Moreover, planters requested specific ethnic groups for specific tasks. Rice planters, for example, sought to purchase slaves from the **Gold Coast** who were already familiar with the intricacies of rice cultivation. Ibos reportedly made excellent house servants, and Whydahs served as capable field hands. Regardless of the specific **ethnicity** planters sought, all looked for subservient and docile Africans who were unlikely to revolt.

The Stono Rebellion of 1739, however, proved that Africans slaves were as prone to revolt as their Caribbean brethren. Bound for freedom in Florida, 60 to 100 Catholic Kongolese slaves launched a revolt, which ended with the deaths of sixty whites and thirty blacks. The following

Slave rebellion in the southern United States. Courtesy of Anti-Slavery International.

year, Charleston authorities placed a £100 prohibitive tax on all imported foreign slaves in the hopes of pricing slaves out of the reach of most planters and thus decreasing the slave population. Consequently, only 1,562 slaves passed through the port in the 1740s, a drastic drop from the 12,589 slaves imported between 1735 and 1740. Despite such a radical reduction, white fear continued to develop and deepen in South Carolina as slaves continued to outnumber whites. As a result, the state formally ended the foreign slave trade for a period of three years in 1787 and outlawed the interstate slave trade in 1792. State representatives renewed the 1787 act for a second three-year term. In 1802 and 1803, demand for rice outstripped supply and South Carolina opted to reopen the domestic as well as foreign slave trades. Roughly, 40,000 foreign slaves passed through the port of Charleston between 1803 and 1808, when the federal government mandated the closing of the foreign slave trade. During the nineteenth century, however, rice prices continued to increase and, in addition to the continued illegal importation of foreign slaves, South Carolinians began to discuss formally reopening the foreign slave trade. Although never officially reopened, South Carolinians often ignored foreign slave importations. In 1858, the slave ship, *Echo*, arrived in Charleston Harbor with a full **cargo** of African Slaves. Perhaps, in retaliation for the Fugitive Slave Act, Charleston authorities refused to convict the ship's **crew** of violating federal law. The 1866 passage of the Thirteenth Amendment permanently ended the foreign as well as domestic slave trades. *See also* Abolition of the Slave Trade, United States; Ports.

Further Readings: Edgar, Walter. *South Carolina: A History.* Columbia: University of South Carolina Press, 1998; Littlefield, Daniel C. *Rice and Slaves: Ethnicity and the Slave Trade in Colonial South Carolina.* Chicago: University of Illinois Press, 1981; Morgan, Kenneth. "Slave Sales in Colonial Charleston." *The English Historical Review* 113 (1998): 905–927.

Cheryl A. Wells

Children

Many African children were deeply affected by the Middle Passage. Some of the younger and weaker children were left behind in Africa when their mothers, fathers, and older brothers and sisters were forced to board the ships. They suffered pangs of loss, difficulties in development, and emotional problems ranging from loneliness to serious depression.

Other children were forced to accompany their parents on the Middle Passage voyages. Many children had never seen men with light colored skin before and they were not familiar with the **languages** spoken by the ship's **crew**. Most of the children had never been on the large ships. These unfamiliar aspects caused great fear in the children, fear which was exacerbated by the terror seen on the ships during the voyage.

Unlike the male slaves who were forced into cramped spaces below the deck, the children on the ships were usually allowed to roam about freely. However, many of the children suffered abuse at the hands of the crewmen. Some children were forced to perform for the men; others were teased, poked, and prodded to entertain the crew.

Boys as young as eight to ten years old were sometimes forced to remain with the other male slaves in the **hold** areas below the decks. The men were shackled together and stacked into small crowded areas, with barely enough room to turn around. The younger boys were sometimes crushed or smothered because of the weight of the grown men they were shackled to and their inability to **escape**.

Many children died during the Middle Passage voyages. The Africans were not used to sailing in the large vessels and seasickness from the rough waters and cramped quarters was extremely common. The ship rations did not allow for extra water or **food** to feed the ill slaves and many children died from **dehydration** or starvation.

Disease was also common on the ships. There were many outbreaks of contagious diseases during the Middle Passage voyages. Because the ships were designed to carry **cargo**, not human passengers, they lacked the necessary rooms and methods for disposal of human waste. The slaves were forced to share buckets to relieve themselves, and sometimes these buckets overflowed for days before being emptied. This contributed to the spread of contagious diseases. Without the proper food, rest, medical treatment, and sanitary **conditions**, the younger and weaker children had little chance of surviving.

The children were usually fed twice daily. Large numbers of slaves died during the early Middle Passage voyages, and many of the **captains** and **investors** believed it was because the slaves were eating foreign foods that their bodies could not tolerate. In later voyages, the captains purchased large quantities of yams that the African bodies were familiar with. Some slaves were given corn, rice, and palm oil, but only enough to sustain them, not enough for them to actually thrive. Because the voyages were meant to be profitable, many captains did not purchase enough food to sustain all of the slaves for the entire journey. The ships did not have adequate food storage areas, so the yams and other perishable items began to rot after only a short time at sea. Because there were no other provisions on board, the rotten foods were often served to the children, adding to the illness and death rates of these young passengers.

As the ships neared the **ports** to trade goods, the crew began preparing the slaves for their new lives. The goal was to achieve top dollar for each slave, so the slaves had to look clean, healthy, and ready to work. The children were usually forced to huddle together on the deck while the crew threw numerous buckets of icy sea water on them. The crewmen attempted to remove the disease and filth that the children had been subjected to during the voyage. Many children were brutally scrubbed with large brushes primarily used for ship-cleaning tasks, harming their skin and frightening them.

The children were subjected to intense physical scrutiny. The crew inspected their eyes, ears, mouths, noses, underarms, private areas, muscles, and bone structure. The children who looked healthier and stronger would be traded for larger amounts of **firearms**, **textiles**, and other items. These invasive procedures often traumatized the children.

After the long voyages at sea, the children's clothing was usually ripped, torn, and dirty. Rather than display the children in the rags, the crew stripped the children and forced them to remain naked for the inspection process. The ragged clothing would have given the buyers a glimpse of the inhumane conditions aboard the ships, and the buyers would want to see the slaves' entire body before making a decision to purchase. Again, this caused trauma to the children, resulting in lifelong difficulties.

Once the ships arrived at their ports, the children sometimes had to wait days before they were able to leave the ship. The strong male slaves were in high demand, as were the female slaves who had experience in spinning thread or domestic duties. These slaves were taken off of the ships first, and the children had to wait while the negotiations for the adult slaves were made. Separated from their **families**, in a foreign country where they did not understand what was going on, and unsure of what would happen next, the children waited in fear.

The children who accompanied their parents and siblings on the Middle Passage voyages sometimes never saw their relatives again after the ships docked at the ports. Fathers, mothers, teens, and children were not kept together as families. Sometimes the slaves were traded or sold as lots, but many times the slaves were all taken to auction houses and purchased by different owners from different locations.

After leaving the ships, the children were subjected to more physical inspections. The potential buyers would perform head-to-toe examinations of the children, determining whether the child's size, health, and stature would be suited to the work the child would perform. In some cases, the children were examined again and again as buyers made their decisions.

Throughout the long journey, the children did not know their fate. Because they didn't understand the language of the crew, they did not know where they were headed. They did not know what would happen when they arrived at the ports. They did not understand why they were forced to be examined or what would happen when they were purchased or traded.

The children rarely stayed with the master by whom they were initially purchased. As the children grew and each master's needs changed, the children were traded again and again. It was not uncommon for a child slave to have had at least five different masters by the time he or she reached adulthood. This continuous disruption kept the children from settling into a stable life even after the damaging trek across seas was completed. *See also* Cargoes; Mortality, Slave; Overcrowding.

Further Readings: "The Middle Passage." Africa in America. PBS Online Web site: http://www.pbs.org/wgbh/aia/part1/1p277.html; "The Middle Passage." University of Michigan Web site: http://www.umich.edu/ece/student_projects/slavery/middlepassage.html.

Kathryn Vercillo

Christianity

The forced transportation of millions of Africans across the Atlantic Ocean did not take place in a vacuum. The Middle Passage arose out of centuries of doctrinal and practical interaction of the Christian church with the institution of slavery. The trans-Atlantic slave trade needs to be examined in this larger theological and historical context.

Christianity was born in a Mediterranean world long familiar with the practice of slavery. The scriptures of ancient Israel, which formed the Christian Old Testament, had made an allowance for the ownership of other humans, but stipulated a much milder form of the master-slave relationship than predominated in Greco-Roman societies. In his ministry, Jesus made no explicit condemnation of slavery and generally did not comment on the political and social conditions of his time, but the overall tenor of his message exuded an ethic of neighborly love that undercut slaveholding's underlying social assumptions. The rest of the New Testament exuded an eschatological egalitarianism that leveled social distinctions within the church, but that did not directly challenge slavery as an institution. The book of Philemon best exemplifies the ambiguity that would come to characterize the Christian attitude toward human bondage. In this short personal letter to a slaveholder whose home hosted a Christian church, Paul advises what should be done with Philemon's **runaway** slave Onesimus. Legally, Philemon was entitled to the life of this unfruitful runaway, but Paul intervenes on behalf of "my child." The apostle refrains from issuing a direct command, but calls Philemon to a higher standard in which he is to treat Onesimus "no longer as a slave but more than a slave, a beloved brother" (Philemon 1:16). Paul's directions typified the early Christian approach to slavery in that it accorded slaves full acceptance into the community and expressed an ultimate hope in the end of slavery, but which also accepted slavery as a ubiquitous part of this present age. The church continued this gradualist approach to the end of slavery throughout the imperial period and into the Middle Ages.

Christianity and the Creation of the Trans-Atlantic Slave Trade

As slavery and serfdom in Christian Europe waned, new forms of human bondage arose to feed the burgeoning economies of modern states.

Christianity's first encounter with the sub-Saharan slave trade came in the context of the re-conquest and hostile engagement of the Western **Islamic** world. Exploration further fueled the desirability of trading in slaves. The discovery of the New World and its subsequent colonization provided the stimulus for extending African slavery across the ocean. As native American and Caribbean populations dropped dramatically because of **disease** and oppression, Spain and Portugal sought new sources of labor. Building on the Portuguese experience on islands off the African coast, the Spanish turned to African slaves for their colonies in the new world. In 1501, Ferdinand granted permission to import slaves from Africa into **Hispaniola**. Emperor Charles V supported the further expansion of the trade granting a 1517 patent to a Flemish corporation to transport 4,000 Africans a year to Spanish holdings in the West. The Middle Passage had been born.

The church responded to these new forms of slavery with its primal inclination toward freedom but tempered its response in light of sixteenth-century circumstances. Just decades after Hispaniola imported its first African slaves, Christianity witnessed its greatest division since the schism of the Eastern and Western churches. The Protestant Reformation redrew the religious and political map of Europe and in turn influenced the shape of trans-Atlantic African slavery. The needs of theological warfare mitigated the moral response and critique of trans-Atlantic slavery and its abuses. Roman Catholic and Protestant churches alike became dependent on the protection and patronage of the civil sphere, which in turn needed new sources of wealth to feed these wars of **religion**.

The rise of trans-Atlantic slavery caught Western Christianity at a vulnerable moment in which ethical scruples gave way to ecclesiastical survival. In 1517, Pope Leo X issued a Papal Bull that declared the Christian religion opposed to slavery. Two decades later, Paul III solidified this church position with the Bull "Sublimis Deus," which threatened excommunication for those who captured and sold slaves, but these decrees seem only to have been applied to the trafficking of native populations in the Americas whose plight was reported to the Vatican by men such as Bartolomé de Las Casas. Neither man applied these condemnations to the actions of the Spanish monarchy or the Holy Roman Emperor in stimulating the trans-Atlantic slave trade. Their patronage proved crucial in thwarting Protestants. The needs of the Africans did not come to the forefront of the church's antislavery stance until centuries later, after the religious wars had ended.

"Christianization"

Protestants and Catholics both fully participated in the forced transportation of millions across the Atlantic, but their spiritual response to these "souls" differed. Initiation into the Christian faith through the rite of baptism furnished the major visible distinction between Roman Catholics and Protestants. Both Spanish and Portuguese legal codes stipulated that entrants into their colonies be certified as Christian. Baptism became obligatory whether received upon departure from Africa or arrival in the New World. At a minimum, this "baptism" involved priests indiscriminately splattering holy water dispensed from the same troughs that would later be used to feed slaves en route to the Americas. More often, baptism took its place as part of the bureaucratic procedure of processing a human **cargo** for transport. Portuguese created an official position of catechist for slaves (*cat-equizador dos negros/dos escravos*) who were responsible for providing religious instruction to those awaiting transport.

Whether or not enslaved Africans understood or remembered receiving Christian baptism, other accompanying ceremonies left a longer lasting impression. The Portuguese branded slaves to demonstrate ownership and offer proof that the necessary duties had been paid. Attempts to enforce the legal requirements for baptism more rigorously led to an added cross brand providing a visible sign of baptism. This searing of human flesh left a painfully visible reminder of the official entry into Christendom. The humane desire to bring African slaves into the Christian faith ironically led to their increased pain and suffering.

Protestantism with its emphasis on the necessity of personal faith for Christian salvation denigrated Catholic baptism of slaves as a perfunctory ritual devoid of substance. Proper instruction into the doctrines and mores of the faith formed a necessary prerequisite to Christianization for Protestants. Therefore, only an extensive program of education and enculturation could overcome the linguistic and cultural differences between Protestants and their slaves. During the era of the legal trans-Atlantic trade, few Protestants made the needed personal and economic investment to bring Africans to their faith. Furthermore, lingering doubts about the legal status of baptized slaves made most owners extremely reluctant to allow missionaries to operate among their slave populations. Many felt the egalitarian aspects of the Christian message would make their slaves haughty and increase acts of defiance. Through the end of the eighteenth century, most slave owners preferred to use the religious divide to maintain a clear barrier between them and their slaves, putting **profit** margins ahead of Christianization.

Christianity Aboard Slave Ships

Few logbooks expressed residual doubts about the morality of the slave trade, but their opening stanzas often explicitly linked the name of God with the nature of their enterprise. Like masters aboard other types of vessels, slave ship **captains** maintained an official record of their voyage to demonstrate their competency if called into question afterward. Frequently, captains acknowledged the uncertainty of their endeavors with a formulaic call on the divine. Roman Catholic slavers widened these formulaic appeals to include the Virgin Mary or one of the saints associated with the maritime trades. The Latin phrase "De Majorem Dei Glorium Virginis q: Maria" (To the greater glory of God and the Virgin Mary) boldly began Robert Durand's journal of the slave ship *Diligent*. Sometimes slavers made these implied prayers in prevoyage inscriptions explicit by the addition of an "Amen." The logbook of the Rhode Island slave captain Nathanael Briggs affords an example of this usage, "the Good Ship Cald the Cleopatra Nathl Briggs Master and Bound for the Coast of Africa So God Send the Ship to her desired port with safety Amen" (Andrews and Gates, 1998). These supplications indicate confidence on the part of Christian mariners that God supported their endeavors in the taking and transporting of slaves across the Atlantic.

In **Brazil**, Portuguese **slave merchants** formed a religious brotherhood, and thus formally enrobed their traffic in humans in the protective garment of the church. These Roman Catholic slave traders acknowledged Saint Joseph as their patron saint and protector of their ships. The saint himself made a Middle Passage of sorts, when the Portuguese transferred his long-revered image from the West African slave depot of São Jorge da Mina to the church of Santo Antônio da Barra in Bahia. Such practices assured both traffickers and ordinary Catholics that God paid attention to the needs of slave traders and blessed their enterprise. Mariners acknowledged "the help of God" needed "to sell our blacks and make our return" but gave little thought to the prayers offered by their human **cargoes** (Harms, 2002, xi).

For some Protestants, the Christian aspects of the Middle Passage moved beyond mere supplication into opportunities for praise. When John Newton's ship safely entered port and discharged its human cargo, he ended his account with the words "Soli Deo Gloria." The floating tombs sometimes became a locus of worship. However, only a few Anglo-American slave ships, with religiously inclined masters, allowed Christian worship on their decks. Newton noted in his journal that he led services on deck twice each Sunday when weather permitted. Whether or not the slaves aboard witnessed Christian rites, he did not say, but the slaves on some ships did observe such performances. James Albert Ukawsaw Gronniosaw admired the seriousness of his ship's captain who "used to read prayers in public to the ship's **crew** every Sabbath day" (Andrews and Gates, 1998, p. 40). Generally speaking, public expressions of Christian worship were few aboard slave vessels.

Roman Catholics faced even greater challenges in regard to worship aboard ships. Baptized African captives were entitled to receive the other rites of the church. The murderous conditions of the Middle Passage necessitated that the sacrament of extreme unction be available. Catholic nations such as Portugal and France passed laws requiring ships to carry chaplains who countersigned the captain's "death book" demonstrating that the proper rituals had been performed. Ship owners chaffed at such **regulations** that mandated the presence of an unproductive mouth to feed aboard ship. Some ships falsely reported their tonnage to escape the regulation to carry a chaplain, while others simply reported that they failed to find priests willing to make the passage.

The language of Christianity imbued even mundane aspects of the Middle Passage. Slavers generally applied the names of the biblical first parents to the first slaves aboard ship, asserting their power to create identity. For example, Samuel Gamble referred to the first slave—a four-foot, four-inch boy—who stepped aboard the *Sandown* as "Adam" (Mouser, 2002, p. 64). James Arnold described a clever and intelligent teenage girl who "was promptly named Eve, for it was usual on slave ships to give the names of Adam and Eve to the first man and woman brought on board" (Dow, 1970, p. 172). In this way, trans-Atlantic slave ships used the Middle Passage as an ironic recreation of Africans into the Christian narrative.

Eventually, the Christian emphasis on love and freedom fueled a more active approach toward slavery's abolition. The steady protests of Catholic and Protestant advocates brought an end to the trans-Atlantic slave trade. In some cases, the critiques offered by African Christians, such as **Olaudah Equiano**, helped to awaken the moral conscience of Europeans and encouraged them to move beyond mere Christianization. *See also* Abolitionism; Claver, Saint Peter.

Further Readings: Andrews, W. L., and Gates, H. L., Jr., eds. *Pioneers of the Black Atlantic: Five Slave Narratives from the Enlightenment.* Washington, DC: Counterpoint, 1998; Berry, Stephen R. "Seaborne Conversions, 1700–1800." Ph.D. dissertation, Duke University, 2005; Dow, George Francis. *Slave Ships and Slaving.* Westport, CT: Negro Universities Press, 1970 [reprint of 1927 edition]; Goldenberg, David M. *The Curse of Ham: Race and Slavery in Early Judaism, Christianity, and Islam.* Princeton, NJ: Princeton University Press, 2003; Harms, Robert. *The Diligent: A Voyage Through the Worlds of the Slave Trade.* New Haven, CT: Yale University Press, 2002; Harrill, James A. *Slaves in the New Testament: Literary, Social, and Moral Dimensions.* Minneapolis: Fortress Press, 2006; Maxwell, John F. *Slavery and the Catholic Church: The History of Catholic Teaching Concerning the Moral Legitimacy of the Institution of Slavery.* Chichester: Rose, 1975; Miller, Joseph C. *Way of Death: Merchant Capitalism and the Angolan Slave Trade, 1730–1830.* Madison: University of Wisconsin Press, 1988; Mouser, Bruce L. *A Slaving Voyage to Africa and Jamaica: The Log of the Sandown, 1793–1794.* Bloomington: Indiana University Press, 2002; Newton, John. *The Journal of a Slave Trader (John Newton) 1750–1754,* eds. Bernard Martin and Mark Spurrell. London: The Epworth Press, 1962; Sweet, James H. *Recreating Africa: Culture, Kinship, and Religion in the African-Portuguese World, 1441–1770.* Chapel Hill: University of North Carolina Press, 2003.

Stephen R. Berry

Claver, Saint Peter (1580–1654)

Peter Claver (San Pedro Claver), apostle to all blacks and self-proclaimed "slave of slaves" was the first monk to be canonized in the New World as a result of his tireless work among newly arriving African slaves. He is the patron saint of African missions, African Americans, and slaves.

Born in Verdu, Spain, in 1580, Claver, after entering the Jesuit College at Barcelona and taking his final vows in 1604, left to study under Saint Alphonsus Rodriguez on the Spanish island of Majorca. Rodriguez, who would later be canonized at the same time as Claver, influenced the young priest to pursue missionary work in the Americas. In 1610, Peter arrived in New Granada at the city **Cartagena** (present-day Columbia) to begin a lifetime of service that lasted for more than four decades in an effort to alleviate the plight and conditions of African slaves as well as provide for their salvation.

Cartagena was considered a leading slave market in the New World and during this period more than a thousand slaves a month arrived in the city. Under the guidance of Father Sandoval, his predecessor in Cartagena, and braced with a progressive understanding that all men were brothers under Christ, Claver saw an immediate need to not only help the sick and poorly treated captured Africans but also consider them as equals, worthy of **Christian** love and sympathy. Claver began his work almost immediately as soon as the ships entered the harbor by rowing out to them to provide **food** and **water**. Once on land, he placed the sick and infirm in a hospital he helped build while also arranging for the burial of the dead. His endeavors included instructing the slaves in the gospel of Christ and resulted in more than 300,000 baptisms among the Africans brought to the Americas.

Declared venerable by Pope Benedict XIV in 1747, beatified by Pope Pius IX in 1850, and finally canonized in 1888 by Pope Leo XIII, Claver's life was marked by a single love and compassion for the transported African slaves that is significant both in its depth and for the period in which he lived. He is buried in the San Pedro Claver Church in Cartegana where he lived and worked.

Further Reading: Thomas, Hugh. *The Slave Trade: The Story of the Atlantic Slave Trade, 1440–1870.* New York: Simon & Schuster, 1997.

William Morgan

Closure of the Slave Trade

The movement to end the trans-Atlantic slave trade began in the eighteenth century, but effective measures to suppress the trade were not implemented until the nineteenth century. Closure of the slave trade was seen as a means to end the worst abuses of slavery, and most abolitionists believed that suppression of the trade would lead to the end of slavery. Although Great Britain led the early efforts to end the trade, it was only after the United States began enforcement of antislave-trade measures that the sale and transport of West African slaves were effectively ended.

In 1792, Denmark was the first European state to outlaw the slave trade by its citizens. However, it was not until Great Britain abolished the trade in 1807 that significant efforts to suppress the trans-Atlantic trade were initiated. Great Britain had been the largest participant in the trade because of its North American colonies. Although bills to end the trade were introduced in Parliament as early as the 1780s, a powerful block of Caribbean planters and merchants were able to defeat successive antislave-trade legislation. Finally, in 1805, the leaders of the abolitionist movement in the House of Commons, **William Wilberforce** and Thomas Clarkson, were able to gain passage of a bill to end the trade. The bill went into force in 1807 and was subsequently followed in 1811 by another measure that made involvement in the slave trade a felony.

The legislation empowered the Royal Navy to stop and seize suspected slave ships. The government paid a bounty for each slave ship captured and for each freed slave. Newly freed slaves were transported to **Sierra Leone**. The colony eventually became the center of British efforts to suppress the trade. Freetown, the colony's capital, was the headquarters for the naval squadron charged with suppressing slave transports and the site of the courts that tried suspected slavers.

The Napoleonic Wars constrained the ability of the British to station forces to suppress **slave traders**. In 1808, two Royal Navy vessels were stationed in Sierra Leone; however, it was not until the continental wars ended in 1815 that the British significantly increased the size of the antislavery flotilla, known as the West **African Squadron**. Concurrently, the British worked to convince other countries either to abolish the slave trade within their territory or to allow the British to stop and arrest non-British citizens who were engaged in the acquisition or transport of slaves. In 1817, a British court ruled in the *Le Louis* case that Royal Navy ships could only stop foreign vessels with the permission of the ship's home country.

In 1815, Portugal outlawed participation in the slave trade, north of the equator, and agreed to allow the British to stop, search, and, if necessary, seize Portuguese ships involved in the trade north of the equator. By the mid-1820s, most major powers previously engaged in the slave trade had granted the British the right to enforce the ban on the slave trade. The main exception to the trend was the United States. To further aid in their suppression efforts, the British also negotiated "equipment clauses" in their antislave-trade treaties. These agreements allowed the British to seize empty slave vessels if the ships were equipped to transport slaves. Other countries, including France and eventually the United States, also stationed naval forces along the West African coast to suppress slave traders. By the mid-1830s, the various naval forces were able to capture an average of thirty slave vessels per year and free approximately 5,000 slaves. During the same period, some 80,000 to 100,000 slaves continued to be transported.

The main destination for many of these slaves continued to be the United States. In 1794, Congress banned building or outfitting ships for the slave trade and, in 1800, U.S. citizens were forbidden from engaging in the slave trade between two foreign countries. Furthermore, the United States banned the slave trade in 1807. These measures were only sporadically enforced, however, and the penalties initially failed to deter participants from **smuggling** slaves into the country. In some Southern **ports**, the arrival of slave ships was not even masked in the 1820s. In addition, the United States remained the main source of slave ships. Into the 1850s, two out of every three captured slave vessels had been built in the United States.

By 1835, the British had secured search rights in treaties from all of the major European states. The 1841 Quintuple Treaty, between Great Britain, France, Russia, Prussia, and Austria, centered around an equipment clause to allow the British to search suspected slave ships of the major powers. Even when Texas became an independent country in 1836, it granted the British the right to stop suspected slave ships sailing under the Texan flag. A common component of the antislave-trade treaties was the creation of mixed courts so that suspected slavers were tried by both British officials and representatives of their own country. Mixed courts were established in Sierra Leone, **Havana**, and other ports.

Unlike most of the European states, the United States refused to allow the British the authority to stop and search American vessels. One result was that many foreign slave ships would sail under the American flag to avoid interference from British or French patrols. Instead, successive U.S. administrations made uneven efforts to suppress the trade unilaterally. In 1819, the United States enacted measures that made participation in the slave trade a felony equivalent to slavery and punishable by death. In addition, in 1820, a four-ship flotilla was dispatched to Western Africa to enforce the American prohibition against the trade. The squadron was withdrawn in 1824, however, following tense negotiations between the United States and Great Britain on a treaty for joint efforts to suppress the trade (the treaty's provisions were substantially weakened after the Senate added amendments that essentially stripped the agreement of any real enforcement power). In 1837, the British invited the United States and the French to form a three-party antislavery naval squadron to be stationed in Western Africa. The French agreed and developed a joint squadron with the British, but the United States refused.

Concurrent with the joint French patrols, the British government initiated a more vigorous program to try to cut off the supply of slaves. The British began offering subsidies to African chiefs who ended their tribe's involvement in the slave trade. Those chiefs who did not voluntarily stop participation faced the possibility of direct military action by the British. When the king of **Lagos** refused to end the slave trade, the British conquered the territory. A blockade by the Royal Navy was instituted around **Dahomey** to stop its participation in the slave trade and the British purchased the former Danish slave colonies in 1850 to completely end their involvement in slavery.

In 1842, the Webster-Ashburton Treaty between the United States and Great Britain marked a breakthrough in the efforts to suppress the slave trade. The treaty pledged that the United States would again dispatch a naval squadron to Western Africa to patrol alongside the British and to stop and search suspected slavers flying the American flag. The initiative was dubbed "joint cruising" and proved successful at interdiction; however, within the United States, officials often refused to act on intelligence or information about suspected slave ships. For instance, even as late as 1860, twenty slave ships were outfitted in New York without interference from customs officials.

The Webster-Ashburton Treaty included a provision to provide restitution for freed slaves at U.S insistence. The British agreed only to compensate owners for slaves freed when a slave ship wrecked on British territory. The United States did accept a provision for extradition in the treaty.

Ultimately, it was the U.S. Civil War that effectively ended the major slave trade. With the Union blockade of Southern ports, the number of slaves imported into the Western Hemisphere dropped from 25,000 per year to 7,000 (destined mainly for **Brazil**). In addition, the Washington Treaty (1862) allowed the British to seize suspected slave ships sailing under the American flag. The Washington Treaty also created mixed Anglo-American courts in New York, Capetown, and Sierra Leone for cases involving U.S. citizens.

Slavery continued in **Cuba** until 1886 and in Brazil until 1888, but the enhanced capability of the British antislavery patrols essentially ended the Atlantic slave trade by the 1870s. In addition, European prohibitions on slavery in the African colonies eliminated the major supplies of slaves and ended the external slave trade by 1900, although as late as 1920 a slave ship was seized in the Persian Gulf. Only the formal abolition of slavery as an accepted institution throughout Africa effectively ended the slave trade. *See also* Abolitionism; Abolition of the Slave Trade, Brazil; Abolition of the

Slave Trade, France; Abolition of the Slave Trade, Great Britain; Abolition of the Slave Trade, Spain; Abolition of the Slave Trade, United States; African Rulers and the Slave Trade; British Caribbean; British Navy; British Slave Trade; Danish Slave Trade; Dutch Slave Trade; French Slave Trade; Illegal Slave Trade, Brazil; Illegal Slave Trade, Spanish Caribbean; Portuguese Slave Trade; Slave Coast; Slavery in Africa.

Further Readings: Alpers, Edward. *Ivory and Slaves.* Berkeley: University of California Press, 1975; Lovejoy, Paul E. *Transformations in Slavery: A History of Slavery in Africa.* New York: Cambridge University Press, 2000; Mannix, Daniel Pratt, with Cowley, Malcolm. *Black Cargoes: A History of the Atlantic Slave Trade, 1518–1865.* New York: Viking, 1962; Miers, Suzanne. *Britain and the Ending of the Slave Trade.* New York: Longmans, Green and Company, 1972; Northrup, David, ed. *The Atlantic Slave Trade.* Boston: Houghton Mifflin, 2002; Ward, W.E.F. *The Royal Navy and the Slavers: The Suppression of the Atlantic Slave Trade.* New York: Pantheon, 1969.

Tom Lansford

Clotilda, The

The *Clotilda* is one of the last American-built vessels to **smuggle** a **cargo** of African captives into the United States, in violation of federal laws. The *Clotilda* embarked on her trans-Atlantic smuggling expedition in 1860, during the height of the "illegal" period in the slave trade.

The Slave Trade Act (1807) criminalized the importation of Africans into the United States after January 1, 1808, inaugurating the "illegal," "illicit," or "clandestine" period in the slave trade. American citizens, however, continued to plan and launch smuggling expeditions, despite the implementation of the Piracy Act (1820), which defined smuggling as "piracy" and that imposed the death penalty on violators. The lucrative nature of the smuggling industry, the rise of cotton as the dominant cash crop, and the admission of new Slave States to the Union comprised the nexus of events that increased the demand for African laborers. American smugglers endeavored to meet that demand, defying all federal statutes legislated to end slave smuggling on land and at sea.

The Webster-Ashburton Treaty (1842) sanctioned the establishment of independent squadrons of U.S. and British naval vessels for the mutual suppression of slave smuggling in Atlantic waters, particularly along the West African coast. "Joint-cruising" was negligible, at best. Efforts to apprehend slave-laden vessels at sea were undermined by advances in maritime technology in the form of schooners and clippers that were designed for speed, allowing smugglers to elude sluggish federal cruisers and to "clip," or decrease, the sail time between West Africa and North America. Although federal cruisers overhauled some slavers, their **captains** escaped prosecution, primarily because of the quid pro quo, proslavery relationships that they shared with the law enforcement officials and judges selected to adjudicate cases involving libeled and condemned vessels.

In 1860, Captain William Foster and his co-smugglers fitted-out the sleek, two-masted schooner *Clotilda* for a trans-Atlantic smuggling expedition, in violation of Section 2 of the Slave Trade Act of 1807. Subsequently, Captain

Foster sailed the *Clotilda* to the city-port of **Ouidah**, located in the Bight of Benin. Ouidah played a central role in the political economy of the Kingdom of **Dahomey**, controlled by powerful Fon warriors who sold millions of African captives to European and American buyers who called at the port well into the second half of the nineteenth century. The *Clotilda* is one of the last American slavers to call at Ouidah where Captain Foster purchased 125 West African captives, transporting 110 of them to Mobile, Alabama.

Like most of their predecessors, Captain William Foster and his co-smugglers escaped conviction for the crimes of smuggling West Africans into the United States and fitting-out a ship for that purpose. With no prospects for returning to West Africa and forced to live the balance of their lives in Alabama, thirty members of the *Clotilda*'s cargo founded a community called **AfricaTown, Alabama** where some of their descendants currently reside as living testaments to the *Clotilda*'s infamous voyage. *See also* Abolition of the Slave Trade, United States; Lewis, Cudjo.

Further Readings: Du Bois, W.E.B. *The Suppression of the African Slave Trade to the United States of America, 1638–1870.* New York: Longmans, Green and Company, 1904; Hurston, Zora Neale. "Cudjo's Own Story of the Last African Slaver." *Journal of Negro History* 12 (October 1927): 648–663.

Natalie Suzette Robertson

Coffle

The term "coffle," in common usage across the Atlantic world, is derived from the Arabic term *qāfila*, or caravan. It is uncertain where and when the term was transferred into the English language, but from its first appearance in print it referred specifically to mobile caravans of captives linked together by yokes or **chains**. Seventeenth- and eighteenth-century records from the English Company of Merchants Trading to Africa commonly use the term to describe processions of slaves arriving on the coast, but not to refer to slaves enclosed in coastal forts and **barracoons** or aboard ship. The word made its way intact to the Caribbean and mainland America at the latest in the eighteenth century, where it similarly referred to a bound procession of slaves. Coffle technology differed widely. In Africa, slaves marched along long-distance trade routes were often secured by iron fetters roped together. Wooden yokes secured by iron bolts were seldom used and were sometimes reserved for punishment. Often chains were added at night. The poor health of the enslaved in the last stages of a long march to markets often made it possible, and indeed necessary, to sever the bonds entirely. This was especially for those who were deemed too weak to run away. Additionally, African coffles were distinguished by the frequent requirement that captives also act as carriers of trade goods being transported to the coast. In the Americas, by contrast, coffles of slaves were habitually chained and shackled in heavy irons. This additional burden was possible largely because of the generally shorter distances covered by newly arriving slaves. *See also* Slavery in Africa.

Further Readings: Park, Mungo. *Travels in the Interior Districts of Africa.* London: Mungo Park, 1799; Tondut-Sene, Mame Kounda. "The Travel and Transport of Slaves." In

Captured Africans being forced to march to the coast for sale to Europeans. Millions of Africans died resisting capture in Africa, during their transport to the coast, or while being held in slave forts or other holds before making the trans-Atlantic crossing. Courtesy of Anti-Slavery International.

Doudou Diene, ed. *From Chains to Bonds: The Slave Trade Revisited*, 15–21. Paris: UNESCO Publishing, 2001.

Trevor Getz

Congo River

The Congo River (Zaire River) provided a strategic communication system between the central African region and the Atlantic world. Congo River, more than 2,729 miles (4,375 kilometers) long, is the fifth-longest river in the world and second only to the Nile River in Africa. It flows through the Democratic Republic of the Congo (DRC), the People's Republic of the Congo, the Central African Republic, **Angola**, Cameroon, and Zambia to the Atlantic ocean. The great river was known to the outside world in 1482 through the visit of the Portuguese navigator, Diogo Cao. The navigation launched commercial links between the Kingdom of **Kongo** and Portugal. The trade started with commodity exchange and blossomed into a trade in slaves. In 1816, a British force under Captain J. K. Tuckey traced its lower course. The upper headwaters were navigated by David Livingstone in 1871. Henry Stanley's transcontinental journey discovered that the head-waters were tributaries of the Congo River and not sources of the Nile.

The Kingdom of Kongo flourished on the Congo River. It was a confeder-ation of provinces under the *manikongo* (the king; *mani* means black-smith, denoting the early importance and spiritual power of iron working). Before the fifteenth-century contact with Europeans, extensive trading net-works was already developed along the Congo River especially in natural resources and ivory, copperware, metal goods, raffia cloth, and pottery. The Portuguese attention was drawn to the trading opportunities that the excel-lent communication system of the Congo River offered. The Congo River became strategic to Portuguese trade in salt, copper, shells, and cloth, which they attempted to dominate and developed. A direct communication link was established between the Kingdom of Kongo and Portugal for Chris-tianization and trade monopolization.

The slave trade flourished on the Congo River as slaves captured from the hinterland were transported to the European forts at the coast where they were exchanged for **firearms**, cloth, and alcohol. Estimates of slaves exported annually from the region of Congo and Angola in the early seven-teenth century was 15,000 per year. In Congo, as in many African commu-nities, European **slave traders** preferred to buy men. The human reservoir for slaves in Congo and Angola was inhabited by the Bantu-speaking people. By the sixteenth century, the slave trade became more organized and domi-nated the Kongo trade. In 1526, the king of Kongo, Afonso, attempted to ban all trades and expel all Europeans except priests and teachers. This became difficult because the slave trade and slave raiding was also carried out by some of the Bakongo chiefs. Yet, Afonso resisted the unregulated slave trade that undermined his authority and created general insecurity. The Portuguese strengthened their monopolistic control over the **ports** of the Congo River. In 1678, São Salvador, the capital of Kongo, was sacked, depopulated, and abandoned. The Portuguese benefited from the chaos as more slaves were obtained and the Portuguese established control. *See also* Christianity; Portuguese Slave Trade; Trade Commodities.

Further Readings: Curtin, P., Feierman, S. Thompson, L., and Vansina, J., eds. *African History: From Earliest Times to Independence.* London: Longmans, Green and Company, 1998; Fage, J. D. *A History of Africa.* London: Routledge, 1997.

Rasheed Olaniyi

Cowry Shells (Cowries)

Cowry shells (also referred to as "cowries") have been used on almost ev-ery continent as adornments, spiritual tools, medicine, or currency. Exten-sive use of cowries has been common in Africa and Asia. Evidence indicates that cowries were most often used as currency, especially during the trans-Atlantic slave trade.

The shape, size, weight, and durability of these shells have made them attractive since prehistoric times. As adornments, cowries have been used as jewelry, on art work, and on clothes. As spiritual tools, cowries have served as oracle implements and have systems bearing their name. Cowries have been deemed necessary additions to certain sacred objects. Their calcium content provides medicinal remedies.

Cowries are marine gastropods, in the same class as snails. There are more than 200 species of cowries found in the Indian and Pacific oceans. The two most common types of cowries are *Cypraea moneta* and *Cypraea annulus*. Cowries can grow up to one-and-a-half inches long. The shells are solid and easily last hundreds of years. Once processed, cowries are typically a creamy white color and are sometimes lustrous.

As money, cowry shell use dates back to the fourth century C.E. Although cowries were present in North, East, and Central Africa, they were most extensively incorporated into West African societies. Since approximately the thirteenth century, cowries were part of the trans-Saharan trade. With the advent of the trans-Atlantic trade, cowry importation multiplied in West Africa (and, to a lesser degree, in Central Africa).

Europeans imported cowries before disembarking to Africa. For 1,000 years, the world's number one suppliers of cowries were the Maldive Islands off the coast of India. The shells were ideal **cargo**, especially considering the distance they traveled. On average, 400 cowries equaled one pound. Cowries placed in barrels for shipping had no kingdom or cultures branded on them, and were virtually impossible to counterfeit.

During the trans-Atlantic trade, billions of cowries were imported into West Africa. It has been estimated that, for a period, cowries accounted for 20 to 35 percent of what was exchanged for enslaved people in the Bight of Benin region. In 1790, one enslaved person was worth approximately 80,000 cowries. This money was used alongside gold, silver, and (later) paper notes. Nonetheless, Europeans and Arabs only traded cowries *to* Africans, they did not accept them as payment in return.

Cowries were imported via trade for enslaved people, then circulated into many West African societies. Africans used cowries as legal tender for items such as **food**, cloth, and spiritual offerings, and for payment for services (like a haircut). It is no wonder that cultures around the world have associated cowries with fertility, not only because they were highly reproductive animals, and the "feminine" shell shape, but also because trading cowries permitted purchasing power.

Toward the end of the slave trade, cowries were in oversupply in West Africa. Thus, their value depreciated. Furthermore, during the late nineteenth and early twentieth centuries, colonists created schemes to intentionally diminish the cowry as currency in Africa. Cowries can still be found in Africa today, although they rarely are used as currency. *See also* Trade Commodities.

Further Readings: Thomas, Hugh. *The Slave Trade: The Story of the Atlantic Slave Trade, 1440–1870.* New York: Simon & Schuster, 1997; Thornton, John K. *Africa and Africans in the Making of the Atlantic World, 1400–1800.* 2nd ed. Cambridge: Cambridge University Press, 1998.

Natalie Washington-Weik

Credit and Finance

Credit was crucial to the trans-Atlantic slave trade. It enabled traders to fund their voyages. According to Inikori, credit was extended to slave dealers on the African coast, and to the employers of slave labor in the Americas. To avoid risks, **slave merchants** secured credits in various forms: export credit from the producer of goods for the trade and credit through discounting the voluminous bills of exchange they obtained from the sale of slaves in the Americas. It further stimulated the development of banking and the discount market in Britain. In the trans-Atlantic slave trade, bills of exchange became the preferred form of making payment for slave sales, rather than in specie or produce. The growth of the **British slave trade**, conducted by private merchants, led to procedures such as remitting bills "in the bottom" of ships that had supplied slaves to North American and Caribbean markets and the extension of lengthy credit periods to purchasers. Colonial factors played a role in financing the slave trade as well, acting as agents for coordinating remittances. Secure British merchant houses were deployed as guarantees for payment by bills. The development of credit practices associated with the slave trade, including remittance procedures, helped to strengthen the British economy by providing sound, complex intermediary instruments for the realization of **profits** from international trade. For the period from 1750 to 1807, slave buying and shipping dominated the economy of Britain. As such, slave merchants who were constantly exposed to risks demanded **insurance** coverage, which inadvertently stimulated the development of marine insurance in Britain. **Liverpool** merchants were financed by banks and other financial institutions in the trans-Atlantic slave trade. The bill system sustained British supremacy in the trans-Atlantic slave trade until its abolition in 1807.

By the beginning of the nineteenth century, Liverpool had established its supremacy in trans-Atlantic trade over **Bristol** and **London**. The trans-Atlantic trade in Liverpool was financed by the bill circulation system between the banks of Liverpool and the capital. This credit system, which has been rarely addressed empirically in existing studies, played a key role in the Industrial Revolution by directing capital northward into regional trade and industrialization. The cost of the trade goods exchanged for slaves was covered by London, Liverpool, and Manchester manufacturers and suppliers. In British America, the slave trade was primarily dependent on credit offered by the London finance houses through bills of exchange.

The credit system was replicated in many parts of Africa where a trust system was introduced in the exchange of European goods for slaves. In the Bights of Benin and Biafra, British merchants dominated the slave trade. Indeed, the local credit system was adapted to the slave trade. The local credit system or debt bondage, especially pawnship, became prevalent during the trans-Atlantic slave trade. Local traders obtained goods from European traders at the coast and distributed them in the hinterland to procure slaves. In Old **Calabar,** the monarchy was involved in the credit network and served as an intermediary between the European and African traders who obtained goods on credit. In this way, the credit system sustained the dominance of British traders in the Bight of Biafra and the region became an important supplier of slaves.

The credit system and finance were not limited to financial institutions alone; individuals also funded slave voyages. In 1562, Sir John Hawkins became the first person in England to ship negro slaves to the New World. His profitable voyage attracted the attention of Queen Elizabeth who had publicly denounced the slave trade but secretly invested in Hawkins's subsequent slaving expeditions. The two largest of Hawkins's six ships were owned by the Queen.

Further Readings: Inikori, J. E. "The Slave Trade and the Atlantic Economies, 1451–1870." In V. A. Shepherd and H. McD. Beckles, eds. *Caribbean Slavery in the Atlantic World: A Student Reader.* Kingston: Ian Randle Publishers Ltd., 2000; Morgan, Kenneth. "Remittance Procedures in the Eighteenth-Century British Slave Trade." *Business History Review* 79 (4).

Rasheed Olaniyi

Crew

The crew in a slave ship performed many functions. Perhaps their first major function was to ensure that all the supplies needed for the Middle Passage were complete and in the right order. European ships arrived in the African coast with several manufactured goods, which they exchanged for the slaves. In most cases, **food** and other domestic needs were derived locally from the African coast before ships were loaded with slaves. Although the function of labeling the slaves belongs to the **slave merchants** and slaver owners, who kept them along the coast before the arrival of the ship, there were occasions when the crew performed the function of making inscriptions on the slaves to ensure that their identity in terms of ownership and destination was ascertained.

The crew of a typical slave vessel was under the sole control of the captain who was responsible for making sure that the voyage was successful. The captain kept records of the day-to-day activities during the Middle Passage. The lengthy nature of the Middle Passage made the responsibility of the crew intense, because they had to feed the slaves on a daily basis as well as remove the bodies of dead slaves (who were thrown into the ocean). The ratio of the crew to slaves is one of the most important aspects of the Middle Passage experience. Except for privateers, the slave trade used the largest crew of any maritime trade. The need for sailors was directly related to both the demands of trading and the need to guard the captured slaves. Thus, the crew per ton of some 252 ships that left **Liverpool** for Africa between 1785 and 1787 was 0.17 crewmen per ton, whereas the 249 ships leaving for the West Indies from this same port carried 0.09 crewmen per ton.

Slave ships had to be adequately armed for two principal reasons: to provide protection from pirates and guard against slave mutiny during the Middle Passage. A ship attacked by pirates automatically lost all its slaves and supplies. Shipwrecks exposed slave ships to the highest degree of attack by pirates. A slave revolt on a 1715 Dutch ship claimed the lives of some ten crewmembers. On January 28, 1731, a Massachusetts schooner lost all but three of its crew during a trans-Atlantic voyage slave revolt.

Crew and **slave mortality** rates usually moved together. A study of French slave ships indicates that as crew mortality increased, so did total slave mortality, although at a slower rate. Not all crewmembers who died did so during the Middle Passage. A good percentage of crew mortality took place before embarkation, that is, while the ship was still on African coastal waters, waiting for slaves to be loaded. The death of crewmembers in Africa is largely explicable in terms of the unfavorable nature of the African coastal environment, which until the nineteenth century was regarded as the white man's "grave yard." *See also* Food; Trade Commodities.

Further Readings: Klein, Herbert. *The Middle Passage: Comparative Studies in the Atlantic Slave Trade.* Princeton, NJ: Princeton University Press, 1978; Lovejoy, Paul E. *Transformations in Slavery: A History of Slavery in Africa.* Cambridge: Cambridge University Press, 1993.

Saheed Aderinto

Cuba

Cuba was one of the first large islands seen and explored by Columbus (November–December 1492). The island was divided into territorial chiefdoms of a people later called *arawacs* (*taínos*), *siboneyes*, and *guanahatabeyes*. On the island and between Cuba and other islands existed a type of prisoner-of-war slavery, kin-slavery, and slave-trading in the form of raids. The most known concept for this pre-Colombian kin-slavery is *naboría*, used later by the Spaniards for house slavery, garden slavery, and gold

Church and convent scene, Havana, Cuba, 1839. Special Collections, University of Virginia Library.

mining. From 1511 to 1521, eastern Cuba was the springboard for the expansion to Mayalands and Mexico, as well as a center of the slave trade with captured Native Americans—first from the *Lucayas* (the Bahamas) and parts of Florida. Like in La **Hispaniola**, the first black slaves arrived in Cuba as members of groups of *conquistadores*. Between 1518 and 1530, the first slaves came directly from the **Cape Verde** islands, **São Tomé**, or from the **Kongo** region to Santiago de Cuba, Baracoa, Remedios, Trinidad, or **Havana**, often as highly prized specialists for agricultural works, mining, and smiths—for example, as *esclavos del Rey* (King's slaves) in the copper mines, El Cobre, near Santiago.

At the of the sixteenth century near Havana, the main port of the *Carrera de Indias* developed the first landscapes of **sugar** slavery and mass slavery, first of all with Congo slaves, Mina slaves, or Jolof slaves. Havana, together with **Cartagena** de Indias and Veracruz, rose as a center of trans-Atlantic and inter-American slave trade, slave-**smuggling**, and different forms of house slavery and craft slavery (construction of vessels). The first cultural grouping of slaves was Congo based, constantly renewed with steady **arrivals** of *bozales* (new slaves from Africa) and some minor ethnic groups (Mina-Arará, Mandinga, Carabalí, and Gangá). The other parts and towns of the island remained until 1800 as centers of stockbreeding or local subsistence with slave-smuggling and different forms of small slavery.

From 1740 onward, new forms of mass slavery rose in the region of Havana, financed by the **profits** of tobacco exports, smuggling, and *situados* (silver from the royal treasury of Mexico). The new and dynamic economy of western Cuba was aided by the British occupation of Havana in 1762–1763, the **British slave trade** to Cuba (and the slave-smuggling of Americans and Dutch), the slave revolution of **Saint Domingue**, and the pressure of the elite of Havana. The crown started the demonopolization of the slave trade to Havana and later to other **ports** of Cuba (1789–1804). Initially with the strong participation of Americans there developed a substantial slave trade. Ships brought African slaves to the efficient and technologically advanced regions of sugar and coffee production.

From 1820 until around 1870 this trade functioned as slave-smuggling, often as a combination of coastal transport and hidden trans-Atlantic trade. The slave trade and smuggling facilitated the establishment and development of cultures of the African diaspora in Cuba, the many different forms of resistance (*palenques, cimarronaje*), and transculturation (*santería, palo monte*, and so on). During the era of slave trade and slave-smuggling of the nineteenth century between 600,000 and 1 million Africans came to Cuba. From approximately 1846 through 1870, 140,000 Chinese coolies arrived on Cuban shores as well, mainly as workers of the most modern sugarmills, but also as house, craft, and transportation slaves. The slave trade and smuggling was officially forbidden by British pressure in 1820 (treaties of 1817, 1822, and 1835, and the mixed court of Havana) and Spanish laws (1844, 1845, 1856, and 1866), but remained one of the main sources of capitalization of sugar production and modernization until the beginnings of the anticolonial Ten Years' War in 1868. *See also* Abolition of the Slave Trade, Spain; Haitian Revolution, The; Religion.

Further Readings: Falola, Toyin, and Childs, Matt D., eds. *The Yoruba Diaspora in the Atlantic World.* Bloomington: Indiana University Press, 2004; Ferrer, Ada. *Insurgent Cuba. Race, Nation, and Revolution, 1868–1898.* Chapel Hill and London: University of North Carolina Press, 1999; Fuente, Alejandro de la. "Sugar and Slavery in Early Colonial Cuba." In Stuart B. Schwartz, ed. *Tropical Babylons: Sugar and the Making of the Atlantic World, 1450–1680,* 115–157. Chapel Hill: University of North Carolina Press, 2004; Heywood, Linda, ed. *Central Africans and Cultural Transformations in the American Diaspora.* Cambridge: Cambridge University Press, 2002; Rosa Corzo, Gabino la. *Runaway Slave Settlements in Cuba: Resistance and Repression,* trans. Mary Todd. Chapel Hill: University of North Carolina Press, 2003; Scott, Rebecca J. *Slave Emancipation in Cuba: The Transition to Free Labor, 1860–1899.* Princeton, NJ: Princeton University Press, 1985 [reprinted, Pittsburgh: University of Pittsburgh Press, 2000]; Zeuske, Michael. "Hidden Markers, Open Secrets: On Naming, Race Marking and Race Making in Cuba." *New West Indian Guide/Nieuwe West-Indische Gids* 76, 3–4 (2002): S. 235–266.

Michael Max P. Zeuske

Cugoano, Quobna Ottobah (c. 1757–1803)

Born in approximately 1757, Cugoano was an African abolitionist most famous for authoring *Thoughts and Sentiments on the Evil of Slavery and Commerce of the Human Species*, a literary masterpiece that blamed all British people for the continued existence of slavery while issuing a plea for slave rebellion.

Hailing from the southern coast of Ghana, Cugoano was born to the same Fante people who would go on to form a confederacy that would aid the British in wars against the **Asante** during the nineteenth century.

At the age of thirteen, Cugoano was kidnapped and sold into slavery. He was first shipped to the West Indies, but wound up in Britain two years later. In 1773, he was baptized as "John Stuart." He would quickly develop a strong reliance on his **Christian** faith, which explains the numerous religious references found in his work. Therein, he countered those who used the bible to justify the morality of slavery by asserting that God intended all men to be equal.

One year after his baptism, he was hired as a servant by Richard and Marie Cosway, two miniaturists of the Regency era. It was primarily through this association with the Cosways that Cugoano was able to infiltrate Britain's high society. There he met **Olaudah Equiano**, a fellow African intellect who would go on to write *The Interesting Narrative of the Life of Olaudah Equiano, or Gustavus Vassa, the African*. Cugoano and Equiano were both active members of the Sons of Africa, an abolitionist group that frequently wrote condemnations of slavery to British newspapers.

Their points against the **British slave trade** were compelling. Between 1662 and 1807, British ships transported 3.25 million Africans across the Atlantic. By the last quarter of the eighteenth century, the British were shipping more than 40,000 Africans each year. Cugoano, a vocal leader among his peers, believed the scope of slavery-related problems was expanding exponentially as a result of colonialism in the Americas, where slaves were needed to work the vast number of **plantations**.

Cugoano thought that slavery made no economic or ethical sense. He argued that all slaves who had been held in the colonies for at least seven years should be emancipated, that all other colony slaves should be prepared for freedom, and that a naval blockade should be used to prevent any further plundering of West Africa. He was a strong proponent of relocating Africans from Nova Scotia and New Brunswick to a community for **London**'s black poor in **Sierra Leone**.

The initial edition of Cugoano's book, published in 1787, displayed scholarly diction and complicated postulations, as he attempted to persuade Britain's intellectual elite to bring about social change. It has been speculated by some that Equiano helped revise the first draft of this work, although the ideas expressed within most certainly came from the author himself. In 1791, Cugoano released an abridged version aimed at a slave-based audience.

Little is known about his life after that final publication, although one of his peers claimed that Cugoano married an English woman. He died in approximately 1803. *See also* Abolition of the Slave Trade, Great Britain; Returnees to Africa.

Further Readings: Cugoano, Quobna. *Thoughts and Sentiments on the Evil of Slavery and Commerce of the Human Species.* London: Dawsons Pall Mall, 1969; Walvin, James. *Atlas of Slavery.* Great Britain: Pearson Education Limited, 2006.

Michael Lombardo

Curaçao

The Caribbean island of Curaçao was an important market for the slave trade. Especially during the last half of the seventeenth and the first decades of the eighteenth century, this tiny Dutch colony off the coast of modern-day Venezuela served as a meeting point for Dutch merchants and buyers from all over the New World. More than 90,000 enslaved Africans were shipped to the port of Willemstad by the Dutch West India Company (WIC) between 1634 and 1730 (Jordaan, 2003).

The Spanish were the first Europeans to set foot on Curaçao, in 1499. The Dutch, looking for a defendable port near the important trade routes, conquered the island in 1634. Since they were fighting Spain for their independence (1560–1640), settling in front of the Spanish American mainland and attacking Spanish merchant ships was also a way of strategic warfare. After peace was signed (1648, Munster), prohibiting the Dutch from traffic with the Spanish colonies, Curaçao became the perfect transit port to evade this restriction. For the WIC, which brought bonded Africans to the Caribbean, it meant avoiding Spanish customs. For buyers, having a central market was easier than having to deal with several localities and traders.

Wanting to control imports, Spain introduced the ***asiento***: a contract that monopolized the delivery of slaves to Spanish colonies. Some merchants, however, subcontracted the WIC, thereby ensuring a steady market for the company. Rivalry with English and French **slave traders**, both pirates and *asentistas*, led to a declining market for the WIC from the eighteenth century on. The Company lost its Dutch **monopoly** during the 1730s. Independent merchants, such as Middleburg's Commercial Company, gradually stepped in. **Interlopers** had been illegally involved in the slave trade all along, delivering up to 40,000 slaves during the period from 1600 to 1795 (Jordaan, 2003; Postma, 2003).

No records were kept in Curaçao regarding the origin of the enslaved. **Ports** of embarkation of the WIC ships indicate that the majority of slaves were boarded in the Guinea region, primarily the **Gold Coast (Elmina,** Bercu) and the **Slave Coast** (Ardra, Fida). Another significant part came from the **Angola-Loango** region. More than half of the embarked were men, about a quarter women, and the rest were children, mostly boys (Gibbes, 2002; Jordaan, 2003). During the Middle Passage, an average of 16 percent succumbed to dysentery, smallpox, scurvy, and tuberculosis, and another 1 percent died immediately before or after disembarkation, because of the time spent aboard the ship in the harbor, which could amount to three weeks (den Heijer, 1997; Jordaan, 2003).

The survivors were marked, examined, classified, and branded. Those in apparent good health, possessing all of their teeth and limbs, between fifteen and thirty-five years of age and at least four feet nine inches tall, were labeled *Piezas de India*. Minors ages four and up, counted as part of a *pieza*; infants who remained with their mother were not counted. The impaired, elderly, and ill were labeled ***manquerons*** and separated to be sold in public auction. *Piezas* were destined for the *asentistas* (Gibbes, 2002; Jordaan, 2003). Other, mainly local, buyers bought smaller quantities. Although Curaçao had no **plantation** economy or mining industry, slaves outnumbered free whites for a long time. In 1789, for instance, the island counted 3,964 whites, 12,804 slaves, and 2,776 free men (Gibbes, 2002). To this day, the inhabitants' heritage is strongly influenced by the African presence. *See also Asiento*; Dutch Slave Trade; Monopoly.

Further Readings: "A Reassessment of the Dutch Atlantic Slave Trade." In Postma, J., and Enthoven, V., eds. *Riches of Atlantic Commerce: Dutch Transatlantic Trade and Shipping, 1585–1817.* Leiden: Brill, 2003; Heijer, Henk den. *Goud, Ivoor en Slaven: Scheepvaart en Handel van de Tweede Westindische Compagnie op Afrika, 1674–1740.* Zutphen: Walburg Pers, 1997; Gibbes, F. E., Römer-Kenepa, N. C., and Scriwanek, M. A. *De Bewoners van Curaçao: Vijf Eeuwen van Lief en Leed, 1499–1999.* Willemstad: Nationaal Archief, 2002; Jordaan, Han. "The Curaçao Slave Market: From *Asiento* Trade to Free Trade, 1700–1730." In Postma, J., and Enthoven, V., eds. *Riches of Atlantic Commerce: Dutch Transatlantic Trade and Shipping, 1585–1817.* Leiden: Brill, 2003; Klooster, Wim. "The Curaçao Slave Market: From *Asiento* Trade to Free Trade, 1700–1730." In Postma, J., and Enthoven, V., eds. *Riches of Atlantic Commerce: Dutch Transatlantic Trade and Shipping, 1585–1817.* Leiden: Brill, 2003; Postma, Johannes. "Curaçao and the Caribbean Transit Trade." In Postma, J., and Enthoven, V., eds. *Riches of Atlantic Commerce: Dutch Transatlantic Trade and Shipping, 1585–1817.* Leiden: Brill, 2003.

Valika Smeulders

D

Dahomey

Dahomey, located in one of the poorer regions of the West African coastal region, was one of the smaller Aja group of states. Founded by a clan or ruling dynasty that claimed membership of the royal house of **Allada** to the south, Dahomey emerged in the early seventeenth century in the region between the Volta Basin and Yorubaland. This ruling family, the Aja, migrated north from the coastal trading state of Allada (founded in 1575) inland because of a disputed succession and Dutch intervention on the coast. Under the leadership of Do-Aklin, the Aja settled among the Fon on the Abomey plateau (about sixty miles from the coast) around 1620. Over the next two decades, the Aja imposed their authority over the loosely organized Fon. Thus, the new Kingdom of Dahomey was founded as an inland kingdom with its capital at Abomey and Wegbaja as king around 1650. Dahomey lasted through the nineteenth century before conquest by the French.

Expansion and Trade

King Wegbaja (1650–1685) and King Akaba II (1685–1708) maintained their control over the area around Abomey and also embarked on wars of expansion and conquered areas south and southeast of Abomey.

To take advantage of trade with Europeans, especially the slave trade, Dahomey conquered Allada and **Ouidah** in the early 1720s, and eventually replaced Allada as the dominant slaving community in the Aja region. Some scholars, however, believe that **Agaja Trudo** (1708–1732), who conquered Allada and Ouidah, wished to end the slave trade to secure greater political stability in the region. Others claim that he wanted Europeans to establish **plantations** and use slave labor in Dahomey, thus keeping slaves in Africa, but the Europeans did not heed his advice. Be that as it may, the need for **firearms** made Dahomey one of the major participants in the slave trade—raiding the hinterland in the eighteenth century.

Coronation of the King of Whydah, Dahomey, April 1725. Tracy W. McGregor Library, Special Collections, University of Virginia Library.

Political System

Wegbaja and his successors strengthened royal power in Dahomey through the establishment of the system of primogeniture. However, only sons born of royal wives during their father's reign were eligible to succeed. By instituting succession by the king's eldest son, Dahomean rulers sought to prevent succession disputes and the accompanying anarchy that attend succession wars. Similarly, when a king came to the throne at an advanced age, only a few children were in all likelihood born, ensuring that rival claimants to the throne were sometimes limited in number. Additionally, the system of primogeniture was meant to reduce the influence of the village chiefs in the choice of a successor to the king.

Dahomean rulers developed a cult around the institution of kingship. This cult involved annual human sacrifice to honor deceased members of the royal family and to supply them with a new group of servants at the "Annual Custom." Several European visitors to the Dahomey court reported on these human sacrifices, which were also designed to demonstrate the omnipotence of royal power.

The Dahomean constitution was similar to that of Oyo and lasted until the early eighteenth century when it was subverted by a new group of rulers who converted Dahomey into a centralized state. According to the Dahomean constitution, the king or *Oba* was the supreme political leader, but he was more like a primus inter pares than an autocratic ruler. Although many of the highest offices of state were hereditary, many others (political and military officials) were appointed by the king. The king also controlled state **taxes**, tribute, and **profits** from the slave trade, and property inheritance was validated through his court.

The king was assisted in the performance of his duties by councils of officials who acted as a check on his authority or power. One council consisted of kingmakers who chose the king from the royal lineage; another council could request the king to commit suicide, much like the Oyo Mesi of the Yoruba Kingdom of Oyo.

The king performed his duties with the assistance of state officials such as the *migan* or prime minister who was also the commander-in-chief of the army. Other officials included the *meu* or minister in charge of taxes and commander of the left wing of the Dahomean army, and the *to-no-num*, the chief eunuch and minister in charge of taxes. Taxes were assessed in the form of income tax, customs duties, tolls, and proceeds from royal estates and tax on agricultural production (including livestock). Other officials included the *yovo-gan* or Viceroy of Whydah and the *tokpo* or minister of agriculture. These top officials of Dahomey were in charge of central government functions and were also commanders of different branches of the army. The king had a private bodyguard that included the celebrated Amazons, an all-female contingent noted for their bravery and fearlessness. This was unique in Africa.

In the early eighteenth century, the Dahomean constitution was subverted by a new group of rulers. Under these rulers, Dahomey became an absolute monarchy with a highly organized central government. Using their control over firearms, they made the kingdom of Dahomey an all-powerful state. This began with Agaja Trudo. One by-product of this centralization was Dahomey's ability to shift from economic dependence on the slave trade to extensive oil palm plantations after suppression of the trade. A kingship cult of sacrificial offerings was developed to support the centralized state system.

To facilitate efficient administration, Dahomey was divided into six provinces with each province under a provincial chief or governor. The provincial governor was assisted by village heads in the execution of his duties and could be summoned to the capital, Abomey, at any time. The king stationed representatives in the offices of the provincial governors to inform him about all activities. In addition to this, the King and his officials (central government) communicated with the provincial governments by utilizing a "carrier corps" of runners known as the *half-heads*. Stationed at relay stations throughout the kingdom, these runners kept the channel of communication open and active between the central government and the provinces.

The Dahomean kings also introduced a unique element into the provincial system of government. They implemented a system known as Dahomeanization. By this policy, the Kings of Dahomey largely abolished the ruling families of conquered states and appointed governors for conquered towns. The laws and customs of Dahomey were made to take precedence in these conquered states. By this policy, Dahomey sought to completely integrate all the conquered states into the Dahomean polity. In this way, Dahomean laws took root in all parts of the kingdom and thus all conquered people were made to become part of the kingdom with a view to achieving homogenization of laws, customs, and institutions. In consonance with this policy, citizenship was not based entirely on blood relationships. Foreigners could become citizens of Dahomey through participation in a "citizenship ceremony" in which the state and national will were represented by a perforated calabash filled with water. Dahomeans and the foreigner seeking citizenship placed their fingers in the holes and thus stemmed the spillage of the water in the perforated calabash. This symbolic action was designed to impress on the candidate for citizenship that withdrawal of a finger from the perforated calabash would lead to water draining from the calabash in much the same way that an act of treason would lead to a weakening or even collapse of the state. A similar ceremony was enacted when individuals were ennobled, thus stressing good citizenship.

Dahomey and Oyo

For all its importance, Dahomey was a relatively small kingdom about seventy miles from north to south and fifty miles from east to west. Its relationship with its larger and stronger neighbor to east, Oyo, proved problematic. Between 1726 and 1740, Oyo attacked and raided Dahomey to keep the former's control over the southwestern trade routes to the coast. Despite Agaja's efforts to secure Dahomean independence from Oyo, Dahomey continued to be a tributary state, a status that was confirmed by a 1730 treaty. Dahomey's tributary status meant heavy annual payments in return for which it kept its army and was not subject to the watchful eyes of an Oyo resident official. It was not until Oyo was occupied with the Fulani wars that first Adandoza (1797–1818) and later Gezo (1818–1858) wrested Dahomey from Oyo overlordship.

Dahomey and the Slave Trade

Dahomey is one of the few African states that owed its prominence to the slave trade. It built a well-trained army that increased in size and efficiency until the mid-nineteenth century. In 1727, the army was estimated at 3,000 regulars and 10,000 militia and by 1845 had increased to 12,000 regulars and 24,000 militia. A carrier corps of young men supplied the army. With this army, Agaja conquered the areas northwest of Dahomey and, between 1724–1727, the coastal states of Allada and Ouidah. Scholars do not agree on the motivation for the conquest of the coastal states, but there is no denying the fact that control of the coastal region brought Dahomey into contact with the Dutch (prominent in Allada), the French, and the English (prominent at Whydah) and made slavery the cornerstone of the Dahomean economy.

Dahomey traded for guns and **gunpowder** with slaves and, in turn, used the weapon for raiding north and northwest for captives. Agaja's successors Tegbesu IV (1732–1774), Kpengla V (1774–1789), and Agonglo (1790–1797) continued the wars of expansion along the southeast and southwest of Dahomey, in the Upper Weme, Mono, and Porto Novo areas. When Gezo (1818–1858) broke free of Oyo in 1821, he used the army to raid the Mahi people north of Dahomey. In 1841 and 1851, Gezo attacked the Oyo provinces of Ketu and Abeokuta. His successors Glele (1858–1889) and Benhazin (1889–1894) attacked Ketu and Abeokuta.

Rivalry between Dahomey and Oyo in the eighteenth century was instrumental in generating a large number of captives who were sold into the Atlantic slave trade. Systematic annual raids also resulted in large numbers of slaves. The Dahomean state exported slaves obtained in the wars of expansion. Slave exports became a state **monopoly** and profits of slave dealers were taxed by the state. The state also depended on large plantations worked by slave labor.

For most of the nineteenth century, during the suppression of the slave trade, Dahomey gradually turned to oil palm plantations for sale to Europeans and overcame the crisis of adaptation that attended the suppression of the slave trade. *See also* African Rulers and the Slave Trade; Allada; Slavery in Africa.

Further Readings: Boahen, A. Adu. *Topics in West African History.* London: Longmans, Green and Company, 1966; July, Robert W. *A History of the African People.* 5th ed. Prospect Heights, IL: Waveland Press, 1998; Shillington, Kevin. *History of Africa.* 2nd ed. New York: Palgrave Macmillan, 2005; Webster, J. B., and Boahen, A. Adu, with Idowu, H. O. *The Growth of African Civilization: The Revolutionary Years—West Africa Since 1800.* London: Longmans, Green and Company, 1968.

Edmund Abaka

Daily Schedule

A captive's life assumed a pattern on reaching the **barracoons**. These were enclosures where the enslaved were kept before boarding a slave ship. The slaves were freed from their shackles twice a day for meals and **exercise**. On the west coast, comprising the **Gold Coast**, the **Slave Coast**, and the Ivory Coast, the slaves were usually fed bread and **water** at the expense of the **slave traders**. **Food** was definitely for sustenance and not for the health of captives. Similarly, exercise was not to ensure the physical fitness of a slave. Both food and exercise were intended to reduce the likely incidence of morbidity or **mortality**, which hunger and immobility might cause.

Each of the major players in the trade insisted that they possessed the best regimen for African slaves as they were transported along the Middle Passage. For instance, the Dutch claimed to have fed their slaves three times a day with "good victuals" that were better than their African food, while the English often criticized the Portuguese of mishandling slaves. On the whole, there appeared to have been a general pattern. Slaves were fed twice a day. On English ships, it was usually mid-morning (around 10:00 A.M.) and early evening (around 4:00 P.M.). They were usually allowed up on deck in pairs. Most slavers shackled slaves together in pairs or in threes. A chain was passed through a ring in their **chains**. This, in turn, was locked down to the ringbolts. These were then fastened, at intervals, to the deck. These precautions were thought necessary because all of the slaves would be on deck at the same time, which presented opportunities for a mutiny or jumping overboard. The sailors serving them the food stood at arms. On other ships, they got to the deck as early as 8:00 A.M. while they were served breakfast at 9:00 A.M. **Women** and relatively young boys were usually allowed to roam on the deck without chains. This was common on most ships.

The meals were usually crude fare. On ships bringing captives from the Windward coast, it was boiled rice, millet, or corn meal. This was sometimes cooked with a few lumps of salt beef taken from the sailors' rations. On ships bringing captives from the Bight of Biafra at the east end of the Gulf of Guinea, the food was stewed yam. Water was seriously rationed, and each slave was given half a pint of water served in a pannikin.

After the morning meal came what the slavers referred to as "**dancing the slaves.**" There was no joy with the dance. It was a cross between torture and compulsory exercise. This ritual was designed to lift their spirits against suicidal tendencies and to prevent scurvy. The exercise proved to be torture for those with swollen limbs. Slaves in irons were ordered to stand up and dance within the limits permitted by their shackles while leaving enough room for those without chains to dance around the deck. This sadistic ritual did not evoke any joy. The men in irons had to forcibly do this until their knees bled. Failure to do so would mean flogging from sailors holding "cats" (whips). Those who could perform this unhindered dance were usually women and children. **Music** was provided by either a drum, an upturned enamel jug, or an African banjo. Sometimes a sailor with a bagpipe or a fiddle supplied the music. Slavers had been known to advertise for fiddlers to come on the voyage with them to Africa. Part of the reason was to supply music when they danced the slaves. On the last days of voyage, when land was sighted, the women were bedecked with the castoffs of the sailors' clothing, and everyone was expected to dance in thankfulness for surviving the Middle Passage.

While some sailors enforced the dance ritual on deck, others went below deck to clean the **hold** where the slaves slept. This was not a pleasant task because the dirt and stench in the hold were almost unbearable. This degree of cleanliness was to ensure having enough **cargo** for sale in the Americas. Similarly, before the slaves came up in the mornings, the deck was holystoned. Most ships added rinsing the mouth of slaves with vinegar and trimming their nails. The latter was usually to prevent them from using their nails as weapons. The general hygiene was primarily for the health of the seamen and slave traders.

In the afternoon, slaves were given their second meal, which was often the same as breakfast. Sometimes, a change in diet included the addition of horse beans, the cheapest European provender. The beans were boiled down to a mash. It was then topped with a mixture of palm oil, flour, water, and red sauce. The sailors referred to this food as "slabber sauce."

As soon as they finished eating, they were herded below deck. The process of stowing the slaves for the night then commenced. The freedom to go on deck was subject to good weather. In bad weather or rainy days, the slaves were left in the hold for the whole day. Sometimes, they stayed there for days until the weather improved. They were served their meals in this confined space.

Further Readings: Curtin, Philip D. *The Atlantic Slave Trade: A Census*. Madison: University of Wisconsin, 1969; Dow, George Francis. *Slave Ships and Slaving*. New York: Dover Publications, 1970; Howard, Thomas. *Black Voyage*. Boston: Little, Brown, 1971; Kay, F. George. *The Shameful Trade*. London: Frederick Muller Ltd., 1967; Klein, Herbert S. *The Middle Passage: Comparative Studies in the Atlantic Slave Trade*. Princeton, NJ: Princeton University Press, 1978; Meltzer, Milton. *Slavery: From the Renaissance to Today*. Chicago: Cowles Book Company, 1972; Plimmer, Charlotte, and Plimmer, Denis. *Slavery: The Anglo-American Involvement*. New York: Harper and Row, 1973; Rawley, James A. *The Transatlantic Slave Trade*. New York: W. W. Norton, 1981; Thomas, Hugh. *The Slave Trade: The Story of the Atlantic Slave Trade, 1440–1870*. New York: Simon & Schuster, 1997.

Oyekemi Olajope Oyelakin

Dancing and Exercise

"Dancing the slaves" was a daily ritual that took place on board most slave ships during their trans-Atlantic crossing. One of the first accounts of dancing the slaves was written in the log of the slaver Hannibal in 1694. **Surgeon** Falconbridge's famous account also describes this practice. This forced ritual was performed on the deck of most slave ships after the first meal of the day. Shackled slaves (mostly men) were forced to jump up and down, twist, and simulate joy under the gaze of the **crew** for an hour or two. Those who could move more freely (generally the **women** and **children**) would circulate around them. The slaves who were reluctant to "dance" or who did not show enough enthusiasm were brutally flogged by crewmembers using a "cat o' nine tails." This was a powerful whip with nine leather or tarred cotton strings attached to the handle. The ships' surgeons (who were in charge of the **food** allocation) imposed this practice, which they also described in their logs, but it was the **captains** or the crewmembers who supervised. It was a widespread ritual performed on all slave ships. Ironically, the physical restraint imposed on the slaves' bodies (forced immobility) on the lower deck was a violent contrast to the forced motion (forced exercise) on the upper deck.

Because the slaves endured cramped conditions and had to crouch all day and night down in the unventilated and soiled lower deck (or in specific quarters, as was the case for the women), "dancing the slaves" was seen as one way, among others, to decrease the high **mortality** rate among slaves and, as such, was motivated by greed. The high mortality rate on slave ships, because of ill treatment and dysentery, murder, and **suicide**, was a real concern since every slave who died represented a loss of **profit** for the slavers' **captains**. Some of them took out **insurance** on their human **cargo**, but most insurance companies only reimbursed losses following revolts or suicide. "Natural" death did not exist within their clauses. In addition, fit slaves could be sold at a better **price** and "dancing the slaves" was believed to keep them in better shape, as a way to exercise their muscles or stimulate blood circulation. Some accounts suggest that this widespread practice was believed to "lift the spirits" of the slaves, alleviate anxiety caused by their condition, and therefore lower the level of **violence** on board.

Some accounts suggest that the slaves were forced to dance at night to entertain the crew and that the best dancers were rewarded with small privileges or alcohol. Slaves were also forced to sing and these simulations of African rituals were sometimes accompanied by the sound of a banjo, drum, or kettle. This practice was so common that musicians were often hired to play on the ships as well. Once at their destination, the slaves were still forced to perform dances, but this time it was to be for the enjoyment of their **plantation** masters, in particular in the United States. *See also* Music, Songs, and Singing; Torture.

Further Readings: Falconbridge, Alexander. *An Account of the Slave Trade on the Coast of Africa*. New York: AMS Press, 1973 (1788); Smithsonian Institution Press, in association with Mariners' Museum. *Captive Passage: the Transatlantic Slave Trade and the Making of the Americas*. Washington, DC: Smithsonian Institution Press; and Newport News, VA: Mariners' Museum, 2002.

Carole Maccotta

Danish Slave Trade

The Danish slave trade, centered around the Danish West Indies and the **Gold Coast** of Africa, began in 1649 and lasted until 1803. Denmark was the first colonial power and European country to outlaw the slave trade. In 1792, its king issued an ordinance declaring the end of the Danish slave exports beginning January 1, 1803.

Although the first recorded Danish slave ships in Africa appeared in 1649, the first charter for a Danish slave-trading company went to the Glückstadt Company in 1651. The success of the *Neldebladet*, the first Danish vessel to carry slaves from Africa to the West Indies, encouraged Danish participation in the Atlantic slave trade when the ship returned to Europe with **sugar**, ivory, gold, and palm oil.

Denmark's involvement in Africa centered on the Gold Coast where it founded strongholds on the coast such as Fort Frederiksborg in 1660 and Christiansborg Castle in 1661. Other later important establishments included Fort Fredensborg (Old Ningo), Fort Kongensten (Ada), and Fort Prinsensten (Keta). During the seventeenth century, the Danes traded slaves from Popo and Ardra in **Dahomey** in exchange for gold along the Gold Coast, where mines needed an inexhaustible supply of labor. In the eighteenth century, the Danes expanded their influence on the eastern Gold Coast in an effort to control trade at the Volta delta and on the western **Slave Coast** (today, Togo and **Benin**). They founded a string of trade lodges just east of **Accra** to Aflahu on the present border between Ghana and Togo.

In the New World where Spain regulated the slave trade by granting **licenses** to trade in slaves, Danish traders initially found little access to the slave markets. Spain withheld its licenses, regarding the Danish companies as weak and unable to handle the contracts with security. After Spain stopped granting licenses in 1773, Danish slavers carried Africans directly to the Spanish colonies, although the Danish presence there was never large.

In 1671, the Danes made their appearance in the West Indies, which would become their main sphere of trading, when Christian V of Denmark granted a charter to his subjects to establish **plantations** on the unoccupied islands of St. Thomas and St. John. From 1680, the Danish West India Company exercised control over the sugar trade on these islands before the Danish Crown took over the task in 1754. In 1733, Denmark bought St. Croix, which became the largest of the Danish sugar islands. As a minor colonial power, Denmark limited its tropical empire to the three West Indian islands of St. Croix, St. Thomas, and St. John. The production of sugar on these islands was not spectacular and, by 1725, less than 5,000 slaves lived on St. Thomas and roughly 1,500 slaves lived on St. John. Together with the Dutch and Swedish Caribbean, the Danish Caribbean imported roughly 6 percent of the slaves who came from Africa. Slave rebellions plagued the Danish West Indian colonies until Denmark abolished slavery there following a rebellion on July 3, 1848. In 1917, the United States bought the three West Indian islands and renamed them the U.S. Virgin Islands.

Before abolishing slavery in 1848, Denmark declared the end of Danish slave exports in January 1792, but with the proviso that the ordinance would not go into effect until January 1, 1803. Because of this proclamation, Denmark was the first European nation to abolish its export slave trade. However, the export of some 30,000 Africans during the last decade of legal commerce in slaves—a sharp increase over previous years—tainted its reputation. Illicit slave-trading continued from Danish forts, particularly Fort Fredensborg, until the 1830s and 1840s. Exact figures are unavailable, but the Danish slave trade exported an estimated 85,000 slaves from Africa between 1660 and 1806.

In 1803, when Denmark abolished its export trade in slaves, it attempted to find an alternative economic base in the Gold Coast by developing cotton and coffee plantations and by turning trade to "legitimate" export products such as palm oil. By 1850, however, Denmark had dropped its colonial ambitions and had sold all its establishments in West Africa to Britain. *See also* Escapes and Runaways (Maroonage); *Fredensborg*, The; Minor European Nations.

Further Readings: Reynolds, Edward. *Stand the Storm: A History of the Atlantic Slave Trade*. London: Allison & Busby, 1985; Thomas, Hugh. *The Slave Trade: The Story of the Atlantic Slave Trade, 1440–1870*. New York: Simon & Schuster, 1997; UNESCO (United Nations Educational, Scientific and Cultural Organization). "Danish-Norwegian Slave Trade." [Online, October 2006]. The Slave Ship Fredensborg Project Web site: www.unesco.no/fredensborg/danish_norwegian_slave_trade.

Leslie Wilson

Decentralized Societies

Decentralized societies are sometimes referred to as "stateless" or "acephalous" societies. In such societies, the largest political unit was the village or a confederation of villages. A range of positions of authority often existed, but within villages and confederations, no person or group had an exclusive claim to the right to exercise coercive force. In face-to-face meetings involving many people, representatives from households sat together to decide matters affecting the whole. Sometimes, influential leaders emerged, becoming "chiefs" or "big men." However, there were no ascriptive authority positions. Simply put, there were leaders but no rulers.

Decentralized societies on states' frontiers sometimes fell victim to powerful armies, their people enslaved and shipped to the New World. Such was the case in the area of present-day **Angola**. Other decentralized societies formed hierarchies as strong rulers capable of protecting people from threatening outsiders emerged. Such was the case on the Island of Bussis on the Upper Guinea Coast, where in the late sixteenth century people submitted themselves to the rule of a warrior who transformed the island into a militarized state. Political centralization was, then, one way people restructured institutions to defend against slavers.

Many decentralized societies refused to adopt centralized political systems yet found ways to respond to outside threats. Across West Africa, five broad patterns emerged. First, when politically decentralized societies were threatened with **violence** associated with slaving, members relocated to easy-to-defend locations. For example, in northern Togo, Kabre moved to mountainous areas to escape the armies of Ashanti and **Dahomey**. In central Nigeria, pagans threatened by **Muslim** raiders retreated to the Jos Plateau, finding refuge in the broken country. In coastal Guinea-Bissau, the Balanta moved to the dense mangrove forests of coastal rivers.

Second, where the terrain provided no defense from raiders, members of decentralized societies concentrated in walled settlements. Walls protected Sikasso from Samori and his powerful armies in 1888 and 1889. In West Africa's Sahel, the Samo's thick-walled *banco* houses, which were connected one to the next, provided no entry to attackers. Chamba, too, built walled settlements on plains where they were forced to go to cultivate crops, and some **Igbo** constructed walls in southeast Nigeria. In Guinea-Bissau, the palisades that protected politically decentralized communities were known as *tabancas*, a word that eventually came to mean village in the Creole **language** of the region.

Third, in the era of the Atlantic slave trade, people living in decentralized societies engaged with the Atlantic market to gain access to valuable imports, most especially weapons, which were needed for protection. Because decentralized societies did not possess broad institutions that regulated exchange in state-based societies, they often relied on **women** to make contact with outsiders and to conduct exchange. In decentralized regions, marriages between women and foreign traders were particularly important in cementing bonds of trust. Thus, in politically decentralized stretches of the **Congo River**, as well as in Igbo and Ibibio areas of southeast Nigeria, male merchants took wives from great distances and relied on marriage to facilitate trade. In Anlo-Ewe areas of the **Slave Coast**, the trading family of Gbodzo established itself when a foreign merchant called Tettega married the daughter of a local. On the Casamance River, Floup women visited trading centers, carrying goods in canoes.

Fourth, in many decentralized regions, people produced and traded slaves, and they did so to gain access to imports. On the Congo River, Bobangi communities often approved of the sale of adulterers, thieves, and witches, and they organized raids to produce tradable captives. Similarly,

Igbo and Ibibio villagers conducted raids and judicial proceedings, generating captives who they traded for weapons and iron, which had great use in warfare. Finally, Montagnards in northern Cameroon produced slaves by staging kidnappings and raids that resembled feuds between lineages.

Finally, because decentralized societies could not amass tremendous armies, they most often sent relatively small groups of men to produce tradable captives. Because raiding parties were small, they more often than not targeted relatively weak females and children and killed men who resisted, or they retreated empty handed when resistance was great. How decentralized societies produced slaves meant that the **gender** and age ratios of the captive populations they sold for export were different from the gender and age ratios of the captive populations sold from state-based regions. State-based armies could more easily subdue strong men than could smaller raiding parties. Hence, a high proportion of child and female captives were shipped from the Cameroon grass fields, Igboland, and Guinea-Bissau. *See also* African Rulers and the Slave Trade; Slavery in Africa; Wars, African.

Further Readings: Lovejoy, Paul E. *Transformations in Slavery: A History of Slavery in Africa.* New York: Cambridge University Press, 1993; Perbi, Akosua Adoma. *A History of Indigenous Slavery in Ghana: From the 15th to the 19th Centuries.* Accra: Sub-Saharan Publishers, 2004; Thornton, John K. *Africa and Africans in the Making of the Atlantic World, 1400–1800.* 2nd ed. Cambridge: Cambridge University Press, 1998.

Walter Hawthorne

Destinations

Slaves who were captured throughout Africa traveled to multiple destinations. Some of these destinations were located within the African continent and others in cities and **ports** in the New World where slaves were dispersed strategically to different **plantations**. **Slavery in Africa** did not resemble slavery in the Americas. In Africa, slavery was based on mutual arrangements made by kings, chiefs, or community leaders. Therefore, it was a common practice for slaves captured from warfare, disputes, and ethnic conflicts to be placed in locations within a community or region in Africa. Tensions and hostilities among communities, ethnic groups, religious groups, and kingdoms sometimes created **violence** and increased the population of the captives. Because of the mutual understanding that often existed among these kingdoms, families, neighbors, rivals, and friends alike, arrangements were made to keep slaves within a reasonable distance within communities in Africa. Slaves who found themselves under such conditions had different responsibilities. Slaves who served in royal palaces performed different duties such as guards, servants, and other prestigious jobs at times. In other African communities, slaves worked as farm laborers producing **food** to serve their masters. Other slaves were relocated to nearby towns, villages, or communities to serve in similar positions as arranged by the leaders of the community. Such practices were widespread during the period when **Muslims** enslaved Africans. This era was known to be associated with the period of Islamic *jihad.*

The destinations for slaves in the New World were different from those for the domestic slaves in many areas in Africa because of the complex money-making ventures that existed during the period of slavery between the sixteenth and nineteenth century. With the support of African chiefs and local slave traders, Europeans traders increased the number of captives. **Slave merchants** did so through batter trading—a system in which European goods and weapons were supplied to African chiefs and slave traders for slaves. Armed with weapons from the Europeans, African slave traders invaded villages and towns rapidly and captured more slaves to satisfy European demands. The negotiations between the two groups expanded the slave trade and made innocent Africans more vulnerable to **enslavement**. Moreover, the new slavery project changed the dynamics that existed domestically. In fact, the introduction of European slavery convinced many local Africans to abandon domestic slavery.

The future destinations of slaves in Africa and the New World were shaped by economic, religious, political, and social elements beyond the control of slaves. In eighteenth-century Africa, as Europeans gained more control over the terms of trade and the destinations of slaves, Europeans made strategic arrangements to capture and disperse slaves according to their skills and **gender**. Therefore, slaves who were captured from the hinterland in the **Gold Coast**, the Bight of Benin, the **Dahomey** Kingdom, **Angola**, and other regions in Africa were forced to walk thousands of miles to new locations that included **barracoons** or slave pens and slave dungeons along the coastlines of Africa. These pens and dungeons, and other locations, served as temporary destinations as slaves waited for weeks and sometimes for months until the slave ships arrived along the coast. Feeble slaves who were not able to complete the journey to their destinations were abandoned along the way. Many slaves who were captured and were taken to coastlines, such as the slave dungeons in **Elmina** and Cape Coast in the Gold Coast region, and **Gorée Island** in **Senegal**, died along the way. In the dungeons, rebellious slaves were separated from passive slaves and held in new destinations such as cells within the compound of the slave-holding castle until they died of starvation.

Other slaves whose journey did not end on the shores of Africa but in the New World were dispersed based on the preferences of slave masters and slave merchants. For example, as rice cultivation increased in the wetland regions in sub-Saharan Africa, slave merchants in North America set up strategic systems to import slaves from countries with abundant skills in rice cultivation. Between 1782 and 1810 as the number of slaves who were captured along the Guinea Coast, Senegal, Gambia, and Angola reached its zenith, many slaves found new homes in South Carolina and Georgia. Here, planters invested heavily in rice production and relied on the skills and labor of African slaves, especially **women** who had expertise in rice planting and cultivation. Thus, through the strategic selection of slaves, new destinations were created in rice-based communities such as the Gullah Islands in South Carolina. The strategic importation and distribution of slaves resulted in the creation of new African communities with similar cultures, skills, and ethnic backgrounds throughout North America. Slaves from

Angolan and Congolese territories were transported to Louisiana, while slaves from the Gold Coast and Nigeria found Virginia, Maryland, Massachusetts, New York, Rhode Island, Louisiana, Mississippi, and other locations to be their final destinations in America.

The demand for special African skills characterized many plantations in the Caribbean and South America where European merchants and traders invested heavily in rice, coffee, and **sugar** production in Kingston, **Jamaica**; **Havana, Cuba**; and other regions of Mexico, Puerto Rico, Panama, Surinam, and Guyana. Slaves from Nigeria and Angola mined gold and worked in coffee plantations in Bahia, Minas Gerais, and Rio de Janeiro in **Brazil**; **Cartagena** in Columbia; and **Buenos Aires** in Argentina, as well as other destinations in South America. In Europe, port cities such as **Liverpool** and **London**, England; Marseille, France; **Lisbon**, Portugal; and Amsterdam, Holland received many African slaves. Overall, slaves had multiple destinations. In slave plantations all over the Americas and Europe, **families** suffered isolation and separations whenever slaves were sold to new owners at different times and were sent to different destinations. *See also* Entrepôts; Slavery in Africa.

Further Readings: Carney, Judith. *Black Rice: The African Origins of Rice Cultivation in the Americas.* Cambridge, MA: Harvard University Press, 2001; Curtin, Philip D. *The Atlantic Slave Trade: A Census.* Madison: University of Wisconsin Press, 1969; Gomez, Michael. *Exchanging Our Country Marks: The Transformation of African Identities in the Colonial Antebellum South.* Chapel Hill: University of North Carolina Press, 1998; Klein, Herbert. *The Middle Passage: Comparative Studies in the Atlantic Slave Trade.* Princeton, NJ: Princeton University Press, 1978; Lovejoy, Paul E. *Transformations in Slavery.* New York: Cambridge University Press, 1983; Nishida, Mieko. *Slavery and Identity: Ethnicity, Gender and Race in Salvador.* Bloomington: Indiana University Press, 2003; Solow, Barbara, ed. *Slavery and the Rise of the Atlantic System.* New York: Cambridge University Press, 1991; Thomas, Hugh. *The Slave Trade: The Story of the Atlantic Slave Trade, 1440–1870.* New York: Simon & Schuster, 1997.

Kwame Essien

Disease

The trans-Atlantic slave trade was a lucrative international business from which many nations benefited economically. As a result of its oppressive nature, it also caused notorious death and destitution at every stage. Exact **mortality** rates for the Middle Passage are elusive; however, scholars generally agree that mortality rates declined as the trade evolved. Seventeenth-century slave voyages probably killed about 20 percent of the slaves. By the late eighteenth century, modest improvements in **food**, **water**, and cleanliness gradually cut the mortality rate to 10 to 15 percent.

During the Middle Passage, the greatest killer of Africans was disease. Copious factors affected the number of slave deaths during the ocean voyage: the time spent along the African coast trading for slaves to fill the **cargo holds**, the length of the journey across the ocean, the extent of crowding aboard the slaver, the quantity and quality of food and water during the voyage, the care, or lack thereof, provided by the captain and **crew**, and the ever-feared outbreak of an epidemic disease.

Many Africans fell ill even before the trans-Atlantic voyage began. Often they had walked long distances under harsh conditions from the African interior to the coast and thus were not healthy enough to resist disease. The weeks held captive in the dungeons or **barracoons** waiting to be sold to the European traders further weakened their immune systems and increased their chances to fall prey to disease. Scholars have suggested that the majority of deaths on the voyage across the Atlantic occurred during the first couple of weeks and were often a result of malnutrition and disease encountered during the forced marches and subsequent internment at slave camps along the coast.

The cramped, unsanitary, and deplorable conditions on board slave vessels allowed sickness and disease to flourish. The floors of the cargo hold were filled with blood, human waste, parasites, and vomit. Toilet and washing facilities for the Africans on board slave ships were inadequate at best, doing more to spread disease than to prevent it. Slaves had to share toilets that were nothing more than tubs placed at various places in the holds that were difficult, at best, to reach. To reach the facilities, the captives, who rarely had room to sit upright let alone stand and walk to the tubs, would have to crawl over each other. Those who were too ill to move were forced to lie in their own urine and excrement.

The prevalence of disease at sea required that **captains** maintain some measure of cleanliness and provide some medical attention for their human cargo. At intervals, the slaves had their mouths rinsed with vinegar or lime juice and were given a dram of the juice as an antidote to scurvy. During good weather, slaves would be brought up on deck to eat, get fresh air, and **exercise**. While on deck, captains would have the cargo holds cleaned and the slaves themselves washed down in an effort to keep disease and death at bay. In bad weather, the slaves remained in the cargo holds and the ship's crew did not have time to clean the slave decks. The ship's port holes were covered during **storms** to stop water from getting in and this made the conditions even more unbearable and bred disease. Given the varying incubation periods for disease, longer voyages increased the chance of illness and death.

Slave captains remarked that, excluding mortality caused by epidemics such as smallpox, the prime cause of mortality during the Middle Passage was dysentery and that the length of stay along the coast to pick up cargoes usually increased the death tolls. If bad weather prolonged the voyage, the normal ration of water and either boiled rice, cornmeal, millet, or yams was cut in half, resulting in starvation and illness. Malnourished slaves were prone to fevers and more susceptible to disease. Scholars have noted that a relationship between epidemic disease and **season** existed, with autumn and winter being the worst. Dysentery was the highest cause of death after epidemics of contagious diseases, so the availability of various kinds of food in relationship to season might also account for this relationship between season and mortality.

Slave cargoes were afflicted by smallpox, measles, dysentery and other gastrointestinal diseases, malaria, hookworm, fevers, eye infections, and body sores. Ophthalmia, an inflammatory disorder of the eye, was a highly contagious disease that spread quickly on slave ships and often resulted in complete blindness and death. Untold numbers succumbed to dysentery, which was then called the flux or bloody flux, while in the hold. Indeed, fever and flux were the terms most used to describe common causes of death aboard slave ships. European diseases such as syphilis and gonorrhea were often passed on to African **women**, who were the victims of **rape**. The **branding** that many slaves were subjected to before embarking on the Middle Passage sometimes became infected in the unsanitary conditions of the holds, inducing fevers and gangrene.

These and other terrible ailments could rapidly afflict an entire cargo of slaves, as well as the crew, in a matter if days if left unchecked. Epidemics of disease spread like wildfire in the tightly packed cargo holds and could wipe out hundreds at a time. Smallpox was particularly disastrous because there was no cure. One English vessel, the *Hero*, lost 360 slaves to an outbreak of smallpox. Slaves showing the slightest sign of smallpox or other deadly diseases were thrown overboard, alive, to prevent an epidemic aboard the ship, which could cost the trader tens of thousands of dollars. In 1819, the captain of the *Le Rodeur* ordered thirty-nine slaves who had been blinded by an outbreak of ophthalmia thrown into the sea rather than bring unsellable slaves to the marketplace. With an outbreak of dysentery on board, the captain of **the Zong** ordered 132 weak and sick Africans thrown overboard.

In 1788, in its effort to reduce mortality rates, the British Parliament required each ship to have a certified surgeon or **doctor** on board. The law provided a bonus to the doctor and the ship's captain if no more than three slaves per hundred died during the Middle Passage. Unfortunately, given the **overcrowded** and unsanitary conditions aboard slave vessels, even capable, conscientious surgeons could do little to stem the spread of communicable diseases. Surgeons sometimes kept death books with the number of slaves who died at sea and journals in which they vividly described the disease and death aboard the slavers. One surgeon, **Alexander Falconbridge**, in an account of his voyages, wrote of boils resulting from slaves lying in their own excrement, of seasickness so bad that it resulted in death, and of the bloody discharge of those slaves suffering from dysentery. His account provides evidence of the devastating affects of disease. He made note of one slave ship that took on board more than 600 slaves and, without encountering storms or experiencing a longer voyage than normal, nearly half of the captives died.

The conditions aboard the ships show the extreme callousness of those involved in the slave trade and the gross inhumanity with which the Africans were treated. Nevertheless, evidence to suggest intentional maltreatment to the point of death is sparse because it was not to the economic advantage of the slavers to neglect or starve their captives or to deny them medical treatment. Only live slaves could be sold for a **profit**. Upon arrival in the New World, slaves would be emaciated from the ravages of the shipboard conditions and the lingering effects of malnutrition and disease. Slaves would continue to die in the days and weeks following their landing as the effects of their mistreatment took its toll. *See also* Ventilation and Suffocation.

Further Readings: Alden, Dauril, and Miller, Joseph C. "Unwanted Cargoes: The Origins and Dissemination of Smallpox via the Slave Trade from Africa to Brazil, c. 1560–1830."; In Kenneth Kiple, ed. *The African Exchange: Toward a Biological History of the Black People*, 35–109. Durham, NC: Duke University Press, 1987; Buxton, Thomas Fowell. *The African Slave Trade and Its Remedy.* London: John Murray, 1840; Curtin, Philip D. "Epidemiology and the Slave Trade." *Political Science Quarterly* 83, 2: 196–216; Falconbridge, Alexander. *An Account of the Slave Trade on the Coast of Africa.* New York: AMS Press, 1973 (1788); Klein, Herbert S. *The Middle Passage: Comparative Studies in the Atlantic Slave Trade.* Princeton, NJ: Princeton University Press, 1978; Klein, Herbert S. "The Trade in African Slave to Rio de Janeiro, 1795–1811: Estimates of Mortality and Patterns of Voyages." *Journal of African History* 10, 4: 533–549.

Sharon A. Roger Hepburn

Doctors and Surgeons

Slaves' first contact with surgeons was on the coast before embarkation. The captain and the ship's surgeon gave naked slaves a thorough physical examination. They looked at limbs, teeth, feet, eyes, genitals, and the overall physical condition of slaves to detect any ailment. The old and infirm were weeded out. Such were called "mackrons." Despite this, sick slaves with no apparent symptoms still got on board. Therefore, ships carried medicine and normally one surgeon on every ship. Nevertheless, medical treatment was either ineffective or sometimes impossible. The sick were separated from the fit and confined to a room. Common ailments were often treated violently through severe bleeds and purges. These treatments caused further damage to the slaves' health and often, within a few days, they would be thrown overboard. A slave ship was not a place to treat epidemics, and the economic interest of the **captains** was a major factor in the administration of treatment.

After the ship anchored, it was left to the surgeons to help sell the human **cargo**. **Chains** were removed from slaves and they were allowed fresh air in the open and fed good **food**. These measures were to enhance the sale value of slaves and were not undertaken out of concern for their wellness. For ill health that could not be overcome by these simple measures, the surgeon camouflaged. For instance, yaws would be covered up using a concoction of iron rust, lime juice, and **gunpowder**. After sale, the yaws would break out and would be practically incurable. Again, the appearance of yaws and other sores were literally removed by washes. Blackening and palm oil were then used to cover the scars. Venereal **diseases** were treated with astringent injections.

This unprofessional handling of patients may be better understood by looking at the position of surgeons. They were in the same social order as barbers. They fell well below the status of physicians. The slave ship surgeons were more or less those who could not make an adequate living on the mainland given the competition between them and the apothecaries and unorthodox medical practitioners. From 1790, slaving companies stopped paying percentages based on trading **profits**. They started paying bonuses based on the **mortality** rates on vessels during the voyage. When the rate was less than 2 percent, the captain got £100 and the surgeon got £50. If the mortality rate rose to 3 percent, they each got half of their amount. Captains and surgeons got around this by falsifying the quantity of their human cargo.

Doctors from the mainland sometimes accompanied buyers to the sales. Older slaves were brought to speak with new slaves in their own tongue to determine whether there were any camouflaged diseases.

In the New World, **plantation** owners always had surgeons who could be called to treat both his family and slaves. By 1792, it had become a legal requirement in **Jamaica** by the enactment of the Consolidated Slave Act. When a slave became ill, the owner first attempted a treatment at home. Sometimes slaves also passed off their ailments as not being serious. They preferred the native African treatment. In both cases, it was when home remedies failed that the surgeon was summoned. Both parties had their different reasons. Some plantation owners did not trust "regular" surgeons. They believed more in the efficacy of "irregular" medical practices like botanic remedies, homeopathy, and hydropathy. Thomsoniasm was a popular self-help treatment used widely in South America. It was a method of restoring lost heat to the body through herbal and steam treatment.

Plantation doctors were paid a per capita fee. The standard rate was 4 shillings. They got paid whether or not a treatment was given. Although the number of slaves on a plantation decided their earnings, most surgeons earned between £2,000 and £4,000 annually. It was only because slaves were economic investments that masters summoned these surgeons. The doctors of the times were such that they did not understand the illnesses and thus were unable to correctly diagnose most tropical diseases. Surgeons got away with their inadequacies in diagnosis and treatment by claiming that slaves were malingering or that injuries were self-inflicted. John Trapham, a doctor on a Jamaican plantation, claimed in 1679 that yaws in Africans were due to their being an "animal people."

Most slaves dreaded the process of medical treatment. Medical practice of the eighteenth to nineteenth century followed the "fallacy of the fours," which was based on the Humoral Theory. Doctors concluded that any **disease** ranging from hookworm to cancer was due to an excess of one of the four humors (fluids) in the body. The aim of medicine was to ensure that all four were balanced. The methods of balance were through bloodletting, salivation, blistering, and purging. Apart from the remedy of the fours, doctors used two dangerous substances for treatment: mercury and opium. Although the former was used effectively to some degree for the treatment of "the pox," its side effects were health damaging. The latter was an effective pain killer with strong addictive side effects. There were few spectacular breakthroughs in medicine during this period. It was more the harsh treatment that killed them than the ailments.

A surgeon's knife was hardly ever put to use in surgery except for the occasional emergency amputation. Planters preferred the services of African midwives in normal deliveries to the high fees of doctors. Again, most farms were very remote and there was hardly a quick mode of communication or transportation. It usually took a doctor hours or even a day to turn up after being summoned. *See also* Falconbridge, Alexander.

Further Readings: Falconbridge, Alexander. *An Account of the Slave Trade on the Coast of Africa.* New York: AMS Press, 1973 (1788); Miller, Randall M., and Smith, John David, eds. *Dictionary of Afro-American Slavery.* Westport, CT: Greenwood Press, 1997.

Oyekemi Olajope Oyelakin

Doldrums

The "doldrums" are also known as "calms." They occur when air movement is reduced to light winds or even completely still air. Squalls, heavy rainfall, or severe thunderstorms sometimes break the calms. The doldrums occur primarily in the equatorial band that circles the globe. This region of unpredictable air currents is also known as the Intertropical Convergence Zone, or ITCZ. For centuries, sailors have known the relative location of the doldrums zone (varying in latitude between 5° and 30° above and below the equator); however, it was, and largely still is, impossible to foresee when the calms would occur. One location essentially in the middle of this zone is located in the Gulf of Guinea and on the west coast of Africa. The presence of the doldrums zone in this location particularly concerned those involved in the trans-Atlantic trade, because westward voyages were notoriously prone to encountering the doldrums.

Being caught in the doldrums was one of the sailors' worst nightmares, particularly before the invention of the engine or electric motor. Being caught in the doldrums meant ships drifted at the mercy of currents that could cause them to stray far off course, which sometimes resulted in dire consequences. Becalmed ships, stalled for hours, days, and even weeks, either had to wait for a breeze or **storm** to propel them out of the zone or use the ships' boats (oared by crewmen) to literally pull the ship along its course. Naturally, having people pull the ship in these smaller boats proved not to be terribly practical for crossing the Atlantic Ocean, and in most situations, the ships were forced to simply wait for the wind.

Stalled ships, typically not well provisioned at the best of times, ran the risk of running out of provisions, and even well-stocked vessels could face serious shortages. This was a potentially deadly situation for ships carrying large numbers of newly enslaved Africans. It was not unheard of for a ship caught in the calms to lose up to 50 percent of the slaves on board. As provisions grew scarce, more and more slaves (as well as sailors) died, primarily from lack of fresh drinking **water**. Additional deaths occurred from starvation and related illnesses. Quite apart from physical health, people were usually hot, bored, and easily irritated, causing squabbles and additional problems on board.

The infamous doldrums figure prominently in tales such as Samuel Taylor Coleridge's "Rime of the Ancient Mariner." In this poem, a sailor, driven to boredom and madness as a result of being caught in the doldrums, shoots a revered albatross and is cursed for it. Although Coleridge's poem is only a tale, the doldrums were indeed an all too present reality for those who dared to traverse seas. *See also* Crew; Food.

Further Readings: Hair, Paul E., Jones, Adam, and Law, Robin, eds. *Barbot on Guinea: The Writings of Jean Barbot on West Africa 1678–1712*. London: The Hakluyt Society, 1992; Mayer, Brantz. *Captain Canot, an African Slaver*. New York: Arno Press and the *New York Times*, 1968; Pope-Hennessy, James. *Sins of the Fathers: The Atlantic Slave Trade 1441–1807*. New Jersey: Castle Books, Edison, 2004 (1967); Walvin, James. *Black Ivory: A History of British Slavery*. Washington, DC: Howard University Press, 1994.

Rachel Horlings

Door of No Return

The main departure point through which thousands of enslaved Africans passed through on the way to the New World, this site marked the beginning of the Middle Passage across the Atlantic.

Located on **Gorée Island**, three kilometers from Dakar, **Senegal**, the Door of No Return is part of a larger slave complex known as the *Maison des Esclaves* (House of Slaves). Built by the Dutch in 1776 and used as a warehouse to hold and process slaves for both domestic use as well as the larger and more profitable external trade, this depot was one of many on the island and throughout the coast of western Africa that represented the final stop before being loaded onto ships bound for the Americas. This particular site was recognized by UNESCO (United Nations Educational, Scientific and Cultural Organization) as a world heritage monument in 1978.

Although the precise number of slaves that actually were sent through this gateway is indeterminable (estimates range from 25,000 to 60,000), the Door of No Return is symbolic for these and all the other millions of slaves forcibly incorporated into the Middle Passage and never to return. *See also* Dutch Slave Trade; Entrepôts; French Slave Trade; Historical Memory; Volume.

Further Readings: Northrup, David, ed. *The Atlantic Slave Trade*. Boston: Houghton Mifflin, 2002; Thomas, Hugh. *The Slave Trade: The Story of the Atlantic Slave Trade, 1440–1870*. New York: Simon & Schuster, 1997.

William Morgan

Drownings

Death on the passage from Africa to the Americas came in many forms. In addition to **disease** and starvation, drowning was not uncommon during the Middle Passage. The two principal causes of slave drownings were **suicide** and what amounted to murder, slaves being forced overboard by their captors. Accidents or acts of nature, although rarer, involved larger numbers of victims per incident.

The crowded and filthy conditions of the **cargo hold**, combined with the heat and stench, to say nothing of the psychological trauma of their harrowing capture, transport, sale, and unknown horrors of their future, caused many Africans to fall prey to melancholy and despair and attempt suicide by jumping overboard. To prevent such loss of life, not for humanitarian sake but for economic reasons, **captains** of slavers made concerted efforts to prevent their human cargo from taking their own lives. Slaves were shackled together when above deck with their leg irons often attached to a chain running the length of the deck. Extra crewmen were kept on hand to physically stop slaves from flinging themselves over the edge of the ships, and nets were secured to the ship's hull to prevent slaves from reaching the depths of the ocean if they succeeded in breaking free from their captors. Despite such precautions, an unknown number of despondent slaves succumbed to the waters, their remains forever trapped within the ocean's depth.

Despite such suicides, more slaves drowned at the hands of their captors than by their own. Some slave captains ordered one or more slaves thrown overboard as examples to others to prevent mutinies or possible slave revolts, either at the outset of their journey or upon hearing rumors of discontent or increased despondency among the captives. Because captains had incentives to deliver only saleable slaves to the markets, extreme circumstances could lead to mass murder at sea. When the captives seemed so sick that they might not survive, they might be hurled into the sea. Shortages of **food** or potable **water** might similarly lead to mass execution to conserve the ship and at least some of its cargo and stave off economic disaster. On particularly long trips, when provisions were low and disease was rampant, some captains threw sick slaves overboard. In 1819, the captain of the *Le Rodeur* ordered thirty-nine slaves who had been blinded by an outbreak of ophthalmia thrown into the sea rather than bring unsaleable slaves to the marketplace.

Insurance policies often covered death by drowning but not by starvation or disease, so captains who threw slaves overboard often sought reimbursement from insurance companies for such losses. In one case, **the Zong**, out of **Liverpool**, carried 440 slaves to **Jamaica** from the African coast. With an outbreak of dysentery on board and a shortage of food and water, Captain Luke Collingwood ordered 132 weak and sick Africans thrown overboard during the course of several days. When the ship's owners tried to claim the insurance money, the insurance company refused to pay and the case went to court in England. No one in the *Zong* case was prosecuted for murder. And in the end, the court ruled for the owners, declaring the slaves' drowning a loss of merchandise.

Another murderous incident occurred when Captain Homans of the slaver *Brillante*, surrounded by four British vessels trying to implement the ban on the slave trade, brought his 600 slaves on deck and tied them to the large anchor chain. To prevent the slaves from being found on board, Homans then ordered the anchor dropped into the sea, dragging the 600 slaves to the bottom. By eliminating the evidence, the captain avoided capture and prosecution. In 1827, a Spanish slave ship, **the *Guerrero***, pursued by the HMS *Nimble* and under fire from the British vessel, slammed against a coral reef a few miles off North Key Largo, drowning 41 of the more than 550 slaves aboard who were shackled below deck.

Accidents or **storms** on the high seas were responsible for large numbers of slave drownings. One Danish slaver, the *Kron Printzen*, sank in a storm in 1706 with more than 800 slaves on board. In 1738, the Dutch slaver *Leuden* became stranded off Surinam during a storm. To prevent panic, the

crew locked the hatches to the slave decks and abandoned ship. More than 700 Africans drowned. After an accident befell the *Phoenix* in the fall of 1762, the crew abandoned the leaking ship and left the 332 Africans to sink with her. *See also* Accidents and Explosions; Chains.

Further Readings: Shyllon, Folarin O. *Black Slaves in Britain.* New York: Oxford University Press, 1974 Thomas, Hugh. *The Slave Trade: The Story of the Atlantic Slave Trade, 1440–1870.* New York: Simon & Schuster, 1997.

Sharon A. Roger Hepburn

Duration of Voyages

It took from three weeks to three months for a trading company to load a **cargo** of 450 slaves. It took from four to ten months for a slaving ship sailing the West African coast to load a similar cargo. Once the ship was supplied, provisions taken on board, and accounts settled, preparations were made to set sail. The slaves were then treated to a large meal. Their heads were shaved and the slaves stripped for, presumably, health reasons. Then the medical and moral ordeals of the Middle Passage would begin. The duration of voyages could be anywhere between 18 and 150 days on the sea. The number of days depended on the point of departure, the route, and the weather at sea.

The percentage of slave ships leaving South East Africa averaged about 5 percent; **Angola** had a departure percentage of about 12 percent, Senegambia had an average of about 18 percent, and the **Gold Coast** had the high of about 34 percent. This high percentage was due to the fact that the West African coast had the largest supply of slaves. One of the most frequent crossings was that of a ship from **Luanda** to **Brazil.** Crossing from Luanda to Recife took an average of thirty-five days. From there to Bahia took another forty days, while the trip from Bahia to Rio de Janeiro took an average of two months.

The more days a ship was at sea, the more deaths (of both slaves and sailors), the more provisions ran low, and the greater the dangers of running into a tempest. Thus, a captain would try to cut short his voyage. One such method was to navigate on a straight course, while at the same time trying to replenish provisions. For instance, the captain may have taken his supply of slaves from **Bonny**, Old Calabar (or any port southward). He might have stopped at one of the Portuguese Islands in the Gulf of Guinea to replenish his stock of **food** and fresh **water** to ensure that he had enough to last for some three months (by which time his voyage would end). If he had traded northward, he would have navigated his vessel straight to the West Indies. This route was usually 4,000 to 5,000 nautical miles. If the passage was from Angola to Virginia, then he had more miles to go.

The shortest passage across the Atlantic was from the **Gambia River** to Barbados. With good weather, the voyage could be made in three weeks. A longer course and unfavorable winds would mean longer than three months on the Atlantic. Stops along other **ports** might also be made for reasons other than supply of provisions.

There was a particularly tedious part of the Middle Passage called the "sea of thunder." A ship would sail westward along the equator for about 1,000 miles, then navigate northward toward the **Cape Verde** islands. This stretch of the ocean was reported as being fatal to navigators. If the calm came on the sea here, it was usually too long. These long calms would keep the vessel under an unfriendly cloud. The clouds themselves were described as electric. The rains usually came down in torrents. It was on this part of the journey that mortal **diseases** were most rampant for both slaves and sailors. This "sea of thunder" was avoided by slave ships as much as possible when approaching the coasts of Africa and those of the Americas.

The **mortality** rate did not strictly correlate with **overcrowding**. Both large and small ships experienced a similar mortality. The actual length of a particular voyage and the consequent risk of the increased incidence of an infectious disease had a greater effect than overcrowding. The duration of the Middle Passage averaged sixty days, with a majority of the slavers accomplishing the journey within forty to seventy days. The reduced rations necessary during long voyages lowered the resistance of the slaves, and longer voyages increased the chance of an infected person exceeding the incubation period and showing signs of disease. Furthermore, the longer the voyage, the greater the chance of epidemics spreading in the unhealthy cramped **holds**. Not only did bad weather lengthen the voyage, but it also prevented the slaves from coming on deck for fresh air and further obliged the **crew** to cover the gratings and close the air ports to prevent the ship from taking in water.

The Middle Passage was often interrupted for a few days as the slavers called at St. Thomas or Princess Islands in the Caribbean to take on water and stores. During this time, the slaves were given a spell in which to recuperate from the horrors of the journey. Far from being motivated by humanitarian considerations, slave **captains** realized that this actually improved both the physical and mental state of the slaves and enabled them to fetch higher **prices** at their sale. Slavers bound for **Jamaica** and places further west called at the Lesser Antilles to take on fresh provisions. Cases of scurvy showed an improvement during this regime; however, many ships arrived in Jamaica with serious epidemics on board, and the inhabitants were infected with the diseases carried by the slaves. *See also* Doldrums; Storms; Ventilation and Suffocation.

Further Readings: Falconbridge, Alexander. *An Account of the Slave Trade on the Coast of Africa.* New York: AMS Press, 1973 (1788); Eltis, David, Behrendt, Stephen D., Richardson, David, and Klein, Herbert S., eds. *The Trans-Atlantic Slave Trade: A Database on CD-ROM.* Cambridge: Cambridge University Press, 1999.

Oyekemi Olajope Oyelakin

Dutch Slave Trade

The Dutch dominated the East African slave trade and were major participants in the West African trade through the eighteenth century. Beginning in the late 1500s, the Dutch undertook a broad campaign to supplant the

Portuguese in Africa. Spearheading the effort were the Dutch East India Company (DEIC), formed in 1602, and the Dutch West India Company (DWIC), created in 1621.

The success and profitability of the DEIC in the slave trade and trade in Oriental goods led to the formation of the DWIC. The DWIC absorbed the existing United New Netherlands Company, which had been trying to establish colonies in North America, and began formal operations in 1623. The company was a semiautonomous entity that was nominally under the control of the Dutch government, but in reality, it operated as an independent branch of the government (although it could not undertake military campaigns without the government's approval). The DWIC was given a **monopoly** on colonies and general trade in the Western Hemisphere. It also received a monopoly on the slave trade in Africa and with the European colonies in North and South America. Without prior arrangements with the company, no Dutch citizens could engage in trade in any part of Africa from the Tropic of Cancer south to the Cape of Good Hope or in the Western Hemisphere between Newfoundland and the Straits of Magellan.

Like the Portuguese before them, the Dutch came across pre-existing systems of slavery, including trade patterns, and adapted them to conform to their economic interests. Throughout the 1600s, the Dutch were at war with various European powers. One purpose behind the formation of the DWIC was to take market share away from the Portuguese who were allied with Spain through the Iberian Union during the Thirty Years' War (1618–1648). Under the mercantilist principles of the day, the Dutch perceived that the optimum way to increase their national wealth and power was to cut into the economic resources of other European states.

In the 1620s and 1630s, the DWIC established a number of colonies in the New World, including New Amsterdam, which included regions of present-day New York, Connecticut, Delaware, and New Jersey. The DWIC also founded colonies in the Caribbean and South America and conquered Portuguese territories in **Brazil**. Significantly, the Dutch took over Portuguese colonies and trade posts along the African coast. By the 1640s, the Dutch had overtaken the Portuguese as the leading **slave traders** in Western Africa. Although the Portuguese had traded for a number of other goods in addition to slaves, the Dutch concentrated almost solely on the slave trade. By 1705, a Dutch official in Africa reported that local rulers had abandoned trade in other items, such as gold or ivory, and instead focused exclusively on the trade in slaves because of the **volume** and the perceived high **profits**.

The Dutch played a major role in establishing the slave trade with the European North American colonies. In 1628, the company decided that a shortage of workers limited the profitability of New Netherlands and prevented the expansion of the colony. To attract settlers, the company introduced the "patroon" system in which land was granted to Dutch settlers who agreed to stay and work the land for a designated period. In addition, the DWIC began importing large numbers of slaves into the colony to supplement the work force and to provide the new settlers with a labor pool. Large slave camps were established outside of present-day Manhattan. The Dutch also found that they could sell slaves to the British colonies in the

South. In some Dutch colonies, slaves were able to purchase certain free-doms and liberties by paying the DWIC an annual payment.

In 1642, the Dutch captured **Elmina**, the main Portuguese slave-trading post on the **Gold Coast**. Like the Portuguese, the Dutch relied on local brokers to capture slaves and bring them to the various slave forts along the coast. There were sporadic clashes between the Dutch and local chiefs and rulers, and those stationed in the forts faced **disease** and heat. The result was a high **mortality** rate among the Dutch in Africa. During the height of the Dutch trade, approximately 5,000 slaves per year were trans-ported from West Africa by Dutch slavers. During the entire period of the Dutch slave trade, some 900,000 were transported to colonies in the West-ern Hemisphere.

At its peak, the DWIC maintained a fleet of forty trade ships that trans-ported slaves to the Western Hemisphere and brought back goods such as **sugar**, gold, and silver. In Africa, the Dutch avoided large-scale colonization attempts and instead developed a series of trade posts. In other areas, such as South America, the Dutch did not engage in efforts to convert natives, as had the Spanish, but instead concentrated on economic exploitation of resources. The DWIC also engaged in privateer operations and even out-right piracy on Spanish gold and silver ships.

The ascendancy of the Dutch was short-lived. In 1654, the Portuguese captured Dutch colonies bordering Brazil, and the British took over New Amsterdam in 1664. Meanwhile, the British, the French, and other Euro-pean powers took over most of the Dutch outposts in Africa. The DWIC was dissolved in 1674, and a new, reformed company was launched to supersede the venture. The new company concentrated mainly on the slave trade, providing slaves to the Dutch Caribbean colonies and Suriname, as well as the colonies of other European powers. The Dutch were shut out of the slave trade with British colonies, however, when a monopoly on the trade was granted to the British **Royal Africa Company** in 1660. In addi-tion, the Treaty of Utrecht (1713) granted the British the right to supply slaves to the Spanish colonies in the Western Hemisphere, further reducing the Dutch share of the slave trade. One result was that the Dutch increas-ingly concentrated on the **Indian Ocean** slave trade and looked to Asia as a source of slaves. Between 1680 and 1731, 30.2 percent of slaves trans-ported by the DEIC came from Indonesia, 24.8 percent were from India, and only 22.1 percent were from Africa (mainly Madagascar).

Following the conquest of Suriname by the British, the DWIC was perma-nently dissolved in 1791 and its possessions were taken over by the Dutch government. Through the late 1790s and early 1800s, the Dutch faced a series of slave revolts that ultimately led to the abolition of the slave trade. The most significant of these revolts occurred in the colony of **Curaçao** in 1795. Slaves on the island were inspired by the rebellion on Haiti. The insurrection lasted two weeks and it took another month for Dutch author-ities to recapture the **runaway** slaves. During the rebellion, slaves were able to capture muskets, ammunition, and even a small cannon. They defeated two militia forces, but ultimately were defeated by a superior mili-tia force. Following the rebellion, twenty-six slaves were hanged, and several dozen others were banned from Curaçao and transported to other colonies. The colonial government did try to alleviate some of the harsh conditions that marked Dutch slavery in the Caribbean. Rules were established that required owners to feed and clothe their slaves and the more harsh forms of punishment were limited. In addition, slaves were ordered to have Sunday free from work, and field slaves could not be forced to start work before 5:00 A.M. and had to end their work before dusk.

Some slaves on the continent were able to escape into the interior. The maroons of Suriname eventually numbered more than 20,000. They were able to defeat successive military expeditions to bring them back into bondage and, in 1760, the colonial government even acknowledged their autonomous status, although further military campaigns were waged against the **maroons.**

Although the Atlantic slave trade was greatly diminished by 1800 as a result of the loss of colonies in Africa and the Caribbean, the Dutch continued transporting slaves to their Asian colonies after the other major powers banned the slave trade. Powerful commercial elites were able to lobby to retain the trade. The Netherlands did not outlaw the slave trade until 1814, and even after its abolition, the prohibition on the transport of slaves was only loosely enforced. The proslave lobby was even more effective in defeating successive efforts to end slavery. Slavery continued in the Dutch colonies for twenty years after it had been abolished by other European states. The first ban on slavery was enacted by a Dutch colonial legislature in Saint Maarten in 1848, not by the national government. Complete abolition in the Dutch colonies did not occur until 1863. *See also* Abolitionism; African Rulers and the Slave Trade; Angola; British Caribbean; Cape Coast Castle; Closure of the Slave Trade; Enslavement and Procurement; Haitian Revolution, The; Mozambique; Trade Commodities; Trade Forts; Triangular Trade.

Further Readings: Arasaratnam, S. *Ceylon and the Dutch, 1600–1800.* Ashgate: Aldershot, 1996; Craton, Michael. *Empire, Enslavement and Freedom in the Caribbean.* Princeton, NJ: Markus Wiener, 1997; Geggus, David, ed. *The Impact of the Haitian Slave Revolt in the Atlantic World.* Columbia: University of South Carolina, 2001; Genovese, Eugene D. *From Rebellion to Revolution: Afro-American Slave Revolts in the Making of the Modern World.* New York: Vintage Books, 1981; Postma, Johannes Menne. *The Dutch in the Atlantic Slave Trade, 1600–1815.* New York and Cambridge: Cambridge University Press, 1990.

Tom Lansford

E

Elmina

Elmina, a port city located on the Atlantic Ocean in Ghana, was one of the most famous **entrepôts** in West Africa. It was a center of the slave trade, supplemented by a fishing industry. It was the first major European settlement in the region. In 1482, the Portuguese established São Jorge da Mina Castle, which created the commercial basis for the foundation of Elmina. The Portuguese used Elmina for trade purposes, and a small attempt was also made to spread **Christianity**. The Portuguese castle at Elmina started as a military fort, built as a precast and shipped to West Africa from **Lisbon**. The original aim of the castle was to obtain access to gold. The castle was to double as a fortress and factory to mine gold obtained from the hinterland. The major trade concern shifted to slaves, however, and the castle acquired its importance as a slave depot. Elmina became the oldest and biggest slave castle in West Africa. The Portuguese turned the place into their commercial headquarters for many years. In 1637, the Dutch West India Company captured Elmina and made it the trading capital of their West African trade empire until they passed it to the English in 1872.

Elmina had a huge warehouse, which was able to keep more than a thousand slaves. There were male and female dungeons. The European sailors and slave dealers did not come with their wives, and they relied on the local female population to address their sexual demands. They abused these **women** in various ways, including rampant cases of **rape**. So-called difficult women were punished, sometimes tied to poles until they either succumbed to the demands or were too depleted to survive. A small biracial population emerged, living in various houses at Elmina. A thriving commercial population developed at Elmina. The Elmina castle is the oldest European building in sub-Saharan Africa, and its Portuguese and Dutch architecture has been preserved until today. *See also* Dutch Slave Trade; Monopoly; Portuguese Slave Trade.

Further Readings: Thomas, Hugh. *The Slave Trade: The Story of the Atlantic Slave Trade, 1440–1870.* New York: Simon & Schuster, 1997; Thornton, John K. *Africa and*

Elmina Castle, on the West African coast, served as a slave-trading outpost for the Portuguese and, after 1637, for the Dutch. Courtesy of Manuel Barcia.

Africans in the Making of the Atlantic World, 1400–1800. 2nd ed. Cambridge: Cambridge University Press, 1998.

Toyin Falola

Enslavement and Procurement

Slavery has always been a part of the human condition. Aristotle, Plato, and other thinkers of antiquity often pondered and discussed the subject in their writings. Thus, within ancient African societies, slavery was a common practice. Compared with the European or Arab-**Muslim** enslavement of black Africans, African forms of servitude and slavery were relatively benign and were an extension of lineage and kinship systems. Slaves and servants were often well treated and could rise to power and exalted positions in households and communities. Slaves were usually war captives. Their social status and conditions of servitude were mitigated by extended kinship networks, which were based on community, clan, and family affiliations. In the forest regions of West Africa (**Benin** and Congo, for example), slavery was an important institution before the European arrival. **African rulers** enslaved other African groups, rather than their own people, to project their wealth and prestige, as well as to control labor. Although they symbolized wealth and power, slaves also had rights and were not regarded as property. They could, and did, intermarry with their conquerors.

Conversely, the African slave trade, as practiced by western European nations (including, for example, Portugal, France, Britain, Spain, Sweden, Denmark, and Holland) from the mid-fifteenth to late-nineteenth centuries,

Enslaved Africans being carried to a slave ship, Gold Coast, late seventeenth century. Tracy W. McGregor Library, Special Collections, University of Virginia Library.

was a much more sordid and dehumanizing practice. It was rooted in notions of racial inferiority of Africans, particularly the peoples of sub-Saharan Africa. Human beings were regarded simply as property and were disposed of as such through commercial exchange and with absolute disregard for their humanity.

The Roman Catholic Church, the most powerful institution in fifteenth-century Europe, provided strong ideological support for European enslavement of the black peoples of Africa. In their attempts to enlist converts and rally support against **Islam's** rapid expansion into Western Europe, Popes Nicholas V and Calixtus III granted the Portuguese royalty the right to subdue and enslave native, non-Christian peoples in Africa and the New World. Three important church documents—the *Dum Diversas* of 1452, the *Romanus Pontifex* of 1455, and the *Inter Caetera* of 1456—provided the moral, legal, and political justification for the western European trade in African human beings. These Papal Bulls granted the Catholic nations of Europe (Spain and Portugal) dominion over "discovered" lands during the Age of Discovery. In addition to sanctioning the seizure of non-Christian lands, the church encouraged the enslavement, in perpetuity, of native, non-Christian peoples in Africa and the New World.

For the purpose of comparison, Arab-Muslim enslavement of black Africans predates that of western Europeans. Even then, it was an equally devastating experience for black Africans and their communities. Arabs had dominated the trafficking in African slaves from about the eighth century. For several centuries thereafter, sub-Saharan East Africa was a source for slaves who were captured and sold in the Middle East, India, and regions of Central Asia. Although these slaves were forcibly converted to Islam, the procurement of slaves was solely for **profit**. *Razzias*, or raids, on African communities were carried out by marauding bands (an eerie precursor to modern-day Sudanese *janjaweed* and their activities, which have included pillaging African villages in southern Sudan and enslaving young, and non-Muslim black Africans). In the Mediterranean, millions of Africans were captured and sold as slaves during the Middle Ages—just as would be the case with western European slaving in latter periods. Casualty rates were high. Most male slaves died from being castrated en route to their masters' lands. Most were used as soldiers. These raids typically involved the plundering of villages and the massacre of as many men and older **women** as possible. Young women and children were then captured by the raiders. The young women were targets because of their value as concubines or sex slaves, while the boys were turned into eunuchs and workers in wealthy Arab and Mediterranean homes. In fact, the **gender** ratio of slaves in the Islamic trade was two females to every male, while in the Atlantic slave trade, the ratio was reversed: two males to every female. Large numbers of slaves were used for domestic purposes. Concubinage was for those who could afford it, and there was no stigma attached to having women as sexual objects.

Enslaved Africans did not just quietly accept their fate. Indeed, beginning in 869 C.E., and for almost two decades, the *Zanj*, or black African slaves of Basra, Iraq, rebelled against their exploitation and living conditions on southern Iraqi **plantations**. During the fifteenth and sixteenth centuries, Arab-Muslim slave raiders continuously plundered sub-Saharan African territories of the Middle Niger, including Mali and Songhai, for slaves. The Arab trade in African slaves continued well into the nineteenth century. For example, Tippu Tip, a Zanzibari merchant, was an infamous Afro-Arab **slave trader** of this period. Some justified slavery in this part of the world by claiming that Islam and the Qur'an sanctioned it. Today, slavery persists in the Islamic world, notably in Mauritania and Sudan.

In his economic history of medieval Mediterranean societies, S. D. Goitein seems to portray the Arab-Muslim enslavement of Africans as less of a collective effort to treat them as property and exploit them for industrial or agricultural activity—as was the case in European enslavement—than as an individual activity in which wealthy Arab merchants owned slaves as symbols of their economic status and power. Nonetheless, the brutality and egregiousness of pre-European enslavement of Africans (especially the **rape** on a massive scale of young African women), when compared with the European slave trade that followed, differed in time but not in consequence for black Africans. Thus it is possible, historically, to speak of two Middle Passages for black African slaves: the Asian, or trans-Saharan trade in the medieval era; and the Western, or trans-Atlantic trade in the modern period. The massive and profound cultural, psychic, and social disruptions are well documented by historians and other scholars. In both trades, the African slaves had no control whatsoever over their persons and destiny.

The slave trade is also known as the triangular slave trade, because the shipment of African slaves followed a tricontinental and triangular route—Europe to Africa to the Americas. Slavers often sailed from western European slave **ports**, including **Lisbon**, **Seville**, **Nantes**, Boulogne, Plymouth, and **Liverpool** (the largest slave port between 1700 and 1807). European capital, African labor, and American land resources combined to supply European markets with goods like **sugar**, **rum**, coffee, tobacco, rice, and later cotton products. American slavers and colonists made direct trips to Africa for slaves to replenish the indigenous population that had been decimated by imported **diseases** and forced labor. They did not follow the triangular route. After 1800, there was a considerable increase in this trade, particularly from **Brazil**, which had several times the number of slaves as the United States. During this era, the main product going out of Africa was slaves.

Regarding the European procurement of African slaves, three major phases have been identified. The first was slaving by piracy and raids reminiscent of the Arab-Muslim *razzias* of the medieval period. In the 1440s, Europeans captured Africans in raids on communities in the coastal areas. The technology of **firearms** played a major role in the slave trade, because the gun functioned as an instrument of power and terror—power in the hands of slavers, and terror in the minds of the captured.

The second phase was slaving through warlike alliances. Europeans desperate for slaves offered goods that African kings and chiefs coveted, including firearms, horses, alcohol, trinkets, and metal bracelets. In return, black slavers sold Africans they had captured through wars. African kings formed alliances with Europeans against their African enemies during wars. Defeated and captured Africans were considered war booty and sold to Europeans. Progressively, African chieftains became major players in the slave trade, and they formed alliances to raid weaker neighbors for slaves. Over time, the trade in slaves evolved into a third phase of peaceful trading partnerships with European slavers. From the sixteenth century onward, Africans sold Africans to European slavers for profit. Slavery had become an industry and an economic system that forever changed the destinies of all peoples. It financed Western Europe's Industrial Revolution, as well as the British Empire, for England traded in African slaves for more than three centuries.

The gathering of slaves covered a wide swath of African territory, beginning from modern-day **Angola** to **Senegal** in West Africa. Slaves were housed in different parts of West Africa, including **Gorée Island** in Senegal, where the Dutch built a House of Slaves in 1776; **Elmina** in Ghana, where a fort was built by the Portuguese in 1482 and captured by the Dutch some two centuries later; and **Ouidah** (Hweda/Whydah) in ancient **Dahomey**, the modern-day Republic of Benin. Over time, the slave procurement zones would extend around the Cape of Good Hope at the southernmost tip of the African continent and would encompass **Mozambique** and the island of Madagascar. **Captains** of slave ships traded directly with African chiefs or through European agents known as "factors" (often free Africans) who were in charge of slave-collecting centers. At these centers, the slaves were kept in enclosed areas known as **barracoons** or in cages to be loaded onto slave ships for the journey to the New World. Slaves were taken mainly from the interior of African towns and villages because the coastal areas were less populated. The enslaved were forcibly marched in **chains** and leg irons and in **coffles** (groups of four shackled together) to the western coasts of Africa for shipment to Europe and European colonies in the Americas, where they were exploited as forced labor to replace the dying labor force of native Indians. African slaves were used in mines, and on rice, tobacco, sugar, and cotton plantations. In transit, captured slaves were detained in forts along the coast constructed by the Portuguese, English, French, and Danish. These forts were warehouses for the human **cargo** en route to the Americas. Thousands died mid-passage from disease and **violence**, and at their own hand as a result of the simple human yearning for freedom from enslavement. Today, some of these slave ports have become monuments and **museums** memorializing the evil of the slave trade and its irreversible consequences.

The voyage across the Atlantic Ocean generally took more than two months. The passage between Africa and the Americas was one of untold misery for the slaves. The slavers had to subdue the Africans to facilitate the shipment of their human cargo. This they did through a process of violence and dehumanization, which was both physical and psychological. From African ports of origin to final **destinations** in the Americas, this process entailed **branding**, beatings, **torture**, physical confinement and brutalization, change of name, rape, death, and forced mixing with other Africans of unrelated **languages** and cultures. The whole journey was designed to make the Africans forget their origins or their very humanity. Once in the Americas, those Africans who had survived the journey were off-loaded, sold, and put to work on sugar and cotton plantations.

Recently, scholars have begun to examine and address African participation in the procurement and enslavement of Africans and its consequences. Some have called for **reparations** from the nations involved. Slavery generated massive profits for African kings and rulers. For example, from 1774 onward, Abiodun, the ruler of the Oyo Empire in Yorubaland, derived much of his political and economic power and influence from trading in captured slaves in Dahomey and its environs. He bought slaves from his northern neighbors and resold them in the south at the large slave market of Abomey-Calavi. Likewise, Madame Tinubu of Badagry (today's **Lagos**, Nigeria) was a prominent slave dealer. King Tegbesu of Dahomey reportedly earned a quarter of a million British pounds around 1750. He sold more than 9,000 slaves a year to the French and Portuguese. Francisco Felix de Souza, another Dahomean, dominated the trade in the mid-1800s. In the **Gold Coast** (now Ghana), the Ashanti traded slaves and gold with the Dutch from about 1705. Babatu was another African slaver in what is now northern Ghana. He sold slaves at the Salaga slave market in the nineteenth century. King Alvare of the Congo region is yet another African leader who sold other Africans as slaves. The African role in the Atlantic slave trade is a highly charged and emotional topic, which is often an undercurrent in relations between recent African immigrants in the United States and their African American neighbors. Indeed, those who attempt to admit and discuss the African involvement are sometimes criticized as apologists for Euro-American slavers.

Regarding the number of slaves bought from Africa, the exact figures are unknown, but scholars and experts generally agree that between 15 and 20 million were taken from Africa. It is estimated from records kept by the traders— merchant banks, **investors**, ship manifests, and **insurance** companies—that some 11 million landed in the Americas alive. At the start of the 1600s, the Senegambia region of West Africa was the major source of slaves for the trans-Atlantic trade because it had a long history of providing slaves for the Islamic sub-Saharan trade. By the mid-seventeenth century, the Kingdom of **Kongo** begun exporting slaves to Europe, and Kongo and Angola would continue to be huge exporters of slaves until the nineteenth century. In the 1670s, the **Slave Coast** (today's Nigeria) saw a rapid growth in the trade in slaves, which lasted until the end of the slave trade in the nineteenth century. In the Gold Coast (modern-day Ghana), slave exports rose markedly in the eighteenth century, but it dropped considerably when Britain abolished slavery in 1808. From the 1740s, the Bight of Biafra (on the Niger Delta and the Cross River) became a significant procurer and exporter of slaves. Together with the Bight of Benin, this area produced two-thirds of the number of slaves captured and sold in the first half of the nineteenth century. In Europe, the trans-Atlantic slave trade declined during the Napoleonic Wars (1799–1815), but it quickly rebounded thereafter.

In the United States, African slaves and their uncompensated labor were important factors in the county's rise as a world economic power. For almost three centuries, African slaves in America, through their labor and skills, laid the foundations of American wealth while they were treated as their owners' property. The enslavement of Africans was the main cause of the American Civil War between 1861 and 1865. In today's America, the grave consequences of slavery continue to affect the lives of all Americans, especially African Americans. For example, various demographic indexes show the parlous nature of black life through the legacy of enduring racism, high unemployment, intractable poverty, and other social pathologies. African Americans have still not recovered from the trade in human beings, which officially ended at the turn of the nineteenth century. The negative effects of the Middle Passage still persist for the American descendants of African slaves.

In Africa, the end of the slave trade led to a new era of European subjugation of Africans. The same western European nations that sold African peoples as commodities began to see Africa as a different resource—one for its land, minerals, and cheap labor. The slave trade was followed by the scramble for Africa and subsequent colonization, which was legalized by the Berlin Conference of 1884. *See also* Christianity; Religion; Slavery in Africa; Trade Commodities; Triangular Trade; Volume.

Further Readings: Davidson, Basil. *The African Slave Trade*. Rev. ed. Boston: Little, Brown, 1980; Engerman, Stanley L., and Gallman, Robert E., eds. *The Cambridge Economic History of the United States: Volume 1, The Colonial Era*. New York: Cambridge University Press, 1996; Engerman, Stanley L., and Gallman, Robert E., eds. *The Cambridge Economic History of the United States*, Vol. 2: *The Long Nineteenth Century*. New York: Cambridge University Press, 2000; Genovese, Eugene D. *Roll, Jordan, Roll: The World the Slaves Made*. New York: Pantheon, 1974; Goitein, S. D. *A Mediterranean Society*. Vol. I: *Economic Foundations*. Berkeley: University of California Press, 2000; Gordon, Murray. *Slavery in the Arab World*. New York. New Amsterdam Books, 1989; Inikori, Joseph E., and Engerman, Stanley L., eds. *The Atlantic Slave Trade: Effects on Economies, Societies, and Peoples in Africa, the Americas, and Europe*. Durham, NC: Duke University Press, 1992; Manning, Patrick, and Anderson, David, eds. *Slavery and African Life: Occidental, Oriental, and African Slave Trades*. New York: Cambridge University Press, 1990; Quarles, Benjamin. *The Negro in the Making of America*. New York: Simon & Schuster, 1996; Thomas, Hugh. *The Slave Trade: The Story of the Atlantic Slave Trade, 1440–1870*. New York: Simon & Schuster, 1997; United Nations Commission on Human Rights. "Abduction and Forced Labour in Sudan." [Online, July 2006]. Anti-Slavery International Web site: http://www.antislavery.org/archive/submission/submission2005-sudan.htm; Von Glahn, Richard. "GE 22B: Globalization of Labor Markets, 1500–1900." [Online, July 2006]. UCLA College of Letters and Science Web site:

http://www.sscnet.ucla.edu/classes/cluster22/lectures/lecture3/sld004.htm; Walvin, James. *The Trader, the Owner, the Slave*. London: Jonathan Cape Ltd., 2006; Wintle, Justin. "The African Slave Trade." In *The Timeline History of Islam*, 328–329. New York: Barnes & Noble Publishing, 2005.

'BioDun J. Ogundayo

Entrepôts

Entrepôts were warehouses where slaves were kept before shipment. These were trading centers where slaves and other products could change hands. Entrepôts were located along the African coastline where they were an essential part of port cities. For the overwhelming majority of slaves, it was the last time they would see their home regions. It was the beginning of a life of hardships. They were **chained** to prevent **escape** and some received cuts on their faces and bodies for identification purposes. For the slave dealers, entrepôts provided opportunities for trade and relaxation. For local merchants and chiefs, the control of entrepôts was a lucrative business. Chiefs struggled for power in part to control the entrepôts and in part to establish monopolies over trade and dealings with foreign merchants. Struggles among chiefs could degenerate into political instability, as was the case of **Lagos** during the nineteenth century. *See also* African Rulers and the Slave Trade; Barracoons; Ports; Slavery in Africa.

Further Reading: Thomas, Hugh. *The Slave Trade: The Story of the Atlantic Slave Trade, 1440–1870*. New York: Simon & Schuster, 1997.

Toyin Falola

Gorée Island served as an entrepôt for slaves departing for the Americas. Courtesy of Manuel Barcia.

Equiano, Olaudah (1745–1797)

Olaudah Equiano, also known as Gustavus Vassa (1745–1797), is renowned for his *Interesting Narrative* (1789), in which he recounts his abduction from Essaka, Eboe, in Guinea with his sister and his subsequent journey across the Middle Passage to the New World. At ten, he traversed Europe, the Americas, the Caribbean, and the Mediterranean, following his purchase by Michael Pascal. Equiano's credentials include ship steward, explorer, hairdresser, gauge, minister and **Christian** missionary, **slave trader** and owner, abolitionist, Commissary of Provisions and Stores for the **Sierra Leone** resettlement project, and author. Equiano's multiple identities have been noted as "fraud, a plagiarist, an apologist, a hero, a capitalist, and a guerrilla fighter" (Sabino and Hall, 1999, p. 5). In 1792, Equiano married an Englishwoman named Susanna Cullen and had two daughters, Ann Marie and Johanna.

Olaudah Equiano was a former slave who bought his own freedom. He wrote one of the best-selling books of his time and became one of the most influential abolitionists in Britain. Courtesy of Anti-Slavery International.

Slave narratives like Equiano's not only embody a people's fears and critique inhuman policies and practices but also testify to human resilience. The abolitionists used these narratives to illustrate the inhumanity of the institution and counter the stereotype of inferior or uncivilized Africans and a heathen land depicted in racist travel journals by William Bosman, John Harris's *Collection of Voyages*, Linnaeus's *Systema Naturae*, and Buffon's *Histoire Naturalle*. Equiano's narrative went through eight editions during his lifetime and twenty others by 2003; with nine text selections; seven contemporary reviews and accounts; two nineteenth-century commentaries; thirty-seven twentieth-century commentaries; and five twenty-first-century commentaries, including five language translations and the 1995 BBC documentary, *A Son of Africa: The Slave Narrative of Olaudah Equiano*. The narrative also appears in anthologies of African American literature.

Equiano's development reflects a recurring theme of multiple identities, a process of reclamation, and a restoration of an African cultural identity and political subjectivity. His travels transform him from nobility to slave, from African slave to Atlantic slave to English slave and later subject, from English slacker to Christian surveyor and missionary, from Christian advocate to antislavery writer, and from abolitionist to autobiographer. Finally, the husband and father culminates into an African, American, and British ancestor. Equiano's African childhood is integrated and remembered through a Western lens, although never at its expense. His assimilated English culture helps him to reclaim his African identity: *Oluadah* signifying "favored one" and *Embrenche* meaning "noble lineage."

Reflective of Equiano's enterprising **Igbo** identity and fate, or Christian predestination, he survives otherwise ominous threats (such as snakes,

European tricksters and exploiters, **shipwrecks**, **drowning**, starvation, shelling, fires, and so on). His visionary world of spirits validated his success in the New World. Equiano published and promoted his narrative to nobility (including the Prince of Wales and eight dukes) and on lecture tours across Europe, which were supported by abolitionists. Equiano's achievements have been attributed to his Igbo culture.

> On board ship and in England, Equiano becomes literate and learns arithmetic. When sold into life on a sugar plantation, he capitalizes on these achievements to become his owner's right-hand man. Nor is Equiano satisfied with achieving his own freedom and amassing individual wealth—worthy goals in the eyes of the West. Rather he emerges as a leader of the London African community, a position of respect from which he could work to better the lives of comrades. (Sabino and Hall, 1999, p. 14)

Equiano eventually relinquishes his earlier racial stereotypes of man-eating, red-faced, and loose-haired whites for an essentialist worldview of Igbo-Jewish-English cultures. The disputes and crimes Equiano's father handled are not unique to his people. Despite differences in skin color, Africans and Jews share a similar lineage with similar laws and rules under a hierarchical patronage. And, like the British, Eboe lifestyle is prescribed by a social code, with "historical traditions, customs and geneology in common with European readers" (Caldwell, 1999, p. 277). In raping and separating **families**, slave traders violate not only African virtues of family and decency but also civic humanism in civilized cultures.

Paradoxically, the Muskito Indian Prince questions the abominations of literate whites, excepting the assimilated Equiano. Equiano presents himself as a more humane slave dealer and even advocates for a recaptured free African, appealing to Christian and humanistic values. His apologetics of African humanity and culture, however, reflects a marginal non-Western identity. Atlantic slavery is extreme. Enslaved or free, blacks are apprehensive of whites. In the end, Equiano speaks for the status quo in reenvisioning Britain's colonial empire.

Questions persist of Equiano's African origins, particularly considering that his baptismal and Navy records locate him in South Carolina and St. Croix. Later editions of the *Interesting Narrative* refute such claims. Equiano's generic portrayal of his African roots reflects an African childhood, but also draws extensively from existing slave narratives and travel journals by Jonathan Edwards, Anthony Bezenet, James Albert, Ukawsaw Gronniosaw, **Quobna Ottobah Cugoano**, and Ignatious Sancho. Deliberations of his true origins show little sign of abating.

Further Readings: Caldwell, Tanya. "Talking Too Much English: Languages of Economy and Politics in Equinao's The *Interesting Narrative.*" *Early American Literature* 34 (1999): 263–282; Costanzo, Angelo, ed. *The Interesting Narrative of the Life of Oaludah Equiano or Gustavus Vassa, The African, Written by Himself.* Ontario, Canada: Broadview Literary Texts, 2001; Adams, Francis D., and Saunders, Barry. *Three Black Writers in Eighteenth-Century England.* Belmont, CA: Wadsworth Publishing Company, 1971; Hochschild, Adam. *Bury the Chains: Prophets and Rebels in the Fight to Free an Empire's Slaves.* Boston: Mariner Books, 2004; Langley, April. "Equiano's *Landscapes*: Viewpoints and Vistas from the Looking Glass, the Lens, the Kaleidoscope." *The Western*

Journal of Black Studies 25, 1 (2001): 46–60; Sabino, Robin, and Hall, Jennifer. "The Path Not Taken: Cultural Identity in the Interesting Life of Olaudah Equiano." *MELUS 24* (Spring 1999): 5–19.

Namulundah Florence

Eric Williams Thesis (1944)

Eric Eustace Williams's influential scholarship has prompted generations of scholars to examine new approaches to the Middle Passage and slavery in the New World. Born in 1911 in Trinidad and educated at Tranquility Intermediate School and Queens Royal College, Williams won the coveted Island Scholarship in 1931, allowing him to pursue a doctorate in history at Oxford University between 1932 and 1938. After Oxford, Williams taught at Howard University in the United States before returning to Trinidad and Tobago. He eventually formed its first modern political party in 1956, the People's National Movement, the party that led Trinidad and Tobago to independence in 1962. Williams was the head of the government of Trinidad and Tobago from 1962 until his death in 1981.

The author of more than 600 books, monographs, and a host of articles and lectures, Williams was instrumental in shifting West Indian **historiography** away from its traditional Eurocentric approach. Through his writings and influence on future generations of intellectuals, Williams fostered a new historiography of the Caribbean from Caribbean perspectives. In the context of scholarship on the slave trade, Williams is best known for his Williams Thesis, articulated in *Capitalism and Slavery* (1944). The book has been translated into eight languages, among them Chinese, Japanese, Russian, and Korean (in 2006).

The Williams Thesis consists of two central premises. First, **profits** derived from the Atlantic slave trade and American slave **plantations** provided the necessary capital accumulation to finance Britain's Industrial Revolution. Second, economic interests rather than **humanitarian** interests succeeded in destroying the slave system. After the American Revolution, the slave system declined in importance to the British economy, prompting business interests, the very groups who benefited from the rise of the system, to first abolish the slave trade and later American slavery. This second premise directly challenged the role of humanitarians in the abolition of the slave trade.

Williams provoked several decades of study concerned with placing the slave system in its proper context in British economic development.

Eric Eustace Williams. The Eric Williams Memorial Collection, University of the West Indies, Trinidad and Tobago.

Much of the work over the past thirty years has challenged the first premise of the Williams Thesis. The current consensus is that slave trade profits were not abnormally large and could not have financed the Industrial Revolution. Detractors posit that it was internal factors that explain the Industrial Revolution. Recently, continuing the debate, Joseph Inikori's *Africans and the Industrial Revolution* (2002) shifted the debate away from a concentration on the role of profits, arguing rather that it was slavery-induced Atlantic commerce that stimulated the Industrial Revolution.

The second premise has also been contested. The critics' argument is best articulated in Seymour Drescher's *Econocide* (1977), a work confronting Williams's thesis on the decline of slavery and the slave trade after the American Revolution. Instead, Drescher argued that the system remained profitable and vital to the British economy. Selwyn Carrington's work *The Sugar Industry and the Abolition of the Slave Trade* (2002) counters Drescher's assumption of the continuing vitality of the slave system, arguing that it was indeed declining in importance and that economic interest groups were central in its abolition.

Despite the criticism of his work, most scholars agree that *Capitalism and Slavery* is a crucial starting point for the study of the slave trade. Linking events on several continents, Williams shifted discussion away from Anglocentric approaches to British economic growth. Recent historiographical trends demonstrate the continued relevance and impact of the Williams Thesis on slave trade scholarship. *See also* British Caribbean; Triangular Trade.

Further Readings: Cateau, Heather, and Carrington, Selwyn, eds. *Capitalism and Slavery Fifty Years Later: Eric Eustace Williams: A Reassessment of the Man and His Work*. New York: Peter Lang, 2000; Palmer, Colin. *Eric Williams and the Making of the Modern Caribbean*. Chapel Hill: University of North Carolina Press, 2006; Paquet, Sandra Pouchet, ed. "Special Issue: Eric Williams and the Postcolonial Caribbean." *Callaloo* 20 (1997); Solow, Barbara, and Engerman, Stanley, eds. *British Capitalism and Caribbean Slavery: The Legacy of Eric Williams*. Cambridge: Cambridge University Press, 1987; Williams, Eric Eustace. *Capitalism and Slavery; with a new introduction by Colin A. Palmer*. Chapel Hill: University of North Carolina Press, 1994 (1944).

Joseph Avitable

Escapes and Runaways (Maroonage)

From the 1500s until the end of slavery in the Americas, there were always a number of Africans who made their escape or attempts at flight. Before their appearance in the Western Hemisphere, Africans collectively fought slavery, individuals fled bondage, and captives struggled to free themselves from slave ships on the Middle Passage. Those who escaped from slavery found temporary refuge or long-term freedom in rural and urban areas. To chroniclers, they were known by a variety of names, mainly runaway slaves or maroons. By the sixteenth century, the English borrowed the word "maroon" from their Spanish colonial rivals. The Spanish originally called cattle and hogs that escaped from ranches to mountains and forests *cimarrones*, meaning "wild or untamed" creatures. *Cimarron* was first imposed on Native Americans, because they were the first to be enslaved in the Americas. Maroon towns—known as *palenques* in Latin America, *manieles* in **Hispaniola**—emerged almost anywhere that slavery existed. Brazilian settlements called *quilombos* were some of the largest of the Americas; the towns of *Palmares* are estimated to have contained thousands of inhabitants. People of African descent who absconded from bondage are significant historic figures because of their success in attacking **plantations** and liberating slaves. They also circumvented laws that discriminated against them in matters such as trade and collaborated in wars with international adversaries of slavery societies.

A wide range of evidence informs our view of past maroon lives. Government records, military papers, and slave catchers' accounts describe population counts, names, and environments. Descendants in the mountains of **Jamaica** preserve oral traditions that discuss spiritual beliefs, military feats, and the ever-present role of ancestors. In **Brazil** and the Dominican Republic, archaeologists discovered the creativity and self-sufficiency of maroons who produced pottery and pipes, some with intricate geometric decoration. Maroon archaeological sites illustrate undocumented

This picture of a poor fugitive is from one of the stereotype cuts manufactured in this city for the southern market, and used on handbills offering rewards for runaway slaves.

THE RUNAWAY.

Depiction of a runaway slave that was often used in notices offering a reward for a runaway's return. Courtesy of Anti-Slavery International.

aspects of life such as the acquisition of European pottery, which came from "contraband" (as authorities saw their trade) or raids against plantations. Ethnographic studies of the riverine Saramaka maroons of Suriname have illustrated their ancestors' struggles with new environments, as well as their historic migrations, **gender** relations, and politics.

All kinds of people fled from slavery: men, **women**, children, and the elderly. In some cases, couples escaped; in others, Africans left captivity in groups that shared a cultural identity. Newspaper advertisements and travelers' accounts suggest that (especially for the earliest centuries) maroons were mostly male, unskilled laborers, ethnically diverse, and young (for example, eighteen to twenty-five years old). This imbalanced sex ratio is one cause of maroon contacts with Native Americans, fostering intermarriage. Eventually, women of African descent became a significant proportion of maroon societies. Harriet Tubman and Nanny (venerated in Jamaica) illustrate how women armed themselves and led antislavery resistance.

Maroons' interactions with people on frontiers or seas, and in urban areas, were complex. Enslaved people were potential spies and covert trade partners or informers who betrayed the maroons to the slaveholders. Native American and African people's various attitudes and interests caused them to interact in myriad ways, in kinship, conflicts, and military alliances. Native Americans helped maroons understand local environments. Maroons' knowledge of introduced domesticates (that is, rice) and Euro-American politics, warfare, and economics were valued by Native Americans. Although they were mostly adversaries, Euro-Americans occasionally allied with maroon traders and raiders, in defiance of their international enemies.

Countless forces worked against *marronage* (the French colonists' word for escaping slavery). Government slave codes required Africans to carry passes to leave plantations. Slavery systems established slave patrols, carried out punishments, and compensated slave catchers. In the intellectual realm, proslavery proponents concocted mental illnesses, such as "drapetomania," to pathologize "fugitives" who refused to endure bondage.

Research reveals evidence for various aspects of maroons' everyday life. Zooarchaeological study of the Spanish-maroon alliance that led to the founding of Fort Mose, in eighteenth century Florida, demonstrates how inhabitants' foodways were based on wildlife, such as (shell)fish, more so than domesticated animals, such as cattle. Documented practices, such as honey collection, hunting, and agriculture, were other important means of subsistence and exchange. Structural remains have been difficult to recover in many archaeological sites, because of the short duration of many maroon settlements and the perishable nature of building materials. Maroons' built environment included houses, gardens, watchtowers, walls, and pit traps. Pottery, metal items (that is, gun or kettle parts), and glass bottle remains, in combination with site features (that is, trash pits or post holes), indicate the general size and specific location of settlements. The metal conical ear-bob recovered from Pilaklikaha (Florida) was a rare find. Metal working has been uncovered by historians examining maroon towns in Jamaica and Brazil. Archaeologists who found iron slag at Jose Leta (Dominican Republic) suggest other evidence for maroon metallurgy. Kaolin pipes, a common find at maroon sites, provide clues to mundane practices (tobacco smoking) and possessions. Beads and buttons, which were sewn on clothes or worn as necklaces, hint at dress and aesthetics of the self-emancipated Africans. Archaeological remains are often excavated in extremely inhospitable locations, such as the Dismal Swamp (North Carolina, Virginia).

From the sixteenth to the nineteenth century, Africans and black people escaped from slavery in all parts of the Americas. Maroons are a complicated subject to understand because they exhibited such great diversity in their relations with enemies and allies, their settings, their group compositions, and their political-economic circumstances. Studies of world history have established the fact that there have always been freedom seekers. For example, Africans known as Zanj rebelled against their **Muslim** captors more than 1,100 years ago in what is today Iraq. They and their Muslim allies established communities and kept the armies of one of the world's mightiest empires at bay for nearly two decades. In the Americas, maroons and their descendants' struggles manifested various levels of success. Some took their chances on networks such as the Underground Railroad, while others sought independence by building new towns. To understand the complexities of maroon life, the student and scholar must seek multiple lines of evidence: material culture, archival texts, oral traditions, and ethnographic observations.

Note: The identity label "maroon" is a biased, and some would say denigrative, term. The author has attempted to use various terms to challenge this and other terms that chroniclers have passed down to modern scholars. Descendants differ in their acceptance, usage, and preference, on the issue of maroon versus other self-ascribed labels of cultural identity.

Further Readings: Franklin, John Hope, and Schweninger, Loren. *Runaway Slaves: Rebels on the Plantation.* New York: Oxford University Press, 1999; Price, Richard. *Maroon Societies: Rebel Slave Communities in the Americas.* New York: Anchor Books, 1979; Weik, Terrance. "The Archaeology of Maroon Societies in the Americas: Resistance, Cultural Continuity, and Transformation in the African Diaspora." *Historical Archaeology* 31, 2 (1997): 81–92.

Terrance Weik

Ethnicity

The trans-Atlantic slave trade involved different people of different geographic, cultural, and historical backgrounds. Cultural diversity is complex because of the involvement of different peoples of the above-mentioned parameters. Ethnicity in the trans-Atlantic slave trade can simply be defined as the relationship among people of the same race and between one race and another. The ethnic factor in the trans-Atlantic slave trade was fluid and never static. It kept changing because Afro-European relations during the period between 1500 and 1800 went through a great deal of transformation. Relations between one European nation and another were dictated by a multiplicity of factors. The most prominent factor seems to have been economic, because the purpose of trade in human beings was related to the need to accumulate wealth through **plantation** agriculture.

The British, Portuguese, Dutch, Spanish, and French were the major European nationalities that bought slaves from Africans and transported them to the Americas. Each of these nations established plantation agriculture in the Americas. Although some of the plantations were owned by national government, private landowners owned others. The goal of all European nationalities in Africa was uniform, that is, the need to explore different parts of Africa and to buy and transport slaves to the Americas. Tension between these countries was inevitable on various grounds. All of them needed the best parts of Africa to get slaves. They also had to look for markets and plantations where the slaves would work in the Americas. Sea pirates' activities increased as the **profit** made from trade in human beings soared. An attacked slave ship automatically lost its slaves and other supplies. The activities of pirates caused tension between European countries. It was common for one country to blame another for attacking its slave ship. In 1750, pirates along Offra, a port of **Allada**, attacked a wrecked French ship. The French government suspected British pirates and ordered similar attacks. Retaliation was common among Europeans who felt that other nationalities did things that were inimical to their slave-trading interests.

A good percentage of slaves that went to the Americas through **Lagos** and Badagry in the nineteenth century were Yoruba. The Yoruba civil wars of the nineteenth century produced a lot of slaves from the war-raged hinterland. Generally, the question of one ethnic group enslaving another was a prominent aspect of interethnic relations between the sixteenth and the nineteenth century. Coastal communities were traditionally seen as "enslavers" of the people from the hinterlands because they had the gateway to the Americas where the slaves were needed.

For Africa, the trans-Atlantic trade in human beings intensified existing differences between one African state or empire and another. The nature of interethnic relations changed dramatically as the result of the introduction of the trans-Atlantic slave trade. Interstate wars, which are as old as the history of state and empire building in the continent, were intensified. The need to acquire slaves for the Americas escalated the nature of warfare among the people of different parts of Africa. In the Bight of Biafra, wars and raiding of villages were carried out to acquire slaves for the Atlantic voyage. The intensified nature of warfare among the Aja-speaking people of West Africa is explicable in terms of the need to get slaves as spoils of war.

Ethnicity played a significant role in the figures or number of slaves transported from specific parts of Africa. Of the 4 million slaves whose coastal origin is known, 38 percent or about 1.51 million came from the Bight of Benin along the **Slave Coast**; 18 percent or about 730,000 came from the Akan area along the **Gold Coast**, another 21 percent or about 850,000 came from the interior of the Bight of Biafra. The remainder, perhaps another 910,000, came from the western coast as far north as the Senegambia basin. This figure is for the seventeenth and eighteenth centuries.

The number of people of African origin who were transported to the Americas as slaves continues to be controversial. One aspect of slave culture that is undisputable, however, is the ethnic factor. Obviously, people can be physically enslaved but cannot be spiritually enslaved. African slaves went to the Americas with their culture, which included **music**, dance, **food**, and **religion**. The resilience of African culture in the Americas—most notably, **Brazil**, which had the highest number of blacks outside the African continent—demonstrates that culture and ethnicity are aspects of human behavior that cannot be enslaved. Ethnicity played a significant factor during the numerous slave revolts in the Americas. People of the same ethnic groups were able to talk among themselves and fashion ways to improve their condition. Ethnic solidarity therefore performed a significant role in facilitating slave resistance both during the Middle Passage and on slave plantations in the Americas. *See also* African Rulers and the Slave Trade; Decentralized Societies; Languages and Communication; Slavery in Africa; Volume; Wars, African.

Further Readings: Klein, Martin. *Historical Dictionary of Slavery and Abolition.* Lanham, MD, and London: The Scarecrow Press, Inc, 2002; Law, Robin. "Slave Raiders and Middlemen, Monopolists and Free-Traders: The Supply of Slaves for the Atlantic Trade in Dahomey, c. 1715–1850." *The Journal of African History* 30, 1 (1989): 45–68; Lovejoy, Paul. *Transformations in Slavery: A History of Slavery in Africa.* Cambridge: Cambridge University Press, 1983; Ross, David. "The Career of Domingo Martinez in the Bight of Benin 1833–1864." *The Journal of African History* 6, 1 (1965): 79–90.

Saheed Aderinto

Europe, Enslaved Africans in

An estimated 80,000 Africans were enslaved from the areas between the Sahara and **Kongo** about fifty years before Columbus's discovery of the New World. Out of these, 25,000 had European **destinations**, especially to Portugal, which served as the major point of **re-export** to Castile, Andalucia, Valencia, and Barcelona and, in the early sixteen century, to the Antilles. By 1466, there were considerable numbers of Ethiopians in Portugal, especially in Oporto and Guanches, and Moorish slaves were supplanted by black slaves. In the fifteenth century, there was an estimated black population of 35,000 (32,370 slaves and 2,580 freedmen), about 25 to 30 percent of the Portuguese population. Black slaves were engaged in agriculture, clearing forests, draining marshes, and public works, and worked as vendors, fishermen, ferrymen, artisans, and porters. Some earned money for their masters while others were engaged as personal servants.

The Portuguese attitudes toward black slaves were influenced by religious and social differences as well as racial consideration. In Spain, slavery had been part of the society long before their colonization of the Americas and most Africans were legally imported directly after the Spanish re-conquest. They were referred to as *ladinos*, Africans who had either lived or were born in Spain. Some were prisoners, or descendants of prisoners, captured in the long wars against the Moorish Kingdoms in southern Spain and forced to adopt **Christianity**. Others had reached Spain over the numerous slave routes that crossed the Sahara desert. An estimated 10,000 *ladinos* lived in **Seville** in 1492, and *ladino* crewmen worked alongside free sailors on the Spanish expeditions of the fifteenth and sixteenth centuries, or as "companions" or "assistants" to the *conquistadors* (the Spanish conquerors of the Aztec and Inca Empires). The Spanish granted the *ladinos* certain privileges, including the right to buy their freedom. Their independent spirit worried the Spanish colonists, however, who pinned their hopes on the more docile and stable ***bozales*** (African born slaves). Legal imports of *bozales* were sanctioned in 1518, but they proved to be just as determined to resist their oppressors and win back their freedom as the *ladinos*. Black Africans in Europe served as pirates, landowners, literati, members of urban confraternities, **galley slaves**, and craftsmen, as well as in many other socio-economic roles between 1440 and 1600 in England, Portugal, and northern Europe.

Many slaves were owned by **plantation** owners who lived in Britain. The legal position of enslaved Africans in Britain before the abolition of slavery was ambiguous. Revolutionary uprisings demanding natural justice rocked America in 1776 and France in 1789, but the principles of political and social freedom had limited application, particularly in the case of slaves. Plantation owners in the Americas depended on slaves to ensure high profitability. In Britain, eighteenth-century laws were designed to support a trade in slaves that was sanctioned by the king and Parliament. A decision by the Solicitor General stated that "Negroes" ought to be "esteemed goods and commodities within the Trade and Navigation Acts." Such a ruling permitted slave owners to use property law with regard to their slaves "to recover goods wrongfully detained, lost or damaged: as they would any other property."

The British courts made a series of ambiguous rulings on the legality of slavery, which encouraged several thousand slaves to flee the newly independent United States as refugees along with the retreating British in 1783. The British courts ruled in 1772 that such slaves could not be forcibly returned to North America, and the British government resettled them as free men in **Sierra Leone**. Most plantation owners lived in Britain. They brought their household slaves back with them from trips to the Americas and used them to perform domestic duties in Britain.

James Somerset, a young African slave, was purchased by Charles Stuart in Virginia in 1749. Stuart was involved in English government service and traveled, accompanied by Somerset, as part of his duties. In 1769, Stuart and Somerset traveled to England. While in England, Somerset associated with the antislavery movement in England, including with the well-known activist Granville Sharp. Somerset was christened with the name James in a church ceremony. In 1771, Somerset ran away. Stuart posted a reward and Somerset was recaptured. Stuart then had Somerset put on board a ship bound for **Jamaica** where Somerset was to be sold. Somerset's godparents from the christening ceremony discovered Somerset's condition and location. Going before the King's Bench, the highest court in England, they obtained a writ of *habeas corpus* requiring the ship's captain to produce Somerset in court, which was done. By this time in England, the general public had a poor opinion of the institution of slavery and the time was ripe for a decision to be forced as to whether slaves in England were in fact free. Somerset, who was supported by antislavery groups, sued for his freedom from Stuart, who was supported by planters from the West Indies who were interested in continuing the practice of slavery. The case was heard in a trial before the King's Bench.

Although Somerset's case provided legal precedent that slavery was unlawful in England itself, having died out there centuries before, it did not end British participation in the slave trade or slavery in other parts of the British Empire. It was not until 1807 that Parliament moved to suppress the slave trade; however, slavery continued to exist in various parts of the British Empire until it was finally abolished by Act of Parliament in 1833.

Law reports provide ample evidence of enslaved people in England bringing actions to obtain discharge from enforced employment. Well aware of the brutalities of plantation life, they would often do anything they could to avoid returning to the colonies with their masters. But the judgments they received were often contradictory and did not bring slavery in Britain to an end. *See also* Abolition of the Slave Trade, Great Britain; Lisbon; Portuguese Slave Trade.

Further Readings: Russell-Wood, A.J.R. "Before Columbus: Portugal's African Prelude to the Middle Passage and Contribution to Discourse on Race and Slavery." In V. Shepherd and H. McD. Beckles, eds. *Caribbean Slavery in the Atlantic World: A Student Reader*. Kingston: Ian Randle Publishers Ltd., 2000; Earle, F., and Lowe, K.J.P., eds. *Black Africans in Renaissance Europe*. Cambridge: Cambridge University Press, 2005.

Rasheed Olaniyi

F

Falconbridge, Alexander (?–1792)

A British surgeon, politician, and author, Alexander Falconbridge worked as a **doctor** on four travels in slave ships from **Bristol** to Africa between 1780 and 1787. Disgusted with the treatment of slaves, he left the trade and became an abolitionist. His 1788 account left us with an enduring account of the conditions of slaves in the Middle Passage. His book, *An Account of the Slave Trade on the Coast of Africa*, published in **London** in 1788, points to the desire of slaves in the Middle Passage to resist. The slaves hated the hardships and bemoaned the loss of liberty. As he explained, the slaves always organized insurrections. The book explains the sources of slaves, as coming from the hinterland where they were bought and sold in the coastal cities. The European merchants, according to him, inspected slaves for their age and health before they paid. The slaves were then transferred to waiting ships where men and **women** were kept in separate rooms and heavily guarded. The men were shackled together in pairs. His descriptions reveal additional cruelty: they had to sleep on their sides as erect positions were not possible; they had to relieve themselves where they slept; the main diet was horse beans, boiled yams, and rice, which were served twice a day, around 8:00 A.M. and 4:00 P.M.; those who refused to eat were force-fed; they were forced to sing and perform **exercises** on the deck to preserve their health; sailors had sex with any woman of their choice; they suffered from seasickness; those who could committed **suicide**; and they suffered from exclusion of fresh air and a poor diet.

His book was well received by the abolitionists in England who used his accounts to popularize the horrors and cruelty of the Middle Passage. An ally of Thomas Clarkson, the famous abolitionist, Falconbridge was encouraged to publish his accounts, which were based on interviews conducted with Richard Phillips (a member of the Anti-Slavery Society) and revealed the gross abuses and inhumanity of the Middle Passage. He was appointed in 1791 as the governor of **Sierra Leone** to reorganize Freetown. He traveled with his young wife, Anna Marie, who did not share his vision and commitment. He failed in his task, and he was dismissed from his appointment after a few months. He died shortly thereafter from excessive drinking in 1792. His wife, who remarried three weeks after his death, wrote her own account of the Middle Passage, *Anna Maria Falconbridge: Narrative of Two Voyages to the River Sierra Leone with Alexander Falconbridge: An Account of the Slave Trade on the Coast of Africa. See also* Abolitionism; British Slave Trade; Disease; Humanitarianism; Narratives by Slave Traders.

Further Reading: Howard, Thomas, ed. *Black Voyage: Eyewitness Accounts of the Atlantic Slave Trade, by Alexander Falconbridge.* Boston: Little, Brown, 1971.

Toyin Falola

Families and Family Separations

Slavery and the slave trade redefined the nature of families and kin. During the four centuries of its existence, the human traffic and the circumstances that led to it had situational effects on African family unity and separation. African families were scattered as wars and raids from stronger neighbors carted off members. From West Africa, former slaves like **Olaudah Equiano** and Ajayi Crowther were kidnapped. Parents lost **children**; siblings lost each other, and children were orphaned as one or both parents were carried off.

Apart from those carried off, a great number of men and **women** within different age-groups were massacred during the wars to acquire captives. Most of those captured were young people in their prime, usually between the ages of sixteen and forty-five. The remnant was a dysfunctional population. The villages were left with the old and the very young. The result was misery and anguish. It was made all the more painful when parents did not know what became of their children, whether they survived the ordeal, and how they were faring. Even when family members were captured in groups, they almost always ended up being sold separately. When recalling his experience, Equiano remembered being separated from his sister after capture. Perhaps the most traumatic moment for him was when he saw her again for the last time in a slave pen. The following morning, they were separated and he never saw her again. At the final slave market in Barbados, he watched as some brothers captured together were sold separately. Whole families were wiped out suddenly through death or captivity as if they never existed. On the vessels at sea, some gave up the will to live as a result of this separation. Some jumped overboard because of the hopelessness of their situation. In the New World, African captives arrived as forcibly separated individuals, who, apart from tribal identity, were not members of the same family.

The families that seemed to escape the ravages of the attacks were the ruling class. They were

The separation of a family of Slaves after being seized & sold upon a Warrant of destraint for their Masters debts, *as described in Bickells West Indies as they are, pages 16 & 17.*

Separation of a slave family in the West Indies. Courtesy of Anti-Slavery International.

the mercenaries behind the organized raids, kidnapping, wars, and criminal judgments. They knew how to protect themselves and members of their families from being captured or sold into slavery. The slave trade was a catalyst in the creation of a new class. This was a group known as the mulattoes, who had African mothers and European fathers. They owed no commitment to either side, but they used both backgrounds to become ruthlessly efficient **slave traders** on the coast.

After being settled on **plantations**, most slaves formed families with great difficulty. One of the first issues was the ratio of male to female slaves. With manual labor in view, male slaves were mostly exported. The number of wives was limited. Some of the men who came from well-to-do backgrounds and who had, or were the sons of men who had, many wives found it difficult to contemplate a monogamous existence. As their numbers multiplied and as the plantation economy calculated a cheaper turnover of investment by procreation, slaves began to enter into legal marriages. Even in this situation, the family unit was not secure and was prone to frequent and sudden separations. Most of the planters claimed to value family life. However, these same owners redefined traditional African family structures and were the cause of family separation in the diaspora. Their idea of what the structure of a slave family should be was basically matriarchal, and they often kept slave mothers together with their children.

The ability to form families varied based on geographic region. It was particularly difficult for African slaves in the Carolinas and Chesapeake region to create families. The latter region had rather compact plantations with farms having between ten and fifteen slaves. Given the size of the population, creating families was difficult. Larger farms housed their slaves in separate quarters, and married slave couples lived on separate plantations. In the Carolinas, more of the slave population lived together. There were usually between twenty-five and thirty slaves on a farm, but there was still the common factor of the unwillingness of "native born" and acculturated slaves to marry the new **arrivals**. This notwithstanding, families were gradually created. Family procreation was furthered because of the few children born of slave parents who survived infancy into adulthood and then went on to marry. In both the Chesapeake region and the Carolinas, the ratio of both sexes in the slave population had evened out by the middle of the eighteenth century.

In contrast, all over the Americas, the native born easily created families. They had acculturated and formed their own Afro-American kinship ties. These slaves did not have a firsthand experience of Africa and could not easily relate to the new arrivals. As the slave population grew with the new arrivals, both groups expanded. They socialized after work and even visited across plantations.

The economic interest of plantation owners worked against family unity. Plantation owners usually set up farms for their grown children and for the ones getting married. These landed gifts usually came with a well-stocked supply of human labor. In these cases, families were separated, as slaves were moved to the new farms. It was usually male slaves who were moved. The children of plantation owners who were given such presents almost always had their farms nearby. This way, slaves could move to see their families.

Other ways that slaves passed from parents to children could be through the death of owners who stipulated the proportion of inheritance before death. The movement of slaves was usually the same in cases of inheritance. With some separations, slave couples and other members of their families were not permitted to see each other. Sometimes a master might fall on hard times. His losses might be such that he had to sell his slaves. In other cases, a master might die and indicate that his slaves and other property should be sold to offset the costs associated with his death. Women were left behind to rear children alone. These female slaves formed female slave networks. They pooled the help of the female slaves in child care and other tasks.

From the early to the mid-nineteenth century, another development occasioned the movement of slaves in the New World. The early part of the century saw an increase in the **internal slave trade**, particularly in the United States. It declined a bit in the 1840s but rose again by the 1850s. This period was the height of the abolitionist movement. Most owners were not willing to let go of their slaves. As abolitionist movements spread across Europe and the New World, slaves were forced to move with their masters or were sold across the states. By 1860, about a million slaves were compelled to move with their owners to the southwest. Children who were born on the plantation and were lucky to remain there grew up to see couples parted, children separated from parents, and siblings sold off. Knowing that the possibility of seeing their families again was virtually impossible, slaves remarried upon arrival at other plantations. Others who experienced the anguish of forced separations from original homelands, as well as the disruption of the families they created on new soil, were less willing to remarry. Sometimes they were forced to remarry by their owners. Some slaves who could afford to simply stayed out of family life because of the pain of separation. The Marriage Register of the Freedmen's Bureau of Mississippi in 1865 indicated that half of all slave marriages with both spouses still alive had ended by the forcible act of separation. Most of these spouses were in the prime of life. The majority of these had been in stable marriages ranging from five to fifteen years.

Quite a number of slaves joined the **Christian** church, but the church had no power to enforce any obligation on their masters. The church could admonish a master in cases of extreme **violence** to a slave. The Christian church did one thing for slaves that seemed to have a slight impact on the family unity: it intervened to persuade owners to purchase spouses living on other plantations. After the American Civil War, the immediate mission of freed slaves was to seek out separated family members.

Family and kinship ties were important to the slaves. It was what helped them maintain their cultural identities and create a sense of belonging. They tried hard to keep this alive. Those on smaller plantations visited those on larger plantations. This was the only way they knew how to keep the African identity alive. At worst, it was the only way they knew how to incorporate some African elements into the new culture their children had assimilated. The tenacity of slaves to keep their family values alive was what made African elements survive in most parts of the Americas. *See also* Enslavement and Procurement; Slavery in Africa; Suicide.

Further Readings: Miller, Randall M., and Smith, John David, eds. *Dictionary of Afro-American Slavery.* Westport, CT: Greenwood Press, 1997; Shepherd, V., and McD. Beckles, H., eds. *Caribbean Slavery in the Atlantic World.* Oxford: James Curry Publishers, 2000.

Oyekemi Olajope Oyelakin

Fernando Po

Fernando Po is an island in the Gulf of Guinea near the coast of modern-day Equatorial Guinea. Although local African populations did form a complex system of lagoons for travel along the West African coast, few African fishermen ventured from the sight of land. As a result, Fernando Po remained uninhabited until the arrival of the Portuguese. Sailors first sighted Fernando Po in 1471 on one of Portugal's many exploratory excursions along the long coast of Africa. Under a Portuguese royal charter, Fernao Gomes successfully explored the African coast between 1469 and 1475, reaching Fernando Po and crossing the equator.

Toward the end of the slave trade, Fernando Po afforded the British naval squadrons with a port for operations against the slave trade. (By the 1840s, the British established a consul on Fernando Po and signed antislavery treaties with the Duala on the mainland. Late in the nineteenth century, cocoa made its way from America to Fernando Po, with the help of the Spanish, as a **plantation** crop and eventually become the region's major export.

Although Fernando Po is sighted early in Portugal's early explorations down the West African coast, the island never reaches the level of importance as other islands in the Bight of Biafra. The ecology of Fernando Po played a determining role in the failure of European settlement. Along with **diseases** like sleeping sickness, malaria, and other tropical diseases that derailed European efforts to establish a colony, the Bantu-speaking Bubi refused to be conquered by European colonizers. Covered by rough mountains, Fernando Po resembles a steep peak of a submerged volcano making the island inhospitable to farming. Because Fernando Po is difficult to reach by sail, the island remained outside of the burgeoning slave trade. After the 1820s, Europeans finally settled on Fernando Po, encroaching on the Bubi.

Fernando Po was located in the middle of the slave-trading system, but the island served several other functions connected to the Atlantic slave trade. Fernando Po became a **maroon** settlement of escaped slaves from **São Tomé** and Príncipe. Later, the antislave squadrons of the British Royal Navy used Fernando Po as a blockade station, stopping ships that were carrying slaves. Many British warships served in the antislave squadron at Fernando Po from 1827 until 1844. The antislave squadron captured slave ships and released the slaves in **Sierra Leone**. **Slave merchants** could be executed if found guilty. *See also* African Squadrons, The; British Navy; Escapes and Runaways (Maroonage).

Further Readings: Curtin, Philip, Feierman, Steven, Thompson, Leonard, and Vansina, Jan. *African History.* Boston: Little, Brown, 1978; July, Robert W. *A History of the African People.* 5th ed. Prospect Heights, IL: Waveland Press, 1998; Reader, John. *Africa: A Biography of the Continent.* New York: Vintage Books, 1999; Sundiata, Ibrahim K.

From Slaving to Neoslavery: The Bight of Biafra and Fernanado Po in the Era of Abolition, 1827–1930. Madison: University of Wisconsin Press, 1996.

Michael Bonislawski

Firearms and Gunpowder

The introduction of firearms and gunpowder into African society forever altered the course of African history. African indigenous ethnic groups contended for supremacy in commerce, control of the best agricultural lands, dominance in commercial markets, political influence, and control over the slave trade, and as a result, sought out any advantage. One such advantage incorporated the increased use of firearms and gunpowder. European traders desired slaves for sale in the Americas and willingly traded firearms for slaves.

Africa's knowledge of firearms dates to the introduction of firearms into North Africa by the Ottoman Turks. Across the Saharan desert, Africans traded **textiles**, copper, breeding horses, and **cowry shells**. Trans-Saharan traders added firearms in the seventeenth century. The proliferation of firearms in sub-Saharan Africa depended on the frequency of African contact with Portuguese traders and later with Dutch and British merchants. West African imports included cowries, silver coins, copper and brass bars, and glass beads. By 1730, military hardware—including knives, swords, horses, and firearms—became the major imports into West Africa. Firearms and gunpowder dominated West African trade with one fifty-year period totaling the importation of 1.7 million guns along with 22,000 metric tons of gunpowder per year. European **plantation** owners in the Americas desired an unending supply of slave labor. By the eighteenth century, trading firearms proved to be the major means of payment during the slave trade. As European plantation owners increased their demand for labor, the number of slaves exported from Africa accelerated. Increased firearm imports coincided with the rise of internal African warfare and the conversion of war captives into slaves. As local African leaders obtained more firearms, these firearms were, in turn, used to capture more slaves. Despite the poor quality of these imported weapons, guns from Britain and Belgium ranked high as one of the most sought after commodities by African leaders. By design, the weapons sent to Africa were the lowest-quality muskets possible and proved to be just as hazardous to the users as they were to their intended targets. African riflemen continually risked death and maiming as European-manufactured rifles often failed to fire in wet weather and regularly exploded. European merchants supplied the gunpowder required for musket warfare. Like the firearms sold by Europeans, the gunpowder used by Africans was of the poorest quality, which added to the instability of gun use in African warfare. Because African iron-making never advanced beyond primitive hand methods, the harder, denser types of metal for gun-making never materialized; thus sub-Saharan African leaders depended on trading with European merchants to obtain modern weapons. Although European traders undoubtedly rushed to bring guns to African leaders, traders viewed firearms as the most likely commodity the Africans would desire. Some Europeans may have made the connection between trading more firearms and obtaining more slaves, but most traders provided what African leaders wanted in exchange for a lucrative human **cargo** that slavers could deliver to the mines and plantations in the Americas. *See also* Slavery in Africa; Trade Commodities; Violence; Wars, African.

Further Readings: Headrick, Daniel R. *The Tools of Empire: Technology and European Imperialism in the Nineteenth Century.* New York: Oxford University Press, 1981; Lovejoy, Paul E. *A History of Slavery in Africa.* Cambridge and New York: Cambridge University Press, 1983; Shillington, Kevin. *History of Africa.* 2nd ed. New York: Palgrave Macmillan, 2005.

Michael Bonislawski

Folklore

Slavery in the Americas was an industry and a system devoted to a single purpose: the buying, selling, and exploitation of Africans. To make it easier to achieve this goal, the slavers had to deny the Africans what they had in common with them—their humanity. They did this through a process of dehumanization that was both physical and psychological. It was designed to either erase African identity or make the African forget his or her origins, or the very source of their being. From African **ports** of origin to final **destinations** in the Americas, this process entailed **branding**, change of name, **rape**, torture, physical confinement and brutalization, death, and forced mixing with other Africans of unrelated **languages** and cultures. Thus, the trans-Atlantic journey between Africa and the Americas, also known as the Middle Passage, was in many ways a zone of forgetting, a zone of erasure of the African being and self. Irreparable damage was done to kinship and family ties. Folklore was the unbreakable and unbroken umbilical cord that sustained the slaves' connections with their roots. It had the capacity to heal the psyche of enslaved Africans in the Americas.

In their new homelands, folklore connected the Africans to their ancestral home and collective memory. This memory, symbolized by folktales and given expression through the same, gave them a sense of their humanness in spite of the harrowing experience of the crossings. In the New World, folklore restored their spirituality and sense of personhood because it affirmed the ethics and timeless values contained therein. In their new home, descendants of African slaves used folklore to create culture and to bring meaning and vitality to their existence. Folklore became a vehicle for affirmation because it bespoke Africa's diasporan connection to an unforgettable past—a rootedness in humanity. Through language and myth, folklore signaled their participation in the human capacity for the divine and eternal. Thus, folklore gave hope and inspiration to generations yet to come.

Generations of diaspora Africans will internalize the ethics and the epistemologies contained in the folklore from Africa. Through the oral reiteration, performance, and transmission of these folktales, African American capacity for mythmaking was assured. Folklore affirmed Africans' contribution to human civilization because it contained histories—individual and social—that attested to black survival, and consequently, human survival. Folklore was thus the major element that held the germ of rebirth of African, Afro-Caribbean, and African American cultures in the diaspora. The psychological impact of this genre on black life is immense. According to Jennifer Hildebrand, "folktales provided a socially sanctioned psychic release" in the face of untold suffering and pain. Folk songs played an important role in the emerging black spirituality. For example, funeral dirges recalled links with African ancestors, while lullabies rooted in folklore expressed yearnings for a better life (for the next generation) beyond the squalor and misery of slavery. African American **music**—from negro spirituals, by way of jazz, through the blues—is rooted in the lament, protest, and hopefulness of folklore.

Folklore provided a measure of optimism in a rather hopeless world. It empowered Africans to exercise some measure of control over their dire circumstances, because the different forms were pungent and poignant signifiers that encapsulated racial, ethnic, communal, and personal memory. Contrary to the racist assertions of Enlightenment thinkers, Africans had made contributions to human history through their unique, folkloric modes of remembering. In African American life, folklore took many forms. The key form was communal performance. It emphasized orality because slaves had little or no access at all to literacy. Storytelling, often for moral education and communal edification, was accompanied by song and dance, using call-and-response, repetition, riddling, and rhyming.

In antebellum America, the black church was the one key and enduring institution that nourished and sustained African American spirituality in its diverse forms—music, art, politics, discourse, and thought. Its roots are clearly traceable to slave **religion**. Thus, the church, its theology, and its modes of expression can be seen as products of African folklore, with strong influences from European religious modes. Black preaching as a rhetorical and performative act still attests to the power of folklore. Its capacity to mobilize African Americans for social and political change is traceable to the power of folklore. The influence of African traditions is clearly evident in the early black churches. Modes of worship included shouts, hand-clapping, foot-stomping, and jubilee songs, just as they did was in **plantation** "praise houses." Negro spirituals thus were the precursors of today's gospel music—a key feature of worship in the black church.

African American folklore, as expressed through negro spirituals, evolved into a subversive tool in the cry for freedom and salvation, which the slaves developed in response to the suppression of their speech by slave masters. Slaves of southern plantations depended on bible text for verse themes. In the story of Jews in bondage in Egypt, African Americans found a striking parallel to their own status. In this regard, the famous tune "Go Down, Moses" is a pertinent example. In the United States, these songs ultimately became a code or road map to freedom in the northern parts of the country.

In twentieth-century America, folklore, expressed by the powerful performances of Paul Robeson through negro spirituals, became a vehicle for promoting racial and intercultural understanding. Folklore still endures as a versatile template for the reassessment and regeneration of African American heritage and life in modern America. *See also* Christianity; Historical Memory.

Further Readings: Anderson, Paul Allen. *Deep River: Music and Memory in Harlem Renaissance Thought.* Durham, NC: Duke University Press, 2001; Carretta, Vincent, and Gould, Philip, eds. *Genius in Bondage.* Lexington: University Press of Kentucky, 2001; Courlander, Harold. *A Treasury of Afro-American Folklore: The Oral Literature, Traditions, Recollections, Legends, Tales, Songs, Religious Beliefs, Customs, Sayings, and Humor of Peoples of African Descent in the Americas.* 2nd ed. New York: Marlowe & Company, 1996; Gates, Henry Louis, Jr. *The Signifying Monkey: A Theory of African-American Literary Criticism.* New York: Oxford University Press, 1988; Hildebrand, Jennifer. "Folktales." In *Greenwood Encyclopedia of African American Folklore*, 456–459. Westport, CT: Greenwood Press, 2005; Mintz, Sidney W., and Price, Richard. *The Birth of African-American Culture: An Anthropological Perspective.* Boston, MA. Beacon Press, 1992; Raboteau, Albert J. *Slave Religion: The "Invisible Institution" in the Antebellum South.* New York: Oxford University Press, 2004.

'BioDun J. Ogundayo

Food

The meals fed to slaves during their captivity in Africa and during the Middle Passage were monotonous and meager. Their content varied significantly, however, according to the regions from which the slaves were drawn, the nationality of the **slave traders**, and over time. Initially the foods fed to slaves reflected agricultural production in Africa, but sometimes slave traders imported crops from other regions, including Europe. The French imported oats, the English biscuits and horse beans, and the Dutch barley, dried peas, and beans. The basic diet of Africans in Senegambia was *milho* (millet or sorghum) supplemented by rice and beans, while on the **Gold Coast** and Bight of Biafra, yams predominated. In **Angola**, millet and beans were the main staples, although from the earliest days of the slave trade the Portuguese imported *farinha* (manioc flour) from **Brazil**, and by the seventeenth century, they had established manioc **plantations** in Angola. Meanwhile, the cultivation of maize spread widely, particularly in West Africa, where it figured significantly among the provisions provided by English slave traders on the Gold Coast. Rice cultivation in Upper Guinea expanded with slaves being employed on plantations for the months before their shipment to the Americas.

Initially, slave traders favored the use of imported foods for provisions, because although they were not necessarily more nutritious, they often had better storage qualities and took up less space on board ship. This was particularly true of yams that could rot before they were consumed. Slave traders soon became aware that slaves fared better when they were fed foods to which they were accustomed. As a result, more emphasis was placed on indigenous African crops. In the early eighteenth century, the French commercial agent **John (Jean) Barbot** claimed that "a ship [leaving Calabar] that takes in five hundred slaves, must provide about a hundred thousand yams. . . . yet no less ought to be provided, the slaves being of such a constitution, that no other food will keep them; Indian corn, beans, and Mandioca, disagreeing with their stomachs so that they sicken and die apace" (Hair, Jones, and Law, 1992, p. 700). Slave traders on the Gold Coast attempted to provide at least one meal a day based on foods to which the slaves were accustomed, although they still relied heavily on maize. This was not the case in Angola, where manioc cultivation was better adapted to its drought conditions and it continued to dominate slave rations.

Whether the basic diet consisted of cereals, yams, or manioc, these staple foods were administered in the form of a gruel or paste rather than in the form of bread. This was prepared in a large copper pan, seasoned with palm oil, salt, or malaguetta pepper. Pepper was used partly to flavor food, but also because it was thought to stimulate the appetite and prevent dysentery. Small amounts of dried meat or fish might occasionally be added, but fresh fruit and vegetables were rare additions, although they were taken on board whenever ships touched land. Slaves were fed twice a day, once in the morning and once in the afternoon, with the food handed out in large bowls shared by six to eight slaves each possessing a spoon attached to their belts. Administered on board deck, meal times were the most dangerous times for rebellions.

Although meals were monotonous and limited, the slave traders paid considerable attention to the provisions they provided, because it did not make economic sense to cut down on food rations to the extent that they induced nutritional deficiency **diseases**, such as scurvy, or even starvation. This was particularly true because expenditure on food generally accounted for less than 5 percent of the total cost of a slave from captivity to sale. Hence, in 1519 and 1684, the Portuguese laid down **regulations** governing the quantities and types of food that were to be provided for slaves. Whether or not these regulations were adhered to, provisions took up valuable **cargo** space, as did **water**. The regulations specified that each ship carrying 300 slaves should carry thirty-five barrels of water. Because of space limitations, slave ships generally carried only limited amounts of food and water above what was needed for an average journey across the Atlantic. Unexpectedly long voyages therefore would result in significant shortages of food, with much of the remaining food being of poor quality because of spoilage. In these circumstances, sanitary conditions deteriorated and outbreaks of scurvy or dysentery, if they did not result in high **mortality**, meant that slaves arrived in a sick and weakened state. Deficiencies in nutrition were often exacerbated by seasickness. Most evidence suggests that ships' **crews** generally fared little better. By the early seventeenth century, if not before, slave traders had learned that scurvy (caused by a shortage of vitamin C) could be treated effectively with a regular mouthwash of lime juice, but it is not clear how widespread was its use. Shortages of food during the Middle Passage were apparent in the fact that many slaves fell sick upon their arrival in the Americas, when they were faced with the more substantial and richer diets provided by the slave traders as they tried to fatten them up for sale.

The Atlantic slave trade not only affected the diets of slaves in Africa and during the Middle Passage, but also in the Americas. Yams spread widely in the Caribbean, while rice was introduced to Carolina, where it was cultivated on plantations by slaves who brought the techniques of rice cultivation with them from Africa. Many other African crops were not developed commercially, but instead were cultivated as subsistence crops on slave plantations or on small plots in the hills by free Africans. These included such crops as yams, the aubergine, ackee, okras, and the congo bean (pigeon pea), which all feature strongly in Caribbean diets today.

Further Readings: Carney, Judith A. *Black Rice: The African Origins of Rice Cultivation in the Americas*. Cambridge, MA: Harvard University Press, 2001; Hair, P.E.H., Jones, Adam, and Law, Robin, eds. *Barbot on Guinea: The Writings of Jean Barbot on West Afria, 1678–1712*. 2 vols. London: Hakluyt Society, 1992; Hall, Robert L. "Savoring Africa in the New World." In Herman J. Viola and Carolyn Margolis, eds. *Seeds of Change*, 162–171. Washington, DC: Smithsonian Institution Press, 1991; Harms, Robert. *The Diligent: A Voyage through the Worlds of the Slave Trade*. Oxford: Perseus Press, 2002; Kiple, Kenneth F. *The Caribbean Slave: A Biological History*. Cambridge: Cambridge University Press, 1984.

Linda A. Newson

Fort Saint Louis

From the fifteenth century, forts were built by various Europeans nations along the West and Central African coastal areas. These fortresses served as trading posts and temporary settlements. Indeed, some of them developed into large settlements with populations of thousands. Arguin, a zone located at the bay beyond Cape Blanco, was the first part of Africa where a fort was built for intensive slave-trading. It was from here that the Portuguese first took slaves, in the 1440s. The Spaniards were not lax in joining their Iberians counterparts whose influence in Arguin had increased considerably.

The Iberians were not the only Europeans who saw the Arguin as a fertile region for the trade in slaves. The French also extended their trade in ivory and slaves into the south of Arguin. Here, a large, mud-built, badly designed fortress called Saint Louis (located in present-day **Senegal**) protected their trading port. Around the fortress lay a cemetery, a hospital, and a church as well as a few brick houses for the small white and mulatto population. Also located in the fort were numerous huts in which Africans lived. The population of French officers and soldiers and a few European-born residents was estimated to be 600 c. 1780. This figure included the undefined mulattos who were descendants of Portuguese traders and settlers.

The significance of this region for slave-trading was not only that it faced the Atlantic but also that it was also connected by good waterways to savannah country. The savannah had the ancient caravan routes to the Magreb where slaves were bought and transported to the Arguin. There were also artificial and natural saltpans. The Bambuk gold fields were accessible by water, 300 miles inland. The first slaves sold here were said to be Wolofs (Jolofs), the people who dominated the territory. But, as the case of most names in Atlantic Africa, many who were called Wolof in America would originally have come from the far interior, from places well beyond the head of navigation on the Senegal River.

The presence of the fort generated serious rivalry between France and Great Britain during the seventeenth and the eighteenth centuries. Capturing and recapturing took place between the two nations. In 1693, the fort was captured by Great Britain. France later regained it through a peaceful settlement. The English captured it again during the Seven Years' War, but lost it once more to the French in 1779. In 1783, France and Great Britain signed a treaty, which gave the latter the opportunity of gum trading. The two powers agreed to continue to frequent the rest of the coast of Africa in accordance with past usage. *See also* Trade Forts.

Further Readings: David, Eltis, and Walvin, James. *The Abolition of the Atlantic Slave Trade: Origins and Effects in Europe. Africa and the Americas.* Madison: University of Wisconsin Press, 1981; Rawley, James. *The Transatlantic Slave Trade, A History.* New York: W. W. Norton, 1981; Stein, Robert. *The French Slave Trade in the 18th Century: An Old Regime Business.* Madison: University of Wisconsin Press, 1979; Thomas, Hugh. *The Slave Trade: The Story of the Atlantic Slave Trade, 1440–1870.* New York: Simon & Schuster, 1997.

Saheed Aderinto

Fredensborg, The

The *Fredensborg* was a Danish slave ship, which wrecked off the coast of Norway in 1768. It was salvaged by Norwegian divers in 1974, providing a valuable insight into day-to-day life aboard an eighteenth-century slaver. It is the single most intact wreck of a slave ship known. The *Fredensborg* was a 100-foot (31.4-meter) frigate, built as a slave ship in Copenhagen (1752–1753).

Her final journey began in June 1767, when she sailed from Copenhagen for the **Gold Coast**. She arrived fourteen weeks later at Christiansborg, the principal Danish fort in West Africa (modern-day Osu, Ghana), with a **cargo** of brandy, cloth, guns, **gunpowder**, and flints. Over the next seven months, she took on a human cargo of 265 slaves (158 men, 78 **women**, 9 girls, and 20 boys), mostly from the Akwamu, an Akan people living near Christiansborg. During her stay, she was refitted to carry slaves. Three tall cylindrical canvas tubes were installed to provide air for the slaves below deck. A strong partition was built across the deck in front of the mainsail and fortified with cannon, in case the slaves tried to rebel. Four swivel guns were positioned along the decks, and nets were installed to prevent desperate slaves from hurling themselves overboard.

In April 1768, the *Fredensborg* sailed for St. Croix, in the Danish West Indies, with her cargo of slaves, 92.8 kilos (205 pounds) of ivory and 1.25 kilos (2 3/4 pounds) of gold. The toll on her **crew** had been high. In just under seven months on the Gold Coast, eleven men died, out of a crew of forty, including the captain. During the course across the Atlantic passage, yet another crewman died and more fell ill. This forced the new captain (formerly the first mate) to press nine of the slaves into service as impromptu deck hands. Because the slaves on board were from the same area, they were able to communicate with each other. They would have rebelled and tried to seize the ship, but for an African member of the crew who spoke their **language** and warned the captain.

During the voyage, the slaves were each fed a daily ration of beans and grain, with a piece of meat on Sunday. Each slave was allotted a clay pipe, with a bit of tobacco daily, and four cups of brandy each week. The women and **children** were kept aft, apart from the men. In the three-and-a-half-month voyage, twenty-nine slaves (11 percent) died. The total death rate for the Europeans, if the time on the West African coast is counted, was 37.5 percent.

Her last leg of the voyage was from Christiansted, St. Croix, bearing a cargo of **sugar**, dyewood, mahogany, tobacco, cinnamon, and cotton. Overloaded, she wrecked in a storm off of Arendal, Norway. *See also* Danish Slave Trade; Food; Minor European Nations; Shipwrecks.

Further Readings: Svalesen, Leif. *The Slave Ship Fredensborg.* Bloomington: Indiana University Press, 2000; Thomas, Hugh. *The Slave Trade: The Story of the Atlantic Slave Trade, 1440–1870.* New York: Simon & Schuster, 1997; UNESCO (United Nations Educational, Scientific and Cultural Organization) Web site: http://www.unesco.no/fredensborg/index.htm.

Timothy Neeno

Free Trade

The modern system of European slavery had its roots in the mercantilist economic patterns of the contemporary era, but slavery expanded during the period that accompanied the rise of free trade and the laissez-faire system. The trade system in place during the early days of Portuguese slavery in the 1400s revolved around government-sponsored efforts to gain control over markets and establish monopolies. Mercantilism was based on the principles of protection for domestic industries through tariffs and monopolies and control over trade with the goal of creating a favorable balance of trade (or importing less than a country exports). As a country's wealth increased so too would its military power by bolstering the state's ability to spend more on soldiers, ships, arms, and ammunition. The implementation of mercantilist policies resulted in policies that limited free trade.

One manifestation of mercantilism was the issuance of monopolies for government-chartered companies to control a country's slave trade. The **Royal Africa Company** and the Dutch West India Company were examples of such companies. Monopolies became so integrated in international trade that Spain granted monopolies on the supply of slaves (known as an *asiento*). Britain's Royal Africa Company received the *asiento* on slaves through the 1713 Treaty of Utrecht. In addition, countries enacted various legislation to support monopolies and promote exports. The succession of Navigation Acts, put into force by the British in the 1600s, were designed to prevent other countries from trading with British colonies and, instead, forced the colonies to trade exclusively with British companies. Throughout the 1600s and 1700s, most countries considered slaves as goods comparable with other products. One result was intense competition between the colonial powers to control the slave forts along the African coast.

During the eighteenth century, laissez-faire economics, which emphasized free trade, became increasingly popular among elites. In 1776, Adam Smith (1723–1790) published *An Inquiry into the Nature and Causes of the Wealth of Nations*, which described how markets could be self-regulating through the "invisible hand" that operated according to the law of **supply and demand**. For markets to achieve their full potential, government interference had to be limited or eliminated. Contrary to mercantilism, advocates for free trade argued that monopolies had to be eliminated and protectionist tariffs had to be reduced or eliminated.

The independence of the American colonies led to the informal end of British mercantilism. After the Revolution, the British continued to dominate trade with the United States. This convinced many British lawmakers that mercantilism was unnecessary and that they could maintain or expand market share through the free market. Other nations began to adopt free trade policies, although they often retained protectionist policies to support specific industries. The **sugar** industries in countries such as Great Britain, France, and the Netherlands were examples of this tactic. Although the British increasingly advocated free trade, much of Europe was engaged in Napoleon's Continental System, which sought to replace British goods and products with those of the countries allied to, or conquered by, the French. Hence, instead of using sugar from the British colonies, Napoleon endeavored to rely on Dutch imports.

As free trade became popular among elites, the economic approach was used as an argument both in favor of, and in opposition to, slavery. In the United States, the South became increasingly dependent on agricultural exports to Great Britain. Therefore, tariffs and other impediments to free trade were unpopular in the South because they raised the cost of Southern exports. Slave owners in the South were supportive of free trade. Northerners in the United States, however, sought to protect growing industries through duties on imports. The result was a longstanding dispute over national tariffs between the North and South.

Proslavery advocates of free trade argued that slaves were a commodity just like any other product. **Taxes** and duties were paid on imported slaves. The construction of slave ships and the outfitting and provisioning of the vessels employed people, and ship owners usually paid **insurance** on their vessels (insurance was also carried on slaves in some countries). The powerful sugar lobby of the **British Caribbean** planters and Southern **plantation** owners were examples of pro–free trade slave groups.

Pro–free traders were more commonly abolitionists. In Great Britain, people who supported laissez-faire economics and free trade opposed slavery, because it caused the cost of labor to be artificially low. They argued that the money spent on slavery and the slave trade benefited a few elites and removed money from national economies that could otherwise be invested in legitimate industries. Pro–free trade Whigs in Great Britain joined the abolitionists, including Tories such as **William Wilberforce**, to abolish the slave trade. Subsequently, free traders contended that the slave trade had to be abolished throughout the globe or countries that continued to participate in the trade would have an advantage. Similar arguments were used to promote abolition. Free traders argued that slavery limited competition and had to be stopped, especially after countries began to end slavery, otherwise the invisible hand of the market could not work and markets could not self-regulate. *See also* Abolitionism; Abolition of the Slave Trade, France; Abolition of Slave Trade, Great Britain; Abolition of the Slave Trade, Spain; Abolition of Slave Trade, United States; British Slave Trade; Closure of the Slave

Trade; Enslavement and Procurement; Legitimate Commerce; Monopoly; Slave Merchants (Slave Traders); Trade Commodities; Trade Forts; Triangular Trade.

Further Readings: Armitage, David, ed. *Theories of Empire: 1400–1800.* Aldershot, UK: Ashgate, 1998; Diamond, Jared. *Guns, Germs, and Steel: The Fates of Human Societies.* New York: W.W. Norton, 1997; Dumett, Raymond E., ed. *Gentlemanly Capitalism and British Imperialism: The New Debate on Empire.* Harlow, UK: Longmans, Green and Company, 1999; Fieldhouse, David K. *The West and the Third World: Trade, Colonialism, Dependence, and Development.* Oxford: Oxford University Press, 1999; Kaufmann, W.W. *British Policy and the Independence of Latin America, 1804–1828.* New Haven, CT: Yale University Press, 1951.

Tom Lansford

French Caribbean

French merchants, sailors, and pirates became interested in the Caribbean during the sixteenth century, but it was not before the 1620s that the French established colonies in this area and promoted settlement and a **plantation** economy based first on tobacco and indigo and then later mainly on **sugar** and coffee. These colonies became one of the main markets for slave trade ships, notably in the eighteenth century, when 1 million Africans were shipped to the French West Indies. The independence of Haiti (1804) reduced considerably the importance of this area for France, whereas the abolition of slavery (1794–1802, and 1848) and of the slave trade (1814–1815) changed the nature of labor and production in the French Caribbean in the nineteenth century.

After the failure of its colonization projects in the Americas in the sixteenth century, France successfully occupied Saint Kitts in 1626, and Guadeloupe and Martinique in 1635. These colonies became the basis for the conquest of other small islands in the lesser Antilles (St. Martin, St. Barthélémy, and others in the following years), as well as for the first French settlement on the Tortue island and on the northwestern part of **Hispaniola**.

The enterprise of colonization; the organization of migration, settlement, and trade; and the rule of the colonies were originally granted to chartered companies, such as the *Compagnie des Iles d'Amérique* founded in 1635 by the king's main minister A. J. du Plessis de Richelieu. After the 1674 failure of the *Compagnie des Indes Occidentales* (1664–1674), which monopolized the slave trade to New France and the Caribbean, the Navy minister J. B. Colbert put the West Indies directly under the direct control of the crown: a governor and an *intendant* were to rule the colonies in the name of the king. They were assisted by a colonial assembly, which represented the planters' interests. When the Spaniards ceded the western part of Hispaniola (that is, **Saint Domingue**) to France in 1697, at the Peace of Ryswick, this colony, which was to become the most important part of the French West Indies, was put directly under the king's rule.

The end of chartered companies opened the West Indian slave trade and shipping to individual French merchants and provoked an increasing specialization of French **ports** in the Atlantic economy. **Nantes**, **Bordeaux**, La Rochelle, and Le Havre progressively entered the colonial and slave trades, eventually leaving shipping to New Foundland to minor French ports. By the end of the seventeenth century, France dominated a significant and rapidly developing portion of the Caribbean, and French merchants were seizing the opportunities of West Indian trade.

Despite temporary foreign occupations of some of the major colonies in times of war (the British occupied Guadeloupe in 1759 and Martinique in 1762 and gave them back to France in 1763) and the definitive loss of minor islands over time (St. Barthélémy was ceded to Sweden in 1785; St. Vincent became British from 1763 to 1779, and again from 1783 to its independence in 1979), France was successful in maintaining the bulk of its Caribbean possessions throughout the *ancien régime*. This was clearly a governmental priority: in 1763, at the end of the disastrous Seven Years' War, the French king chose to abandon New France to Great Britain so that he could recover his West Indian colonies.

The French Revolution heavily affected French possessions in the Caribbean, as warfare among European powers (1793–1802, 1803–1815) threatened the colonies once more. The loss of Saint Domingue, however, was not so much the consequence of international rivalry among European great powers, but rather of the implosion of the slave system on which colonization relied. The 1791 slave uprising in Saint Domingue, resulting in the independence of Haiti (1804), reduced the French empire in the Americas to Guadeloupe and Martinique, as well as to some of the Lesser Antilles. Most of these colonies are a part of the French Republic today.

From the middle of the seventeenth century to the end of the eighteenth century, the French West Indies played an increasing role for France. The colonies became an important market for slaves and European products, and the development of plantations provided rich return **cargoes** to the mother country.

The plantation economy developed rapidly from the middle of the seventeenth century. From the 1630s to the 1660s, the French Caribbean was a basis for pirates and buccaneers (hunters who smoked meat on wooden frames and sold it), while the first planters grew tobacco and indigo. From the 1650s to the 1660s, Dutch refugees from **Brazil** introduced their knowledge about sugarcane and financed the first sugar plantations. French colonists rapidly abandoned tobacco, because they could not compete against the increasing production of the Chesapeake and the drop in price of this commodity, and instead grew sugarcane. Parallel to these changes in colonial crops, the French made an effective attempt to secure maritime routes, to encourage French shipping and trade, and to exclude Dutch merchants from the lucrative colonial trade.

In 1683, the French Lesser Antilles produced 9,300 tons of sugar. A subsequent significant increase of production was hindered by soil impoverishment and lack of space, so that in 1767, the Lesser Antilles produced a total of 14,000 tons of sugar. In the meantime, Saint Domingue had emerged as the world's leader in sugar production. Saint Domingue planters had begun to grow sugarcane at the turn of the eighteenth century, and they exported 7,000 tons as early as 1714. This island dramatically increased its sugar production through the eighteenth century (43,000 tons in 1743; 73,000 tons in 1767; 86,000 tons in 1789). By 1788, the French West Indies produced half of the world's sugar, and 85 percent of French sugar was grown in Saint Domingue. From the middle of the eighteenth century, coffee production increased consistently, reaching 40,000 tons in 1788. France was the unique legal destination for all ships from the French West Indies, but colonial products were largely re-exported to Northern Europe, mainly to Amsterdam, Hamburg, and the Baltic. Approximately 80 percent of the sugar and coffee imported to Bordeaux in the 1780s left for these **destinations**, thus providing further opportunities to **profit** from shipping activities. The West Indies considerably improved the French balance of payments and intensified the activities of French ports. They were important markets for French agricultural and manufactured goods, such as wines and flour from the Bordeaux region, and **textiles** from Northern France.

The French government obliged colonists to trade exclusively with France, and all the trade had to be carried on French vessels. This monopolistic system (the so-called *exclusif*) was slightly softened in 1767 and again in 1784, when foreign ships were allowed to enter some colonial ports, but the nature of the trade they could conduct was reduced. **Smuggling** continued as before, which allowed colonists to acquire North American supplies and foreign slaves at lower costs.

Colonial trade and production relied on slave labor. The French West Indies were not only an important market for French products, but also they sustained a consistent demand for slaves. The considerable increase of goods produced in the eighteenth century is intimately linked to a rise in the number of slaves living and working in the French Caribbean. Because their **mortality** was higher than their birth rate, the increase in the slave population depended on the intensity of the slave trade, which considerably modified the composition of the population in the French West Indies.

In 1650, there were about 12,000 slaves in the West Indies and 15,000 to 16,000 French, two-thirds of whom were **indentured servants**. The number of indentured servants and their high mortality rate led to a massive recourse to slave labor on plantations. By 1683, slaves already outnumbered the French colonists (28,000 and 19,000 respectively), and the ratio of Africans to Europeans continued to increase throughout the eighteenth century. The slave trade to the French West Indies dramatically increased from the end of the seventeenth century, parallel to the number of sugarcane plantations: 80 percent of the Africans shipped to Martinique in the seventeenth century arrived after 1680. In the 1780s, slaves represented 80 to 90 percent of the total population of the French West Indies. They were approximately half a million in Saint Domingue, 85,000 in Martinique, and an equal number in Guadeloupe. Three-quarters of the whites in Saint Domingue were born in France, and two out of three were men, a factor that contributed to an increasing mulatto population, both free and enslaved. At the eve of the French Revolution, one out of every five Guadeloupan slaves had a white ancestor. In Saint Domingue, the free blacks were, at that time, as numerous as the white colonists.

Although a consistent percentage of the slaves were born in the West Indies, the increase in the slave population relied largely on the slave trade: 3,000 ships carried about 1 million slaves to the French West Indies in the eighteenth century, 15 percent of whom died during the Middle Passage. One slave ship out of three departed from Nantes, which was the main French slave port. More than three out of four ships went to Saint Domingue.

The conditions of slaves in the French West Indies were ruled by the *Code Noir* (1685) or Black Code, which was subsequently modified in the eighteenth century. Slaves were considered the property of their owners, who could sell or rent them. Marriages between a free person and a slave were forbidden, and those among slaves were possible only with the agreement of their masters. The **children** of slave **women** were slaves, although white French fathers tended to free their mulatto children and their mother. Slave children could not be sold separately from their mother until they were fourteen years old. Masters were obliged to provide **food** and clothing to their slaves, to heal the ill ones, and to provide the necessary care to their old and disabled slaves. All slaves should be baptized and instructed in the Catholic faith. Masters could beat their slaves and inflict corporal punishments, but they could not kill or mutilate them. The king's court was to judge slaves for their crimes. They were liable to death if they beat their master and to mutilation if they tried to run away.

In fact, as slaves had no legal status or right to testify, they were largely submitted to their master's arbitrary authority. Both the crown's representatives and the planters' assembly were unanimous in maintaining the slaves under their total subjection, and they did not hesitate to repress harshly any threat to the existing order. Whereas the *Code Noir* clearly distinguished between slaves and free people, it did not make any difference in rights between white people and free mulattos, who were still an insignificant minority at the time the *Code* was issued. The necessity to stress the superiority of the French to maintain slavery led to increasing racial prejudice and segregation. In the eighteenth century, at the request of West Indian planters, the French crown issued laws restricting the rights of free blacks—for example, they were prevented from exercising a profession or craft, and they could not serve in the local militia with white people.

This system, which was based on slave labor, the plantation economy, and the **monopoly** of colonial and slave trade by the mother country, enabled France to increase its participation in the Atlantic economy and increased the prosperity of French ports and their hinterlands throughout the eighteenth century. But it was seriously affected in the 1790s through the 1810s. The slave uprising in Saint Domingue (1791), the first abolition of slavery by the French Republic (1794), and the British occupation of Martinique and some of the Lesser Antilles (1794–) disrupted both production and trade networks for two decades. At the end of the Napoleonic Wars (1815), France had lost Saint Domingue, which became independent Haiti in 1804. Napoleon had reintroduced slavery in 1802 in the French colonies, but France forbade the slave trade in 1814–1815, although the implementation of the law was ineffective until the 1830s. Guadeloupe and Martinique, the main Caribbean colonies of nineteenth-century France, continued to produce sugar in slave-run plantations until slavery was definitively abolished in 1848, but the quantities were less important than French

West Indian production in the 1780s. As in the British colonies after the 1833 abolition, laborers in the second half of the nineteenth century were recruited on a voluntary basis in India. From 1849 onward, however, sugar beet fields in France produced more sugar than those exported to France by the French West Indies. The French Caribbean had ceased to play a relevant role in the French economy. *See also* Abolition of the Slave Trade, France; French Slave Trade; Haitian Revolution, The; Volume.

Further Readings: Adelaïde-Merlande, Jacques. *Histoire générale des Antilles et de la Guyane, des précolombiens à nos jours.* Paris: L'Harmattan, 1994; Butel, Paul. *Histoire des Antilles françaises, XVIIe–XIXe siècles.* Paris: Perrin, 2002; Moreau, Pierre. *Les petites Antilles de Christophe Colomb à Richelieu.* Paris: Karthala, 1992; Pluchon, Pierre, ed. *Histoire des Antilles et de la Guyane.* Toulouse: Privat, 1982; Tarrade, Jean. *Le commerce colonial de la France à la fin de l'Ancien Régime: L'évolution du régime de l'exclusif de 1763 à 1789.* 2 vols. Paris: Presses Universitaires de France, 1972; Thomas, Hugh. *The Slave Trade: The Story of the Atlantic Slave Trade, 1440–1870.* New York: Simon & Schuster, 1997.

Silvia Marzagalli

French Slave Trade

Together with Great Britain and Portugal, France is among the three European countries that together fitted out more than four out of every five slave ships crossing the Atlantic. French merchants took an active part in the Atlantic slave trade from the sixteenth to the nineteenth centuries. Evidence of **triangular trade** from French **ports** to Africa, then to the Americas and back to Europe, existed for the first half of the sixteenth century, although it is not until the seventeenth century and the founding of the first French colonies in the Caribbean that the slave trade was officially recorded as such. French involvement in the slave trade increased throughout the eighteenth century, when French ships were responsible for the transport of a million Africans to the West Indies. Although France forbade the slave trade in 1814–1815, French merchants continued to ship slaves until the end of the 1820s, when a more severe implementation of the ban considerably reduced the chances that a French slave ship would complete its voyage.

No material evidence exists confirming the exact nature of the trade carried out by the French ships sailing from France to Africa and then to **Brazil** or to Spanish America in the sixteenth century, but there are strong presumptions that they carried slaves. If French authorities clearly condemned the sale of slaves in France, as in **Bordeaux** in 1571, they did not prevent French merchants from shipping them to the Americas.

The crown, in fact, openly encouraged the slave trade after France established its first colonies in the West Indies in 1626. The American Islands Company (*Compagnie des Iles d'Amérique*), which the king's main minister A. J. du Plessis de Richelieu founded in 1635, was charged not only with settlement and trade, but also with the shipment of African slaves to the colonies. In the following decades, the French king authorized other chartered companies to ship slaves to the American colonies. In 1664, the existing companies merged into the West India Company (*Compagnie des Indes*

Occidentales), which obtained the **monopoly** of trade to Africa up to the Cape of Good Hope and to the West Indies. The French navy minister J. B. Colbert wished the company not only to introduce 2,000 slaves a year in the French colonies, but also to provide Spanish America with slaves; however, the company, which failed in 1674, was not even able to supply French colonists with a sufficient number of slaves, who were provided instead by Dutch **smugglers**. Other chartered companies, such as the Senegal Company or the *Compagnie de Guinée*, obtained the monopoly of the slave trade on a given portion of the African coast in the last quarter of the seventeenth century. In 1701, the latter merged with the *Compagnie de Saint Domingue* and obtained the Spanish *asiento*—that is, the contract to supply Spanish America with slaves—and kept it until 1713. In 1719, the French finance minister John Law granted to the *Compagnie perpeteulle des Indes* or East Indian Company (1719–1769) a trade monopoly to Africa, Louisiana, and Asia, including the slave trade.

As chartered companies proved unable to provide colonists with the quantities of French goods and slaves they required, the French crown first granted to French merchants the privilege to ship to the colonies, under the condition that they paid duties to the company. It 1717, it then authorized merchants living in major French ports to trade to the West Indies. Similarly, from the second half of the seventeenth century, chartered trade companies occasionally sold the right to trade slaves to individual French ship owners. In 1713, **Nantes** merchants obtained the right to introduce slaves into the West Indies by paying a sum to the *Compagnie de Guinée* for each slave they sold. In 1716, this was possible in Rouen, Saint Malo, La Rochelle, and Bordeaux, and the number of French ports that could outfit slave ships increased. From 1720 to 1726, the East Indian Company perceived 20 *livres tournois* for each slave carried to the French colonies, thereafter the sum was reduced to 10 *livres*. In 1767, this right was first perceived by the state, and then it was suppressed.

The French government tried to encourage the slave trade by different means, as the **plantation** economy developed in the West Indies. No import duties, for instance, were levied on goods imported to France that were reshipped to barter for slaves, and from 1688 to 1767, colonial goods bought with the proceeds of the slave sales in the West Indies paid half of the duties at their arrival in France. In 1776, a bonus of 15 *livres tournois* per slave was granted to those ship owners who traded slaves south of **Angola** or east of the Cape of Good Hope. The bonus was paid to prompt slavers to provide more captives, and hopefully less expensive ones, to the French colonies. From 1784, the crown moderately opened the West Indies to the foreign slave trade, but it increased the incentives to the French. French **slave merchants** received a consistent bonus—up to 200 *livres*—for each slave carried to those parts of the French West Indies that were considered most in want for slaves, such as the southern part of **Saint Domingue** or Cayenne. Meanwhile, foreigners paid a duty of 100 *livres* for each slave they introduced into the French West Indies. The duty was used to pay the bonus for the French slave traders. The French Revolution abolished all bonuses to the slave trade on July 27, 1793, and slavery itself on February 4, 1794.

The French slave trade revived during the peace of Amiens (1802–1803), as Napoleon Bonaparte reintroduced slavery in the French colonies, but it was hindered thereafter by maritime wars. By an additional article to the 1814 peace treaty, Great Britain obliged France to forbid the slave trade within five years and to restrict it to French colonies. Trying to flatter Great Britain, Napoleon banned the slave trade on March 29, 1815, when he came back from the Elba Island. After Waterloo, Louis XVIII confirmed the immediate ban of the French slave trade on July 30, 1815, but no attempt was made to implement the law until the middle of the 1820s. The abolition of slavery in the French colonies (1848) put an end to French participation in the slave trade. The last known French slave ship left Le Havre in 1849 and disembarked its slaves in La Bahia.

The French fitted out approximately 3,500 slave ships from 1714 to 1793, and about 700 from 1814 to 1849. It is likely that from the sixteenth to the nineteenth centuries, French merchants were responsible for the transhipment of 1.5 million Africans to the Americas. The **mortality** rate on French slave ships decreased in the eighteenth century, but it was still 12 percent in the last quarter of the century. The typical **cargo** of a French slave ship would include all sorts of **textiles** (the significant share of Indian textiles could partly explain the relative advantage of Nantes merchants, where the return cargoes of the ships of the East Indian Company based in Lorient were sold), arms, and other manufactured goods, both French and foreign, as well as wines and brandies. The nature of the cargo was determined by the region where the ship intended to acquire the captives.

Nantes was the major French slave port, and its merchants organized 42 percent of the eighteenth-century slave voyages. Their share diminished over time, parallel to the increasing participation of Bordeaux merchants in the slave trade (192 shipments from 1783 to 1792). In 1789, the French slave trade peaked with 130 slave ships. From 1802 to 1804, Bordeaux sent out twenty-one slave ships, eight more than Nantes. With 291 slave voyages from 1815 to 1830 (70 percent of the total French shipments), Nantes recovered its leading role among French slave ports. The loss of **Saint Domingue**, which became Haiti in 1804, and the progressive enforcement of the ban on the slave trade contributed to keeping the number of slave shipments lower than it was at the end of the eighteenth century. Nonetheless, the French averaged some twenty-five shipments a year between 1814 and 1830.

Saint Domingue, particularly its northern coast, was the main destination of French slave ships. The island received 60 percent of the captives shipped on French vessels to the Caribbean in 1714–1721, and approximately 90 percent in the 1780s, when foreign slave ships supplied other French colonies with slaves. By that time, French slave ships frequented all of the African coast from **Senegal** to **Mozambique**, but the bulk of French slavers still went to the region between Senegal and Angola. Half of the 27,000 slaves sold in 1789 in Saint Domingue, for instance, came from Guinea. Some 52 percent were men, 25 percent **women**, 15 percent young boys, and 8 percent young girls. *See also* Abolition of the Slave Trade, France; French Caribbean; Haitian Revolution, The; Trade Commodities.

Further Readings: The Atlantic Slave Trade: New Approaches. Paris: Société Française d'Histoire d'Outre-Mer, 1976; Daget, Serge. *La traite des Noirs*. Rennes: Ouest-France, 1990; Daget, Serge, ed. *De la traite à l'esclavage*. Actes du colloque international. 2 vols. Nantes: CRHMA, 1988; Deveau, Jean-Michel. *La France au temps des négriers*. Paris: France-Empire, 1994; Pétré-Grenouilleau, Olivier. *L'argent de la traite: Milieu négrier, capitalisme et développement: un modèle*. Paris: Aubier, 1996; Saugera, Eric. *Bordeaux, port négrier, XVIIe–XIXe siècles*. Paris: Karthala, 1995; *Les Anneaux de la Mémoire*. Web site: http://www.lesanneauxdelamemoire.com/.

Silvia Marzagalli

G

Galley Slaves

Using prisoners as forced, unpaid labor began in prebiblical times. It was in the 1500s that Europe began enslaving men for hard labor. French literature references go back to 1532, but an act written in 1561 approved the practice. Some time in the 1600s, it became an industry among trading nations.

The year 1628 began a six-year reign of terror upon French ships by Barbary corsairs. The English, Italians, and Spanish suffered no better fate. Men, **women**, and **children** were kidnapped. Women often wound up in harems, young boys in palaces as pages, and men sold for professions, or as laborers. Perhaps the worst off of the lot were those forced onto galleys as oarsmen. They were frequently stripped of all clothing and chained to long rows of benches, where they would spend upward of twenty hours a day struggling with heavy oars. Should the unfortunate fall asleep while pulling the oar, he was flogged until there was no sign of life and then tossed into the ocean. These captives were rarely released without payment of ransom. Seventeenth-century records show that the Spanish and Italians lost nearly 20 percent of their population to the corsair raids.

While the Barbary pirates wreaked havoc, galley slavery was not limited to the Algerians or anyone else. In Italy, it was common for convicts to become galley slaves: right alongside paid oarsmen. Free men could leave the ship. A convict would easily face a sharp edge for escaping his **chains** and possibly lose a nose or ear. Not all criminal acts were egregious; often misdeeds were political (or even had the suspicion of being so).

In an economic move that also satisfied the theologically motivated call for penance, slaves provided the propulsion for navy ships, especially at war. *La peine des galères* is still used to describe the ultimate labor. Retribution for sins was meant to be a preamble to hell.

And so, when Europeans built trading posts along the west African coast, it was a natural transition to receive humans as **cargo**. The trip across the Atlantic was called the Middle Passage. Merchants thought even less of the African slaves than they did of convicted ones. The bodies were lined up and tied or chained together in the ship's **hold**, and in any other space that could be filled. The captured received less favorable treatment than live-stock. Slaves were poorly fed, slept in their own feces, and frequently did not see the light of day until the ship docked at its final destination. It is estimated that 11 million slaves were captured in Africa. Only 9.6 million survived the trip to the Americas. There is no doubt that engaging in such cruelty occurred.

In a twist of fate, the European seafarers frequently became subject to severe treatment by the ship's officers. Many were kidnapped themselves and sold to merchant vessels for the purpose of moving the African commodities. The accommodations for these men were just as harsh as those for the galley oarsmen. *See also* Crew; Mortality, Crew.

> ***Further Readings:*** Lane-Poole, Stanley. *Story of the Barbary Corsairs*. New York: G. P. Putnam's Sons, 1896; Thomas, Hugh. *The Slave Trade: The Story of the Atlantic Slave Trade, 1440–1870*. New York: Simon & Schuster, 1997.

Corinne Richter

Gambia River

The Gambia River served as an important transit route for slaves arriving from the interior and as a point of embarkation for slaves about to cross the Atlantic. It runs for some 1,130 kilometers (700 miles) from the Fouta Djallon plateau in north Guinea westward to the Atlantic Ocean at the city of Banjul. From the Fouta Djallon, the river runs northwest into the Tambacounda province of **Senegal**, where it flows through the Parc National du Niokolo Koba. It is then joined by the Nieri Ko and Koulountou before entering The Gambia at Fatoto. At this point, the river runs generally west, but in a meandering course with a number of lakes. It gradually widens to more than ten kilometers where it meets the sea. The river's initial width of 600 feet is constricted to a twenty-foot channel by the Barrow Kunda Falls.

The river is known largely because of The Gambia, the smallest country in Africa, which consists of little more than the downstream half of the river and its two banks. Near the mouth of the river is James Island. This island was a place used in the slave trade. It is not named after the Dutch nobleman, James, Duke of Courland, who built a fort there in about 1651. It was named for James, Duke of York, after the English captured it in 1661, and the island became known as Fort James or James Island.

Fort James Island is located in the middle of the River Gambia about twenty-five kilometers upriver from Barra and was ideally placed to provide strategic defenses for whomever had control of it. It is in the middle of the River Gambia, about two kilometers south of Jufureh and Albreda. It initially served as a trading base for gold and ivory. The stock in trade then changed to slaves, most notable of whom was the legendary African slave, Kunta Kinte, portrayed in the movie *Roots*. He was one of ninety-eight slaves brought to Annapolis, Maryland, aboard the ship *Lord Ligonier* in 1767.

The island was held by the French, Dutch, and British. The British used the fort as a slave collection point until slavery was abolished. The fort was

Clothing styles, houses, and musical instruments, Gambia River region, early eighteenth century. Tracy W. McGregor Library, Special Collections, University of Virginia Library.

completely destroyed and rebuilt at least three times. The remains of Fort James can be found on this island today. The island was so small that it had to be extended to accommodate other buildings as well the fort. This was done by creating embankments supported by stakes.

Jufureh is another town lying on the north bank of River Gambia, near James Island. This village served as the main trans-shipping post from the mainland to James Island. Albreda was another slave-trading center on the river, and it was the main French post. It became a French trading post in 1681 and, like the English fort on James Island less than one mile away, it played a crucial role in the international competition for trade in the Gambia region. Later, when it came under English rule, many enslaved Africans were shipped from Albreda to the Americas. There are statues and works of art that remember ancestors taken from The Gambia outside the **museum** in Albreda.

The city of Janjanbureh, whose name during the slave trade was Georgetown until it was changed in 1995, is a major port city on Janjanbureh Island. The island on which the city is located was originally called Lemain Island. It is 176 miles (283 kilometers) upstream from Banjul, in central Gambia. It was ceded in 1823 to Captain Alexander Grant of the African Corps, who was acting for the British crown. He established it as a settlement for freed slaves in 1823. The island was renamed for Sir Charles MacCarthy, the British colonial governor (1814–1824). Janjanbureh island is six miles (ten kilometers) long and one-and-a-half miles (two-and-a-half kilometers) wide and is mostly inhabited by the Malinke people.

According to Alex Haley's account, it was the Gambia River that helped him trace his African roots to Juffureh during the 1760s. The Madinka words *Kamby Bolongo* were the few African words he knew to determine that his ancestors referred to the flowing water (*bolongo*) of the Gambia (*Kambya*).

An estimated 3 million slaves were taken from this region during the three centuries that spanned the trans-Atlantic slave trade. The Portuguese had reached this region in the mid-fifteenth century and had begun to dominate the profitable enterprise. Antonio, Prior of Crato, a Portuguese claimant to the throne, sold the trade rights on the river to English traders. In 1618, King James I of England granted a charter to a British company for trade with The Gambia and the **Gold Coast**. Part of Gambia became a colony of the Polish-Lithuanian Commonwealth between 1651 and 1661. It was bought by the Courlandish prince Jakub Kettler. During this period, Courland in modern-day Latvia was a fiefdom of the Polish-Lithuanian Commonwealth. The Courlanders settled on James Island on the Gambia River. They named it St. Andrews Island and used it as a trade base from 1651 until it was captured by the English in 1661.The Gambia itself was handed over to the British by the 1783 Treaty of Versailles, but the French retained a tiny enclave at Albreda on the north bank of the river. This area was finally given over to the British in 1857, which was confirmed by Queen Elizabeth I in patented letters.

During the late seventeenth century and throughout the eighteenth century, England and France struggled continually for political and commercial supremacy in the regions of the Senegal and Gambia Rivers. In 1807, slave-trading was abolished throughout the British Empire, and the British tried unsuccessfully to end slave trafficking in The Gambia. They established the military post of Bathurst (now Banjul) in 1816. In the ensuing years, Banjul was at times under the jurisdiction of the British governor general in **Sierra Leone**. The area was known then as the Senegambia region, and it comprised Senegal, Gambia, Guinea, and Guinea-Bissau. *See also* British Slave Trade; French Slave Trade; Portuguese Slave Trade; Trade Forts; Volume.

Further Readings: Boubacar, Barry. *Senegambia and the Atlantic Slave Trade*. Cambridge: Cambridge University Press, 1997; "Breaking the Silence, Learning about the Slave Trade, Slave Routes." Anti-Slavery International Web site: www.antislavery.org.

Oyekemi Olajope Oyelakin

Garcia II of Kongo (r. 1641–1661)

Garcia II, also called *Nkanga a Lukem*, was the ruler of the **Kongo** Kingdom (in present-day Congo, Democratic Republic of the Congo, and **Angola**) from 1641 to 1661. Don Garcia II based his power on political centralization, intense diplomatic activity with European powers, and state-controlled Catholicism. Under his reign, the Central African Kingdom reached the height of its prosperity and international prestige.

Garcia II seized power with the help of the military after the sudden death of his brother King Don Alvaro VI, passing over the traditional process of election of the Kongo King by high-ranking nobles. His centralized government was based in the great town of São Salvador (also known as Mbanza Kongo), the traditional political, economic, and court capital of the kingdom.

Garcia II elaborated an alliance with Holland at the outset of his reign and the Dutch occupation of Portuguese territories in **Brazil** and Angola from 1641 to 1648. By siding with the Dutch while refusing the establishment of Protestantism in the kingdom, he wished to regain control of the church in the Kongo and to denounce the Portuguese-led slave trade for its disregard for traditional enslavement laws and its bringing political and social instability to the region. During this period, he conducted military campaigns to regain territories previously lost to Portugal.

In 1645, the king, attached to Catholicism, which had been adopted as Kongo's state **religion** by his predecessor Nzinga Nkuwa (also called Affonso I) in 1512, welcomed a delegation of Capuchin priests in São Salvador and facilitated their work in the country. The Italian missionaries were sent by the Vatican's newly created Holy Congregation for the Propagation of the Faith at the demand of several Kongo kings over three decades. They came to revive **Christianity** in the Kingdom after fifty years of limited missionary activity. The Capuchins became active participants in Kongo regional and international diplomatic efforts, reinforced royal power by creating lay Christian congregations supporting the king, and allowed the kingdom more independence from Portugal and its clergy. Through them, Garcia II pursued direct and successful diplomatic relationship with the Papacy, culminating with his 1648 embassy trip to the Vatican through which he obtained, against the will of the Portuguese Crown, the appointment of a new Italian bishop in his capital.

The repossession of Angola by Portugal in 1648 marked the beginning of the decline of Garcia II's power with the unraveling of his alliance with

Holland and the Vatican and the growing control of Portugal over Kongo territories. In the last decade of his reign, Garcia II faced civil war against the rising Kongo province of Soyo and the rebellion of his first-born son Don Afonso, situations announcing the decades of turmoil that would follow his death in 1661. He was succeeded by his second-born son Antonio I (1661–1665) whose short reign ended with his defeat against Portugal in the Battle of Mbwila (1665) and the unraveling of the Kongo Kingdom. *See also* Portuguese Slave Trade.

Further Readings: Hilton, Anne. *The Kingdom of Kongo, Oxford Studies in African Affairs.* New York: Clarendon Press; Oxford: Oxford University Press, 1985; Thornton, John Kelly. *The Kingdom of Kongo: Civil War and Transition, 1641–1718.* Madison: University of Wisconsin Press, 1983.

Cécile Fromont

Gender and Slave Exports

The role of gender in the Atlantic slave trade is reflected in the gender structure of that traffic. Two-thirds of Africans sent into the slave trade from most African regions were males. The explanation of this structure provides some basis for understanding important characteristics of the societies of the Atlantic rim and must take into account both African and Euro-American processes. The well-documented tendency of Euro-American **plantation** masters to prefer male captives to females reinforced the lower trans-Atlantic demand for female captives and the corresponding lower **prices** for which they were sold in trans-Atlantic markets. But the African role went beyond merely assembling and delivering captives in the perfect combinations demanded in the external markets. The Atlantic market was only one of three overlapping slave markets. The two other markets were the domestic and the Saharan markets, where African captives were sold for **enslavement** in Middle Eastern and **Indian Ocean** societies. Atlantic buyers prized men, Saharan buyers prized **women**, and domestic buyers prized both women and **children**. The fact that women and children entered the Atlantic market at all underscored the mediating influence of internal African processes on that market, as in the other two. Interregional variations in the sex ratio were greater on the African side of the Atlantic than the American, suggesting a greater diversity in attitudes toward gender in Africa as well as a greater impact on the sex composition of the Atlantic slave trade.

The high male ratio of the captives exported to the Americas reflected women's important productive and reproductive roles in African societies. Despite the important role women came to play in the Americas, American plantation

Female clothing styles, Nigeria, 1820s. Special Collections, University of Virginia Library.

masters were reluctant to buy African women. This attitude reflected European notions of women's weakness, but protection from physically exerting labor normally given to European women was not extended to African women in the Americas, where labor and legal regimes treated them as harshly as men. Europeans exploited the labor of African women but underappreciated that labor in the slave market. This ambiguous attitude bespeaks the influence of culture and ideology on the slave trade, as well as fundamental differences in gender constructions between Europeans and Africans.

Africans placed a high premium on female labor, and this was more significant in shaping the gender composition of American-bound captives than Euro-American preferences. The widespread and extensive roles women played in African agriculture largely explain why most African societies sent relatively small numbers of females to Atlantic slavery. Evidence from much of western Africa overwhelmingly shows that women performed far more agricultural labor than men.

In the Bight of Biafra, however, the gender division of labor differed significantly from the above scenario. This difference explains why the pattern of female departures from the region deviated from the general pattern in Atlantic Africa. Both males and females contributed significantly in agriculture in the region, but the division of labor by sex was particularly clear-cut among the two groups that supplied the overwhelming majority of the region's captives—the **Igbo** and Ibibio. Although females performed a wide range of tasks, such activities as tilling the ground, planting and stemming yam, building, and climbing trees were exclusively for males. Unlike in most other regions, men in the Bight of Biafra played a key role in agriculture.

As the above case indicates, division of labor was primarily an ideological construction. The Igbo valorization of yam as the king of crops and its allocation exclusively to men shaped the slave trade in the region. Yam was a measure of wealth, had wide ritual functions, and was the most preferred **food**, although the so-called subsidiary crops surpassed yam in both quantity and nutritional quality. Yam agriculture was relatively labor-intensive and drew on some female labor, especially in weeding and harvesting. Because women did not primarily work yam, and were not acknowledged as important in its production, this region would have shown a greater willingness to dispense with its female labor. Conversely, women were vital to the production of the key agricultural products in the **Gold Coast**, Upper Guinea Coast, and West Central Africa, which sent lower proportions of females into the Atlantic slave trade. In Yorubaland, where men also did most agricultural work, the influence of the female-oriented Saharan market and different methods of enslavement would have kept the proportion of female departures low. In the Bight of Biafra, the Saharan market was marginal and the specialist warrior societies focused on headhunting, decapitating their male victims as a matter of honor. Surviving prisoners tended to be women and children rather than men.

The sex ratio of enslaved Africans had a notable impact on the African population. The departure of a high proportion of men left a preponderance of women and reinforced women's importance in the economies of

Atlantic Africa. The effect was negative because population growth is at an optimum when the sex ratio is close to parity. As historian John Thornton observes from his analysis of an eighteenth-century census in **Angola**, which is about the only place where a census count was taken during the slave trade era, the export of overwhelmingly male captives increased the dependency ratio for all working people, and the burden of producing for the dependent population fell heavily on women. It also affected the gendered division of labor. Because there were now 20 percent fewer males, women came to perform some exclusively male tasks or else these tasks were left undone. This development burdened women with basic subsistence production at the expense of production for the market and collateral economic activities. The model also demonstrated that the more balanced the sex ratio of the captives leaving a particular society, the more balanced the sex ratio of the population left behind, which allowed those staying to escape some of the ruptures in the division of labor.

Did the trade create a surplus of women and encourage polygyny in Africa? Information from eighteenth-century life in **Benin**, **Dahomey**, Upper Guinea Coast, and the Gold Coast suggests that polygyny was widespread in these regions, but European fascination with the institution gave it exaggerated prominence in European sources. In truth, however, polygyny does not appear to have been an automatic consequence of the high male ratio of the slave trade and was not as widespread as often supposed. Men married women primarily because of women's labor and reproductive resources and not simply because women were surplus. In one West Central Africa society, where the existence of a baptismal register for the years 1774 and 1775 permits a precise statement, the majority of marriages were monogamous. This is similar to the situation in the Bight of Biafra; however, although West Central Africa sent the second-lowest proportion of females into the Atlantic slave trade (after Upper Guinea Coast), the Bight of Biafra sent the highest.

Among the factors that shaped the gender structure of the Atlantic slave trade, the division of labor appears to have been critical. The productive roles of gendered persons in freedom and slavery are located within the gender division of labor, which is frequently at the core of gender construction. Differences in the ways societies allocated gender roles were reflected in differences in conceptions of gender, both among African regions and between them, on the one hand, and the Americas, on the other. The proven high work rate of African women, in both Africa and the Americas, never seemed to change Euro-American planters' ideas that enslaved men were more productive in plantation labor than their women counterparts, and not even significantly lower prices for females persuaded the planters that female captives were of much value. Although Africans placed greater value on female labor, like Euro-Americans, their attitudes to gender drew on both economic calculations and cultural bias, with culture probably being the stronger influence. *See also* Slavery in Africa; Trans-Saharan Slave Trade.

Further Readings: Eltis, David, and Engerman, Stanley. "Was the Slave Trade Dominated by Men?" *Journal of Interdisciplinary History* 23 (1992): 237–257; Eltis, David, and Engerman, Stanley. "Fluctuations in Sex and Age Ratios in the Transatlantic Slave Trade, 1663–1864." *Economic History Review* 46 (1993): 308–323; Greene, Sandra. *Gender,*

Ethnicity and, Social Change on the Upper Slave Coast. Portsmouth, NH: Heinemann, 1996; Morgan, Jennifer. *Laboring Women: Reproduction and Gender in New World Slavery*. Philadelphia: University of Pennsylvania Press, 2004; Nwokeji, G. Ugo. "African Conceptions of Gender and the Slave Traffic." *William and Mary Quarterly* 58, 1 (2001):47–66; Robertson, Claire, and Klein, Martin, eds. *Women and Slavery in Africa*. Madison: University of Wisconsin Press, 1983; White, Deborah Gray. *Ar'n't I a Woman?: Female Slaves in the Plantation South*. Rev. ed. New York: W. W. Norton, 1999.

G. Ugo Nwokeji

Gold Coast

During the trans-Atlantic slave trade, the term "Gold Coast" was used by European and American **slave traders** to refer to the stretch of West Africa's coast that roughly corresponds to that of modern-day Ghana. Portuguese traders gave the area its name in the 1400s when their explorations along the West African coast revealed that Africans in this area had abundant quantities of gold and were willing to trade it for slaves and foreign goods. European commercial interests in this part of West Africa focused primarily on gold for more than 200 years following the first Portuguese trade on the Gold Coast. The trade in enslaved Africans superseded the gold trade around 1700.

The slave-trading companies of England and Holland had the most active presence on the Gold Coast during this period, but significant numbers of enslaved Africans were also sold to traders from Denmark, Portugal, France, and the United States.

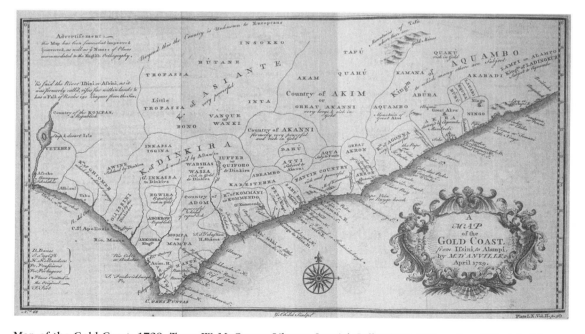

Map of the Gold Coast, 1729. Tracy W. McGregor Library, Special Collections, University of Virginia Library.

Gold Trade

The societies living near the Gold Coast and in its hinterland have been dramatically shaped by the gold deposits in the ground upon which they live. The gold mines of what is now Ghana were first integrated into the expanding trans-Saharan trade around 1400 C.E. The population of the forest region, which was later the center of the **Asante** empire, grew increasingly wealthy as a result of this long-distance trade. At the same time, between 1400 and 1700, trade between the forest region and the coast also increased. Trade between Gold Coast Africans and Europeans traveling by sea developed later and much more slowly than the northbound trade across the Sahara Desert. Nevertheless, by 1500, the king of Portugal was taking in about 22,500 ounces of gold annually from the Gold Coast. During the 1600s, Dutch, Swedish, Danish, English, and Brandenburg traders established fortified outposts on the Gold Coast to secure their involvement in this lucrative trade. The bulk of gold exports from Ghana's forest region continued over land into Saharan and Mediterranean markets, but the trade on the coast established an important precedent for the trade in enslaved people that developed in the later decades of the 1600s.

Slave Trade

The Gold Coast economy became fully engaged in the trans-Atlantic slave trade later than adjacent regions of West Africa because European traders knew that the development of slave-trading on the Gold Coast would impede the gold trade there. Although neighboring **Benin** and Nigeria saw a sharp increase in the export of enslaved Africans in the final decades of the 1600s, Ghana's coast became primarily a **Slave Coast** only in the early decades of the 1700s. Over the course of the trans-Atlantic slave trade, the Gold Coast was the place of embarkation for approximately 1 million enslaved Africans entering the Middle Passage, roughly 9.4 percent of the total number of Africans forcibly removed from Africa.

Fante Society

The rise of the slave trade in Ghana's coastal towns profoundly influenced the societies living nearest to the coast. Today, these people are known as the Fante. As slave-trading increased in coastal markets, the Fante transformed their government from a string of sovereign mini-states into a coalition of chiefs who were able to regulate the **price** of goods and enslaved people along most of the Gold Coast. As a result, the coastal population became more culturally unified during this period and was able to defend itself against conquest by their neighbors and rivals, the **Asante** empire. Some Fante merchants and chiefs profited from their activities as intermediaries in the trade between Asante and the coast.

Asante Empire

In the hinterland of the Gold Coast, the Asante empire ruled over an area roughly the size of modern-day Ghana from the early 1700s to 1896. The Asante state was created in the heart of Ghana's forest region toward the end of the seventeenth century when a chief named Osei Tutu claimed leadership over several prominent families in the area. Osei Tutu raised a powerful army and began defeating neighboring states, taking control of the major gold mines and trade routes. In 1701, Osei Tutu declared himself king of all the conquered people and declared a golden stool to be the symbol of his divine kingship. As European and American traders on the coast began to buy an increasing number of enslaved Africans in the 1700s, the Asante empire began to export large numbers of people into the Atlantic slave trade. Enslaved people sold by the Asante empire to coastal merchants were primarily prisoners of war seized by the Asante army in its many wars of conquest and re-conquest. Other people became slaves of the Asante empire through a system of taxation that required subject territories within the empire to give human beings to the Asante king as a form of tribute.

Forts and Castles

The Gold Coast is a unique part of West Africa's coastline because it is the site of an unusual number of fortified trading outposts built by European trading companies. Within a 300-mile stretch of coastline, more than sixty such structures once stood. Most of these forts were constructed before 1700 during the era in which gold still dominated coastal exports to European traders. The structures were built to house administrators and soldiers whose principal duty, aside from trade, was to prohibit competitors and **interlopers** from trading at sites claimed by the company. The largest and most well-known are **Elmina** Castle, former headquarters of the Dutch West India Company; **Cape Coast Castle**, former headquarters of the English **Royal Africa Company** and Company of Merchants; and Christiansborg Castle (**Accra**), former headquarters of Danish company trade in Africa.

Gold Coast Colony

The Gold Coast was the site of one of the earliest movements toward colonial acquisition by a European power in sub-Saharan Africa. After abolishing the slave trade in 1807, Great Britain began to pursue commerce in palm oil and other tropical products on the Gold Coast. As this trade developed, Britain extended its influence in political and military affairs among the African population of the Gold Coast. Throughout the 1800s, British troops allied with coastal societies in numerous wars intended to limit the extent of Asante control of the coastal region. Along the way, Britain declared the Gold Coast a Protectorate in 1874. After many other bloody wars, Britain finally conquered Asante and expanded what was by then known as the Gold Coast Colony to include the former Asante Empire in 1896. *See also* African Rulers and the Slave Trade; Barbot, John (Jean); British Slave Trade; Dutch Slave Trade; Elmina; *Fredensborg*, The; Slavery in Africa; Trade Forts.

Further Readings: Daaku, Kwame Y. *Trade and Politics on the Gold Coast, 1600–1720: A Study of the African Reaction to European Trade*. London: Oxford University Press, 1970; Fynn, John Kofi. *Asante and Its Neighbors*. Legon History Series. Evanston: Northwestern University Press, 1971; Hernæs, Per O. *Slaves, Danes and African Coast Society: The Danish Slave Trade from West Africa and Afro-Danish Relations on the Eighteenth-Century Gold Coast*. Trondheim: Norwegian University of Science and

Technology, 1995; Meredith, Henry. *An Account of the Gold Coast of Africa, with a Brief History of the African Company.* 1967 ed. London: Cass, 1812; Van Dantzig, Albert. *Forts and Castles of Ghana.* Accra: Sedco Publishing, 1980; Yarak, Larry W. *Asante and the Dutch 1744–1873.* New York: Oxford University Press, 1990.

Rebecca Shumway

Gorée Island

Gorée Island is a major visitation destination for people of African descent, especially from the black Atlantic societies of North America and the Caribbean, because of its prominent role in the Atlantic slave trade. Gorée is a small island off the Senegalese harbor in the capital city of Dakar. Roughly about forty-five acres or so, it is about a kilometer from the Senegalese mainland. One half of a huge monument to slavery stands like a colossus on the island, while the other half of the same monument stands on the seafront of the Senegalese coastline. In September 1989, the United Nations Educational, Scientific and Cultural Organization (UNESCO) designated Gorée Island a world heritage site.

On one part of the island is the infamous *Maison des Esclaves* (House of Slaves) from which about a million plus Africans were shipped to the New World during the Atlantic slave trade. On another part of the island stands Fort D'Estrees, probably the only circular fort in Africa. On the highest point of the island stands the castle, where a few heavy guns and batteries stand fearlessly. Although looking outdated and frozen in time, it ominously stares down at visitors and harks back to the European struggle for hegemony in West Africa among the Portuguese, Dutch, French, and English. A huge bunker below this gun connects with trenches constructed by the French and turned into a fort during the colonial period.

Fifteenth-century Portuguese exploratory voyages in search for the "gold of Guinea" and the legendary Prester John, the Christian king of Abyssinia, brought the Portuguese down the western coast of Africa. They landed on Gorée Island in 1444. In 1588, the Dutch captured Gorée Island from the Portuguese during a period of intense struggle for supremacy between the Dutch and the Portuguese on the West African coast. By this time, the United Provinces had rebelled against Spain and had embarked on a period of consolidation and expansion that culminated in the creation of the largest commercial empire in the seventeenth century. Gorée Island later changed hands between the Dutch and Portuguese before the British Admiral Robert Holmes captured it in 1664 as part of the British attempt to take Dutch possessions on the West African coast. The French eventually took the island in 1677 and made it an important center of the slave-trading activities of **Nantes** and **Bordeaux** merchants. These two French cities would eventually reap rich dividends in the eighteenth century from the Gorée Island slave trade. The French continued to hold the island into the colonial period, and from 1850 onward, especially in the 1880s, Gorée became the base from which the French military would launch their invasion of West Africa. In fact, the French fortified the island, built bunkers, and installed some of the heavy artillery that litter the island to this day.

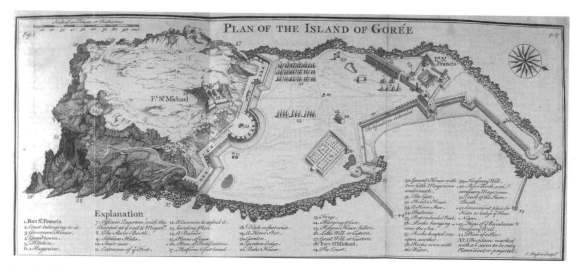

Gorée Island, 1728. Tracy W. McGregor Library, Special Collections, University of Virginia Library.

Using the island as a base, Louis Faidherbe (1818–1889) and later, Luis Archinard, Borgnes Desbordes, and other members of the *officiers sudanais* embarked on the creation of a French West African empire from Gorée, which extended all the way across Mali, Chad, and Mauritania. In the process, they initiated the establishment of the tirailleurs sénégalais, the first battalion of Senegalese infantrymen in 1857.

The House of Slaves is one of the major significant architectural edifices on the Island of Gorée. This red building epitomizes the slave trade and thus chronicles the role of Gorée as the transit point in the Atlantic slave trade. From the sixteenth to the nineteenth century, more than a million plus men, **women**, and **children** were shipped from the House of Slaves on Gorée Island. Some historians dispute the assertion that millions of slaves were shipped from the House of Slaves because it looks so small compared with the huge Cape Coast, **Elmina**, and Christiansborg Castles. But the House of Slaves compares favorably with most of the slave forts on the **Gold Coast** (now Ghana), including Fort de Santo Antonio de Axim, Fort São Sebastião, and several others. The Portuguese, Dutch, French, and English all struggled for control of the Island of Gorée during the Atlantic slave trade and thus Gorée was not inconsequential.

The House of Slaves was reportedly built in about 1786 by an Afro-French family described by some as the half-caste descendants of Jean Pépin, a navy **surgeon**. Gorée was a bustling slave port and the Senegambian region became an important slave-trading locale in the first two-and-a-half centuries of the slave trade. Like the forts and castles of the Gold Coast, the holding pens of the House of Slaves, all of them on the ground floor of the structure, could hold up to 200 slaves at any particular time. A porchway led to an open courtyard with rooms for domestic slaves, separate dungeons for male slaves, female slaves, and child slaves as well as a place for slaves considered recalcitrant or troublesome. Many were shackled to forestall rebellion or **escape**. The top floor of the House of Slaves, like similar slave pens elsewhere, had a wooden floor and, here, "palavers" were held between slaveholders and slave dealers. Buyers and sellers haggled over the **price** of slaves like commodities or cattle. There were also quarters for the European officials or merchants who lived there at the time, almost always with a small detachment of soldiers.

Besides the *Maison des Esclaves*, a number of other houses on Gorée Island were used as slave houses. Slaves from Gorée went to France, the French colonies, and areas under French control such as Haiti and Martinique. The French also supplied slaves to other European powers. Slave-trading from Gorée was stopped in 1794, resumed in 1802, and stopped again in 1807. The first stoppage was due to the impact of the French Revolution and the declaration of the Rights of Man and the Citizen by the French National Assembly. The slave trade from Gorée came to a halt until 1802, when Napoleon Bonaparte, under pressure from the French **sugar** barons of the Caribbean, decreed a resumption of the trade. However, the British later took Gorée Island and effectively banned slave-trading. In 1831, the British made Gorée the headquarters of the Africa naval squadron, which was tasked with checking illegal trading and **smuggling** of slaves.

In 1895, when Dakar became the capital of the colony of **Senegal**, Gorée was one of the four communes created by the French who sought to put in place the administrative system known as assimilation. The people of the communes of Gorée, Rufisque, Dakar, and Saint Louis could attain French citizenship and could be represented in the French Chamber of Deputies in Paris. Bliase Diagne would play this role through the World Wars. Gorée lost its importance and population to Dakar and, in 1944, Gorée was registered on the list of natural monuments and sites. *See also* African Squadrons, The; British Navy; Door of No Return; Entrepôts; French Slave Trade; Historical Memory; Museums; Tourism; Trade Forts.

Further Readings: Camara Abdoulaye, and Benoist, Joseph Roger de. *Goree: The Island and the Historical Museum*. Dakar: IFAN-Cheikh Anta Diop, 1993; Webster, J. B., and Boahen, Adu, with Idowu, H. O. *Revolutionary Years, The Growth of Afrian Civilisation: The Revolutionary Years—West Africa since 1800*. London: Longmans, Green and Company, 1968.

Edmund Abaka

Guerrero, The

The *Guerrero* (formerly the *San Jose*), under Captain José Gomez, was a **Havana** slave ship that wrecked off Key Largo, in the Florida Keys, on the night of December 19, 1827. It wrecked while being pursued by HMS *Nimble*, commanded by Lieutenant Edward Holland. The slaver was carrying a **crew** of 90, with 561 captive Africans, when she struck the Florida Reef, killing 41 Africans. The *Nimble* grounded on the reef five minutes later, just two miles away.

The next morning, American wreckers *Thorn*, under Captain Charles Grover, and *Surprise*, under Captain Samuel Sanderson, found the vessels. They were joined by the fishing smack *Florida*, under Captain Austin Packer.

The *Guerrero* had turned over on her side during the night and was full of water. The survivors were rescued and Packer set sail for Key West. En route, the twenty Spaniards aboard hijacked the *Florida* to Santa Cruz, **Cuba**.

The *Surprise* towed the British warship off the reef, but she could not sail, having lost her rudder. That night the *Thorn*, with fifty-four Spaniards aboard, was also hijacked to Santa Cruz. The 252 Africans aboard the *Thorn* joined the 146 from the *Florida* on the Cuban shore, the 398 people doomed to a life of slavery.

The *Thorn* and *Florida* were released by Gomez and arrived at Key West on Christmas Day. The repaired *Nimble* and the *General Geddes*, another wrecker whose crew had fitted the rudder of the slaver to the *Nimble*, had arrived Christmas Eve. The *Surprise*, with 121 male Africans aboard, had arrived on December 23.

The Collector of Customs, William Pinkney, claimed the Africans were under the protection of the Americans for they had landed in American territory. A demand by the wreckers for an immediate salvage award through their Court of Arbitrators drove Holland from Key West. The actions of the "court"—made up of wreckers—in tiny Key West had been notorious for years. Salvage awards were 50 to 90 percent of the ships' value. Holland would not submit to any proceedings at Key West and, with a 24-hour notice, sailed away on December 27 without paying the wreckers and leaving the Africans with the Americans.

That began a saga of heroics by U.S. Marshal Waters Smith of St. Augustine, and of inaction by Washington officials, primarily Secretaries of the Navy Samuel L. Southard and John Branch. Smith, unable to support so many freed Africans, rented those who could work to area **plantations**, including the Kingsley Plantation, now a National Park Service property. Finally, after Smith had traveled twice to Washington to see President John Quincy Adams, Branch arranged passage and all but three of the survivors, twenty having died in Key West and North Florida, sailed for **Liberia**. They left Amelia Island, North Florida, on September 30, 1829, in the *Washington's Barge*, having spent twenty-three months in Florida.

After eighty-eight days at sea, the *Washington's Barge* came into Carlisle Bay, Barbados, in distress. Governor James Lyon made arrangements for the continuance of the voyage on a Barbados vessel, the *Heroine*. On March 4, 1830, the ninety-one who had survived the voyage (nine did not) arrived at Liberia. There, their American-given names were recorded and they were settled in New Georgia, with the **re-captives** rescued by a U.S. revenue cutter off Florida from the slaver *Antelope*.

The remains of their floating prison, the *Guerrero*, still lay in the shallow tropical waters off Key Largo. *See also* Drownings; Havana; Returnees to Africa; Shipwrecks.

Further Reading: Swanson, Gail. *Slave Ship Guerrero*. West Conshohocken, PA: Infinity Publishing, 2005.

Gail Swanson

H

Haitian Revolution, The

The Haitian Revolution was the only successful slave rebellion in the Western Hemisphere. Beginning in 1791 in the French colony of **Saint Domingue**, it was prosecuted by the enslaved and *affranchi* (mulatto) populations of the island. The revolution was actually a series of conflicts between 1791 and 1804 involving transient alliances between these two groups, native whites, and French, British, and Spanish armies.

Saint Domingue was founded in 1697 when Spain ceded the western third of the Caribbean island of **Hispaniola** to France. During the eighteenth century, it became one of the wealthiest French colonies. **Sugar** was the primary export, but indigo, coffee, cocoa, and cotton were also produced. The deadly conditions associated with sugar cultivation made **plantations** heavily dependent on the import of African slaves and, by the end of the 1700s, the enslaved population numbered around 500,000, dwarfing the 32,000 white French colonists and 24,000 free mulattoes. Whites and *affranchis* were entitled to own property (although racial laws curtailed the privileges of the latter), but bondspeople on Saint Domingue were afforded no legal rights.

French revolutionary rhetoric, with its earnest promises of liberty and equality, had a visceral resonance for the colony's nonwhites. But there was a more local spark to the revolt. *Grands blancs* (the wealthiest whites) desired representation in the French national assembly to the exclusion of mulatto free men. As a statement of intent, whites increased racial acrimony by barring *affranchi* representatives from colonial assemblies. In late 1790, mulatto dissatisfaction produced a rebellion. Led by Vincent Ogé, a wealthy *affranchi*, it followed his unsuccessful appeal to the French assembly for voting reform. The insurgency was immediately crushed, and Ogé was brutally executed. Although he did not fight to end slavery as such, enslaved rebels later named Ogé's treatment as a motivation for their August 1791 uprising.

This first slave revolt enabled restive bondspeople to redress long-held frustrations. Plantations were burned, and brutal atrocities were committed on all sides—slave, *affranchi*, and free—in what came to resemble a civil war. Rebellious bonds-people murdered many mulattoes, who owned one-third of the colony's enslaved labor. In this, the slaves had outside succor. They were supported by Spanish colonists in Santo Domingo (on the eastern side of Hispaniola, later to become the Dominican Republic) and by British troops from **Jamaica**. In April 1792, in an attempt at appeasement, the French assembly granted citizenship to all *affranchis*. In 1793, Léger Félicité Sonthonax, sent from France to restore order, offered to free those slaves who joined his army. He soon abolished slavery altogether, and the following year the French government affirmed his decision.

The revolution's most notable leader was Toussaint L'Ouverture, a self-educated former domestic slave. In May 1794, General Étienne Laveaux convinced Toussaint to fight for the French Republic and expel the Spanish and British from Hispaniola. This expedition was successful. In 1795, Spain ceded Santo Domingo to France, although war in Europe prevented the transfer. In 1797, Toussaint was appointed commander in chief of all French troops on the island and from then on, to the consternation of Paris, Toussaint sought to rule Saint Domingue as an autonomous entity. By 1801, he had captured Santo Domingo, the eponymous capital of the former Spanish col-

Toussaint L'Ouverture, Haitian independence leader. Courtesy of Anti-Slavery International.

ony; declared all slaves in Hispaniola free; and issued a new constitution that provided for colonial autonomy and made Toussaint governor for life.

In retaliation, Napoleon sent a force of 70 warships and 250 men. By a ruse, Toussaint was kidnapped and imprisoned in France, where he died in 1803. The French had little further success, however. Their army was decimated by yellow fever (to which its leader, General Charles Leclerc, succumbed), subjected to rebel attack, and menaced by the Royal Navy. Leclerc's successor, the Vicomte de Rochambeau, pursued a campaign of such brutality that many loyalists defected to the rebels. Jean-Jacques Dessalines, former slave and one of Toussaint's generals, finally defeated the French at the Battle of Vertrières in 1803.

On January 1, 1804, Dessalines declared Haiti (the island's original Arawak name was reprised) the first free black republic. The country's immediate history was marked by invasion, interregional strife, and its leaders' assumption of monarchical powers. The unbearable **reparations** that it was forced to pay to former slaveholders interminably crippled Haiti. Yet its revolution would long represent a portent for New World planters and a beacon of hope for their slaves. *See also* Abolition of the Slave Trade, France; French Caribbean; French Slave Trade; Violence.

Further Readings: Geggus, David P., ed. *The Impact of the Haitian Revolution in the Atlantic World.* Columbia: University of South Carolina Press, 2001; Ott, Thomas O. *The Haitian Revolution, 1789–1804.* Knoxville: University of Tennessee Press, 1973.

Tristan Stubbs

Handbooks for Slave Traders

Handbooks or other forms of instruction manuals for **slave traders** provided guidance on various aspects of the slave trade, including the procurement, transportation, and sale of slaves. Depending on the handbook, instructions or advice would relate to daily activities, overseeing and managing slaves, discipline measures, caring for the sick, proper amount of **food** rations, and housing for slaves. Other handbooks discussed the business side of slave-trading, such as **profit** margins, overhead, and business practices at slave markets.

Slave traders, ship **captains**, and slave owners would consult handbooks. One manual carried aboard the nineteenth century slave ship *Bricbarca Lavigilante*, dating to 1822, included illustrated pages showing the preferred distribution of slaves on the slave decks, as well as placement of manacles, **chains**, beds, and other equipment. Edward Telfair, governor of Georgia and owner of a slave-trading firm in the late 1700s, discussed in his writings the management of slaves, their purchase and sale, the problem of **runaway** slaves, slave **mortality** rates, the difficulty of selling related slaves, and the relationship between whites and free blacks.

Further Readings: Hochschild, Adam. *Bury the Chains: The British Struggle to Abolish Slavery.* New York: Houghton Mifflin Company, 2005; "The Slave Period." [Online, November 2006]. Duke University Web site: http://library.duke.edu/specialcollections/franklin/collections/af-am-mss/slavery.html; Thomas, Hugh. *The Slave Trade: The Story of the Atlantic Slave Trade, 1440–1870.* New York: Simon & Schuster, 1997.

Leslie Wilson

Havana

The city of Havana was founded in the south coast of the island of **Cuba** in 1514 by Spanish Conquistador Diego Velázquez. In 1519, the city was moved to its current location in the north coast. From the sixteenth century, African slaves constituted a constant presence in the village, as the records from the Iglesia Parroquial Mayor—nowadays kept in the archive of the Cathedral of Havana—testify.

It was not until the mid-eighteenth century, however, that the number of slaves in **Havana** and its surroundings began to grow significantly. The expansion of **sugar** cultivation to the east of Havana and the British occupation of the city between 1762 and 1763 affected the future of the Spanish colony. Already in the late 1780s, Cuban planters began pressing for a Royal Order that would allow them to import African slaves freely. The economic collapse of the neighboring French colony of **Saint Domingue** gave them

Three Kings Day festival, Havana, 1850. Marion duPont Scott Sporting Collection, Special Collections, University of Virginia Library.

the perfect excuse to obtain more and more privileges. Following the outbreak of **the Haitian Revolution**, Cuba replaced Saint Domingue as the leading producer of sugarcane in the world, while African slaves constituted the labor force used to achieve this status.

During these years, the slave trade to Cuba, and particularly to Havana, intensified to unprecedented levels. The trade was carried out mostly by British (until 1807), American, and Danish slave ships. After 1803, however, Cuban-Spanish merchants entered the business and, within a few years, eventually became the main traders. In the countryside around Havana, large **plantations** defined the rural landscape. In Havana, slaves worked mostly as domestic servants. Those who managed to get their freedom settled down in the outskirts of the city—mostly in the Manglar neighborhood—and worked in different types of crafts.

After 1820, the slave trade was prohibited and a new, illegal trade flourished. Once again, Havana, alongside Matanzas, constituted the main destination for slave vessels. Well into the second half of the nineteenth century, slave **cargoes** arrived in the city and its surroundings.

The slave population in Havana was composed of several different African ethnic groups, most of them from West and West Central Africa. Notably Lucumi, Carabali, and Congo slaves left a huge cultural and historical legacy. For instance, most of the slave conspiracies and revolts that occurred in Havana during the first half of the century counted Lucumi slaves among their leaders and participants. The most famous slave movements of the period in the capital were the Aponte conspiracy of 1812, the Lucumi revolt of 1836 in the neighborhood of El Cerro, the revolt of the

Lucumi slaves of Domingo Aldama in 1841, and the Great Conspiracy of La Escalera in 1844.

The legacy of slavery in Havana is enormous. **Music**, religious practices, common wisdom, and several other aspects of the daily life in the city bear the manifest signature of the cultures brought by the slaves from their distant African places of origin. *See also* British Slave Trade; Danish Slave Trade; Ethnicity; Spanish Caribbean.

> ***Further Readings:*** Barcia, Manuel. "Revolts amongst Enslaved Africans in Nineteenth-Century Cuba: A New Look to an Old Problem." *The Journal of Caribbean History* 39, 2 (2005): 173–200; Bergad, Laird W., García, Fe Iglesias, and del Carmen Barcia, María. *The Cuban Slave Market, 1790–1880*. Cambridge: Cambridge University Press, 1995; Childs, Matt D. *The 1812 Aponte Rebellion in Cuba and the Struggle against Atlantic Slavery*. Chapel Hill: University of North Carolina Press, 2006; Eltis, David, Behrendt, Stephen D., Richardson, David, and Klein, Herbert S., eds. *The Trans-Atlantic Slave Trade: A Database on CD-ROM*. Cambridge: Cambridge University Press, 1999; Paquette, Robert. *Sugar Is Made with Blood: The Conspiracy of La Escalera and the Conflict between Empires over Slavery in Cuba*. Middletown, CT: Wesleyan University Press, 1987.

Manuel Barcia

Henrietta Marie, The

The **shipwreck** site of a small English slave ship, the *Henrietta Marie*, was located in 1972 on New Ground Reef by the well-known American salvage company Treasure Salvors about thirty-five miles west of Key West, Florida. A small collection of diagnostic artifacts was recovered in 1972 and 1973 under the auspices of the State of Florida's salvage program. The site then lay undisturbed for a decade after which the wreck was once again investigated. Archaeological control was initiated in 1983 and the site identified when the ship's bell was located with the embossed inscription "The *Henrietta Marie* 1699," which allowed historical research to be focused on one particular identified vessel and time frame.

Artifacts recovered in 1972–73, 1983–85, and 1991 provide a rare glimpse into the material culture of both a typically small West Indian merchant vessel and a vehicle associated with the notorious African slave trade. Perhaps the most diagnostic items recovered from the site are the dozens of wrought iron manacles or shackles last used in 1700 to restrain as many as 400 enslaved Africans within the confines of the ship's **hold**. Other artifacts include copper cauldrons for preparing meals for **crew** and human **cargo**, thousands of glass trade beads, various types of weapons, numerous tools, scale and scale weights, elephant tusks, logwood, "Voyage iron" or iron barstock, and perhaps the largest archaeological assemblage of William III era pewterware ever recovered from one archaeological site.

The artifacts represent a wide variety and large cross-section of late-seventeenth-century shipboard furnishings and slave trade merchandise. The first leg of *Henrietta Marie's* voyage from **London** to Africa is represented by pewter, trade beads, iron bars, and guns. These items were identified as cargo through examination of manifests and accounts from the same period as *Henrietta Marie*. Many of the pewter bowls were recovered still stacked (seventeen in one instance) with remnants of paper and straw packing material between each. Most of the recovered pewter, including large bowls, tankards, bottles, plates, and spoons, had maker's touchmarks stamped on them that have been traced to several artisans in London, England, and dating between 1694 and 1702. This tentatively identified the vessel as being of English origin and probably sailing during the late seventeenth to early eighteenth century.

Perhaps the most common types of slave-trading merchandise are the many styles, sizes, and colors of beads that the African natives highly prized. Most slave ships carried an abundance of these beads, and this vessel was no exception. A sampling of more than 10,000 trade beads have been recovered from the site, some found encrusted to various other artifacts, but the majority were found scattered throughout two separate areas of the site buried within bottom sediments. Most are composed of glass and are colored blue, white, yellow, or green. A few beads were the larger, striped varieties commonly called "gooseberries."

The journal of another slave ship provides a clue as to why *Henrietta Marie* had so much of this type of cargo left after visiting the African coast and perhaps even a clue as to where that visit took place. Another London slaver, *Albion Frigate*, sailed for Africa in January 1699, approximately eight months before *Henrietta Marie* left the same port. **John (Jean) Barbot**, *Albion*'s supercargo or person in charge of slaving operations, kept an account that mentions that there was little demand at that particular time among the Africans for wrought pewter or for the yellow and green beads. They chose, instead, the brass or copper rings called manillas that were worn around the legs and arms. It is reasonable to assume that two privately owned slavers registered in the same port might naturally tend to trade at the same locations along Africa's Guinea coast. Because such a large **volume** of pewterware remained on the ship and more than 80 percent of the more than 10,000 recovered beads were yellow or green, it would seem that *Henrietta Marie* probably ran into the same demanding trade conditions that *Albion* had experienced earlier in the year. Interestingly, Barbot's father by the same name was recorded as placing commodities aboard *Henrietta Marie* in London shortly before her final voyage in 1699.

Several examples of small lead mirror or picture frames have been recovered from the site. Various manifests indicate that mirrors or "looking-glasses" were carried by the dozens for trading purposes, and so it is probable that *Henrietta Marie* was also carrying them. Perhaps the most indicative of all the artifacts recovered from the site are the many sets of iron leg and arm shackles used to manacle the slaves during the Middle Passage or the second leg of the voyage from the Guinea coast to the West Indies. A large number of these shackles will usually indicate that a ship was involved in the slave trade.

In addition to the recovery of shackles and trade goods and the historical research made possible by the discovery of the ship's bell, further evidence suggests that the *Henrietta Marie* had been in Africa. In addition to slaves and perhaps gold dust when available, slavers were instructed to obtain as much ivory as they could afford. These "elephant teeth" brought high

profits in England, and the *Henrietta Marie* had a small number on board when she sank. The only evidence indicative of the vessel's last leg from the West Indies to England are numerous examples of dyewood or logwood, commonly used as a red or purple dyestuff. This wood was normally harvested around the Yucatan region of Mexico and present-day Belize, and shipped to **Jamaica** and other islands for eventual sale and transport back to Europe. The other cargo items listed as being carried by this vessel in various shipping records—that is, cotton, indigo, and **sugar**—were readily perishable and probably disintegrated shortly after the vessel sank and broke up.

In addition to the many artifacts associated with actual slave-trading practices that have been recovered from the wreck of the *Henrietta Marie*, many representative items of ship's furnishings and fittings have been excavated, including rigging elements, cannon, anchors, and a substantial section of one of the vessel's bilge pumps. Perhaps the single most significant artifact associated with the shipwreck, however, is the remaining wooden hull structure. A relatively intact section of the slaver's lower stern provides insight into the construction practices of shipwrights during the late seventeenth century and reveals valuable clues into the architecture of a little-recorded class of ship, the smaller trans-Atlantic merchant vessel. The configuration of the stern suggests a situation long suspected by some historians and archaeologists—that **slave merchants** frequently used faster-than-normal sailing vessels to facilitate higher profits because of the inherent problem of delivering live human cargo across the Atlantic.

Historical records indicate that the *Henrietta Marie* was a square-sterned, foreign-built vessel of 120 tons burden and registered in London. Archaeological evidence along with the fact that the English captured almost 1,300 prizes during recently concluded hostilities with France (King William's War, 1689–1697) suggest a French origin for the ship. The earliest identified date of operation as an English slaver (1697) is provided by one of six wills located of people associated with the *Henrietta Marie*. Sailing as a separate trader and therefore an **interloper** in 1697, the slaver departed England and made her way to the West African coast on the first of two known voyages. She arrived in Barbados in July the following year, taking on 114 hogsheads of sugar after offloading her cargo of 250 Africans. In 1698, the **monopoly** on the English trade in slaves held by the **Royal Africa Company** was thrown open to those who agreed to pay a 10 percent duty to the Company on those goods used for trade in Africa. Hereafter, the *Henrietta Marie*, while still a separate trader, sailed legally as a "ten-percenter." She appears to have wrecked a few weeks after departing Jamaica in July 1700 on the third leg of her second-known slaving voyage.

In 1991, the National Association of Black SCUBA Divers (NABS) in association with the Mel Fisher Maritime Heritage Society placed a bronze memorial plaque on the site near the hull structure to commemorate the millions of lives lost during the trans-Atlantic slave trade. In December of 1995, an international traveling exhibition containing many of the *Henrietta Marie* artifacts began touring the United States and the Caribbean. As of 2006, they had been viewed by an estimated 2 million people.

In June 2001, another expedition took place on the site of the *Henrietta Marie*, which was undertaken by the Mel Fisher Maritime Heritage Society, RPM Nautical Foundation, Inc., and the National Geographic Society. The research design entailed performing a more detailed examination of the remaining hull structure than had previously been possible. These efforts eventually resulted in a pictorial article in *National Geographic Magazine* (August 2002).

The shipwreck and its associated artifacts preserve an irreplaceable archaeological record that lends direct support to and complements a large historical data bank that survives relating to the trans-Atlantic slave trade through various letters, accounts, manifests, and other contemporary documents. The physical remains of the *Henrietta Marie* represent a rare collection of tangible evidence from the notorious Guinea trade and provide a unique look into one of the most dramatic eras of our past.

Further Readings: Donnan, Elizabeth, ed. *Documents Illustrative of the History of the Slave Trade to America.* 4 vols. New York: Octogon Press, 1965; Hair, P.E.H., Jones, Adam, and Law, Robin, eds. *Barbot on Guinea: The Writings of Jean Barbot on West Africa 1678–1712.* 2 vols. London: Hakluyt Society, 1992; Moore, David D. *Anatomy of a 17th Century Slave Ship: Historical and Archaeological Investigations of "The Henrietta Marie 1699."* Unpublished master's thesis. Greenville, NC: East Carolina University, 1989; Sullivan, George. *Slave Ship, The Story of the Henrietta Marie.* New York: Cobblehill Books, 1994; Steinberg, Jennifer. "Last Voyage of the Slave Ship *Henrietta Marie.*" *National Geographic* 202 (August 2, 2002): 46–61. National Geographic Web site: http://magma.nationalgeographic.com/ngm/0208/feature4/index.html; "A Slave Ship Speaks." Mel Fisher Maritime Heritage Society Web site: http://www.melfisher.org/henriettamarie/.

David D. Moore

Hispaniola

La Hispaniola is the name given by Columbus to the island today mostly known by the names of the two states Haiti and the Dominican Republic. Before the arrival of the Iberians under Colón or Nicolás de Ovando, a local form of kin-slavery, called *naboría*, existed between the Indigenous peoples. The Castilian, Genoese, and German elites of Santo Domingo used the indigenous as house slaves and as slaves for gold digging.

La Hispaniola was the first center of Spanish dominion in America, known as *Las Indias*, and from 1493 until 1508, it was the only one. From around 1495, La Hispaniola was the base for further expansion to other parts of America (including Puerto Rico, **Cuba**, **Jamaica**, Venezuela, Colombia, Panama, Florida, and Mexico) and for the establishment of slavery and the first **sugar**-*ingenios* near Santo Domingo and Azua. The first documented blacks arrived to Santo Domingo as slaves, servants, and members of the households of the *conquistadores* in 1502, coming as "Christian blacks" from the South of the Iberian peninsula. Santo Domingo became the first center of slavery and the slave trade in the Americas, and between 1518 and c. 1580, the island developed its first landscape of sugar-*ingenios* and mass slavery.

At the end of the sixteenth century, Santo Domingo and Hispaniola were losing their place as a slave center and only relatively few slaves from Africa or other parts of the Spanish empire were sold as house slaves to the elites of the island, primarily to Santo Domingo, headquarters of the Caribbean *audiencia* and archbishop. From the beginning of the seventeenth century very few slaves came in the transports of official **slave traders** to the towns of the eastern part of the island, where a new agriculture of stock-breeding arose. Most of the slaves arrived in the sixteenth century became freedmen (*libres de color*) and part of the peasantry of the island (mainly in the northern region of Cibao). The house slaves of the bigger centers were bought from **smugglers** from other islands (Jamaica, Saint Maarten, or **Curaçao** or, later, from the French parts of the island).

Although the Spanish crown attempted to eliminate smuggling and privateering in the northwestern and western parts of Hispaniola, French corsairs, pirates, and buccaneers started to occupy coastal parts of the island. From 1697, **Saint Domingue**, as the western portion of the island came to be known, became an official French colony. Both parts, Saint Domingue and Santo Domingo, established an economic, social, and cultural symbiosis, complementing each other. In 1795, the crown in Madrid temporarily resigned the whole island to the French under Napoleon. In 1802 (under Toussaint L'Ouverture) and 1822 (Jean-Pierre Boyer), the French-Haitian abolition of the slave trade was extended to slavery in Santo Domingo. *See also* French Caribbean; Haitian Revolution, The; Plantations; Spanish Caribbean.

Further Readings: Moya Pons, Frank, "The Establishment of Primary Centres and Primary Plantations." In Pieter C. Emmer and Germán Carrera Damas, eds. *General History of the Caribbean*. 6 vols. Vol. II: *New Societies: The Caribbean in the Long Sixteenth Century*, 62–78. London: UNESCO Publishing, 1999; Rodríguez Morel, Genaro. "The Sugar Economy of Española in the Sixteenth Century." In Stuart B. Schwartz, ed. *Tropical Babylons: Sugar and the Making of the Atlantic World, 1450–1680*, S. 85–114. Chapel Hill: University of North Carolina Press, 2004; Turits, Richard Lee. "Foundations of Despotism: Peasants, the Trujillo Regime, and Modernity in Dominican History." Stanford: Stanford University Press, 2003; Vila Vilar, Enriqueta, and Klooster, Wim. "Forced African Settlement. The Basis of Forced Settlement: Africa and its Trading Conditions." In Pieter C. Emmer and Germán Carrera Damas. *General History of the Caribbean*. 6 vols. Vol. II: *New Societies: The Caribbean in the Long Sixteenth Century*, 159–179. London: UNESCO Publishing, 1999; Watts, David. *The West Indies: Patterns of Development, Culture and Environmental Change since 1492*. Cambridge: Cambridge University Press, 1987.

Michael Max P. Zeuske

Historical Memory

History was traditionally considered an objective account of the past. That view is now challenged. Memory, considered closer to human experience, is gaining importance. Both are important considerations in the new approach toward the trans-Atlantic slavery past.

Individuals in a globalizing world are looking for their identity. Especially in affluent parts of the world, historical **tourism** has grown tremendously (Dorsman, 2000). People want to learn about their past and want to be able to identify the role their "group" has played in it. This calls for an approach to the past coined "heritage" (Lowenthal, 1996) or "memory" (Nora in Dorsman, 2000). Until recently, history primarily accounted for the past as seen through the eyes of those in power; heritage and memory are more democratic concepts. They are considered authentic, while history is increasingly viewed as artificial, cold, and partial (Nora in Dorsman, 2000; Peckham, 2003). For those who want to learn more of the experience of the enslaved, that partiality is extra meaningful: history was traditionally produced by those who established trans-Atlantic slavery.

That which is passed down through generations to become part of history or heritage is introduced into a new social context, which alters it. One could say that what we call tradition is in fact what our contemporaries have chosen to symbolize their culture and their past. Many "old traditions" have been invented during the forming of nation-states, a time when people invented their group identity (Anderson, 1985; Burke, 1997). Three agencies are distinguished in the passing down of history and traditions: namely, the selective view of those who produce memory; the interests of those who consume it; and the persistence of cultural traditions, which frame the representations of the past (Kansteiner, 2002). In memory, two types are perceived. The first, "cultural memory," includes the body of reusable texts, images, rituals, buildings, and monuments that stabilize a society's self-image, which is intended for the long term. "Communicative memory" comes into being in everyday communications. It is not organized and has a limited temporal horizon of 80 to 100 years (Asmann in Kansteiner, 2002). Because cultural memory of the slavery past, in this sense (like tangible history and images), is strongly influenced by Europeans, communicative memory is an important part of reinterpreting trans-Atlantic history.

The concept of *lieux de memoire*, or sites, events, and dates that form memory and identity, originally proposed for a nation-state (Nora), can be applied to groups as well. As groups differ in their interpretation of the past, *lieux de memoire* can become heavily contested areas of history (Van Stipriaan, 2004). This is certainly the case in the African diaspora: with the arrival of Caribbean and African migrants, the former colonizing countries became involved in the legacy of slavery, as did the other involved countries and transnational organizations such as UNESCO (the United Nations Educational, Scientific and Cultural Organization). The trans-Atlantic slavery past has enjoyed a renewed contemporary interest because of its enduring legacies, such as the widely divergent economic situations of the three continents involved, racism, and the African diaspora (Oostindie, 2005).

Because the debate about the trans-Atlantic past is important for politics and ideas about social and economic justice today, several subjects are shunned. Naming just a few, these subjects include "the participation of Africans on the supply side," "the background to abolition and its widely divergent timings," and "the issue of trauma borne in the African diaspora and its consequences in contemporary societies" (Oostindie, 2005, p. 68). Because memory and identity are so closely linked, subjects that a purely academic, historic debate would not evade have explosive results in a politicized, moralistic "memory context." "Heritage ... has become a field of political struggle," "memory has become a site of power where restitution turns the losers into winners," and "Europeans are being asked to remember what they were taught to forget: the acts of **violence** and the losses upon which Europe's prosperity has been dependent" (Peckham, 2003, p. 210). "One consequence of this may be the dissolution of a unified past into multiple local pasts, where ghettoized and antagonistic styles of remembrance, reflecting different group interests, compete" (Peckham, 2003, p. 214).

It seems as if, after a period of relative silence, the subject of the trans-Atlantic slavery past is now reborn in an arena of dissonance. This is a reaction that can be seen in other traumatic events in history like the Second World War (Landzelius in Peckham and Cole, 1999). A plausible theory is that these transitions are needed before groups are able to overcome the past. Another factor is the changing meaning of the concept of trauma. Before the Second World War, the word was primarily used in physiological context. After the war, it came to refer more to psychological wounds (Peckham, 2003, p. 206), gaining importance in the display of heritage.

Historians are moving closer to the fields of psychological and spiritual guidance and justice, disturbing the idea that critical historical research and emotional memorial rites are barely compatible (Dorsman, 2000, p. 197). Out of this recognition of trauma follows several public statements of regret pronounced by world leaders on world stages. The questions remain: What do these apologies mean? Can the past be pronounced closed? Can guilt be bought off?

Several authors agree that the past should never be put in the past. Both memory and critical, objective historical research should be kept alive, as should the debate between the two. Some state it is the basis for new and just states, built on the memory of the crimes committed in the past. An unfinished memorial can guarantee that these questions will continue to be asked (Griffin, 2000). An ongoing debate about contested heritage, especially in a globalizing world, is needed to remind participants that there is no "winning" argument.

Today, *lieux de memoire* of the trans-Atlantic slavery past range from private initiatives as rituals, awards, and beauty pageants (reminiscent of the cunning and courage of female enslaved) to national and transnational initiatives. Former colonies celebrate different aspects of the past in festive processions on traditional occasions, commemorating the official abolition of slavery or, in a proud twist of agency, commemorating rebellion and marooning. Monuments are erected all over the Black Atlantic. The United States, the Caribbean, and even Europe cannot ignore the presence of descendants of the enslaved in its midst. In 2002, the Netherlands erected a commemoration monument and, as of 2006, France similarly commemorated its slavery past. *See also* Folklore; Museums; Oral History.

Further Readings: Anderson, Benedict. *Imagined Communities: Reflections on the Origin and Spread of Nationalism.* London: Verso Editions and NLB, 1985; Burke, P. *Varieties of Cultural History.* Cambridge: Polity Press, 1997; Dorsman, L. *Het zoet en het zuur: geschiedenis in Nederland.* Amsterdam: Wereldbibliotheek, 2000; Griffin, M.

"Undoing Memory." *PAJ: A Journal of Performance and Art* 22, 2 (2000): 168–170; Kansteiner, W. "Finding Meaning in Memory: A Methodological Critique of Collective Memory Studies." *History and Theory* 41, 2 (2002): 179–196; Lowenthal, D. *Possessed by the Past: The Heritage Crusade and the Spoils of History.* New York: The Free Press, 1996; Oostindie, G. "The Slippery Paths of Commemoration and Heritage Tourism: The Netherlands, Ghana, and the Rediscovery of Atlantic Slavery." *New West Indian Guide* 79, 1&2 (2005): 55–77; Peckham, Robert Shannan. *Rethinking Heritage. Cultures and Politics in Europe.* London: I. B. Tauris & Co. Ltd., 2003; Peckham, Robert Shannan, and Cole, Tim. *Selling the Holocaust: From Auschwitz to Schindler. How History Is Bought, Packaged, and Sold.* New York: Routledge, 1999; Van Stipriaan, A. "July 1, Emancipation Day in Suriname: A Contested Lieu de Memoire, 1863–2003." *New West Indian Guide* 78, 3&4 (2005): 269–304.

Valika Smeulders

Historiography

In its broadest sense, historiography is the systematic examination of the records of human lives, societies, and how historians have attempted to explain, reconstruct, understand, and give meanings to humanity's past. With written, oral, and archaeological sources as its primary tools, historiography seeks to understand and give meanings to events in relation to people, society, and the socio-economic and political milieu that surround them. Unarguably, the historiography of the Middle Passage poses the greatest challenge to historians, because records, be they written or oral, regarding the Atlantic crossing are nonexistent or, when available, grossly inadequate.

The task of historians of the Middle Passage is to collect and record facts about the conditions of not only the human **cargoes** aboard the slave vessels, but also of the **crew**, merchants, vessels, sea, and kinds of experiences witnessed by all concerned during the voyages. Only through the systematic applications of reports, accounts, memoirs, testimonies of living witnesses, narrative records (such as previous histories, letters, and imaginative literature), legal and financial records of vessels and **ports**, and unwritten information derived from physical remains of past civilizations (including their relics and memorabilia, arts and crafts, and so on) can the historians of the Middle Passage make meaning of a drowned past. The relationships between evidence and facts about the Middle Passage are rarely simple and direct. Records may be decidedly biased, deliberately distorted, wholly fragmentary, or nearly unintelligible because of the peculiar nature of the voyages. Historians, therefore, have to assess their evidence with a critical eye and purge themselves of biases and subjectivity.

For nearly two centuries, slaves remained the most important reason for contact between the Europeans and the Africans. As Europeans colonized the Americas, a steady stream of Europeans migrated to the Americas between 1492 and the early nineteenth century. Demographic problems associated with the meeting of Europeans and the Amerindians greatly reduced the numbers of Amerindian laborers and raised the demand for labor drawn from elsewhere, particularly Africa. The shipping of enslaved Africans across the Atlantic was the largest transoceanic migration of a people anywhere in the world, and, while it lasted, it was morally indistinguishable from shipping **textiles**, wheat, or even **sugar**. Although it provided the Americas with a crucial labor force for their socio-political and economic development, it nevertheless led to population hemorrhage in Africa. Able-bodied African men and **women**, the very active life of the continent, were forced away from their places of habitual residence to become enslaved in Europe and the Americas. The Atlantic slave trade is a vital part of the history of some millions of Africans and their descendants who helped shaped Europe and the modern Americas socially, economically, and culturally.

The task of the historians in the reconstruction of any part of this forced migration and the effects it had for the enslaved Africans and the slave-owning Europeans and for the Americas covers the three continents on which the effects of the ignoble trade were felt. This occurred in an era when there was massive technological change, as well as dramatic shifts in perceptions of good and evil. Most records contain thousands of names of ships, ship owners, and **captains**, but no names of the millions of the enslaved Africans. **Plantation** records; church records of births, marriages, deaths, baptisms, and confirmations; and judicial and military records do offer lists of names, usually indicating the African national identity of these slaves. None of these records, whatsoever, have directly provided genealogical information on Africans who arrived in the Americas at any given time and any given place or on their African American descendants.

Through the available shipping records, not minding their inadequacies, historians must develop new insights into the history of peoples of African descent; the forces that determined their forced migration; and cultural, demographic, and economic changes in the Atlantic world from the late sixteenth to the mid-nineteenth centuries. Additionally, historians use these records to examine the relationships among slaving communities, warfare in Africa and Europe, political instability, climatic and ecological change, and other forces that determined the history of people of African descent.

The Middle Passage experience was not limited to the official records of one such crossing alone. It deals with the treatment of the human cargoes, who were separated and held in stuffy and unsanitary quarters that were not high enough to allow an individual to sit upright. During these horrendous journeys, which took between two and four months, Africans were shackled, **chained** wrist to wrist and ankle to ankle in pairs, and forced to lie naked and crowded together. They had to lay on their backs with their heads between the legs of others enduring smallpox, dysentery, yellow fever, and other illnesses. Because medical facilities were inadequate, some of the diseased were thrown overboard into the Atlantic to prevent wholesale epidemics.

For historians to make meaning and give explanations to these experiences, it requires more than merely shifting evidence from facts. Fact-finding is only the foundation for the selection, arrangement, and explanation that constitute historical interpretation and explanation. The historiography of the Middle Passage informs all aspects of historical inquiry, starting with the selection of subjects, themes, and experiences to be investigated, as the choice of a particular experience over the other is in itself an act of passing judgment that asserts the importance of such subjects, themes, and experiences. Once chosen, the subject, theme, or experience itself suggests a provisional model that guides the study and assists historians as they assess and classify the available evidence and present convincing, intellectually sound, and satisfying explanations and interpretations. *See also* Eric Williams Thesis.

Further Readings: Bentley, Michael. *Modern Historiography: An Introduction.* New York: Penguin, 1998; Collingwood, R. G., and Van Der Dussen, W. J. *Idea of History.* N.p.: Newman, 2000; Shotwell, James T. *The History of History.* N.p.: Harold, 2005; Eltis, David, Behrendt, Stephen D., Richardson, David, and Klein, Herbert S., eds. *The Trans-Atlantic Slave Trade: A Database on CD-ROM.* Cambridge: Cambridge University Press, 1999.

Oyeniyi Bukola Adeyemi

Hold

The hold is a storage area below the main (top) deck of a ship designed to store (or hold) **cargo**. In a restricted sense, the hold refers only to the area below the orlop, or lowermost deck of the ship, but the term is typically used to refer to any storage area in a ship. What is designated as the hold also varies by ship type. Although the area below the orlop deck is generally the primary hold, it may be divided into different compartments and store rooms, depending on the function of the vessel. Most historic vessels had multiple decks with parts or entire decks designated as holds. Various holds were designed to store different goods, from ship equipment such as anchors and water casks to trade goods to slaves.

For ships involved in the trans-Atlantic trade, the hold variously held manufactured goods from Europe (for trade in Africa), slaves and ivory (destined for the Caribbean or the Americas), or **sugar**, **rum**, and various other goods from the Caribbean (en route back to Europe). When ships were outfitted for voyages to Africa, the holds were designed to be large and spacious to make room for bulky goods. Once the ships arrived at port in Africa, the holds were converted for "stowage" of slaves. This generally entailed fitting dividers between decks and even adding extra shelves halfway between the floor ceiling of the deck to accommodate more people in the hold. Separate areas of the hold were designated for the men, **women**, **children**, and sick, and these areas were heavily controlled to prevent mutinies among the slaves.

Regardless of location in the ship, holds had notoriously poor **ventilation**. As a result, goods stored in the hold often rotted and spoiled, including the slaves. What little circulation there was in the hold generally came from a few port holes and ventilation shafts from above. These port holes rarely supplied enough air for the massive numbers of people (sometimes more than 600) who were crammed into the hold. The lack of air in the hold created a stifling atmosphere that, combined with the rocking motion of the ship, greatly exacerbated the illness and discomfort of the slaves. Some ships had better designs and allowed more airflow, but these were the exception rather than the rule.

As a general practice in calm weather, the holds were washed out at least once a day and sprinkled with vinegar or "purified" with smoke in attempts to mask the inevitably putrid smell from so many people forced into such small confines. Rough weather, however, not only made it impossible to clean the holds, but also the portholes and vents were shut to keep out the water, rendering the holds even more vile and unbearable.

When the ships docked in the Caribbean or America, the holds were once again modified to accommodate bulk goods for the voyage back to Europe. *See also* Trade Commodities.

Further Readings: Inikori, Joseph, and Engerman, Stanley L., eds. *The Atlantic Slave Trade: Effects of Economics, Societies, and Peoples of Africa, the Americas and Europe.* Durham, NC: Duke University Press, 1992; Mouser, Bruce L. *A Slaving Voyage to Africa and Jamaica: The Log of the Sandown, 1793–1794.* Bloomington: Indiana University Press, 2002; Pope-Hennessy, James. *Sins of the Fathers: The Atlantic Slave Trade, 1441–1807.* Edison, NJ: Castle Books, 2004 (1967); Walvin, James. *Black Ivory: A History of British Slavery.* Washington, DC: Howard University Press, 1994.

Rachel Horlings

Humanitarianism

Humanitarianism condemned slavery and the slave trade as inhuman and created a movement that fought for the abolition of the trans-Atlantic slave trade. When the British Parliament passed an act in 1807 to make the slave trade illegal, abolitionists, acting within the framework of humanitarianism, declared victory. A more sympathetic view of people and the world began to emerge in the second half of the eighteenth century. In England, humanitarians stressed the rights of the individual and spoke about the principles of liberty and equality. Abolitionists called for an end to slavery, arguing that it violated the fundamental rights of human beings.

William Wilberforce, a member of Parliament, with Thomas Clarkson and Granville Sharp, founded the Committee for the Abolition of Slave Trade in 1787. The antislavery campaign was vigorous for twenty years. Critical support came from **Christian** evangelicals and Quakers, many of whom gathered around the Clapham Sect and the able leadership of Wilberforce. Wilberforce and the evangelicals mobilized public opinion against the slave trade and worked to win the sympathy of the British Parliament and Prime Minister William Pitt. In the British Parliament, those opposed to slavery established the Abolition Committee, which lobbied to end the trade. Prime Minister Pitt became convinced that the trade was evil and a disgrace to Britain.

In the United States, the Quakers took a humanitarian position against slavery. The church questioned the morality of slavery and asked its members not to own slaves. Humanitarian religious dissenters established in 1775 an antislavery society. Abolitionists in the United States established links with those in England. They promoted the spread of **slave narratives**, such as that of **Olaudah Equiano (1749–1797)**, who spoke eloquently about the horrors of the Middle Passage and the brutalities in the **plantations**.

Humanitarianism was a moral campaign that recognized other important dimensions. First, abolitionists knew that slaves resisted bondage and were prone to **violence**. Resistance by slaves showed permanent hostility toward the institution and their own inhuman circumstances. Indeed, the humanitarians encouraged freed slaves to speak about their conditions. Furthermore, the abolitionists benefited from changes in the economy. The Industrial Revolution began to be felt in Britain from the second half of the eighteenth century, creating conditions in which production did not have to rely on slave labor. The aim of industrialists shifted to the search for new markets for their manufactured products, and it was contended that the trans-Atlantic slave trade actually constituted an obstacle. New industrial centers required more raw materials from abroad. Oceangoing vessels previously used for the slave trade were now being converted to carry cotton, palm oil, and other raw products. Changes in the economy in Britain and the **British Caribbean** led to the alternative explanation, credited to Eric Williams, author of *Capitalism and Slavery*, that abolition was possible not because of what the humanitarians did but because of the need to respond to a new set of economic circumstances.

Humanitarians did not talk about the economy. Rather, they spoke about moral values, Christian benevolence, and God's providence. They portrayed slavery and the slave trade as a moral failure and a deliberate act of wickedness. These humanitarians were successful in disseminating their views. They were able to provide written and visual evidence to support their antislavery propaganda. In Britain, between 1787 and 1792, they obtained about 1.5 million antislavery signatures, out of a population of 12 million, making this the most successful petition at the time. The impact of the humanitarians on antislavery was a major one, although the ultimate success of abolition must account for the economic changes of the eighteenth century. *See also* Abolition of the Slave Trade, Great Britain; Abolition of the Slave Trade, United States; Christianity; Closure of the Slave Trade; Eric Williams Thesis; Religion.

Further Readings: Anstey, Roger. *The Atlantic Slave Trade and British Abolition 1760–1810*. London: Macmillan, 1975; Coupland, Reginald. *Wilberforce: A Narrative*. Oxford: Oxford University Press, 1923; Solow, Barbara L., and Engerman, Stanley L., eds., *British Capitalism and Caribbean Slavery: The Legacy of Eric Williams*. Cambridge: Cambridge University Press, 1987.

Toyin Falola

I

Igbo

The Igbo refer to the people and language of a major African ethnic group whose homeland is in southeastern Nigeria. They are particularly well known as traders and entrepreneurs. In other parts of Nigeria, they are often the second-largest group after the native ethnic group, and significant numbers of Igbo reside across West Africa. Estimates of the Igbo population range widely from 18 to 35 million. Igbo-speaking people accounted for at least 60 percent of all captives that departed from the Bight of Biafra during the Atlantic slave trade era, with proportionately high numbers of them going to the **British Caribbean**, Haiti, and Virginia.

With some exceptions, the Igbo social organization was characterized by noncentralized political arrangements that gave prominent civic roles to elders, age-sets, and, in some instances, secret societies. Before the twentieth century, Igbo **religion** was dominated by a belief that espoused "Chi" (personal god), ancestors, and a pantheon of localized deities, all subordinated to "Chukwu" (Grand God). The Igbo believed in life after death, where good people enjoyed and bad ones suffered. This cosmogony seems to have contributed to the frequently reported Igbo tendency to commit **suicide** under American slavery, to speed up their transition to better life. The Igbo overwhelmingly became **Christians** during the course of the twentieth century.

Although the Igbo region has been continually occupied since Neolithic times, it is unclear when and how a self-identifying Igbo group emerged in present Igboland. Existing explanations usually seek a single origin, but these narratives of ethnogenesis are misleading and often ahistorical. Invariably, waves of immigrants—irrespective of origins and specific periods of arrival—would have met people in the region, and some groups who were not Igbo became so over time. Some claim that the Igbo ethnic identity was forged in the Americas through the activities of the Igbo diaspora and that this identity strengthened during twentieth-century British colonial rule. Indeed, many groups that have become Igbo in the nineteenth and twentieth centuries were not Igbo in earlier times, but the existence of pre–Atlantic slave trade towns of Amaigbo (Igbo Square) and Igboukwu (Grand Igbo) indicates that people of central Igboland, or at least some of them, had identified themselves as Igbo for many centuries and that notions of an Igbo identity would have trickled from Igboland to the Americas rather than the other way around. The Atlantic slave trade and colonialism merely facilitated the expansion of the modern Igbo identity.

The Igbo were relative latecomers to Western education, but they made up rapidly in the first half of the twentieth century, attaining prominence in civil service and the military. The Nigerian civil war of 1967–70 and the defeat of the Igbo-dominated secessionist Biafra were major turning points in the Igbo experience. The war resulted from the Igbo quest for security and self-determination in the wake of massacres of Igbo residents in northern Nigeria, which was a reaction to a 1966 bloody military coup led by mostly Igbo army officers. The defeat of Biafra resulted in a declining Igbo influence in Nigeria, leading some borderland groups to repudiate Igbo identity. *See also* African Rulers and the Slave Trade; Aro; Arochukwu; Slavery in Africa.

Further Readings: Afigbo, Adiele E. *Ropes of Sand: Studies in Igbo History and Culture.* Ibadan: University Press, 1981; Harneit-Sievers, Axel. *Constructions of Belonging: Igbo Communities and the Nigerian State in the Twentieth Century.* Rochester, NY: University of Rochester Press, 2006; Isichei, Elizabeth. *A History of the Igbo People.* New York: St. Martin's Press, 1976; Nwokeji, G. Ugo. "The Atlantic Slave Trade and Population Density: A Historical Demography of the Biafran Hinterland." *Canadian Journal of African Studies* 34 (2000): 616–655; Uchendu, Victor C. *The Igbo of Southeastern Nigeria.* Toronto: Holt, Rinehart & Winston, 1965.

G. Ugo Nwokeji

Illegal Slave Trade, Brazil

Technically, the illegal slave trade to Brazil commenced in 1815 when the Portuguese government signed a treaty with Britain to cease all trade in slaves north of the equator. Although this treaty was to a certain extent aimed at checking the slave trade between the Mina coast and **Brazil**, it was violated right from the start. The disregard for the 1815 treaty soon compelled Britain and Portugal to sign an additional agreement in 1817, which provided for the enforcement of the partial ban on the slave trade. This measure did not also end the traffic. Rather, like the earlier treaty, it stimulated both legal and illegal slave-trading much to the frustration of the British. In view of the failure of these pioneering antislave-trade agreements, Britain ultimately had to negotiate directly with Brazilian authorities. Thus, in 1828, it pressured the latter into signing a treaty to end the slave trade to all areas within its jurisdiction by 1831. Despite this new initiative, however, the illegal slave trade to Brazil expanded and, by 1836, it had gained sufficient acceptance to permit vessels engaged in the business to obtain **insurance**. By this date, illegal **slave traders** were also emboldened and scornful of authorities. For instance, they published announcements of their activities with impunity.

Accordingly, hundreds of thousands of Africans were transported into Brazil over the course of the illegal slave trade. To achieve this scale, slave ships and slave merchants used diverse tactics to frustrate the enforcement of relevant legislations. For instance, they bribed government officials, assassinated magistrates, used flags that gave them immunity from arrest on slave ships, and illegally established **barracoons** and escarpments suitable for disembarking slaves at many points on the irregular coast of the province of Rio de Janeiro and elsewhere. It must be noted, however, that illegal slave traders were not solely responsible for the failure of various antislave-trade legislations. Other factors include a strong general conviction that slavery and the slave trade were essential to the Brazilian economy, the resentment of British interference in the internal affairs of Brazil, the unpopularity of the steps that the Brazilian government had taken (voluntary or otherwise) to suppress the trade, and the continuing demand for slaves in the Brazilian market (particularly in the coffee-growing provinces). Simply put, custom and economic forces generally made the Brazilian government, among others, reluctant to end the illegal slave trade.

Given the reluctance of the Brazilian government to end the illegal slave trade, Britain continued to take independent measures to check the business. Thus, in 1846, it ultimately passed a bill (popularly known as the Aberdeen Bill) that authorized its navy to deal with slave ships as if they were pirate ships and approved the trial of arrested traffickers in Britain. Although this British effort subsequently contributed to the end of the illegal slave trade in 1851, other factors, such as the escalating **prices** of slaves and the increasing moral revulsion against the business within Brazil, influenced the process. *See also* Abolition of the Slave Trade, Great Britain; Internal Slave Trade, Brazil; Portuguese Slave Trade; Supply and Demand.

Further Reading: Conrad, Robert Edgar. *World of Sorrow: The African Slave Trade to Brazil.* Baton Rouge: Louisiana State University Press, 1986.

Mohammed Bashir Salau

Illegal Slave Trade, Spanish Caribbean

After the abolition of slave trade in 1807, Spaniards were allowed to trade south of the equator until May 20, 1820; however, they engaged in the slave trade much longer. Following demand in Great Britain and the United States, **sugar** estates increased significantly from 1,000 in 1827 to 1,650 in 1850. The exponential growth in the sugar **plantations** prompted demand for slave labor. Attempts by Cuban planters toward mechanization of the sugar industry could not mitigate the labor needs. The profitability of the trade equally provided a stimulus for the importation of slaves. **Cuba** was the main destination of the illegal slave trade and thousands of Africans were brought there, despite British efforts to stop the trade and knowledge by Cuban authorities. The slave population in Cuba continued to soar. This was because many Cuban planters opposed interdiction of the illegal slave trade that could drain plantations of their labor supply. An estimated 372,449 slaves were imported to Cuba before the slave trade legally ended, and at least 123,775 were imported between 1821 and 1853. The system of slave trade suppression was less effective in Cuba.

Despite British efforts to end the slave trade, Spanish and Portuguese ships carried slaves to Cuba after the suppression in 1820. The British government suggested that slaves continued to be imported because the demand for slaves was still high. Slave ships used fraudulent and clandestine means to traffic Africans to the Caribbean. On June 28, 1835, the Anglo-Spanish agreement on the slave trade was renewed and enforcement was tightened. British cruisers were authorized to arrest suspected Spanish slavers and bring them before mixed commissions established in **Sierra Leone** and **Havana**. Vessels carrying slaving equipment were declared prima facie to be slavers. In 1841, Nicholas Trist was dismissed as U.S. consul in Havana amid allegations that he connived in, or took no effort to suppress, frequent illegal sales of U.S. vessels to Spanish **slave traders**. Later,

Parliament ... proposed a uniform set of punishments for all those captured on the high seas while engaged in the illegal slave trade. There were seven punishments listed:

1. Captain, Master, Pilot, and Crew of any Spanish vessel involved will be found guilty of piracy and be sentenced to ten years at the galleys.
2. Captain, Master, Pilot, and Crew of a vessel being prepared to pick up slaves will serve two years in prison if they have not left port. If they are at sea but have not done anything involved with the slave trade yet, they will be sentenced to four years at the galleys. If negotiations have taken place for the purchase of slaves, they will spend six years at the galleys.
3. The owner(s) of a vessel engaged in the slave trade will be punished like the Captain, unless they can prove that the object they proposed for the vessel did not involve slave trade, and the object and cargo of the vessel changed after her departure from port.
4. The purchaser of African Negroes will be sentenced to six years at the galleys.
5. The owner(s) of a vessel that knowingly equip her for another fitter-out to go on a voyage to Africa will suffer half the punishment to be indicted on the fitter-out.
6. All African Negroes are declared free when landing in Spanish possession.
7. Crimes against Africans on ships will be punished with penalties established by Spanish laws against such offenses when committed against free white Christian peoples. (Irwin, "The Illegal Slave Trade to Cuba after Emancipation")

These consequences, if implemented, could have helped stop the slave trade. This list of punishments came from Britain, however, and the punishments were supposed to be implemented in Spanish territories. The Spanish government would not let the sovereignty of their government be challenged, so they seldom enforced these punishments.

The illegal slave trade to Cuba was no secret. It continued for many years, until it was finally stopped in the 1860s. *See also* Abolition of the Slave Trade, Great Britain; Closure of the Slave Trade; Spanish Caribbean.

Further Readings: Irwin, Lynsey. "The Illegal Slave Trade to Cuba after Emancipation." University of Miami Digital Library: http://scholar.library.miami.edu/emancipation/trade1.htm; Martniez-Fernandez, L. "The Sweet and the Bitter: Cuban and Puerto Rican Responses to the Mid-Nineteenth Century Sugar Challenge." In V. A. Shepherd and H. McD. Beckles, eds. *Caribbean Slavery in the Atlantic World: A Student Reader*, 506–517. Kingston: Ian Randle Publishers Ltd., 2000).

Rasheed Olaniyi

Indentured Servants

Indentured servants were people contracted to work for a specific amount of time in exchange for training, living expenses, land, or some other form of compensation. Like slaves, they were viewed as property and, as such, could be sold or traded like any other commodity. Their fate, however, was more favorable in that they regained their freedom upon completion of their term of service. Terms were usually seven years long but varied conditionally.

Indentured servitude was a result of rampant unemployment in England early in the seventeenth century. Many Englishmen wanted to relocate to America in search of better financial opportunities but lacked the means to make such a trek plausible. Men and **women** of varying ages, experience, and financial backgrounds looked upon this as a prime opportunity, although the most common type of servant was the single male between his late teens and early twenties. Also, as the English economy began to improve, servants started coming from additional regions such as Scotland, Ireland, Wales, and Germany.

Although indentured servants volunteered for their posts, not all ended up there as a result of their own free will:

> Labor recruiters promoted Virginia as a paradise on earth and an open society where laborers were sure to become landholders. Yet in 1623, Richard Frethorne ... made the bitter claim that many Englishmen would give one of their limbs to be back in England. ... It is a reminder that after a decade-and-a-half of settlement, indentured servants were far from realizing the dream ... that had lured many to mortgage their futures. (Shifflett, "Indentured Servants and the Pursuits of Happiness")

It was around 1620 when the Virginia Company first organized the indentured servant infrastructure. Company agents sponsored the transportation of Britons across the Atlantic and arranged for them to be sold to planters in Virginia. The planters then reimbursed the Company for transportation costs.

The Company managed to convince hundreds of thousands of struggling Britons that indentured servitude was a worthwhile endeavor by pitching it as an investment in one's future. But if those considering a term of servitude knew exactly what they were getting into, they likely would have been disinclined to acquiesce. Instead of working in pleasant venues such as gardens and orchards where they could hone their craft—which is what most were promised—they were sent to do grueling manual labor in the tobacco and **sugar** fields of Virginia and Maryland. Their masters often scolded them and beat them in an attempt to force them to work more efficiently. Many servants died in these inhospitable conditions; those who survived often attempted to flee. That was a risky venture, though, as unruly servants were punished by having their contracts extended against their will.

In fact, masters frequently turned to underhanded tactics such as impregnating their female servants and accusing the males of stealing to justify the enforcement of a contract extension. This created an uncomfortable living dynamic, because the servants usually stayed in the homes of their masters.

The rights of indentured servants were severely limited. They were not allowed to marry, travel, vote, or barter without the consent of their owners. Female servants were often **raped** or otherwise sexually assaulted by their masters, often with no legal recourse. It is not as if their rights were completely nonexistent, though. They could own property, bring suit, and testify in court.

Although the inhumane conditions that many indentured servants endured evoke comparisons to slaves of the same era, the two groups were certainly on different planes. Servants entered into their contracts voluntarily and were respected more because of that autonomy. Some servants were respected more than others. Certain skilled adults would enter into a service contract to help traverse rough financial times. Those contracts could be as short as four years and involve less labor-intensive work. On the other end of the spectrum, unskilled adolescents would agree to contracts as they tried to support themselves until they were old enough to marry; those contracts could run more than ten years in length and demanded physically challenging fieldwork. Additionally, those who had agreed to contracts or "indentures" with American colonists before the trans-Atlantic passage were far better off than those who were merely assigned to contracts upon their arrival. Those subject to auction would be advertised in the *Virginia Gazette* in what is equivalent to a modern-day classified ad. A sample headline would read, "Just arrived at Leedstown, the Ship Justitia, with about one Hundred Healthy Servants, Men Women and Boys. . . . The Sale will commence on Tuesday the 2nd of April."

Servants played a vital role in the development of America's economy. At first, servants were used primarily to harvest sugar and tobacco. As those markets began to boom, planters began to use cheaper slave labor to do the fieldwork while the servants moved into supervisory roles. As slaves became more competent in managing this fieldwork, they began to take over those lead roles, forcing indentured servants to ply their services in a new craft. Some servants branched out into fields like construction, iron making, and shipbuilding, while others moved into precision or semi-artistic trades.

Indentured servitude essentially ended in America by 1800. Part of the reason for that is that trans-Atlantic fares became much more affordable, thereby diminishing the need to sell one's self into servitude to afford the journey. Another reason was the growing racial tension in America between African slaves and their Caucasian masters. Slaves were being looked down on as pitiful specimens, and so to volunteer for a term of servitude would be equitable to choosing such a supposedly pitiful existence.

Indentured servants who made it successfully to the end of their contracts were provided by their masters with clothing, two hoes, three barrels of corn, and fifty acres of land, although those specific allotments depended on the servant's colony of residence. More servants died in poverty than ever achieved financial security or elite social stature. It has been estimated that 75 percent or more of Virginia's seventeenth-century settlers were servants. *See also* Ethnicity.

Further Readings: Dabney, V. *Virginia: The New Domain.* Virginia: University of Virginia Press, 1971; Galenson, D. W. *White Servitude in Colonial America.* New York:

Cambridge University Press, 1981; "Indentured Servants' Experiences 1600–1700." January 2006. [Online, November 2, 2006]. TeacherVision.com Web site: http://www.teachervision.fen.com/slavery-us/american-colonies/3848.html; Menard, Russell. "Indentured Servitude." October 30, 2006. [Online, November 2, 2006]. Answers.com Web site: http://www.answers.com/topic/indentured-servant; Shifflett, Crandall. "Indentured Servants and the Pursuits of Happiness." Folger Shakespeare Library: http://www.folger.edu/html/folger_institute/Jamestown/c_shifflet.htm; Smith, A. B. *Colonists in Bondage*. Chapel Hill: University of North Carolina Press, 1947.

Michael Lombardo

Indian Ocean

The Indian Ocean had a longer history of the slave trade when compared with its Atlantic counterpart. The history of slave-trading in the Indian Ocean dates back to about 1,000 years before the trans-Atlantic slave trade began in the fifteenth century. As early as the eighteenth dynasty (1580 B.C.), ships were sailing from Egypt to northern Somaliland with the specific aim of obtaining slaves. There is reference to the trade in slaves from East Africa to Alexandria in the early second century C.E. The large number of black slaves in the Persian Gulf area attests to the presence of a slave trade, which precedes the rise of **Islam**. The slave trade was intensified as Islam grew. Arab traders established posts on the East African coast as far as Zanzibar, probably as early as the ninth century. Slaves were captured and sold by Arabs whose influence in the development of the Swahili civilization of East Africa remains undisputed. The integral position that slavery occupied in medieval Islamic societies was a factor that facilitated the buying, selling, and transportation of slaves along the Indian Ocean. Slaves from East Africa found their way to the Middle East where they were called *Zanj*. Some were also shipped to India, China, and Indonesia.

As the trans-Atlantic slave trade was beginning in the fifteenth century, it marked the gradual decline of the ancient slave trade, which dates back to the early second century C.E. The ancient slave trade did not disappear completely, but rather went hand in hand with the new trade. The Indian Ocean slave trade, which began to appear from the sixteenth century, is called "colonial" because it was carried out by French, Portuguese, Danes, and British.

The Portuguese were instrumental in pioneering the colonial slave trade in the Indian Ocean. Their initial motives for exploring the Indian Ocean were similar to that of the Atlantic, that is, the quest for gold and spices. When they visited the towns along the East African coast at the beginning of the sixteenth century, they noted that slaves wore simple loincloths. They reported that the buildings were beautiful and that the social elites wore silk and jewels. The Portuguese, through the intermediary of Malagasy chieftains, acquired slaves from the northern part of the island. They tended to prefer the northwest part of the coast because it was a layover point between **Mozambique** and Goa.

The Portuguese were later joined by the French, Dutch, British, and Danes. The Bay of Antongli (in Madagascar) was transformed by the Dutch into a veritable port for the **enslavement** and transportation of slaves along the Indian Ocean. Their settlement in Mauritius in 1638 and on the Cape in 1652 added greater impetus to their role in the Indian Ocean slave trade. The Dutch, from the mid-seventeenth century, began to import slaves into the Cape of Good Hope. The wide range of procurement areas in the Indian Ocean included the Indonesian archipelago, Sri Lanka, Madagascar, Mauritius, and the East African mainland. In 1793, there were 14,747 slaves in the colony compared with 13,830 Europeans. Slaves had to be imported, because—unlike the European segment of the colony's population—the Cape slaves did not reproduce.

The Danes's slavery activities were noticed at their outpost, located at Transquwbar, while the French settled in Fort Dauphin. Driven out of the West Indies by the advance of colonialism, hundred of freebooters took refuge in the Great Isle. They became the brokers of the slave trade until about 1726. They bought Malagasies and resold them to the English of **Bristol**, the Dutch of Batavia, and the French of Martinique. They also resold slaves to the Arabs of Biona and Majunga. The corsairs delivered their own merchandise and slaves to the neighboring island of Bourbon. Here, the French governor signed a contract with the natives. This contract gave the governor the opportunity to buy slaves from and resell them to the people under his administration.

The need for manpower in the West Indies and on the American continent facilitated an increase in the activities of slave dealers and voyages in the Indian Ocean. The period between 1675 and 1725 represents a peak of the Indian Ocean slave trade. During that period, an estimated 12,000 inhabitants of Madagascar went to the New World in servitude. In 1785, about 3,000 to 4,000 slaves were provided by **Mozambique** to **Saint Domingue**.

The multiplier effect of the intrusion of the Europeans in the Indian Ocean slave trade is best seen noticed in the Mascarene Islands. The colonization of Bourbon and Mauritius gave rise to the need, as in the West Indies, for additional manpower. The French government turned to the Gulf of Guinea. **Cargoes** of slaves were brought from Madagascar. Slaves were taken into Mauritius from these places for more than fifty years.

The Portuguese with their trading stations South of Cape Delgado seem to have monopolized the Indian Ocean slave trade. In the second half of the eighteenth century, slaves were purchased from the **Muslims** on the Zanguebar coast that runs from Cape Delgado to the Gulf of Aden. From 1670 to 1810, the Mascarene Islands appeared to have imported approximately 160,000 slaves, 115,000 of them between 1769 and 1810.

The early nineteenth century marked a significant period in the history of the Indian Ocean slave trade. The British extended their abolitionist campaign to the Ocean. It was not easy getting the Portuguese, the French, and the Arabs to give up the slave trade. At the end, the scramble for Africa and the eventual partitioning of East African states and empires was needed to put an end to the trade. The colonization of East African states did not terminate the Indian Ocean slave trade because the economy of some parts of the Middle East was closely connected to slave labor. Until the early twentieth century, African slaves were still clandestinely recruited for a variety of tasks:

as workers in the Red Sea **ports**, in the date gardens of Medina, and in the coffee region of the northern Hijaz. *See also* Danish Slave Trade; Dutch Slave Trade; French Slave Trade; Portuguese Slave Trade.

Further Readings: "The African Slave Trade from the Fifteenth to the Nineteenth Century." Report of the papers of the meeting of experts organized by UNESCO. Paris: UNESCO, 1979; Dorsey, Joseph. *Slave Traffic in the Age of Abolition*. Gainesville: University Press of Florida, 2003; Patterson, Orlando. *Slavery and Social Death*. Cambridge, MA: Harvard University Press, 1982; Scarr, Deryck. *Slaving and Slavery in the Indian Ocean*. London: Macmillan, 1998; Solow, Barbara, ed. *Slavery and the Rise of the Atlantic System*. Cambridge: Cambridge University Press, 1991; Thomas, Hugh. *The Slave Trade: The Story of the Atlantic Slave Trade, 1440–1870*. New York: Simon & Schuster, 1997.

Saheed Aderinto

Insurance

Insurance reinforced the slave trade by making high-risk voyages financially viable. By purchasing insurance, ship owners transferred their financial losses to the insurers when a voyage went wrong. Owners typically insured the vessel and its slave **cargo**, as well as the ship's original outward-bound cargo. Less commonly, **captains** and crewmembers insured the "privilege" slaves whom they were entitled to transport and sell privately.

The cost of insuring a slave voyage depended on the age and condition of the ship, the competence of the captain and **crew**, the route, **season**, and state of geopolitics, among other factors. Policy purchasers provided letters of reference and detailed descriptions of the vessel and cargo, particularly where underwriters could not carry out their own inspection.

Premiums ranged from as little as 2 percent to as much as 50 percent of the value of the slave cargo. Peacetime premiums did not normally exceed 10 percent. During war, they climbed to 20 percent and above. The abolition of the slave trade by various governments and the rise of the abolitionist movement increased premiums, as did the likelihood of hitting the West African or Caribbean hurricane season. Some insurers offered refunds of up to 10 percent of the premium for successful voyages.

Although some ship owners purchased coverage for their entire voyage, most insured only part of the value of their cargo, or for the second leg alone—from Africa to the New World. Partial coverage became standard practice because of the high cost of premiums and despite the availability of loans from insurers.

Policies normally covered all losses with key exceptions. Insurers would not cover losses caused by "natural death" or "common mortality." Death by negligence, accident, **suicide**, malnutrition, and **disease** fell under these headings. In the late eighteenth century, English law only permitted ship owners to insure slave cargo against loss by "perils of the sea," piracy, insurrection, capture by the king's enemies, barratry by the master or crew, and destruction by fire. Compensation could not be claimed if slaves died as a result of ill treatment or if they were thrown overboard.

English underwriters' willingness to cover loss by insurrection increased over the course of the eighteenth century. Generally, they only covered losses exceeding 5 to 10 percent of the cargo's value. By the late eighteenth century, many French policies also covered insurrection and even collective suicide. Where insurrection could be attributed to the crew's negligence, underwriters attempted to deny compensation on the basis that this was a loss by "common mortality."

During the period when the slave trade was legal, insurers generally excluded losses caused by prohibited trade. After 1807–1808, when the slave trade was criminalized in the United States and the British Empire, some insurers continued to underwrite illegal voyages. Only in 1815 did American courts rule that insuring an illegal slave voyage was illegal.

Slave deaths by **drowning** were generally covered. **Storms** or **shipwreck** might cause these deaths. Less commonly, death by drowning could be covered as a "danger incident to navigation" or "peril of the sea." The throwing overboard of 132 sick slaves in 1781 by the captain of the British *Zong* was a deliberate attempt to maximize compensation from insurers: drowning was covered by the *Zong's* insurance policy, while death by illness was not. The English courts rejected the captain's claim to compensation. The incident became the *bête noire* of the abolitionist movement. It prompted legislation and was the subject of J.M.W. Turner's oil painting, "The Slave Ship" (1840).

Permissible routes were carefully specified. Parts of the Barbary coast and the Caribbean were high-risk regions because of piracy. Seizure by foreign powers was also a threat in many areas, particularly after the abolition of the slave trade by British and American governments. Some insurers imposed penalty fees of up to 20 percent of the cargo's value for deviation from the approved course. Others refused to insure any losses resulting from deviation. Destination markets and time limits were also set by the original agreement.

In Britain, the insurance of the slave trade was dominated by underwriters at Lloyds of **London**. A campaign to sue Lloyds for insuring the slave trade is currently being led by descendants of African slaves. Other British insurers operated out of **Liverpool** and **Bristol**. Before American independence, British insurers underwrote slave voyages originating from the American colonies. After 1776, American insurers in Boston, Newport, Providence, New York, Philadelphia, **Charleston**, and elsewhere underwrote American slave voyages. **Nantes, Bordeaux**, and Marseilles were French centers for slave-trade insurance. Until at least the eighteenth century, Dutch underwriters in Amsterdam, Rotterdam, and Middleburg insured slavers. Other European insurers of the slave trade were based in Hamburg, Barcelona, and Cadiz. *See also* Credit and Finance; Reparations; Slave Merchants (Slave Traders).

Further Readings: Coughtry, Jay. *The Notorious Triangle: Rhode Island and the African Slave Trade 1700–1807*, 90–102. Philadelphia: Temple University Press, 1981; Weisbord, Robert. "The Case of the Slave-Ship *Zong*, 1783." *History Today* 19, 8 (August 1969): 561–567; Williams, Eric. *Capitalism and Slavery*, 104–105. Chapel Hill: University of North Carolina Press, 1994.

Mitra Sharafi

Interlopers

The term, "interloper," was used during the trans-Atlantic slave trade to refer to people or ships that illegally purchased or carried enslaved Africans from an African port that was under **monopoly** control by a European nation or trading company. The first European monopoly on the African coast was Portugal's claim to exclusive trading rights on the so-called **Gold Coast**, beginning in the 1470s. Therefore, the first interlopers of the slave trade were traders from England and other countries who purchased or kidnapped Africans on the Gold Coast in violation of the Portuguese monopoly there. A famous early interloper was the Englishman John Hawkins, who made three slaving voyages and left an account of his journeys. Throughout the era of the trans-Atlantic slave trade, interlopers literally intercepted the trade that trading companies intended for themselves.

In general, the ships that carried enslaved Africans through the Middle Passage can be divided into two categories: those in the service of a company and those that operated on behalf of a private individual. During the first two centuries of the slave trade from Africa, the cost to outfit a ship for the journey from Europe to Africa and, finally, the Americas, and the risks associated with such voyages, were beyond the reach of individuals. Slaving voyages in this period were sponsored by governments and royal families using state funds. As Europe's merchant class accumulated its own capital during the course of the seventeenth and eighteenth centuries, private businesses were able to launch slaving enterprises and compete with the company trade. Another segment of the "private trader" category consisted of those who made an occupation of seizing and confiscating ships and merchandise on the high seas. These are generally referred to as pirates. From the point of view of company traders, either type of private ship would be considered an interloper if it conducted trade at a company port.

Interlopers had an advantage over company traders because they could purchase their **cargo** of human beings in a shorter time by purchasing slaves wherever they were available on the coast. By contrast, company traders were required to purchase slaves only at company posts, which often involved stopping at several **ports** on the West African coast and sometimes dropping anchor and waiting for the **trade forts** to accumulate enough slaves to fill the ships. In addition, private traders were not hindered by the costs of maintaining forts and personnel on the African coast. Consequently, private traders usually offered higher **prices** for slaves and lower prices for imported goods—especially cloth, **rum**, and tobacco—than the company traders.

Interloper trade has been much more difficult to quantify than company trade, because private traders and pirates were less likely to keep detailed records and correspondence. Historians must therefore speculate as to the number of private voyages and the composition of the human cargo they brought to the Americas. *See also* British Slave Trade; Portuguese Slave Trade.

Further Readings: Eltis, David. *The Rise of African Slavery in the Americas.* New York: Cambridge University Press, 2000; Rediker, Marcus Buford. *Villains of All Nations: Atlantic Pirates in the Golden Age.* Boston, MA: Beacon Press, 2004.

Rebecca Shumway

Internal Slave Trade, Brazil

After the trans-Atlantic slave trade to Brazil finally ended in the early 1850s, an internal slave trade began, affecting thousands of **women** and men. At that time, the coffee economy of Rio de Janeiro province was booming, soon to be followed by that of São Paulo and then southern Minas Gerais. Meanwhile, the international price of **sugar** stagnated and then fell precipitously, depressing the economies of **Brazil's** northeast, especially that of Bahia and Pernambuco, provinces that for three centuries had been the principal destination of Africans shipped to the New World. The result was a massive transfer of human beings from one part of the country to the other.

It is likely that in the 1850s and 1860s the number of slaves coming south from the northeast averaged 5,000 to 6,000 per year. This trade became even more intense in the 1870s, probably averaging 10,000 per year. In the 1880s, for reasons discussed below, the trade dwindled to a trickle until the abolition of slavery in 1888 ended it altogether. In all, more than 200,000 slaves were bought and sold from one province to another after 1850. In addition, within each province, a great movement of slaves occurred from the cities, from general farming areas, and from the gold and diamond fields (where the veins had run out) to coffee **plantations**. If this intraprovincial trade were also tallied, the number of those in the internal trade would probably be double.

Inevitably, given the large number of slaves shipped from Africa to Brazil's northeast in the previous twenty years (some 150,000), many of those who were taken from one province to another had already suffered the trans-Atlantic trade. Twenty-eight percent of those who arrived in Rio in 1852 were recorded as having been born in Africa, and there is reason to suppose that even some of those said to be Brazilian-born were actually African. For them, the nightmare of the Middle Passage had begun again. Over time, the proportion of those born in Brazil increased and, by the late 1870s, they were almost the only slaves still young enough to be worth shipping from province to province.

Given the lack of good inland roads, the principal route for the trade remained a coastwise one. In the 1850s, slaves were typically shipped from **port** to port in small groups, often in lots of four or so, presumably along with other commercial **cargo**, that is, not on slaving ships. An 1854 newspaper in Bahia advertised the departure for Rio of a ship that "has good rooms both for passengers and slaves" and of a schooner that "takes on small cargo and slaves." By the 1870s, however, much larger numbers of slaves traveled together, and there are examples of 51, 78, and even 232 slaves carried on a single ship. Still, in 1880, a white passenger complained that "one cannot travel on the [steam] packets of the Brazilian Company except in the company of this human cargo destined for sale in the South." So strictly slaving ships do not seem to have been the rule. A trip by sea from Bahia to Rio lasted approximately four days by steamship (the preferred mode of transport by the 1870s), much less than the six weeks or so that the trade from Africa had required, although the slaves were perhaps still **chained**. After slaves arrived in a southern port they were forced to walk long distances to interior plantations, a minimum of 125 miles over a steep escarpment that rose more than 2,500 feet.

Although many women were caught up in the internal slave trade, the great majority were men, especially young men. By 1884, males in the coffee-producing provinces accounted for 55 percent of the slave population while in the exporting provinces of the northeast their percentage was only 49. In short, most women remained behind while men were sent south.

Sale almost always was marked by a moment of wrenching separation and grief. A Brazilian politician decried this business, saying it was a horror "to see children yanked from their mothers, husbands separated from wives, parents from children! Go to the [slave market] and you will be indignant and stricken with the spectacle of so much misery!" Mothers, sisters, mates, and **children** left behind must have been devastated by the gaping absence of those sent away, and those shipped south found themselves isolated from their accustomed human contacts.

Relatively young, overwhelmingly male, no longer stitched into the social life of a particular place, and forcibly denied the contacts with family and friends that could have exerted a moderating influence on behavior, the transported men were probably angry, resentful, anxious, less constrained by social expectations, and certainly volatile. Males alone had always had less to lose by active resistance than those with wives and children. Masters who purchased such slaves could sense the disquiet among them.

Eventually, more and more coffee planters began to have doubts about the wisdom of importing slaves from the northeast and, in 1880–1881, they persuaded their legislatures to impose a prohibitive **tax** on those bringing slaves across provincial borders. Lawmakers made their reasons clear, speaking of how this causes situations in small towns where robbers and assassins keep those families in a constant state of alarm.

Another political leader declared that the slaves brought south in the internal trade "brought to the plantations neither the resignation nor the contentment with their lot that are essential to good discipline," and he hoped that restricting the trade would help maintain "order and tranquility on rural establishments." The new tax virtually ended the internal slave trade.

The measure did not put an end to slave unrest, however, and in 1887 and early 1888, slaves contributed specifically and decisively to the final end of slavery in Brazil. In those years, a massive flight of slaves from plantations to the cities took authorities by surprise; completely overwhelmed by their sheer numbers, every effort was made to stanch the flow. At first, fleeing slaves left stealthily in the night, but soon they did so openly, sometimes even confronting the authorities with **firearms**. When the army was summoned to help maintain order, its leaders disdainfully declared that they did not wish to be charged "with the capture of poor blacks who flee slavery." Faced with a *fait accompli*, the national Parliament, when it met in May 1888, hastily passed a law abolishing slavery.

The major area of these slave actions was the province of São Paulo, the province that had been most prominent in importing slaves from other regions. Another place witnessing direct action—and more spectacular because here the slaves burned the cane fields—was a sugar-producing county in the province of Rio de Janeiro. It was one of the few non-coffee areas of the province to have experienced a growth in the number of slaves between 1873 and 1882. No such mass flight or generalized sabotage occurred on the sugar plantations of the northeast, where the slaves had grown up and remained more securely attached to local society and culture. In short, the dislocation brought on by the internal slave trade powerfully contributed to the actions of those in the south and thus to the end of slavery. *See also* Abolition of the Slave Trade, Great Britain; Escapes and Runaways; Families and Family Separations; Portuguese Slave Trade.

Further Readings: Bethell, Leslie. *The Abolition of the Brazilian Slave Trade: Britain, Brazil and the Slave Trade Question, 1807–1869.* Cambridge: Cambridge University Press, 1970; Conrad, Robert Edgar. *World of Sorrow: The African Slave Trade to Brazil.* Baton Rouge: Louisiana State University Press, 1986.

Richard Graham

Internal Slave Trade, United States

The internal slave trade in the United States, or the Second Middle Passage, was part of a vast forced migration of slaves in the seventeenth and eighteenth centuries. Forced migration transferred slaves to Georgia and South Carolina in the early nineteenth century, but the "Cotton Kingdom" that stretched across Alabama, Mississippi, Louisiana, and Texas became the primary destination for slaves after 1810. It is estimated that between 1810 and 1860 more than 1 million slaves were forced to leave behind family and familiar surroundings and begin life anew in the Deep South.

It was the acquisition of new land and the declining agriculture in settled land that created the necessary conditions for the interstate slave trade. Indians gave up territory that would become the "Black Belt" and whites who moved there were hungry for laborers who would convert the virgin lands to productive farms and **plantations**. They found these laborers in the Chesapeake region, where Virginia and Maryland slaveholders were making the transition away from tobacco cultivation. These new agricultural forms demanded fewer slaves, and so masters along the Atlantic seaboard were eager to sell their slaves.

The internal slave trade, which accounted for 50 to 60 percent of all forced migrations, was the largest enterprise in the South outside of the plantation enterprise. Roving speculators scoured the countryside in the Chesapeake. They visited farms and plantations, buying up slaves who had become disposable or who proved intractable. **Slave traders** could also be seen at auctions, acquiring slaves in an estate sale or purchasing **runaways** from the sheriff on the courthouse steps. By the 1840s, slave traders set up their own auction houses that specialized in buying, selling, and renting slaves.

Slave traders were looking for specific kinds of slaves and tailored their purchases accordingly. They broke up **families**, and most slaves in the Upper South knew of the sale of at least one close family member. Slaves had a 30 percent chance of being sold to the Deep South until they were in their mid-twenties. Speculators typically purchased slaves between the ages of nineteen and twenty-five who appeared to be in good health. These "No. 1 Men," as they came to be called in the slave market, might sell for $1,500 in Richmond in 1860. Slaves with specific skills such as **carpenters** or blacksmiths were worth even more in the slave market. The slaves who commanded the highest **prices** were known as "fancy girls." These attractive young **women**, often biracial, became reluctant concubines of their new masters and sometimes sold for $1,700.

Once purchased, the slaves were taken to pens or jails found in cities like Baltimore, Alexandria, Norfolk, and Richmond. They might wait for anywhere from one day to several weeks before beginning the journey to the southwest. Most jails had a main office where slave traders might serve wine to prospective customers. Behind the office was an open yard where slaves could be assembled, either for **exercise** or inspection before sale. Large rooms abutted the yard, and here slaves slept on the ground, men in one room and women in another. The tall walls around the jails kept slaves in and curious stares out.

Once slave traders gathered a sizable number of slaves, they arranged for transportation to the slave markets of the Deep South. The most common, and visible, way to move bondservants was a **coffle**. Anywhere from 50 to 150 slaves comprised a coffle, which was essentially a three-month forced march to Mississippi or Louisiana. Young male slaves were manacled together in pairs, a set of handcuffs cutting into the wrist of each person. A rope or chain was threaded through the handcuffs, so the slaves moved in two parallel lines. They typically remained in handcuffs around the clock for a week or so, until the threat of escape diminished. Women, children, and older slaves trudged alongside the coffle if they could maintain the pace, or they rode in supply wagons. Slaves slept on the ground at night and ate meager provisions from the slave trader's supplies.

Speculators also transported slaves in other ways. The coastwise trade, travel in sailing vessels along the Atlantic seaboard, Florida, and the Gulf of Mexico, was a fast and reliable way to send slaves from the Chesapeake to **New Orleans**. During the two-week voyage, bondservants were packed tightly in cargo **holds** and normally not allowed on deck. Speculators also transported slaves on the rivers. Slaves from the Chesapeake marched to the western edge of present-day West Virginia and boarded flatboats for a voyage to Natchez. By the 1850s, slave traders used railroads to send their slaves to the Deep South.

Once slaves arrived in the slave emporiums of the Deep South, slave traders prepared them for sale. Speculators increased the diet of these slaves and dressed them in better clothing to give the appearance of humane treatment. William Wells Brown, a slave who worked for a slave trader, recalled how he plucked grey beards, rubbed a blackening substance on grey hair, and put grease into the creases of the slaves' faces. He recalled that slaves looked decades younger after he was through with them. Because a slave's value declined with age, a slave trader might earn a greater **profit** by using such tactics. Speculators also coached slaves on what to say and how to present themselves to prospective buyers.

Slave traders quickly, and rightfully, gained a reputation for double dealing, and so prospective buyers were wary in their purchases. Whites customarily examined slaves before purchasing them. Male slaves might have to jump, run, or climb stairs to prove their vigor. Females opened and closed their hands quickly to show they could easily pick cotton. Potential buyers squeezed muscles, poked abdomens, and examined teeth, all in the hopes of determining the truth about slaves. Slaves, women included, customarily stripped to the waist for such inspections; buyers perceived scars on a slave's back as evidence of difficulty or unruliness. Women might also undergo a rude gynecological exam to determine whether or not they were capable of bearing children.

Slaves who suffered these indignities were not merely passive actors in the sale. They often actively influenced their purchasers. When a potential buyer seemed too harsh or unappealing, slaves sulked or performed requests with a minimum amount of exertion. In contrast, when slaves encountered a potential buyer who seemed favorable, they presented a much more appealing front. Slaves also shared gossip and information in the slave markets. A number of slaves ran errands for slave traders and had access to outside information. It seems that slave markets became collection points for the transmission of information, and news and rumors spread to various plantations through the slave market.

The internal slave trade had significant consequences for white and black southerners. The slave population of the "Cotton Kingdom" was a youthful one. In Alabama, for instance, nearly 40 percent of slaves were under the age of twenty-five, a figure significantly higher than the established states of the South. The domestic slave trade unified slave culture by softening regional differences. Dialects and practices that were noticeable in eastern Virginia or Savannah became indistinguishable in Louisiana. Slaves caught in the coils of the internal slave trade had to drop their regional identification and rely on one another to survive the shock of transportation to the Deep South. In this fashion, the "Second Middle Passage" closely approximated the first journey across the Atlantic Ocean. *See also* Languages and Communication.

Further Readings: Deyle, Steven. *Carry Me Back: The Domestic Slave Trade in American Life.* New York: Oxford University Press, 2005; Gudmestad, Robert. *A Troublesome Commerce: The Transformation of the Interstate Slave Trade.* Baton Rouge: Louisiana State University Press, 2003; Johnson, Walter. *Soul by Soul: Life Inside the Antebellum Slave Market.* Cambridge: Harvard University Press, 2000; Tadman, Michael. *Speculators and Slaves: Masters, Traders, and Slaves in the Old South.* Madison: University of Wisconsin Press, 1989.

Robert Gudmestad

Islam and Muslims

Slavery was practiced in Islamic societies for more than 1,400 years, and Muslims played an integral part in the trans-Atlantic slave trade. Modern European slavery had its roots in the Muslim slave culture of North Africa and the Ottoman Empire. In addition, Islamic chiefs and merchants often served

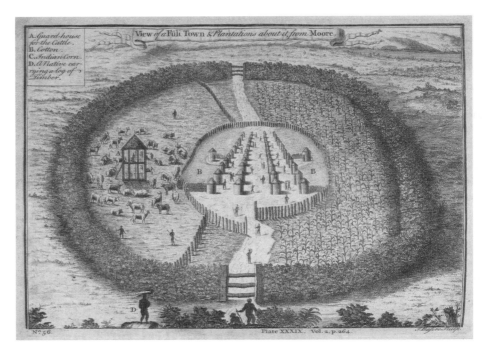

Fulani settlement and surrounding gardens, eighteenth century. Tracy W. McGregor Library, Special Collections, University of Virginia Library.

as suppliers to European **slave traders** along the West coast of Africa. Slavery continued in some parts of the Arab world through the twentieth century.

As is the case with the bible, the Qur'an, the holy book of Islam, contains numerous passages that deal with slavery. For the most part, the Qur'an neither endorses nor objects to slavery, but rather deals with a range of practical issues related to conversion, manumission, and the integration of slaves into society. Mohammad, Islam's founder and major prophet, owned slaves, although some Islamic scholars argue that he advocated freedom for slaves that converted to Islam. Traditional Islamic law specifically details the treatment of slaves, including allowances for enslaving non-Muslims and punishments for owners who mistreat their slaves (manumission of the injured slave was one such punishment for cruel masters). Islamic law also allowed the use of slaves for their master's sexual pleasure and dictated that **children** born to a male owner and female slave were free of bondage.

Slaves in Muslim societies could gain a high degree of social status. For instance, warrior slaves were often given political appointments while other slaves rose to be powerful advisors to ruling monarchs. Military slaves (commonly known as "janissaries") enjoyed greater status than household servants. Large numbers of slaves were used as domestic servants, body guards, and concubines. There were also large numbers of military slaves. For instance, the first Muslim leader of Egypt had an army of 24,000 Arab and European slaves and 45,000 black slaves. Finally, some rulers and elite merchants had thousands of slaves working in mines, in large-scale agriculture, and on trade routes.

Under Islamic law and tradition, there were a range of ways in which people could become slaves. Children of slaves could become slaves under certain circumstances. In addition, captives from war or conquest could be made slaves, especially if they were not Muslim. Captured soldiers were often made into slaves, although it was customary to allow warriors to be ransomed. Civilian **women**, men, and children who were captured during raids or the conquest of territory were made slaves (there were numerous historical examples in which the men of a captured area would be killed and the women and children turned into slaves). Finally, non-Muslims could be sold into slavery.

Through the 1800s, Muslim societies gained most of their slaves by conquest. Initially, slaves from Europe and Russia were highly sought after; however, as the military prowess of the European powers increased with the Renaissance and Reformation eras, Muslim rulers increasingly turned to Africa for slaves. Muslim slave traders organized large raids into Africa to capture blacks who were then sold in large slave bazaars. Until the height of the European slave trade in the early 1800s, the world's largest slave bazaars were in Mecca, Baghdad, and Tripoli.

The demand for African slaves accelerated as the **trans-Saharan slave trade** routes became increasingly profitable. Slaves were needed to transport goods along the routes and the high **mortality** rate of the trip necessitated a constant supply of new slaves (some contemporary accounts suggested that slaves on the routes or working in the salt mines had life expectancies of less than five years). The harsh conditions and high mortality rates led to several major slave revolts. One of the largest was the Zenj revolt in present-day Iraq. The revolt lasted from 863 to 883 C.E. and involved African slaves who had been transported to the Middle East to work on large farms.

Islamic traders conducted a highly developed slave trade from the East African coast. Slaves were acquired through a variety of means, including raids, and as tribute to rulers from lesser chiefs. Beginning in the 700s C.E., slaves were transported and sold to owners in India, Ceylon, and China. In exchange for slaves, Arab traders received spices, gold, and silver. The East African slave trade continued until European suppression in the nineteenth century.

The Portuguese first interacted with modern slavery in their trade relations with the Arab rulers of North Africa. As Portuguese merchants established trade outposts along the African coast, they began to engage in the profitable transport of slaves for Islamic rulers, especially in the shipment of slaves from the southern outposts to points north where slaves could be used in the trans-Saharan routes. By the 1480s, the Portuguese were trading with local Muslim chiefs and merchants for gold, pepper, and ivory, in exchange for trade goods, guns, and the transport of slaves. The Portuguese and later European slavers established forts or trading posts along the coast and relied on locals to raid and capture slaves from interior villages or opposing tribes. The Europeans also traveled further south beyond the

Islamic traders to bypass their higher costs. Nonetheless, Islamic traders remained an important part of the trade.

Muslim rulers resisted European efforts to suppress the slave trade. After Great Britain abolished the slave trade within its empire, Muslim traders continued to raid and capture slaves and sell them to illegal slavers. Through blockades, direct military action, and the conquest of territory, the West African slave trade was ended by the late 1800s. *See also* Abolition of Slave Trade, Great Britain; Accra; African Rulers and the Slave Trade; Calabar; Closure of the Slave Trade; Dahomey; Enslavement and Procurement; Mozambique; Portuguese Slave Trade; Rape and Sexual Abuse; Slave Coast; Slavery in Africa; Wars, African.

Further Readings: Esposito, John L. *Islam: the Straight Path.* New York: Oxford University Press, 1991; Lewis, Bernard. *Race and Slavery in the Middle East: An Historical Inquiry.* New York: Oxford University Press, 1990; Peters, Rudolph. *Jihad in Classical and Modern Islam.* Princeton, NJ: Markus Wiener, 1996.

Tom Lansford

Ivory Wreck, The

A **shipwreck** offshore of the Middle Florida Keys, Florida, was determined in 1948 to be that of a slaver. The wreck is located four miles offshore of Key Vaca, at Delta Shoal, a mile east of Sombrero Key Lighthouse, in a spur and groove reef formation just to the south of the shoal. This formation has canyons leading out to the open sea. In one of those canyons, at a depth of twenty-five feet, the first artifacts were discovered.

The wreck is one of seven slave ships known to have wrecked at the Florida Keys, a chain of tiny islands along the sailing route to Europe from **Havana**, the Gulf of Mexico, and the Western Caribbean. The others are (1) a Portuguese vessel returning from Cartegena, Columbia, which wrecked at the Dry Tortugas in a 1622 hurricane; (2) the English slaver **the *Henrietta Marie***, which wrecked near the Marquesas Keys in a **storm** in 1700, returning from **Jamaica**; (3) the English vessel *Nassau*, which was returning to **Bristol** from Jamaica, at an unknown location on "the Martins" (the Martires, the old Spanish name for the Florida Keys), in 1741; (4) the English slaver *Fly*, en route to Africa from Jamaica, which burned off "Cape Florida" in 1789; (5) the American coastal slaver *Cosmopolite*, which ran aground and was lost in a storm off Key West in 1821 with twenty-seven enslaved aboard (all survived), bound from **Charleston** for **New Orleans**; and (6) the Spanish slaver **the *Guerrero***, which wrecked off Key Largo in 1827 (520 of the 561 captives aboard survived).

Local fishermen generally knew of the wreck on Delta Shoal, but none had investigated it. Some interest was generated in the wreck after a seventeen-year-old spear fisherman, Charlie Slater, came into the village on the island, Marathon, with an elephant's tusk. Two cannons at the site were found (with one brought to the surface) by Marathon resident Halley Hamlin, after they had been shown to him by bottom fisherman Harry Reith.

Young Slater brought the tusk to famed treasure diver Art McKee. McKee owned the Museum of Sunken Treasure in the Upper Florida Keys, and he was interested in the find. The tusk, he knew, meant the site was certainly the wreck of a slave ship. After **slave traders** loaded ivory and human beings in Africa, and sold the captives in the New World, they returned to Europe and sold ivory for additional **profit**.

The day before Slater and McKee traveled to Marathon to charter a boat to the site, a Cleveland couple George ("Barney") and Jane Crile and their children discovered the unraised cannon while doing underwater photography. The Criles were vacationing on the Keys, and when the owner (Bill Thompson) of the Marathon guest cottages where they were staying learned of their desire to dive on wrecks, he suggested some off Marathon. Thus, on the day the Criles intended to salvage the cannon they had found the day before, McKee, a veteran hardhat diver, and Slater arrived at the site. Earlier that same day, Barney Crile found a tusk near the cannon.

Jane Crile wrote in her popular 1954 book, *Treasure Diving Holidays*, of the fantastic coincidence of McKee's presence that day. McKee found a musket barrel encased in coral, with the brass trigger guard visible. There were two brass coral-covered cooking kettles, one badly crushed, manufactured in the "spun brass" technique. Also found were stacks of brass pans, stuck together. Other finds included dozens of round lead musket balls and waterworn pebbles, three-pound cannon balls, bar shot, a piece of a pewter spoon, a metal dinner plate and serving dish, partially burned stove wood, blue and white china fragments (later identified by the Smithsonian Institution as part of a delftware ale mug made in Bristol, England), and a 1500s or 1600s "Cardinal Bellarmine" wine jug, a broken clay pipe, sheets of lead sheathing, and a lead piece marked "XI." Twelve tusks (in addition to the one Slater recovered) and a bronze breechblock for use with a swivel gun were recovered. Later, Bill Thompson found a pewter mug in perfect condition, and Hamlin located a 24-pound bronze breech cup, which would have carried the powder in breech-loading cannon. In later years, others found leg irons, brass bowls, scale weights for precious gems, a small copper cannon, brass dividers, and five ornate decorations that once adorned musket stocks, in the form of sea dragons.

In 1948, Hamlin and McKee winched the cannon, which had a yellow seafan growing from its muzzle, free of the reef and onto a barge for the Criles. The iron gun was a saker, seven-and-a-half feet long with a three-and-a-half inch bore. Once ashore, markings were found on the cannon after an inch of coral was chipped off: the letter P, beneath that, in script, JN and the numbers 170 1/11 24.

A written agreement was made between Bill Thompson, Art McKee, and George Crile as to the division of the artifacts. After the Criles returned to Cleveland, McKee and partner Wesly Bradley discovered more ivory, which was divided between McKee and Thompson. None of the writers of the discovery mentioned ballast rock, so only a part of the vessel may have been found. In his 2001 book, *Galleon Alley*, Bob Weller wrote of Miami salvor Art Hartman's discovery of four tusks, African-copper coinage, and "slave bracelets" (*manillas*, used as trade items for captive people) in another location off the southeastern side of Key Vaca. That site had a ballast pile.

A quarter mile away from Delta Shoal, inventor and explorer Ed Link, with the Criles in 1951, raised a Spanish cannon dated 1617. It too was iron, but with different markings. Although there are no fewer than seven wrecks on Delta Shoal, it may have been from the slaver. Link recovered a small piece of tusk, now in the Edwin A. Link Underwater Archaeological Collection at the Roberson Center for the Arts and Sciences in Binghamton, New York.

The Criles shipped their cannon to Cleveland. Their artifacts were displayed at the Cleveland Museum of Natural History and the Criles made a color film on the wreck, which was shown in the area. Their four tusks, brass kettles, and the cannon were then placed in their Cleveland home. Untreated, flake by flake, Jane Crile wrote, the cannon was disintegrating. In his 1971 book, *Diving to a Flash of Gold*, Martin Meylach wrote that there was not much visible of the first wrecksite, and that the wreck was scattered and mostly buried. He observed that a second part of the wreck was on the shoal, where two more tusks had been found.

As recently as April 2000, still another tusk was found by a Marathon diver, and after photographing it and reporting the find to the Florida Keys National Marine Sanctuary office, it was reburied at the site. Between 2000 and 2006, two **museums** in the Florida Keys obtained additional artifacts. The Museums at Crane Point Hammock, Marathon, obtained a tusk recovered long ago, and the Mel Fisher Treasure Museum, Key West, purchased two brass bowls and two tusks from Karen McKee, daughter of the late Art McKee. Some day, perhaps, the wreck can be identified by name through the markings on the cannon. Since 1948, it has been named simply "The *Ivory* Wreck."

Further Readings: Crile, Jane and Barney. *Treasure Diving Holidays*, 160–176. New York: Viking Press, 1954; McKee, Arthur, to Ben Hibbs. December 24, 1953, in Ed Link Correspondence File, Edward A. Link Collection, Special Collections, University Libraries, State University of New York, Binghamton, New York.

Gail Swanson

J

Jamaica

An island nation of 4,207.5 square miles in the Caribbean Sea, Jamaica was once the largest of the British colonial possessions in the Caribbean. In 1962, it gained independence and derived its name from the Arawak word meaning "land of water and wood." Following Christopher Columbus's first landing in 1494 on the island, to which he gave the name Santiago, Jamaica became a Spanish colony in 1509. It was later wrestled from the Spaniards by the English in 1655 and formally became a British colony in 1670. In an effort to enslave the indigenous inhabitants, the Tainos, the Spaniards decimated the population by working them to death either on farms or in unyielding gold mines. The demand for labor on **sugar** and tobacco **plantations** in the New World occasioned the importation of Africans as slaves beginning from the early sixteenth century. When the English fought to gain control of the island in 1655, the Spaniards freed the African slaves who fled to remote regions on the island where they lived in quasi-independent **maroon** communities. With the advent of British rule, the importation of African slaves increased exponentially and Jamaica not only became the largest producer of sugar (770 tons per year), but also served as a hub for slave ships en route to South Carolina, Barbados, and New York.

The trans-Atlantic slave trade brought about many demographic and cultural changes to the island over time. It is estimated that in 1770 there were 40,000 African slaves to 7,000 English denizens, and by 1800, the slave population had grown to 3 million. Although other immigrants from Asia and Europe arrived on the island largely after the abolition of the trans-Atlantic slave trade and slavery, the African presence was, and still is, predominant: about 90.5 percent of the population is of African ancestry. The majority of the slaves taken to Jamaica were from what is referred to as the **Slave Coast** (present-day Western Nigeria, **Benin**, and Togo) and the **Gold Coast** (Ghana), creating a diverse linguistic, religious, and cultural group. As a result, certain forms of polytheistic religious practices (Obeah) and of expression (Creole) are partly rooted in the cultural orientation of this group.

Slave rebellions in Jamaica, as in other slaveholding societies in North and South America, and in the Caribbean, took many forms: arson, foot-dragging, and running away. Historians believe that the frequency of slave revolts in Jamaica was unparalleled because of the huge slave population, the number of African-born slaves, and the maroon communities. Led by figures such as Cudjoe, Accompong, Nany, and Quao, the maroons waged a guerrilla war of emancipation against the English for more than fifty years. When the English outlawed slavery in 1833, an estimated 311,000 slaves became free in Jamaica. The trans-Atlantic slave trade, which forcibly took many Africans through the Middle Passage to Jamaica, also brought religious, cultural, and linguistic diversity to the island nation. *See also* British Caribbean; British Slave Trade; Escapes and Runaways (Maroonage).

Further Readings: Knight, Franklin W., and Palmer, Colin A., eds. *The Modern Caribbean*. Chapel Hill: University of North Carolina Press, 1989; Shepherd, Verene, and McD. Beckles, Hilary, eds. *Caribbean Slavery in the Atlantic World*. Kingston: Ian Randle Publishers, 2000; "Slave Movement During the Eighteenth and Nineteenth Centuries." Data and Information Services Center, University of Wisconsin-Madison Web site: http://dpls.dacc.wisc.edu/slavedata/index.html.

Mawuena Logan

K

Key West African Cemetery

In 2001, a State of Florida historical marker was placed at a cemetery previously unmarked for 141 years, on a public beach in Key West, Florida Keys. Buried there in 1860, and then forgotten, were 295 Africans, all victims of the slave trade.

In 1859, the U.S. antislave-trade squadron was moved to **Angola** from the **Cape Verde** islands and four steamships added as a second net for the slavers not caught off Africa. The orders from U.S. Secretary of the Navy Isaac Toucey to the commanders were to proceed to the coast of **Cuba** and patrol, "the immediate object in view being the suppression of the slave trade between that island and Africa, so far as carried on by citizens or under the flag of the United States."

Since 1808 it had been illegal for any U.S. citizen to equip or finance any slave ship operating from any U.S. port. The law was ignored by ship owners and **captains** because of the immense **profit**. In 1860, a human being purchased in Africa for $10 to $34 could be sold to the planters in Cuba for $1,000.

On December 16, 1859, the Amesbury, Massachusetts-built clipper *Wildfire* (Captain Philip Stanhope, Pierre L. Pearce, owner) sailed from New York for the **Congo River**, where, on March 21, 1860, 608 Africans were forced into the ship's **hold**. Most were between the ages of six and twenty. The *Wildfire* had been at sea for thirty-five days when the USS *Mohawk* (under Lieutenant T. Augustus Craven) sighted her. The *Wildfire* captain believed the *Mohawk* to be a British cruiser and ran up the American flag.

The bark was towed into the nearest American port, Key West, where the 507 surviving Africans were delivered to a surprised U.S. Marshal Fernando J. Moreno. Moreno acted with all haste in getting quarters and a hospital built for the Africans. Many were sick or blind from **diseases** brought on by the conditions that they had endured **chained** in the hold—blind from ophthalmia, and ill from lung disease, typhoid fever, and dysentery.

This capture was followed by the capture nineteen days later of the *William* (under Captain William Weston alias Washington Symmes, of Philadelphia, Thomas W. Williams of Baltimore, owner) by USS *Wyandott* (under Lieutenant

Fabius Stanley) and 513 more Africans were brought to Key West. Fourteen days later the USS *Crusader* (under Lieutenant John N. Maffitt) captured the *Bogota* (under Captain Faukner, owned in New York). With her human "cargo" a total of 1,433 Africans were brought to Key West.

The diseases continued their courses unabated, despite the care given. The dead were buried at a point of land now named Higgs Beach, an established burial ground since the 1830s. The survivors were taken to **Liberia**.

The Civil War began the next year, but Key West remained in Union hands. In anticipation of the building of fortifications, James C. Clapp drew a detailed map of Key West for Captain E. B. Hunt, Army Corps of Engineers, in 1861. On the map, discovered in Washington by Keys historian John Viele in 1994, Clapp had marked, "African Cemetery." When ordered to build a battery, West Martello Tower, on the cemetery, Hunt objected. His superior in Washington, Joseph G. Totten, overrode it. Most of the remains were moved in 1862, possibly to an area about two blocks away where many human bones were found during a 1940s piping project.

In 1992, a receipt for the burial of 294 Africans was uncovered. Two years later, Viele forwarded the map and this tragic location was discovered. It was marked five years after being made public in the March 2, 1997, issue of the *Key West Citizen*.

A nondisturbing ground-penetrating radar survey around the battery was conducted in 2002 by Lawrence B. Conyers. Conyers discovered an area that contained at least nine more undisturbed burials. *See also* Abolition of the Slave Trade, United States.

Further Readings: Lynch, Marika. "Beneath the Beach, Bones of Slaves." *Miami Herald*, February 22, 1998; Blevin, Kip. "History Hidden under Higgs [Beach]." *Key West (Florida) Citizen*, May 8, 2000; Jenkins, Robert N. "Freed, then Forgotten." *St. Petersburg (Florida) Times*, December 26, 2003.

Gail Swanson

Kongo

The Kongo are a Bantu-speaking group from West Central Africa (in present-day Congo, Democratic Republic of the Congo, and **Angola**). The Kongo consolidated in the fourteenth century into a centralized kingdom shaped by their close contact with Europeans and **Christianity** since the late fifteenth century until their unraveling at the turn of the nineteenth century. The word Kongo also refers to an array of cultural and religious practices shared by a large number of people in Central Africa and the Americas since the era of the Atlantic slave trade.

The origins of the kingdom are traced back in **oral history** to a civilizing hero, military champion, inventor of blacksmithing and magic, the first Kongo king or *manikongo*, called Lukeni lua Nimi, who presumably lived at the turn of the fourteenth century. In the following two centuries, under the leadership of the royal matrilineal lineage, the Kongo group consolidated a large territory of vassal provinces, agglomerated by force or willful alliance, around their capital city of Mbanza Kongo (later São Salvador). At the height of its power, the kingdom extended from beyond the **Congo River** in the north to the Kwanza River in the south, and from the Atlantic Ocean to the

Residence of the king of Kongo, late seventeenth century. Tracy W. McGregor Library, Special Collections, University of Virginia Library.

west to past the Nkisi River eastward. Its economy was based on the production and trade of agricultural goods, copper, and iron and was organized in a system of hierarchical taxation and tribute payments ultimately controlled by the king's house. Its political system was formally organized, hierarchical, and centralized in the hand of the *manikongo*. In 1482, with the arrival of the Portuguese explorer Diogo Cão, the Kongo Kingdom entered into European history. In 1512, the *manikongo* Nzinga Nkuwa adopted Catholicism as the state **religion**, took the Christian name of Afonso I, and built an economic and diplomatic relationship with Portugal and the Papacy. The involvement of Kongo in the Atlantic slave trade in response to the need for labor in the Brazilian lands, which were controlled in turn by its European allies Portugal and Holland, varied from province to province. It is generally admitted that a limited number of Kongo people were sold as slaves while they supplied men and **women** from the hinterland to the coastal slave market. Although not opposed to the trade, the various *manikongo* objected to its disruptive effects on the political and social structures of the kingdom and to the European disregard for traditional rules of **enslavement**.

After a century of prosperity culminating with the brilliant reign of King **Garcia II of Kongo (1641–1661)**, the kingdom started to suffer from the combined disruptive effects of waves of invasions from neighboring peoples, civil war, and the growing Atlantic slave trade. Following the decisive battle of Mbwila (1665), lost by the Kongo to the Portuguese, the centralized, urban kingdom unraveled and became a predominantly rural monarchy ruled by a provincial aristocracy and a weakened king. Strategic use of Christian rituals and the **profits** derived from the slave trade allowed the nobles to sustain their privileges and political status quo through the mid-nineteenth century. In 1885, Kongo's territories were divided by European colonial powers between Portuguese Angola and the Belgian crown.

As a part of the larger Bantu cultural and linguistic area, the Kongo share with the neighboring African populations key religious, linguistic, and social features. *Kikongo*, the **language** of the Kongo people (or *bakongo*), is a Bantu idiom and is related to the adjacent Kimbundu (Angola), Lingala (Congo), and Swahili (South Eastern Africa) languages, and to a small extent, they are mutually understandable. Kongo religion is centered on ancestor worship and a belief in the relationship between the world of the living and the world of the dead. The centuries-long relationship with European traders and missionaries has shaped the Kongo belief system and religious art, both of which integrate traits and icons of Christianity into their discourse. Socially, one of the long-lasting effects of the mixing of Christianity and the Kongo world view in Central Africa has been the proliferation of prophetic or messianic politico-religious movements from the early eighteenth century Antonians to 1920s Kimbanguism.

The larger Kongo region had been one of the main gateways for the deportation of Africans to be sold as slaves in the Americas. On the New Continent, Bantu slaves from Central Africa recreated a culture based on the common social, linguistic, and religious traits of their groups of origin, a phenomenon that they identified by the word "Kongo." Kongo has taken different forms in various parts of the Western Hemisphere, but it has remained, through the centuries of the slave trade to contemporary times, the common identifying name for the diverse vibrant manifestations of shared beliefs. Kongo's spiritual and cultural heritage manifests itself in the use of such religious artifacts as *paquets congo* in Haiti, bottle-trees in the U.S. South, or *prendas* in **Cuba**. Kongo has also served as a rallying name for social, cultural, and political movements of empowerment among the members of the African diaspora. In **Brazil**, as well as in Cuba and Haiti, distinct groups have formed, calling themselves Kongo Nations and symbolically electing their own kings during week-long festivals. *See also* Dutch Slave Trade; Portuguese Slave Trade.

Further Readings: Balandier, Georges. *Daily Life in the Kingdom of the Kongo from the Sixteenth to the Eighteenth Century.* 1st American ed. New York: Pantheon Books, 1968; Hilton, Anne. *The Kingdom of Kongo, Oxford Studies in African Affairs.* New York: Clarendon Press; Oxford University Press, 1985; Thompson, Robert Farris, Cornet, Joseph, and National Gallery of Art (U.S.). *The Four Moments of the Sun: Kongo Art in Two Worlds.* Washington, DC: National Gallery of Art, 1981; Thornton, John Kelly. *The Kingdom of Kongo: Civil War and Transition, 1641–1718.* Madison: University of Wisconsin Press, 1983.

Cécile Fromont

Kormantyn

The name Kormantyn comes from a West African town that is now located in the town of Abandze in modern Ghana. This town is the site of Fort Amsterdam, a large fortified structure built by the Dutch West India Company in the 1660s for protection of the Dutch gold trade. It was later used for that company's trade in enslaved Africans. The term "Kormantyn" (spellings vary) was used between the seventeenth and nineteenth centuries to refer to enslaved Africans presumed to be from the **Gold Coast** region of West Africa.

The first European outpost at Kormantyn was built by the English "Company of Adventurers of London Trading to Guynney and Binney" (Guinea and **Benin**). The English built a fort at Kormantyn in 1631 in hopes of improving England's gold trade on the Gold Coast. The structure built by the English was destroyed by fire in 1640 and subsequently rebuilt. The new fort at Kormantyn contained what was possibly the first slave prison built on the Gold Coast. Kormantyn was the headquarters of the English company trade until 1664, when the English fort was captured by the Dutch. Fort Amsterdam continued to function as a Dutch trading fort during the era of the trans-Atlantic slave trade on the Ghana coast, but it was never as important to European trade on that coast as it had been in the mid-seventeenth century.

During the middle decades of the seventeenth century, when Kormantyn was under English control, English **plantation** owners and slave buyers in the Americas—especially **Jamaica** and Barbados—began to refer to all slaves purchased on the Gold Coast as *Coromantese* or *Coromantines*. So-called Coromante slaves accounted for the majority of the slave population in Jamaica from the late 1600s to mid-1700s and played significant roles in slave rebellions in Barbados and Jamaica.

References to Gold Coast slaves as Coromantese, after Kormantyn, are misnomers in two ways. Enslaved persons sold at Kormantyn or anywhere else on the Gold Coast most likely originated from a town or village far inland from the coast and had cultural backgrounds quite different from the Fante people of **Kormantyn** itself. More important, by labeling enslaved persons sold on the Gold Coast as belonging to the Coromante ethnic group, record-keepers in the British West Indies created the false impression that enslaved persons sold on the Gold Coast had a common ethnolinguistic or cultural background. In fact, enslaved people sold on the Gold Coast were captured or purchased in villages and markets ranging beyond the boundaries of modern-day Ghana. They represented dozens of distinct linguistic and cultural groups.

There are many alternate spellings of this term. In addition to those used above, one may encounter the following spellings: Kormantine, Kromantse, Cormantyn, Cormantyne, Cormantin/Kormantin, Cormentin, Coromonteen, and Koromanti. *See also* British Slave Trade; Dutch Slave Trade; British Caribbean; Trade Forts.

Further Readings: Craton, Michael. *Empire, Enslavement and Freedom in the Caribbean.* Princeton, NJ: Ian Randle Publishers, 1997; Postma, Johannes Menne. *The Dutch in the Atlantic Slave Trade, 1600–1815.* New York and Cambridge: Cambridge University Press, 1990; Van Dantzig, Albert. *Forts and Castles of Ghana.* Accra: Sedco Publishing, 1980.

Rebecca Shumway

L

Lagos

The port of Lagos (Nigeria) was one of the most important ports of the **Slave Coast**. Its emergence is often explained as a consequence of its geographic position in relation to the inland Lagoon routes. It was situated at the only permanent outlet from the inland lagoons to the sea and between the River Volta in the west and the Mahin River (known to the earliest European navigators as the Rio Primeiro, or First River) to the east.

Oral and written sources indicate that the first set of European traders came to Lagos during the reign of Akinsemoyin, the fourth *Oba* (king) of Lagos. The date of Akinsemoyin's reign is not certain, but it is known that his successor, Ologun Kutere was on the throne in the 1780s and 1790s. It was during this period that trade in human beings developed into a veritable economic enterprise. Although, a latecomer in the trade in human beings when compared with her Dahomean neighbors, Lagos developed into a major slave port in the first half of the nineteenth century. Yoruba civil wars of the nineteenth century produced most of the slaves transported to the West Indies through Lagos.

The British interest in Lagos during the first half of the nineteenth century can best be appreciated within the framework of its role in providing the market and facilities for the trade in human beings. "Gun-boat politics," the British official policy of policing the West African waterways to free captured slaves, was extended to the port of Lagos. The second and third decades of the nineteenth century were characterized by unhealthy relationships between the British, on one hand, and Africans and other European nations who wanted the slave trade to continue, on the other.

In 1845, events in Lagos developed into an episode, which tested the profundity of the British policy toward the slave trade and African local politics. A succession dispute broke out between two princes, Akintoye and Kosoko. The British interpreted the rivalry predominantly in terms of the struggle between pro- and antislave-trade parties. Meanwhile, chieftancy rivalry was a traditional problem that occurred whenever new kings or chiefs were to be enthroned in Africa. Just as African chiefs had long exploited the jealous rivalries of European traders on the coast, European traders of various nations had similarly exploited chieftaincy disputes. The British supported Akitoye who had been crowned as the king in 1841, but in 1845, he was overthrown by Kosoko, a slave dealer detested by the British.

Between 1845 and 1851, when Kosoko reigned, his relations with the British were unpalatable because he continued to trade in slaves. Events took a completely different turn when the British bombarded Lagos in 1851 and reinstated Akitoye as the king because he assured them that he would outlaw the slave trade. *See also* Abolition of the Slave Trade, Great Britain.

Further Readings: Law, Robin. "Trade and Politics behind the Slave Coast: The Lagoon Traffic and the Rise of Lagos, 1500–1800." *The Journal of African History* 24, 3 (1983): 321–348; Lovejoy, Paul. *Transformations in Slavery: A History of Slavery in Africa.* Cambridge: Cambridge University Press, 1983; Rawley, James. *The TransAtlantic Slave Trade, A History.* New York: W. W. Norton, 1981.

Saheed Aderinto

Languages and Communication

By the sixteenth century there had developed a trading language on the West African coast. It was called "pidgin," and it started as "sailors' jargon," a language of communication used among sailors on a ship. It transformed into a "shore jargon" on arriving on the African coast. This was the acutely Africanized version of the language. It was the last stage of a metamorphosis of native African and European languages. The earliest version of pidgin had a great Portuguese influence.

Notwithstanding its varied forms, the vocabulary of trading languages differed in content from place to place on the West African coast. The intensity of a particular European language's influence depended on the presence of that nation on that stretch of the coast. For instance, where the English traded, there developed "pidgin-English" as found in the towns of the Niger estuary. The development of this language from a convergence of different languages is now known as Creole. The most common was the Creole-Portuguese. It was mostly spoken in **Angola** and Congo, stretching all along the coast from **Senegal** to **Sierra Leone**, largely because they were the first Europeans who made contact on the African coast. The Portuguese kind of Creole spoken in Guinea, Senegal, and **São Tomé** has similar features to that spoken in **Curaçao** and Bonaire of the West Indies.

Few Africans could speak a European language fluently. Those who could were usually the sons of African chiefs sent to live with European merchants in their factories or **trade forts** along the coast. Some were even reported to have been sent overseas for education in a period when their fathers sold other people's **children** into slavery in the same region. For captives, language was a major barrier when they got to the coast, because the enslaved were usually from different ethnic backgrounds. Some slaves acquired other native African languages. **Olaudah Equiano** was one who claimed that these dialects were not so difficult to learn and bore similarities unlike those of the Europeans. That was to be expected because the intonation of Africans would have been a lot easier to comprehend than that of Europeans. Some of the captives also acquired a few European words while waiting for embarkation. This was hardly adequate for communication.

On board, slave ship **captains** segregated slaves into tribal groupings for manageability. Nevertheless, there were language barriers between slaves of different ethnic groups and between slaves and their masters. First-generation slaves spoke with people of like tongues, but not to slaves of other tribes when they were all mixed. They arrived on European or American soil speaking their languages. On arrival, they were called *bozales* in Latin America and "**saltwater negroes**" in the South. Fluency in any language that was not European offered no advantage. Apart from language differences, different faiths—either **Islam** or traditional African **religions**—were looked on as fetishism, even by their predecessors who had learned their masters' language and culture.

These humiliations necessitated devising a means to communicate with their fellow slaves and masters. This also enabled new slaves to fit in. These new slaves had a hard time speaking with Portuguese, English, Spanish, or whatever other language their masters spoke. This led to the development of the pidgin languages that are particular to slaves of different colonies. As African slaves developed these pidgins, the masters too often understood these languages as a means of communicating with them. The pidgins were derived from European languages like Portuguese, Spanish, French, and English, and were not whole derivatives from languages spoken on the African coast. At the same time, the pidgins in the diaspora were not totally different from languages spoken on the African coast.

Over time, the pidgins came to replace native African languages. The native languages that were not so easily wiped off were those spoken in areas with a large number of speakers of the same tongue and with little European influence. With the differences in African dialects, it was easier to adopt European pidgin as a common language for slaves. Language barriers between slaves and between slaves and masters slowly crumbled.

The Afro-American pidgins that developed are known as Creole languages. The development of Creoles led to the formation of a black community in the Americas. Gullah was a Creole dialect of the slaves along the coast of South Carolina and Georgia. This language was a convergence of common elements in their native tongues with influences from European languages. A strong influence was the Wolof dialect. Other significant influences came from the Fante, Ga, Kikongo, Kimbudu, Mandinka, Twi, Ewe, Ibo, and Yoruba. As native dialects contributed to its makeup, so too did other European languages. Of them, English had a strong influence on Gullah. The different Creole languages were widely spread. Afro-English Creole was spoken in Barbados, Antiqua, Guyana, **Jamaica**, Suriname, South Carolina, and Georgia. Afro-Portuguese Creole was spoken mainly in **Brazil** and Curaçao. Afro-Spanish Creole speakers were in **Cuba**, Puerto Rico, and Colombia. Afro-French Creole speakers were in Louisiana, French Guiana, Haiti, Guadeloupe, and Grenada, while Afro-Dutch Creole was spoken in the Virgin Islands.

These were what the children of first-generation slaves took as their native languages. They still spoke native languages when they met other Africans with the same tongue and as the opportunity arose. Given this, first-generation African slaves were fluent in their native tongues and Creole. As older slaves acculturated, they kept their native tongues. These African languages were used to communicate with new slaves. It was through the medium of language that African slaves preserved what they could of their culture, added to it, and passed it down to generations of their children.

Further Readings: Knight, F. W., ed. *General History of the Caribbean.* vol. III. London and Basingstoke: UNESCO Publishing, 1997; Miller, Randall M., and Smith, John David, eds., *Dictionary of Afro-American Slavery.* Westport, CT: Greenwood Press, 1997.

Oyekemi Olajope Oyelakin

Leeward Islands

The Leeward Islands are a line of Caribbean islands constituting the northern end of the Lesser Antilles. In the seventeenth century, the islands were colonized by the French, British, Dutch, and Danish. Some of the islands, especially some controlled by the British and French, became important **sugar** producers. Until the nineteenth century, hundreds of thousands of slaves were imported from various parts of Africa to work on the sugar **plantations** and in other economic activities. By the eighteenth century, the populations of all the habitable islands had large majorities of slaves.

From north to south, the group includes the nonvolcanic Anguilla, Saint Martin, Saba, and Sint Eustacius; and the volcanic Saint Kitts, Nevis, Antigua, Barbuda, Montserrat, Guadeloupe, and Dominica (the last is sometimes included as part of the **Windward Islands**). The Virgin Islands are not geologically part of the Lesser Antilles, but they are usually included in the group because of their proximity.

The Leeward Islands were discovered by Europeans as early as the journeys of Columbus. None, however, became major colonies until the 1620s when the French, British, and Dutch began to settle some of them. By the end of the seventeenth century, all of the islands had been claimed. The British controlled the northeastern Virgin Islands, Anguilla, Saint Kitts, Nevis, Antigua, Barbuda, and Montserrat; the Danish controlled the southwestern Virgin Islands; the Dutch controlled part of Saint Martin, Saba, and Sint Eustatius; and the French controlled the other part of Saint Martin and Guadeloupe.

From the very beginning, some African slaves were brought to the new colonies. In the early years, however, whites made up the majority of settlers (some 55 percent as late as 1678 in the English Leeward Islands). In the last quarter of the seventeenth century, the English Leeward Islands began to adapt the Barbadian methods of sugar production, creating a large market for slaves. By 1708, 76 percent of the residents of England's Leeward Islands were enslaved. French Guadeloupe and Saint Croix in the Danish Virgin Islands also became major sugar producers. Many other islands did not have the appropriate environment for large-scale sugar production and produced only small crops of sugar or other commodities, remained economically unimportant, or became trade **entrepôts** (for example, Sint Eustatius). Regardless, virtually all of the islands had slave majorities (if fewer in absolute numbers) by the end of the eighteenth century.

Because of the low fertility and high **mortality** among African slaves in the sugar colonies, thousands of slaves had to be imported annually just to maintain the required labor forces. For the English Leeward Islands, slave imports grew from an estimated 1,300 per year in the last quarter of the seventeenth century to more than 3,000 per year after 1730. The total number of slaves imported to England's Leeward Islands has been estimated as more than 340,000. The slave population peaked at only 81,000. Similarly, Guadeloupe imported an estimated 291,000 slaves while having a peak slave population of nearly 100,000. Other parts of the Leeward Islands imported only a few tens of thousands of slaves. An estimated 7 percent of all slaves transported from Africa were brought to the Leeward Islands (Curtin, 1969, pp. 59, 62, 78, 80, 88).

Records suggest that the single-largest African region of origin for slaves imported directly to the English Leeward Islands was the Bight of Biafra (more than 40 percent), which seems to have dominated the trade after an initial period in which Africans from the **Gold Coast** were the most common. Still, a diverse group of Africans came to the Leeward Islands with sizeable contingents from the Gold Coast (15 percent), **Windward Coast** (12 percent), and **Angola** (10 percent). Direct imports of slaves to Guadeloupe seem to have been even more diverse with the two largest groups coming from Angola (29 percent) and the Bight of Biafra (27 percent). Other well-represented groups included the Bight of Benin (13 percent) and Senegambia (10 percent). Earlier trade was characterized by a greater balance between the Bight of Benin and the Bight of Biafra with Angola excluded. Only in the later part of the eighteenth century did Angola become important and the Bight of Benin fall off as a supplier. Many of the slaves in the English Leeward Islands and Guadeloupe were probably not imported directly but transshipped from other European colonies making their origins unclear (African origins calculated from Eltis, Behrendt, Richardson, and Klein, 1999). *See also* British Caribbean; French Caribbean; Trans-Atlantic Slave Trade Database.

Further Readings: Curtin, Philip D. *The Atlantic Slave Trade: A Census*. Madison: University of Wisconsin Press, 1969; Dunn, Richard S. *Sugar and Slaves: The Rise of the Planter Class in the English West Indies, 1624–1713*. Chapel Hill: University of North Carolina Press, 1972; Eltis, David, Behrendt, Stephen D., Richardson, David, and Klein, Herbert S., eds. *The Trans-Atlantic Slave Trade: A Database on CD-ROM*. Cambridge: Cambridge University Press, 1999; Stinchcombe, Arthur L. *Sugar Island Slavery in the Age of Enlightenment*. Princeton, NJ: Princeton University Press, 1995.

Patrick Luck

Legitimate Commerce

"Legitimate commerce," also known as legitimate trade, is a term used to distinguish trade in African products, such as hides, palm oil, peanuts, and gold dust, from the slave trade during the late eighteenth and nineteenth centuries. British abolitionists of the time hoped legitimate commerce would cause the decline and eventual end of the Atlantic slave trade.

In the 1790s, early support for legitimate commerce developed in Great Britain and sprang from the belief that trade in legitimate goods could not coexist with trade in slaves, because the greater competitive advantage of legitimate trade would drive out the slave trade. Abolitionists predicted that legitimate commerce would stimulate local economies to such an extent that it would replace the need for the slave trade and also create an greater market for European imports. In reality, both legitimate commerce and the slave trade expanded in tandem until the 1830s when the slave trade began to decline.

Most abolitionists by the early nineteenth century supported military or political intervention to end the slave trade, but the theory of legitimate commerce remained influential. Advocates such as Swanzy and Hutton, British merchants on the **Gold Coast**, argued that legitimate commerce allowed large-scale participation by ordinary people unlike the slave trade, which limited itself to a narrow elite. By the mid-nineteenth century, official British colonial circles advocated the liberating potential of legitimate trade. Benjamin Campbell, British Consul at **Lagos**, and Richard Hutchinson, Consul for the Bight of Biafra, were notable key figures.

Other factors contributed to the expansion of legitimate commerce. European maritime and domestic laws abolishing the slave trade hastened the transition, as did military interventions. The new demands of the Industrial Revolution meant that European traders turned their attention to commodities like palm products, peanuts, cloves, rubber, and cotton. Peanut and palm products went into manufacturing cooking oils, machine lubricants, soaps, and candles, further facilitating the expansion of European urban centers and their industries.

By 1830, palm oil had become the most lucrative commodity obtainable from the West Coast. The Ijo and Efik areas of the Niger Delta, once the centers of slave-trading activity, were the most productive areas. Regions that already had an economy for such exports were excellently positioned to take advantage of new trading opportunities. The Bight of Biafra, which had long established a small trade in palm oil, saw regular exports to Britain beginning in the late eighteenth century. The trade continued to grow steadily through the turn of the century, increasing greatly from the 1820s onward. Despite this growth in legitimate trade, while British merchants had switched from slaves to palm oil, African merchants continued to engage in both trades simultaneously.

Between 1842 and 1850, Great Britain negotiated more than forty treaties to encourage **African rulers** to refrain from participating in the slave trade and to turn toward an economy based on other commerce. Many African leaders, however, found it difficult to honor the treaties because legitimate trade yielded fewer dividends than the slave trade. Other African rulers, such as **Agaja Trudo**, one of the great kings of **Dahomey**, had little sympathy for the slave trade. One of his motives for invading the coastal Aja kingdoms was to restrict and eventually stop the slave-trading and replace it with legitimate commerce. He implored tailors, **carpenters**, smiths, and other trade workers to come to Dahomey in the hopes of attracting trade other than the slave trade. Throughout the nineteenth century, European powers signed treaties with regional African rulers to gain rights to lands and waterways, which led to the beginning of commercial empires.

In some areas in Africa the expansion of agricultural commodities empowered peoples of slave origin as they acquired independent incomes, but legitimate commerce had negative side effects in other regions. European observers of the day expressed the view that, in some instances, legitimate commerce produced more inequality and servitude within Africa. Richard Burton, British Consul for the Bight of Biafra from 1861 to 1864, argued that the end of the overseas slave trade and the rise of the commodities export trade had strengthened the institutions of domestic slavery and worsened the conditions for slaves. The expansion of new trade industries required labor to grow crops, to produce palm oil and kernels, to carry loads, to paddle canoes, and to work as trading assistants. In many societies, **enslavement** satisfied the labor demand whenever possible.

The expansion of legitimate commerce had fundamental political, economic, and social impacts on Africa. The abolition of the slave trade, the economic mainstay of the coastal states, precipitated a radical change in the economic sphere, which led to major social and political changes, including revolts in which former slaves demanded political and economic rights. The economic crisis of the 1870s in Europe caused falling **prices** in African commodities, in turn causing turmoil in areas dependant on those commodities. Such upheavals do not exhaust the many manifestations of the transformation from slavery to legitimate commerce. Worldwide, slavery continued to exist alongside legitimate trade for economic reasons until the beginning of the twentieth century, when continued military intervention enforced abolition. *See also* Abolition of the Slave Trade, Great Britain; African Rulers and the Slave Trade; Closure of the Slave Trade; Slavery in Africa.

Further Readings: Bowman, Joye L. "'Legitimate Commerce' and Peanut Production in Portuguese Guinea, 1840s–1880s." *Journal of African History* 28 (1987): 87–106; Korieh, Chima J. "The Nineteenth Century Commercial Transition in West Africa: The Case of the Biafra Hinterland." *Canadian Journal of African Studies* 34, 3, Special Issue: On Slavery and Islam in African History: A Tribute to Martin Klein (2000): 588–615; McPhee, Allan. *The Economic Revolution in British West Africa*. London: F. Cass, 1971 (1926); Northrup, David. "The Compatibility of the Slave and Palm Oil Trades in the Bight of Biafra." *Journal of African History* XVII, 3 (1976): 353–364; Reynolds, Edward. *Stand the Storm: A History of the Atlantic Slave Trade*. London: Allison & Busby, 1985.

Leslie Wilson

Lewis, Cudjo (?–1935)

Cudjo Lewis, one of 110 West African captives **smuggled** into the United States aboard the slaver *Clotilda*, co-founded and governed **AfricaTown, Alabama**, making important contributions to the social, economic, and political life of that community.

Slave raiders captured Lewis during the height of the Yoruba civil wars in the territory contemporaneously referred to as Nigeria, evacuating him to the coastal city of **Ouidah** where Fon warriors sold him to Captain William Foster, commander of the *Clotilda*. In violation of Section 4 of the Piracy Act, Captain

Foster smuggled Lewis and his co-captives into Alabama where Foster and his co-smugglers distributed the captives among themselves, selling the balance of the cargo to several buyers. Timothy Meaher, the reputed mastermind of the *Clotilda* smuggling scheme, kept thirty captives for himself, including Lewis, depositing them on his property located three miles north of Mobile.

Land ownership was tantamount to the captives' survival, especially during the Reconstruction period when former Slave States designed Vagrancy Laws to entrap and re-enslave landless, penniless blacks, forcing them to labor on **plantations** in lieu of paying fines or imprisonment. Land ownership offered blacks a modicum of protection against imprisonment, re-enslavement, and domestic terrorism perpetrated against them by klansmen and other white supremacists. Lewis and his **shipmates** preferred a life of freedom in their West African homelands rather than a life of **enslavement** in a foreign place. With no prospects for returning to their West African homelands, however, they aimed to establish an African town for themselves and their posterity in Alabama. Realizing the importance of land to the captives' protection and survival, Lewis led efforts to acquire land from Meaher. In 1868, Lewis co-founded a community that was designated AfricaTown.

Lewis garnered respect from individuals in, and outside of, AfricaTown where he built a one-room house and established a family. Lewis served as one of AfricaTown's governors, helping to maintain moral and social order among its residents. Like his West African ancestors, Lewis was a skilled agriculturalist who cultivated one of the most productive gardens in Africa-Town. Individuals who knew Lewis described him as a generous individual who shared **food** with others. Indeed, AfricaTown is rooted in communalism and other West African ideals that contributed to its viability. In 1872, Lewis played a key role in the establishment of The Old Baptist Church, serving as its caretaker for several years thereafter. Extant as Union Baptist Church, the edifice is the architectural cornerstone of AfricaTown. Its congregation is still composed of the descendants of AfricaTown's founders.

Lewis crossed over into ancestorhood in 1935, the last survivor of the *Clotilda* smuggling expedition. Although he was a victim of a federal crime, forced to live the remainder of his life in a land that did not recognize or respect his intelligence or humanity, Lewis lived his life as an upstanding individual of exemplary character. Cudjo Lewis was an astute leader, a **humanitarian**, and a model resident of AfricaTown upon which he left an indelible mark.

Further Readings: Falola, Toyin, and Oguntomisin, G. O. *Yoruba Warlords of the 19th Century.* Trenton: Africa World Press, 2001; Hurston, Zora Neale. "Cudjo's Own Story Of The Last African Slaver." *Journal of Negro History* 12 (October 1927): 648–663.

Natalie Suzette Robertson

Liberia

The establishment of Liberia as an American colony in 1821 was the culmination of converging efforts to return free African Americans to their ancestral homeland. By the early nineteenth century, a considerable number of free people of color were living in the United States, having been manumitted for economic or moral reasons. Among many Southern whites, there was a pervasive fear that these free blacks were apt to incite slave revolts, citing the 1800 Virginia insurrection led by Gabriel, and similar plots in South Carolina, New Jersey, and New York. Many Southerners feared that increased interactions between whites and freed people of color would lead to miscegenation. Urban Northerners resented the competition that free African Americans posed in the labor market. To address these issues, a group of white Americans met in Washington, DC, in December of 1816 and founded what became known as the American Colonization Society (ACS). The ACS's primary goal was to establish a colony on the West African coast and to convince Congress to provide funds to facilitate the removal of willing African Americans. The ACS found support among white abolitionists, suggesting that the repatriation of African Americans to Africa would help to undo some of the wrongs committed by slavery. Missionaries saw an opportunity to spread **Christianity** to Africa. Most African Americans opposed African colonization outright, but a small number saw repatriation to the newly created colony as an opportunity to escape oppression and embarked on the first voyage in 1820. Increasing numbers of free blacks would embrace the idea of settling in Liberia as it became clear that full protection under the law in the United States was a long way off.

Upon their arrival in Liberia, the settlers, products of Victorian society, were intent on building a similar society in the West African colony. They continued the African American tradition of establishing benevolent, occupation-based, fraternal organizations, and missionary activity was encouraged. Freemasons, for instance, figured prominently, as lodges became a forum for political issues and members acted as models of Christian values. The Liberian government supported moral behavior through the legislation it enacted. Divorces, for instance, were subject to legislative approval and unwed childbirth was penalized.

Although the settler population was mainly composed of African Americans who had been free in the United States, settlements were confined to the Atlantic coastline and existed largely apart from the native African population. Those Africans who did live in their midst were required to wear Western clothing and adhere to the settlers' social norms. Orphaned African youths were assimilated through apprenticeships with settler families. In part because of the contributions of their charges, the American Liberians were able to become more self-sufficient through agriculture. Liberia gained its independence from the United States and the administration of the ACS in 1847.

Further interaction between settlers and native Africans increased with the arrival of free, educated West Indians. Men such as Edward Wilmot Blyden followed different traditions from those who had previously settled. Wanting to create an exclusively black republic, many of the **arrivals** during the 1850s advocated the economic and social integration of inland areas. This brought them into conflict with the older generation of settlers who wished to remain essentially separate from the peoples of the interior and who wanted to restrict commerce to the coastline settlements to maintain their grip on power. Such tensions would characterize the volatile political situation facing Liberia during the late nineteenth and early twentieth century.

Meanwhile, however, American Liberians and missionaries were pushing for **rum** and tobacco bans, recognizing that these commodities were instrumental to the slave trade. After the importation of slaves in the United States was abolished, Liberians took in Africans who had been liberated from ships captured by the U.S. Navy, incorporating them into settler communities through missions or the apprentice system. In these respects, the establishment of Liberia proved important to challenging the system of the **triangular trade** of slaves. In addition, the nation, along with Haiti and Ethiopia, provided a powerful example of black rule that was rare at the time. *See also* Returnees to Africa.

Further Readings: Moses, William J. *Liberian Dreams: Back-to-Africa Narratives from the 1850's.* University Park: University of Pennsylvania Press, 1998; Schick, Tom. *Behold the Promised Land: A History of Afro-American Settler Society in Nineteenth-Century Liberia.* 2nd ed. Baltimore: Johns Hopkins University Press, 1980; Smith, James. *Sojourners in Search of Freedom: The Settlement of Liberia by Black Americans.* Lanham, MD: University Press of America, 1987.

Carmen Lenore Wright

Licensing

Licensing was a part of the trans-Atlantic slave trade, which took different forms. In its crudest form, it represented the form of authority given to a company that or a person or group of people who were involved in slave-trading activities. Slave-trading activities included ownership of vessels or **plantations** and transporting, buying, and selling of slaves.

As the trans-Atlantic slave trade transformed into a veritable economic enterprise, the home countries of individuals and groups of merchants began to establish principles and laws related to the activities of their citizens in Africa and the Americas. Big slave trade merchant companies were required to collect licenses from their home country before they could engage in the trans-Atlantic slave trade in Africa. **Trade forts** and slave ships were owned by individual traders or companies, which acted in the interest of their home country.

The most significant aspect of licensing in the trans-Atlantic slave trade was that authority and approval were required if another country demonstrated interested in trading at a fort or post that the other considered as its sphere of influence. Therefore, licensing allowed fort owners to preserve their ownership and **monopoly** of the trading port. The desire of one nation to trade in a fort or trading post that belonged to another without approval or a license caused tension and rivalry during the period of the trans-Atlantic slave trade. A classic example is **Fort Saint Louis** (located in present-day **Senegal**), which generated serious rivalry between France and Great Britain during the seventeenth and eighteenth centuries.

The list of chartered slave trade companies is long and inexhaustible. One of the most influential was a British joint stock company named the Royal Adventurers into Africa. This company was chartered in 1651 to deliver 3,500 slaves to the Spanish colonies each year. By 1672, the company had run into severe financial difficulties and had to fold. Its demise paved the way for the emergence of a more formidable slave-trading company called the **Royal Africa Company**. The Royal Africa Company was licensed to monopolize the **British slave trade**. The license gave the company the opportunity of asserting sole control of territories between Cape Blanco in the north and the Cape of Good Hope in the south. As a monopoly company, it could seize the ships and prosecute illegal traders operating in its sphere of influence.

The Dutch West India Company carried out the official policy of the Dutch government in Africa and the Americas. Chartered in 1621, the company, like her Royal Africa Company counterpart, built and maintained forts across the West, East, and South African costal waters. It monopolized the trade in human beings until the eighteenth century when attempts were made to give individual traders the opportunity to buy and sell slaves.

The Dutch were not the only European nations that saw the need to allow their nationals to trade freely in slaves. In fact, they came after the French and the English who had by 1672 and 1689, respectively, allowed individual merchants to buy and sell slaves. The only condition was that individual **slave traders** in the case of the British had to pay 10 percent of their proceeds to the government. *See also* Dutch Slave Trade.

Further Readings: Engerman, Stanley, and Genovese, Eugene. *Race and Slavery in the Western Hemisphere: Quantitative Studies*. Princeton, NJ: Princeton University Press, 1975; Palmer, Colin A. *Human Cargoes: The British Slave Trade to Spanish America, 1700–1739*. Urbana: University of Illinois Press, 1981; Postma, Johannes. *The Dutch in the Atlantic Slave Trade 1600–1815*. New York and Cambridge: Cambridge University Press, 1990.

Saheed Aderinto

Life Expectancy

"If few die the profit is certain, but if many are lost so also is their owner." This dictum profoundly influenced the way slavers adopted measures to prevent high **mortality** rates in the Middle Passage. There were nutritional and epidemiological odds against slaves and sailors, which affected their life expectancy. Generally, slave deaths during the Middle Passage caused by sickness, **suicide**, depression, and rebellion averaged 13 to 15 percent.

There were two schools of thought among the English slaving **captains**, the "loose-packers" and the "tight-packers." Loose-packers opined that by giving the slaves a little more room, better **food**, and a certain degree of liberty, they reduced the death rate and received a better **price** or **profit** for each slave in the West Indies. Conversely, the tight-packers pointed out that, although the loss of life might be greater on each of their voyages, so too were the net receipts from a larger **cargo**. If the survivors were weak and emaciated, they could be fattened up in a West Indian slave yard before being offered for sale in the slave market. For many years after 1750, the tight-packers were in the ascendant.

Many factors influenced life expectancy during the Middle Passage. They included time spent in embarkation, mutinies, **disease**, suicides, provisions, hygiene, and melancholy. Taking on slaves was a process that could take up to a year depending on the geographic location. The **crews** were often exposed to malaria, the revenge of angry natives, attacks of pirates, and the constant threat of a slave mutiny. Mutinies were frequent and some of them were successful. The mutinies that failed often resulted in heavy losses among the slaves and the sailors. There are fairly lucid accounts of 55 mutinies from 1699 to 1845 and passing references to more than 100 others. The Middle Passage record reveals that Africans did not submit tamely to being carried across the Atlantic.

The cargo could be swept away by disease. The more days at sea resulted in a greater number of deaths among the slave cargo. Therefore, the captain often strived to shorten the voyage by ensuring an ample supply of food and fresh **water**, at least three months' worth. Slaves from the **Windward Coast**, **Liberia**, and **Sierra Leone** were fed with rice, millet, or corn meal sometimes cooked with a few lumps of salt beef. Those from the Bight of Biafra, at the east end of the Gulf of Guinea, were fed stewed yams. Slaves from Congo and the Angolas preferred manioc or plantains. They were all provided with a pint of water, served in a pannikin. After the breakfast followed a "joyless ceremony" called "**dancing** the slaves." The slaves in irons were told to dance around the deck. Dancing was prescribed as a therapeutic measure against suicidal melancholy. Slaving captains sometimes advertised for "A person that can play on the Bagpipes for a Guinea ship." The slaves were told to sing. Their **songs** were not for amusement but rather about songs of sorrow, sickness, fear of being beaten, their hunger, and the memory of their country.

Housekeeping was carried out in an effort to promote good health and a proper diet. This approach was to ensure fewer slaves were lost in the Middle Passage. Some captains with filthy vessels ran the risk of losing their slaves. While the slaves were on deck, they were monitored against committing suicide. The propensity for suicide was high. Some slaves committed suicide by willfully **drowning** themselves or starving themselves to death. They believed that when they died they would return to their own country and friends again. This belief was popular among the **Igbo** slaves of eastern Nigeria. To discourage the widespread dissemination of this idea, captains often cut off the heads of those who died, thus intimating that they must go without heads in their next life. This was carried out in the presence of the slaves.

Another deadly scourge was a phenomenon called "fixed melancholy" in the Guinea cargoes. In the Guinea cargoes, slaves who were well fed, treated with kindness, and kept under some measure of good sanitary conditions would often die because they simply lost the will to live. Fixed melancholy was a contagious sickness among the slaves. Its symptoms were lowness of spirits, despondency, and the hunger strike. Some human cargoes were crowded, filthy, undernourished, and terrified out of the wish to live.

Perhaps the greatest cause of mortality during the Middle Passage was illness. The Middle Passage was a marketplace for diseases. From Europe came smallpox, measles, gonorrhea, and syphilis. The African diseases included yellow fever, dengue, blackwater fever, and malaria, as well as amoebic and bacillary dysentery (the bloody flux), Guinea worms, hookworm, yaws, elephantiasis, and leprosy. Smallpox was much feared because the vessel could be infested, although dysentery often caused more deaths in the aggregate.

The average mortality in the Middle Passage is impossible to state. Some voyages were made without the loss of a single slave. The English Privy Council in 1789 arrived at an estimate of about 12 percent for the average mortality among slaves in the Middle Passage. The mortality among slaves in the Middle Passage was arguably not greater than that of white **indentured servants** or even free Irish, Scottish, and German immigrants in the North Atlantic crossing. The increasing sophistication of transporting slaves was reflected in the declining rates of mortality especially in the post-1700 period. Ships often claimed 10 percent mortality because of standardization adopted in the trade, particularly the specially constructed slave vessels.

The increasing demand for slaves was attributed to the low life expectancy of the African American slave population. It was noted that African American slaves lived an average of seven years. Joseph Miller has pointed out the crucial impact of age and sexual imbalance among Africans as causal factors for the negative population growth of the slave labor force. Yet, recent studies reveal a positive rate of population growth among native-born slaves and a life expectancy beyond the average of seven working years in all American societies. The average life expectancy of slave males was in the upper twenties in **Brazil**, and in the mid-thirties for the United States, which suggests an average working life of at least twenty years in Brazil and twenty-five years in the United States. The average working life was, at a minimum, twenty-five years for Brazilian slaves and thirty years for North American slaves.

There was a high death rate among the newcomers. This was referred to as the **"seasoning"** process in which newcomers become accustomed to the climate. Many of the young slaves in the American tropics died at about twice the rate expected for their peers in Africa. Europeans with less resistance to yellow fever and malaria died at ten times the expected death rate in Europe. This partly explains why planters preferred Africans to Europeans. Slaves were imported to supply the shortfall between births and deaths. *See also* Overcrowding.

Further Readings: Cowley, Malcolm, and Mannix, Daniel P. "The Middle Passage." In David Northrup, ed. *The Atlantic Slave Trade*. Lexington, MA: DC Heath and Company, 1994; Miller, Joseph C. "Deaths before the Middle Passage." In David Northrup, ed. *The Atlantic Slave Trade*. Lexington: DC Heath and Company, 1994.

Rasheed Olaniyi

Lisbon

During the Portuguese Age of Exploration (1415–1478), Portugal initially ruled, along with its neighbor Spain, the Atlantic Ocean with its many ship fleets and colonies along the West coast of Africa and the Americas. By the 1470s, Lisbon became the country's main slave port. The Portuguese slave trade started then not as a trans-Atlantic trade but as an Old World trade, supplying slaves to Lisbon and hence onward to Spain and Italy. In 1539, 12,000 slaves were sold in the city's markets. Lisbon thrived off the businesses associated with slavery, with Portuguese goods exchanged for slaves, goods traded for slaves, and goods produced by the slaves. People invested in, and profited from, the trade, and the Royal family took its share through taxation. African slaves were employed in a variety of occupations, but increasingly they were to be found in urban employment such as domestic service. On January 8, 1455, a Papal Bull entitled "Romanus Pontifex," issued by Pope Nicholas V, was read in both Latin and Portuguese in Lisbon Cathedral. This document, one of enormous importance, justified slavery. From the reading of this document, Prince Henry was permitted to invade, search out, capture, and conquer all non-Christian-believing subjects— specifically those living in West Africa. Deemed enemies of Christ, these groups of people were reduced to perpetual slavery.

Prince Henry the Navigator, the third son of the King of Portugal, was pivotal to early Portuguese exploration from Lisbon. He helped finance and organize many expeditions, such as the one in 1415 to the North and West coasts of Africa, from which he learned about trade in spices, gold, and silver. In 1441, the first groups of black slaves were brought to Lisbon for Prince Henry. Initially, slaves were captured through cruel means, including kidnapping and banditry. Prince Henry, however, ordered a change of practice, thus creating a new system of trading slaves between Africans and Europeans. Prince Henry also established a slave market and fort in Arguin Bay in the year 1445. It was from this fort that black slaves were brought back to Lisbon and then distributed, if necessary, to nearby Portuguese cities.

Slavery's long tradition in Portugal dates back to the time of the twelfth and thirteenth centuries when **Muslims** were taken as prisoners and then enslaved by **Christians** in wars. Although the **enslavement** of Muslims declined in subsequent centuries, a new trade in sub-Saharan African slaves became established in the early fifteenth century. Initially the slave trade developed with Portugal as the center of commerce, with goods and human cargo traded to and from Lisbon. Black slaves worked not only in Lisbon, but also in Évora and the Southern region known as the Algarve. During the mid-sixteenth century, more than 32,000 African slaves resided in Portugal, with the majority owned by the aristocracy, legal and religious officials, and religious institutions. Yet, because of the declining number of slaves in Portugal, the country's African population—especially in Lisbon—decreased. Ultimately, Brazil's economic importance—which was fundamentally linked to slavery—overtook that of Portugal.

Slave fortresses were established on small islands off the coast of West Africa, the most important being **Cape Verde** and **São Tomé**. These two islands were used to collect slaves traded from the mainland, and who were then sent to Lisbon. The development of **sugar** cultivation on São Tomé provided the blueprint for the larger **plantation** economy of the Americas.

Without a doubt, Lisbon was certainly involved in the Atlantic slave trade quite early, at least by 1512, and indeed it was frequently Portuguese traders who supplied African slaves to Spanish colonists and **slave traders**. The Portuguese established the first trading fort in West Africa (**Elmina**) in present-day Ghana, and were taking Africans to work in the plantations in Madeira and São Tomé. Over the centuries, ships from Lisbon carried more slaves to the Americas than any other European port. *See also* Europe, Enslaved Africans in; Portuguese Slave Trade.

Further Readings: Thomas, Hugh. *The Slave Trade: The Story of the Atlantic Slave Trade, 1440–1870.* New York: Simon & Schuster, 1997; Williams, Eric Eustace. *Capitalism and Slavery; with a new introduction by Colin A. Palmer.* Chapel Hill: University of North Carolina Press, 1994 (1944).

Nicholas Jones

Liverpool

Liverpool, England, emerged as the dominant British slave-trading port by the 1750s and was the premier slaving port in the trans-Atlantic world in the decades thereafter. Lying at the juncture of the Mersey River and the tidal inlet known as the Pool, Liverpool was an unpromising site for an oceangoing port. In addition to a growing trade with Northern Europe, especially Sweden and Russia, the Mediterranean littoral, and other parts of the continent, Liverpool merchants began to develop a keen interest in trans-Atlantic trade after 1660, particularly the West Indian **sugar** and Chesapeake tobacco trades.

Liverpool trade grew slowly from the mid-sixteenth century to the early eighteenth century, in part, because commercial development was hampered by an almost total lack of wharves, docks, and other basic harbor facilities, a deficiency that was addressed with the opening of the first wet dock in 1715. In the decades that followed, an unparalleled system of docks and wharves, roads, and canals was built, a development that aided the expansion of the slave trade during the course of the eighteenth century. Liverpool's first **slave traders** were **interlopers** who often employed chicanery to bypass the slave-trading **monopoly** of the **Royal Africa Company**. Although the demise of the Royal Africa Company in 1712 led to explosive growth in the British traffic in slaves, the Liverpool slave trade remained insignificant for many years thereafter. Although Liverpool's slave traders did not pose a serious threat to their **Bristol** competitors before 1740, a decade later, by 1750, Liverpool had eclipsed both Bristol and **London** to become the premier slaving port in the Atlantic world.

This dominance was especially marked between 1751 and 1775, when 1,713 slave ships cleared Liverpool for West Africa, while only 485 ships departed for Africa from Bristol, and 458 departed from London. Between 1695, when the first-known slaving vessels departed Liverpool for Africa, and the abolition of the **British slave trade** in 1807, more than 4,800 slaving ventures cleared the port of Liverpool. Traditional interpretations of the rise of the Liverpool slave trade are many and varied. Some attribute the rise to ready access to the industrial products of Lancashire and the Midlands, while others point to the construction of a system of docks; an expansive regional trade in coal, salt, fish, and Irish goods; the safety of the

North Channel during wartime; the availability of investment capital; the low cost of slaving operations; the role of commercial and social relationships; and a long maritime tradition on Merseyside. Important as these factors were, however, the rise of the Liverpool slave trade can be attributed equally to the appearance of a diverse group of slave-trading entrepreneurs after 1700, men whose commercial acumen, social relationships, business connections, and wealth yielded a competitive advantage over their rivals in France, the Netherlands, Portugal, and elsewhere in Britain. Often described as a fishing village before 1700, the rapid rise of the Liverpool slave trade by 1750 was one of the great socio-economic developments of eighteenth-century British history.

Further Readings: Clemens, Paul G. E. "The Rise of Liverpool, 1665–1750." *Economic History Review* 29 (1976): 211–225; Francis, Hyde, Parkinson, Bradbury, and Marriner, Sheila. "The Nature and Profitability of the Liverpool Slave Trade." *The Economic History Review* (1953): 368–377; Parkinson, C. N. *The Rise of the Port of Liverpool.* Liverpool: Liverpool University Press, 1952; Williams, Gomer. *History of the Liverpool Privateers and Letters of Marque with an Account of the Liverpool Slave Trade.* London: F. Cass, 1966 (1897).

Brian W. Refford

Loango

By the fifteenth century, the **Vili** kingdom of Loango extended along the West Central African coast from the **Congo River** to Cape Lopez in the north. The earliest accounts of Loango come from European explorers and traders in the fifteenth and sixteenth centuries, who describe a highly centralized kingdom comprising four provinces ruled by a powerful *Maloango* from the royal capital Buali, near present-day Pointe Noire. Although never a source of slaves on the scale of its southern neighbor, **Angola**, Loango nonetheless furnished European traders with many thousands of slaves primarily for Caribbean markets during the eighteenth century. With the decline of the trans-Atlantic slave trade in the nineteenth century and a corresponding rise in **legitimate commerce**, the kingdom's political structure became increasingly fragmented. The wealth and power of merchants and traders replaced that of the *Maloangos*, setting the stage for the kingdom's demise and French colonization in the 1880s.

Early European traders encountered well-established trade networks linking villages on the Loango coast with those in the interior. Regional specialization and production provided Vili merchants with a wide range of products, including sugarcane, redwood, palm nuts, salt, copper, and ivory. Especially after the founding of **Luanda** in 1576, Vili traders engaged in regular commerce with European merchants. What began as a small trade in cloth, ivory, and copper with Portuguese and Dutch traders in the early seventeenth century, by the 1670s, had become largely a trade in slaves. Increasingly, the Portuguese encountered competition from other European powers for its share in the Loango trade. By the eighteenth century, the English, followed by the French, had surpassed the Portuguese and Dutch as Loango's greatest trading partners. As demand for slaves increased during the eighteenth century in North and South America and the Caribbean, Loango became an important source for New World labor. By the 1780s, Loango accounted for nearly two-thirds of the **French slave trade** (10,000 to 15,000 slaves per year), which secured labor for the booming **sugar** industry in **Saint Domingue** and other Caribbean islands. Portuguese trading in Loango increased during the first half of the nineteenth century, however, as American, Brazilian, Cuban, and Spanish **slave traders** joined Portuguese **smugglers** in attempting to dodge British and American navy squadrons that were patrolling against trans-Atlantic slave voyages.

The kingdom's three major trading **ports**, Loango Bay, Malemba, and Cabinda, drew slaves from various regions, including Mpumbo, **Kongo**, and Angola. A highly structured, hierarchical organization of the slave trade in Loango allowed Vili rulers to trade with Europeans largely on their terms. The *Maloango* generated revenue by taxing the sale of slaves through a system that authorized local officials (*mafouks*) to regulate local brokers who gained exclusive negotiating rights with Europeans. Despite attempts by the Portuguese to undermine this system, Vili rulers succeeded in creating a **free trade** zone that welcomed (and profited from) trade with a number of European powers for three centuries. *See also* Portuguese Slave Trade.

Further Reading: Martin, Phyllis M. *The External Trade of the Loango Coast 1576–1870.* Oxford: Oxford University Press, 1972.

Edward D. Maris-Wolf

London

The earliest center of the **British slave trade**, London was the largest slave-trading port in Britain until it was eclipsed by **Bristol** after 1725. According to the **Trans-Atlantic Slave Trade Database**, the first known slave ship to depart London for Africa, the *Dragon*, sailed in 1633; while two others, the *Bonadventure* and the *Mary*, set out in 1644 and 1645, respectively. After the mid-seventeenth century, the growing profitability of the African slave trade inspired a group of primarily London **investors** to found the Royal Adventurers of England Trading to Africa (1662). Although granted a royal **monopoly** of trade from Sallee to the Cape of Good Hope, the Royal Adventurers were never profitable, and the company ceased trading in 1672. A group of creditors and shareholders from the Royal Adventurers combined in 1672 to establish the London-based **Royal Africa Company**, a royally sanctioned slave-trading monopoly.

The greatest portion of the slave trade, whether under the Royal Africa Company or free traders, remained in London until well after 1700. Although London continued to dominate the British slave trade after 1700, by 1725, Bristol had overtaken London as the dominant **port** in the trade. Although surpassed by Bristol after 1725, London remained the center of slave trade financing for the outports (both Bristol and **Liverpool**), the primary source for East Indian **textiles** and other goods traded for slaves, and the principal market for tropical produce imported from the West Indies by returning **slave traders**. In fact, London remained the principal port in the British trans-Atlantic trade throughout the eighteenth century, although never specializing in the slave trade as did Bristol or, later, Liverpool. However, London's share of the slave trade did not decline as much for the period 1726–1776 as previously thought. Recent historians, such as James Rawley, have argued that London's role in the trans-Atlantic slave trade has long been underestimated.

Between 1676 and 1725, more than 1,140 slaving ventures departed London, while only 399 departed Bristol. This changed in the half-century that followed. Between 1726 and 1776, only 880 ventures departed London, while more than 1,380 set out from Bristol. After 1750, especially after 1776, the London slave trade experienced a resurgence, supplanting the Bristol trade after 1776. All told, 2,700 slaving ventures cleared London for Africa between 1633 and 1807, a figure that compares favorably to the 2,060 that left Bristol between 1676 and 1807 (**Trans-Atlantic Slave Trade Database**) Home of **William Wilberforce** and the Clapham Sect, as well as parliamentary defenders of the slave trade, London emerged as the center of the British abolitionist movement after 1775. *See also* Abolition of the Slave Trade, Great Britain.

Further Readings: Eltis, David, Behrendt, Stephen D., Richardson, David, and Klein, Herbert S., eds. *The Trans-Atlantic Slave Trade: A Database on CD-ROM.* Cambridge: Cambridge University Press, 1999; Klein, Herbert. *The Middle Passage: Comparative Studies in the Atlantic Slave Trade.* Princeton, NJ: Princeton University Press, 1978; Rawley, James. *London, Metropolis of the Slave Trade.* Columbia: University of Missouri Press, 2003; Richardson, David. *Bristol, Africa, and the Eighteenth Century Slave Trade to America.* Vol. 1: *The Years of Expansion, 1698–1729.* Gloucester: Produced for the Bristol Record Society by A. Sutton Pub., 1986.

Brian W. Refford

Luanda

Founded in 1575 by the Portuguese explorer Paulo Dias Novais, Luanda was the main hub of a profitable and extensive slave trade to Brazil and the West Indies from c. 1550 to c. 1850. By the early 1600s, the Portuguese developed the port of Luanda, turning the expanding city into a main repository of the slave trade: Luanda became a terminus where slaves captured in the interior were gathered for sale to traders heading for **Brazil**. The Portuguese government officially put an end to the slave trade in 1836. Unfortunately, as long as there was a demand from Brazil and **São Tomé** slaving continued.

The Mbundu inhabited the area surrounding Luanda, which the Portuguese referred to as **Angola**. Beset with internal instability, the Mbundu leaders failed to control the local chiefs leading to civil war. The Portuguese created deceptions and maneuvering among the rival groups compounded the increasing social and economic tensions within Angola. Internal warfare intensified, bringing social disintegration that led to increased trafficking in slaves. By the 1570s, Portugal attempted to establish a formal colony in Angola by appointing a royal governor and building forts. Portuguese control eventually weakened, making the colony susceptible to the military incursions of the Dutch in the 1640s. The expanding demands of the Atlantic slave system, internal strife among local chiefs, and competition among foreign powers meant a constant state of confusion for Angola, which seeped into Luanda throughout its history, finally subsiding by the First World War. Slavery and the slave trade dominated 88 percent of all commercial and economic activities in Luanda at least until the end of the eighteenth century.

Luanda attained the distinction of becoming a "complete" African slave **port**. Portuguese merchants provided the credit that slavers needed to purchase **food** and other supplies for the expeditions inland to procure slaves. Merchants in Luanda supplied the financing to acquire African-owned slaves. Although African slavers owned the slaves during the trans-Atlantic voyage, Brazilian shippers carried and delivered their **cargo** to slave markets in South America.

Luanda's beginning as a major slave port is connected to the history of the island of São Tomé. A small island located off the coast of Africa in the Gulf of Guinea, São Tomé became an integral part of the trans-Atlantic trade. Serving as a **sugar plantation**, São Tomé also served as a staging area for the slave trade with slaves originating mainly from the **Kongo**. In the sixteenth century, conflict erupted between official Portuguese **slave traders** and private traders. To avoid taxation by the Portuguese crown, **interlopers** moved their slaving operations to Luanda. In 1576, the Portuguese crown wanted to contain the interlopers and established a base at Luanda allowing the crown to increase its share of the trade. Luanda became a major gateway into the interior, providing several thousand slaves per year and shipping the human cargo directly to the Americas.

Similar to the slave trade in general, slaves were acquired through tribute paid by a subordinate chief to other African elites or to Portuguese traders or officials. Luanda shipped slaves from the immediately surrounding area. As slaving depleted the closest inhabited areas around Luanda, slavers moved further inland to meet the increased demand for labor in the Americas. As the demand for slaves increased, **African rulers** established slave markets in the interior, but the constant warfare produced most of the slaves. Neither the local African kings, the Portuguese slavers, nor the Imbangala war chiefs could maintain order. The need to procure more captives led to increased internal strife between the monarch and his tributary kings. Nobility in need of cash would raid their own peasants pressing them into slavery. Even pawning as payment of debt could lead to slavery and exportation. Constant turmoil among the three groups not only created political and economic instability, but also increased the confrontations that produced occasions for **enslavement** on a colossal scale. Portuguese slavers supported opposing African factions leading to heightened conflict.

Throughout the seventeenth and eighteenth centuries, local African states and the Portuguese administrative colony at Luanda attempted to regulate the slave trade. An intense commercial rivalry developed that created a trading network with its major export terminus at Luanda. Interior African states each in turn developed as a source of slaves. Other goods like **textiles**, salt, and copper changed hands, but many slaves found their way to the waiting European ships at Luanda. Foreign ships searched the West coast to obtain slaves for transport and found other points of entry, but the Portuguese successfully kept control of Luanda and thus their **profits** remained quite high. Plenty of slaves seemed to be available for sale elsewhere, but Luanda remained crucial as a valuable source for captives.

Historical sources vary on the number of slaves exported from Luanda and the surrounding Angolan environs; however, 4 million slaves or an average of 11,000 slaves per year for 350 years remains a reasonable estimate. With these estimates, it seems that Luanda exported more slaves than any other port during the period of the Atlantic slave trade. *See also* Portuguese Slave Trade.

Further Readings: Curtin, Philip, Feierman, Steven, Thompson, Leonard, and Vansina, Jan. *African History*. Boston: Little, Brown, 1978; Henderson, Lawrence W. *Angola: Five Centuries of Conflict*. Ithaca, NY: Cornell University Press, 1979; July, Robert W. *A History of the African People*. 5th ed. Prospect Heights, IL: Waveland Press, 1998; Lovejoy, Paul E. *Transformations in Slavery: A History of Slavery in Africa*. New York: Cambridge University Press, 1993; Manning, Patrick. *Slavery and African Life: Occidental, Oriental, and African Slave Trades*. African Studies Series, ed. J. M. Lonsdale. Cambridge: Cambridge University Press, 2000.

Michael Bonislawski

M

Manqueron

Manqueron, also *makron* or *macron*, is a term that refers to an African slave who was considered unsellable by Dutch **slave traders**. Africans from the **Gold Coast** and **Angola** were transported by the Dutch West India Company via slave ship to the island of **Curaçao** off the coast of Venezuela in the Lesser Antilles. There, slaves were sold according to the rules of ***asiento***, the **monopoly** permissions given by the Spanish to sell slaves to their American colonies. Under the terms of this agreement, Africans were valued in *pieza de India*. The standard value for a healthy individual between the ages of fifteen and twenty-five was one *pieza*, or a *peça*. Those between eight and fifteen or twenty-five and thirty-five were valued at two-thirds *peça*. Those who appeared to be older than thirty-five and those who had physical or psychological impairments were classified as *manquerons*. The number of Africans imported to the Americas and classified as *manquerons* by the Dutch is estimated to be close to 20 percent, although 10 percent is considered to be a more accurate figure. Many Africans who could not be sold were given time to recuperate from their trans-Atlantic voyage and then re-evaluated to see whether they might meet the conditions of the Spanish. Many of the Africans who did not meet these conditions were sold elsewhere in the Americas or illegally at discounted **prices** to Spanish colonies. These Africans sold illegally by the Dutch would have been priced low in terms of *pieza de India*. Africans who could not be sold to the Spanish at any price were sometimes earmarked for delivery to other locations, although it is not clear whether these deliveries always took place. A significant number of African *manquerons* did remain on Curaçao. These Africans were often used as domestic servants by the island's colonists. After slavery was abolished by the Dutch in 1863, many of these former slaves emigrated elsewhere in the Caribbean in search of work. The contributions of *manquerons* were important to the creolization of the islands of the Lesser Antilles. In terms of **music**, their participation in Caribbean cultural production led to the creation of the Antillean waltz. The Papiamentu **language**, spoken in Aruba, Bonaire, and Curaçao, combines elements of the *manquerons'* West African languages with Dutch,

Portuguese, Arawak, and other languages. The modern-day population of Curaçao reflects this Creole history, as nearly 85 percent of the population identifies having African ancestry. Many of these ancestors were presumably *manquerons*. *See also* Dutch Slave Trade.

Further Reading: Postma, Johannes Menne. *The Dutch in the Atlantic Slave Trade, 1600–1850*. New York and Cambridge: Cambridge University Press, 1990.

Eric Covey

"Middle Passage" (1966)

"Middle Passage" is a poem by Robert Hayden, former Poet Laureate of the United States and **Senegal**. Written in 1945 and revised several times before its final publication in 1966, it is a fictionalized history of the circumstances surrounding **the *Amistad*** mutiny of 1839. Hayden's research provided the backbone for the stories within the poem. The depositions, ship logs, and ledgers that Hayden referenced while writing his poem lent validity to his speakers' words. What "Middle Passage" achieves with this material, however, are vague characters, ambiguous themes, and an indefinite sequence of events. The historical event is retold in three parts with a distinctively modern ironic distance, and incorporates European voices to disempower them and discreetly unravel justifications for the slave trade.

Hayden was aware of how African American identity and history are shaped by an inherently hegemonic language. Therefore, rather than attempting to resituate the events of "Middle Passage" by assigning that language to a non-European, Hayden assigned words to the **slave traders** whose speech and writings give the poem direction. No Africans are directly heard from in "Middle Passage"; the reader is merely given a sense of the turmoil experienced and is informed of what is said by way of translators or hearsay. Rather than presenting good's triumph over evil, "Middle Passage" illustrates how the slave trade self-destructed.

"Middle Passage" is about several aspects of the Middle Passage: its historical and conceptual existences, a particular event that occurred during it, and its reversal. Themes and devices throughout the poem echo this difficult combination of meanings. The prominent concepts of life and death are almost impossible to consistently decipher in relation to one another. Indeed, in the poem's first stanza, the first mention of life by way of death is immediately followed by an account of African **suicide**.

The sense of time and space is complex, because of the various settings afforded to speakers and action. The final stanza of the poem comes after the missing climax, and introduces the poem's hero, Cinquez, who is not afforded speech, description, or action. "Middle Passage" is essentially about the transformative undoing of the Middle Passage. This notion is subtly hinted at in the first part, during the second log excerpt, in which the units of time that are written about decrease from eight, to four, to three, while the actual quantities increase from hours, to days, to weeks.

Hayden struggled with issues addressed by his "Middle Passage," including personal identity and history. In addition to the historical Middle Passage that was the origin of Hayden's existence as an African American, he was concerned with life's metaphorical Middle Passages. By virtue of his race, Hayden was considered a black poet. Because he did not view art primarily as a tool for social change, however, many members of the African American literary community of the mid-twentieth century questioned Hayden's blackness. Certainly, "Middle Passage" is exemplary of the influence that poets such as T. S. Eliot had on Hayden's style, and the poem's literary allusions are to Shakespeare and Coleridge. Therefore, his literary persona was not definable; he was concurrently marginalized and rejected by that margin. This struggle for a professional identity was compounded by a similar lack of personal identity, as he continually faced issues linked to his adoption, including a midlife discovery that "Robert Hayden" was not his legal name. *See also* Historical Memory.

Further Readings: Fetrow, Fred M. *Robert Hayden*. Boston: Twayne Publishers, 1984; Kutzinski, Vera M. "Changing Permanences: Historical and Literary Revisionism in Robert Hayden's 'Middle Passage.'" *Callaloo* 26 (1986): 171–183; Murphy, Jim. "'Here Only the Sea Is Real': Robert Hayden's Postmodern Passages." *MELNUS* 27 (2002): 107–127; Nelson, Cary, and Smethurst, Jim. "Robert Hayden." [Online, January 2006]. Modern American Poetry Web Site: http://www.english.uiuc.edu/maps/poets/g_l/hayden/hayden.htm.

Jessica M. Kubiak

Middle Passage, The (2000)

The Middle Passage (2000) represents one of the few attempts in the French-speaking world to tackle the painful topic of slave trade. This movie, directed by Guy Deslauriers, tries to give a realistic account of the trans-Atlantic trade based on a script written by famous Antillean novelist and Prix Goncourt winner Patrick Chamoiseau and author Claude Chonville. The story is told through the voice-over of a dead African slave who narrates the journey of a slave ship traveling from **Senegal**, on the west coast of Africa to the Americas. The voice used for the French version is that of Maka Kotto; the English version features the voice of Walter Mosley. The title of the movie evokes the infamous Middle Passage, so called because it was the middle leg of a three-step journey that began in Europe, from where the vessels left to reach the west coast of Africa. The second leg consisted of going to America—the focus of this movie. The third part of the voyage was the return to Europe from the colonies, thus the usual triangular shape attributed to the trade.

The movie opens with the view of a tropical beach, with a child staring at the sea, a symbol of a new generation of African and Caribbean people who might not be familiar with the history of slavery. The didactic purpose of the movie is clear from the very beginning. It is, to use the words of Toni Morrison, "a story to pass on."

Through the eyes of the anonymous slave, the spectator travels through a journey of torture, **sexual abuse**, starvation, and despair. The story starts with the selling of slaves by an African prince and goes on to show the horrors of the journey on vessels going to America. The depiction of the eighteen-week trip alternates between scenes shot inside the boat and, less frequently, scenes from the deck where the enchained slaves are taken to "get some exercise" and **dance** for the **crew**. There are occasional moments of hope and visions of Africa that remain in the slaves' mind throughout the journey, until it becoming a faint memory.

Passage du Milieu (the original French title) was first shown in North America in 2000 at a film festival in Toronto (Canada) and is now used by many teachers throughout America as a documentary on slavery. Although *The Middle Passage* is technically a French movie (Martinique being a part of France), it has not encountered a lot of success there, because discussion of the role of French **ports** such as **Bordeaux**, **Nantes**, and La Rochelle in the slave trade is still taboo.

For Guy Deslauriers, the goal of the movie was twofold: (1) to inform a population that might not know much about the conditions in which these trans-Atlantic voyages occurred and (2) to engrave specific images in the viewer's mind, acknowledging the fact that these ships are still part of the collective unconscious. The movie succeeds in creating a haunting atmosphere that lingers long after the movie is over as the voice of the narrator successfully articulates the fears of millions of Africans. *See also* Historical Memory.

Steve Puig

Minor European Nations

The minor nations involved in the trans-Atlantic trade included Sweden, Denmark, Norway, and the Netherlands. Initially, there was trade competition between Sweden and Denmark during the sixteenth century.

Sweden

On the part of Sweden, it was at the behest of King Gustav III when he ascended the throne in 1771. He wanted Sweden to restate itself as a world power. Economically, he longed for the same kind of huge **profit** Denmark was making on its colonies in the West Indies. Both nations set up trade posts on the West African coast. In 1784, Gustav bought the West Indian island of Saint Barthélemy from the king of France. After this transaction, he informed a surprised Swedish Privy Council that Sweden now owned an island in the West Indies. However, the report of the council on the island was that it was not economically viable. Its only good feature was a good harbor. The report recommended that it be made into a **free trade** zone. Because France had some difficulties getting slaves across to its colonies, Gustav saw this as a profitable venture.

In 1786, the Swedish West India Company was established. In March 1790, Saint Barthélemy was given another boost by a new tax law and constitution. **Slave traders** could sell slaves directly to the island without paying a **tax**. Traders buying slaves from the island would, however, pay a fee.

At this time, agitation for the abolition of the trade in England was growing. England feared that after its abolition other nations would expand their own trade in slaves. The king sent a letter to Gustav imploring him not to encourage his subjects to engage in the trade. Gustav's reply was that not one of his subjects was engaged in the trade. Shortly after, Sweden abandoned the slave trade to pursue different economic goals. The nation never contributed anything significant to the trade.

Denmark and Norway

Denmark, on the other hand, continued its trade. The Danes set up their first **trade fort** on the **Gold Coast** in 1658, but they were reported to have entered the trade in 1651. It was really a Danish-Norwegian venture. Fort Frederiksborg (Kpompo), the commercial headquarters, was built near **Cape Coast Castle** near Fetu. Fort Christiansborg followed at Osu in 1661. In 1685, after the British took over Frederiksborg, Christiansborg became the commercial headquarters. There were other forts such as Fort Fredensborg in Old Ningo, which was built in 1736, Fort Kongensten in Ada, built in 1783, and Fort Prinsensten in Keta, built in 1784. Augustaborg was built at Teshie in 1787 and an equally small fort, Isegram, was in the making in Kpone. Christiansborg extended its influence in the eighteenth century as far as the eastern Gold Coast.

The Danes aimed at controlling as far as the Volta delta and the western Gold Coast (now known as Togo and **Benin**). To this end, they established lodges all along the coast from Labadi, Teshie, and Kpone to Aflahu on the present-day Togo-Ghana border. During the first half of the century, the trade was in gold, but by 1660, the dominant trade was in slaves.

Like other European nations, the Danish were anxious to send African slaves to their holdings in the West Indies. Between them, Danish and Norwegian slave ships transported between 85,000 and 100,000 African captives, making 340 voyages across the Atlantic in the process. This was in the period between 1660 and 1806. The trade in humans lasted until 1802. Ernst Schimmelmann, who was the minister of finance for Denmark between 1784 and 1813, observed that there was a decline in the slave trade. He then suggested having **plantation** economies in the African colonies. Some attempt was made to develop cotton and coffee plantations around Fort Frederiksborg. However, neither this nor the trade in "legitimate" exports flourished. This venture and the forts were finally abandoned. Denmark also lost Norway in 1814, and the nation sold all of its interests on the Gold Coast to Britain in 1850.

The Netherlands

The Netherlands was a small country that was the center of European trading activities in the seventeenth century. The Dutch could transport more slaves faster and at lower costs than other European counterparts because of great advancements in navigation and because they had a lot of financial backing for their trade. The first recorded trade was made in 1619 when a trader sold twenty African slaves to Virginia in Northern America. The Dutch trade took on commercial proportions in 1630, when they responded to the acute demand for slaves on the plantations of Northern Brazil. The Dutch acquired quite a lot of territory on the West African **Slave**

Coast during their confrontational wars with Portugal between 1620 and 1655.

The Netherlands decided to join the human trade late. The Dutch West India Company, believed to be the largest single trader in slaves, was established in Amsterdam in 1621. Their first good in trade was African gold. It was the capture of the **sugar** plantations in Northern Brazil that made them realize that slave trade was lucrative. To establish their presence, they had to struggle with the Portuguese, particularly in the quest to conquer its commercial headquarters, São Jorge da Mina on the Gold Coast. This was captured in 1637. It was renamed **Elmina**. It was not as prosperous as they expected, and the Dutch looked farther afield. This led them to **Angola** and as far as **São Tomé**. Even after the return of the Brazilian colonies to Portugal in 1654, the Dutch still controlled the supply of slaves to other European nations, especially to Spain until the 1690s. Their influence extended from the Cape of Good Hope to the Indonesian Archipelago. Incessant wars between the Netherlands and other nations like France, Britain, and Spain weakened the nation. Its control on the trade began to slip, and by 1795, it had stopped trading altogether. By the end of the slave trade and slavery in 1863, Dutch traders had exported 540,000 African slaves to the Americas. *See also* Abolition of the Slave Trade, Great Britain; Danish Slave Trade; Dutch Slave Trade.

Further Reading: "Breaking the Silence, Learning about the Slave Trade, Slave Routes." Anti-Slavery International Web site: www.antislavery.org.

Oyekemi Olajope Oyelakin

Monopoly

The European concept of monopoly during the slave trade era was to possess a "balanced set of colonies," with unrivalled access to slaves, provisions, and shipping and **plantations** for the metropole. For two hundred years, 1440–1640, Portugal enjoyed a monopoly on the export of slaves from many parts of Africa. It is estimated that during the period of the trans-Atlantic slave trade, Portugal alone transported more than 4.5 million Africans (about 40 percent of the total slaves). When the African slave trade was beginning in the late fifteenth century, the Portuguese and the Spanish dominated it. Portugal claimed a monopoly over the slave trade in the South Atlantic because of their settlements in South America, especially **Brazil**. Spain claimed a monopoly on the trade in the North Atlantic because of their earlier exploration of the islands of the Caribbean Sea. England and many other European countries tried to compete in the highly profitable trade in the northern Atlantic. For a long time, Portugal sustained its monopoly, but Spain could not contain England for long.

By the eighteenth century, when the slave trade had transported more than 6 million Africans, Britain was responsible for almost 2.5 million. France and Britain had colonies in North America and tropical America as well as slave-trade posts on the African coast. Many European countries exercised monopolies over the slave trade by granting permits and **licenses** to a single, chartered, joint-stock company empowered with government laws and **regulations** as well as subsidies. It was expected that companies would use their monopoly **profits** as a subsidy to offset the cost of running fortified trading posts in Africa. Monopoly rights were less effective because planters preferred to purchase slaves cheaply from private traders rather than pay monopolistic **prices**. The most enduring challenge to monopoly was by private traders, both African and European. They often infringed on monopoly regimes by conducting their transactions outside of the control of chartered companies. The competition with **interlopers** led to the collapse of chartered companies that could not maintain their **trade forts**. The Portuguese could not wholly enforce the royal monopoly over their own nationals and other Europeans. After 1530, the English and French challenged the monopoly the Portuguese had enjoyed for the past fifty years. By the seventeenth century, the independent shippers who competed among themselves carried out the bulk of the slave trade.

Further Readings: Curtin, Philip D. *The Image of Africa: British Ideas and Action, 1780–1850.* Madison: University of Wisconsin Press, 1973; Curtin, Philip, D. "The West African Coast in the Era of the Slave Trade." In P. Curtin, S. Feierman, L. Thompson, and J. Vansina, eds. *African History: From Earliest Times To Independence.* London: Longmans, Green and Company, 1995; Russell-Wood, A.J.R. "Before Columbus: Portugal's African Prelude to the Middle Passage and Contribution to Discourse on Race and Slavery." In V. Shepherd and H. McD. Beckles, eds. *Caribbean Slavery in the Atlantic World: A Student Reader.* Kingston: Ian Randle Publishers Ltd., 2000.

Rasheed Olaniyi

Mortality, Crew

Although mortality is one of the most scrutinized areas of the history of the trans-Atlantic slave trade, little has been written about the crews of the slave ships.

A large amount of data have been scanned into the Du Bois Institute data set, which permits analysis of crew mortality during the five stages of slaving voyages: the outward passage, time on the African coast, the Middle Passage, time in the Americas, and the homeward passage. Findings to date demonstrate that there were variations in crew mortality by year, voyage leg, **season** of sail from Africa, and region of trade on the African coast.

It is clear that **disease** was the greatest killer: the vast majority of deaths resulted from fevers (yellow fever and malaria), scurvy, smallpox, and "fluxes" (dysentery, mainly). A small number were **shipwrecked**, **drowned**, or killed by slaves.

Some routes were known to be particularly hazardous to the health of the crew. For instance, mortality and morbidity on the Middle Passage soared after French crews had gone to the Bight of Benin and West Central Africa. The **Gold Coast** and southeast Africa (Madagascar and **Mozambique**) had much lower health risks. Those slavers present in Africa during the rainy season (when disease was more rampant) were at a significantly higher risk of mortality during the Middle Passage. British slavers who sailed to the **Gambia River** were three times more likely to die than those trading along the Gold Coast.

Not surprisingly, of the crew, **surgeons** were the most likely to die while experienced seafarers were the least likely. The former had the most contact with the sick, and experienced mariners likely built up immunity to many of the diseases.

Although there are important differences based on nationality (British crews died at greater rates than their French counterparts), overall crew mortality did decline in the eighteenth century. This was due in part to concerted efforts to improve shipboard conditions to obtain maximum **profits**. Thus, there were improvements to provisions and shipboard conditions. It was common for slave ships to carry surgeons, but they were powerless to curb infectious diseases. The British Parliament passed Dolben's Act (1788) along with later amendments; this Act reduced crowding among slaves, which meant that fewer seamen were needed. Fewer people may have reduced the level of contagion between slaves and crew. The Act also decreed that sailors receive a regular diet (although it still did not fend off malaria or yellow fever) and that at least half the crew should be allowed to sleep below deck. This Act allowed for better qualified ships' surgeons. Other changes limited the time crews spent ashore in Africa, which helped preserve their health.

The biggest factor in the decline in mortality seems to have been changing routes.

Both French and British slavers shifted their attention away from the Senegambia region and the Bight of Benin for the lower-mortality Angolan coast during the eighteenth century. Nonetheless, crews of slaving voyages still had higher rates of mortality than crews on other types of voyages. With good reason, abolitionist Thomas Clarkson claimed that the slave trade was not a "nursery of seamen" but rather a "grave." *See also* Mortality, Slave.

Further Readings: Behrendt, Stephen D. "Crew Mortality in the Transatlantic Slave Trade in the Eighteenth Century." *Slavery and Abolition* 18, 1 (1997): 49–71; Cohn, Raymond L. "Maritime Mortality in the Eighteenth and Nineteenth Centuries: A Survey." *International Journal of Maritime History* 1, 1 (1989): 159–189; Haines, Robin, Shlomowitz, Ralph, and Brennan, Lance. "Maritime Mortality Revisited." *International Journal of Maritime History* VIII (June 1996): 133–172; Klein, Herbert, Engerman, Stanley L., Haines, Robin, and Shlomowitz, Ralph. "Transoceanic Mortality: The Slave Trade in Comparative Perspective." *William and Mary Quarterly* 58, 1 (2001): 93–117; Steckel, Richard H., and Jensen, Richard A. "New Evidence on the Causes of Slave and Crew Mortality in the Atlantic Slave Trade." *Journal of Economic History* 46 (March 1986): 57–77.

Cheryl Fury

Mortality, Slave

Slave mortality is one of the most controversial aspects of the study of the trans-Atlantic slave trade. The abundance of opinions and theories demonstrate that there is little consensus among scholars about how best to analyze the extant data or how to interpret the findings. Exact numbers continue to be elusive and estimates vary widely.

Especially contentious is the debate concerning mortality during the Middle Passage, whether it decreased over time, and the factors that may have affected that decrease. Some historians assert that mortality was scandalously high and remained so until the trade was abolished. Other scholars accept the notion that mortality fell, especially after the mid-eighteenth century, although it may have increased after 1830. Some vessels reported shipboard losses of a third or more of their slaves; on more fortuitous voyages, losses were measured in single digits. When the slave trade was abolished in the nineteenth century, however, conditions deteriorated and death rates rose again. Among scholars who accept a decrease in the "lost in transit" numbers, there is great divergence of explanations for why this occurred.

It is difficult, if not impossible, to disentangle causes of slave mortality in the Middle Passage from its antecedents: to what extent did prevoyage conditions affect mortality at sea? After their capture, slaves might change hands several times as they marched to the coast for transit; their conditions would likewise vary. Some slaves were made to carry goods as well. Distance covered, diet, and exposure to different disease environments were important variables. The nature and length of their containment before boarding were significant determinants of their overall health. Crowded, unsanitary conditions combined with ill treatment, malnourishment, exhaustion, and exposure to new **diseases** could be a lethal combination. There was a much greater chance of illness and death if this occurred during the wet **season**. In addition, factors such as age, **gender**, socio-economic circumstances before **enslavement**, and place of origin (as well as climate) were key variables.

Abolitionist Thomas Fowell Buxton constructed one of the earliest studies of the human costs of slaving; he analyzed slave mortality connected with capture, the march to the coast, detention before sailing, the Middle Passage, and subsequent **"seasoning"** (entry into New World slavery). Buxton and some later historians argue that losses during this initial phase of slavery were as substantial as those at sea.

For the survivors, their treatment during the early phase of their enslavement would have a significant impact on their ability to endure the Middle Passage. Poor treatment before sailing may well have predetermined high mortality at sea. Conversely, those who were healthy at the beginning of the voyage stood a better chance of survival.

Conditions on board had an impact on slaves and the ship's **crew**. All sea travel was risky during the early modern period, but slave ships had some of the highest rates of mortality, per voyage, per day.

Enslavement caused such anguish that some committed **suicide**. Rebellious slaves could expect harsh treatment. It was, however, in the interest of the crew to preserve the health of as many slaves as they could. Disease was the biggest cause of shipboard mortality. Some slaves brought illness with them on board. Scurvy was the plague of all trans-Atlantic travelers until well into the eighteenth century. Bacterial infections, smallpox, yellow fever, and malaria were perennial threats; they were more rampant in the wet season and in certain geographic areas. Most slavers carried medical personnel, but they were generally ineffective.

Scholars have analyzed the various routes plied by slavers and found that the time of sailing and the route itself were important determinants in mortality. Stopovers and shorter voyages were beneficial. In addition, proper provisioning and shipboard conditions were critical to preserving the health of the slaves.

As the slave trade flourished, improvements were made to lower mortality and yield greater **profits**. A number of scholars agree that the drop in mortality after the mid-eighteenth century was the result of a complex interplay of variables. For instance, measures were taken to fight disease. Some slaves were inoculated for smallpox, but inoculation was in its infancy and its impact is questionable. Furthermore, in some circumstances, inoculations were not administered until there was an outbreak at sea.

There were concerted efforts to procure better **food** and **water** and to keep the ships clean. Levels of cleanliness varied from ship to ship; crews of competing nations boasted they had the highest standards. Vinegar, tar, and whitewash were all used as part of a strategy to improve sanitation and **ventilation**.

To some extent, faster ships and changes in technology in the eighteenth century facilitated speedier voyages. Copper sheathing of the hulls made the ships slightly faster and reduced dampness within the ship.

Efforts to decrease crowding may have had an impact as well. Dolben's Act (1788) and its subsequent amendments did improve the lot of slaves on British ships. This Act can be seen as part of a larger drive by Europeans to regulate the trade by determining the carrying capacity of ships, amount of provisions, and medical care on board. Not all Acts were enforced or affected mortality, but it is clear that the trade was being scrutinized by legislators, **investors**, and abolitionists.

In addition to these improvements, mortality rates at sea were lowered by being more selective about who was transported. Bonuses for crews of ships with low death rates provided more incentive to look after the slaves. Shorter voyages to and from **destinations** with reduced probability of disease were also significant. Even with these changes, mortality and human misery on such voyages exceeded other types of trans-Atlantic migrations. *See also* Abolition of the Slave Trade, Great Britain; Mortality, Crew; Overcrowding.

Further Readings: Buxton, Thomas Fowell. *The African Slave Trade and Its Remedy.* London: Dawsons, 1968 (1840); Cohn, Raymond L. "Deaths of Slaves in the Middle Passage." *Journal of Economic History* 45 (September 1985): 685–692; Gemery, Henry A., and Hogendorn, Jan S. *The Uncommon Market: Essays in the Economic History of the Atlantic Slave Trade.* New York: Academic Press, 1979; Haines, Robert, McDonald, John, and Shlomowitz, Ralph. "Mortality and Voyage Length in the Middle Passage Revisited." *Explorations in Economic History* 38 (2001): 503–533; Klein, Herbert, Engerman, Stanley L., Haines, Robin, and Shlomowitz, Ralph. "Transoceanic Mortality: The Slave Trade in Comparative Perspective." *William and Mary Quarterly* 58 (2001): 93–117; Steckel, Richard H., and Jensen, Richard A. "New Evidence on the Causes of Slave and Crew Mortality in the Atlantic Slave Trade." *Journal of Economic History* 46 (March 1986): 57–77.

Cheryl Fury

Mozambique

African tribal chiefs, Arab traders, and the Portuguese traded slaves within Mozambique. Portuguese merchants purchased gold and slaves along the Mozambique coast in the early seventeenth century. Because early Portuguese explorers and traders lacked sufficient capital and manpower, they failed to establish permanent settlements in Mozambique until later in the seventeenth century. By the nineteenth century, this Portuguese colony on the east coast of Africa became an important source of valuable human commodities destined to be transported to the Americas as **plantation** and mining labor.

The desire of Europeans to circumvent the **Muslim**-controlled Mediterranean route to India led to Vasco da Gama's voyage around the Cape of Good Hope (the southern tip of Africa) in 1498. The end of the fifteenth century marked the entry of Europeans into the **Indian Ocean** trading system. Because of the high cost of transporting slaves from Mozambique to the Atlantic slave trade, the Portuguese main interest resided in obtaining gold. After establishing a trading depot and fortress on Mozambique Island, the Portuguese added a steady supply of ivory to the shipments of gold sent to India in exchange for spices.

Europeans and Africans practiced slavery on the East coast of Africa, but the transportation of slaves outside of Mozambique did not occur until the middle of the eighteenth century. Inhambane became known for its exports of ivory, pitch, amber, rice, and other lesser products; however, Inhambane's commercial success can be attributed to the port becoming the first Mozambique port to export slaves. By the 1760s, French **sugar** plantation owners on the Island of Reunion in the French Indian Ocean purchased slaves at Inhambane in Mozambique. **Slave traders** also transported slaves from Quelimane to **São Tomé**, Madagascar, Mauritius, Reunion, and Comoros. Slave exports rose to 3,000 per year in the 1780s. Although Mozambique became a major exporter of slaves, Portuguese slavers failed to bring slaves to Rio de Janeiro on the coast of **Brazil** until 1797. Over the next fourteen years, Portuguese slavers managed to bring 3,800 slaves from Mozambique to Rio de Janeiro. During the Middle Passage, the high **mortality** rate of 24 percent deterred slave transportation from Mozambique to Brazil.

Increases in the exportation of slaves can be traced back to the 1560s during which time drought and famine fostered increased migrations that touched off armed raiding. Famine played a pivotal role in filling the **barracoons** on the coast of Mozambique. With a dwindling **food** supply, the inland population migrated toward the coast. In addition, the purchase of food by the slave ships decreased the amount of food available for local Mozambicans. Plantation owners in Mozambique were more interested in supplying the commercial market than producing food for local consumption. The series of severe droughts and internal migrations that followed generated an increased supply of war captives. Besides war captives, *mocambazes* (slave merchants) obtained slaves in a similar manner as Atlantic slave traffickers. Slave sources included kidnapping, raiding, and purchase. Tribal chiefs, who raided warring tribes, sold their captives to the slavers.

Slaving in Mozambique developed a unique twist when strange sea vessels appeared off the coast in 1800. Raiding fleets of thirty-foot-long canoes assembled at the northern tip of Madagascar. These raiding fleets attacked along the Mozambique coast from Kilwa to as far north as Mozambique Island. By 1808, the raiding fleet grew from three boats in 1800 to 500 war boats and 8,000 armed raiders. Sea raiders attacked and harassed the Mozambique coast for twenty years. Attacks by the Nguni chiefs produced an unusual set of circumstances. The Afro-Portuguese, Indian, and Swahili coastal inhabitants grew accustomed to making a living from the slave trade and never experienced the misery and war that accompanied slavery. Mozambique's coastal communities gained firsthand experience in the ferocity and inhumanity of the slave trade at the hands of slave-raiding pirates. The events inside of Mozambique gave rise to coastal raiding. Drought, famine, and migration led to the destabilization of coastal societies making them easy prey for sea raiders.

After 1800, the New World's demand for slaves increased and slavers viewed Mozambique as a vital source of slaves. The Portuguese government responded to the availability of increasing amounts of slaves coupled with increased demand and rising **prices** by allowing Brazilian slavers **free trade** along the East African coast. In a five–year period (1825–1829), eighty-five ships arrived in Rio de Janeiro from Mozambique carrying more than 48,000 slaves. Mozambique exported 9,000 in 1790. By the 1830s 15,000 Mozambican slaves were exported per year. After 1811, slavers transported more than 380,000 to the Atlantic slave system, making Mozambique the third-largest supplier of slaves in the nineteenth century. Overall, the East African slave trade accounted for 400,000 slaves in the eighteenth century. Slavers transported about 270,000 slaves to the Muslim world, while the remaining 130,000 slaves found themselves in the Mascarene Islands or the Americas. In the 1770s, slave exports increased from a bare trickle to an average of 5,400 per year in the 1780s (Curtin, 1978, pp. 393–394; Lovejoy, 1993, p. 60). *See also* Enslavement and Procurement; Portuguese Slave Trade.

Further Readings: Curtin, Philip, Feierman, Steven, Thompson, Leonard, and Vansina, Jan. *African History.* Boston: Little, Brown, 1978; Klein, Herbert S. *The Atlantic Slave Trade.* Cambridge and New York: Cambridge University Press, 1999; Lovejoy, Paul E. *Transformations in Slavery: A History of Slavery in Africa.* New York: Cambridge University Press, 1993; Newitt, Malyn. *A History of Mozambique.* Bloomington: Indiana University Press, 1995.

Michael Bonislawski

Museums

History as shown in museums can never be complete or cover all perspectives: it is a selection of a selection. Heritage has a personalizing factor: it is appropriated by people to identify themselves with a certain group, detaching themselves from others. Heritage in museums therefore is bound to tell the story of a certain group, from a certain perspective. In a globalizing world, however, audiences are more diverse and more demanding. Museum curators are confronted with the difficult task of dealing with diverse expectations and sensitivities.

Museums that deal with the trans-Atlantic slave trade and slavery are found all over the Black Atlantic. What is shown by those institutes varies. Because the idea of a museum is a European invention, traditional museums have always painted the world from a Western point of view (Kreps,

2003). Traditionally, museums displayed history that was seen as relevant by those in power. Thus, exhibitions contained the (technical) economic history and those "heroes" who had contributed to the economic and political success of the country. To be able to portray the history from the perspective of the African diaspora, museums needed to reinterpret the objects they possessed, and complement their collection with new objects and research.

In the United States, where the formerly enslaved lived side by side with former enslavers, and where a continuing struggle for further emancipation was taking place, changes in museum representation can be seen as early as the 1950s, but only in small museums. Twenty years later, the Smithsonian was the first major museum organizing an African American exhibition, working with African American advisors and managers. Colonial Williamsburg, in 1979, was the first to touch on the subject of slavery. In 1994, forty such attractions were inventoried in the U.S. South (Dann and Seaton, 2001).

In Europe, the arrival of Caribbean immigrants initiated changes in heritage policy. Their presence prompted the need to represent them in exhibitions and to attract them as visitors. Starting in the 1990s, museums in the United Kingdom and the Netherlands changed the tone of their regular exhibitions and dedicated (temporary) exhibitions to the theme of slavery. How to narrate history that included all constituent variants equitably soon became a subject of debate. Some museums argued that keeping the dissonance in heritage (debates about ownership, control, and representation) alive would eventually heal the diverse community.

In the Caribbean, a central question is the authenticity of the exhibitions. Mass **tourism**, being an important source of income, sets the tone, resulting in an often nostalgic representation of the colonial past. Some museums do exactly the opposite: confronting visitors with the horrors of the slave trade.

The biggest changes may be taking place in Africa. As tourism to the continent is growing faster then ever before, museums are struggling to accommodate diverse audiences. In post-Apartheid South Africa, this growing diversity is also apparent within the country, because of a higher level of democracy than was experienced during the Apartheid regime. Museums that want to attract African Americans have to choose between putting the trans-Atlantic experience central or depicting it as an occurrence in their general history. *See also* Historical Memory; Historiography.

Further Readings: Bruner, E. *Culture on Tour: Ethnographies of Travel.* Chicago: University of Chicago Press, 2005; Dann, G., and Seaton, A. V. *Slavery, Contested Heritage and Thanatourism.* New York: The Haworth Hospitality Press, 2001; Duncan, James. "Presenting Empire at the National Maritime Museum." In Robert Shannan Peckham, ed. *Rethinking Heritage. Cultures and Politics in Europe.* London: I. B. Tauris & Co. Ltd., 2003; Kreps, Christina F. *Liberating Culture: Cross-Cultural Perspectives on Museums, Curation, and Heritage Preservation.* London: Routledge, Taylor & Francis Group, 2003; Lowenthal, D. *Possessed by the Past. The Heritage Crusade and the Spoils of History.* New York: The Free Press, 1996.

Valika Smeulders

Music, Songs, and Singing

A people's music, songs, and singing not only nurture their particular traditional beliefs, but also reflect their collective and individual ambitions, especially in times of dislocation and crisis. Music has always been a crucial component in the lives of Africans on the continent. During the Middle Passage its significance expanded.

Many of the Africans transported as slaves originated from cultures that placed emphasis on oral, aural, and musical activity as part of ceremony, religious ritual, and everyday life. The creation and delivery of songs was a public and expressive phenomenon, but it was also a private and covert activity. The cultures of Africa that lost their citizens to the trans-Atlantic trade created music for marriage ceremonies, for deaths, for war, and for private activity like courtship. Commentators on African music and song have highlighted the role of praise songs, satirical songs, dirges, and historical compositions to African society. When slaves were captured and taken to the point of departure, they were confined to a newly defined physical place and space. The experience of bondage had a traumatic impact on their physical, psychological, and cultural disposition. Because music, songs, and singing were critical components of African life, however, it was impossible for physical bondage to silence their outer and inner voices.

Slaves were able to retain vital aspects of their cultural practices in spite of the traumatic experience of **enslavement**. The dilapidated environment, the close surveillance of slaves on board, and the cramped storage of people of diverse linguistic, religious, social, and cultural traditions militated against the proliferation of singing and music-making, but individual slaves responded to their incarceration in a variety of ways. These responses included singing, moaning, screaming, and tapping rhythms while still enchained below deck, during the six- to eight-week voyage.

The slaves sang religious songs, and songs of despair, defiance, and lamentations throughout the Middle Passage. Despite (indeed, because of) the cramped conditions below deck, any available implement was a potential musical instrument. The enslaved used their voices as the dominant instrument, sometimes masking their songs of defiance amid the roar of the ocean beating against the side of the slave ship. The work-song singing of the ship's **crew** often rang out on and below deck. Some slaves when taken on deck were forced to dance, sing, and drum. According to some written accounts of the Middle Passage, drumming was done on a one-headed drum.

The prevalence of African tone **languages** and the differences between African and Western musical scales led some Western observers to interpret African songs as nothing more than lamentations, cries, and groanings. Not all of these songs were such. During the Middle Passage, some slaves masked their inner ambition and plots beneath audible sounds. For instance, while a measured rendition of some songs would be interpreted as a "melancholy lamentation of their exile from their native country" (Falconbridge, 1788), this rendition could mask the singer's intention to affect mutiny on board.

Musical group, Brazil, 1846. Special Collections, University of Virginia Library.

It is this same subversive strategy that became prevalent among slaves even after they left the slave ship and were forced to work on **plantations**. The Middle Passage was therefore the birthing space for renewed performance by Africans who sought to come to terms with their confinement. The slaves were forced to negotiate their survival while confined to the bowels of the slave ship. Some used song, music, and singing as a survival mechanism to keep their spirits up and to survive the Passage. Others used these activities to shield their inner plan of revolt.

Olaudah Equiano's *Interesting Narrative* (despite questions about Equiano's birthplace) recounts the horrors of the Passage as well as the bathos and endurance of many African survivors who carried their songs and customs across the Atlantic. Sir **John Newton**'s experience as a sea captain and the impact of the slaves' songs of lamentation influenced his composition of the reflective song "Amazing Grace."

Scholars have debated the extent to which the Middle Passage has affected African culture when it was transported to the New World. Some have suggested that the trauma of the Passage resulted in the dislocation and discontinuity of traditional activities, such as singing and music-making. Others have argued that the Middle Passage facilitated the strengthening of traditional practices and forged even newer forms of musical expression.

The songs, music, and singing of slaves that were nurtured (and in some cases reconfigured) during the Middle Passage found a range of locations, contexts, and situations in which they survived, thrived, and transformed in the New World. **Historiography**, **oral history**, and maritime accounts have helped us to better understand the nature of African musical continuities. Because the Middle Passage did not destroy the cultural practices of the slaves, many actions of slaves in the Americas reveal some truths about music during the Middle Passage. Although **slave traders** and plantation owners were aware of the use of songs and music for **communication**, the range of challenges associated with managing a slave ship rendered it impossible to have prevented the slave from such activity. Work songs and spirituals were sometimes viewed by the slave masters as having some positive impact on the experience of slaves and on their psychological state of being. Hence, scheduled singing and drumming was encouraged among slaves on some slave ships.

The revolutionary quality of some African songs is well documented. Music and singing are considered central activities within mass covert uprisings and revolts. At the individual and interpersonal level, slave songs are well regarded for their deception, their employment of wit and satire, veiled threats, and gracious curses.

Some New World music genres are considered to have evolved out of African traditional forms that experienced some level of transformation en route to the Americas. These forms have evolved through contact with music forms of European and other cultures that cohabited the slave ship. Music and singing forms such as the blues, negro spirituals, rumba, and calypso are a few of the New World genres and styles that were born and reconfigured during the Middle Passage.

Some of the characteristics of traditional African song can also be found in some of the musical genres that have continued to evolve over the centuries. Polyrhythm, syncopation, call and response, and free improvisation are some of the defining features of African music styles that expanded via the Middle Passage. A musical form like calypso, for instance, still bears some similarity to African music. Calypso is remarkable for its use of lyrical wordplay and its use of call and response, among other features. A defining feature of such African–New World genres is the tendency to mask their subversive intent.

If the experience of the Middle Passage forced many Africans to retreat to the solace of song, it also forged a music that encapsulated the intense emotions of a people who were determined to use every strategy to regain total liberation. *See also* Dancing and Exercise; Falconbridge, Alexander.

Further Readings: Equiano, Olaudah. *The Interesting Narrative of the Life of Olaudah Equiano, or Gustavus Vassa, the African.* Essex: Longmans, Green and Company, 1789; Diedrich, Maria, Gates, Henry Louis, and Pedersen, Carl, eds. *Black Imagination and the Middle Passage.* Oxford: Oxford University Press, 1999; Falconbridge, Alexander. *An Account of the Slave Trade on the Coast of Africa.* New York: AMS Press, 1973 (1788).

Curwen Best

N

Nancy, The

The *Nancy* was a Rhode Island brig that experienced an unsuccessful shipboard slave revolt while crossing the Atlantic from Senegambia (West Africa) to Paramaribo (Suriname) during an illegal slave voyage of 1793. The revolt was one of just three Middle Passage revolts to occur on Rhode Island slavers between 1730 and 1807, and it was publicized in newspapers across **New England**. It occurred some time between August 6 and October 29, 1793. Four of the original 121 slaves on board were killed. Another eighteen died of other causes during the Middle Passage. Rhode Island banned the slave trade in 1787, but the legislation remained largely unenforced until the 1808 federal abolition of the trade.

The *Nancy*'s captain, Joseph B. Cook, was a slave **captain** of moderate experience, having undertaken only one slave voyage before the 1793 trip. The average Rhode Island slave ship captain made an average of 2.2 slave voyages during his lifetime. Cook would make at least three.

Three factors may have contributed to the revolt's occurrence. First, the slaves on board were probably of Upper Guinean origins. Ethnicities like the Fulbe, Wolof, Serer, and Malinke of the Senegambia region exhibited the highest rate of insurrection of all West Africans, a rate three to five times higher than the average. One explanation may have been the prevalence of **Islam** in the area: Muslim slaves may have banded together to revolt despite ethnic differences. Second, at least three out of nine of the *Nancy*'s crewmembers

Slave revolt on board a trans-Atlantic slave-trade ship. Courtesy of Anti-Slavery International.

were black. It is possible that they identified with the enslaved Africans and facilitated the revolt. Third, Captain Cook's ship logbook suggests that he maintained poor **crew** discipline on the *Nancy*. It is possible that disorder and insubordination by crewmembers gave the slaves an opportunity to rebel.

Rhode Island slave ships normally carried a single-product **cargo** of **rum** to Africa for the purpose of purchasing slaves. Rhode Island rum was so sought after in the region that West African slave **prices** were often expressed in gallons of rum. Unusually, the *Nancy* carried a mixed cargo of goods, including rum, on its 1793 voyage.

The *Nancy* made at least one other slave voyage. Joseph Cook carried 121 slaves from the **Gold Coast** of West Africa to the Caribbean in 1795–1796, losing sixteen during the Middle Passage. The rest of the *Nancy*'s seafaring was probably spent in the coasting trade, exchanging livestock and dried goods from Rhode Island for molasses, **sugar**, and coffee in Suriname.

The brig was a medium-size slave ship by Rhode Island standards. It weighed 110 tons and measured sixty-three feet two inches long, twenty feet four inches wide, and ten feet five inches deep. It was built in North Providence in 1784, nine years before its 1793 voyage. The *Nancy* was not registered with the District of Providence until six years after it was built, on July 13, 1790. Registration was required for all vessels engaged in foreign trade. It is therefore unlikely that the *Nancy* transported slaves across the Atlantic before this date. At the time of the 1793 voyage, the *Nancy* was owned by Providence merchants Zachariah and Philip Allen. By 1801, it had been sold to Providence mariners Cornelius G. Bowler and John Cook, and had a new captain, Benjamin Taylor, Jr. In 1803, the nineteen-year-old brig was surrendered to port authorities for unseaworthiness in Savannah, Georgia.

Further Readings: Behrendt, Stephen D., Eltis, David, and Richardson, David. "The Costs of Coercion: African Agency in the Pre-modern Atlantic World." *Economic History Review* 54, 3 (2001): 454–476; Coughtry, Jay. *The Notorious Triangle: Rhode Island and the African Slave Trade 1700–1807*, 151, 157, 266, 268. Philadelphia: Temple University Press, 1981; Eltis, David, Behrendt, Stephen D., Richardson, David, and Klein, Herbert S., eds. *The Trans-Atlantic Slave Trade: A Database on CD-ROM.* Cambridge: Cambridge University Press, 1999; Sharafi, Mitra. "The Slave Ship Manuscripts of Captain Joseph B. Cook: A Narrative Reconstruction of the Brig *Nancy*'s Voyage of 1793." *Slavery and Abolition* 24 (April 2003): 71–100.

Mitra Sharafi

Nantes

A commercial town on the Loire, in Western France, Nantes was the major **French slave trade port**. Its merchants fitted out a total of 1,424 slave ships during the eighteenth century—that is, 42 percent of the total French slave ships—and were responsible for the shipment of 450,000 African captives. About one out of five ships fitted out in Nantes during the eighteenth century was a slave trader. This percentage is consistently higher than those of other contemporary ports. Nantes kept its primacy as a slave trade port during the first half of the nineteenth century, and fitted out 290 slave ships from 1815 to 1830 (70 percent of French slave ships), at a time when France had already forbidden the slave trade.

The city had been a lively port since the Middle Ages, trading primarily in salt, wine, and cereals. By the seventeenth century, Nantes sold these commodities from Southern Spain to the Baltic. The local merchant community, however, ventured mainly in local and regional trade that, together with Newfoundland fisheries, provided for a regular, although not spectacular, increase in fortunes and commercial know-how. Nantes's long-distance trade was still in the hands of foreign merchants and ships.

It was the slave trade that enabled the city's merchants at the end of the seventeenth century to take a more active part in the rising Atlantic economy and to venture into long-distance trade and shipping. Nantes fitted out eight slave ships from 1688 to 1698. The emergence of Nantes as the main slave trade port of eighteenth-century France is intimately linked to the rise of the **plantation** economy in the French West Indies in the 1660s and 1670s and to the contemporary reinforcement of the French politics excluding foreigners, notably the Dutch, from French colonial trade. French West Indian planters had demanded African slaves since the beginnings of colonization, and by the 1660s, black slaves were as numerous as white colonists. The development of **sugar** production provoked a consistent increase in the number of slaves at the end of the seventeenth century, when the French West Indies imported 5,000 captives each year. Foreign ships provided the majority of these slaves, but French ships had begun to enter the slave trade, and Nantes was emerging as the leading port.

In the first two decades of the eighteenth century, Nantes fitted out about two out of every three French slave ships. Until the 1730s, most of Nantes's slave ships went to **Ouidah**; thereafter, they increasingly frequented the coasts between to the River Niger and **Angola**. In the 1780s, almost three-quarters of Nantes's slave ships acquired captives in this region. At that time, 85 percent of ships sold their human cargo in **Saint Domingue**.

The majority of **captains** and **crew** came from the region around Nantes; so, too, did the capital to fit out the ships, which merchants sometimes collected on a larger basis through the sale of shares. Two out of three Nantes ship owners were sons or grandsons of merchants. Eighteen percent were sons of captains or artisans, and 14 percent were noble. For the impoverished nobility of Brittany, the slave trade in Nantes provided a means to acquire both social status and fortune. *See also* Bordeaux; French Caribbean.

Further Readings: Meyer, Jean. *L'armement nantais dans la deuxième moitié du XVIIIe siècle.* 2nd ed. Paris: EHESS, 1999; Pétré-Grenouilleau, Olivier. *L'argent de la traite: milieu négrier, capitalisme et développement: un modèle.* Paris: Aubier, 1996; Pétré-Grenouilleau, Olivier. *Nantes au temps de la traite des Noirs.* Paris: Hachette, 1998; Thomas, Hugh. *The Slave Trade: The Story of the Atlantic Slave Trade, 1440–1870.* New York: Simon & Schuster, 1997.

Silvia Marzagalli

Narratives by Slave Traders

Trading in human beings, who were snatched from their homelands on the African continent, did not represent the kind of activity that the organizers of this trade wished to see published in the popular literature of the day. Yet, here and there, across the centuries, enslavers and **slave traders** chronicled their activities, sometimes in all the stark dehumanizing details that were associated with their business. These narratives of the slave trade provide perspectives other than the conventional viewpoint and help provide a more comprehensive view of the realities that governed this trade in Africans.

The various narratives available cover the several nationalities that were involved in the trade. For example, there are the letters of Paul Erdman Isert, a Danish slave trader. His narrative was first published in German and later translated into English. Then, there is the account of **John (Jean) Barbot**, a Frenchman, at one time on self-imposed exile to England because of prejudice against his Protestant faith. Barbot wrote a journal of his voyages in the African waters in the 1680s. His first voyage took place sometime between 1681 and 1682, following which he submitted a journal to the ship's owners. Although this journal appears to have been lost, Barbot chronicled the events of his voyage in a later publication. Barbot began this work in 1683, and completed it in 1688.

In addition to the narratives by Isert and Barbot, there is the narrative of Captain Theodore Canot, an Italian who was employed by an American company in their slave-trading ventures to Africa. Canot's account was dictated during a series of interviews granted to a Brazilian journalist, Bratnz Mayers. Mayers subsequently published this narrative in the form of a biographical history, written in the first person. Apparently, he had access to Canot's journals and to other written accounts that helped to verify much of what this slave trader wrote about conditions on the African coast and about the slave trade. Other narratives that were available for this brief survey include the following: **John Atkins** (1721), **John Newton** (1750–1754), Samuel Gamble (1793), and **Alexander Falconbridge** (1792).

One of the commonalities spread throughout the various narratives is that they are mostly written by traders in command of ships, owned by others, or they are written by other employees on such ships, for example, by the **surgeons**. In the latter case, they are written generally in the format of a ship's log intended to report to the owners on various aspects of the voyage(s). Therefore, these accounts include much description of natural phenomena, for example, navigation hazards off a coastline and, in some cases, as in Barbot's account, descriptions of the flora and fauna of the African coast. Indeed, his account is accompanied by several sketches of birds and fish peculiar to West Africa. Once the ship was on the Middle Passage to the New World, the descriptions were generally accompanied by references to the latitude and longitude of the ship at various points of the journey and to statistical data such as the number of deaths of the enslaved.

It is not to be expected that as slave traders, the narratives would express any sympathy to the human **cargo**. Any descriptions of the conditions on board a slaver tended to be written more from the viewpoint of a businessman interested in the bottom line than from a social issues perspective. Yet, as recorded in John Newton's narrative, the human suffering that the conditions on a slaver engendered could not fail to attract the attention of any but those whose consciences had been seared by long involvement in the trade. Newton was writing some thirty years after his last voyage and, even then, the memories were so strong that he found it difficult to write with "coolness" on the subject. He was forced, finally, to describe the slave trade as an iniquitous, cruel, oppressive, and destructive business.

These various narratives represent firsthand accounts by people who were deeply involved in the trade and, as such, they add to the understanding of how the trade operated. As further research continues on what some refer to as the "African holocaust," such narratives will—along with other accounts that were written from other perspectives, including those of the enslaved who suffered in the **holds** of slavers—remind all of human's capacity to treat life as a mere economic commodity.

Further Readings: Atkins, John. *A Voyage to Guinea, Brazil and the West Indies.* London: Frank Cass, 1970 (1735); Falconbridge, Alexander. *An Account of the Slave Trade on the Coast of Africa.* New York: AMS Press, 1973 (1788); Hair, P.E.H., Jones, Adam, and Law, Robin, eds. *Barbot on Guinea: The Writings of Jean Barbot on West Africa 1678–1712.* London: The Hakluyt Society, 1992; Martin, Bernard, and Spurrell, Mark, eds. *The Journal of a Slave Trader (John Newton) 1750–1754.* London: The Epworth Press, 1962; Mayer, Brantz. *Captain Canot, an African Slaver.* New York: Arno Press and the *New York Times*, 1968; Mouser, Bruce. *A Slaving Voyage to Africa and Jamaica: the Log of the Sandown, 1793–1794.* Bloomington: Indiana University Press, 2002; Wisnes, Selena Axelrod, ed. and trans. *Letters on West Africa and the Slave Trade: Paul Erdman Isert's Journey to Guinea and the Caribbean Islands in Columbia.* Oxford: Oxford University Press, 1992.

Pedro Welch

Nbena

Nbena, an Ndombe woman and native of Katumbela near Benguela, was a slave owner who regularly dealt in agricultural produce. In June 1817, during the course of one of her business trips to Benguela, an old slave woman tricked her and her daughter into slavery. Specifically, the old slave in question tactfully presented them to her master, Antonio Leal do Sacremento, as her replacement. The following day after this incident, however, both mother and child fled from Sacremento's estate, where they were detailed to perform servile duties, back to their village. About six months after this escape, Nbena and her daughter once again set out for Benguela to sell produce. This time, they successfully arrived at their destination. Sacremento, however, who learned about their presence in Benguela, soon re-enslaved them there. In addition, he ultimately sold Nbena and her daughter to Joao de Oliveira Dias, **captain** of a **Lisbon** slave vessel soon to depart to **Brazil** via **Luanda**.

The Ndombe community strongly challenged the **enslavement** and shipment of Nbena and her daughter out of Benguela. Indeed, the Ndombe initiated a public hearing against Sacremento. During the process, they argued that Nbena and her daughter were freeborn, hence unlawfully enslaved. Partly influenced by this argument, the Portuguese governor of Benguela, Mello e Alvim ordered Sacremento to have Nbena and her daughter returned from Luanda (where they were then located) without delay, at his own expense. He also took further administrative actions, which ultimately led to the successful return of Nbena and her daughter to Benguela. Sacremento was not pleased with the governor's decision and therefore persistently challenged it. Eventually, his actions led not only to the detention of the two female subjects but also to a long-lasting legal debate on the applicability of the principle of "original freedom" upon which they proclaimed their liberty in the ongoing case against them.

Sacramento's spirited efforts to regain possession of what he perceived were his slaves subsequently led to direct confrontation between him and Mello e Alvim. It also sparked a conflict between this particular governor of Benguela and his counterpart in **Angola**, Motta Feo. In the course of these engagements, Mello e Alvim freed Nbena and her daughter partly to foster his personal commercial interests in Benguela. Several months after that development, however, Motta Feo established that the 1796 instructions upon which Mello e Alvim officially based his release of Nbena and her daughter in 1818 were not in force and had not been for twenty years. Following this discovery, Mello e Alvim was removed from office, and subsequently was arrested and transported to Luanda for further actions. Taken together, the story of Nbena provides insight into the relationship between **ethnicity** and the mechanisms for protection against enslavement during the Atlantic slave trade era. It also reveals the transmutability of ethnicity in that period. For, assuming Nbena was successfully shipped to Brazil, her ethnic identity would have been most probably known as "Benguela." *See also* Portuguese Slave Trade.

Further Reading: Curto, José. "The Story of Nbena, 1817–1820: Unlawful Enslavement and the Concept of 'Original Freedom' in Angola." In Paul E. Lovejoy and David V. Trotman, eds. *Trans-Atlantic Dimensions of Ethnicity in the African Diaspora*, 43–64. London: Continuum, 2003.

Mohammed Bashir Salau

New England

Notwithstanding romantic notions of congenitally antislavery Puritans, New England was a vital hub in both England's and North America's involvement with the Atlantic slave trade. This involvement had enormous consequences, not only for the West Indian colonies it fed with labor and the slaves involved, but also for New England itself. Although slave labor and the slave trade were not necessary for New England's survival, historian Edgar McManus put it aptly when he wrote that they "transformed shaky outposts of empire into areas of permanent settlement" (1973, p. 17).

New England's first recorded involvement with the oceanic traffic in souls was in 1638, when traders exchanged Native American slaves taken in the Pequot War of 1637 for black slaves from Providence Island and the Tortugas. This 1638 trade initiated a long-running connection between New England and the West Indies via the slave trade. The more typical connection involved the **triangular trade**, wherein New Englanders traded **rum** for African slaves, then sold them in the West Indies for molasses, which they then took back to New England to distill into rum.

Such were the **profits** of this trade that New Englanders proved to be intrepid **slave traders** on their own account. As early as 1644, Boston merchants attempted to link up with Africa directly to procure Africans to sell in Barbados. They were so determined to exploit the West Indies' demand for slaves that they went to Madagascar as early as 1676 to circumvent larger slaving companies' sway in West Africa.

These seventeenth-century forays would prove to be only the beginning. As England's participation in the slave trade grew in the next century so too did New England's. Massachusetts and Rhode Island emerged as the leading slave-trading centers, but an increasing number of industries throughout the region came to revolve around fitting out ships for and processing the produce of the triangular trade. The social prominence of the chief slavers in these colonies was one measure of how lucrative and important it was. Especially in the port towns of Massachusetts and Rhode Island, most of the first families participated in the slave trade.

As moral and political discomfort with slavery arose with the American Revolution, many New Englanders faced a serious struggle between economic interest and the principles they now proclaimed. Yankees' divisions over this issue came to light, especially in their varying responses to the compromise in the Constitution of 1787, which allowed for the Atlantic slave trade to continue until at least 1808. Many of them—especially but far from limited to Quakers—refused to support the proposed Constitution because of this clause. These people against slavery supported various state and federal measures in coming years to restrict or ban America's participation in the trade. But New England votes in the Convention had been vital to securing this delayed abolition in the first place, because it served the interests of both the Lower South and New England. Individual Yankees flouted the restrictions on pursuing this commerce in the years after the restrictions passed. It was, in short, not as simple as some modern readers would imagine for New England to sever its extensive and lucrative connection to the traffic in African souls. *See also* British Caribbean; *Nancy*, The.

Further Readings: Coughtry, Jay. *The Notorious Triangle: Rhode Island and the African Slave Trade, 1700–1807.* Philadelphia: Temple University Press, 1981; Donnan, Elizabeth, ed. *Documents Illustrative of the Slave Trade to America.* Vol. 3: *New England and the Middle Colonies.* Washington, DC: Carnegie Institution of Washington, 1930–1935; Greene, Lorenzo J. *The Negro in Colonial New England, 1620–1776.* New York: Columbia University Press, 1942; Kaminski, John P., ed. *A Necessary Evil? Slavery and the Debate over the Constitution.* Madison: Madison House, 1995; Manus, Edgar J. *Black Bondage in the North.* Syracuse, NY: Syracuse University Press, 1973.

Matthew Mason

New Orleans

New Orleans' involvement with the slave trade went through three phases between 1718 and 1860. Between 1718 and 1730, the French West Indies Company imported nearly 6,000 slaves from Africa into its fledging Louisiana colony through New Orleans. The trans-Atlantic slave trade went into a steep decline after 1730, and only in the 1760s did planters revive the international slave trade to New Orleans. Between 1810 and 1860, New Orleans' involvement with the slave trade entered a third distinct phase, as it became a main terminal for the "second Middle Passage," which carried slaves from the Upper South to the Deep South.

In 1718, the French Company of the West Indies established the town of New Orleans to serve as the center for its Louisiana colony. Between 1718 and 1730, planters and company officials imported roughly 6,000 slaves, hoping to quickly establish a profitable, **plantation**-based staple economy. Despite these importations, New Orleans' plantation economy languished. New Orleans was simply too far removed from the main currents of trade in the colonial Atlantic world, a situation exacerbated by Native American and African resistance to the plantation regime. By 1731, crown officials had taken control of the colony away from the bankrupt Company and then all but abandoned it. France now focused on providing slaves to its more lucrative Caribbean colonies. The trans-Atlantic slave trade to New Orleans virtually ended between 1730 and the 1760s, with only a few hundred slaves imported into New Orleans from the Caribbean.

New Orleans and its hinterlands began the transition to a full-blown plantation economy dependent on the slave trade only after Spain took control of Louisiana in 1763. From then through 1815, the international slave trade was both irregular and sporadic. Spanish officials encouraged the expansion of the plantation economy and the slave trade, but the increases in both proved modest until the 1790s. Perhaps 3,800 slaves were imported to Louisiana between 1763 and 1785, with most purchased in small groups of twenty to thirty slaves from Spanish and French traders in the Caribbean.

After 1790, the expansion of **sugar** and cotton production into the lower Mississippi Valley led to the explosive growth of plantation slavery in the region. From 1790 through 1815, New Orleans became the main port for African slaves imported to the lower Mississippi Valley. Perhaps 3,000 additional slaves were imported between 1785 and 1803, with most again purchased from traders in the Caribbean. It was only after the United States took possession of Louisiana in 1804 that the trans-Atlantic slave trade became somewhat regularized. Between 1804 and 1808, **slave traders** from **Charleston**, South Carolina, became the main suppliers of African slaves to New Orleans' slave markets. Charleston slavers imported nearly 40,000 slaves between 1803 and 1808, and many were immediately shipped to New Orleans in vessels carrying anywhere from 70 to more than 200 slaves. The United States prohibited the international slave trade in 1808, but by 1810, the slave trade and natural increase had boosted the slave population around New Orleans to more than 55,000.

After 1815, American slavery shifted from the Chesapeake to the Deep South. A domestic slave trade quickly emerged. The slave markets of New Orleans became the main destination for slaves caught up in what the historian Ira Berlin has called "the second Middle Passage," that is, the massive transfer of perhaps 1 million African American slaves from the Upper South to the Deep South between 1790 and 1860. In the domestic slave trades' "second Middle Passage," slaves experienced the same harsh, degrading conditions of the first Middle Passage. *See also* Internal Slave Trade, United States.

Further Readings: Berlin, Ira. *Generations of Captivity: A History of African-American? Slaves.* Cambridge, MA: Belknap Press, 2003; Ingersoll, Thomas N. *Mammon and Manon in Early New Orleans: The First Slave Society in the Deep South, 1718–1819.* Knoxville: University of Tennessee Press, 1999.

John Craig Hammond

Newton, John (1725–1807)

Born in **London** in 1725, John Newton's early life was tied to the sea. He came to be known as a slave ship **captain**, minister, hymn writer, and abolitionist. His father was a merchant shipmaster who frequently took his son to the Mediterranean following the death of John's mother. After a brief troublesome stint aboard a British naval vessel and three years on the African coast, Newton underwent a Christian conversion experience. Married in 1750, Newton made three more voyages to Africa and the Caribbean as a slave ship captain before leaving the trade in 1754. After a brief career as customs agent for the port of **Liverpool**, Newton entered the Anglican ministry in 1764, serving parishes in Olney and London. Newton displayed his attachment to the rising evangelical movement, particularly with his composition of the *Olney Hymns* in 1779, which included his most famous work, "Amazing Grace." While in London, Newton enlisted in the rising abolition movement. His death in 1807 coincided with Britain's making the slave trade illegal.

John Newton's importance for the study of the Middle Passage derives from his multiple **narratives**, which provide glimpses into the material and mental circumstances of slave ships. In 1763, Newton published his autobiography, *The Authentic Narrative of Some Remarkable and Interesting Particulars in the Life of John Newton*. Mainly a conversion narrative, the account provides no details regarding the experience of slaves but does demonstrate Newton's activities, including studying Latin and the bible. He also conducted personal and public worship during the trans-Atlantic crossing. His shipboard letters to his wife, published in 1793, provided a darker picture, describing the ship as overcrowded and filthy.

The most insight into slave ships comes through Newton's logbooks as captain, first published in 1962 as the *Journal of a Slave Trader*. Newton's daily entries provide a stark account of buying and transporting Africans. In addition to the quantified descriptions of illness and death, Newton records attempts at mutiny by the **crew** and rebellion by the enslaved **cargo**. During his third and final voyage as a slave ship captain, Newton became extremely ill and was confined for the entirety of the Middle Passage. This illness coupled with his weariness of being a "jailor" furnished Newton with his outward reasons for retiring from the slave trade. Although he expressed no theological scruples while engaged in the slave trade, in his later life, Newton's **Christianity** led him to advocate its end. At the age of 63, Newton published his final reflection on the Middle Passage, an influential tract entitled, *Thoughts upon the African Slave Trade* (1788). In this work, Newton combined his "public confession" and "humiliating reflection" with the major emphases of the British abolitionist movement—the moral and physical damage the slave trade wrought on Africans and Europeans alike. *See also* Abolition of the Slave Trade, Great Britain; Slave Merchants (Slave Traders).

Further Readings: Hindmarsh, Bruce. *John Newton and the English Evangelical Tradition.* New York: Oxford University Press, 1996; Newton, John. *The Journal of a Slave Trader*, eds. Bernard Martin and Mark Spurrell. London: Epworth Press, 1962; Newton, John. *The Works of the Rev. John Newton.* London: Hamilton, Adams & Co., 1820.

Stephen R. Berry

O

Oral History

The oral tradition in history relates to the verbal transmission of informational data germane to the day-to-day welfare of society. The oral tradition is as old as time itself. It was the first kind of history and has long established itself as a historical source of a special nature. This special nature is derived from the fact that it is an unwritten source of information couched in a form suitable for oral transmission. Its preservation depends on the powers of retention of successive generations of human beings.

The social importance of some oral traditions resulted in the creation of reliable systems for handing them down from generation to generation with a minimum of distortion. Such practices as group testimony on ritual occasions, disputations, schools for teaching traditional **folklore**, and the recitations on taking office could preserve the exact texts through the centuries, including archaisms even after they had ceased to be understood.

Traditions of this type resemble legal documents, or sacred books, and their bearers became highly specialized officials in many African royal courts.

African oral tradition can be divided into the following five categories:

- Formulae
- Poetry
- Lists
- Tales
- Commentaries

Formulae

Formulae are stereotype phrases used in various special circumstances. Formulae consist of titles, slogans, didactic formulae, and ritual formulae. Titles are formulae describing a man's status. They preserve a memory of the past. These formulae often contain eulogistic features. Usually slogans are recited on occasions when the special characteristics of the group are highlighted. There is no guarantee as to the accurate reproduction of their content given their frequent repetition. Slogans can often only be understood in the light of accompanying explanatory commentaries. They are a source from which information can be extracted about the family, clan, district, or country that they characterize.

Didactic formulae are proverbs, riddles, sayings, and epigrams. They are the store house of ancient wisdom. They are meanings in themselves and sometimes contain historical information.

Ritual formulae are used in religious or magic rites. It is commonly believed that if they are not repeated word for word supernatural sanctions will fall on everyone involved in the ceremony. They are learned with special care and are usually spoken by specialists such as priests, water-diviners, and sorcerers.

Poetry

Poetry includes all traditions in fixed form, the form and content of which are considered to be of artistic merit in the society within which they are transmitted. Poetry is meant to fulfill aesthetic demands. Its preservation and transmission are often in the hands of specialists, and the mode of expression must comply with certain fixed laws or conventions. Poetry, in the main, includes the following forms: historical poetry, which provides an account of historical events and often is composed for propaganda purposes; panegyric poetry, a poem of praise composed during the lifetime of the person concerned or immediately after their death; religious poetry, which includes stereotype forms or prayer, hymns, and dogmatic texts; and personal poetry, composed to give free expression to the feelings of the person who composes it.

Lists

Lists contain the names of places or people and are usually preserved by specialists belonging to some institution. These lists are pronounced on the occasion of some public ceremony, such as the death or the accession of a chief. They generally form an official tradition intended as a historical record, although the facts recorded are mostly used to support claims to political, social, and economic rights. Lists are normally the only available sources for compiling a chronology.

Tales

Tales are a form of testimony with a free form of text—that is, they are composed in prose. This category contains diverse types, their common thread being that they are all in narrative form. To some extent, their main aim is to instruct, edify, give pleasure, or vindicate rights. Tales are the only sources that give detailed accounts of a series of events. They are usually recited by specialists on ceremonial occasions and are transmitted within a particular social group. Three types can be distinguished: those concerning general history, those concerning local history, and those concerning family history. They attempt to explain the world, the culture, and the society. When such explanations are given in terms of religious causes, the tale in question is called a myth.

Commentaries

Traditions of this kind have two features in common: (1) they are presented in the form of brief pieces of information, and (2) they are supplementary to other sources or are closely connected with a particular situation and only transmitted in the context of that situation. They are never primarily aimed at recording history, but rather have either a legal or a didactic purpose.

Each type of oral tradition has its bias and limitations. They can be garbled and exaggerated. They are remote in time and have problems with semantics and archaisms. They can be difficult to understand when taken out of context. But their very diversity makes it possible to surmount the particular failings of each by comparing the information that can obtained from the different types.

All oral traditions are, to a greater or lesser extent, linked with the societies and the cultures that produce them. Therefore, all are influenced by the culture and society concerned, upon which their very existence depends. *See also* Historical Memory.

Further Readings: Carretta, Vincent, and Gould, Philip, eds. *Genius in Bondage: Literature of the Early Black Atlantic.* Lexington: University Press of Kentucky, 2001; Diedrich, Maria, Gates, Henry Louis, and Pedersen, Carl, eds. *Black Imagination and the Middle Passage.* Oxford: Oxford University Press, 1999; Rice, Alan. *Radical Narratives of the Black Atlantic.* New York: Continuum, 2003.

Reginald Clarke

Ouidah

Throughout the eighteenth century, Ouidah, also spelled Whydah and originally called Ajuda, became the main **port** of embarkation on the **Slave Coast** for millions of enslaved Africans removed from their homelands and communities and shipped to the New World. The Portuguese who first arrived at Ouidah in 1580 were followed by the Danes, the English, and the French. These European powers built forts (some of which are still standing today or renovated into **museums**) to protect their slaving endeavors. It is estimated that between 15 percent and 20 percent of all Africans sold into slavery came through the port of Ouidah.

Both Ouidah and **Allada** were coastal kingdoms that controlled the export of slaves until the eighteenth century when the hinterland kingdom of **Dahomey**, under King **Agaja Trudo** (1708–1732), conquered both kingdoms, in 1724 and 1727, respectively, to gain access to the coast, monopolize the supply of slaves to European slave ships, and gain access to the gun market. The king's army began to expand the kingdom, encouraged by the availability of rifles and other **firearms** traded with the French and Spanish **slave traders** for war captives.

The kingdom of Dahomey had long been at odds with the neighboring kingdom of Oyo, which it tried in vain to subjugate; Dahomey later conceded defeat and became a tributary to Oyo. Historians have argued that the slave trade in Dahomey was mainly state controlled because the kingdom only sold prisoners of war. Apparently, it was against custom to sell anyone from Dahomey, and King Wegbaja (1645–1685) made it a capital offence to do so. William Snelgrave, an English slave trader, concurred that the king of Dahomey never sold slaves on his farms unless they were found guilty of serious crimes. Research also shows, however, that besides selling its prisoners of war and foreign slaves, Dahomey, through the seaport of Ouidah, sold imported slaves from the hinterland to European slavers. With the conquest of the seaport of Ouidah, Dahomey became the main supplier of slaves on the Slave Coast as the kingdom developed into an authoritative military slave-raiding state in the region after the collapse of the Oyo Empire.

It was during the battles to conquer Ouidah that King Agaja started the female military unit known as the Amazons, after his regular all-male army had taken heavy casualties. The Amazons trained for battle through energetic **dancing** and hunting, and were prohibited from having children or becoming pregnant. Recent scholarship indicates that, although the empire flourished during the reign of Agaja, the raids and disciplined military were designed for self-protection and for control of the slave trade that threatened to engulf the kingdom. In fact, after Dahomey, under Agaja, took partial control of the trade, the number of Africans transiting through Ouidah dwindled from 20,000 to 5,500 per year. Unable to get European traders interested in any kind of trade besides slaves, however, King Agaja fell back on the sale of humans. His immediate successor, Tegbesu IV, tried to revive the slave trade during his reign and made Ouidah the principal port of departure for the enslaved Africans, but in the 1760s, Dahomey and the port of Ouidah declined rapidly and were supplanted by other ports such as Porto Novo.

Ouidah is significant for reasons other than being a notorious gateway for slaves en route to the New World. Ouidah has been dubbed the Voodoo (Vodun) capital of the world, where Voodoo sympathizers and believers, mainly from the diaspora (the United States and Brazil), and curious tourists celebrate Voodoo, a belief in life that is driven by physical and spiritual forces. Once suppressed, banned, and considered a barbaric **religion** by both the colonial administrators and Mathieu Kerekou's Marxist regime (1973–1991), the government in 1996 gave recognition to this religious observance and inaugurated a National Voodoo Day. A member of the Voodoo Supreme Chief family underlines the importance of Ouidah and Voodoo specifically to those whose ancestors went through the **Door of No Return** at Ouidah when he says that "the annual celebration is an occasion for us in Ouidah to remember the hundreds of thousands of Blacks deported to the Americas as slaves."

Ouidah has inspired historical, fictional, and travel **narratives**, including Frank Yerby's *The Man from Dahomey* (1971), Bruce Chatwin's *The Viceroy of Ouidah* (1980), and Sharon Caulder's *Mark of Voodoo: Awakening to My African Spiritual Heritage* (2002). Chatwin's historical novel tells of a Brazilian slave trader who helped a prince from Dahomey accede to the throne, but ended up dying poor and destitute even though he had been granted a **monopoly** of the slave trade in the kingdom. *Mark of Voodoo* is an autobiographical travel narrative, which documents the author's physical and spiritual journey to Ouidah. Although knowledgeable about Voodoo and a practitioner, Caulder found her spiritual roots in Ouidah: the Voodoo Supreme Chief became her mentor.

The legacy of Ouidah is not an enviable one given its role in the trans-Atlantic slave trade; it stands today as a testimony to both the dehumanization of Africans and the commemoration of the spirits of those who took the journey into the unknown. *See also* Returnees to Africa; Slave Coast; Trade Forts.

Further Readings: Caulder, Sharon. *Mark of Voodoo: Awakening to My African Spiritual Heritage.* St. Paul, MN: Llewellyn Publications, 2002; Chatwin, Bruce. *The Viceroy of Ouidah.* London: Penguin Books, 1980; Dalzel, Archibald. *History of Dahomey, an Inland Kingdom of Africa.* London: Heinemann, 1793; Falola, Toyin, and Childs, Matt D., eds. *The Yoruba Diaspora in the Atlantic World.* Bloomington: Indiana University Press, 2004; Law, Robin. *Ouidah: The Social History of a West African Slaving Port, 1727–1892.* Athens: Ohio University Press, 2005; Yerby, Frank. *The Man from Dahomey.* London: Heinemann, 1971.

Mawuena Logan

Ounce Trade

The term "ounce trade" refers to a particular type of transaction that emerged as West Africa switched from a gold-exporting to a gold-importing region. By the sixteenth century, gold was already a recognized currency between European merchants of the Atlantic and coastal African societies, largely because Europeans had initially bought large quantities of African gold. Thus, ounces of gold, and one-sixteenth of an ounce divisions (or *ackies*), were understood mediums of exchange that were easily transferred over to the slave trade. By the early seventeenth century, buyers and sellers in many regions habitually negotiated an ounce value for each captive.

The ounce trade was, however, far more complex, because in most cases gold did not change hands. European and American merchants recognized that the demand for trade goods was higher in West Africa than the demand for currency, and that they could earn greater **profits** by employing arbitrage to sell **firearms**, alcohol, manufactured goods, and above all cloth in West Africa at a higher **price** than it cost to buy these goods in Europe. Africans, however, did not continuously or ubiquitously value all of these goods at the same price. Instead, each time a European (or American) ship engaged an African community or individual in trade, the value of the goods they had to offer had to be negotiated between the ships' officers and community leaders or **slave traders**. This created the need for a method to establish the value of slaves in terms of trade goods. The solution was to develop an artificial trade unit, the "trade ounce." Through negotiation, each commodity offered by the merchants was assigned a value in trade ounces. Each captive for sale, similarly, was assigned a value in trade ounces. Generally, the seller could then select the goods that would make up the payment for individual slaves.

The economics of the ounce trade were complex and reflected agency on the parts of both the buyers and the sellers. The objective of the ships' officers, **investors**, and **captain** was to buy cheap goods in Europe and establish a high value for them in Africa. This effort was sometimes confounded by Africans' selectivity in the goods that they would accept, which was based on their personal needs and potential resale value in the interior. In addition, competition could shift the balance. The arrival of competing ships, for example, sometimes enabled African participants to force buyers to value the trade ounce quite high in terms of its goods. As a last resort, European and American buyers would sometimes offer to include gold in the trade ounce. This was undesirable, however, because the price of gold in Europe was similar to its value in Africa, and thus the profit from arbitrage disappeared. Pricing was similarly complicated by the overall **supply and demand** of slaves and by the health, age, and **gender** of the captives.

In addition to direct payment for slaves, the trade ounce facilitated negotiation of the "custom," a fee paid to African administrators and elites by ship captains to secure the right to trade in that region. *See also* Trade Commodities.

Further Readings: Metcalf, George. "Gold, Assortments and the Trade Ounce: Fante Merchants and the Problem of Supply and Demand in the 1770s." *The Journal of African History* 28, 1 (1987): 27–41; Polyani, Karl. "Sortings and 'Ounce Trade' in the West African Slave Trade." *The Journal of African History* 5, 3 (1964): 381–393.

Trevor Getz

Overcrowding

Having been captured, transported to the coast, and sold to European traders, the next harrowing experience for African slaves was their boarding on the slave ships and the horrific ocean voyage across the Atlantic. Once aboard the ships, the human **cargo** would be packed or stored below decks, often according to the vessel's "stacking plan," which was designed to pack the maximum number of slaves in the cargo **holds**. Ships were packed from bow to stern with men, **women**, and **children**.

In the big business of the slave trade, slavers often debated the merits of packing strategies, trying to squeeze as much **profit** as possible out of each voyage across the ocean. The trader's goal was to cram as many slaves as possible into the holds of the vessels and to get as many of the slaves across the Atlantic alive and healthy for maximum resale. These two goals were not necessarily compatible with one another. Slave **captains** generally fell into one of two categories on the issue. One school of thought, the "loose-packers," reasoned that providing the slaves a little more room and better **food** would reduce the **mortality** rate of the Middle Passage and land healthier slaves who would sell at a higher **price**, yielding a greater profit. Most slavers, however, were "tight-packers" who jammed the holds as full as possible, often wedging slaves so close together that they were obliged to lie one upon another, without so much room as in a coffin. This allowed for larger slave cargoes, but loss of life on these voyages was often greater than on ships with smaller cargoes. Tight-packers calculated that, despite the higher mortality rate, the larger cargoes would offset the deaths and thus net larger profits overall. The great demand and the high price for slaves by the mid-eighteenth century worked to ensure that most slave captains were willing to risk great loss of life to transport as many slaves as possible.

Before regulatory laws were passed to control the person-to-ton ratio of slave ships, scholars estimate that for every ton of cargo space there were habitually four more slaves transported. The infamous slaver **the Brookes** was a 320-ton vessel whose stacking plan showed where 451 slaves could be stowed by using every available space. Yet evidence shows that on several voyages, the *Brookes* carried more than 600 slaves. Another British slaver out of **Liverpool** took nearly 700 slaves, more than three slaves to each ton, for its passage across the ocean. Such tight-packing was the norm rather than the exception as traders tried to reap the riches of the trade in human beings.

Overpacking led to severe physical and emotional stress. Slaves, packed below decks and forced into such proximity with their fellow sufferers, kicked and even bit each other in their attempts to maneuver enough space for themselves. Rough weather made a dreadful situation

Slave deck on the bark *Wildfire*, 1860. Special Collections, University of Virginia Library.

even more appalling because slaves were not brought out of the holds to spend time on the decks. As they were held captive below the decks, they were thrown against the ship and each other, bruising with each punishing ocean wave. Slaves packed in such manner, without enough room to even sit upright, were forced to crawl over one another to reach the toilet buckets. Few would bother to try, and thus slaves would lay in their excrement and other bodily fluids. Such **conditions** encouraged the spread of **disease** and led to mortality death rates between 10 and 20 percent, depending in part on the length of the voyage and the extent of the overpacking.

In an effort to reduce mortality, the British Parliament passed the Dolben's Act of 1788, limiting the person-to-ton ratio of slave ships to five slaves per three tons up to 200 tons, and one slave per ton after that. In 1799, a revised law required minimum space standards for each slave carried. Male slaves were to be provided six feet by one foot four inches; women, five feet ten by one foot four; boys, five feet by one foot two; and girls, four feet six by one foot. Overcrowding of slavers continued, however, as unscrupulous traders circumvented the space requirements by changing the registered tonnage of the ship or blatantly ignoring the **regulations**. In 1814, the Spanish 200-ton brig, *Carlos*, was captured with 512 slaves on board, nearly 180 more than the complement allowed according to law. That same year, another slaver, the 40-ton schooner *Aglae*, was captured with a cargo of 152 slaves, nearly four to each ton. The high profit margin of the Atlantic slave trade ensured that traders would continue to overpack their cargo holds despite any regulatory laws and regardless of the suffering and death of their victims.

Further Readings: Dow, George Francis. *Slave Ships and Slaving.* New York: Dover Publications, 1970; Eltis, David. *The Rise of African Slavery in the Americas.* New York: Cambridge University Press, 2000; Garland, Charles, and Klein, Hebert S. "The Allotment of Space for Slaves aboard Eighteenth-Century British Slave Ships." *William and Mary Quarterly* 42 (1985): 238–248; Northrup, David, ed. *The Atlantic Slave Trade.* Boston: Houghton Mifflin, 2002; Rawley, James A. *The TransAtlantic Slave Trade: A History.* New York: W. W. Norton, 1981.

Sharon A. Roger Hepburn

P

Phillips, Thomas

Thomas Phillips was the captain of a slave ship called *"Hannibal"* which made a voyage to Whydah (**Ouidah**) in 1693–1695. He was a member of the cartel that owned the ship. Thomas Phillips kept an account of the voyage, entitled "A Journal of a Voyage made in the *Hannibal*," which provides excellent source material for reconstructing the history of the slave trade, most importantly, the Middle Passage experience.

His ship went to Whydah with European manufactured goods, most notably Welsh cloth. In his journal, he notes that a slave **captain** did not commence trade without paying customs, and that it was customary for the captains to buy the king's slaves before buying from other African merchants. Other people whom the captain needed to make payments to included the interpreter, the person who guarded the ship's supplies, the porters who carried the supplies to the seaside, and the people who rang the bell that signaled the commencement of trade. Phillips purchased some 692 slaves. Apart from barter, another means of payment as recorded by Phillips was **cowries**. He mentioned that smaller cowry shells were more valuable than the bigger ones.

Phillips described how slaves were packed in the ship and forced to dance at night. The slaves were made to dance not primarily for entertainment purposes but to make them agile. Like most slave vessels, Phillips's *Hannibal* also suffered casualties. He lost about 300 of his slaves, and noted the economic misfortune of that loss. The slave captain lost £10 for each slave who died. *See also* African Rulers and the Slave Trade; Mortality, Slave; Narratives by Slave Traders; Trade Commodities.

Further Readings: Rawley, James. *The TransAtlantic Slave Trade: A History.* New York: W. W. Norton, 1981; Stein, Robert. *The French Slave Trade in the 18th Century: An Old Regime Business.* Madison: University of Wisconsin Press, 1979; Thomas, Hugh. *The Slave Trade: The Story of the Atlantic Slave Trade, 1440–1870.* New York: Simon & Schuster, 1997.

Saheed Aderinto

Plans and Diagrams

Among the most powerful and chilling records depicting the cold-hearted and calculating nature of those who controlled the **profit**-driven trans-Atlantic slave trade are the plans and diagrams drawn up and consulted by slave **captains** for the loading and storage of human **cargo** aboard their vessels for the voyage across the Atlantic Ocean to the slave societies of the New World. Often referred to as the "stacking plan," these records attest to the suffering endured by those Africans forcibly removed from their homeland and carried to the New World as slaves. Slave vessels were outfitted to best hold their human cargo, and great care was taken to use every available space. Because slaves were considered trade goods, their owners kept relatively accurate manifests for each ship and followed their stacking plan to literally jam as many slaves in the **holds** as possible.

The space assigned to human cargo, as illustrated in the stacking plans, was determined through precise mathematical calculations, with the primary concern being that of maximum profit. In allocating spaces, particular attention was paid to size. The taller slaves were to be placed in the area of the greatest breadth of the ship, while those who were shorter were lodged near the bow. To maximize the number of slaves to be transported, specially built shelves, or platforms, divided the cargo holds so that the normal four to five feet space between decks was halved. Slaves were thus not even allowed the room to sit upright. The mathematical calculations used to design the stacking plans typically allotted a space of six feet by sixteen inches for males, and five feet ten inches by sixteen inches for females.

Many of the diagrams were used by abolitionists in their campaign to end the Atlantic slave trade to illustrate the horrors endured by the victims of the trade. The most notorious of the stacking plans was that of **the *Brookes***, used by the Plymouth committee of abolitionists in a 1788 leaflet to document the vile nature of the trans-Atlantic slave trade. The plan of the *Brookes* showed where 451 slaves could be stowed below the decks of the slaver, seemingly without an inch to spare. Nevertheless, an Act of Parliament allowed the *Brookes* to carry 454, so the stacking plan concludes that three more slaves could be wedged in among the number represented in the plan to reach full capacity.

Slavers' diagrams were drawn up in accordance to the **regulations** set out by those European nations controlling the slave trade; however, adherence to these laws was often lax. Slave vessels often carried more slaves than permitted by law and shown in the stacking plan. The plans and diagrams of slave vessels dispel any doubt as to the inhumanness of the centuries-long business of trading in human lives.

Further Readings: Clarkson, Thomas. *The History of the Rise, Progress and Accomplishment of the Abolition of the African Slave-Trade by the British Parliament*. 2 vols. London: Cass, 1968 (1808); Donnan, Elizabeth, ed. *Documents Illustrative of the History of the Slave Trade to America*. 4 vols. Washington, DC: Carnegie Institution of Washington, 1930–1935; Garland, Charles, and Klein, Hebert S. "The Allotment of Space for Slaves aboard Eighteenth-Century British Slave Ships." *William and Mary Quarterly* 42 (1985): 238–248; Dow, George Francis. *Slave Ships and Slaving*. New York: Dover Publications, 1970; Northrup, David, ed. *The Atlantic Slave Trade*. Boston: Houghton Mifflin, 2002.

Sharon A. Roger Hepburn

Plantations

The plantation was an economic unit where the profitable crops of **sugar**, tobacco, and cotton, among other crops, were grown and processed beyond the subsistence level. A large landowner, also a slave owner, raised crops solely for **profit** considerations. The source of profit was based on extensive and exploitative use of slaves or indentured labor. The slaves could be organized as gang labor, a situation in which they worked in groups and were confined to specific locations for a duration of time. Others worked as peasants and were given daily tasks to perform.

In **Brazil** and the Caribbean, African slaves worked on sugarcane plantations. A plantation economy, based on sugarcane cultivation and the production of sugar in factories known in Brazil as *engenho* (the "engine"), exploited slaves to their maximum capacity. In the southern states of the United States, slaves produced cotton, tobacco, rice, and some other crops. The slave master lived in the plantation house where he had close access to the supervision of slaves. Business was also transacted in plantation houses—selling products, including slaves, and manufacturing small items. Plantation houses were the sites to discipline slaves and perform social events.

A combination of plantations gave rise to what is known as a plantation economy based on large-scale profitability. Such crops could be traded within national boundaries or converted to manufactured items for international trade. The majority of slaves involved in the Middle Passage ended up on the plantations. They were part of a global Atlantic economy that involved Europe taking manufactured goods to Africa in exchange for slaves. The slaves were then taken to plantations to produce items that circulated in the Americas and in Europe.

Many of the extreme brutalities of slavery occurred on plantations. The work hours were long, the supervision intense, and the rewards to slaves no more than the cabins where they slept. Growing and picking cotton,

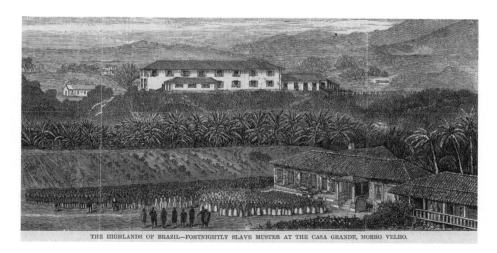

THE HIGHLANDS OF BRAZIL.—FORTNIGHTLY SLAVE MUSTER AT THE CASA GRANDE, MORRO VELHO.

Master of plantation slaves, Brazil, 1867. Special Collections, University of Virginia Library.

separating the seeds from the fluff (ginning), and baling the cotton took hours on end. To produce more cotton, a slave owner needed more labor, which in turn created greater demand for slaves. Because many of the slaves had been farmers in Africa, they adapted to the plantations, with a number of slaves even introducing new ideas for rice cultivation.

Plantations had cottage industries where slaves could work as artisans producing baskets, ceramics, utensils, and other small items. Also to be found were those who did household tasks such as child rearing, sewing, and dairying. Slaves with skills as craftsmen were the most valued because their owners could make more money from their products and could even rent their services to other plantations. An apprenticeship system developed that enabled slaves to transfer their skills to their **children**.

Slaves, where conditions permitted, raised **families** in plantations, although their children were also slaves. The children were co-opted early into the labor force, as early as seven years old when they could be asked to run errands all day long. When a plantation owner died, or because of other economic exigencies, slaves could be dispersed for good. Slaves survived on rations of small **food**, which they could supplement by growing vegetables and raising livestock. Slaves had a minimum of clothing and enjoyed only minimum privacy. *See also* British Caribbean; Cuba; French Caribbean; Hispaniola; Indentured Servants; Saint Domingue; Spanish Caribbean.

Further Readings: Hamilton, Virginia. *Many Thousand Gone: African Americans from Slavery to Freedom*. New York: Alfred A. Knopf, 1991; Hopkinson, Deborah. *Sweet Clara and the Freedom Quilt*. New York: Alfred A. Knopf, 1993; Lester, Julius. *To Be a Slave*. New York: Scholastic, 1968.

Toyin Falola

Ports

A network of ports constituted an indispensable component of the trans-Atlantic trade in enslaved Africans. The major ports engaged in the trade were in Europe and **profits** were invested in commercial ports and industrial areas. The system of the trans-Atlantic trade in enslaved Africans interconnected the Americas, Africa, the Mediterranean and parts of Asia. Key elements of business in many European Atlantic ports were based on Atlantic connections tied to the dependence on slavery during the eighteenth century.

English ports involved in the trans-Atlantic trade in enslaved Africans included the ports of **London**, **Bristol**, and **Liverpool**, which grew with the increase in trade between 1700 and 1800. Banks were opened by merchants who did well, thus facilitating trade in Britain and overseas. Liverpool was making £1 million each year from the trade by 1700.

In such port communities, the principal slavers were the financial leaders, and they ascended to the summit of political office and became influential in policy making both locally and at times nationally. This was the case of leading slavers in London, Liverpool, Manchester, and Bristol. Slavers in Bristol sent out 14 percent of all ships leaving the port during the last quarter of the eighteenth century. In the case of Liverpool, 33 percent of the ships leaving the port in the 1770s were slave ships from the town.

Ships sailed from British ports such as Liverpool to the west coast of Africa where they would unload the goods brought from Britain and exchange them for enslaved Africans. Liverpool was a port where ships were specifically designed and constructed for the sole purpose of ferrying Africans across the Atlantic. These vessels, however, could be easily adapted to carry other types of **cargo**.

The economic development of areas beyond Liverpool was nurtured by the slave trade. Manchester's manufactured products such as cotton, for example, made it famous, and the city was heavily involved in the trans-Atlantic trade in enslaved Africans. The trade saw Manchester grow to become a major export town.

Nantes and La Rochelle were examples of slave-trading ports in France that were integrated into the global trade system. The ports of La Rochelle, Nantes, and **Bordeaux** have been described as elegant reminders in urban settings of the labor of enslaved Africans in the French West Indies, the exports from which were increasingly valuable.

By 1789, the slave trade became indispensable to the Nantes economy. Investments in slavery surpassed investments in other business activities and the trade sustained Nantes as a key distributor of goods from the colonies. Bordeaux also became an important port, having a huge **re-export** trade fueled by the colonial economy. This trade enabled Nantes to keep pace with Bordeaux. The industrial development of Nantes was also stimulated by the trans-Atlantic trade in enslaved Africans. In the 1770s, Nantes stood out as France's largest ship-building port. Slavers had heavy investments in **textile** and ship-building industries and local hardware financed by profits from the trans-Atlantic trade in enslaved Africans. *See also* Entrepôts; Shipyards.

Further Readings: Byrom, Jamie. *Minds and Machines; Britain 1750–1900*. London: Longmans, Green and Company, 1999; McD. Beckles, Hilary, "Slave Voyages, the Transatlantic Trade in Enslaved Africans." Unpublished manuscript prepared for the UNESCO Associated Schools Project Network Transatlantic Slave Trade Education Project. Paris: UNESCO, 2000; Walvin, James. *Black Ivory: A History of British Slavery*. Washington, DC: Howard University Press, 1994.

Sandra Ingrid Gift

Portuguese Slave Trade

The inception of the Atlantic slave trade was a secondary result of Portuguese Atlantic expansion in the first half of the fifteenth century. Despite this fact, the slave trade became a significant interest for Portugal and its merchants in the next four centuries, contributing to the making of the Portuguese Atlantic Empire.

As part of a complex project—involving religious, political, and economic concerns—Portugal sponsored southward navigation in the Atlantic Ocean starting in the early fifteenth century (its success owed much to foreigners such as the Genoese sailors). After the discovery of the Atlantic Islands—Azores, Madeira, and **Cape Verde**—the Portuguese continued in search of African gold, which they found on the Guinea Coast, on a coastal stretch soon known as the **Gold Coast**.

The first slaves purchased on the Gold Coast by Portuguese traders were transported to Portugal to work as domestic servants. In the first 200 years of the Portuguese slave trade, the slaves came from two main regions: Guinea Coast (West Africa) and Congo and **Angola** (West Central Africa). From the former region, the slaves came from the mainland (Senegambia), but almost all went through the Cape Verde Archipelago and increasingly thousands were channeled from southern **ports**, chiefly from the Bight of Benin, through **São Tomé** Island. For this reason, Portuguese traders and settlers early spoke about Africa as "Guinea" and about Africans as "Guinea Negroes."

It was in the Atlantic Islands (primarily Madeira and São Tomé) since the middle of the fifteenth century that Portugal prefigured the **plantation** model of the New World colonial economy, which was made up of large-scale **sugar** production based on African coerced labor. This pattern was further improved in Portuguese South America. **Brazil** turned into the mainstay of the Portuguese overseas empire from the middle of the seventeenth century, but it already was one of two major Portuguese slave trade destinations since the last quarter of the sixteenth century.

Between the years 1620 and 1640, the Portuguese slave trade became steady from Congo and Angola, turning West Central Africa into the major Atlantic slave-exporting region. From **Luanda**, the Portuguese penetrated the backland and mixed with the native people, originating a Portuguese-speaking African population. The Portuguese control over Luanda and, later, over the Benguela slave trade owed partially to the formation of that mixed population, which supported the increasing demand for slaves on Brazil's sugar plantations.

During the unification of the Spanish and Portuguese Crowns under the Habsburg kings (1580–1640), Portuguese traders controlled the supply of slaves to Hispanic South America through contracts or *asientos*, granted by the king. Brazil's plantation owners had to compete with Spanish South American miners in purchasing slaves from Portuguese-speaking traders, as sugar became a rival to silver in this period of high **prices** in the European market. At this time, the crown regulated the slave trade to its colonies by granting *licenças* (**licenses**) to trade slaves in Iberian overseas possessions.

The rebellion of 1640 against the Habsburg king restored a Portuguese dynasty to the Portuguese throne and gave rise to an Iberian war with overseas consequences. To Portugal's slave trade the foremost result was the loss of the *asiento*, which deprived the Portuguese of immediate access to the Spanish South American market and hence to the source of the silver. Only in the last years of the seventeenth century did the slave commerce with Spanish South America become important once again.

Meanwhile, the slave trade between Brazil and Africa became increasingly important, given the necessity of Portuguese-Brazilian plantations for slave labor, not provided in appropriate scale by metropolitan merchants more attracted to South American silver. From Bahia, Rio de Janeiro, and Recife, humble Portuguese migrants newly settled as merchants in Brazil's harbors invested in the direct import of forced African migrants. The appointment of Brazil's settlers and former governors of captaincies to rule Angola in the later half of the seventeenth century was also an important means of penetration of Portuguese-Brazilian interests in the slave trade.

This tendency, initiated about 1650, was reinforced by the combined effect of the downward trend of the Portuguese-Brazilian economy and hard competition with the Northern European powers (in the sugar market and therefore in the Atlantic slave trade) in the latter half of the century. Portuguese dealers had difficulty providing a varied assortment of manufactured goods (most not produced in the kingdom) at the lowest prices required by African **slave merchants**. Therefore low-cost goods produced in Portuguese South America replaced metropolitan consumer goods in the Portuguese slave trade. Brazilian sugarcane alcohol (*jeribita*) took over the role of wines and liquors in Angola, and third-grade tobacco began to be exported to West Africa as well.

This pattern of trade had distinct features according to the African region of slave exports. In Guinea Coast, particularly in the cluster of ports known as *Costa da Mina* (Mine Coast or Bight of Benin), Portuguese and Luso-Brazilians rivaled with Dutch, English, and French slave traders. Although these rivals had several factories and fortresses in the region, a Portuguese fortress was not built until 1721. Nobody could monopolize the trade, however, because the local kingdoms and merchants exercised control over the flow of slaves.

Portuguese traders from Brazil, who prevailed in this branch of Brazilian slave imports, furthermore, were subject to **tax** exaction from the Dutch, paying 10 percent of their **cargoes** as grants. Notwithstanding, Luso-Brazilian traders exchanged tobacco and gold to buy manufactured goods from European rivals so that they could procure slaves.

In spite of the minimal interest of **Lisbon** merchants in this branch of trade, the metropolitan government tried to increase official control over Brazil's trade with *Costa da Mina*. Concerned with the **smuggling** of tobacco—and later of gold—to European rivals on Africa's shores and the unlawful colonial import of manufactures in return, as well as with Luso-Brazilian prominence in Luanda, Portugal issued a pioneer law in 1684. This law restricted the permitted number of slaves loaded per ship's **hold** space (*lei da arqueação*) and later (1699) set the number of ships authorized to buy slaves on the *Costa da Mina* (24 from Salvador and 12 from Pernambuco). Ironically, although the former law was successful in its aims, the latter rule resulted in strengthening the **monopoly** of a few Bahian merchants over the *Costa da Mina* slave market. Only in 1756 did this branch of the slave trade become free for all of the king's subjects within the Portuguese Atlantic Empire.

In Angola, where Portugal held effective control over the exports and some backland regions, metropolitan and colonial traders shared slave exports to Brazil. The former exercised its control over Luanda's exports mainly during the Brazilian gold boom, providing cheap manufactures and long-term credit to local slave dealers, whereas Luso-Brazilian merchants, whose chief goods were sugarcane alcohol and smuggled manufactures, moved to Benguela, which, in turn, became one of the major slave exporters in the two last decades of the eighteenth century.

The settlers on Luanda also had an important role in the trade. Supported by Portuguese credit, they organized the caravans and fairs in the backland to buy captives. In the eighteenth century, nevertheless, the Portuguese Crown became increasingly troubled at colonial settlers' share (Luso-Brazilians and Luso-Africans) in the Angolan trade. To protect metropolitan interests in Luanda, the Portuguese ministers put into place some mercantilist measures such as the priority to load slave cargoes to those whose vessel and cargo belonged to the same owner—usually Lisbon traders.

The most straightforward royal attempt to guarantee the metropolitan control over some branches of the Angola-Brazil slave market was the formation of two chartered Royal Trade Companies during Prime Minister Marquis of Pombal's government. The *Real Companhia do Gão-Pará e Maranhão* (1755) and the *Real Companhia de Pernambuco e Paraíba* (1759) had the monopoly on the slave trade bound to these Brazilian captaincies (Pará, Maranhão, Pernambuco, and Paraiba). The latter trade company carried out most of its trade in Luanda. Thus, the Portuguese slave trade in Angola showed the classic triangular pattern in addition to a bilateral colony-to-colony trade.

After the independence of Brazil (1822), some Portuguese merchants—the majority of whom likely were settlers in African colonies—continued with the slave trade to Brazil and **Cuba** even with the pressure of the British abolitionist movement and the strong Brazilian competition. The Portuguese flag could be seen on the slavers' ships at least up until 1836 when Portugal abolished the slave trade to its colonies.

Metropolitan and seaborne Portuguese slave merchants carried out a great share of the Atlantic slave trade for some 400 years, bound to Europe, the Atlantic Islands, and the Americas. The slave exports to Portuguese South America from the middle of the sixteenth century until the break of Brazil's colonial ties numbered nearly 2,900,000 souls, almost one-third of all people deported as captives in the course of the Atlantic slave trade.

Further Readings: Alencastro, Luiz Felipe de. *O trato dos viventes: a formação do Brasil no Atlântico Sul*. São Paulo: Companhia das Letras, 2000; Curtin, Philip D. *The Atlantic Slave Trade: A Census*. Madison: University of Wisconsin Press, 1969; Klein, Herbert S. *The Atlantic Slave Trade*. Cambridge: Cambridge University Press, 1999; Miller, Joseph C. *Way of Death. Merchant Capitalism and the Angolan Slave Trade, 1730–1830*. Madison: University of Wisconsin Press, 1988; Verger, Pierre. *Trade Relations between the Bight of Benin and Bahia from the Seventeenth to Nineteenth Century*. Ibadan: Ibadan University Press, 1976.

Gustavo Acioli Lopes and Maximiliano Mac Menz

Potosí

African slaves resided in Potosí, a silver mining city 13,000 feet up in the Andean plains, within several years of its 1545 founding. Until the 1590s, the African population was generally criollo, born in **Seville**, Santo Domingo, Panama, Lima, or Mexico City. After the 1590s, African-born Angolan slaves dominated the city. These slaves sold for an average **price** of 500 pesos. Silver was the main business of Potosí, and Spanish mine owners typically rejected costly slave labor in favor of the crown-supported indigenous labor draft. General opinion held that slaves could not adjust to the high altitude or mine labor. Instead, slaves ranked as symbols of wealth for their owners and labored in domestic service, artisanry, or bakeries. Although few mined silver, slaves in Potosí had the unique job of making silver coins. Some fifty slaves worked in Potosí's mint (*Casa de la Moneda*), the only one in Peru from 1572 to 1683.

The slaves' journey to Potosí shifted over time. Sixteenth-century slaves, mainly Wolof and Biafra, arrived via an official route through crown-approved **ports** (like Nombre de Dios in Panama) where slavers paid crown **taxes**. This was a lengthy and often deadly journey from Africa or Spain through Panama and down the Pacific Coast. Slaves who arrived to Potosí from the Pacific were equally likely to have been born in the Spanish Americas as in Africa. In some instances, African-born slaves paired up during the journey and arrived to Potosí anticipating the birth of a child.

By 1580, a growing circuit of illicit trade between Potosí and the Atlantic coast changed slaves' journeys to Potosí and dramatically increased the number of African-born slaves. Tucuman became a bridge between the Atlantic and silver-rich Upper Peru, and Brazilian merchants known as *peruleiros* traversed this path. In 1592, the Spanish crown awarded traders permission to sell some slaves from the port of **Buenos Aires**. By 1600, an estimated 450 African slaves entered Potosí annually from the Atlantic.

This new route meant a shorter journey for slaves, yet it remained extraordinary in its demands. Traders ferried Angolan slaves to **Brazil** and then to Buenos Aires. Once on land, slaves traversed more than 1,000 miles. En route the slaves had plentiful beef on the grasslands, and good water sources in the forest, but little sustenance through the mountains. Passing through cities like Salta, Jujuy, and Tucuman, slaves encountered Spaniards and indigenous peoples like the Guaraní. The new route bypassed Spain and Panama and offered a more gradual ascent on the eastern side of the Andes, thus making altitude sickness less debilitating. The trip, on boat and land combined, took more than 120 days. After 1623, the crown again suppressed this Atlantic route, because it hurt Panamanian merchants.

The numbers of Africans (free and slave) peaked at 6,000 when Potosí reached its height of 120,000 inhabitants around 1620. Reasons of distance, price, and labor needs account for the small percentage of Africans in Potosí. Although Africans never became fully incorporated into mining, they fulfilled significant roles in the urban economy and influenced the emerging colonial society of Potosí.

Further Readings: Boxer, C. R. *Salvador de Sá and the Struggle for Brazil and Angola, 1602–1686.* London: University of London, the Athlone Press, 1952; Wolff, Inge. "Slavery and the Trade of Blacks in Upper Peru 1545–1640." *Jahrbuch fur Geschichte von Staat, Wirtschaft und Gesellschaft Lateinamerikas* 1 (1964): 157–186.

Jane Mangan

Price

There was no common trading currency throughout the Atlantic World. The value of slaves was determined by local peculiarities and economic systems. For example, on the **Windward Coast**, slaves and European imports were commonly valued in relation to bars of iron; on the Ivory Coast, to pieces of cloth; on the **Gold Coast**, to gold dust; between **Accra** and Keta, to **cowry shells**; on the **Slave Coast**, to both iron and copper bars; in the Oil Rivers, to brass basins; and in the Cameroons, to pieces of cloth. Iron and copper were imported from Europe in standard size bars. On the Slave Coast, cloth was imported in standard lengths. Except for cowry shells and gold dust, these modes of exchange were commodities that could be consumed and they varied in accordance with the extent of the need for them.

More often, the process of bargaining in slaves was complicated and lengthy. Large trading companies that had depots where they kept enough stock of imports tried to fix prices. The price could be upset if an **interloper** came to the coast and his or her trading caused a glut in guns or bars. Again, African taste in European goods tended to change, so the maintenance of stock might be a dicey business. Because of the variation in **supply and demand** from time to time and place to place on the coast as well as the complicated system of trading, it is difficult to establish a representative example of prices paid by Europeans for slaves in West Africa. At the beginning of the eighteenth century, the equivalent of £3 was the price of a fit male slave in the prime of life, at the beginning of the nineteenth century, perhaps an equivalent of £25. The purchase price of a slave was paid in goods, the value of which on the coast might bear little relation to their cost in Europe.

The prices of slaves in Africa were low in relative terms. It was possible to buy 18 Moors for one house at Arguin in 1455. Half a century later, a horse would only purchase twelve negroes near **Senegal**. At Rio dos Sestos, the price of one slave rose from two shaving basins to four or five. The native merchants of Porto d'Ali demanded a horse for six slaves in 1505.

The first batch of negroes was purchased in **Lisbon** for the West Indies in 1510 and a **licensing** system was inaugurated three years later. An edict of March 15, 1518, regulated the price of slaves and forbade merchants to penetrate into the interior of Guinea to get them. The original form of currency had been a kind of cowry shell, known as *njimbu* or *zimbo*, which was found on the island of **Luanda** and imported extensively from **Brazil**. The *zimbo* was gradually supplanted by the use of panos or palm leaf cloth and by rock salt, brandy, **gunpowder**, and other European goods of relatively small value.

Profits in slaves between West Africa and South America were immense, as all foreign visitors to Brazil and Peru noted. Slaves who sold for a few squares of palm cloth in Angola fetched from 400 to 600 pesos in Peru, according to age and condition.

But profit differed in the different markets and localities. In the southern states of the United States, a male cost $325 in 1840 and $500 in 1860. In Cuba, the average price was £20 in 1821 and £125 in 1847. In 1847, the Brazilian price was £50. Ten years later when suppression was becoming effective, the Cuban price rose to £200. On the other side of the Atlantic, a slave could be purchased on the Gold Coast in 1847 for £1.10, but in Whydah (**Ouidah**) in the same period, a slave cost £10. The price of slaves in Africa rose fivefold between 1680 and 1840s. *See also* Interlopers; Slave Merchants (Slave Traders); Textiles; Trade Commodities.

Further Readings: Curtin, P., Feierman, S., Thompson, L., and Vansina, J., eds. *African History: From Earliest Times to Independence.* London: Longmans, Green and Company, 1998; Fage, J. D. *A History of Africa.* London: Routledge, 1997; Inikori, J. E. "The Slave Trade and the Atlantic Economies, 1451–1870." In V. A. Shepherd and H. McD. Beckles, eds. *Caribbean Slavery in the Atlantic World: A Student Reader*, 290–308. Kingston: Ian Randle Publishers Ltd., 2000; Martinez-Fernandez, L. "The Sweet and the Bitter: Cuban and Puerto Rican Responses to the Mid-Nineteenth Century Sugar Challenge." In V. A. Shepherd and H. McD. Beckles, eds. *Caribbean Slavery in the Atlantic World: A Student Reader*, 506–517. Kingston: Ian Randle Publishers Ltd., 2000.

Rasheed Olaniyi

Profits and Investors

The slave trade was pivotal to the early accumulation of capital. The profits from the slave trade occupied a prominent place in the Portuguese trade with west and central Africa and stimulated the search for new areas for trading in the sixteenth century. Many of the European investors profited hugely from the slave trade. For every slave that landed alive in the new world, a huge profit was made for the slavers. The profits were so great that hardly any **captain** refrained from loading his slave vessel to its utmost capacity. There was no profit on a slaving voyage until the slaves were landed alive and sold. Because of the high level of profitability, many slave captains took great care of the **cargoes**. In 1826, Theophilus Conneau (also called Canot), made a profit in four months of more than $41,000 (after a capital outlay of more than $39,000).

Apart from individual investor's profits, European nations derived huge profits from the slave trade. Investors in the slave trade made careful records and afforded detailed attention to the births, deaths, morbidity, fecundity, and natal care that determined the reproduction of the slave population and the **plantation's** profits. The dominant decision was the calculation that it was cheaper to work a slave to death and buy a new replacement from Africa than to offer nutrition and care that promoted biological reproduction of the labor force. Indeed, the perceptions of profits did not entirely obliterate abuse in the slave trade. To ensure low **prices**, the **slave traders** and investors bought slaves in bulk and stored them on the African coast to await shipment. To avoid high risk to investment, slave traders tried to purchase when prices were low and to ship when conditions favorable and prices high.

The Atlantic slave trade marked a "rosy dawn" in the era of capitalist production. Although it has been acknowledged that the profits from the slave trade were fabulous, they could not be quantified by the actual monetary profits made by Europeans. In Central and South America, gold and silver mined by Africans was indispensable in the minting of coins for the money economy of Western Europe.

Slaves produced the raw materials (for example, fish, indigo, cam wood, Brazil wood and cochineal, gum, and ivory) that were vital to the manufacturing sector in Europe and the Americas. The Atlantic slave trade was responsible for advances in maritime technology and served as a training ground for

British seamen. Spectacular features of slavery's profits include the rise of seaport towns—**Bristol**, **Liverpool**, **Nantes**, **Bordeaux**, and **Seville**—the emergence of manufacturing centers and the Industrial Revolution.

Profits in the suppression period were quite high as well. At every stage of the **triangular trade** there were profits for the European merchants who invested in the voyage. Cheap European goods, especially cotton cloth and guns, were exchanged for slaves. The dependence on European goods inevitably contributed to the decline of African indigenous industries and resumed the supply of slaves captured during wars. For most of the seventeenth and early eighteenth centuries, prices of slaves were static, but the increasing European competition provided the impetus for a rise in the price of slaves in the 1780s. In the New World, slaves were sold for two or three times their cost in Africa. By the 1780s, all European nations exported about 75,000 slaves per year from West Africa, about half of them carried by British merchants. The annual average "official" value of British exports to Africa in 1783–1787 was £691,000. The gross income from the sale of slaves in America was nearly twice the value of exports to the coast, about £1 million a year.

Scholar Herbert Klein has argued that slave trade profits were not extraordinary by European standards. To him, the average 10 percent rate of the eighteenth-century French and English slave traders was considered a good profit rate at the time but not out of the range of other contemporary investments. In the nineteenth century, the profits doubled because of the rising slave prices in the United States, which were accentuated by the British suppression of the slave trade.

Investors required high initial costs of entrance and a long period to fully recover profits (about five years of slaving voyages), which implies that only highly capitalized firms could enter the trade. Slave merchants often spread their investment by offering stock in slaving voyages to insure themselves from catastrophic loss. The costs of entrance and the complexity of negotiations and contacts limited the number of slave merchants. Major studies show that the industrial capital in Europe was locally derived from agriculture and European commerce. Some aspects of European trade, especially the French armaments industry, were overwhelmingly dependent on the African trade and were paid for by slave exports. Some English industries were dependent on the African market, and these markets also sustained the growth of some European infant industries. The number of slave ships provisioned for the African trade in Bahia, Rio de Janeiro, and Rhode Island signified a dramatic growth in local capital.

When considering the influence on British capital formation, it was suggested that only 15 percent of Britain's gross investment capital expenditures during its Industrial Revolution could have been generated from the profits on all of Great Britain's overseas trades, including that of the Atlantic slave trade. The slave trade was a profitable trade, but it was not the single largest capital-generating trade of the Europeans during the Industrial Revolution. It has been argued that the slave trade and American slavery were important in providing the capital for the Industrial Revolution in Britain. Indeed, overproduction and a fall in the selling price of **sugar** combined with higher prices for the sale of slaves reduced the profit levels of European investors. Slave dealers could no longer redeem their debt to European bankers. The banking sector had invested in sugar and the slave trade and found it more lucrative and profitable to invest in manufacturing industries in Europe. *See also* Abolition of the Slave Trade, Great Britain; Eric William Thesis; Insurance.

Further Readings: Cowley, Malcolm, and Mannix, Daniel P. "The Middle Passage." In David Northrup, ed. *The Atlantic Slave Trade.* Lexington: DC Heath, 1994; Holt, Thomas C. *The Problem of Race in The Twenty-First Century.* Cambridge, MA: Harvard University Press, 2000; Klein, Herbert S. "Profits and the Causes of Mortality." In David Northrup, ed. *The Atlantic Slave Trade*, 112. Lexington: DC Heath, 1994; Rodney, Walter. "How Europe Became the Dominant Section of a World-wide Trade System." In V. A. Shepherd and H. McD. Beckles, eds. *Caribbean Slavery in the Atlantic World: A Student Reader.* Kingston: Ian Randle Publishers Ltd., 2000; Russell-Wood, A.J.R. "Before Columbus: Portugal's African Prelude to the Middle Passage and Contribution to Discourse on Race and Slavery." In V. Shepherd and H. McD. Beckles. *Caribbean Slavery in the Atlantic World: A Student Reader.* Kingston: Ian Randle Publishers Ltd., 2000; Sanneh, Lamin. *Abolitionists Abroad: American Blacks and the Making of Modern West Africa.* Cambridge, MA: Harvard University Press, 1999.

Rasheed Olaniyi

R

Rape and Sexual Abuse

Rape is any form of sexual intercourse against a person's will. Most experts believe the primary cause of rape is an aggressive desire to dominate the victim rather than an attempt to gain sexual fulfillment. Rape was considered an act of **violence** rather than principally a sexual encounter. Sexual abuse occurs when adults use **children** for sexual gratification or expose them to sexual activities. Sexual abuse may begin with kissing, fondling of the breasts, and progress to more intrusive sexual acts, such as oral sex and vaginal or anal penetration. During the Middle Passage, the term used to describe the trans-Atlantic slave voyages between Africa and the Americas that claimed the lives of approximately 1.8 million slaves over a period of about 350 years, cases of rape and sexual abuse abounded.

The Middle Passage was, indeed, a physical and psychological **torture** for the estimated 15 million slaves who were packed like animals aboard slave vessels. This second leg of the trans-Atlantic slave trade marked the beginning of a terrifying experience.

Typically, slaves were shackled in pairs, and men were separated from **women** and confined below deck and in slave quarters in the ship's belly. These quarters were no more than 1.8 meters (6 feet) long and were not high enough to allow an individual to sit upright. Conditions were miserable and slaves were forced to lie naked on wooden planks. Many developed bruises and open sores and the human waste and vomit produced an overpowering stench in the unbearable heat below deck. These unsanitary conditions became breeding grounds for **diseases** such as dysentery, smallpox, and measles, spreading like wild fire among the hapless Africans. An estimated 5 percent of the slaves aboard these vessels died from these diseases, while many more died of malnutrition.

Women and children were often permitted to roam freely, a practice that opened unhindered and unlimited opportunities for the ship's **crew** and some **slave merchants** to sexually abuse the children and rape the women. Under this unlimited and unhindered access to women and children, rape and sexual abuse served as means of gratifying the aggressive desire to dominate the victims as well as satisfying the sexual pleasure of the crew.

It has been suggested that the institutionalized pattern of rape during the Middle Passage, and even during slavery in the New World, reflected nothing about men's sexual urges; rather, it was an aberration that has nothing to do with any dysfunctional behavior. But, when viewed from the perspective that the crew and slave merchants have been away from their homes where they could have easily gratified their sexual desires and may have been filled with pent-up desires for many months, then it becomes apparent that sexual abuse and rape during the Atlantic voyage served both the purpose of letting off the steam as well as gratifying the desire to dominate the Africans. Although this rings true for rape and sexual abuses during the Middle Passage, it cannot explain miscegenation in the New World.

Just as today, cases of rape and sexual abuse are hardly reported and therefore precise and reliable data concerning them are not available. During the Middle Passage, the crew as well as the slave merchants assaulted the slaves but no official record exists other than a tacit mentioning in some vessels' reports. Slaves' accounts, however, are replete with stories of rape, sexual abuses, and sex-related sports that crew and slave merchants practiced en route to the Americas.

Sexual abuse could be described as sexual intercourse with a person who has not reached the age of consent. According to the W.E.B. Du Bois Institute for Afro-American Research's database on the trans-Atlantic slave trade, in a voyage sample of 25,686 slaves, 3,088 were girls. This, when checked against the estimated 15 million Africans transported from Africa, excluding those who died during the slave raids, on the journeys to the coast, and the long wait before the Middle Passage, amounts to a total female population of about 27.90 percent. How many of these women and girls were sexually abused and by whom?

The percentage of women who have passed the age of consent and who would have rejected such sexual advances and would have done everything possible to prevent being forcibly violated if they had had the chance must have quadrupled those of children below the age of consent. In another sample of 2,281,690 African slaves, 28.70 percent were women. The fact that they were enslaved negates the argument that the only condition in which cases of rape could be established exist when the rapist forcibly subdued the victim. African slaves were not only forcibly raped and sexually abused but forcibly taken away from their places of habitual residence to places other than their own.

Under normal circumstances, rape and sexual abuse, as perpetrated against Africa slaves, would have constituted serious crimes. The practice was accepted as the norm, however, because the slaves were obtained for primarily nonsexual purposes and rape and sexual abuses were used as weapons of domination and repression, whose covert goal was to extinguish the slave woman's will to resist, and in the process, to demoralize the men.

Further Readings: Eltis, David, Behrendt, Stephen D., Richardson, David, and Klein, Herbert S., eds. *The Trans-Atlantic Slave Trade: A Database on CD-ROM.* Cambridge: Cambridge University Press, 1999; McElroy, Guy C. *Facing History: The Black Image in*

American Art 1710–1940. San Francisco: Bedford Art Publishers, 1990; Morgan, Edmund S. *American Slavery, American Freedom: The Ordeal of Colonial Virginia*. New York: W. W. Norton, 1995; Mullane, Deirdre, ed. *Crossing the Danger Water: Three Hundred Years of African-American Writing*. New York: Anchor Books/Doubleday, 1993; Mullin, Michael, ed. *American Negro Slavery: A Documentary History*. Columbia: University of South Carolina Press, 1976; Newton, John. *The Journal of a Slave Trader (John Newton) 1750–1754*, eds. Bernard Martin and Mark Spurrell. London: The Epworth Press, 1962; Owen, Nicholas. *Journal of a Slave-Dealer*, ed. Eveline Martin. London: George Routledge and Sons, 1930.

Oyeniyi Bukola Adeyemi

Re-Captives and Liberated Africans

Before the formal launching of the colonial enterprise in Africa, **Sierra Leone** had had contact with Britain as early as 1787 when the first batch of freed slaves was repatriated to this settlement through a treaty signed between the indigenous Temne who owned the land and British philanthropists (*Sierra Leone Weekly News*, 1892–1895). The repatriation of these ex-slaves to this newly acquired territory opened the way for further philanthropic experiments in Sierra Leone. After the resettlement of this first group of freed slaves, often referred to as the black poor because of their destitute situation while in Britain, a total of three additional groups of freed slaves were repatriated to this settlement. The settlement, later referred to as Freetown by the settlers, became a Crown Colony of Britain in 1808 (Crooks, 1903, pp. 10–30). With the formal abolition of the slave trade in British-controlled territories in 1807, the British government was determined to end the trade at all costs. It therefore signed treaties with other governments that empowered it to patrol the international waters in search of slave **cargoes**. With the signing of these treaties, the British also established Courts of Mixed Commission in Sierra Leone to try **captains** and slavers carrying slaves to Europe and the Americas. The naval squadrons that the British government unleashed to patrol the Atlantic Ocean, in particular, resulted in the capture of numerous slave ships containing slaves (Alldridge, 1910; Bangura, 2001, pp. 12–18). The British impounded these ships and freed the slaves in Freetown, while the captains of these ships were tried in the Courts of Mixed Commission. The freed slaves—who were referred to as re-captives because they had been captured once by slavers to be sold in Europe and America and then re-captured by British philanthropists who set them free in Freetown—became one of the progressive set of settlers. Between 1808 and 1860, the British resettled more than 40,000 re-captives making them the fourth and final group of freed slaves to be repatriated to the Sierra Leone colony (Wyse, 1989). The presence of these ex-slaves changed the socio-religious and politico-economic dynamics in the colony. The progressive nature of the re-captives led to their full acceptance into the wider Freetown society, which eventually led to intermarriage among them and the earlier settlers, who had previously neglected them because they perceived the re-captives as lacking any European orientation. The children born out of the intermarriage between the re-captives and the early settlers produced a unique society referred to as Creoles. This group dominated part of colony life until Sierra Leone attained independence in 1961 (Horton, 1857, pp. 62–64; Porter, 1963, pp. 3–10). *See also* Abolition of the Slave Trade, Great Britain; African Squadrons, The; Returnees to Africa.

Note: The use of the term "Creole" has generated some controversy in Sierra Leone **historiography**, and many scholars prefer the term "Krio" to Creole. The historical documents describe Creole society as descendants of ex-slaves, while the Krio is a matter of dialectical variation referring to the same people.

Further Readings: Alldridge, T. J. *A Transformed Colony, Sierra Leone as It Was and as It Is.* London: Seeley, 1910; Bangura, Joseph Jusuf. *Ethnic Invention and Identity Formation in Sierra Leone: A Case Study of the Sierra Leone Creoles, 1870–1961.* Master's thesis, Dalhousie University, 2001; Crooks, J. J. *A History of the Colony of Sierra Leone: Western Sierra Leone.* London: Browne and Nolan, Ltd., 1903; C.S.O. Treaty Between the Governor of Sierra Leone and King Tom. London, 1801; Horton, James Africanus Beale. *West African Countries and Peoples, British and Native.* London: W. J. Johnson, 1857; Porter, Arthur. *Creoledom: A Study of the Development of Freetown Society, 1787–1870.* London: Oxford University Press, 1963; *Sierra Leone Weekly News,* April–June, 1892–1895; Wyse, Akintola. *The Krio of Sierra Leone: An Interpretive History.* Freetown: W. D. Okrafo-Smart Publishing Co., 1989.

Joseph Jusuf Bangura

Re-Export

Scholars use the economic term re-export to refer to the sale of and forced movement of enslaved Africans from the first **port** of disembarkation to second and subsequent **destinations** in the era of the Atlantic slave trade. Generally, re-exportation happened shortly after their arrival at islands off the coast of West Africa, in southern Europe, specifically Iberia, and the Caribbean islands. Hence, enslaved Africans were disembarked in a slave **entrepôt** (transshipment center) such as the islands of **Fernando Po**, **São Tomé**, Príncipe, or **Gorée** in West Africa. In the early phase of the slave trade to the Americas, port towns in Spain and Portugal were used as commercial slave markets for enslaved Africans. In the Americas, slave entrepôts existed in Barbados, **Curaçao**, **Jamaica**, and Martinique.

Upon their arrival, the enslaved were temporarily housed and put to work or they were refreshed before embarking on the next slave vessel. In the first case, enslaved Africans were forced to work on nearby **plantations** controlled by a specific European chartered company or they were hired out to a local plantation in the entrepôt. If they were ill or sick because of the crowded and unhealthy conditions onboard vessels, however, they were sent to an infirmary to recover from their illness. In this instance, the entrepôt functioned as a "refreshment" station. Generally, the enslaved did not reside longer than a year in these places. Dutch, English, French, Spanish, Portuguese, and other **slave traders** regularly traveled to the entrepôt to purchase enslaved Africans. Many enslaved Africans were re-exported in **smuggling** rings, so that the slave trader would avoid paying **taxes**.

Further Readings: Elbl, Ivana. "The Volume of the Early Atlantic Trade, 1450–1521." *Journal of African History* 38, 1 (1997): 31–75; Palmer, Colin A. *Human Cargoes: The*

British Slave Trade to Spanish America, 1700–1739. Urbana: Illinois University Press, 1981; Postma, Johannes, and Enthoven, Victor, eds. *Riches from Atlantic Commerce: Dutch Transatlantic Trade and Shipping, 1585–1817*. Leiden: Brill, 2003.

Nadine Hunt

Regulations

The trans-Atlantic slave trade was conducted in accordance with some set of rules, regulations, and conditions. These rules were laid down by all the different categories of people involved in the trade. The nature and character of conditions and regulations associated with the slave trade changed over time. All the parties involved tended to understand the need to adjust the character of business in accordance with prevailing market conditions.

In Africa, the generally accepted trend was that European manufactured goods were exchanged for slaves either along the coast or in the hinterland. The most important of these European goods included salt, gin, and ammunition. Before these goods were exchanged for slaves, **taxes** and other forms of levies were paid to the king or chiefs of the coastal area. European manufactured goods were sometimes given in advance for the exchange of slaves. This type of slave trade transaction was called the "trust system." The European merchants entrusted their goods to Africans under the condition that they would receive slaves. Goods were mostly entrusted to trustworthy and popular intermediaries. It was through the trust system that intermediaries in places such as the Bight of Biafra got the wealth that allowed them to wield power and influence. Europeans also paid for slaves in **cowries**. Trade by barter, however, was the most prominent method of economic transaction.

European trading companies had guidelines, which governed the pattern of their relations with Africans along the coast. Some of these regulations had their origin in the need to avoid scuffles between African chiefs and their European trading partners. Willem Bosman, a Dutch factor stationed at **Elmina**, had some guidelines and principles, which he used in dealing with the African coast. In 1699, some of these regulations include a payment of six slaves to the king before the commencement of the transaction. This payment represented a form of duty. Another payment in the form of two slaves was made to the chiefs while the person who announced the commencement of trade got a pitcher of cowries.

Sailors were expected to abide by certain rules and regulations before and during the Middle Passage. The rules were spelled out to enhance a problem-free voyage and to increase the level of proceeds accrued from slave trade. The **captain** of a Dutch vessel, *De Nieuwe*, was instructed in 1715 to ensure that slaves did not revolt during the voyage and that female slaves were not defiled or maltreated by members of the **crew**. The captain was also instructed to keep the vessel clean while the **doctors** were supposed to check the eyes of the slaves every morning for **disease**.

The place of construction of vessels and their owners, age, and tonnage were part of the data that sailors were expected to keep. All European nations involved in the slave trade had navigation laws popularly called Acts. Navigation or Maritime Acts were promulgated to regulate trade and enhance profitability. Tonnage of ships tended to constitute a serious problem between merchant companies and home governments. The size of vessels and the tonnage were used to determine duties paid before the vessel set sail from Europe to America and when it finally arrived in the Americas with slaves. Merchant companies and ship owners doctored the sizes of ships, numbers of slaves carried, and tonnage to reduce the duties paid to the government.

The Middle Passage experience, in all its ramifications, was associated with the highest degree of suffering. **Mortality** was recorded in the slave ship partly because the slaves were packed like sardines. This allowed them to have limited space for comfort during the long voyage to the Americas. Slave mortality was sometimes caused by the outbreak of diseases such as dysentery. Also, slaves had limited chances of escaping during **shipwrecks** and **explosions**. The eighteenth century saw attempts by **slave merchants** to reduce mortality rates by observing better safety regulations. **Humanitarian** gestures, most notably in Great Britain, came partly as a result of the need to reduce the hardship on the slave ship. Regulations established the number of slaves that ships should carry and the provision of welfare services during the Middle Passage. The Dutch Maritime Law of 1684 sought to make a clear provision for the *argueacao*. The law demanded that officials should provide adequate space for slaves on the vessels.

In Great Britain, Dolben, a member of Oxford University, sponsored a bill that would increase the medical care provided aboard slave ships. This came about as the result of a visit to a slave vessel during which he discovered the high medical risk that slaves faced. Dolben's Act of 1788, as it is popularly called, had a decisive effect on the **British slave trade**, for it reduced the slaves-per-ton ratio. The act provided that vessels should carry only five slaves per registered ton of shipping. Every captain had to carry a **surgeon**, who was to attend to the medical needs of slaves and keep records of mortality.

Further Readings: Galenson, David. *Traders, Planters and Slaves: Market Behavior in the Early English America.* Cambridge: Cambridge University Press, 1986; Gemery, Henry, and Hogendorn, Jan, eds. *The Uncommon Market: Essays in the Economic History of the Atlantic Slave Trade.* New York: Academic, 1979; Richardson, David. *Bristol, Africa and the Eighteenth-Century Slave Trade to the Americas.* 4 vols. Gloucester: Bristol Records Society, 1986–1996; Postma, Johannes. *The Dutch in the Atlantic Slave Trade 1600–1815.* New York and Cambridge: Cambridge University Press, 1990.

Saheed Aderinto

Religion

Despite the various social and cultural traumas of the Middle Passage and the various acculturation and **"seasoning"** processes, African slaves maintained and redefined their religious beliefs to survive and endure the brutal realities and harsh treatment of slave living. Many Africans arrived to the shores of New World colonies and settlements in the Caribbean and North and South Americas with their own religious beliefs, which often varied with geographic and ethnic origin. Often those religious beliefs included **Islam**, **Christianity**, and religious practices indigenous to the peoples of Western Africa: Yoruba, Mandinges, **Igbo**, Akan, **Dahomey**, and others.

Once upon the shores of the North, South, and Central Americas and the Caribbean Islands, traditional West African religious practices encountered, commingled, and fused with the religious beliefs of Native Americans, Roman Catholics, and various denominations of Protestantism. The result was the creation of a variety of religious sects and denominations that represent, remember, and speak to the socio-cultural encounters that occurred throughout the Americas. From Santeria in **Cuba**, to Candomble in **Brazil**, and Vodun in Haiti, to Pentecostalism and African Methodist Episcopalians in the United States, the religious communities formed provided not only emotional support but also opportunities to create and imagine lives that existed outside of the harsh realities of lived conditions.

Roman Catholicism and the Americas

The story of Roman Catholicism in North America begins with the creation of Spanish and French settlements along the coast of the Atlantic Ocean and the Gulf of Mexico. Despite the later debates about the importance of slave baptism and conversion among the British, the French and the Spanish often baptized their slaves. The conversion of non-Christians was an impetus for the creation of colonial settlements. It was not the only reason that these colonial settlements were established. Missionary work did provide the French and Spanish with the moral authorization necessary to establish socio-political systems of slavery. Among the Spanish, African converts emerged in the sixteenth century not only in Mexico but also throughout the western sections of North America. In Mexico, African slaves would in fact blaspheme their Catholic faith to gain freedom. Denouncing Catholicism allowed them to appear before a judge, and by doing so, many slaves were provided with the opportunity to describe their living conditions. Many successfully won their freedom by describing their horrendous treatment, which did not correspond with the ethical tenets of Catholicism.

As the population of these settlements and colonies increased so too did the number of African converts. There was a fairly large community of African Catholics that lived in Louisiana and Florida. During violent conflicts with the English, both the Spanish and the French lured African slaves to Catholicism with the promise of freedom. Despite the growing numbers of African Catholics in these colonies and later states, there were not many ordained preachers and established and recognized African-centered Catholic churches. It was increasingly difficult for African men to become ordained priests. Furthermore, it was often difficult for African **women** to participate in the ministerial activities of the church. Scholars attribute the first African women to enter successfully into Catholic religious life to a small group known as the Oblate Sisters of Providence around 1830. This group established a school in Philadelphia in 1863.

Although England had denounced Roman Catholicism during the reign of King Henry VIII, there were several colonies established with sizable Catholic populations, including Maryland and Pennsylvania. Although Protestant African-centered churches, such as the African Methodist Episcopalian, emerged in these areas, there still existed a small number of African Catholics. By the end of the eighteenth century, nearly 3,000 African Catholics lived in Maryland. The first African Catholic Church was established in Pittsburgh in 1844.

With the emergence of the United States as an independent nation, Africans and African Americans continued to create spaces that allowed them to worship as Catholics. Despite their persistent confrontation with discrimination on the part of the Archdioceses, African Americans maintained their Catholic faith.

Protestantism and British North America

The story of Protestantism in British North America and the conversion of African peoples begins during the seventeenth century and the early eighteenth century. For centuries, Christianity, specifically Roman Catholicism and later Protestant denominations, had been used by Europeans to justify the conquest of non-Christian peoples. As the dependence on enslaved African labor grew in the Americas, there was much debate among **plantation** owners and theologians about the promotion of conversion among Africans. The debate was often divided along geographic and denominational lines. The **New England** region often supported the conversion of Africans, while the mid-Atlantic and the southern colonies sought to inhibit religious practices. The latter areas depended on larger numbers of African slaves and the threat of rebellion was quite real. The suppression of religious practices and religious conversion was considered an effective means of preventing slave rebellion.

In New England, where the slave population was small and also confined to urban areas or small rural farms, many Africans were provided with opportunities to join, hear, and participate (although participation was segregated) in church activities. Cotton Mather in 1706, published his essay *A Negro Christianized: An Essay to Excite and Assist the Good Work, the Instruction of Negro-servants in Christianity*, which encouraged the conversion of Africans. A decade earlier, Mather wrote the Rules for Society of Negroes (1693) in Boston, which also advocated conversion. The document outlines the rules of the Society of Negroes—a local group that sought to create a community among the local African population. The rules outline the behavioral requirements for participation. These requirements include obedience to one's master, active participation, attendance at church, and the recitation of catechisms from the New England or the Negro Christianized catechisms. Even as religious and community leaders, such as Cotton Mather, advocated for conversion, others throughout the New England community and further south used their Christian faith to support the **enslavement** and the dehumanization of African peoples.

On the burgeoning farms in the Carolinas and Georgia and on plantations throughout the mid-Atlantic region, slave masters resisted baptism and conversion among Africans. Conversion and baptism were associated with a freedom only to be afforded to whites and an equality that would undermine the master-slave power structure. There was a growing fear that conversion would encourage a sense of equality between the slave and his or her master. These fears often became realized in violent forms of resistance. Colonies in North, South, and Central America and the Caribbean were plagued by small- and large-scale slave revolts. To ease the fears of masters concerned about the literal freedom of slaves by conversion, during the seventeenth century, colonial governments began to include clauses that prohibited the manumission of baptized slaves. The religious services of slaves, both Christian and otherwise, were localized to specific hours of the day and entirely prohibited in the evening hours. Furthermore, West African religious practices were quelled because they were understood to be counter to the tenets of Christianity and a threat to European masters who had limited knowledge of the various faiths and the ritual practices.

Despite these earlier debates about conversion and its impacts on the African populations, throughout the eighteenth and nineteenth centuries many Africans and their descendents converted to Christianity, more specifically Protestantism. With the help of social organizations and missionaries, Africans were converted slowly to various denominational beliefs: Moravians, Anglicans, Methodists, and Baptists. Missionaries not only traveled throughout various regions but also founded missions on plantations in the south. These missions helped convert many living on plantations who were unable to travel the longer distances to neighboring churches.

One of the first organizations created with an investment in African conversion was the Anglican group, the Society for the Propagation of the Gospel in Foreign Parts (SPG). The purpose of the society was not specifically African conversion, but it played an important role in missionary work among slave populations. The SPG helped encourage masters to convert their slaves, particularly in the South. Their missionaries promoted the idea that conversion would make slaves more obedient to their masters. In many ways, the SPG echoed the sentiments of Cotton Mather in his essays on the christianization of Africans. Christianity served two purposes for the society. It redeemed the souls of Africans and made them more submissive to the social hierarchies that sought to dehumanize them.

With the growth of Enlightenment theories of racial and cultural inferiority or superiority, many Europeans doubted both the existence and the quality of the African soul; in turn, they doubted the validity of baptizing slaves. Despite these debates and concerns, the first Great Awakening in the mid-eighteenth century helped convert large numbers of African slaves. The first Great Awakening was heavily criticized for its emphasis on enthusiasm and enthusiastic preaching. Despite those who sought to prohibit enthusiastic revivalism, like Charles Chauncey, minister Jonathan Edwards helped lead several revivals that brought increased numbers of Africans into the church. As the numbers of Africans attending these revivals increased, their cultural influence in many ways helped Africanize the religious practices. Free and enslaved Africans began to participate in church activities; they became informal and formal preachers, teachers, and exhorters not only to African but also to white congregants. The Africanization of Protestantism not only informed the establishment of the African churches but also helped promote the emotional enthusiasm that marked the revivalistic experience: the ring shout and the love feasts. The reintroduction of emotion into the church services, the water baptisms, and the increased significance of the Holy Spirit and its possession of the body speak to the various cultural influences of the many West African peoples who attended the services.

George Whitefield's itinerant preaching along the coast and inlands of British North America also brought the gospel to many. Whitefield's evangelicalism was not only emotionally moving and spiritually satisfying, it also emphasized the importance of an individual's relationship to God. The intimacy between God and believer often attracted more converts because it was not interested in the formalism of church structure as such.

Furthermore, Whitefield's preaching and his large numbers of African conversions benefited from the financial support of Selina Hastings, Countess of Huntington. Hastings not only helped fund Whitefield's missionary work, she also financially supported the creation of black churches—one in particular built in Nova Scotia, pastored by John Marrant. She supported and promoted the spiritual **narratives** and writings by a number of converted Africans, including Ukawsaw Gronniosaw, John Marrant, **Phillis Wheatley**, and Ignatius Sancho. Whitefield and Hastings were a part of a community of English men and women who sought to save the souls of many Africans living in the Americas.

As the numbers of African converts increased in British North America, African-centered churches and theological revisions of various denominational ideologies emerged. In protest to the discriminatory policies of the predominantly English St. George Methodist Church, Richard Allen and Absalom Jones created an organization, the Free African Society, designed to encourage the development of a cohesive religious and social community. The Free African Society, created in 1787, preceded the establishment of the African Methodist Episcopal Church, in 1816. Richard Allen, who had been ordained by the Methodist Society in 1799, became the first bishop of his new denomination. Absalom Jones established the St. Thomas African Methodist Episcopal Church. In other cities, churches and church-related organizations emerged. George Liele and David George established churches in Savannah, Georgia, and **Jamaica**. John Marrant with a number of former loyalist slaves left the former colonies and headed to Canada to found a settlement at Birchtown in Nova Scotia. He founded a church as well, which attempted to return its African congregants to West Africa, specifically **Sierra Leone** to continue their missionary work. Zilpha Elaw, Julia Foote, and Jarena Lee were black women who found a space within these early churches to preach and minister, despite the sexism that initially prevented them from entering into ministerial roles.

As African and, later, black churches continued to develop throughout the United States, there emerged a black theology that emphasized the importance and relevance of African Americans cultural contributions. Several denominations created by Africans and African Americans, such as African Methodist Episcopalian (1816), African Methodist Episcopalian Zion (c. 1820), and Colored Methodist Episcopalian (c. 1867), sought to unite and maintain a cohesive black community in their respective locations. As churches developed, they became centers of social and political action for both men and women. Literary organizations formed. Political protests were organized. Opportunities for social interaction were encouraged.

West African Spiritualities and the Diaspora

The large population of West Africans, particularly from the Senegambian, Dahomean, and Nigerian regions, brought with them religious practices that were indigenous to their native regions. Despite the social and legislative prohibitions, West African slaves continued to find innovative ways to practice their faith in secret. For example, plantation overseers and slave masters encouraged slaves to have community activities and festivals to energize and boost morale. These public festivals served as opportunities to enact some of the ritual practices that were so much a part of their faith. To mask their activities, certain West African religious figures were often disguised as Catholic saints. Although many converted to Christianity, Christianity, more specifically Catholicism, did not counter or vanquish their original faith but rather subsumed itself into the original beliefs. Christianity offered a complement to their former religious practices and therefore became a part of their religious experiences.

Throughout the Caribbean and South America, various communities of Africans were able to preserve their religious beliefs for several reasons: the secret practice of religious rituals, the creation of community faith-based groups that helped sustain cultural practices, and a population of West African peoples that was larger than that of the Europeans. Despite the distance between these geographic locations, various religious sects had remarkable faith-based similarities to the Yoruba and Dahomean religious practices. The Yoruba brought with them a resilient faith in a transcendent deity, Olodumare, and *orishas*, the lesser spirits who served as divine mediators between Olodumare and the believers. The Dahomey, Igbo, and Mandinges also brought faith and ritual practices with them that endured similar prohibitions. Despite the religious differences that mark the faith of these groups, among them all was a reverence for ancestors as well as an appreciation for nature. With the continued growth of the slave population over the years, there emerged a distinctive religious culture that combined elements from the Yoruba and the Dahomey, Igbo, Mandinges, the Roman Catholic, and the Native American populations. In Haiti, Vodun emerged. In Brazil, it was Candomble, and in Cuba there was Santeria. In many of the other neighboring islands, there were similar religious equivalents.

Vodun

Vodun comes from the Fon word, vo-du, which means God. Fon is the language of the Dahomey people, from present-day **Benin**. As a result of the commingling of religious practices, Vodun emerged and was maintained by the priests, *houn'gans* and priestesses, and *mam'bos* of the religion. Both the deities and the practices borrow heavily from those of the Dahomey. Similar to Santeria, Vodun and its deities (*loas*) offer the faithful balance and protection. This faith and the quest to restore balance helped motivate slaves in Haiti to rebel against their masters in the late 1790s. Empowered by *loas*, Haitian slaves reclaimed the island and their freedom. The result was one of the first large-scale successful revolutions.

Santeria

In Cuba, African slaves maintained their faith by creating religious communities and participating in activities and festivals that strengthened their commitment to ritual practices. The result was Santeria, also known as the way of the saints. The *orishas* of their Yoruba faith were masked with the names of Roman Catholic saints. For example, Oludomare, the transcendent God, is represented by Jesus Christ. Obatala is the Virgin of Mercy, and Ogun is characterized as St. Peter. Santeria promotes a commitment to honor and revere one's ancestors. Appropriate acknowledgement of ancestors, through worship and sacrifice creates a balance through which *ashé* or a manifestation of life's energy can flow properly. *See also* Christianity; Cuba; Saint Domingue.

Further Readings: Brooks, Joanna, and Saillant, John. *"Face Zion Forward:" First Writers of the Black Atlantic, 1785–1798.* Boston: Northeastern University Press, 2002; Fulop, Timothy E., and Raboteau, Albert J. *African-American Religion: Interpretive Essays in History and Culture.* New York: Routledge, 1997; Genovese, Eugene D. *Roll, Jordan, Roll: The World the Slaves Made.* New York: Pantheon, 1974; Pinn, Anthony B. *The African American Religious Experience in America.* Westport, CT: Greenwood Press, 2006; Raboteau, Albert J. *Slave Religion: The "Invisible Institution" in the Antebellum South.* New York: Oxford University Press, 1978.

Tara Bynum

Reparations

Increased public awareness of slavery has been accompanied by the recent demand for reparations for slavery, advocated by the Nairobi-based Organization for African Unity. This demand has been supported by black organizations in Britain, the United States, the Caribbean, and other parts of the African diaspora. The demand for reparations represents a growing movement for justice for enslaved Africans and their descendants, and the growing interest in reparations is stimulated by recent successes of other peoples in their demand for reparations.

Philosophers and legal theorists understand "reparation" as referring to what is owed victims by the perpetrators of injustice. Reparation concerns the restoration of moral balance. This is achieved by taking from perpetrators their unjust acquisitions and returning to victims what was taken away from them. Justice requires that perpetrators redeem to victims the value of their losses and may even include providing redress to victims for other harms related to the wrongs committed against them. It is thought that reparations are owed for forced labor and **enslavement**.

The earning capacity of those who were enslaved, had they been free, should inform decisions about compensation, and various scholars believe that reparations are due for the injustice done to family lines because the system of slavery was based on the enslavement of **families**. This is of moral significance as family histories are important to individuals and, in Western societies, emphasis is placed on individuals' entitlements and obligations. Public acknowledgment of wrongs and reconciliation acts do not rule out material compensation being demanded by most of those in favor of reparations for enslaved Africans and their descendants.

There are varying conceptions of the form that reparations might take and of the most effective means of ensuring success. The reparations discourse takes account of a number of key considerations, including moral, legal, political-cultural, and practical-political considerations. The moral consideration acknowledges the need to right the wrongs of the past. Legal considerations entail identifying approaches for the pursuit of reparations based on constitutional, statutory, or international law. Political-cultural considerations address the issue of national reconciliation facilitated by public acknowledgment of and atonement for past injustices, and practical-political considerations are focused on the aims, strategies, and consequences of the demand for reparations. *See also* Historical Memory.

Further Readings: Gift, Sandra. "Selected Teachers' Pedagogical Content Knowledge of the Transatlantic Slave Trade." Ph.D. dissertation, University of the West Indies, 2005; McCarthy, Thomas. "Remarks on the Morality and Politics of Reparations for Slavery." Paper presented at the Seventh Annual Gilder Lehrman Center International Conference at Yale University, New Haven, Connecticut, October 2005. The Gilder Lehrman Center for the Study of Slavery, Resistance, and Abolition Web site: www.yale.edu/glc/justice/mccarthy. pdf; Thompson, Janna. "Memory and the Ethics of Reparation." Paper presented at the Seventh Annual Gilder Lehrman Center International Conference at Yale University, New Haven, Connecticut, October 2005. The Gilder Lehrman Center for the Study of Slavery, Resistance, and Abolition Web site: www.yale.edu/glc/justice/thompson.pdf.

Sandra Ingrid Gift

Returnees to Africa

Throughout the history of the Atlantic slave trade, the dream of a return to Africa remained in the minds of many in the diaspora. As early as the colonial period, as the slave trade was well under way, small numbers of Middle Passage trips were actually returning peoples of African descent to their homeland.

The prospect of repatriation encouraged many African Americans to support the Loyalist cause during the American Revolution. Following the British defeat, significant numbers of African American slaves were **smuggled** out of the colonies during the troops' mass evacuations of the 1790s. Although most of those evacuated were taken to Nova Scotia and the West Indies, thousands of blacks settled in the West African territory controlled by the Sierra Leone Company.

Also joining the African American returnees to Africa were many of the sizable numbers of blacks living in England at the time. Free blacks from the British colonies often found their way to England, seeking education or employment. Many Britons lamented what they saw as a degeneration of British society and a flooding of the labor market as more and more blacks filled **London** neighborhoods during the late eighteenth and early nineteenth centuries. Suffering from discrimination and yearning for their ancestral homeland, many took advantage of the chance to return to Africa offered by the Sierra Leone Company.

In the United States, increasing numbers of freed African Americans contributed to growing competition for jobs, particularly in the North. In addition, many whites feared that a rising free population would lead to a mixing of the races, and that free blacks would encourage slave uprisings. Their calls to return the free black population to Africa found support among abolitionists and missionaries, who felt that doing so would help to bring **Christianity** and "civilization" to native Africans. These personal motives aside, thousands of African Americans—although a proportionately small amount—accepted the opportunity to escape the racial intolerance that pervaded American society at the time. Beginning in 1820, they headed to the newly created colony of **Liberia**, located next to **Sierra Leone**.

Although the black settlers were generally of the professional, privileged classes, as the nineteenth century progressed, more diverse groups arrived to the West African coast. Once slavery had been banned in the United States and Great Britain, the West African settler colonies took a significant role in suppressing the trade. As renegade ships were apprehended, settler populations were made responsible for repatriating former captives. New Georgia, a Liberian settlement near the Stockton river, missions received these recaptured Africans who had been liberated by U.S. naval forces. Although most would flee, seeking their homelands, many were absorbed into settlement communities and educated in church-run schools.

From the 1850s on, a large number of West Indians settled in West Africa. Most were born free and were well educated, but found little economic opportunity at home. To them, however, the prospect of returning to Africa held more of a spiritual significance. Many of these settlers regarded the West African colonies as a "promised land" and saw themselves as a chosen people to be delivered from oppression in the New World. They were some of the first to move away from the settlements along the Atlantic coastline in an attempt to integrate the interior and establish trade with Africans. By the 1870s, the Caribbean immigrants in Liberia would come into conflict with earlier settlers over issues of expansion and commerce.

As the twentieth century began, peoples of African descent throughout the New World were gaining a collective consciousness that manifested itself in a number of movements, including Pan-Africanism. Liberia was heralded as a rare example of black rule on the continent, and many blacks became increasingly disgusted with the racial climate present in the United States and the British colonies. Bishop Henry McNeal Turner of the African Methodist Episcopal Church and Marcus Garvey were among the many who advocated a return to Africa during the 1910s and 1920s. Aside from commercial objectives, Garvey envisioned his ill-fated Black Star Line, and its successor, the Black Cross Navigation and Trading Company, as modes of transportation for African Americans to return to Africa. In 1920, the Liberian government tentatively agreed to assist in this effort, as it stood to benefit from investment. Meanwhile, Garvey was petitioning the League of Nations for a free black state in Africa to which those in the diaspora could return.

However, outside pressures eventually turned the Liberian government against a colonization effort. By 1924, representatives from the Universal Negro Improvement Association, who had arrived in Liberia to create housing accommodations for prospective colonists, were promptly deported. Meanwhile, the Back-to-Africa movement received criticism from most African Americans and blacks in Latin America and the Caribbean who preferred integration to black separatism. Most had come to see themselves in more nationalistic terms and sought to secure rights for themselves in a patriotic nationalist context. By then, blacks' connection to Africa was becoming increasingly less direct. Although few persons of color settled in Africa at this point, the Back-to Africa movement came to be seen in more figurative and psychological terms. *See also* African Squadrons, The; Returnees to Africa.

Further Readings: Harris, Joseph, ed. *Global Dimensions of the African Diaspora*. 2nd ed. Washington, DC: Howard University Press, 1993; Lewis, Rupert, and Bryan, Patrick, eds. *Garvey: His Work and Impact*. Mona, Jamaica: University of the West Indies, 1988; Schick, Tom. *Behold the Promised Land: A History of Afro-American Settler Society in Nineteenth-Century Liberia*. 2nd ed. Baltimore: Johns Hopkins University Press, 1980.

Carmen Lenore Wright

Royal Africa Company

The Royal Africa Company was the main English trading organization involved in the trans-Atlantic slave trade during the last quarter of the seventeenth century and the first quarter of the eighteenth century. This company's ships traveled between West Africa, the British West Indies (Caribbean), and England in a **triangular trade** intended to benefit royal and private English **investors**. The Royal Africa Company was founded in 1672 as a joint-stock company to replace the failed Company of Royal Adventurers. It, too, ended in bankruptcy and was replaced in 1752 by the Company of Merchants Trading to Africa.

The company's trade with Africa consisted of two parts. Some of the trading ships filled a **cargo** of African products that were destined directly for England. These included gold, ivory, dyewood, hides, and wax. The remaining ships primarily purchased enslaved Africans who were transported across the Atlantic and sold in the British colonies at Barbados, **Jamaica**, Nevis, St. Christopher's, Antigua, Montserrat, and Virginia. The **Gold Coast** was the headquarters of the Royal Africa Company in Africa. Its administration there was based in **Cape Coast Castle**, a **trade fort** built by Swedes in 1653 (formerly known as Fort Carolusburg) and seized by the English in 1664.

From its establishment until 1698, the Royal Africa Company was granted a royal **monopoly** on English trade with Africa. The monopolistic approach of chartered companies, however, gave way to more liberal ideas at the turn of the eighteenth century. In 1698, the Royal Africa Company was forced to open up trade to private traders, provided that the latter paid a 10 percent fee to the company. By 1712, the Africa trade was open to everybody in England. Similarly, the Dutch West India Company opened its monopoly to free traders in 1730.

The Royal Africa Company struggled throughout its existence to generate **profits** for its shareholders. Political changes and poor management in England interfered with the company's success. In West Africa, the company faced intense competition from other European and American traders and suffered a number of incompetent administrators. Financial crises in the West Indies and changes in the price of **sugar** also destabilized the company over time. By 1715, the Royal Africa Company was economically

The Cape Coast Castle housed the headquarters of the Royal Africa Company on the West African Coast. Courtesy of Manuel Barcia.

paralyzed and beginning a slow descent into bankruptcy. *See also* British Caribbean; British Slave Trade.

Further Readings: Daaku, Kwame Y. *Trade and Politics on the Gold Coast, 1600–1720: A Study of the African Reaction to European Trade.* London: Oxford University Press, 1970; Davies, K. G. *The Royal African Company.* London: Longmans, Green and Company, 1957; Eltis, David. *The Rise of African Slavery in the Americas.* New York: Cambridge University Press, 2000.

Rebecca Shumway

Rum and Cachaça

Rum and cachaça are distilled, sugar-based alcoholic beverages that played a major role in the slave trade both as finished products that were traded for slaves and as agricultural goods that were part of the slave-based economy in the Western Hemisphere. Rum has its origins in Asia, and variations of the drink have been distilled for thousands of years. Modern rum was discovered in the 1600s when people began distilling molasses, a byproduct of the process of converting raw sugarcane into **sugar**. Like rum, cachaça is a byproduct of sugar production. While rum is made from molasses, cachaça is distilled from the juice of the sugarcane.

Cachaça predates modern rum. The first cachaça was produced in **Brazil** in the 1530s. Initially, the drink was used as a cheap alcohol to give to slaves. Soon, however, it became popular among the colonial elites. Portugal tried to suppress the manufacture and sale of cachaça, but in 1756, the colonial government gave up and instead began to heavily **tax** the product.

By the 1700s, cachaça became a common trade good that Portuguese slavers used to procure slaves for Brazil.

Rum became popular quickly in the European Caribbean colonies. The colonies already used slaves to grow and harvest sugar for European markets, and the appeal of rum created a need for additional labor to produce more sugarcane for rum. Rum became an important component of the **triangular trade**. **Plantations** in the Caribbean produced molasses that was shipped to **New England** to be distilled into rum (the first rum distillery in what is now the United States was established on Staten Island in 1664). The manufacture of rum became one of New England's most profitable industries. For instance, by 1760, Rhode Island had twenty-two distilleries and Massachusetts had sixty-three. Rum was then shipped throughout the colonies and Great Britain.

Rum was used as a libation and often as a medicine (it was used to alleviate pain and treat colds and the flu). By the mid-1700s, the average American consumed about four gallons of rum per year. A large percentage of rum was shipped to Africa, however, where it was used to trade for slaves who were then shipped to the Caribbean sugarcane colonies. Rum was prodigiously used by the **British Navy**. Beginning in 1655, British sailors were issued a daily ration of rum (a practice that continued until 1970).

French colonies in the Caribbean produced a less expensive and less potent form of rum known as tafia. Tafia was produced mainly for domestic consumption in the French islands of the Caribbean where, like cachaça, it was given to slaves and sold to local merchants as a way to bolster **profits** by plantation owners. *See also* African Rulers and the Slave Trade; British Caribbean; British Slave Trade; Enslavement and Procurement; Free Trade; French Caribbean; French Slave Trade; Legitimate Commerce; New England; Portuguese Slave Trade; Trade Commodities.

Further Readings: Broom, Dave. *Rum.* New York: Abbeville Press, 2003; Coulombe, Charles. *Rum: The Epic Story of the Drink That Changed the World.* Sacramento: Citadel Press, 2004; Pack, James. *Nelson's Blood: The Story of Naval Rum.* Annapolis: Naval Institute Press, 1982.

Tom Lansford

S

Saint Domingue

Saint Domingue (today's Haiti) was the name of the western part of the Caribbean island of **Hispaniola**, which was officially a French colony from 1697 to 1804. In the second half of the eighteenth century, Saint Domingue was the world's first **sugar** and coffee producer, and it was the main destination for slave ships within the Caribbean. Some 685,000 slaves disembarked in the island during the eighteenth century.

Christopher Columbus had claimed the island for Spain as early as 1492, but Spaniards rapidly neglected it once they conquered the American mainland. In the first half of the seventeenth century, French pirates and some colonists settled in the western part of Hispaniola, which Spain officially ceded to France in 1697 at the Peace of Ryswick.

Although the French had introduced tobacco and slaves in Saint Domingue during the second half of the seventeenth century, the recognition of French sovereignty over the island, and the transfer of the Spanish crown to the Bourbon family after the War of Spanish Succession in 1713–1714, spurred the onset of sugar **plantations** in Saint Domingue, because planters could invest in costly infrastructure without fearing that Spain would eventually drive them away. Whereas Martinique and Guadeloupe could not consistently increase their production in the eighteenth century, because the uncultivated soils were poor and the good ones impoverished over time, Saint Domingue's sugar production grew consistently throughout the century, reaching 86,000 tons in 1789. From the middle of the eighteenth century, Saint Domingue became a leader in the coffee production as well (40,000 tons in 1789).

Depiction of the successful slave rebellion of Saint Domingue. Courtesy of Anti-Slavery International.

Such production was possible only through the extension of a plantation economy and a sharp increase in the number of slaves. Official statistics state that there were 5,000 slaves in 1700, 240,000 in 1774, and 480,000 in 1790, and about 25,000 French colonists and as many free people of color. At the eve of the French Revolution of 1789, there were more slaves in Saint Domingue than in the whole **British Caribbean**. Whereas until the 1770s the slaves born in Saint Domingue outnumbered those having experienced the Middle Passage, this was no longer the case in the 1780s, when a significant number of captives (29,000 in 1788) arrived each year to Cap Français and to the other main **ports** of the islands.

The rapid increase in the slave population contributed to make the situation in Saint Domingue explosive. The precarious balance of powers between the different groups of the colony's population was seriously affected by the ongoing debates over the political rights of free people of color at the beginning of the 1790s in revolutionary France. Tensions between planters and free blacks and mulattos weakened the capacity of repression against slave revolts. The great slave uprising in August 1791 opened a period of great turmoil, leading to the independence of Saint Domingue, which became Haiti, in 1804. *See also* Abolition of the Slave Trade, France; French Caribbean; French Slave Trade; Haitian Revolution, The.

Further Readings: Blancpain, François. *La colonie française de Saint-Domingue*, Paris: Karthala, 2004; DuBois, Laurent. *Avengers of the New World: The Story of the Haitian Revolution*. Cambridge: Harvard University Press, 2004; Geggus, David Patrick. *Haitian Revolutionary Studies*. Bloomington: Indiana University Press, 2002; Rogers, Dominique. *Les libres de couleur dans les capitales de Saint-Domingue: fortune, mentalités et intégration à la fin de l'Ancien Régime (1776–1789)*. Ph.D. dissertation, University of Bordeaux, France, 1999.

Silvia Marzagalli

"Saltwater Negroes"

African captives who were newly transported to the slave **plantations** in the Americas were referred to as "saltwater negroes." They underwent a period of **"seasoning"** for at least twelve months. Acclimatization and acculturation were difficult for them. So slave owners always had a **doctor** who gave advice on the treatment of new slaves.

For most of the eighteenth century, black people in the lowcountry regions of South Carolina and Georgia, unlike those in Maryland and Virginia, resided in an immigrant society. "Country-born" or "native-born" slaves frequently distinguished themselves from the saltwater negroes who arrived annually on slave ships. They often had concerns about the new **arrivals** and hesitated before developing any kinship alliances with them. The arrivals were unable to speak English and were not at all familiar with the habits of the inhabitants of the land. Most significant, they did not know the grueling routine of American slave life.

By the middle of the eighteenth century, the expansion of the slave trade was such that there was a continuous influx of saltwater slaves. With some reluctance, the native black population of the lowcountry began to create families with the new arrivals and the number of African Americans grew. In South Carolina, by 1730, the number of Africans (or saltwater negroes) and native-born African Americans, many descendant from West Central Africans, exceeded the white population. *See also Bozal.*

Further Readings: Baseler, Marilyn C. *"Asylum for Mankind": America, 1607–1800.* Ithaca: Cornell University Press, 1998; Berlin, Ira. *Many Thousands Gone: The First Two Centuries of Slavery in North America.* Cambridge, MA: Belknap Press, 1998.

Oyekemi Olajope Oyelakin

São Tomé

São Tomé is a small island located in the Bay of Guinea about 175 miles off the coast of Gabon in Africa. Along with the smaller island of Príncipe and a number of islets, São Tomé is part of the Democratic Republic of São Tomé and Príncipe. The Portuguese arrived in São Tomé in 1469, although some sources place the date of arrival in 1477. There is no evidence to suggest that São Tomé was inhabited when the Portuguese arrived, and by 1486, a colonial slave society had emerged. Along with the early colonists came Augustinian priests who established **Christianity** on the island. Capuchin monks from Italy would arrive several hundred years later. In the last decade of the fifteenth century, more than 2,000 Jewish children between the ages of two and ten were kidnapped from Portugal during the Spanish Inquisition and brought to São Tomé to work with imported African slaves on the island's **sugar plantations**.

By the time Columbus arrived in the Caribbean in 1492, colonists in São Tomé were already exporting sugar to Europe. By 1500, at least a thousand Africans were present on the island. At about the same time, São Tomé was supplying African slaves from the Bight of Benin to the Portuguese colony of São Jorge da Mina on the **Gold Coast** in Ghana. These Africans were used to transport gold from the interior of Africa to the coast, where it could be sent to Europe.

Slave rebellions were frequent on São Tomé in the sixteenth century. The most serious occurred in 1595 and was led by an African named Amador. Many accounts hold that Amador was an *Angolar*, a distinct group of Africans whose oral tradition identifies them as survivors of the wreck of a slave ship from Angola. However, some sources do not place the *Angolars* in São Tomé until the early eighteenth century. This 1595 uprising was eventually suppressed and its leaders executed. In the twentieth century Amador was touted as a nationalist icon and his image appears on São Tomé's currency. *Angolar* societies continued to live free in the southern mountains of the island until 1875 when they were forced off their land by the encroachment of coffee plantations. Confined to a narrow coastal strip, they established a fishing-based economy. *Angolars* still exist as a distinct ethnolinguistic group on São Tomé.

The sixteenth century marked a period of decline for São Tomé. The Dutch occupied São Tomé City from 1641 to 1648, but it eventually surrendered the island back to the Portuguese. The slave rebellions of the previous century, conflicts with other European colonial powers, and the export of higher-quality sugar from America to Europe led to a decline in São Tomé sugar exports. Thereafter, São Tomé took on a new role in the trans-Atlantic slave trade. By 1809, São Tomé had become one of the busiest slave markets in the world, importing 33,000 slaves for sale between 1809 and 1815. Many of these Africans were sent to **Brazil** and **Cuba**. São Tomé served as an important stopover point for slavers traveling from Africa to the Americas. Here they could take on provisions for the long Middle Passage.

Slavery continued to be important in the nineteenth century as cocoa and coffee became important exports. Although it was made illegal by 1869, slavery continued into the early twentieth century on São Tomé in the form of forced wage labor. In 1953, anger over abuses of African laborers led to a general uprising in which several hundred blacks were killed. The "Batepa Massacre," as it is known today, is marked by a government holiday. On July 12, 1974, São Tomé and Príncipe realized their independence from Portugal. *See also* Portuguese Slave Trade.

Further Reading: Shaw, Caroline S. *World Bibliographical Series, São Tomé and Príncipe*. Oxford: Clio Press, 1994.

Eric Covey

"Seasoning"

Seasoning was the process by which slaves were introduced to a new environment and their new status. After **arrival**, African slaves would have to adjust to a new climate, work regime, **food**, clothing, and **language**. There was no single method by which the seasoning process occurred. It varied according to time of arrival and master, and each of these aspects would vary depending on where the slaves were sold. For example, there would have been a sharp difference between the climate in the northern United States and **Brazil** or the Caribbean. Location also determined work regime. Slaves in the northern United States may have participated in mixed agriculture, while slaves further south would have participated in various enterprises such as tobacco, cotton, rice, and sugarcane. In the Caribbean and Latin America, slaves would have worked on primarily sugarcane and coffee **plantations**. Each of these crops has its own planting and harvest schedule, and each would have varied in the difficulty of tending. Slaves also learned their new positions in society during the process of seasoning. In the New World, African slaves, and later their descendents, were subordinate to white slave owners. Whiteness became synonymous with power, while blackness came to represent the absence of power. Perhaps one of the most important aspects of seasoning was learning a new language, whether French, Spanish, English, or another European language. It was through language and punishment that Africans learned their place in society and what behavior was appropriate to that position. Physical punishment also served as a way to attempt to break the will of slaves so that they would not rebel. It also played a role in communicating what work was to be done. *See also* Bozal; "Saltwater Negroes."

Further Readings: Gomez, Michael A. *Exchanging Our Country Marks: The Transformation of African Identities in the Colonial and Antebellum South*. Chapel Hill:

University of North Carolina Press, 1998; Morgan, Philip D. *Slave Counterpoint: Black Culture in the Eighteenth-Century Chesapeake and Lowcountry.* Chapel Hill: University of North Carolina Press, 1998.

Lauren Whitney Hammond

Seasons

Supply and demand are two basic aspects of every trade, including the trade in human beings. In all ramifications, several factors determined the demand for slaves in the Americas and supply from Africa. The factors that determined supply and demand include but are not limited to the following: African crop and weather patterns, Atlantic winds and current conditions, and the American work demands based on harvest cycles. Local weather and sailing conditions also played an important role in determining the speed of the Middle Passage. The length of the Atlantic voyage tended to affect the supply of slaves. Typically, slave vessels from parts of West Africa such as the **Windward Coast** arrived in the Americas earlier than those from the Bight of Benin.

Seasons had a serious impact on the demand and supply of slaves because the slaves were needed for **plantation** agriculture, which was affected by seasonal variation. This implies that different parts of the Americas had different periods of rises or drops in the number of slaves imported. The highest demand for slaves in the Caribbean was January though June when plantation owners needed slaves for harvest. The months from August to January, in the case of **Brazil**, represent higher arrivals of slave ships, while a drop was witnessed between February and July.

Sailing during the stormy season directly affected the safety of slave vessels. The Atlantic environment naturally produced heavy winds. Catastrophic ones were usually recorded during the rainy season. Heavy **storms** lowered the speed of vessels and exposed them to the risk of **shipwreck**.

Seasonal variations also had serious impacts on the health and **mortality** of European **crews** in Africa. The months of heavy rains from February to May constituted serious medical hazards for the crew who fell sick and died of tropical African **diseases**, such as malaria. The longer they stayed waiting for their ships to be loaded with slaves, the higher the risk of dying of African tropical diseases. In another vein, diarrhea was a disease that posed a medical hazard to the slaves and the crew during the Middle Passage. It spread quickly through dirty **water** and the problems of sanitation on the slave vessels. During the rainy season, the incidence of this disease was higher as a result of the higher humidity occasioned by the heavy rainfall.

Further Readings: Eltis, David. *Economic Growth and the Ending of the Transatlantic Slave Trade.* Oxford: Oxford University Press, 1987; Hogendorn, Jan, and Johnson, Marion. *The Shell Money of the Slave Trade.* Cambridge: Cambridge University Press, 1986; Klein, Martin. *Historical Dictionary of Slavery and Abolition.* Lanham, MD: The Scarecrow Press, 2002.

Saheed Aderinto

Senegal

During the 1700s when the Atlantic slave trade was flourishing, West Africans accounted for roughly two-thirds of the African captives shipped to the Americas. The coastal **ports** where these Africans were assembled, and from where they were exported, are located in the present-day Senegal and Gambia on the northwest to Gabon on the southeast. From Ceuta, Morocco, Tangiers, Madeira, and Azores, the Portuguese caravels reached Senegal by 1460 and explored the Gulf of Guinea and its islands (notably **São Tomé** and Príncipe) in the 1470s. The Portuguese established a permanent presence at Fort Byhurt in Senegambia during the early fifteenth century. From the trading posts and forts, the Portuguese "policy of expansion" enabled it to explore the interior of West Africa for trading purposes. By the mid-1450s, Portuguese **slave traders** moved into Senegal and **Cape Verde**, and the trade in slaves became preeminent in these areas. The Wolof at the coast and the interior of southern Senegal signed treaties with the Portuguese for the supply of slaves. Before the end of fifteenth century, between 200 and 400 slaves per year were traded from the Senegal River. The Wolof exchanged Africans with items supplied by Portuguese caravels that sailed up river to the trading fair at Tuculor. About 5,000 slaves were estimated to have been exported from Senegal and **Sierra Leone** in the decade from 1450 to 1460. The slave trade coast extended from Benguela in **Angola** to Saint Louis at the mouth of the Senegal.

The Senegambia, along the shores of Senegal and Gambia, was the first West African region to participate in the maritime contact with Europe, serving as the major **port** of the slave trade before 1600. After the seventeenth century, slave exports from Senegambia were obtained from the hinterland areas. The Portuguese abandoned Senegal for Cape Verde and the **Gambia River** and organized their trade with the region from there. This led to the emergence of an Afro-Portuguese community who became the major traders and identified themselves as Portuguese and Catholic. They traded in slaves and ivory for export overseas, and brought down iron, cotton **textiles**, and kola nuts for Senegambia in return for Senegambian mats and textiles for distribution in the interior. The French held the dominant position in Senegal from their base on the island of Saint Louis, but their position was often threatened by commercial rivals and pirates. Senegal, unlike the Gambia, was not tidal and therefore was less important as a transport route. Seaborne ships could hardly proceed beyond Saint Louis. The Senegal route also lacked the Afro-Portuguese community that could serve as intermediaries between the coastal areas and the hinterland. This led to the emergence of an Afro-French community in Saint Louis. In the

Blacksmith at work, Senegal, 1780s. Special Collections, University of Virginia Library.

eighteenth century, the coastal trade at Senegal was controlled by the Wolof merchants of Saint Louis. The growing importance of Senegambia in the slave trade was short lived following the breakup of the Jolof empire.

In the eighteenth century, Senegambia ceased to be a major source of slaves. The *Maison des Esclaves* (House of Slaves) on **Gorée Island** was built in 1776 by the Dutch and was one of several sites on the island where Africans were brought to be loaded onto ships bound for the New World. The owner's residential quarters were on the upper floor. The lower floor was reserved for the enslaved Africans who were weighed, fed, and held before they were taken on the Middle Passage across the Atlantic. The *Maison des Esclaves*, with its famous **Door of No Return** has been preserved in its original state. Between 1650 and 1900, the number of slaves exported was 479,900, accounting for 4.7 percent of the trans-Atlantic slave trade. Senegambia, Upper Guinea, and Sierra Leone, were closest to the Caribbean and to the United States, and the voyage was much more swift. The Africans from Senegal were highly prized in many places in the Americas, and this was another reason why there was a clustering. Africans from Senegal came earliest to the Americas. Throughout the 1500s into the 1600s, these were the main Africans brought the Americas. Once an African culture was established, including on **plantations**, the masters wanted to bring in people whom their existing slave force could communicate with, talk to, and socialize in the ways they were supposed to behave in this new environment. Africans from the same places were brought to particular regions over many, many decades, even centuries.

In the early stages of the slave trade to Louisiana, people were almost entirely from Senegal and Guinea because of the rice industry and indigo cultivation, which the Africans from that region introduced. The **captains** of the first slave-trade voyages that brought slaves to Louisiana were instructed to bring Africans who knew how to cultivate rice and rice for seeding. African technology was introduced in the production of rice and indigo cultivation. This accounted for the growing rate of Atlantic slave-trade ships coming from Senegal and Upper Guinea to the rice and indigo production regions. *See also* French Slave Trade; New Orleans; Portuguese Slave Trade; Fort Saint Louis; Trade Forts.

Further Readings: Curtin, Philip D. "The West African Coast in the Era of the Slave Trade." In P. Curtin, S. Feierman, L. Thompson, and J. Vansina, eds. *African History: From Earliest Times to Independence*. London: Longmans, Green and Company, 1995; Richardson, David. *Shipboard Revolts, African Authority, and the Atlantic Slave Trade*. Williamsburg, VA: Institute of Early American History and Culture, 2001; Russell-Wood, A.J.R. "Before Columbus: Portugal's African Prelude to the Middle Passage and Contribution to Discourse on Race and Slavery." In V. A. Shepherd and Hilary McD. Beckles, eds. *Caribbean Slavery in the Atlantic World: A Student Reader*. Kingston: Ian Randle Publishers Ltd., 2000.

Rasheed Olaniyi

Seville

The year 1492 marked significant political, socio-racial, and religious changes—while also introducing new beginnings—throughout the Iberian kingdoms that are now Spain. The following transformations took place:

the publication of the first grammar of the Spanish language (*Gramática castellana*) by Antonio de Nebrija (born in Lebrija, a province of Seville); the fall of Nasrid Granada; the expulsion of Jews, **Muslims**, and black *ladinos* (a sub-Saharan African who is "Latinized" and culturally Hispanicized); and the first voyage of Christopher Columbus. Thereafter, Seville served as an important seaport for the early modern (late fourteenth to early eighteenth centuries) trans-Atlantic world. Throughout the sixteenth century *Sevillano* merchants exported, imported, and traded a variety of commercial goods such as gold, fabrics, spices, silver, tiles, and wine. The city also stood as the principal central distributor of sub-Saharan slaves who, initially, were sent to the Spanish Kingdoms of Aragon, Barcelona, Basque Country, Castile, and Valencia, as well as to the Italian **port**, Genoa, and many other southern Italian cities. As an international city, Seville's sixteenth-century slave trade attracted many foreigners, especially Florentines from Italy. Christopher Columbus's friends the Berardi brothers, for example, stationed their headquarters in Seville. Bartolommeo Marchionni—an early **Lisbon** Florentine beneficiary and entrepreneur—and his *Sevillano* agent Piero Rondinelli, took a decisive part in the Spanish slave trade. Evidence of Marchionni's privileged role in the slave trade can be witnessed from his trading of slaves on the Slave River, **Benin**, between 1486 and 1493, and in the "rivers of Guinea" (what is now today known as the Senegambia region) between 1490 and 1495. Initially, Seville participated in domestic trade throughout the Iberian Peninsula. Seville's significant conversion into a major exporter and player of the exportation and importation of African slaves began during the second decade of the sixteenth century. The city, as a result, became conditioned to responding to the Spanish American colonies' high demand for black slaves in the Caribbean, Mexico, and South America.

Spain's speedy occupation of the West Indies and Central and South America proved to be devastating for the indigenous populations. By 1501, black African slaves were imported into the Spanish colonies throughout the Americas to work not only in the coffee and **sugar plantations**, but also in the mines where precious minerals presided. Lacking a viable presence on the West African coast, Spain was forced to grant **licenses**, the majority to **monopoly** traders, for the transportation of slaves to Spain's new world colonies. The crown declared **free trade** in slaves in 1789.

The origins and development of black African slavery in Spain were closely connected to the city of Seville. Dating back from 1276, Medieval Spanish texts tell us that sub-Saharan African slaves—often referred to as *privados*, *esclavo moros*, or *esclavos negros*—were transported to Andalusia via a variety of routes, including along the Saharan gold and salt posts, the coast of Guinea, the Canary Islands, and the Balearic Islands. During the sixteenth century, Seville reigned as a cosmopolitan and prosperous city that constituted a group of people who came from diverse racial makeups and varied social conditions. Seville was one of the two (Lisbon, Portugal, the second) western European cities with the oldest slave colonies in the New World. During this time period, 6 percent of Seville's inhabitants were of direct African lineage. To this day, Seville's riverfront neighborhood,

Arenal, is recognized as one of the principal sections of the city where black *Sevillanos* and their descendants once lived. *See also Asiento*; Europe, Enslaved Africans in; Hispaniola; Spanish Caribbean.

Further Readings: Anti-Slavery International Web site: www.antislavery.org; Franco Silva, Alonso. *La esclavitud en Andalucía, 1450–1550*. Granada: Universidad de Granada, 1992; Thomas, Hugh. *The Slave Trade: The Story of the Atlantic Slave Trade, 1440–1870*. New York: Simon & Schuster, 1997; Williams, Eric Eustace. *Capitalism and Slavery; with a new introduction by Colin A. Palmer*. Chapel Hill: University of North Carolina Press, 1994 (1944).

Nicholas Jones

Shipmate

Life aboard slave ships effectively brought together varying groups of people—merchants, **slave traders**, seamen, and African captives. For enslaved populations in particular, despite the horrors of the trade that severed former familial and communal ties within their homelands, this process of **enslavement** initiated the beginnings of bonds as shipmates, or *malungos* (Portuguese word). These bonds helped to forge friendships and, more important, ties of survival among fellow captives. Shipmate is defined as the association of those captives transported on board the same slave ship bound for the Americas. These connections many times extended beyond lines of age, **gender**, and **ethnicity** as diverse groups of Africans were collectively placed at the centerpiece of this system of trade and capital gain.

Once **chained** and led on board vessels of their captors, the process of shipmate became set into motion among the enslaved. These particular relationships were often of a two-person orientation, owing largely to the separation of men and **women** on ships. Close relationships among the enslaved were not always easily developed because of the presence of varying ethnicities within the trade. Being collectively thrust within a system of brutal enslavement, however, and often being chained side by side within the **holds** of ships, these ethnic animosities often quickly dissolved throughout the progression of the Atlantic voyage. The term "shipmate" was understood among many enslaved to signify a relation of the most endearing nature. As ties of friendships were borne out of these shared experiences of hardship and oppression, a consciousness of common fate was further solidified, which allowed captives to move beyond the anguish and pain they endured to reach out emotionally to their fellow shipmates.

The bonds of shipmate not only existed onboard ships crossing the Atlantic, but also became transplanted into **plantation** societies throughout the Americas. The experience of the auction block for African captives sought to deny deeper bonds of friendship as planters freely bought and sold incoming African **cargo**, effectively splitting apart friends and **families**. Yet, despite the probability of never seeing their former shipmates, many enslaved held onto the memories of their fellow shipmates and their ship experiences. As shipmates, many of the enslaved viewed themselves within a bond of formal kinship much like an interfamilial link, quite invisible to traders and masters, that helped sustain their ultimate survival of slavery.

Following placement within a plantation community, some enslaved Africans held on to these previous feelings of emotional attachment for their fellow cohorts, which were reserved not only for other survivors on board the same ship crossing the Atlantic, but also toward descendants of their shipmates, their wives, and their husbands.

Placed within the sphere of the domestic slave trade, many Africans quickly recognized the necessity of collective unity needed to survive the conditions of enslavement. The relationships as shipmates often provided the foundation of survival, kinship, and communal identity forged among communities of African-born enslaved populations. Within New World societies, these same ties as shipmates also became the principal factors in the social organization that was maintained among the enslaved spanning both decades and generations.

Further Readings: Conrad, Robert. *World of Sorrow: The African Slave Trade to Brazil.* Baton Rouge: Louisiana State University Press, 1986; Lovejoy, Paul. "The Origins of Muslim Slaves in Bahia." *Slavery and Abolition* 15, 2 (1996): 151–180; Mintz, Sidney, and Price, Richard. *The Birth of African-American Culture: An Anthropological Perspective.* Boston, MA: Beacon Press, 1992; Nishida, Mieko. *Slavery and Identity: Ethnicity, Gender, and Race in Salvador, Brazil. 1808–1888.* Bloomington: Indiana University Press, 2003.

Sowande' M. Mustakeem

Shipwrecks

Shipwrecks were an inherent risk of the Atlantic slave trade because of the distances involved, conditions at sea, and the shipbuilding technology of the times. Although precise Atlantic figures are lacking, an estimated 8.5 percent of French slave ships wrecked during the latter half of the 1700s. This might roughly correspond to losses from other nations participating in the slave trade.

Slave expeditions were high-risk ventures. **Storms** routinely sank ships and others foundered off reefs or shoals. A few such wrecks have become famous. After a storm in 1738 left the Dutch vessel *Leuden* stranded on rocks off the Suriname coast, the crew escaped but left behind 702 slaves to **drown**. The Danish *Kron-Printzen* sank in 1706 in a storm and all 820 slaves on board perished. The *Trouvadore*, a Spanish slave ship that wrecked off the Turks and Caicos Islands in 1841, faired better. Its cargo of 193 slaves was freed when they escaped to East Caicos, a British island that had abolished slavery.

Nature did not cause all wrecks. A few were engineered. In 1766, slaves aboard the Dutch ship *Meermin* rebelled. The crew kept alive to navigate them home secretly set course for Cape Town, South Africa. When a struggle broke out after the slaves discovered the plot, the **captain** cut the anchor and the *Meermin* drifted into the sand. The slaves surrendered and were sold in the Cape Town slave markets.

The modern discovery in 1972 of the English merchant vessel **the *Henrietta Marie*** off Key West in Florida opened the slave trade as a field of study to maritime archeologists. In 1700, shortly after selling a shipment of

190 slaves in **Jamaica** the *Henrietta Marie* sank at sea. The rare collection of shackles, cannons, Venetian glass beads, ivory, and other goods salvaged from the ship represent one of the largest early artifact finds of the slave trade, providing a wealth of information about a pivotal period in African, European, and American history.

Worldwide the number of discovered slave ship wrecks are few. Researchers have identified fewer than ten wrecks, and the *Henrietta Marie* is the only wreck excavated from the Americas. Projects for locating ships such as the *Trouvadore* and *Meermin* are under way, as are searches for *La Cybele*, a French ship carrying slaves from **Senegal** in 1756, and the Portuguese vessel *St. José*, which sank in 1794 with slaves from **Mozambique**. Such finds would permit researchers to draw comparisons between the conditions aboard the vessels of different slave-trading nations and uncover secrets about the complex maritime slave trade. *See also* Accidents and Explosions; *Fredensborg*, The; *Guerrero*, The; *Ivory* Wreck, The.

Further Readings: Lindow, Megan. "In Shipwrecks, New Clues to a Buried Past." *The Christian Science Monitor.* July 29, 2004; Mel Fisher Maritime Heritage Society. "A Slave Ship Speaks: The Wreck of the Henrietta Marie." [Online, November 2006]. Mel Fisher Maritime Heritage Society Web site: http://www.melfisher.org/henriettamarie; "Slave Ship Trouvadore." [Online, November 2006]. Trouvadore Project Web site: http://www.slaveshiptrouvadore.com; Thomas, Hugh. *The Slave Trade: The Story of the Atlantic Slave Trade, 1440–1870.* New York: Simon & Schuster, 1997.

Leslie Wilson

Shipyards

Ships or vessels are the lifeblood of maritime trade. There is a deep relationship between the development of the slave trade and the development of shipbuilding industries in Europe and the Americas. The major European slave-trading countries developed shipbuilding technology, which suited both the natural trading environment and the modus operandi of loading and transporting slaves from Africa to the Americas. In the Americas, shipyards were owned and maintained by both the imperial government and individual **slave merchants**. The good percentage of shipyards in Europe were owned by the huge slave trade companies such as the **Royal Africa Company** and the Dutch West India Company. The names given to ships sometimes depict the place they were constructed or the name of their designers.

In the fifteenth century, the Portuguese had founded the trans-Atlantic slave trade using the single-docked caravel, with square or lateen sails. These types of vessels were only big enough to accommodate 50 to 100 slaves. The Portuguese also used smaller vessels of twenty to twenty-five tons for transporting slaves between **Benin** and **Elmina** and Benin and **São Tomé**.

Yet, shipbuilding technology developed through the centuries. In the eighteenth century, vessels build in European shipyards by merchant companies were state of the art. Slave merchants were convinced that ships should be built in a manner to enhance their **profits**. The smaller the space allotted to slaves the higher the number of slaves a vessel could accommodate. Dutch ships were believed to be the most generous in terms of space and comfort given to slaves.

The major threat to the durability of ships build in European yards was the presence of barnacles or shipworm. It was only in the late eighteenth century that ships built in northern Europe began to be given copper-sheathed hulls. This innovation did not protect vessels from shipworm but did increase their speed.

The Portuguese were also said to have manufactured ships in Africa. Cacheu was for a time in the seventeenth century a major boat-building place for the Portuguese. The abundance of a tree called *Cabopa* that yielded planks known to resist shipworm may have contributed to making Cacheu a major Portuguese shipyard in Africa. *See also* Dutch Slave Trade; Portuguese Slave Trade.

Further Readings: Eltis, David, and Richardson, David, eds. *Routes to Slavery: Direction, Ethnicity and Mortality in the Transatlantic Slave Trade.* London: Frank Cass, 1997; Gemery, Henry, and Hogendorn, Jan, ed. *The Uncommon Market: Essays in the Economic History of the Atlantic Slave Trade.* New York: Academic, 1979; Postma, Johannes Menne. *The Dutch in the Atlantic Slave Trade 1600–1815.* New York and Cambridge: Cambridge University Press, 1990; Richardson, David. *Bristol, Africa and the Eighteenth-Century Slave Trade to the Americas.* 4 vols. Gloucester: Bristol Records Society, 1986–1996.

Saheed Aderinto

Sierra Leone

Sierra Leone was first encountered in the mid-fifteenth century by the Portuguese explorer Pedro da Cintra. Between the sixteenth and the eighteenth centuries, the slave trade in the area was successfully carried out, mainly by the British, the Dutch, and the French. Bunce Island and the Gallinas and Sherbro Rivers were the main places of export.

After 1787 things changed. Under the tutelage of Granville Sharp, a British abolitionist, a new colony was founded along the south bank of the Sierra Leone River. Granville Town soon became Freetown, and new waves of black émigrés arrived, including around 2,000 black loyalists from Nova Scotia and then a few hundred Jamaican **maroons**.

After the abolition of the slave trade by the British Parliament in 1807, **Sierra Leone** was transformed into a base of operations to enforce British antislave-trade laws off the coast of Africa. With this aim, the British forced other slave-trading nations to stop their involvement in the trade and to participate actively in bringing the trans-Atlantic slave trade to an end. Courts of Mixed Commission for the abolition of the slave trade were created in various Atlantic **ports**. Particularly important were those established in Sierra Leone, **Havana**, and Rio de Janeiro.

The Court of Mixed Commission of Sierra Leone lasted until 1871, but it was the period between 1819 and 1845 when it played a prominent role in the abolition of the slave trade, processing 528 slave ships during those years. After 1845, its responsibilities were transferred to the Vice-Admiralty Court, and as a consequence, it presided only over a few cases from that date onward. The significance of Sierra Leone in the abolition of the trans-Atlantic slave trade cannot be dismissed. The Sierra Leone commission court alone freed 64,625 Africans who were bound for the New World as slaves. The resettlement of these thousands of African men and women was a new problem per se for the local authorities in the colony.

Still in the mid-1880s, after returning from Freetown to England and long after the slave trade had been finally abolished, T. R. Griffiths published an interesting account of the population of this British West African colony. Among the several ethnic groups he accounted for, Griffiths mentioned the Yoruba, the **Igbo**, the Coromantee, the West Indian negroes, and another large number of individuals whose ethnic backgrounds could not be determined. This population of West African, West Indian, and unknown origin was to a large extent the result of the establishment of the Court of Mixed Commission of Sierra Leone in the second decade of the century. Nineteenth-century Freetown was characterized as disorderly due to its multiethnic population.

Sierra Leone continues to be the result of these migrations. The main language spoken throughout the country, the Krio, is a combination of English with local dialects and words taken from the many different **languages** of the various groups of immigrants that arrived in the area throughout the nineteenth century. Their cultures, values, and **religion** are present today among their descendants. *See also* Abolition of the Slave Trade, Great Britain; Closure of the Slave Trade; Returnees to Africa.

Further Readings: Asiegbu, J.U.J. "The Dynamics of Freedom: A Study of Liberated African Emigration and British Antislavery Policy." *Journal of Black Studies* 7, 1 (1976): 95–106; Bethell, Leslie. "The Mixed Commissions for the Suppression of the Transatlantic Slave Trade in the Nineteenth Century." *The Journal of African History* 41, 1 (1966): 79–93; Campbell, Mavis C. *Back to Africa: George Ross and the Maroons: From Nova Scotia to Sierra Leone.* Trenton: Africa World Press, 1993; Clarke, Robert. *Sierra Leone: A Description of the Manners and Customs of the Liberated Africans.* London: James Ridgway, 1843; Peterson, John Eric. *Province of Freedom: A History of Sierra Leone, 1787–1870.* London: Faber and Faber, 1969; Probyn, Leslie. "Sierra Leone and the Natives from West Africa." *Journal of the Royal African Society* 6, 23 (1907): 250–258; Walker, James W. *The Black Loyalists: The Search for a Promised Land in Nova Scotia and Sierra Leone, 1783–1870.* New York: Africana Pub. Co., 1976.

Manuel Barcia

Slave Coast

The Slave Coast (also referred to as the Bight of Benin), so named by European **slave traders** for its role in the trans-Atlantic slave trade that lasted for almost four centuries, covers the coastal areas of present-day Togo, **Benin**, and Western Nigeria. Along this West African coastline, European traders, slavers, and pirates built numerous forts to protect their commercial interests. Although the Gold Coast (Ghana) is not traditionally referred to as the **Slave Coast** because of its prominence in the gold trade, it nevertheless was one of the main **ports** of departure for the slaves: **Elmina** and Cape Coast were as busy as the ports at **Ouidah**, **Lagos**, Popo, Benin, and **Allada** on the Bight of Benin. In the 1720s for instance, the Gold Coast supplied about

25 percent of the Anglo-French export of slaves; this figure dropped to 8 percent toward the end of the century when Ouidah, Allada, and Lagos became the main suppliers of slaves. Although European trade relations with Africa began with commodities such as gold, metals, ivory, cloth, hides, and alcohol before the trans-Atlantic slave trade, slaves, guns, and ammunition came to dominate trade relations during the sixteenth through the eighteenth centuries. The Portuguese were the first to build a **trade fort** at Elmina (Ghana) in 1481 to tap into the gold trade with the Gold Coast. Other European countries followed suit: in all, twenty-seven forts were built on a coastal distance of 220 miles. But when **legitimate commerce** turned into trade in humans, these forts were reinforced to serve as slave depots throughout the Slave Coast and elsewhere along the coastal towns down to **Luanda** (Angola).

On the Slave Coast proper, in the Bight of Benin, ports like Ouidah, Allada, Popo, Benin, Lagos, Onim, Porto Novo, Epe, Offra, Jakin, Badagri, and Apa served as the major points of embarkation between 1650 and 1860 for the majority of Africans who crossed the Atlantic to the New World.

There is a diasporic dimension to the Slave Coast that needs to be stressed: the so-called Atlantic community. Even before the trade was outlawed, a new hybrid community of mixed "race" and culture was slowly coming into being. This community included mostly ex-slaves who had returned to the coastal areas (predominantly from the Slave Coast) to settle or to participate in the slave trade. This community was powerful and wealthy enough during the slave trade to challenge local chiefs who tried to control the trade. These **returnees** were not the first to return to Africa as free individuals. English and U.S. ex-slaves and their descendants, voluntarily or under the auspices of **humanitarian** and abolitionist organizations, had resettled in **Sierra Leone** and **Liberia**, respectively. From **Brazil** (and to a lesser degree from **Cuba**) historians have identified a much larger group of Creoles (ex-slaves) who had returned to the Slave Coast after the Bahia slave rebellion in 1835, which prompted a massive deportation of about 200 suspected individuals to the Slave Coast. Repatriation from Brazil also occurred on an individual and voluntary basis. Over the years, a community of Afro-Brazilians developed along the Slave Coast who took up residence in present-day Togo, Benin, and Nigeria. Like the slaves who took their culture with them to the New World, the returnees brought back to the coastal regions their Creole culture. Today, the de Souza and d'Almeida families are descendants of these Afro-Brazilians who had returned "home" and remained connected to Brazil and Portugal. These descendants are politically active and powerful in their new homes across political boundaries.

The abolition of the trans-Atlantic slave trade in France in 1794 and in Britain in 1808 diminished the Atlantic community's presence on the Slave Coast as France and England closed down the slave forts at Ouidah. Trade in slaves and commodities such as palm oil between Brazil and the Slave Coast continued into the 1850s. The end of the slave trade also brought to the fore a decline in commercial activities along the Slave Coast when Britain annexed Lagos in 1861 and drove out all foreign slave traders in an attempt to provide security for trade in palm oil. *See also* Abolition of the Slave Trade, France; Abolition of the Slave Trade, Great Britain.

Further Readings: Berlin, Ira. "From Creole to Africa: Atlantic Creoles and the Origins of the African American Society in Mainland North America." *William and Mary Quarterly* 53 (1996): 251; "Europeans Come to Western Africa." Africans in America. PBS Online Web site: http://www.pbs.org/wgbh/aia/part1/1narr1.html; Falola, Toyin, and Childs, Matt D., eds. *The Yoruba Diaspora in the Atlantic World.* Bloomington: Indiana University Press, 2004; Manning, Patrick. *Slavery and African Life: Occidental, Oriental, and African Slave Trades.* Cambridge: Cambridge University Press, 1990; Verger, Pierre. *Flux et reflux de la traite des nègres entre le Golfe de Bénin et Bahia de Todos os Santos, du XVIIe au XIXe siècle.* Paris: Mouton, 1968 (translated by Evelyn Crawford as *Trade Relations between the Bight of Benin and Bahia from the Seventeenth to the Nineteenth Century).*

Mawuena Logan

Slave Merchants (Slave Traders)

Like all other types of economic enterprises, the slave trade required merchants and slave owners who were responsible for the buying and selling of slaves. The career patterns of slave merchants varied based on race, **ethnicity**, class, and geographic location.

In Africa, slaves were chiefly owned and sold by kings or rulers and important dignitaries such as the military aristocratic class. The **oral history** of rulers and important dignitaries in precolonial Africa is replete with reference to their status as owners, buyers, and sellers of slaves. Some of these rulers had thousands of slaves who worked on their farms. Domestic slaves were sometimes disposed at will in exchange for European manufactured goods and ammunition. The patriarchal nature of most African societies meant that the largest percentage of slave dealers were men. Nevertheless, some women were involved in the buying and selling of slaves. Efuntesan Aniwura, the *Iyalode* of Ibadan, and Madam Tinubu of Abeokuta were two powerful nineteenth-century women who derived part of their wealth and political status from trade in slaves.

Most of the slaves sold to the Americas came from the hinterland of the **Slave Coast**, the heavily populated area that stretched from modern Togo to Cameroon and included the Bight of Biafra. States and empires located in the hinterland required the cooperation of their coastal neighbors before slaves could be bought and sold. Not all slave owners bought the people they enslaved. Kings and the military had the power to embark on raids of neighboring communities for the purpose of getting slaves. Most of the kingdoms that did this were chiefly encouraged by the insecurity posed by their neighbors and the need to use slaves to acquire European-manufactured ammunition. The Kingdom of **Dahomey** is perhaps the most classic examples of a slave-dealing kingdom that embarked on sporadic wars to acquire slaves. During the abolitionist movement, the wealth that slavery brought to the king of Dahomey was the principal reason the kingdom refused to adhere to the British abolitionist agenda. Kosoko, mid-nineteenth century king of **Lagos**, incurred the bad favor of the British because he would not give up the trade in human beings after it had been outlawed.

On the European end, a noticeable trend is that slave merchants were sometimes big companies who traded in both slaves and European-manufactured articles such as ammunition, **rum**, salt, iron bars, silver coins, and **textiles**. All of these commodities were exchanged for slaves. The range of commodities changed over time as the European and African technology and societies transformed. In the nineteenth century, **firearms** seemed to be the most important article of exchange along the Slave Coast.

The **Royal Africa Company** had a history of monopolizing British slave-trading along West African coastal waters until the closing decade of the eighteenth century. Most of these big companies were based in influential **port** cities such as **Liverpool** and Manchester of Great Britain. European slave-trading companies were responsible for implementing their government's official policy toward buying and selling of slaves. European slave merchants, however, required the services of another type of merchant: local chiefs and other non-Africans, who were responsible for buying and gathering the slaves from the hinterland and assembling them along the coast. These intermediaries were quite important because European merchant activity before the nineteenth century was confined to the coast. It was natural for the local chiefs to protect their **monopoly** by preventing the Europeans from venturing into the hinterland and buying the slaves directly from slave owners. The medical threat that the African coastal environment posed to the Europeans was another reason they avoided venturing into the hinterland in search of slaves.

Brazilians seem to have occupied the most important position as non-European slave merchants along the Slave Coast. The most readily cited of the first generation Brazilian slave dealers was Francesco Souza. He was responsible for making **Ouidah** (Whydah), part of the kingdom of Dahomey, the most popular slave port during the second and the third decades of the nineteenth century. King Ghezo made Souza the sole middleman between his kingdom and the Europeans because of the role he played in facilitating the 1818 revolution, which paved the way for his enthronement. Another popular nineteenth-century slave merchant of Brazilian origin was Domingo Martinez. Martinez was a major problem for the British during the abolitionist years, which saw the introduction of the so-called **legitimate commerce**.

Slave merchants in the Americas completed the process of the Atlantic journey of the slaves. West Indian slave merchants usually were the suppliers to **plantations** that needed frequent importations of slaves to work the land. These merchants were consistently exposed to the problems of health of slaves and changes in the world **prices** of **sugar**, the major plantation agricultural product. Slave resistance in terms of mutiny and revolt also exposed merchants to a high degree of insecurity. A merchant who experienced a slave revolt often lost his total investment. *See also* African Rulers and the Slave Trade; Interlopers; Trade Commodities.

Further Readings: Klein, Martin. *Historical Dictionary of Slavery and Abolition*. Lanham, MD, and London: The Scarecrow Press, Inc, 2002; Law, Robin. "Slave Raiders and Middlemen, Monopolists and Free-Traders: The Supply of Slaves for the Atlantic Trade in Dahomey, c. 1715–1850." *The Journal of African History* 30, 1 (1989): 45–68; Lovejoy, Paul. *Transformations in Slavery: A History of Slavery in Africa*. Cambridge: Cambridge University Press, 1983; Ross, David. "The Career of Domingo Martinez in the Bight of Benin 1833–1864." *The Journal of African History* 6, 1 (1965): 79–90.

Saheed Aderinto

Slave Narratives and Slave Autobiography

The slave narrative is a genre within the African American literary tradition that describes the experiences of a formerly enslaved individual, born in either the United States or Africa. The term "slave narrative" encompasses a wide range of literary materials published primarily in the eighteenth and nineteenth centuries. Those literary materials may include life stories, published orations, captivity and conversion tales, confessions, letters, and other texts that capture the experiences of Africans and African Americans. There are three distinct time periods that altered the form and content of these narratives: the eighteenth century, the antebellum and Civil War era, and the twentieth century. The events of these periods greatly influenced the **language** with which Africans and Americans tell their stories and portray their lives.

The slave narratives of the eighteenth century were most often stories of conversion and divine providence, which were published in England or in colonial America, particularly **New England**. Eighteenth-century narratives articulate the lives of Africans and African Americans living in American both before and after the Revolutionary War. They represent the development of intellectual and writing communities that were aware of slavery but far more interested in saving souls than in abolition.

Scholars attribute the first narrative to Briton Hammon, an African mariner who left his New England master to travel and work on a ship in the Caribbean. Briton Hammon's *Narrative of the Uncommon Sufferings, and Surprizing Deliverance of Briton Hammon, A Negro Man* was published in Boston in 1760. Hammon's text is a captivity narrative, which described his capture by Indians and the means by which divine providence delivers him. The captivity narrative was a common genre of the colonial period and was appropriated within slave narratives by other African Americans, such as John Marrant. The conventions of Hammon's text highlighted the style and format common to eighteenth-century narratives, in particular the role of divine providence, salvation, conversion, and the amanuensis or editor. Most of these narratives were dictated to an amanuensis that edited the story for style, grammar, and content errors. Those that were not dictated still included a preface, which authenticated the story and stated the reasons why the narrative had been published. Despite the fact that many of these narratives were dictated, most of the narrators and authors, such as John Marrant, James Albert Ukawsaw Gronniosaw, and **Olaudah Equiano**, were literate.

Together with the editor, these authors chronicled their individual pursuit of **Christianity** and their quest for salvation. Beginning with a statement that acknowledged the author's birth and birthplace, these narratives emphasized their experiences before and after conversion, with a particular attention to the actual conversion. Their lives before their conversion were mired with sinfulness, a sense of doom and an inability to answer life's questions. Conversion happened the moment at which they acknowledged and accepted Christianity as the basis of their religious beliefs. It was characterized by intense emotional responses such as fainting, weeping, elation, and tears. The conversion experience for some took place aboard the slave ship or during a church revival. For others, it came as they read their dying confessions while speaking their last words. Once converted, the narrators emphasized the importance of God within their lives. As His delivered subjects, it then became their mission to spread his word by recounting and publishing their stories. Their texts, along with public speaking engagements, served as the primary means by which these authors ministered to their brethren.

The nineteenth-century narratives revise and reimagine the genre established by the eighteenth century. Instead of emphasizing conversion, these narratives were much more invested in literacy and freedom. There were several prominent nineteenth-century narratives that have helped scholars define the genre, including those by Harriet Jacobs, Frederick Douglass, and William Wells Brown. According to many scholars, Frederick Douglass's first autobiographical account, *The Narrative of Frederick Douglass, An American Slave*, published in 1845, represents the height of African American narrative ability because of its narrative intricacy and his use of complex literary techniques to describe his life.

Like the eighteenth-century narratives, these texts included a preface that introduced the life story and authenticated the experiences of the author. Instead of describing conversion or salvation, they were a part of the discourse within the abolitionist movement, which sought to represent the horrors of the slave experience. As an integral component to the representation of slavery, these narratives often included a statement of birth and place, a description of the moment at which the author acquires literacy and the story of their individual flight to freedom.

Authors maintained the traditional conventions of this narrative genre, such as beginning with the statement, "I was born," and chronicling the life of the individual through his or her **enslavement**. Because of the usefulness of these narratives to **abolitionism**, the inaugural moment, "I was born," had a different resonance than the earlier narratives. This statement initiated the development of the individual's subjectivity and located them within the human community. In doing so, the subject acknowledged his or her own validity and authenticity as a human being who, in fact, was born in a specific location. It also contradicts the socio-political assertion that African American slaves were neither human nor worthy of the respect afforded to the citizenry.

As the former slave described his or her life, there was a particular emphasis placed on the acquisition of literacy. Literacy further validated the humanity of writers. Despite the editorial supplements, these nineteenth-century narratives emphasized that the authors had written their narratives by themselves. Many of the titles end with the declaration that the narrative had been written by himself or herself. Literacy provided the means by which many of these authors found both literal and metaphoric freedom.

During the Depression, President Franklin D. Roosevelt authorized the development of the Works Progress Administration, which financially supported artists and writers. With the support of these federal funds, a large group of writers traversed the South to interview and transcribe interviews conducted with former slaves. These interviews were published in a variety of volumes. Stories range from several pages to short paragraphs. *See also* Baquaqua, Mahommah Gardo; Wheatley, Phillis.

Further Readings: Foster, Frances Smith. *Witnessing Slavery: The Development of Ante-bellum Slave Narratives.* Madison: University of Wisconsin Press, 1994; Pierce, Yolanda. *Hell without Fires: Slavery, Christianity and the Antebellum Spiritual Narrative.* Gainesville: University Press of Florida, 2005; Sekora, John, and Turner, Darwin T. *The Art of the Slave Narrative: Original Essays in Criticism and Theory.* Macomb: Western Illinois University, 1982; Stepto, Robert. *From Behind the Veil: A Study of Afro-American Narrative.* Urbana: University of Illinois Press, 1991.

Tara Bynum

"Slavers Throwing Overboard the Dead and Dying—Typhon Coming On" (1840)

This painting, a masterpiece by English artist J.M.W. Turner (1775–1851), is the most direct, visceral, and ultimately influential of all contemporary paintings of the Middle Passage. First exhibited at the Royal Academy, **London**, in 1840, it may have arisen in Turner's mind as a subject as early as 1833 when the abolition of slavery in the colonies was reconsidered by the British Parliament. Although slavery had been banned in Great Britain in 1807, its more widespread abolition in British territory did not come into effect until 1838. At this time, the issue of slavery was being widely discussed in the London press, in particular through the publication of a second edition of Thomas Clarkson's *History of the Abolition of the Slave Trade* (1839) and of Thomas Fowell Buxton's *The African Slave Trade* (2nd ed., 1839). Five extracts from Clarkson's book were published in *The Times* in the summer and autumn of 1839, and, furthermore, a biography of **William Wilberforce** appeared in the same year. In the meantime, Buxton founded the Society for the Extinction of the Slave Trade, under the Presidency of Prince Albert. Its first conference was held in London at the time of the showing of the Royal Academy exhibition.

Other literary work that Turner knew, such as Thomas Gisborne's *Walks in the Forest* (1794), bitterly attacked the cruelties of slavery, so there were a number of motives that drove the artist to choose the subject. One was Turner's lifelong fascination for subjects that reflected contemporary issues; another was his understanding of the sea in all its moods and colors; a third was his passionate concern for history and humanity, and his characteristic expression of landscape, seascape, and natural forces as emblems of human activity, achievement, and suffering. Turner was in his mid-sixties when he painted "Slavers," all too aware of the brevity of life, and had established a powerful voice as an artist. He knew well that whatever he exhibited would be sure to touch a large audience and would be noticed and widely discussed. In taking the horrors of the Middle Passage as his subject, it is clear that the artist was registering a howl of protest against slavery and all its machineries, which would be seen by many and, by some, understood.

The purpose of the painting was largely missed or mocked at its first exhibition. W. M. Thackeray perhaps came closest to an understanding of it when he wrote in *Fraser's Magazine* (June 1840) that it was "the most tremendous piece of colour that was ever seen.... Ye Gods, what a Middle Passage." But coming as it did in 1844 into the ownership of John Ruskin (1819–1900), "Slavers" rapidly became one of the best-known, though least-seen, modern paintings of its time. It has been noted that for many years Ruskin's paragraphs in *Modern Painters*, volume 1, part 2, section 5 (1843) became a surrogate for the painting (McCoubrey, 1998, pp. 319–353):

> Purple and blue, the lurid shadows of the hollow breakers are cast upon the mist of night, which gathers cold and low, advancing like the shadows of death upon the guilty* ship as it labours amidst the lightning of the sea, its thin masts written upon the sky in lines of blood, girded in condemnation in that fearful hue which signs the sky with horror, and mixes its flaming flood with the sunlight, and, cast far along the desolate heave of the sepulchral waves, incarnadines the multitudinous seas. (Ruskin, 1843, chapter 3, paragraphs 39 and 40)

Ruskin reduces the main subject of the painting to a footnote: "*She is a slaver, throwing her slaves overboard. The near sea is encumbered with corpses." Such detachment is not shared by Turner, and by focusing his attention on the color, the ship, and the seascape, Ruskin distorts Turner's purpose. It has further been noted that the hands raised from the water by the dying slaves derive from the figure of the freed slave appearing on the medal commemorating the 1836 abolition of slavery in the British colonies. The floating **chains** may suggest that in death the slaves have found a new freedom and that the evidence of evil will not go away. Turner accompanied the painting, as was his frequent practice, with lines of his own inscrutable poetry, which ended "Hope, Hope, fallacious Hope!/Where is thy market now?"

Sold by Ruskin in 1872, the painting came immediately to the United States and entered the collections first of the New York lawyer John Taylor Johnson and subsequently in 1876 of the abolitionist Alice Hooper of Boston. Hooper exhibited the work in New York and Boston, where it and Ruskin's description helped to give a new momentum to the antislavery campaign. "Slavers" was purchased in 1899 from its final private owner by the Boston Museum of Fine Arts, where it has remained. *See also* Abolition of the Slave Trade, Great Britain; Drownings.

Further Readings: McCoubrey, John. "Turner's 'Slave Ship': Abolition, Ruskin, and Reception." *Word & Image* 14, 4 (1998): 319–53; Ruskin, John. *Modern Painters*. vol. 1. New York: Knopf, 1987 (1843).

James Hamilton

Slavery in Africa

Throughout its history, slavery has been an integral part of African life affecting internal economics, politics, agriculture, and society. Slavery existed in African societies in an assortment of varieties long before the Atlantic slave trade. Indigenous African slavery, including clientage, pawnship, serfdom, debt bondage, apprenticeship, and household slavery, existed as part of Africa's subsistence economy and can be seen as vital to the African agricultural system. In Africa, a number of paths could lead a freeborn person into dependency for which the word "slavery" is commonly used; however, slavery was decidedly different within Africa than the commercial slavery introduced from outside of Africa.

It is reasonable to conclude that African communities sold slaves for export, but they sold slaves at levels that would not damage their own communities. In the early period of the slave trade, Europeans captured slaves by sailing along the coast and capturing whoever appeared. By the eighteenth century, however, European slavers procured slaves from established **African rulers** or from African **slave merchants** who were permitted to engage in the slave trade by royal **license**. African rulers needed to make a decision: were they to build their own local labor force or trade away some of that labor force for goods they could not produce as efficiently or at all? Europeans offered cloth, metal, and hardware that Africans could produce, but Europeans could offer these goods more cheaply, or they offered **firearms** that Africans could not produce. Africans viewed firearms as emblems of power that were quite useful in procuring more slaves as well as useful in agricultural productivity by keeping down wild animals.

During the course of the slave trade, many African rulers decided to strike a bargain with European traders who would bring the goods they desired. In **Benin**, the kings decided in 1516 to stop the uncontrolled export of slaves. If significant portions of the population became enslaved and sold to the European slavers, then the state of Benin should benefit. When attempting to control the slave trade within **Dahomey**, King **Agaja Trudo**, actually diminished the trade. When his successor came to power in 1740, however, the only commodity that Europeans would accept in exchange for guns and **gunpowder** was slaves, and the Dahomey kings desperately needed to acquire weapons for warfare.

Slavery existed in Africa in many different forms, but most slaves originated from outside the society that sold them. Slavery exists based on the use of force, and to acquire a slave or to maintain a slave requires coercion. But other forms of slavery can exist in situations in which coercion is not used. Those Africans sold into slavery may be termed "unfortunates" or misfits. They may have offended a person in a position of power, committed an antisocial act causing them to be shunned by their extended family, or had no kin or friend to prevent their kidnapping and sale. People sold as slaves may include the mentally deficient, someone who had been convicted of a crime or witchcraft, or they may be enslaved as payment of a debt. The other people who were sold into bondage were obtained by force, usually raiding or warfare. In the early stages of the European slave trade the captors normally kept their slaves. On occasion, captives could be executed if they were

" Remember them in bonds."

Africa slaves awaited the trans-Atlantic crossing in dungeons on the coast. Courtesy of Anti-Slavery International.

criminals or war captives. They could also be sacrificed or sold to other Africans and, as the trade progressed, they could be sold to Europeans.

Africans and African rulers believed that the most important resource they could possess was the productive power of people. Agricultural production diminishes, the mining of minerals decreases, and goods cannot be manufactured without the human labor to accomplish those tasks. Feudal lords in Western Europe needed a system of peonage to bind labor to their estates. Similarly, kings of the new centralizing states in Africa desired a committed, reliable workforce to take advantage of the rising demand for gold, salt, copper, and ivory. In Africa, however, this relationship between kings and bound labor was labeled slavery. Organized on the village system, traditional African societies are based on close kinship ties that were engaged in subsistence agriculture. This system of social organization reached its limits by the sixteenth century. Kinspeople moved from agricultural production into mining, the military, and politics, creating a need for people to fill the void. Strong kings emerged unifying several smaller kingdoms into one and forcing other kings to pay tribute. These new kings became strong enough to add more people to their own kinship group through peonage, clientage, tributaries, and slavery.

Slaves who were added to another social group suffered the stigma of **enslavement** for the remainder of their lives; however, in time, they could become essential members allowing them to attain positions of authority and responsibility. Although a hardship, the social status of a slave could be ameliorated. As a unit of social organization, Africans became part of a social group. A group could be based on membership in a village, extended family, or lineage. Each member of the group contributed to the strength and success of the group through their own social and biological reproduction. Because a group could face extinction, a slave who desired assimilation into a group could be readily accepted, and in return for the slave's productive capacity, the group would offer the slave protection. As part of a social group, slaves could marry, obtain property, and become trusted traders, soldiers, or court officials.

The most important element of indigenous African slavery is that slaves were not a commodity or article of commerce, but rather slaves were used to expand the social group more quickly than through natural kinship ties. Indigenous African slavery was a rapid response to the need for an expanding population. As long-distance trade expanded, African kings attempted to accumulate enough goods to attract foreign traders. Without enough gold, salt, or other trade goods, trading slaves for the desired goods became a viable alternative. Slaves were valued much lower than the preferred goods. It was a result of this process that human beings were assigned an economic value, with their value compared to that of a horse, a gun, or a bundle of produce. Once assigned an economic value, people could be freely traded at the whim of the king and ruling elites. Foreign powers and other kings assessed the might of African kings by the amount of slaves the kingdom possessed and the once-unattainable items, horses from the Sudan and muskets from Guinea, that were well within the reach of the king.

Without question, an indigenous African slavery system existed before Europeans made contact in the fifteenth century. Because indigenous

African slavery was rapidly absorbed by the trans-Atlantic slave system, and earlier Arabic writings describe the trans-Saharan trading system including that of slaves, it is quite possible to skip over the indigenous African trading system and conclude that African slavery is simply part of the trans-Saharan and trans-Atlantic systems.

The trans-Atlantic slave-trading system quickly absorbed the fate of powerful states like Oyo and Dahomey in the Gulf of Guinea. The history of Oyo and Dahomey became part of the history of the trans-Atlantic slave-trading system. These two African states built their wealth and power from slavery, rising into strong states. In the same West African area, the **Asante**, one of the minor allies of the Akwamu, rose to a powerful centralized state when the slave trade was prevalent.

Oyo emerged in the last half of the seventeenth century as a key African state in the interior of the Bight of Benin. Among the Oyo, slavery existed in the eighteenth century. Oyo kings and leading chiefs and many of Oyo's aristocrats drew the main portion of their wealth from slavery; however, in addition to the sale of slaves, the Oyo added large numbers of slaves to their households as administrators and to serve military and economic functions. Working for the state, slaves served as common soldiers and horse handlers and trainers. Oyo's strength as an empire rested on its superb cavalry and the expertise of its horse handlers. The Oyo bureaucracy employed slaves in various capacities. Slaves maintained **tax** rolls, collected caravan tolls, and could be found governing provincial towns. The varied positions that slaves could occupy suggests that not all slaves were treated the same. Palace slaves served the empire holding important positions in the kingdom and received privileges for their work. Religious slaves served as priests and priestesses and could be severely punished for violating any of the religious taboos, but they also enjoyed many privileges. Although not identical, similar elements can be used to describe the states that emerged along the Gulf of Guinea.

The centralized states of Oyo, Dahomey, and the Asante, among others, profited from the Atlantic slave trade. Asante became a major state on the west coast of Africa in c. 1701. Asante grew and strengthened itself to the point at which it became the largest exporter of slaves in the eighteenth and nineteenth centuries. Even though the Asante traded large amounts of slaves, they also exported gold because they controlled much of the Akan gold fields. The Asante rulers retained some of the war captives for gold mining and, at other points, had to import slaves to gather gold.

Traveling inland away from the aforementioned coastal states to another centralized state, the institution of slavery was part of life in Cameroon. Cameroon never came under the total influence of the **trans-Saharan slave trade** and it did not feel the influence of the trans-Atlantic trade until the eighteenth century. The forms of servitude (clientage, pawnship, serfdom, debt bondage, apprenticeship, and household slavery) fit into the definition of slavery, and those forms of servitude predate the trans-Atlantic slave trade. It is the presence of that servitude, however, that provided the fertile conditions the allowed the fermentation and development of European-type slavery on the Cameroon grasslands. Before the arrival of

European influences, the culture and politics of the centralized states of Africa produced the necessary conditions to transform indigenous African slavery into European, trans-Atlantic slavery.

Slavery at the coast contrasted with inland slavery. The Hausa city-states to the north of Yoruba and west of Lake Chad participated in the local indigenous slave trade. The Hausa city-states appeared in the twelfth century and developed skills in cloth dying and leather work. The so-called Moroccan leather sold to European traders to the north was manufactured in Hausa. By the sixteenth century, Zazzau, the southernmost Hausa city-state, became a major source of slaves after it raided the Kwararafa region just north of the Benue River. The Hausa city-states used many of the slaves captured in Kwararafa and exported others to Borno, which is around Lake Chad; some captives were traded in North Africa for horses, harnesses, and guns. Participation in the indigenous African slave trade by the Hausa city-states can be traced to 891 C.E., when al-Ya kubi recorded the movement of slaves. In the 1050s there were also indications of both the import and export of slaves out of Kano. The Kwararafa were compelled to send slaves as tribute payments to Yaji (c. 1349–1385) and his son. During one war, Galadima Dawuda sent Kano 1,000 slaves every two months. In return, Kano sent horses and clothing. At the end of the military campaign, Dawuda had accumulated 21,000 slaves in what some historians believe was an organized slaving expedition in the 1440s.

Slavery within Africa cannot be understood without connecting internal slavery with external slavery. European buyers captured those Africans who came out to the coast to meet the European ships. This practice by European slavers ended quickly, and European slavers soon depended on African slave agents for the procurement of slaves. African merchants willingly participated in bringing slaves from the interior and the interior kingdoms supported these African merchants and agents. Europeans learned to deal with the **regulations** established by states to purchase slaves. For example, the kingdom of Whydah on the **Slave Coast** required slave traders to pay a **tax** for the right to trade, and the state required Europeans to deal directly with a given set of African slave brokers who also required a payment of a sales commission. These common practices existed along the west coast of Africa.

In West African societies, royalty, nobility, warriors, peasants, servants, and slaves attended the royal court. By the time of the arrival of Europeans in the fifteenth century, West African society had established varying classes within their prevalent use of slaves. Individuals reached the state of slavery because they were pawned for debt, captured during war, or purchased. As the external demand for slaves increased, the frequency of slave procurement and the internal use of slaves also increased, becoming a rudimentary aspect in African daily life. Depending on whether captives were destined for sale outside of Africa or to be sold internally, slavery in Africa varied by region and by circumstance. During the 400 years of the Atlantic slave trade, more than 11 million slaves disembarked from the West coast of Africa destined for the Americas. This rapid depopulation altered traditional hierarchical relationships with well-defined classes and groups. Although

quite different than external trans-Atlantic slavery, increased internal indigenous African slavery also altered African society. *See also* Decentralized Societies; Gender and Slave Exports; Islam and Muslims; Trade Commodities;
Violence; Wars, African.

Further Readings: Agiri, Babatunde. "Slavery in Yoruba Society in the 19th Century." In Paul E. Lovejoy, ed. *The Ideology of Slavery in Africa*. Beverly Hills: Sage Publications, 1981; Fage, J. D., and Tordoff, William. *A History of Africa*. 4th ed. New York:
Routledge, 2002; Fomin, E.S.D. *A Comparative Study of Societal Influences on Indigenous Slavery in Two Types of Societies in Africa*. Lewiston: The Edwin Mellen Press,
2002; Henderson, Lawrence W. *Angola: Five Centuries of Conflict*. Ithaca: Cornell University Press, 1979; Jewsiewicki, Bogumil, and Mumbanza mwa Bawele. "The Social Context of Slavery in Equatorial Africa during the 19th and 20th Centuries." In Paul E.
Lovejoy, ed. *The Ideology of Slavery in Africa*. Beverly Hills: Sage Publications, 1981;
Klein, A. N. "The Two Asantes: Competing Interpretations of Slavery in Akan-Asante Culture and Society." In Paul E. Lovejoy, ed. *The Ideology of Slavery in Africa*. Beverly Hills:
Sage Publications, 1981; Klein, Herbert S. *The Atlantic Slave Trade*. New York: Cam-
bridge University Press, 1999; Laya, D. "The Hausa States." In B. A. Ogot, ed. *UNESCO-
General History of Africa: Africa from the Sixteenth to the Eighteenth Century*. vol. 5.
Berkeley: University of California Press, 1992; Shillington, Kevin. *History of Africa*. 2nd
ed. New York: Palgrave Macmillan, 2005.

Michael Bonislawski

Smuggling

The period after 1807 ushered in a new epoch in the history of the slave
trade and smuggling. This period, which is officially known as the abolitionist period, was characterized by the desire of the British government to end
the slave trade. Smuggling of slaves intensified because it was no longer
legal for slaves to be bought and sold. With the introduction of the British
West **African Squadron** in West African coastal waters and frequent
attacks and freeing of slaves, new techniques of acquiring and transporting
slaves had to be developed.

Different parts of West Africa were affected in different ways by British
attempts to halt the slave trade. For instance, when the naval blockage
became effective in **Bonny**, a part of the **Slave Coast** located in Niger
Delta region of present-day Nigeria, the Portuguese and Spanish slavers
diverted their trading activities to the Brass River, another part of the Niger
Delta region. For more than two centuries, the Brass River had been a Portuguese stronghold and was closed to British commercial influence. It was
therefore easy for slave smugglers to transport slaves to the Americas
through Brass. Geography also played a significant role in making Brass a
safe haven for the smuggling of slaves because it is in the deep recesses of
the Niger valley and approached by creeks with no outlet in the Atlantic.
The organization of the underground traffic was a closely guarded secret
never fully probed by the **British Navy** and merchants. The man in charge
of the network that linked the mainland trade with the slavers at sea and
who was himself resident at Brass was Don Pablo Frexas. With the Bonny
and the chiefs of Brass, he was a leading architect of the smuggling ring
and worked in alliance with Pareira at Princes Islands. The **oral history** of

Bonny and Brass people is replete with references to the methods that their forefathers used in smuggling slaves and negotiating the British Naval Squadron. *See also* Abolition of the Slave Trade, Great Britain.

Further Readings: Dike, Onwuka. *Trade and Politics in the Niger Delta, 1830–1885*. Oxford: Clarendon Press, 1956; Jones, G. I. *The Trading States of the Oil Rivers: A Study of Political Development in Eastern Nigeria*. London: Oxford University Press, 1963; Priestley, Margaret. *West African Trade and Coast Society*. London: Oxford University Press, 1969.

Saheed Aderinto

Spanish Caribbean

The word Caribbean derives from different forms of the concept of *canib/carib/caniba–caníbal*, first written down in the diary of Christobal Colón (Christopher Columbus), and spread by Bartolomé de Las Casas and others. The geographic notion of the Caribbean from the seventeenth century until the 1960s meant the Caribbean sea and some parts of the Guayanas. With the new wave of **historiography** in the 1930s, 1940s, and after the Cuban revolution, the concept acquired two meanings: first, all islands and groups of islands (archipelagos of the Greater and Lesser Antilles, Bahamas, and coastal islands of South and Central America); and, second, the islands and coastal landscapes from St. Augustine to Cayenne. In fact, the Spanish Empire never controlled all these Caribbean regions. Until 1600, however, great parts and, following the Treaty of Tordesillas in 1494, all of the Atlantic coasts of the Americas minus the parts shared with Portugal were under Spanish **monopoly**.

If we define slavery simply as "work forced by violence," then we might say that different concepts and realities of slavery and the slave trade were in force at the time of the colonial intrusion of Europeans into the Caribbean, including different forms of slave exchange, raids, and trade. Slavery in the Spanish Caribbean took three major forms. First, under the Indian concept of slavery, outcasts or war prisoners were enslaved. The Spaniards transformed this type of slavery into urban house-slavery, primarily for **women** (who could not by law be sold). Second, the *encomienda* was a distribution of the vanquished natives among the Spanish soldiers. This type of personal service (initially as carriers) was transformed into the main source of unfree labor of the *conquista*, renamed *repartimiento* after 1512 (a legal form with an old medieval tradition), which by law did not entail slavery, but rather "civilizing by labor." The third concept, familiar to Columbus himself, was a type of "modern" slavery that was similar to slavery of the Portuguese African slaves in **São Tomé** or São Jorge da Mina (Africa).

From 1493 until 1550, in other territories (like Eastern Nueva Andalucia, Cumaná, and other frontier territories) until c. 1650 and in peripheries until the nineteenth century, the Caribbean was a region of slave raids and slave contraband. Columbus started with this kind of raiding, kidnapping Taínos from the Bahamas (*lucayos*) and from **Hispaniola** and sending them to Spain to be sold at the slave markets of Al-Andalus and Algarves (Lisboa, **Seville**, Lagos, Córdoba, and Granada) and Cataluña (Valencia, Barcelona). In Spain, a well-defined and socially accepted slavery existed that was governed by the legal code of the *Siete Partidas*. The Catholic Monarchs, Isabella of Castile and Fernando of Aragón, stopped Columbus from carrying out this deal and forbade the legal **enslavement** of Indians—with the exceptions of "man-eating" *Caribs* and prisoners of the *guerra justa* (just war) after 1512. Indians were vassals and had to pay tribute. Despite this effort, descriptions of the first cities and mini-districts founded by the Spanish in the Caribbean are full of slaves and indigenous war captives. When the catastrophic **mortality** of the indigenous began, *baquianos*, a type of slaver, and the institution of raiding supplied the Spanish-dominated islands with slaves from the Lucayas (Bahamas), La Florida, the Lesser Antilles, the coast of Mexico, Honduras, Nicaragua, and the *Tierra Firme* (Panamá to the Guayanas). In turn, many Indian peoples, like the so-called Caribs of the Guyanas and the Lesser Antilles, developed—under pressure and in response to the demands of European settlers and missionaries—their own forms of slavery and slave trade (*poitos*), as did other native peoples of the greater Caribbean (Kuna, Wajúu, Misquito, Comanche, Seminoles, and others).

The first black slaves arrived in the Caribbean from Europe as servants and slaves of the Spaniards. Nicolás de Obando, the governor of Santo Domingo after Christopher Columbus, first refused *negros ladinos* but later experimented with black slaves in mining. After the genocide and demographic catastrophe of the native population of the Greater Antilles, larger groups of enslaved men and women from Guiné, **São Tomé**, the **Senegal** region, and other parts of Africa were brought to Santo Domingo after 1518. In two memoranda (1516 and 1518) about the productivity of "negro" labor under Caribbean conditions, and the impact of forced labor on the native population, Bartolomé de las Casas initially justified the importations of Africans, although he later repented this decision.

The Caribbean, from 1493 to 1886 (including the coastal slaveries of the U.S. South and Florida), formed a core of Atlantic slavery and the slave trade. The first general stage stretched from 1440 to 1600. The first Iberian center of African and Indian slavery on the American side of the Atlantic was the island of Hispaniola (Santo Domingo). The second general stage reached from c. 1600 until c. 1790 and began with the privateering and founding of new centers of slavery and the slave trade in the **British Caribbean (Jamaica** and Barbados), the **French Caribbean (Saint Domingue**, Martinique, and Guadeloupe), and Dutch Suriname (also **Curaçao**). In the Spanish Caribbean, a **plantation** complex of cocoa production was rising with mass slavery first on different parts of *Tierra Firme* (Venezuela) and later with rice and indigo in Louisiana and Florida. About 40 to 45 percent of the 10 to 12 million African slaves who arrived in America alive were sold to the Caribbean, most of them to Jamaica and Saint Domingue or Curaçao. From these islands, English, French, and Dutch **smugglers** and privateers sold slaves to the Spanish Main, **Cuba**, or Puerto Rico. Until 1820, the North American colonies, like Louisiana, the Floridas, and the **New England** states, were effectively peripheries of the Caribbean centers of slavery, supplying wood, rice, tobacco, fish (*bacalao*), and other **foods** and accumulations by privateering and slave contraband. Urban centers of slavery and the slave trade in the Spanish Caribbean included **Havana**, **Cartagena** de Indias, Veracruz, and Nueva Orleans.

An overlapping third stage of expanding slavery begins with the **Haitian Revolution** (1791–1804). Slaves were brought to the Americas, either by the official slave trade (until 1789–1804 in the Spanish empire organized by *asientos*) or in slave contraband, to perform labor. Working in the fields in crop production, they could be readily discerned as bound residents of the plantations. Moreover, after 100 to 300 years of African enslavement in the main American **sugar**, cacao, and rice-producing regions, slavery was mostly by definition a question of race because of this long-standing tradition. In most of the plantation zones until the end of slavery, the class of fieldworkers was overwhelmingly black. Therefore, this work was deemed "black." In the U.S. South and the Caribbean in the nineteenth century, free members of the population of color faced the risk of being identified as "black" and attributed the status of a slave.

The geographic center of the third stage was Cuba (and Puerto Rico), specifically Western Cuba. Cuban slavers and merchants organized a **free trade** in slaves until 1820. After 1820, Spanish-English treaties attempted the abolition of the slave trade. Cubans organized, together with British, American, and other smugglers from different lands, a well-functioning contraband slave trade (like Ramón Ferrer, the captain of **the *Amistad***). The island of Cuba under Spanish colonial rule in the nineteenth century is one of the three great examples of modernization in slavery (together with Brazil and the Southern United States). In the first half of the nineteenth century, Western Cuba's large plantations, sugar, and mass slavery shaped the Western world's most efficient, compact, and admired agriculture. Yet, in Cuban rural slavery, analyzed in terms of Marxist structuralism by Moreno Fraginals and put into literature by Anselmo Suárez y Romero (and others), the portion of slaves in one census alone (that of 1846) reached more than 50 percent of the whole population of the island.

Communities of Caribbean slaves rapidly shaped new identities and cultures, like the Puerto Rican and Santo Domingo popular cultures in the Spanish Caribbean and the Congo culture in Cuba. Caribbean slavery came to an end with the process of emancipation in Puerto Rico (1868–1873) and in Cuba (1868–1886). In Cuba, this process and the first years of postemancipation were accompanied by three wars (1868–1878, 1879–1880, and 1895–1898) and a reconstruction period under Spanish rule (1878–1886). *See also* Abolition of the Slave Trade, Spain.

Further Readings: Casas, Bartolomé de las. *History of the Indies*, ed. Andrée Collard. New York: Harper and Row, 1971; Chaplin, Joyce E. *An Anxious Pursuit: Agricultural Innovation & Modernity in the Lower South, 1730–1815*. Chapel Hill: Institute of Early American History and Culture, University of North Carolina Press, 1993; Dorsey, Joseph C. *Slave Traffic in the Age of Abolition: Puerto Rico, West Africa, and the Non-Hispanic Caribbean, 1815–1859*. Gainesville: University Press of Florida, 2003; Dunn, Oliver, and Kelley, Jr., James E. *The Diario of Christopher Columbus's First Voyage to America, 1492–1493*. Norman: University of Oklahoma Press, 1989; Ferry, Robert. "Trading Cacao: A View from Veracruz, 1629–1645." [Online, February 8, 2006]. Nuevo Mundo Web site: http://nuevomundo.revues.org/document1430.html; Fuson, Robert H. *The Log of Christopher Columbus*. Camden: International Marine Publishing, 1987; Granberry, Julian, and Vescelius, Gary S. *Languages of the Pre-Columbian Antilles*. Tuscaloosa: University of Alabama Press, 2004; Hall, Gwendolyn Midlo. *Slavery and African*

Ethnicities in the Americas: Restoring the Links. Chapel Hill: University of North Carolina Press, 2005; Keegan, William F. "Columbus Was a Cannibal: Myth and the First Encounters." In Herbert S. Klein, ed. *African Slavery in Latin America and the Caribbean.* New York: Oxford University Press, 1986; Knight, Franklin W. "The American Revolution and the Caribbean." In Ira Berlin and Ronald Hoffman, eds. *Slavery and Freedom in the Age of American Revolution,* S. 237–261. Urbana: University of Illinois Press, 1986; Olsen, Margaret M. *Slavery and Salvation in Colonial Cartagena de Indias.* Gainesville: University Press of Florida, 2004; Schwartz, Stuart B., ed. *Tropical Babylons: Sugar and the Making of the Atlantic World, 1450–1680.* Chapel Hill: University of North Carolina Press, 2004; Scott, Rebecca J., and Zeuske, Michael. "Property in Writing, Property on the Ground: Pigs, Horses, Land, and Citizenship in the Aftermath of Slavery, Cuba, 1880–1909." *Comparative Studies in Society and History. An International Quarterly* 44, 4 (October 2002): S. 669–699.

Michael Max P. Zeuske

Storms

The trans-Atlantic voyage is one of the numerous attempts made by human beings to control or manipulate nature to their advantage. The Portuguese explorations of the fifteenth century were landmarks in this respect. The construction of ships that were strong enough to navigate the Atlantic Ocean opened a new era in Afro-European relations. As the world moved from the medieval to modern and as the slave trade and maritime trade in general expanded globally, ships that are capable of withstanding dangerous weather were constructed.

The breakthrough in ship-building technology did not represent a total solution to the danger posed by dangerous weather such as storms. Basic characteristics of Atlantic storms included heavy wind and thunderous lightening. Dangerous storms were an eventuality that was highly dreaded by all sailors. The effect of storms was unquantifiable. The location of the slave ship determined the degree of damage that a storm caused. A vessel hit by a storm while loading slaves along the coast recorded limited loss compared with the one hit in the middle of the Atlantic voyage. This is because the **crew** and slaves could take refuge along the coast and inland. Only few slaves and crew were capable of surviving a **shipwreck**, many of which were caused by storms during the Middle Passage.

The history of trans-Atlantic voyages is replete with the havoc caused by storms. In 1738, the Dutch vessel *Leuden* was hit by a heavy storm around the Suriname Coast. The crew closed the hatches of the slave decks to avoid chaos and then escaped with fourteen slaves who had been helping them while 702 slaves were left to **drown**.

Off **Mozambique**, a Portuguese captain reported,

Suddenly, the weather closes in, and the sea rise so high and forcefully that the ships obey the waves without course or control, at the mercy of the winds.... The clanking of the irons, the moans, the weeping, the cries, the waves, breaking over the side of the ship and then the other, the shouting of the sailors, the whistling of the winds and the continuous roar of the waves." (Thomas, 1997, p. 426)

See also Accidents and Explosions.

Further Readings: Engerman, Stanley, and Genovese, Eugene, eds. *Race and Slavery in the Western Hemisphere: Quantitative Studies.* Princeton, NJ: Princeton University Press, 1975; Palmie Stephan, ed. *Slave Cultures and the Cultures of Slavery.* Knoxville: University of Tennessee Press, 1995; Thomas, Hugh. *The Slave Trade: The Story of the Atlantic Slave Trade, 1440–1870.* New York: Simon & Schuster, 1997.

Saheed Aderinto

Sugar

The trans-Atlantic trade in enslaved Africans was first sanctioned by the Portuguese and the Spanish Imperial crowns. Madeira became a prosperous sugar colony by the 1490s and was dependent on the labor of enslaved Africans. Madeira was the first colony dedicated to a sugar monoculture based on black slave labor and became the prototype for later mercantilist ideals of empire. Having lived for more than ten years in Madeira, Columbus saw the benefit of taking sugar plants from the Canary Islands when he voyaged to the "Indies." Following the shift from Madeira to take advantage of **São Tomé's** fertile and well-watered soil, the Atlantic island and its neighbor Príncipe became extremely successful in sugar production and imported, in the first half of the sixteenth century, more enslaved Africans than did the Americas, Europe, or other Atlantic islands. With São Tomé's good fortune, it became evident that the keys to the imperial power and wealth could be sugar and slaves.

The trade was stimulated by the development of the sugar industry in **Cuba**, **Hispaniola**, and Puerto Rico. The "sugar complex" has been described as being based on forced labor, a monoculture for export to distant markets, and inputs of large capital. Around the 1530s, sugar production for export to Europe first began in northeast **Brazil**. Contributing factors in this regard were that northeast Brazil was the region of the Americas closest to African sources of enslaved labor and to European markets for the export of sugar. By the end of the sixteenth century, Brazil had become the Portuguese holdings of a formidable sugar **plantation** economy with enslaved Africans providing the labor.

For slavers in **Nantes** in France, the refining of sugar proved to be a lucrative business. Nantes slavers imported raw sugar from the Caribbean and refined it for export. The history of slavery was tied up with the history of sugar during the first phase of European imperialism.

Up to the nineteenth century, sugar was a luxury item and used largely for medicinal purposes. The growth of the market for sugar relied on affluent consumers with a liking for sweet

Cane cutters harvesting sugar. Courtesy of Anti-Slavery International.

drinks. Sugar made various hard liquors possible and accessible to Europeans. European population declined in the second half of the fourteenth century and was accompanied by a fall in the **price** of wheat and other **foods**. Surplus money became available and sugar was increasingly consumed and grew in importance in the international trade and finance network. Slave labor, therefore, was used for this trade in sugar. It has been argued that the trade in sugar is a principal reason Europeans considered it necessary and profitable to supply enslaved Africans to the New World. *See also* Rum and Cachaça; Saint Domingue.

Further Readings: Davis, David Brion. *Slavery and Human Progress*. Oxford: Oxford University Press, 1984; Eltis, David, Lewis, Frank, D., and Sokoloff, Kenneth, L., eds. *Slavery in the Development of the Americas*. New York: Cambridge University Press, 2004.

Sandra Ingrid Gift

Suicide

Before and during the Middle Passage, captured slaves committed suicide frequently enough to cause an awful problem for their captors. Captured slaves could attempt to commit suicide repeatedly until they were successful or could resort to other violent means of resistance, such as self-mutilation or the assassination of crewmembers and land-based merchants. **Slave traders** feared such events so seriously that some contemporary writers, such as the Frenchman Jacques Savary, urged **captains** to depart rapidly after loading their ships. Savary justified his recommendation based on his perception of the character of the Africans and their love for their land.

And, indeed, Savary was right. One example to back his opinion took place in 1812, when Captain Felipe Nery wrote that while the ship under his command was entering the River Zaire in West Central Africa, three of the slaves he was carrying threw themselves overboard after being whipped. Although the very fact of being enslaved was perhaps the main reason behind the decision of taking their own lives, various other causes could precipitate the events. Several reports attest to the general fear among the enslaved that their white captors would devour their flesh or suck their blood. These fears led many of them to commit suicide. A remarkable case from 1737 illustrates the strength of these assumptions. Just after docking on the island of St. Christopher, more than 100 of the African slaves on board the *Prince of Orange* jumped into the sea in a collective suicide attempt. A joke made by a local slave had inspired their sudden determination to end their lives: the local slave stated that the newly arrived slaves' eyes would be put out and eaten by their white masters. This idle jest led to the loss of thirty-three human lives. Beliefs in "white cannibalism" and "white vampirism" remained alive throughout the entire history of the Atlantic slave trade.

The punishments given to those who attempted to commit suicide varied from cutting their arms and legs to filling their mouths with boiling lead. But the different measures taken by slave traders to prevent suicides never succeeded in bringing it to an end.

Once the slave ships were at sea, and despite the opinion of Savary and others, the situation did not seem to improve. Rather, the slavers' problems increased because of the slaves' isolation and the poor living conditions onboard ships. Some slave ships were packed with slaves in numbers almost unbelievable for the ship's size. Onboard punishments, compulsory **dancing** and **singing**, epidemics and other health problems, and inadequate **food** all made the living conditions almost intolerable for the slaves.

Once in the Americas, the situation continued to be serious enough, particularly in places like **Brazil** and **Cuba**, where slave suicides were a matter of discussion almost at every level. *See also* African Fears of Cannibalism; Torture; Violence.

Further Readings: Law, Robin. *The Slave Coast of West Africa, 1550–1750: The Impact of the Atlantic Slave Trade on an African Society.* Oxford: Clarendon Press, 1991; Peel, J.D.Y. *Religious Encounter and the Making of the Yoruba.* Bloomington: Indiana University Press, 2000; Piersen, William D. "White Cannibals, Black Martyrs: Fear, Depressions, and Religious Faith as Causes of Suicide among New Slaves." *The Journal of Negro History* 62, 2 (April 1977): 147–159; Schwartz, Stuart. *Sugar Plantations in the Formation of Brazilian Society: Bahia 1550–1835.* Cambridge: Cambridge University Press, 1985; Sheridan, Richard B. "The Guinea Surgeons on the Middle Passage: The Provision of Medical Services in the British Slave Trade." *The International Journal of African Historical Studies* 14, 4 (1981): 601–625; Steckel, Richard H., and Jensen, Richard A. "New Evidence on the Causes of Slave and Crew Mortality in the Atlantic Slave Trade." *The Journal of Economic History* 46, 1 (1986): 57–77.

Manuel Barcia

Supply and Demand

Supply and demand for slaves varied from place to place on the African coast. Slaves were supplied from almost the whole length of the western coast of Africa, from **Senegal** in the north to **Angola** in the south. Initially, the bulk of West African slaves came from Guinea, but by 1600, Congo and Angola had become the major slave-producing regions. The Arguin factory on the West African coast lost its position as the major commercial center as the trade expanded southward. The Senegambia (including **Sierra Leone**) area became a slave-producing region yielding an average of 5,000 slaves in the sixteenth century. Later, it spread to Rio de Casamansa, the Rio de Case, Cape St. Anna, the Rio Dos Sestos, the whole coast of **Benin**, and the Bight of Biafra.

Between 1513 and 1516, more than 7,000 slaves were carried annually to Portugal and Spain from the regions of Congo and Angola. By the early seventeenth century, it had risen to 15,000. The Angolan coastline remained a major slave-supplying region for the duration of the slave trade from West Africa. The **Gold Coast** (from Assini to the Volta) and **Loango** supplied 5,000 and 10,000, respectively, each year during the seventeenth century. The increasing demand for slaves on the **plantations** coupled with the competition among European traders to supply this demand account for the figures.

African slaves were obtained in a number of ways. Criminals in the society were sold into slavery by the kings. Sale of slaves was carried out in "commodity" currency, which was just the barter of slaves for goods on a one-to-one ratio. As the trade and **profit** from it increased, African kings were noted to have tried to lure their subjects into crime, and accusations of unverifiable crimes like witchcraft abounded. There were also cases of kidnapping and raids on weaker neighbors. On the Upper Guinea Coast, the Mande-speaking tribes raided the Susu. In Ghana, the Ashante terrorized the Ga. Congo was noted for its slaving agents (*pumbeiros*) roaming interior regions and purchasing slaves from the kings especially in peace times. When slave stocks were low on the coast, traders usually organized their own raids to scourge the interior. The practice of ransoming war captives back or absorbing them into the captor's society died down. It was more profitable to sell them into slavery.

It was at the time of military expansions of most kingdoms that the supply of captives was at its peak. For instance, Benin sold captives to the Portuguese in the late fifteenth century during its military expansion. During the sixteenth century, the Mande subjugated the highlands of Sierra Leone and sold their captives at the coast. Oyo, **Dahomey**, and **Asante** all produced massive numbers of captives from their wars of expansion during the seventeenth and eighteenth centuries. An estimate of the **volume** of slave exports from Africa through the Middle Passage gives at least 15 million. More recent studies proffer that the numbers may have been a bit lower.

Preference for African slaves was first shown in the low-lying areas, but by the early seventeenth century, they were in demand as far as **Potosí** and High Peru. In Congo, demand for slave labor came from two sources. First, Portugal's sparse population was being stretched to meet the administrative requirements of a growing empire. The shortfall in agricultural labor could only be met by outside help. Second, Congo supplied slaves to **São Tomé**. In the following years, they developed **sugar** plantations, which were manned by African slave labor. Slaves from the Niger Delta and Zaire River region were transported mostly to São Tomé. As for the Senegambia region, captives were transported to the plantations of Southern Spain and Portugal.

Demand for slaves from the West Indies especially **Cuba**, **Brazil**, and the Caribbean Islands was high as well. The colonizers required massive imports to work the gold and silver mines on the mainland and the tobacco plantations on the islands. Another reason for their high demand was that Africans had skill and experience in metal-working, mining, and tropical agriculture.

Another factor generating demand was that the slave population could not reproduce itself. **Mortality** involved in the conditions of slavery was so high that demands could not be satisfied. Slaves recorded an average of 17 percent mortality on trips, but plantation owners recorded about 33 percent mortality during adaptation to new climate and conditions of work. Again, according to the economics of the plantation owners, it was easier to import new slaves than to allow the existing ones to raise their own children. In light of this, in the British colony of **Jamaica**, 750,000 of the enslaved were imported from Africa over a period of 200 years. Jamaica, however, had a population of only one-third of a million. One-third of all slaves died within the first year of captivity and few survived beyond ten years. *See also* African Rulers and the Slave Trade; Enslavement and Procurement; Europe, Enslaved Africans in; "Seasoning"; Slavery in Africa.

Further Readings: Curtin, Philip D., *The Atlantic Slave Trade: A Census*. Madison: University of Wisconsin, 1969; Davidson, Basil. *The African Slave Trade*. Rev. ed. Boston: Little, Brown, 1980; McEwan, P.J.M., ed. *Africa from Early Times to 1800*. London: Oxford University Press, 1976.

Oyekemi Olajope Oyelakin

T

Taxes

The payments of **taxes** or levies is a significant aspect of African culture. Indigenous people who traded in places under the control of chiefs and kings were expected to make some form of payment. In **Islamic** societies of Africa, direct taxation was the largest source of revenue to the state. So, when European contact was established, African kings were used to the idea of taxes and levies. Before the trade in human beings, the early explorers of the fifteenth century narrated how they were made to pay taxes and levies before trade relations were established with Africans along the coast. Payment of such levies was an indication of respect for the territorial integrity of the African coastal waters.

During the period between 1500 and 1800, there is adequate evidence to suggest that Europeans did not contemplate the breach of Africa sovereignty by refusing to pay levies and customs. In the first place, both parties benefited from the trade in human beings. Europeans seemed to be flexible in accepting the terms of trade as dictated by the Africans along the coast. They could not venture into the hinterland and had limited opportunities to influence the levies and customs imposed on them by the African chiefs.

Coastal chiefs traditionally capitalized on the desire of the ship **captains** to set sail as fast as possible because of the unfavorable nature of the African coastal environment. Coastal factors determined **prices** and negotiated the assortment of commodities to be exchanged for slaves. Because the trade along the coast was heavily dependent upon credit—often extended in the form of goods that were taken inland to acquire slaves—numerous payments, ranging from customs fees to anchorage duties, transport services, and outright bribes, were required and had to be added to the sale price for slaves on the account of the European merchants. This payment, sanctioned by tradition, demonstrates the success of local merchant-princes and the strong government in regulating the export business.

In Whydah (**Ouidah**) the king imposed extra taxes on British ships during the War of Spanish Succession. The king set duties when European nations captured each other's ships on his waterways during the war. If the king could impose such conditions on warring Europeans, then he could enforce rules on Afro-European commerce with a greater degree of influence. When John Wortley, of the **Royal Africa Company** attempted to circumvent rules related to taxes and levies in 1682, he was first imprisoned and then expelled. The king's subjects could expect equivalent treatment for similar transgressions. *See also* African Rulers and the Slave Trade; Slave Merchants (Slave Traders).

Further Readings: Eltis, David. *The Rise of African Slavery in the Americas*. Cambridge: Cambridge University Press, 2000; Klein, Herbert. *The Middle Passage: Comparative Studies in the Atlantic Slave Trade*. Princeton, NJ: Princeton University Press, 1978; Solow, Barbara, ed. *Slavery and the Rise of the Atlantic System*. Cambridge: Cambridge University Press, 1991.

Saheed Aderinto

Textiles

Many African groups regularly produced textile products. They planted and harvested crops for use in making textiles and then spun and wove their own blankets, clothing, and other products. Most of the textile items they produced were traded with other African peoples.

When the Africans were introduced to the brilliant colors of the textiles produced in India, England, and Asia, the demand for brightly colored textiles in Africa increased. The textiles produced in Africa were of bland colors and the fabrics were of a thinner consistency than those produced in other countries. To meet the demand for textiles produced in other countries, the Africans began trading slaves for textile products from India, England, and Asia.

Of particular interest to Africa, England, and Indonesia was the cloth produced in India. The textiles produced in India offered a wide variety of patterns such as stripes, checks, and calicos. The muslin fabrics had varying thicknesses, from lighter sheer fabrics to thick, durable weaves. Many of the Indian-produced textiles were dyed in bright, bold colors and some had hand-painted designs.

The East Indies Trading Company purchased large amounts of the Indian-produced textiles, using them as one of the principal goods for trade with Africa, North America, and the Caribbean. Indian textiles with stripes and checks are still commonly referred to as "Guinea cloth" because these cloths were commonly traded with West African areas.

Because the Africans still needed to produce textiles for trade within their own country, the slaves who had experience in spinning and weaving cloth were less likely to be traded than those slaves with other experiences. Female slaves usually worked in spinning the threads, while male slaves typically worked as weavers. It generally took about eight hours of spinning to produce enough thread to keep a weaver busy for one hour, therefore the **women** spinners were considered to be of more value to the textile producers than were the male weavers. These women were either retained for use by the textile producers or were traded for a higher value than other slaves.

African slaves also had a large role in the textile industry in the United States. The slaves made it possible for Southern U.S. farmers to grow large cotton crops and to sell their products to the U.S. textile factories in **New England**, increasing the already lucrative industry of the new slave trade. *See also* Cargoes; Trade Commodities.

Further Readings: "The Middle Passage." Africans in America. PBS Online Web site: http://www.pbs.org/wgbh/aia/part1/1p277.html; "The Middle Passage." University of Michigan Web site: http://www.umich.edu/~ece/student_projects/slavery/middlepassage.html.

Kathryn Vercillo

Torture

For many African captives, torture was a common mode of punishment onboard slave ships crossing the Atlantic Ocean. This form of physical and mental **violence** typically began with the process of **branding** that they endured before boarding their captor's ship. The Portuguese are credited with the early practice of branding (the *carimbo*) in the 1440s, which typically involved the use of a hot silver instrument that left a red mark on the shoulder, breast, or upper arms of enslaved populations. These burned marks generally symbolized proof of paid duties, ownership—through use of the royal coat of arms or the names of companies that purchased captives—and even baptism in which a small cross was burned into an enslaved person's chest.

Upon boarding vessels bound for the Americas, many enslaved were bound by their necks and ankles and quickly transferred to their respective holdings. Males were ushered to the bottom **hold** of the ship, being deprived of both light and fresh air while **women** and **children** were led to separate female holdings apart from their male counterparts. Many traders relied on exercise to maintain the health of all captives on board. Quite commonly many enslaved were forced to **dance**, often being prodded by a whip to do so. Usually they were not released from their irons during these dances for fear of possible rebellion.

In response to their **enslavement**, some African captives sought to liberate themselves through starvation. To effectively quell these attempts, during feeding times, a monitor often was employed to report those captives attempting to starve themselves. If caught, they were severely whipped. If this proved less useful, some captives were subjected to the *speculum oris*, a mouth opener containing hooks and a thumbscrew that was used to force **food** through a funnel into the throat of resistive slaves. A **surgeon** formerly employed in the slave trade, **Alexander Falconbridge**, recounted testimony of his observations noting,

> Upon the negroes refusing to take sustenance, I have seen coals of fire, glowing hot, put on a shovel, and placed so near their lips, as to scorch and burn them. And this has been accompanied with threat, of forcing them to swallow the coals, if they any longer persisted in refusing to eat.... a certain captain in the slave trade, poured melted lead on such of the negroes as obstinately refused their food. (1973, p. 23)

Resistance remained a constant threat captives used against their enslavement. In retaliation, many **slave traders** relied on public torture as a means to thwart future attempts of freedom. While decapitation and castration were common methods of punishment for resistive captives, it was not uncommon for enslaved Africans to have boiling water or fat poured on them. Additionally, to maintain continued obedience of ship rules, some captives were required to either throw over the body of a dead **shipmate**, hold the head or kiss the lips of a decapitated cohort, or even eat the heart of a seaman they may have been responsible for killing during rebellion.

Further Readings: Falconbridge, Alexander. *An Account of the Slave Trade on the Coast of Africa*. New York: AMS Press, 1973 (1788); Robotham, Rosemarie, ed. *Spirits of the Passage: The Transatlantic Slave Trade in The Seventeenth Century*. New York: Simon & Schuster, 1997; Thomas, Hugh. *The Slave Trade: The Story of the Atlantic Slave Trade, 1440–1870*. New York: Simon & Schuster, 1997; Tibbles, Anthony. *Transatlantic Slavery: Against Human Dignity*. London: HMSO, 1994.

Sowande' M. Mustakeem

Tourism

As tourists, audiences of diverse backgrounds make contact with the trans-Atlantic slavery past. By attending places, exhibitions, and cultural events that have a connection to that past, people purposefully or matter-of-factly, consciously or unconsciously, (continue to) form an image of that episode in world history and its implications for the present.

The Middle Passage left a substantial amount of cultural heritage. For a majority of descendants, intangible heritage of the slavery past is very much part of their everyday lives. Tangible heritage, however, is something that for a long time has taken a predominantly European approach. It was produced and conserved by those who introduced trans-Atlantic slavery and, later, transformed into written history primarily by their descendants. In recent decades, the global focus has been shifting to produce academic work and present tangible heritage in such a way that it includes the perspective of the enslaved. Descendants turned into tourists, visiting places and seeing artifacts that played a role in slavery history, experiencing slavery heritage in a way that until recently was neglected. The group that is able to do this and interested in doing this is growing, with African Americans leading the way.

Because of the increasing awareness of the significance of this heritage and its audiences, the number of exhibitions and *lieux de memoire* concerning the trans-Atlantic slave trade is growing. The concept *lieux de memoire* was developed by Pierre Nora and refers to places that inherit the function of living memory. UNESCO (United Nations Educational, Scientific and Cultural Organization) served as a catalyst for this increased awareness by implementing a World Heritage List in 1972 that includes historic sites significant to the slave trade. The list includes such places as the European forts in Ghana; James Island in Gambia; Isle de Gorée in **Senegal**; Willemstad, **Curaçao**, and cities built with slave labor, like Paramaribo, Suriname, and Salvador de Bahia, **Brazil**. In 1993, UNESCO started its Slave Route Project,

Tourists visit the House of Slaves on Gorée Island. Courtesy of Manuel Barcia.

aiming to end the silence around the slavery past and further deepen the knowledge about that past and its heritage and consequences. Furthermore, with its Convention for the Safeguarding of Intangible Heritage in 2003, UNESCO opened up the path for a more general recognition of **oral history**, which enriches the academic knowledge of the slavery experience. Also, a strong lobby for recognition of the past has lead to apologies and greater involvement and commitment from governments in Europe and the United States, which in turn lead to the establishment of monuments, and academic institutions, new learning material in schools, and debate in the public sphere. All these developments incite tourism to slavery sites.

On both sides of the Middle Passage, as well as in Europe, an interesting development is discernible, as presenters of heritage are juggling to accommodate diverse audiences. Although the mass tourist is looking for entertainment and a nostalgic representation of the past, those who are researching their roots feel a strong personal interest in the tragedy. The thanatourist may be fascinated by the horror, but pilgrims want to be able to connect to their ancestors' suffering, requiring a more serene atmosphere of regret and mourning. Some visitors are looking for a quick impression of the past and do not mind achieving that through secondary means, while others adhere to a representation of the past that is historically accurate, precise, and correct. And although some want to focus on the hardships of the enslaved, others want a broader view of black history, ranging from the early African civilizations to an impression of the accomplishments of the enslaved and their descendants. So, debates in tourism and slavery heritage cover topics like authenticity, mass tourism versus pilgrimage, sensationalism, historical correctness, and resilience versus victimization.

Ghana was the first African country to obtain its independence (1957), and the country, known as the **Gold Coast**, inspired great expectations for the future. Many famous African Americans visited the country, including Maya Angelou who chronicled her visit in her memoirs *All Gods Children Need Travelling Shoes*. But it was not until the beginning of this century that the country saw an explosion of tourist arrivals. International tourism receipts grew from 8 million euros in 1995 to an average of almost 370 million between 2000 and 2003. Not only the European forts are well visited, but also newly established *lieux*, like the river at Assin Manso, where captives took their last bath before being led to slavery. The return to Mother Africa for many in the diaspora is a spiritual experience. It is symbolized in the reburial of the remains of two enslaved, Samuel Cassey and Crystall, in African soil, freed from life in the colonies. Symbolic also are the "Door of Return" signs at several forts that are attached above the door through which bonded Africans once left, back then called the **Door of No Return**.

Ghana welcomes tourists, but it struggles with accommodating both those who claim the forts as a sanctuary dedicated to the enslaved and those who are interested in the general history of the country. Among that last group are the Ghanaians themselves, for whom the forts represent part of their economic history and future, as the buildings continue to generate income. Here, the problem of essentializing "the black experience" becomes apparent: "Ghanaians do not identify with contemporary African Americans who visit the sites on the basis of race, but instead feel distinct from them by virtue of economic differences" (Favor, 2003). Conceding to sensitivities, however, restaurants and gift shops at the sites keep a low profile and guides adjust their tours according to the people in the group.

In the United States as well as in the Caribbean, where tourist sites aim to attract a wide audience, history and heritage are often used as entertainment. Consequently, the colonial past is represented in a way that downplays the role of slavery in society, obscuring the existence of the enslaved. This representation is seen in more traditional **museums** and heritage institutions, in shows for tourists, on Web sites and brochures. Sometimes, as in Colonial Williamsburg, that representation is amended because of tourist complaints. Others aim to please an entirely different audience. Like the private museum Kura Hulanda, in Curaçao, which depicts the whole experience of trans-Atlantic slavery. An example of "proud" heritage are the maroon villages in **Jamaica** and Suriname, where tourists get a real taste of the lives of those who escaped slavery. *See also* Bahía; Gorée Island; Historical Memory.

Further Readings: Bruner, E. *Culture on Tour: Ethnographies of Travel*. Chicago: University of Chicago Press, 2005; Dann, G., and Seaton, A. V. *Slavery, Contested Heritage, and Thanatourism*. New York: Haworth Hospitality Press, 2001; Favor, J. Martin. "Souvenirs of a Sordid Past." Interview by Tamara Steinert, 2003. Dartmouth Web site: www.dartmouth.edu/%7Edartfac/features/souvenirs.html; Lowenthal, D. *Possessed by the Past: The Heritage Crusade and the Spoils of History*. New York: The Free Press, 1996; Marcel, J. "Death Makes Holiday." *The American Reporter*. August 26, 2005; Potter, Robert. *The Urban Caribbean in an Era of Global Change*. Aldershot: Ashgate, 2000;

Somashekhar, S. "Black History Becoming a Star Tourist Attraction." *Washington Post.* August 14, 2005; Wesseling, Henk. "Overseas History." In Peter Burke, ed. *New Perspectives on Historical Writing.* University Park: Pennsylvania State University Press, 1992.

Valika Smeulders

Trade Commodities

The trade commodities merchandised in the Atlantic slave trade played a chief role in the purchase of captives by people in the Western Hemisphere. Given that the use of metallic coins was unusual in the African Atlantic economy and that the value of their use was predominate in it, the supply of several foreign trade goods became an unavoidable condition to enter the slave market. Purchasers and suppliers had to gauge slave **price** in trade commodities, but each side had its own assessment about the goods exchanged.

Although a slave vessel **cargo** was made up of tens of different types of trade goods, including **textiles, firearms**, and alcohol, the "large" goods were indispensable to achieving success in the West African slave market. Miscellaneous other commodities such as beads and other personal ornaments, metalware (saucepans, bowls, kettle), mirrors, clocks, hats, umbrellas, and so on, the "small" goods, as well as seaborne shells, tobacco, and metal, the "intermediate" goods, compounded the value of the "bundles" exchanged for slaves.

The proportion of each one of these commodities in slave vessel cargoes varied through four centuries of the Atlantic slave trade and among the different national carriers. Regardless of perceived value, the importance of this cargo was unbroken from the middle seventeenth through the early nineteenth centuries.

Textiles were the first goods imported in large scale through the Atlantic slave trade. Pioneers in the eastward route, the Portuguese were the first to introduce Asian fabrics, most of which came from India, into Western Africa. Indian textiles became irreplaceable for the purchase of African slaves until the early nineteenth century, when they were superseded by British output.

The color pattern and durability of Indian cotton cloth made them preferred by African purchasers, comparing advantageously with local fiber textile and European woolen and linen cloths and their imitations of Indian pattern. The popularity and relevance of textiles were such that they made the Portuguese word *peça* (piece). A *peça* originally was designated as a piece of cloth that was a suitable size to be worn by an adult person and that had the value to buy one slave, which became synonymous with prime slave (that is, an adult male), as the exchange rates evolved and the slave price came to encompass several other goods.

European firearms (the second main Africa import), **gunpowder**, and munitions grew in demand from Senegambia to **Angola** and they traded in larger quantities throughout the mid-seventeenth century. In the second half of the eighteenth century, the import of firearms into West Africa amounted to 300,000 to 400,000 a year, half of which the British made.

Atlantic Africans imported muskets, fuzee, pistols, and rifles of various sorts, a pattern that generally became known as the "gun-slave cycle." Some sort of firearms were linked to certain African slave trade regions, which earned them such peculiar names as the "Bonny Musket" and "Angola Gun."

Early on in the slave trade, alcoholic beverages were exported in exchange for slaves and became highly consumed in Africa. Initially wines, gin, and other European and Atlantic liquors were used to supply the slave trade. Since the mid-seventeenth century, however, the Brazilian *jeribita* (or distilled sugarcane brandy) rose as the main alcoholic beverage imported into Western Africa, specifically into Angola, followed by Caribbean and North America. These beverages were a basic commodity in the slave trade that was carried out by American merchants coming straight from Africa.

Tobacco was another popular luxury good in West Africa. Although produced by settlers in all American regions, the Brazilian variety was preferred by African consumers, mainly along the **Slave Coast**. This trade gave rise to a link between Northeast **Brazil** and that region, a trade that lasted through the extinction of the Atlantic slave trade.

There were some sorts of trade commodities that Africans imported not only as consumer goods but also as currency. This was the case with copper and brass bars, mainly, but iron bars were also minted or used as currency in the African economy. The **cowries**, in turn, brought by Europeans from the **Indian Ocean**, were used as currency along the coast and inland from Senegambia to the Bight of Benin (except along the **Gold Coast**). Small pieces of home- or foreign-made clothing also circulated as currency, specifically in West Central Africa.

The pattern of imports varied according to African region, for some goods were more demanded in one region than in others. Demand for firearms was linked to warfare among the African states or it was directly connected to slaving raids inland. Textiles and beverages were distributed or merchandised inland as consumer goods, but returned captives who were exported. Africa importing of goods resulted in new slaves being exported through the Atlantic slave trade. The role played by those trade commodities in the African economy ranged from consumer goods to capital goods.

For the Western economy, besides generating trade in Africa, these commodities generated the profitability of the European and American slave trade. This profitability level remains a matter of debate. *See also* Rum and Cachaça.

Further Readings: Eltis, David. *The Rise of African Slavery in the Americas*. Cambridge: Cambridge University Press, 2000; Inikori, Joseph E. *Africans and the Industrial Revolution in England*. A Study of International Trade and Economic Development. Cambridge: Cambridge University Press, 2002; Lovejoy, Paul. *Transformations in Slavery: A History of Slavery in Africa*. Cambridge: Cambridge University Press, 1983; Miller, Joseph C. *Way of Death: Merchant Capitalism and the Angolan Slave Trade, 1780–1830*. Madison: University of Wisconsin, 1988.

Gustavo Acioli Lopes

Trade Forts

Trade forts were constructed by European trading companies to protect their commercial interests along the coast of Africa. They functioned primarily as storehouses for goods brought to Africa by European traders, and as living quarters for company employees who carried out the trade and soldiers who provided military protection. European companies gained the permission of local **African rulers** to build their forts and paid rent to local authorities as long as they inhabited the forts. The forts ranged in size and strength from small temporary structures to enormous castles with turrets and cannons. Some of these forts look out over the African shores to this day.

Trade forts are found in the highest concentration along the coast of modern-day Ghana, where more than sixty structures were built within less than 300 miles of coastline. Most of the trade forts in West Africa were built before 1700 and were initially used for Europe's gold trade with Africa. West African gold mines were a source of gold currency in Europe and North Africa long before Europeans began to navigate the African shoreline, thanks to the camel caravan trade across the Sahara Desert. When Portuguese traders began purchasing gold directly from West Africans, especially along the **Gold Coast**, they felt the need to protect this trade from European competitors by constructing fortified outposts in areas where gold could be purchased. The largest trade fort in West Africa, St. George's Castle at **Elmina** (also known as Elmina Castle), was built by Portugal in 1482. It was subsequently enlarged several times while under Dutch ownership from 1637 to 1872.

When the demand for enslaved Africans in the Americas began to escalate dramatically in the seventeenth century, European companies converted the warehouses of most trade forts into slave dungeons, or they expanded the forts to include rooms for this purpose. Most enslaved Africans who were sold into the trans-Atlantic slave trade never passed through a trade fort, because the majority of the trade was carried out by private traders who did not buy slaves at company forts. Nevertheless, the passageway through which slaves who were held in the dungeons of these forts passed before boarding ships bound for the Americas has become a symbol of the traumatic separation of African people from their homeland. This passageway is identified at each of the trade forts as the **Door of No Return**.

Many trade forts can still be seen in Africa. The most commonly visited are the forts at **Gorée Island** in **Senegal**, and **Cape Coast Castle** and Elmina Castle in Ghana. Some forts have been converted into **museums** where the history of the Atlantic slave trade is retold. Visitors can walk through the rooms where the governors and soldiers of European companies lived and step inside the slave dungeons where enslaved Africans waited under horrifying conditions to be taken aboard a ship for the Middle Passage. **Tourism** associated with the trade forts has become an important source of foreign income for the Republic of Ghana.

Further Readings: Daaku, Kwame Y. *Trade and Politics on the Gold Coast, 1600–1720: A Study of the African Reaction to European Trade.* London: Oxford, 1970;

Davies, K. G. *The Royal African Company.* London: Longmans, Green and Company, 1957; Ghana Castle Web site: www.ghanacastle.gov.gh; Van Dantzig, Albert. *Forts and Castles of Ghana.* Accra: Sedco Publishing, 1980.

Rebecca Shumway

Trans-Atlantic Slave Trade Database

In 1999, David Eltis, Stephen Behrendt, David Richardson, and Herbert Klein revolutionized the ability to study and quantify the impact of **slavery in Africa** and the Americas. *The Trans-Atlantic Slave Trade: A Database on CD-ROM* is a useful tool to pursue a demographic study of the enslaved Africans forced to migrate in the era of the Atlantic slave trade. The *Database* provides a basis to learn and explore the Middle Passage, slave ships, the **mortality** of the enslaved at sea, the frequency and timing of revolts, Atlantic sailing times and routes, and patterns of ownership of slave vessels.

In his pioneering study, *The Atlantic Slave Trade* (1969), Philip Curtin set the course for studies of forced migration scholarship of enslaved Africans to the Americas. Since Curtin's publication, a number of scholars, including the creators of the *Database*, as well as Johannes Postma, Jean Mettas, Serge Daget, Jay Coughtry, and José Curto, have collected archival data on slave-trading voyages from archives in England, Spain, France, the Netherlands, the United States, and beyond. In the 1970s and 1980s, scholars created a number of slave ship data sets. By the late 1980s, there were approximately 11,000 individual trans-Atlantic slave voyages stored in individual data sets. The basis for each data set usually was to record the data for a specific European nation or particular **port** where slaving voyages originated.

The *Database* contains records on 27,233 trans-Atlantic slave trade voyages. For statistical purposes, the authors acknowledge that there are several limitations of the *Database*. First, documentation had disappeared and is possibly unrecoverable. Second, many voyages failed to embark slaves, because of capture or **shipwreck** before reaching Africa, or they sank while embarking enslaved Africans and all Africans on board died. Third, some ship **captains** or owners left no information on the outcome of their voyages. Finally, there are voyages that include disembarked slaves in Africa, comprising mainly ships captured in the nineteenth century that were taken to **Sierra Leone** or St. Helena as part of the attempt to suppress the trans-Atlantic slave trade. Thus, nearly 25,000 voyages that did land or could have landed slaves in the Americas are recorded in the database.

The strength of the *Database* lies in its ability to reveal the regional concentrations of the Atlantic slave trade in both Africa and the Americas. Four out of five slaves left from four primary regions: the **Gold Coast**, the Bights of Benin and Biafra, and West Central Africa between 1662 and 1867. Furthermore, 44 percent of all enslaved Africans who disembarked in the Americas landed in **Brazil**; 20 percent landed in the **British Caribbean**; 17 percent landed in the **French Caribbean**, 10 percent landed in Spanish mainland America and its Caribbean possessions, and less than 7 percent landed in the United States. The *Database* is designed to be used as a tool for scholars to trace in detail the principal routes of New World slavery. Geographic trends in the slave trade reveal that enslaved Africans disembarking in Bahia, Brazil, primarily originated in the Bight of Benin; West Central Africa was heavily linked with Brazil; the Gold Coast with Barbados, Suriname, and the Guianas; the Bight of Benin with the French Caribbean islands, excluding Haiti; and the Bight of Biafra with **Jamaica** and the British **Leeward Islands**.

The authors have attempted to correctly fill the historical gap and thus a revised *Database* is scheduled to appear in 2007. The revised database will contain an additional 6,500 slave voyages, and 9,000 slave voyages documented in the first edition have been modified. *See also* Historiography; Import Records.

Further Readings: Eltis, David, Behrendt, Stephen D., Richardson, David, and Klein, Herbert S., eds. *The Trans-Atlantic Slave Trade: A Database on CD-ROM*. Cambridge: Cambridge University Press, 1999; Eltis, David, and Richardson, David. "The 'Numbers Game' and Routes to Slavery." *Slavery and Abolition* 18, 1 (1997): 1–15; Hall, Gwendolyn M. *Slavery and African Ethnicities in the Americas*. Chapel Hill: University of North Carolina Press, 2005; Lovejoy, Paul E. *Transformations in Slavery: A History of Slavery in Africa*. 2nd ed. Cambridge: Cambridge University Press, 2000.

Nadine Hunt

Trans-Saharan Slave Trade

The Sahara desert encompassed an important trade route, the trans-Sahara, which connected West Africa to North Africa and the Mediterranean world. The popularity of this trans-Saharan trade (especially after the introduction of the camel) created a high demand for gold and slaves in exchange for salt and other North African products. The salt-for-gold trade led to the development of major trade centers in the desert, such as Awdaghast, through which slaves were channeled. Although the origins of the trans-Saharan slave trade are obscure and may go back to an earlier period, it is clear that by the tenth century the trade was already well established as the Arab geographer, Ibn Hawqal, noted. By then, there was a regular stream of slaves who were transported across the desert to North Africa.

The slaves who ended up in North Africa and the eastern Mediterranean served in different capacities as soldiers, administrators, harem eunuchs, messengers, doorkeepers, laborers, domestic servants, and concubines. Some of them may have been sent to Andalusia/**Muslim** Spain and Portugal in the Middle Ages, although their numbers were quite small. Later, a number of slaves were acquired by the ethnic groups living in the Sahara desert who depended on them to perform domestic work and other tasks. This partly explains why the inhabitants of this region, extending all the way to North Africa, include people of different shades of skin color (although it is possible that some are native to the area). Over a period of time, the former slaves adapted to their condition by becoming Muslims and members of these ethnic groups. The institution of marriage facilitated the incorporation of outsiders or captives into their host societies. This was partly a function of manumission, which the **Islamic religion** encourages of its followers.

Slavery in North Africa and the Middle East was not defined by race because there were slaves from Eastern Europe, western Russia, and Asia in addition to Africa.

Scholarly research on trans-Saharan slavery (in contrast to the trans-Atlantic trade) is not yet substantial because none of the **slave narratives** or the **plantation** records of the Americas exist, and if they do, their analysis is yet to be carried out. Furthermore, there is a lack of significant local "black" communities in North Africa that live apart from the rest of society and possess distinctive cultures comparable to those of African Americans. Rather, the ex-slaves have been integrated into the local populations (especially through intermarriages and concubinage as most slaves were **women**). These communities share in the local identity, although some have retained particular practices and interpretations of (popular) Islam that have their origins in sub-Saharan Africa.

The demography of slavery and the slave trade in the trans-Saharan context remains relatively underdeveloped. This explains why there are disagreements among scholars over the numbers of people involved. There is, in fact, little hard evidence of numbers, and efforts to quantify the slave trade are at best rough estimates and at worst mere conjectures. Some, for instance, believe that fewer slaves crossed the Sahara in the period between the tenth and the nineteenth centuries than crossed the Atlantic between the sixteenth and the nineteenth centuries, but their numbers were not negligible (a few or several million). Others estimate much higher figures of slaves (when compared with those who crossed the Atlantic) who were taken from sub-Saharan Africa via the Sahara, Red Sea, and the **Indian Ocean** to the Islamic world, although the annual **volume** was much lower. If one accepts this high figure, then the demographic balance today (more than 100 million people of African descent in the Americas compared with only a small fraction of a residual population of Africans living in the Arab-Muslim world) needs to be explained. In any case, what is not contested today is the magnitude of the trans-Atlantic slave trade was much higher (almost two-thirds of the estimated 9 to 12 million slave exports happened between 1700 and 1850) and its consequences much more concentrated (it spanned, for instance, systems of racial segregation as in the United States and left distinct communities in the Americas) and tied to capitalist developments than the longer-lasting trans-Saharan and Red Sea trades. The slaves in Islamic areas, generally speaking, tended to be more a luxury commodity (items of conspicuous consumption) than a means of production.

It is not clear whether there were many slave **escapes** in the trans-Saharan trade and, if so, how the **runaways** could have eluded detection in the difficult terrain of the Sahara, which poses a major obstacle. Would the slaves have wanted to return especially if they had been captured in war, or were they fleeing starvation, or had they been labeled as criminals or outcasts? Again, there is not much to go by by way of escape narratives (particularly for the early period) to allow us to piece together information on these escapades.

Before the 1500s, slavery was not based on skin color but on the misfortune of being a captive of war, a kidnapping, a criminal offense, and so on.

Therefore, slaves of all ethnic and racial backgrounds could be found and suffered the same fate as those who were sold away from their home areas to serve new masters. With the advent of the trans-Atlantic slave trade, however, slavery became increasingly identified with skin color as it involved white masters and black slaves. The idea of racism was born out of this need to justify racial servitude. Similarly, while in Muslim societies, slaves and particularly slave soldiers, white and black, could rise to become officers and commanders and even rulers. Egypt had a Mamluk-slave dynasty first ruling then later sharing power from the mid-thirteenth century to the beginning of the nineteenth century. Increasingly, the terms "black" and "slave" became interchangeable, particularly in the eighteenth and nineteenth centuries when the slave trade reached a peak. The Haratin in Morocco, for example, are an interesting example of a free black people who were enslaved by the Moroccan Sultan Mulais Ismail in the early eighteenth century (because he claimed they were runaway slaves). At the same time, he was asserting that he needed black people to serve in the army. Later when these blacks acquired too much political power by the mid-century they were again re-enslaved. This indicates that the phenomenon of kidnapping for **enslavement** purposes was not isolated and often targeted at dark-skinned people.

The Muslim scholar of Timbuctu, Ahmed Baba, writing in the mid-sixteenth century, condemned the immoral practice of innocent people in West Africa being enslaved, including fellow Muslims, on the pretext that they were not sufficiently Muslim. He claimed this was quite dishonest and that it contravened the laws of Islam. Similarly the nineteenth century Moroccan historian Ahmed b. Khalid al-Nasiri was obliged to issue a polemic against those who believed that being black and living in sub-Saharan Africa was a sufficient reason for enslavement. This indicates that there were some unscrupulous businessmen who sought to **profit** from the slave trade by expanding the group or class of people who could be enslaved. This horrified al-Nasiri who believed that the conditions for enslaving others did not exist any more and that the institution of slavery was no longer acceptable. For him the time had come for the abolition of slavery, but what to do of it and who was to do it?

Despite European attempts to abolish the slave trade, which was outlawed in 1870, Morocco and Benghazi continued to import slaves until the dawn of the twentieth century. The French attempted to end the salt-for-slaves trade in Africa by finding a new supply for salt outside of North Africa. This measure did not achieve the desired result as alternative routes were found in the Nile region into Egypt, Dongola, and Equitoriana where the slave market flourished despite the British ban on the slave trade. Moreover, the desert ethnic groups of the Sahara were still obtaining slaves to work for them. When the Ottoman took steps to abolish slavery in its territories, it had some appreciable effect on undermining the demand for slaves coming from North African coastal centers. By the time European colonial rule was firmly established along much of the Mediterranean coast in Africa in the nineteenth century, the trade was being affected and the socio-economic basis of its existence undermined so that slavery as an institution came to an end early in the twentieth century. There were, however, pockets of resistance to the abolition of slavery—for example, in some rural areas of Mauritania where the institution apparently continues to exist, although no government today officially approves of slavery. *See also* Gender and Slave Exports; Slavery in Africa.

Further Readings: El Hamel, Chouki. "'Race,' Slavery and Islam in the Maghrebi Mediterranean Thought: The Question of the Haratin in Morocco." *Journal of North African Studies* 7, 3 (2002); Lovejoy, Paul, ed. *Slavery on the Frontiers of Islam*. Princeton, NJ: Markus Wiener, 2003; Manning, Patrick. *Slavery and African Life: Occidental, Oriental, and African Slave Trades*. African Studies Series, 67. Cambridge: Cambridge University Press, 1990; Marcel, Dorigny, ed. *The Abolition of Slavery: From L. F. Sonthonax to Victor Schoecher; 1793, 1794, 1848*. New York: Berghahn Book and UNESCO Publishing, 2003; Richardson, David. "Across the Desert and the Sea: Trans-Saharan and Atlantic Slavery, 1500–1900." *The Historical Journal* 38, 1 (1995): 195–205; Savage, E., ed. *The Human Commodity: Perspectives on the Trans-Saharan Slave Trade*. London: Frank Cass, 1992.

Abdin Chande

Triangular Trade

The term "triangular trade" refers to the voyage pattern vessels took in the slave trade between Europe, West Africa, and the Americas. The Atlantic slave trade involved the forced removal and transportation of more than 11 million Africans between the mid-fifteenth century and the mid-nineteenth century. Nine European nations, as well as colonists in the Americas, participated intermittently in the Atlantic slave trade. During this period, Portuguese merchants carried the largest number of slaves to the Americas (5 million), followed by Britain (3.1 million), and then France (1.4 million). More than 84 percent of all Africans were transported to **Brazil** and the West Indies with the rest going to various places throughout the Americas. The voyage patterns of slave vessels from each nation generally resembled that of a triangle, leaving Europe for Africa then the West Indies and back to Europe. The term "triangular trade" has traditionally been applied to the slave trade of the British Empire.

The exact origin of the term is not known. In the second half of the nineteenth century, several American scholars commenced the **historiography** of the slave trade. George Moore's short study *Notes on Slavery in Massachusetts* (1866) is considered the first historical work on the slave trade. Based on more merchant records, two subsequent articles by George Mason (1872) and William Weeden (1887) further uncovered aspects of the slave trade. However, it was W.E.B. Du Bois's doctoral dissertation, "The Suppression of the African Slave Trade to the United States" (1896), that provided a more complete and rigorous discussion of the trade and its impact on the economic development of **New England**. The first actual use of the term "triangular trade" appeared in Charles William Taussig's *Rum, Romance and Rebellion* (1928). Afterward, the usage of the term became more widespread, appearing in American history textbooks and scholarly works on the colonial period. In Britain, the first use of the term seems to have occurred in Charles MacInnes's *England and Slavery* (1934). But, it gained its widest international currency in Eric Williams's *Capitalism and Slavery* (1944), which placed the slave trade within the context of the evolution of the Industrial Revolution.

The slave trade within the British Empire consisted of two separate triangular trades: the **British slave trade** and the British North American (later the United States) slave trade. The British slave trade involved a ship departing for the west coast of Africa carrying alcoholic beverages and manufactured goods like **textiles**, iron bars, tools, and guns. These goods were exchanged for a full **cargo** of slaves. Thereafter, the ship proceeded to the Americas, primarily the Caribbean. The slaves were exchanged for either bills of exchange (a form of payment) or commodities (**sugar**, tobacco, **rum**, or cocoa) or both. Finally, the slave ship left the Americas for Britain. For the most part, the pattern of the trip resembled a triangle. Although some British slave ships moved from island to island or from the islands to the North American mainland, the general contours of the trade formed a large triangle.

Starting in the 1950s, several scholars challenged the existence of triangular patterns in the British slave trade. The major issue in question concerned the final leg of the triangle when the slave ship returned to England carrying West Indian commodities. In particular, scholars investigated whether English slave ships carried American commodities back to England after selling their cargo of slaves. Throughout the eighteenth century, these scholars contend, a developing direct trade between England and the Americas in **plantation** products undermined the ability of slave ships to secure a cargo for the final leg of the journey. Therefore, these scholars assert, rather than carrying commodities, English slave ships returned home empty, carrying only payment for the slaves usually in the form of bills of exchange. This new scholarship raised serious doubts about the validity of the term triangular trade. Countering this argument, Walter Minchinton has shown that slave ships were able to secure cargoes on the return trip to England. Analyzing the **port** records of **Jamaica** and Virginia, Minchinton found that virtually every slave ship left for England carrying American commodities despite the growth of a direct trade between Britain and the Americas. Slave ships may not have carried much sugar, but they did bring back other plantation commodities like tobacco, rum, cocoa, and dyewoods. Providing the most detailed evidence of its existence, Minchinton's study confirms the validity of the term triangular trade.

The British triangular trade became an even more controversial issue after the appearance of Eric Williams's *Capitalism and Slavery* (1944), which claimed **profits** derived from this branch of commerce financed the Industrial Revolution. Williams argued that English merchants earned enormous profits from exchanging manufactured goods for slaves in Africa, selling the slaves in the Caribbean, and selling the plantation commodities upon returning to Britain. This argument assaulted the very foundation of Western economic development, assigning the notorious slave trade primacy in causing the British Industrial Revolution. *Capitalism and Slavery* naturally provoked considerable international discussion. Debunking the **Eric Williams Thesis**, scholars contended that slave trade profits were not overly large, on the one hand, and they were not of sufficient magnitude to finance the Industrial Revolution, on the other hand. Although largely disproved, the Williams Thesis has encouraged scholarship in new directions. Rather than looking at profits, scholars have examined the role of the triangular trade in the settlement of the Americas, which inaugurated a massive expansion of Atlantic commerce. Recently, Joseph Inikori's *Africans and the Industrial Revolution* (2002) linked the expansion of this commerce to the Industrial Revolution.

The second triangular trade of the British Empire consisted of the branch originating in British North America. A ship departed a British North American port for Africa carrying primarily rum and some manufactured goods. This rum was exchanged for slaves, who were carried to the West Indies or the southern mainland colonies. From the West Indies, these slave vessels brought back molasses, which was distilled into rum. Like the British slave trade, the branch originating in British North America resembled a triangle. Totaling about 220,000 slave deliveries, the British North America slave trade represented less than 10 percent of the British slave trade. Rhode Island slave ships represented about 50 percent or more of the total trade.

A spate of works in the 1960s and 1970s directly challenged the British North American triangular trade, calling it a myth, particularly Gilman Ostrander's article "The Myth of the Triangle Trade" (1973). Ostrander, however, did not attack the triangular pattern of British North American slave ships, but the importance this branch of commerce has been given in discussions of colonial America's economic development. Ostrander insisted that the triangular trade was an insignificant branch of commerce and that it played no major role in the development of colonial America. On the contrary, Elaine Crane and Virginia Platt asserted that, although the slave trade may have represented only a tiny portion of colonial American commerce, it was particularly important in the economic development of Newport, Rhode Island. Fostering the development of its mercantile community, shipbuilding, rum distillation, and overall commerce, the triangular trade, these scholars argue, was central to Newport's economy.

Overall, despite assertions to the contrary, there was, indeed, a triangular trade. The recent *Trans-Atlantic Slave Trade: A Database on CD-ROM* covers more than 25,000 vessels engaged in the slave trade between 1500 and 1867. With the exception of the bilateral slave trade between **Angola** and Brazil and the smaller slave trade from the Caribbean to Africa, the voyage pattern of most of these ships resembled a triangle on the map. Although the profitability of the triangular trade has been a contentious issue, the overall voyage pattern that each vessel engaged in is not in question. Arguments suggesting that the trade was a myth are, themselves, myths.

Further Readings: Crane, Elaine F. "'The First Wheel of Commerce': Newport, Rhode Island and the Slave Trade." *Slavery and Abolition* 1 (1980): 178–198; Eltis, David. "The Volume and Structure of the Transatlantic Slave Trade: A Reassessment." *William and Mary Quarterly* 58 (2001): 17–46; Inikori, Joseph. *Africans and the Industrial Revolution in England: A Study in International Trade and Economic Development.* Cambridge: Cambridge University Press, 2002; Minchinton, Walter. "The Triangular Trade Revisited." In Henry Gemery and Jan Hogendorn, eds. *The Uncommon Market: Essays in the Economic History of the Atlantic Slave Trade,* 331–352. New

York: Academic Press, 1979; Ostrander, Gilman M. "The Making of the Triangular Trade Myth." *William and Mary Quarterly* 30 (1973): 634–644; Williams, Eric Eustace. *Capitalism and Slavery; with a new introduction by Colin A. Palmer*. Chapel Hill: University of North Carolina Press, 1994 (1944).

Joseph Avitable

Trudo, Agaja (r. 1708–1732)

Agaja Trudo was one of the greatest rulers of **Dahomey**. He came to power after Wegbaja (1650–1685) and Akaba II (1685–1708) had consolidated the Aja hold over the Fon on the Abomey plateau and established Dahomey as a small inland kingdom.

Agaja was the first of many Dahomean rulers who made expansion a cornerstone of their reign. Cognizant of the need for a well-trained army and a steady supply of guns, Agaja reorganized the Dahomean army and established contact with Europeans at the coast. He set up a military training school for boys who were trained to become the next batch of Dahomean soldiers.

Agaja followed the reorganization of the army with the establishment of the *Agbadjibeto*, an organization that served as an intelligence-gathering unit and a public information outfit by which the king propagated information. Agaja used the Agbadjibeto as a spy organization to gather information about neighbors and enemies alike to help plan the new offensives that he undertook.

Agaja's predecessors, Wegbaja (1650–1685) and Akaba II (1685–1708), had initiated a policy of expansion to districts south and southeast of Abomey. Agaja concentrated first on the northwestern districts. In 1724 and 1727, he conquered **Allada** and **Ouidah**, the coastal principalities that had primacy in slave-trading in the region. As a result, Dahomey gained access to the coast and came into contact with the Dutch, the French, and the English. Scholars disagree on the rationale for the conquest of Allada and Ouidah. Some argue that Agaja wanted to stop the slave trade and urge Europeans to use slaves on **plantations** in Africa. Others believe that Agaja was driven by the desire to trade slaves for guns and **gunpowder** and this set in motion a gun-slave-gun cycle in the region. In either case, Dahomey over time replaced Allada as the dominant slave exporter in the region.

The conquest of these coastal states gave Agaja control of slave ports and his conquests yielded captives who were sold into the Atlantic slave trade. Slaving became a central element of the Dahomean economy, and Agaja became actively involved in the slave trade. The king controlled the **profits** of the trade and taxed the profits of other slave dealers.

Agaja's control of the coast cut into Oyo's considerable profits as Oyo lost the use of Allada as an outlet for slaves. Consequently, between 1726 and 1740, Oyo with its cavalry attacked Dahomey on four occasions. The larger Oyo state was such a nuisance that, despite his best efforts, Agaja was unable to achieve Dahomey's independence. In 1730, he signed a treaty with Oyo acquiescing to Dahomey's tributary status in return for annual payment of tribute. In return for tribute payments, Dahomey was permitted to keep its army, which Agaja used in slave raids. Agaja's successors, Teg-besu IV (1732–1774) and Kpenge V (1774–1789), continued his policy of expansion and slave-trading. *See also* African Rulers and the Slave Trade.

Further Readings: Boahen, A. Adu. *Topics in West African History.* London: Long-mans, Green and Company, 1966; July, Robert W. *A History of the African People.* 5th ed. Prospect Heights, IL: Waveland Press, 1998; Shillington, Kevin. *History of Africa.* 2nd ed. New York: Palgrave Macmillan, 2005; Webster, J. B., and Adu Boahen, A., with Idowu, H. O. *The Growth of African Civilization: The Revolutionary Years—West Africa since 1800.* London: Longmans, Green and Company, 1968.

Edmund Abaka

V

Ventilation and Suffocation

Before embarkation on to the slave ships, African captives were kept in stockades and **barracoons**. They were simply sheds made of heavy piles driven deep into the earth, tied together with bamboo and thatched with palm leaves. For large barracoons, there was a center row of piles with a **chain** on each pile. At about two-foot intervals, there was a large neck link to which two slaves were padlocked. The walls of these enclosures were about four to six feet high. The shaft for ventilation cut into the wall just under the roof at about four feet high. With increasing demand and supply of slaves, these enclosures became more **overcrowded** and ventilation poorer.

After embarkation, slaves were usually stowed below deck. Although some slaving **captains** claimed to be "tight-packers," others prided themselves on being "loose-packers," each with different economic reasons. The **holds** were specially constructed for slaves and were about five feet high. They were composed of little more than shelves barely half a meter above the other. A man was allowed a space of six feet long by sixteen inches wide; a woman had about five feet by ten inches with sixteen inches width; a boy had about five feet by fourteen inches wide and a girl had four feet by twelve inches wide. They definitely could not sit up straight or move freely. It was reported once by a ship **surgeon** that a corpse in a coffin had more room. On some Portuguese ships, the men were shackled to the hold standing. In some ships, they were made to lie on each other's laps like sardines to make room for the entire **cargo**. This kind of packing gave little room for air. The air circulating was unfit for respiration. Massive perspiration, the emission of normal bodily functions, and the attendant stench brought on widespread sickness and death.

Most ships had five or six air ports about six inches long and four inches wide. These ran along each side of the ship between the decks. Only a few ships had what were called "wind sails" to let air into the hold. During heavy rain or rough weather, they were shut. This made the hold unbearably hot. Inhaling toxic air mixed with sweat and effluvia soon produced fevers and fluxes. Sometimes the rooms were covered with their blood and mucus. Apart from the air breathed when they came up to feed during the day, slaves had very little ventilation.

Further Readings: Alderman, Clifford L. *Rum, Slaves, and Molasses: The Story of New England's Triangular Trade.* New York: Crowell-Collier Press, 1972; Curtin, Philip D., *The Atlantic Slave Trade: A Census.* Madison: University of Wisconsin, 1969; Dow, George Francis. *Slave Ships and Slaving.* New York: Dover Publications, 1970; Howard, Thomas. *Black Voyage.* Boston: Little, Brown, 1971; Klein, Herbert S. *The Middle Passage: Comparative Studies in the Atlantic Slave Trade.* Princeton, NJ: Princeton University Press, 1978.

Oyekemi Olajope Oyelakin

Vili

The Vili language is native to the Congo, along the coast between Gabon and **Angola**. It is also spoken in Gabon. Although the people were thought to have migrated to the coast from the inland areas around 1300, the culture derives from a little-known kingdom spanning the fifteenth to nineteenth centuries. It was centered in a city named **Loango**. The realm stretched from the north coast of the **Congo River** to Cape Lopez.

Royalty established strong trading ties with the Dutch and other Europeans, China, India, and some countries in the Mediterranean basin to prosper and grow. The first meeting between African and European traders occurred more than 100 years before the large-scale export of human **cargo**. The coastline was kept intact and free from foreign settlers (mainly in the eighteenth and nineteenth century) who would construct outposts to benefit from the slave trade. The coastline of the Vili region was a fertile resource for slavers, yielding in the neighborhood of 15,000 Africans a year for export. This protectionism by the Loango kings was maintained, even when the demand for slave labor increased. One of the major sources of revenue for the Africans had been ivory, which by the time of a developed worldwide slave trade was becoming scarce. It was then they yielded to their trading partners and altered their merchandising to **profit** in the trade of humans on an industrial scale.

The new enterprise in the nineteenth century heralded the decline of the sovereigns, as their authority, and those of the governors, was challenged by new individuals of wealth. They eventually slipped into economic ruin, along with the Portuguese (who alone were buying and selling between 5,000 and 10,000 slaves a year for Latin America). One of the world's most important slaving markets is now a little-known, and long-forgotten, footnote to history.

The kings of the Vili nation (as well as the rulers of **Benin**, **Dahomey**, Congo, and Ashanti) sold slaves for a number of generations: the European incursion and overwhelming demand for slaves was at the tail end of a tradition dating back centuries. One might think that the practices of the precolonization Vili would disappear with the abolition of slavery in the West, but it did not. Human bondage carried on into the twentieth century with the Dutch rubber harvest and **plantations**. Salt, laboriously transported from the coast inland, was used to trade for slaves, as well. Slavery in the area ceased only when French missionaries, and their government, put an end to it. *See also* Kongo.

Further Readings: Gordon, Raymond G., Jr., ed. *Ethnologue: Languages of the World*. 15th ed. Dallas, TX: SIL International, 2005; Martin, Phyllis M. *The External Trade of the Loango Coast 1576–1870*. Oxford: Clarendon Press, 1972; Thornton, John K. *Africa and Africans in the Making of the Atlantic World*. 2nd ed. Cambridge: Cambridge University Press, 1998.

Corinne Richter

Violence

The system of trans-Atlantic slavery was maintained by a system of violence that sought to ensure the complete domination and suppression of enslaved Africans and their offspring. Slavery in the Caribbean has been described as a totally exploitative system underpinned by force, violence, and racist ideology. It has been argued that enslaved persons were permanently and violently dominated. Facets of the power relation included the use or threat of violence by the slave owner in the control of the enslaved person. Brute force served as the basis of the relationship between slave owners and the enslaved. The slave owner's role was that of "master," whose will was imposed by force and threats. Violence was the means of creating and maintaining the slave system. The whipping of the enslaved was intended to inflict punishment, to dominate them, and to impress on them their state of servitude. **Escape**, rebellion, or abject submission became the alternatives open to the enslaved.

Being mere tools, masters could treat them as they saw fit and availed themselves of an array of physical or symbolic instruments to wield control over the bodies of the enslaved. To dehumanize, degrade, and deprive of personality and identification with free human beings were the objectives of the methods employed. These methods included changing the names of enslaved persons and inflicting corporal punishment and torture.

The interrelated system of violence conceived, sustained, and nurtured the trans-Atlantic trade in enslaved Africans. In such a system, killing an enslaved African was experienced as an economic rather than as a human phenomenon. For the **slave traders** themselves, trading in enslaved Africans was often considered a violent, cruel, inhuman activity, or quite simply, an unattractive occupation.

Although the slave systems of North America and the Caribbean were characterized by violence, it has been argued that it was even more so in the Caribbean. Walvin comments, "The bitterest of slave experiences were to be found in the sweetest of all crops—sugar" (Walvin, 1994, p. 90). Corporal punishment was pivotal to the institution of West Indian slavery. Indeed, it was believed that to tamper with the use of corporal punishment was to destabilize the institution of slavery. White mistresses were part of this system of violence, and they have been equated with the field drivers for their demanding and exploitative ways.

Violence of Sexual Relations

The violence of the legal code and of masters was inflicted on enslaved African men who fought against **women** being violated sexually. The brutality of sexual relations began on the slave ships and continued on the

Whipping or flogging was the most frequent form of punishment and varied in severity. It was possible to die as a result of flogging, for which the perpetrator would often receive nothing more severe than a fine. Courtesy of Anti-Slavery International.

plantations. Enslaved women were used by white men as their "sexual playthings" and were generally subjected to the most base sexual exploitation. White men justified their rapacious violation of enslaved women by convincing themselves that the Africans' morals were different and that they were promiscuous. In the northern colonies, however, there was a legal framework for the castration of enslaved Africans as punishment for the **rape** of a white woman.

Whites formulated justifications for the culture of violence that they instituted against enslaved Africans in the context of the trade, including the following:

- Africans were savages and uncivilized and this could be contained only through violence;
- Africans were lazy, laziness was a racial vice, and only the discipline enforced by the white man could deal with the Africans' laziness; and
- Without, ultimately, the sanction of violence there could be no real discipline.

At that time, unlike today, whipping of a child or "an inferior" was common practice and corporal punishment was accepted, but the enslaved Africans experienced this punishment on a far greater scale. The situation of enslaved Africans was distinguished by "the persistence, the inescapability and the ubiquity of violence in their lives" (Walvin, 1994, p. 238).

Whipping was an instrumental feature in the maintenance of slavery and often resulted in scars that lasted for life. Floggings were brutal. The most minor infraction would bring down on the enslaved a punishment that was instant and often grotesque, which included at times **branding**, tarring, burning, and mutilations. Indeed, it was the issue of corporal punishment that was used by protestors against slavery early in the nineteenth century. Hard work was no guarantee of escape from whippings and, even in the case of men who were deemed considerate, the trans-Atlantic trade in enslaved Africans was a system of debasement and corruption.

Walvin sets out the thinking of slave owners and plantation society concerning the treatment deemed proper for enslaved Africans in the Caribbean: Enslaved Africans were denied the right to a jury when accused of offences; they had no rights; they were subject to corporal punishment and punished by "death without benefit of clergy" (1994, p. 245) for a series of crimes. They were transported out of the island; they had their ears cut off, their noses slit, their faces branded, and even had limbs amputated for thieving or trying to run away without cessation. Slave owners were prepared to kill enslaved persons who transgressed their mandates. This they did using tortuous means such as "progressive mutilation, slow burnings, breaking on the wheel, or starvation in cages" (Craton, in Walvin, 1994, p. 248). This was particularly the case of enslaved Africans who rebelled in the Caribbean and in South America. The punishment meted out to the enslaved Africans was not in proportion to the offences they committed. The slave owners' use of violence in slave societies served as a clear demonstration of the power they wielded.

The critical role of violence in maintaining slavery—whether the slaves were young, old, male, female, skilled, or unskilled—has been emphasized by scholars. The pervasiveness of violence clouded the line between slave owners' normal or abnormal behavior. This violence, while causing the blacks to suffer, at the same time corrupted the whites in that they became dependent on violence to maintain the system, and that violence became for them an addiction—one that became unnoticeable.

The Situation of Enslaved Females

The crews on slavers used female slaves for sexual relief, and these **women** were subject to the whims of white sailors. They were easy targets for **sexual abuse** and were demoralized and defenseless. Sexual exploitation of women was not unique to the trans-Atlantic trade in enslaved Africans, but it is a characteristic of the history of slavery in general. The sexual harassment and violence to which enslaved African females were subjected began on the Atlantic crossing and continued in the Americas.

Barbados was the one slave society that was different because there were more female than male slaves. Furthermore, white planters had access to more white women, which resulted in social relations that were less volatile.

Women slaves endured arduous fieldwork, even when pregnant. In the later years of West Indian slavery, however, in the interest of breeding, pregnant enslaved females were burdened less with such fieldwork. The flogging of enslaved females by drivers, at times, even when they were pregnant, caused negative reactions among the abolitionists. British abolitionist sentiment was fed, in part, by the "putrid details" of the violence against enslaved Africans and their offspring in the West Indies. *See also* Children; Families and Family Separations; Torture.

Further Readings: Oruno, Lara D. "Under the Whiplash." *The UNESCO Courier* October (1994): 8–10; Patterson, Orlando. *Slavery and Social Death.* Cambridge, MA: Harvard University Press, 1982; Walvin, James. *Black Ivory: A History of British Slavery.* Washington, DC: Howard University Press, 1994.

Sandra Ingrid Gift

Volume

One of the most hotly contested issues surrounding the Atlantic slave trade is how many people it thrust into the African diaspora. The estimates have ranged wildly, from a high of 50 million people dragged from Africa to labor in the New World, to a low of 7 or 8 million. The debate feeds on both the nature of the evidence and the high stakes surrounding these numbers. Many of the evidentiary problems center on its secretive nature after European nations began outlawing the trade. **Slave traders** operated openly—indeed, with government encouragement—from the sixteenth century through the late eighteenth. But as official abolition proceeded, the traffic in Africans did not halt; rather, much of it went underground. Although thanks to recent research efforts the record is getting better, especially for the nineteenth century, the truth remains enshrouded in mystery.

The stakes go beyond the scholarly. The question of volume has played into running disputes in the historical literature, but it also has explosive implications for racial politics throughout the Atlantic World. Even the lowest estimates qualify this as one of the great crimes in human history. By 1820, only about 2 million European immigrants had come to the New World, but in that year there was a total New World population of about 12 million whites and 6 million blacks. This contrast tells a horrifying tale of the brutalities of New World slavery, whichever estimate for the slave trade one adheres to. The numbers debate takes on urgency because many people want an accurate assessment of this horror. They share an urge to assess this particular slave trade's place within the annals of man's inhumanity.

One comparison that seems fairer than others is between the Atlantic slave traffic and other examples of large-scale commerce in slaves. These other volume estimates provide perspective for the Atlantic trade. For instance, the Roman Empire's slave markets involved as many as 500,000 new slaves per year for about 100 years at the peak period of its slave trade, which dwarfs the Atlantic slave trade's peak average of 60,000 people per year. Also, slave traders from **Muslim** regions bought and sold as many as 14 million Africans over the course of twelve centuries.

The pioneer in quantifying the Middle Passage was Philip D. Curtin. He provided an estimated total of just under 10 million African victims of the trade. One of his most striking revelations was that British North America (the United States) received less than 5 percent of the total. Curtin demonstrated that the West Indies and **Brazil** were the biggest importers, taking in about 80 percent of the total between them. This was startling given that the 4 million slaves in the United States in the 1860s was roughly half of the total New World slave population at the time. Brazil, which Curtin estimated had received roughly 39 percent of these African slaves, held only 2.5 million slaves in 1850. This disparity underscored the fact that the United States was the only large-scale slave society in history whose enslaved population grew by natural increase. "In the antebellum period," historian Michael Tadman has written in a recent exploration of this issue, slaves in the United States "showed a natural population growth of some 25 percent per decade (and indeed, North American slaves had established a pattern of natural growth by about 1710). In sharp contrast, Caribbean and Brazilian slaves commonly suffered rates of natural *decrease* of 20 percent per decade" (2000, p. 1535).

This insight kicked off wide-ranging debates over the explanations and implications of this disparity. It put on the defensive scholars who had advanced the notion that Latin American slave regimes were a racial paradise compared with those of the British and especially the United States. Unlike what previous generations would have done, however, historians of slavery in the United States were not prepared to trumpet these numbers as proof that slaveholders there were somehow more benevolent. These scholarly disputes have raised central questions such as the role of **disease** and labor regimes in New World slave life, and even what constituted "good treatment" of slaves.

Despite the impact of Curtin's study, it has had numerous challengers in the three and a half decades since it was published. Many have mined new sources and methods unavailable to him. The best examples of this are CD-ROM databases that take advantage of the great leaps forward in computer technology since Curtin did his work in the 1960s. For instance, Gwendolyn Midlo Hall published a database specific to Louisiana in 2000. Most significant, a team of scholars working out of the W.E.B. Du Bois Institute for Afro-American Research presented an even more ambitious effort for the entire Atlantic trade in 1999. Their estimate is that the overall number of Africans forced into the trade was just over 11 million (about 9.6 million of whom actually arrived in the New World), which they recognize is not a massive revision of Curtin's numbers. Similarly, by attending to the trade in Africans *within* the Americas, they have revised Curtin's breakdown of the **destinations** of these slaves, but not radically. For instance, they estimate that Brazil took 40.6 percent of the African diaspora to America rather than Curtin's 39 percent.

Most of the more effective challenges to Curtin's numbers flow not from grand overviews of the whole trade, but rather from close investigation of specific regions. Historian James A. McMillin has provided a recent example of the value of careful attention to a particular corner and period of the trade that had previously appeared only as part of more general surveys. McMillin focuses narrowly on the Atlantic slave trade to the United States between the end of the Revolutionary War and the federal ban beginning in

1808. He subjects all the methods and sources used by past estimators to unflinching scrutiny. He acknowledges and reveals all the difficulties involved in the complex task of making correct estimates. But his methodical critique of past efforts, and his willingness to reveal his own methods and sources (including providing a CD-ROM of his own with his book), make for a convincing case. That case is that the number of foreign slaves brought to the United States between 1783 and 1808 was on the order of 170,000—well above Curtin's estimate of 92,000, but below Robert W. Fogel and Stanley Engerman's estimate of 291,000.

The repercussions of such revised numbers for the overall question of the volume of the Middle Passage are not clear, of course, from one microstudy such as McMillin's. Only as such examinations yield more of these particular insights, and then as an able synthesizer (or group, such as the scholars at the Du Bois Institute who produced such an impressive overall effort) updates Curtin for the whole Atlantic, will we benefit in the aggregate from such work. And even then, it will remain only the latest, greatest estimate. *See also* Historiography; Trans-Atlantic Slave Trade Database.

Further Readings: Bradley, Keith. *Slavery and Society at Rome.* Cambridge: Cambridge University Press, 1994; Curtin, Philip D. *The Atlantic Slave Trade: A Census.* Madison: University of Wisconsin Press, 1969; Davis, David Brion. *Challenging the Boundaries of Slavery.* Cambridge, MA: Harvard University Press, 2003; Eltis, David, Behrendt, Stephen D., Richardson, David, and Klein, Herbert S., eds. *The Trans-Atlantic Slave Trade: A Database on CD-ROM.* Cambridge: Cambridge University Press, 1999; Fogel, Robert William, and Engerman, Stanley L. *Time on the Cross: The Economics of American Negro Slavery.* Boston: Little, Brown, 1974; Genovese, Eugene D. "The Treatment of Slaves in Different Countries: Problems in the Application of the Comparative Method." In Laura Foner and Eugene D. Genovese, eds. *Slavery in the New World: A Reader in Comparative History.* Englewood Cliffs, NJ: Prentice-Hall, 1969; Hall, Gwendolyn Midlo, ed. *Databases for the Study of Afro-Louisiana History and Geneaology, 1699–1860: Information from Original Manuscript Sources (CD-ROM).* Baton Rouge: Louisiana State University Press, 2000; McMillin, James A. *The Final Victims: Foreign Slave Trade to North America, 1783–1810.* Columbia: University of South Carolina Press, 2004; Tadman, Michael. "The Demographic Cost of Sugar: Debates on Slave Societies and Natural Increase in the Americas." *The American Historical Review* 105 (December 2000): 1534–1575; *William and Mary Quarterly* 3rd ser., 58 (January 2001) A special issue updating scholarship on the Atlantic slave trade; Woodward, C. Vann. "Southern Slaves in the World of Thomas Malthus." In *American Counterpoint: Slavery and Racism in the North-South Dialogue.* Boston: Little, Brown, 1971.

Matthew Mason

W

Wars, African

Although slavery is a recognized institution as old as humanity itself, the trans-Atlantic slave trade—which gained momentum after the first human **cargo** of kidnapped Africans arrived in Portugal in 1441—gave a new meaning to the trade in humans. Debates as to how Europeans managed to ship an estimated 10 to 12 million Africans to the New World over four decades still rage today. Historians and scholars have cited African urgency and complicity in the success of the trade. Although this is true, the market for slaves was created by the demand for labor on the **sugar** and tobacco **plantations** in the Americas and the Caribbean.

To broach the question of wars in Africa as these relate to the trans-Atlantic slave trade and the Middle Passage is to discuss the many factors that facilitated the trade in humans. Western **historiography** and scholarship have sought to put the blame squarely on the African urgency, while paying lip service to the fact that the market for slaves was created by the European quest for labor. Clearly the issue of wars is directly linked to that of **supply and demand**.

The so-called African domestic slavery into which European slavers tapped was the traditional punishment for crimes such as adultery, theft, kidnappings, debt, and the misfortune of being a war prisoner. During the trans-Atlantic slave trade, the main source of slaves was from this group. These individuals, in the real sense, were **indentured servants** who could and did return to their societies of origin, or intermarry, own property, and become productive citizens in their new communities. Trans-Atlantic slavery, which involved three continents, and plantation chattel slavery was a far cry from the kind of servitude that was used as a justification for chattel slavery. In the initial stages of the trans-Atlantic slave trade, various criminals and prisoners of war constituted the bulk of individuals sold to European traders. In his autobiography, *The Life of Olaudah Equiano, or Gustavus Vassa the African* (1789), **Equiano**, an ex-slave, underscores this

Two soldiers with weapons, Nigeria, 1820s. Special Collections, University of Virginia Library.

assertion when he tells of the markets in Igboland (Nigeria). These markets were frequented by Europeans who—

generally bring us firearms, gunpowder, hats, beads, and dried fish.... They always carried slaves through our land; but the strictest account is exacted of their manner of procuring them before they are suffered to pass. Sometimes indeed we sold slaves to them, but they were only prisoners of war, or such among us as had been convicted of kidnapping, or adultery, and some other crimes, which we esteemed heinous. (Equiano, 1789, p. 7)

But as the demand for slaves increased, European merchants devised means to augment their pool of slaves. Military campaigns were carried out by European **slave traders** with the help of their African mercenaries, the former providing the military support and ammunition: guns. The introduction of **firearms** into the equation as early as the 1500s enhanced the supply of slaves. Historian Philip Curtin argues that the "availability of firearms set off a gun-slave cycle in which an African state used the arms to capture more slaves, to buy more arms, and so on—forcing African states to take up slave raiding in self-protection, since guns could only be bought with slaves" (1973, p. 274).

The sale and exportation of firearms became a lucrative business in Europe, especially in England and the Netherlands. In the 1780s, the Dutch imported about 6,000 to 7,000 guns into **Luanda** (Angola) alone every year in exchange for slaves. In 1788, Birmingham gun-makers sold 150,000 guns to Africans; the total number of guns exported to Africa from Europe during the second half of the eighteenth century was 300,000 per year. **Gunpowder** was another commodity that was essential to slave raids and thus to the procurement of slaves. Britain exported approximately 1 million pounds of gunpowder to Africa per year, and by 1790 that number had doubled (Thomas, 1998, pp. 324–25). Some historians have argued that the "gun-slave cycle" had a minimal impact on the slave trade, but research shows that these developments fueled ethnic tensions and encouraged wars that furnished European slavers with Africans for sale on the slave blocks of European and American cities.

Like many societies and nations, Africans fought each other for supremacy and territorial expansion before their contact with the Europeans. But these earlier wars were relatively small in scale and less protracted because of the limited arsenal at the disposal of the warring factions. Guns magnified, expanded, and prolonged these conflicts, making more war prisoners available for sale. In 1700, a Dutch official filed this report: "Perhaps you will wonder how it happens that the Negroes get supplies of firearms? The reason is simply that we sell them incredible quantities, so handing them a knife with which to cut our throats" (Davidson, 1978, p. 171). Although African nations used those guns mainly to fight each other, there were instances in which European slavers were gunned down for trading in slaves. The report is significant because it indicates the deliberate Dutch effort to encourage conflict and wars to procure slaves by selling "incredible quantities" of guns.

In spite of the fact that some Africans willingly and greedily took part in supplying Europeans with slaves, many African communities and nations resisted slave raids and European **enslavement**, paradoxically, owing in large measure to the guns they exchanged for slaves. Records documenting African resistance to European enslavement on the African continent remain conspicuously scanty at best, giving the impression that because Africans practiced "slavery" before the advent of Europe on the scene, Africans were willing victims. This line of argument nullifies recent debates about **reparations** for slavery. On the contrary, African resistance had been noted along the slave-trading **ports** in varying degrees, from threats (King **Agaja Trudo** of **Dahomey**) and keeping a watchful eye on the coast to prevent European slave ships from docking (King Ansah of present-day Ghana) to wars against European slave traders and their African collaborators. In 1626 in **Angola**, Queen Nzingha began a thirty-year war against Portuguese slave traders and protected her kingdom until her death in 1663. The resistance was made more difficult, among other things, by what Basil Davidson calls a "one gun, one slave" policy, whereby guns to protect African communities against slave raiders, kidnappers, and hostile neighbors had to be bought, cheaply, with slaves.

It would be simplistic and misleading to assert that wars in Africa during the trans-Atlantic slave trade were primarily for the purpose of securing slaves for the European market. In addition to the "gun-slave cycle," examples of other conflicts abound. The collapse of Oyo Empire (present-day Nigeria) in the late eighteenth century came about as a result of a protracted and long war between Oyo and its neighbors that lasted for centuries. Although these wars provided slaves for European markets well into the early nineteenth century, the conflicts were primarily motivated by territorial expansion and legitimacy. Conversely, the Kingdom of Dahomey, present-day **Benin**, became one of the slave-trading and -raiding states in the region after it failed to convince European traders of any other commodity other than slaves. To remain a trading partner with Europe, the kingdom developed a well-organized army that waged wars against its neighbors for protection and to procure slaves throughout the eighteenth and nineteenth centuries. When King Agaja opposed European slave traders in the 1720s and destroyed their forts and slave camps, the Europeans turned African mercenaries on him. In the Congo, dubious treaties were signed with European slave traders and thus war was averted at the expense of continued slave-trading.

The consequences of these wars among African nations, either to protect themselves or to acquire slaves for the European slave market, took a heavy social, economic, and demographic toll on the continent as a whole.

Although the exact figures may never be known, it is estimated that the continent lost between 50 and 100 million people, but only 10 to 12 million made it through the Middle Passage to the Americas and the Caribbean. Famine, economic decline, and political instability became more noticeable after the trans-Atlantic slave trade ended—a recipe for the problems in postcolonial Africa. *See also* African Rulers and the Slave Trade; Enslavement and Procurement; Igbo; Ouidah; Slavery in Africa.

Further Readings: Agatucci, Cora. "African Slave Trade and European Imperialism." Central Oregon Community College Web site: http://www.cocc.edu/cagatucci/classes/hum211/timelines/htimeline3.htm; Curtin, Philip. *The Image of Africa: British Ideas and Action, 1780–1850.* Madison: University of Wisconsin Press, 1973; Davidson, Basil. *Discovering Africa's Past.* Essex: Longman Publishing Group, 1978; Diouf, Sylviane. *Fighting the Slave Trade: West African Strategies.* Athens: Ohio University Press, 2003; Equiano, Olaudah. *The Interesting Narrative of the Life of Olaudah Equiano, or Gustavus Vassa the African.* Essex: Longmans, Green and Company, 1789; Rodney, Walter. *How Europe Underdeveloped Africa.* Washington, DC: Howard University Press, 1981; Thomas, Hugh. *The Slave Trade: The Story of the Atlantic Slave Trade, 1440–1870.* New York: Simon & Schuster, 1997; Walvin, James. *Black Ivory: A History of British Slavery.* Washington, DC: Howard University Press, 1994.

Mawuena Logan

Washington, Madison (c. 1815–?)

In October 1841, the ship *Creole* set sail from Hampton Roads, Virginia. On board were at least 135 African American slaves destined for sale in the slave markets of **New Orleans**. En route, the slave Madison Washington led a revolt, seized control of the *Creole*, and forced the crew to sail to the British **port** of Nassau, Bahamas, where the slaves received their freedom. Through the American Civil War, black and white abolitionists used Washington and the *Creole* revolt to symbolize African Americans' desire for liberty.

Little is known about Madison Washington. Born in Virginia around 1815, he escaped to Canada in 1839 or 1840 and renamed himself Madison Washington. In 1841, Washington returned to Virginia to aid his wife in escaping to Canada. He was instead recaptured and sold to a Virginia slave-trading firm that moved slaves from the Chesapeake to the bustling slave markets of New Orleans. Washington and the slaves on board the *Creole* entered into what the historian Ira Berlin has deemed the "second Middle Passage," the forced migration of perhaps 1 million slaves from the Upper South to the Deep South between 1810 and 1860. Indeed, by 1840, the intended voyage of the *Creole* had become a routine method for transplanting Chesapeake slaves to the markets of New Orleans, in many ways replicating the first Middle Passage.

Yet the voyage of the *Creole* was anything but routine. On November 7, Madison Washington created a disturbance and then urged his fellow slaves to rebel; eighteen slaves joined him and they soon controlled the ship and its crew. Washington had the vessel sail to Nassau, where the slaves not directly involved in the revolt were soon freed by British officials. The nineteen slaves involved in the revolt, however, were held until British officials could determine whether they should be charged with mutiny and piracy. In January 1842, a British court ruled that the slaves should be freed and cleared of all charges, despite American efforts to have them re-enslaved. Once released, Washington disappeared from the historical record, although he most likely settled in the Bahamas or **Jamaica**.

Madison Washington and the *Creole* revolt was important for several reasons. It complicated ongoing negotiations between the British and American governments that eventuated in the Webster-Ashburton Treaty of 1842. The *Creole* incident also set off a brief but intense debate over slavery in the U.S. Senate when Ohio Senator Joshua Giddings introduced a resolution declaring that the dictates of natural rights and the U.S. Constitution justified the rebellion and prevented any attempt to re-enslave those involved.

Most important, black and white Abolitionists recognized the rich irony of a Virginia-born slave who had renamed himself Madison Washington leading a slave revolt. In 1853, Frederick Douglass used Washington and the *Creole* revolt as the basis of his 1853 novella, "The Heroic Slave." Douglass portrayed Madison Washington as the quintessential Virginian, cast from the same mold as his liberty-loving namesakes. As the fictionalized Washington states as he leads his rebellion, "Liberty I will have, or die in the attempt to gain it." When African American writers began penning their own accounts of black Americans during and after the Civil War, William Wells Brown devoted much attention to Washington in his books *The Negro in the American Rebellion* and *The Black Man, His Antecedents, His Genius, and His Achievements*. *See also* Abolition of the Slave Trade, United States; Internal Slave Trade, United States.

Further Readings: Berlin, Ira. *Generations of Captivity: A History of African-American Slaves*. Cambridge, MA: Belknap Press, 2003; Harrold, Stanley. "Romanticizing Slave Revolt: Madison Washington, the *Creole* Mutiny, and Abolitionist Celebration of Violent Means." In John R. McKivigan and Stanley Harrold, eds. *Antislavery Violence: Sectional, Racial, and Cultural Conflict in Antebellum America*, 89–107. Knoxville, University of Tennessee Press, 1999; Hendrick, George, and Hendrick, Willene. *The Creole Mutiny: A Tale of Revolt Aboard a Slave Ship*. Chicago: Ivan R. Dee, 2003.

John Craig Hammond

Water and Dehydration

Dehydration was the primary cause of **slave mortality** during the Middle Passage. Most slaves were allowed no more than a pint of water per day, although daily two-pint rations of stew did contain some water. A 145-pound male with an inactive lifestyle requires five pints of water daily to sustain himself properly; a minimum of two pints is needed just to replace water lost under normal conditions.

The trans-Atlantic passage typically lasted between thirty-five and seventy days, and it is scientifically remarkable that so many slaves successfully endured the voyage despite such small rations of water—between 80 and 90 percent of slaves survived the trek.

One cause of dehydration was high temperatures. At coastal Nigeria, for example, the average temperature was more than 80 degrees Fahrenheit with humidity around 80 percent. The hottest months in that region were between November and May, which is exactly when slave ships traveled in an effort to avoid hurricane **season**. Additionally, slaves were fed poorly while being transported to their ships, leaving them short on water before the intercontinental journey ever got under way.

The issue of dehydration was only worsened by the difficulties of life at sea. Many experienced sea sickness, causing them to lose water via sweat, vomit, and diarrhea. Such sea-related illness was commonplace because most slaves were unaccustomed to life at sea.

Matters only worsened when the weather turned stormy. Slaves were granted time on deck during clear weather, allowing them **exercise** and fresh air. With the rain, however, came extended stays below the deck where the conditions were violently hot and humid—one **slave trader** estimated that temperatures below deck raised as high as 130 degrees Fahrenheit. Much sorely needed water was lost through perspiration during these times. When the weather cleared, the crew was reluctant to let the slaves on deck again for fear their extreme dehydration would cause them to jump overboard without considering that it was salt water into which they would be jumping.

The effects of dehydration are brutal. Muscle cramps, mental apathy, and anorexia are all common symptoms. The victim's blood pressure drops dramatically, leaving them in a semi-conscious state in which they are not fully aware of their own dire need for water. For those enduring the rigors of Middle Passage, a sudden death was inevitable once they had progressed to that point.

Dehydration can inflict just as much pain on the psyche as it can on the body. Many slaves, suffering from an extreme lack of water, seemingly willed themselves to die. This resulted in the misguided belief that Africans had the unique ability to kill themselves by holding their breath. It has since been discovered that extreme dehydration caused a state of shock, which then led to an involuntary death.

Water serving sizes increased slowly as the journey progressed, as those who died of dehydration had their rations divvied up among the survivors. *See also* Food; Ventilation and Suffocation.

Further Readings: Higgins, Brian, and Kiple, Kenneth. "Mortality Caused by Dehydration during the Middle Passage." *Social Science History* 13 (1989): 421–437. USMA Library, NY. [Online, November 8, 2006]. Journal Storage Web site: http://links.jstor. org/sici?sici=0145-5532(198924)13%3A4%3C421%3AMCBDDT%3E2.0.CO%3B2-3; Walvin, James. *Atlas of Slavery.* Great Britain: Pearson Education Limited, 2006.

Michael Lombardo

Wheatley, Phillis (1753–1784)

Wheatley was the first African American, and one of the first American women, to publish a collection of poetry. She arrived in Boston in 1761 at the age of seven on a ship named the *Phillis*, which departed from **Senegal**. Wheatley was purchased by John and Susanna Wheatley, parents of twins Mary and Nathaniel, and was immediately afforded an informal education by the family. She was emancipated in September of 1773 after publishing a book of poetry, *Poems on Various Subjects, Religious and Moral*. Wheatley married John Peters of Boston in April of 1778 and died during childbirth in 1784, leaving no surviving children.

A prodigious adolescent, with knowledge of several languages, and keenly alert to the social and academic spheres of prerevolutionary Boston, Wheatley began to publish her poetry in 1767 at the age of fourteen. She gained much public attention because of her poetry, which was featured in newspapers across **New England**. In 1772, Wheatley was formally interrogated by scholars, politicians, and clergymen in Boston so that they might validate her ability as a poet. Because slavery advocates justified their position based on the purported intellectual inferiority of Africans (as proven by the lack of a body of African literature), Wheatley's publicly proclaimed status as a legitimate author was of particular social significance. Subsequent claims of the poet's mimicry and parroting came about as a result of the content of Wheatley's poetry and her style of writing, which was greatly influenced by the poetry of Alexander Pope.

Much of Wheatley's poetry is concerned with classical themes, mythology, and **Christian** theology, but some critics find a discreet subversion in even her most seemingly complacent poems, such as the often-anthologized "On Being Brought from Africa to America." One of Wheatley's most scathing accounts of her **enslavement** is found in her "To The Right Honourable William, Earl Of Dartmouth." Indeed, in both her poetry and her correspondence, Wheatley pointed out the hypocrisy of those in power who at once postulated equality for all men and insisted on the inferiority of certain races of men.

In 1773, her collection *Poems* was published in **London**. Between then and 1838, the work was published ten more times in America and Britain (although with varying titles). Advertisements for the first edition emphasized the frontispiece engraving of Wheatley. The illustration was drawn by Scipio Moorhead, the "S. M." of Wheatley's "To S. M., a Young African Painter on Seeing His Works," which extols the talents of a fellow African artist in America. Wheatley's attempts at securing funding for a second volume of poetry were unsuccessful, in part because of the turmoil of a difficult marriage and the American Revolution.

Wheatley's poetry excited the ire of such figures as Thomas Jefferson and the praise of George Washington and Voltaire. Wheatley has maintained such notability because of her unusual status as an eighteenth-century African American slave, woman, and poet. Her poetry itself is exemplary of neoclassical and Romantic poetry, thus perpetuating Wheatley's primarily literary historical persona. In many ways, Wheatley was the forerunner for modern black and women's literary movements. It was during the twentieth century, however, that Wheatley's poetry endured the scrutiny of critics and activists owing to its lack of explicit subversion.

Further Readings: Applegate, Anne. "Phillis Wheatley: Her Critics and Her Contribution." *Negro American Literature Forum* 9, 4 (1975): 123–126; Carretta, Vincent, and Gould, Philip, eds. *Genius in Bondage: Literature of the Early Black Atlantic*. Lexington: University Press of Kentucky, 2001; Gates, Jr., Henry Louis. *The Trials of Phillis Wheatley*. New York: Basic *Civitas* Books, 2003.

Jessica M. Kubiak

Wilberforce, William (1759–1833)

William Wilberforce was a prominent British politician and leader of the abolitionist movement. Wilberforce was born on August 24, 1759, to a wealthy family. His father died while Wilberforce was a youth, and the child was placed under the care of an uncle who was a devout Methodist. Under his guardian's influence, Wilberforce developed a keen interest in social equality and **Christianity** (he later became an evangelical Christian). While at Cambridge, Wilberforce became a close friend with future Prime Minister William Pitt (1759–1806). After college, Wilberforce decided to pursue a career in politics and was elected a member of Parliament in 1780 as a Tory.

Wilberforce quickly became known for his efforts at social reform, particularly trying to improve the working conditions and lives of the poor in Great Britain. His efforts led him to be dubbed the "Renewer of Society." In 1787, he became a firm abolitionist following a meeting with some of the leading antislavery advocates in Great Britain. Wilberforce's **abolitionism** often put him at odds with other Tories who supported the commercial interests in the West Indian colonies, which were economically dependent on slavery at the time. He did, however, enjoy the support of some leading politicians such as Pitt. In 1791, Wilberforce put forth a bill to abolish slavery, but the measure was defeated by a vote of 163 opposed and 88 in favor.

Throughout the remainder of his political career, Wilberforce introduced antislavery measures in each session of the House of Commons. Wilberforce's greatest legislative success occurred in 1805 when Parliament approved a bill to abolish the slave trade within the British Empire. The law went into force in 1807 and forbade the sale and transport of slaves within the empire. Wilberforce and many abolitionists of the time believed that ending the trade would eventually lead to the end of slavery.

Wilberforce subsequently endeavored to bolster support to enforce the prohibition on slavery, including stationing naval forces off of Africa to interdict slave ships. The continuing Napoleonic Wars constrained the availability of forces, and Wilberforce and his allies realized that only a complete ban on slavery would end the practice. Repeated efforts to completely ban slavery failed during Wilberforce's political career. Nonetheless, he was able to continue placing pressure on successive governments to suppress the slave trade. Meanwhile, he was active in other social issues, including initiatives to suppress vice and improve education and health care for the poor. He was a founding member of the Royal Society for the Prevention of Cruelty to Animals. Wilberforce retired from politics in 1825, and it fell to his successors to secure the passage of the Abolition Act, which finally ended slavery in the

Portrait of William Wilberforce, the main parliamentary spokesperson for the antislavery movement. Courtesy of Anti-Slavery International.

British Empire. The act was passed one month after Wilberforce died on July 29, 1833. *See also* Abolition of Slave Trade, Great Britain; African Squadrons, The; British Caribbean; British Slave Trade; Closure of the Slave Trade.

Further Readings: Brown, Ford K. *Fathers of the Victorians: The Age of Wilberforce*. Cambridge: Cambridge University Press, 1961; Coupland, Reginald. *Wilberforce*. London: Collins, 1945; Pollock, John. *Wilberforce*. New York: St. Martin's Press, 1978.

Tom Lansford

Windward Coast

The coastal areas of West and Central Africa produced the largest percentage of the slaves taken to the Americas during the trans-Atlantic slave trade. These coastal areas were given a variety of names by the Europeans. The names given to them help to differentiate between one part of Africa and the other. The Windward Coast is one of the five major coastal regions of West Africa. The remaining four include, Senegambia, **Sierra Leone, Gold Coast**, and **Slave Coast**.

The Windward Coast is located in the territory stretching between Cape Mount in present-day western **Liberia** and Assini in eastern Côte d'Ivoire. Its size is equivalent to the present-day Liberia and the Côte d'Ivoire put

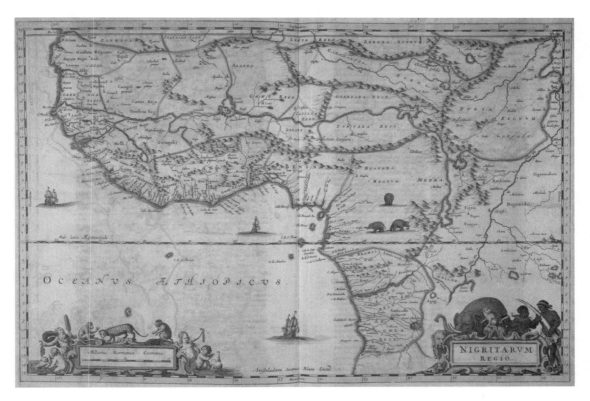

Map of West and West Central Africa, 1662. Tracy W. McGregor Library, Special Collections, University of Virginia Library.

together. The Windward Coast was particularly noteworthy for its malagueta pepper and ivory.

Whether in the Windward, Gold, or Slave Coasts, the general trend in slave acquisition was such that Europeans traders waited along the coast to buy slaves from African and non-African intermediaries. Limited evidence suggests that Europeans unilaterally engaged in slave capturing. One of the few episodes of a European abducting and enslaving an African was found along the Windward Coast. William Snelgrave, a prominent **slave merchant**, observed that in the Windward Coast French and British traders abducted black traders under some slight pretence of having received injury from them.

The slave-trading activities of all Europeans occurred along the Windward Coast. It was one of the longest stretches of coastline where the Dutch traded in slaves. Dutch traders acquired their slaves from a large variety of small trading centers along the coast. Of all these coastal trading centers, Cape Lahous was the most influential. Another prominent part of the Windward Coast was Cape Mesurado. Ethnically, the Caga people were shipped from Cape Mesurado while most of the slaves shipped from Cape Lahou were of Mbato origin. The Dutch seem to have had a longer period of trading along the Windward Coast when compared with their French and British counterparts.

French economic activities became important from the 1720s through 1740s, and then fell off. Both English and Dutch trade reached a peak in the 1760s. Between 1741 and 1782, 40 percent of the Dutch slave traders acquired their slaves from the Windward Coast. By the early nineteenth century, when other coastal regions such as the Gold and the Slave Coasts still supplied slaves, the Windward Coast had dropped considerably as a source of slaves. *See also* Dutch Slave Trade; Senegal.

Further Readings: Engerman, Stanley, and Genovese, Eugene. *Race and Slavery in the Western Hemisphere: Quantitative Studies*. Princeton, NJ: Princeton University Press, 1975; Palmer, Colin. *Human Cargoes: The British Slave Trade to Spanish America, 1700–1739* Urbana: University of Illinois Press, 1981; Postma, Johannes. *The Dutch in the Atlantic Slave Trade 1600–1815*. New York and Cambridge: Cambridge University Press, 1990.

Saheed Aderinto

Windward Islands

The Windward Islands are a line of Caribbean islands constituting the southern end of the Lesser Antilles. From the seventeenth to the early nineteenth century, they were colonized by the British and French and became some of the most important and productive **sugar** colonies in the world. During this time, hundreds of thousands of slaves were imported from Africa to work on the sugar **plantations** and in other economic activities. By the end of the eighteenth century, the populations of all the habitable islands had large majorities of slaves.

From north to south, the group includes the volcanic islands of Dominica (sometimes included as a **Leeward Island**), Martinique, Saint Lucia, Saint Vincent, the Grenadines, and Grenada. Barbados (to the east) and Trinidad and Tobago (to the south) are not a geographic part of the Windward Islands but often are included in the region because of their proximity.

Most of the Windward Islands were discovered by Europeans as early as the journeys of Columbus. None, however, was settled permanently by Europeans until the English colonized Barbados in 1627 and the French colonized Martinique in 1635. All other islands either remained unsettled by Europeans until the eighteenth century or changed hands numerous times over the seventeenth and eighteenth centuries. Ultimately, Britain took control of all the Windward Islands except Martinique.

From the beginning some African slaves were brought to the new colonies. In the early years, however, whites made up the majority of settlers—an estimated 97 percent in Barbados in 1638 (Blackburn, 1997, p. 230). In the 1640s, this began to change as sugar, a lucrative export product, was introduced to Barbados, creating a strong market for slaves. By 1655, nearly 50 percent of Barbados's residents were enslaved. By 1712, more than 75 percent of the population was enslaved (Dunn, 1972, p. 87). A similar pattern, although delayed by about a decade, occurred in Martinique although it, unlike Barbados, diversified somewhat into coffee during the eighteenth century. In the other Windward Islands, sugar was not introduced and slave populations did not increase appreciably until the late eighteenth century when the islands came under permanent British control. By the nineteenth century, these islands also had slave majorities.

Because of the low fertility and high **mortality** among African slaves in the sugar colonies, thousands of slaves had to be imported annually just to maintain the required labor forces. For Barbados, slave imports increased from an estimated 1,300 a year in the 1640s to more than 3,000 by the end of the seventeenth century. The total number of slaves imported to Barbados has been estimated at nearly 390,000, but the slave population peaked at only 82,000. Similarly, 365,000 slaves were imported into Martinique, which had a peak slave population of around 86,000, and some 160,000 slaves were imported into the other Windward Islands, which had a combined slave population of around 95,000 in 1834. An estimated 10 percent of all slaves transported from Africa were brought to the Windward Islands (Curtin, 1969, pp. 55, 59, 65, 68, 78, 80, 88).

For the early period of trade (from 1640 until 1725) records suggest that Barbadian planters mostly purchased slaves from the adjacent regions of the **Gold Coast** and the Bight of Benin (nearly 65 percent) with large contingents also coming from the Bight of Biafra and **Angola**. The Barbadian trade later shifted its emphasis to the Bight of Biafra and then, to a lesser degree, to Angola, while always importing large numbers from the Gold Coast. For Martinique, most direct imports (nearly 60 percent) came from the Bight of Benin until 1750 with more than 20 percent coming from Angola. From 1750, the trade shifted to the Bight of Biafra and Angola (around 30 percent each). Many of Martinique's slaves, however, probably were not imported directly but transshipped from other European colonies. The other, smaller, Windward Islands did not import all of their slaves directly; however,, those that did mostly came from the Bight of Biafra with small groups (around 10 percent) from the Gold Coast, **Sierra Leone**, Angola, and the **Windward**

Coast. Some variability existed between particular islands (African origins calculated from Eltis, Behrendt, Richardson, and Klein, 1999). *See also* British Caribbean; French Caribbean; Trans-Atlantic Slave Trade Database.

Further Readings: Blackburn, Robin. *The Making of New World Slavery: From the Baroque to the Modern, 1492–1800*. New York: Verso, 1997; Curtin, Philip D. *The Atlantic Slave Trade: A Census*. Madison: University of Wisconsin Press, 1969; Dunn, Richard S. *Sugar and Slaves: The Rise of the Planter Class in the English West Indies, 1624–1713*. Chapel Hill: University of North Carolina Press, 1972; Eltis, David, Behrendt, Stephen D., Richardson, David, and Klein, Herbert S., eds. *The Trans-Atlantic Slave Trade: A Database on CD-ROM*. Cambridge: Cambridge University Press, 1999; Stinchcombe, Arthur L. *Sugar Island Slavery in the Age of Enlightenment*. Princeton, NJ: Princeton University Press, 1995.

Patrick Luck

Women

Although men accounted for the majority of captives during the initial stages of the slave trade, women became increasingly valuable to the market. Initially, European enslavers wanted adult men; however, the supply was dependent on the African traders, who brought both men and women (Klein, 1999, p. 162). Soon enough, New World planters realized the high work rates of women, and began to value their labor as much as men (Nwokeji, 2001). The Bight of Biafra was the only region that supplied higher percentages of women into the trade (Nwokeji, 2001). The rest of the coastal regions supplied mostly men. The supply of enslaved women rose significantly during the eighteenth century, as women began making up a significant percentage of the trade (Klein, 1978, p. 149).

Contemporary view of São Jorge da Mina women's dungeon. Courtesy of Manuel Barcia.

There was an increasing demand for women preceding the closing of the British and U.S. trans-Atlantic slave trade (Klein, 1999, p. 162). By the late eighteenth century, the sex ratio was equal in the United States, which attempted to ensure a stable procreation rate throughout the nineteenth century (Gaspar and Hine, 1996, p. 26). Lower percentages of women were brought to the **sugar plantations** throughout the Caribbean and South America than to the United States. The labor demands were fiercer in sugar production, and the **mortality** rates were significantly higher because of the physical demands of the process.

The Middle Passage was exceptionally hard for women. They were often kept on deck and at proximity to the ship crew, who would routinely **rape** and abuse them. The crew would often make them sing and dance as a mode of humiliation and entertainment. This was a practice called "**dancing** the slaves," which occurred regularly during the passage. The **suicide** rates during the Middle Passage were higher for enslaved women, because they chose to jump ship rather than endure the horrors of slavery.

Once in the New World, the **gender** division of labor depended greatly on the region and the individual plantation, although the majority of the time, women and men did similar jobs. It was common for the company that shipped them, as well as for the initial planters, to **brand** the captives. The French were known for placing the brand on the women's chest (Gaspar and Hine, 1996, p. 289).

The cost of an enslaved woman was usually lower than of an enslaved man, except for when the woman was sold as a concubine or prostitute (Gaspar and Hine, 1996, p. 26). The trans-Atlantic slave trade intensified gender inequality as well as diversified women's roles both in the New World and in West African regions (Nwokeji, 2001, p. 36). *See also* Children; Families and Family Separations; Gender and Slave Exports.

Further Readings: Gaspar, David Barry, and Hine, Darlene Clark, eds. *More Than Chattel: Black Women and Slavery in the Americas.* Bloomington: Indiana University Press, 1996; Klein, Herbert S. *The Atlantic Slave Trade.* Cambridge: Cambridge University Press, 1999; Klein, Herbert S. *The Middle Passage: Comparative Studies in the Atlantic Slave Trade.* Princeton, NJ: Princeton University Press, 1978; Nwokeji, G. Ugo. "African Conceptions of Gender and the Slave Traffic." *William and Mary Quarterly* 58, 1 (2001):47–66.

Kelley Deetz

Z

Zong, The

The *Zong* was a **Liverpool** slave ship involved in a notorious incident long cited by British abolitionists as an example of the cruelty of the West African slave trade. It was of average size (107 tons) and had been taken as a prize during the American Revolution. Owned by a partnership group headed by **slave trader** and banker William Gregson (1718–1809), the *Zong* departed Liverpool on March 5, 1781, bound for the **Gold Coast**. After embarking 440 slaves, the *Zong* departed Africa for **Jamaica** on September 6, 1781. Captained by Luke Collingswood, the *Zong* arrived in Jamaican waters in December 1781 and began the sale of its slaves on December 28, 1781. The *Zong* returned to Liverpool on May 20, 1782. En route from Africa, however, **overcrowding** and **disease** claimed the lives of more than half the slaves, and only 208 slaves arrived in Jamaica. To prevent further deaths, and to save dwindling supplies of **water**, Collingswood had ordered 131 slaves be cast overboard, reasoning that they could be claimed as a loss to the **insurance** underwriters.

The terms of the insurance policy taken out by the owners stated that, if slaves died a natural death, the loss would be the owners', but if slaves were thrown overboard alive, the loss would be the insurance underwriters'. Arguing that illness did not constitute a sufficient reason to throw slaves overboard, the insurance underwriters denied the claim. In the resulting court case, *Gregson v. Gilbert*, the jury sided with the ship owners and ordered the underwriters to pay the claim. Despite its implications for the future of the **British slave trade**, the case was decided as a routine business dispute. The case was appealed by the owners and came before Lord Justice Mansfield on May 1783. Counsel for the owners maintained that as a matter of law slaves were chattels, a species of property, rather than human beings. As such, Captain Collingswood had acted within his discretion as master of the ship in throwing the slaves overboard. Necessity had required him to do so to save the crew and the remaining slaves and to ensure the success of the venture for those who had hired him. Justice Mansfield accepted this reasoning, and upheld the lower court ruling. Mansfield understood the importance of the case and ordered a new trial, a trial that was never held.

The *Zong* affair created a public sensation, and was offered as an example of the barbarity of the African slave trade. Possessing all the innate qualities of humanity, abolitionists argued that a slave was a person and could thus never be considered merely property. This notion presented a contradiction, however, that threatened the continued existence of the profitable British slave trade. Abolitionist Granville Sharp attempted to rally public support for prosecuting the crew of the *Zong* for murder, to little avail. The *Zong* case was a powerful indictment of the slave trade that elicited wide public support for the abolition of the British slave trade. *See also* Abolitionism, Abolition of the Slave Trade, Great Britain; Closure of the Slave Trade; Drownings.

Further Readings: Herbert Klein, *The Middle Passage*. Princeton, NJ: Princeton University Press, 1978; Shyllon, F. O. *Black Slaves in Britain*. New York: Oxford University Press, 1974; Walvin, James. *Black Ivory: A History of British Slavery*. Washington, DC: Howard University Press, 1994.

Brian W. Refford

Zulueta, Pedro de

Pedro de Zulueta was the first person tried for allegedly participating in the slave trade while on the United Kingdom's own soil. His was tried and acquitted by a lay jury, in **London**'s central criminal court at the Old Bailey in October 1843.

The case against Zulueta, while called *Regina* (Queen) *v. Zulueta* because it followed grand jury indictments, was prosecuted by Sir George Stephen, an English abolitionist and historian. The U.K. government made strong efforts to enforce antislave-trading laws after 1807, but those efforts did not include prosecutions in its criminal courts. The English government did not have a permanent staff of lawyers to prosecute crimes in the first half of the nineteenth century. This lack of staff was due to a constitutional tradition dating back to abolition of the Star Chamber and England's seventeenth-century revolutions, continued "Saxon" antipathy to any remnant of "the Norman yoke," and fears of potential abuse like Spain's inquisition and France's 1790s guillotinings. Criminal prosecutions were typically maintained by victims or concerned private individuals at their own expense or (after they were formed) by officers of England's new local police forces.

Zulueta, a Basque, was a younger member of the merchant firm of Zulueta and Co., headed by his father, which had been quartered in London since the 1820s. The charges against him arose from Zulueta and Co.'s role with a ship named the *Augusta*.

The *Augusta* had previously been sailing as the *Gollupchick* under the Russian flag, with a Spanish captain named Thomas Bernardos and a Spanish crew, when it was boarded and seized by the Royal Navy as a possible slaver off the West African coast in 1839. It found evidence that the *Gollupchick* was to be used in transporting slaves—extra water casks, a large kitchen, and covered gratings. The joint British-Spanish commission in

Freetown ruled, however, that it could not act against Russian-flagged ships, so the *Gollupchick* was sent on to England and released to the Russian consul in London. The ship was then sold, stripped of its "slaving equipment," and refitted in Portsmouth, registered as the *Augusta* under the U.K. flag, loaded with a new cargo at **Liverpool** and Cadiz, and sent back to the West African coast where the Royal Navy again seized it in early 1841, this time off the Gallinas River.

The second seizure of the *Gollupchick-Augusta* was discussed by the first Select Committee of the House of Commons on the West Coast of Africa in 1842, while it was evaluating the role of the United Kingdom. Zulueta testified before the Select Committee as a representative of Zulueta and Co. in mid-1842. The grand jury's 1843 indictments were largely based on his Select Committee testimony.

The grand jury's specific accusations were that Zulueta had employed a ship and shipped goods to be used in the slave trade, in violation the U.K. 1824 antislave-trading statute, a felony punishable by transportation to Botany Bay for up to fourteen years. Although the *Gollupchick-Augusta*'s new owners were a Captain Jennings and the former *Gollupchick*'s Captain Bernardos, the check for the £650 used to complete the purchase came from Zulueta and Co. Zulueta and Co. had received a mortgage on the ship, supposedly (per Zulueta) as agents for Martinez and Company of Cadiz. Zulueta and Co. had also paid for the *Augusta*'s new **cargo**—tobacco, arms, **gunpowder**, copperware, iron pots, looking glasses, and cloth—also supposedly as Martinez and Company's agents.

Stephen's prosecution of Zulueta was based entirely on circumstantial evidence. The *Augusta* had not reached the Gallinas when it was seized, it was not carrying any slaving equipment, and no slaves were on board. The lawyers Stephen employed as prosecutors were therefore forced to argue that: (1) there was no other business along the Gallinas, and no buildings other than **barracoons**, so the *Augusta*'s only reason for being in its vicinity must have been to engage in slave-trading; and (2) the equipment necessary for shipping slaves could have been purchased onshore.

Stephen's lawyers were unable to effectively counter Zulueta's own testimony that he—thousands of miles away in London—was unaware of any intent of the ship's **captain** and owners to trade the *Augusta*'s cargo for slaves.

After Zulueta's acquittal, he privately published an 1844 book asserting his innocence. Later the same year, the British and Foreign Anti-Slavery Society took and republished his book, with additional sections asserting that other evidence, not presented at the trial, showed him to be guilty.

Stephen brought his case against Zulueta at a time when U.K. abolitionists had become frustrated by their inability to obtain Spanish legislation toughening the ban of the Middle Passage trade, particularly to **Cuba**, as promised in Spain's 1835 treaty with the United Kingdom. It may, or may not, have been a coincidence that Zulueta's first cousin in **Havana**, Julian Zulueta, was a prominent—if not the most prominent—Cuban **slave trader**. *See also* Abolition of the Slave Trade, Great Britain; African Squadrons, The; British Navy; British Slave Trade; Closure of the Slave Trade; Illegal Slave Trade, Spanish Caribbean; Sugar.

Further Readings: Catterall, Helen Tunnicliff. *Judicial Cases Concerning American Slavery and the Negro.* vol. 1. Washington, DC: Carnegie Institution, 1926; Eltis, David. *Economic Growth and the Ending of the Transatlantic Slave Trade.* New York: Oxford University Press, 1987; Hay, Douglas, and Snyder, Francis, eds. *Policing and Prosecution in Britain 1750–1850.* Oxford: Clarendon Press, 1989; Lloyd, Christopher. *The Navy and the Slave Trade.* London: Longmans, Green and Company, 1949; Slave Trading Act of 1824, 5 George IV, chapter 113; Thomas, Hugh. *The Slave Trade: The Story of the Atlantic Slave Trade, 1440–1870.* New York: Simon & Schuster, 1997; Zulueta, Pedro de. *The Trial of Pedro de Zulueta, Jun., on a Charge of Slave Trading.* Westport, CT: Greenwood Press, 1970.

Steven B. Jacobson

SELECTED BIBLIOGRAPHY

The following bibliography represents only a selection of some of the most important works on the Middle Passage. Readers should also consult the numerous additional titles that appear at the end of each entry under the heading "Further Readings."

Andrews, George Reed. *The Afro-Argentines of Buenos Aires, 1800–1900*. Madison: University of Wisconsin Press, 1980.

Barbot, Jean. *Barbot on Guinea*, ed. P.E.H. Hair, Adam Jones, and Robin Law. 2 vols. London: Hakluyt Society, 1992.

Barry, Boubacar. *Senegambia and the Atlantic Slave Trade*. African Studies Series no. 92, ed. J. M. Lonsdale. Cambridge: Cambridge University Press, 1997.

Behrendt, Stephen D. "Crew Mortality in the Transatlantic Slave Trade in the Eighteenth Century." *Slavery and Abolition* 18, 1 (1997): 49–71.

Bergad, Laird W., Fe Iglesias García, and María del Carmen Barcia. *The Cuban Slave Market, 1790–1880*. Cambridge: Cambridge University Press, 1995.

Berlin, Ira. *Generations of Captivity: A History of African-American Slaves*. Cambridge, MA: Belknap Press, 2003.

———. *Many Thousands Gone: The First Two Centuries of Slavery in North America*. Cambridge, MA: Belknap Press, 1998.

Bethell, Leslie. *The Abolition of the Brazilian Slave Trade: Britain, Brazil, and the Slave Trade Question, 1807–1869*. Cambridge: Cambridge University Press, 1970.

———. "The Mixed Commissions for the Suppression of the Transatlantic Slave Trade in the Nineteenth Century." *Journal of African History* 41, 1 (1966): 79–93.

Blackburn, Robin. *The Making of New World Slavery: From the Baroque to the Modern, 1492–1800*. New York: Verso Press, 1997.

Carretta, Vincent, and Philip Gould, eds. *Genius in Bondage: Literature of the Early Black Atlantic*. Lexington: University Press of Kentucky, 2001.

Clemens, Paul G. E. "The Rise of Liverpool, 1665–1750." *Economic History Review* 29 (1976): 211–225.

Conrad, Robert Edgar. *World of Sorrow: The African Slave Trade to Brazil*. Baton Rouge: Louisiana State University Press, 1986.

Corwin, Arthur F. *Spain and the Abolition of Slavery in Cuba, 1817–1886*. Austin: University of Texas Press, 1967.

Costanzo, Angelo, ed. *The Interesting Narrative of the Life of Olaudah Equiano or Gustavus Vassa, the African, Written by Himself*. Peterborough, Canada: Broadview Press, 2001.

Coulombe, Charles. *Rum: The Epic Story of the Drink That Changed the World*. Sacramento, CA: Citadel Press, 2004.

Craton, Michael. *Empire, Enslavement, and Freedom in the Caribbean*. Kingston, Jamaica: Ian Randle Publishers, 1997.

Curtin, Philip D. *The Atlantic Slave Trade: A Census*. Madison: University of Wisconsin Press, 1969.

———. *The Image of Africa: British Ideas and Action, 1780–1850*. Madison: University of Wisconsin Press, 1973.

Davidson, Basil. *The African Slave Trade*. Rev. ed. Boston: Little, Brown, 1980.

Davis, David Brion. *Challenging the Boundaries of Slavery*. Cambridge, MA: Harvard University Press, 2003.

———. *Slavery and Human Progress*. Oxford: Oxford University Press, 1984.

Davis, Natalie Zemon. *Trickster Travels: A Sixteenth-Century Muslim between Worlds*. New York: Hill and Wang, 2006.

Diedrich, Maria, Henry Louis Gates, and Carl Pedersen, eds. *Black Imagination and the Middle Passage*. Oxford: Oxford University Press, 1999.

Dike, Onwuka. *Trade and Politics in the Niger Delta, 1830–1885*. Oxford: Clarendon Press, 1956.

Donnan, Elizabeth, ed. *Documents Illustrative of the History of the Slave Trade to America*. 4 vols. Buffalo, NY: William S. Hein, 2002 (1930–1935).

Dorsey, Joseph C. *Slave Traffic in the Age of Abolition*. Gainesville: University Press of Florida, 2003.

Dow, George Francis. *Slave Ships and Slaving*. New York: Dover Publications, 1970.

DuBois, Laurent. *Avengers of the New World: The Story of the Haitian Revolution*. Cambridge, MA: Harvard University Press, 2004.

Du Bois, W.E.B. *The Suppression of the African Slave Trade to the United States of America, 1638–1870*. New York: Longmans, Green and Co., 1904.

Eltis, David, Stephen D. Behrendt, David Richardson, and Herbert S. Klein, eds. *The Trans-Atlantic Slave Trade: A Database on CD-ROM*. Cambridge: Cambridge University Press, 1999.

Engerman, Stanley, and Eugene Genovese. *Race and Slavery in the Western Hemisphere: Quantitative Studies*. Princeton, NJ: Princeton University Press, 1975.

Falconbridge, Alexander. *An Account of the Slave Trade on the Coast of Africa*. New York: AMS Press, 1973.

Falola, Toyin, and Matt D. Childs, eds. *The Yoruba Diaspora in the Atlantic World*. Bloomington: Indiana University Press, 2004.

Falola, Toyin, and G. O. Oguntomisin. *Yoruba Warlords of the Nineteenth Century*. Trenton, NJ: Africa World Press, 2001.

Gates, Henry Louis, ed. *Oxford African American Studies Center: Encyclopedia of African American History, 1619–1895*. Oxford: Oxford University Press, 2006.

Geggus, David, ed. *The Impact of the Haitian Slave Revolt in the Atlantic World*. Columbia: University of South Carolina Press, 2001.

Gemery, Henry, and Jan Hogendorn, eds. *The Uncommon Market: Essays in the Economic History of the Atlantic Slave Trade*. New York: Academic, 1979.

Genovese, Eugene D. *Roll, Jordan, Roll: The World the Slaves Made*. New York: Pantheon, 1974.

Goldenberg, David M. *The Curse of Ham: Race and Slavery in Early Judaism, Christianity, and Islam*. Princeton, NJ: Princeton University Press, 2003.

Gomez, Michael. *Exchanging Our Country Marks: The Transformation of African Identities in the Colonial Antebellum South*. Chapel Hill: University of North Carolina Press, 1998.

Greene, Lorenzo J. *The Negro in Colonial New England, 1620–1776*. New York: Columbia University Press, 1942.

Gudmestad, Robert. *A Troublesome Commerce: The Transformation of the Interstate Slave Trade*. Baton Rouge: Louisiana State University Press, 2003.

Hall, Gwendolyn M. *Slavery and African Ethnicities in the Americas*. Chapel Hill: University of North Carolina Press, 2005.

Harms, Robert. *The Diligent: A Voyage Through the Worlds of the Slave Trade*. New York: Basic Books, 2002.

Harris, Joseph, ed. *Global Dimensions of the African Diaspora*. 2nd ed. Washington, DC: Howard University Press, 1993.

Hazlewood, Nick. *The Queen's Slave Trader: John Hawkyns, Elizabeth I, and the Trafficking in Human Souls*. New York: HarperCollins, 2004.

Hernaes, Per O. *Slaves, Danes, and African Coast Society: The Danish Slave Trade from West Africa and Afro-Danish Relations on the Eighteenth-Century Gold Coast*. Trondheim: Norwegian University of Science and Technology, 1995.

Hurston, Zora Neale. "Cudjo's Own Story of the Last African Slaver." *Journal of Negro History* 12 (October 1927): 648–663.

Ingersoll, Thomas N. *Mammon and Manon in Early New Orleans: The First Slave Society in the Deep South, 1718–1819*. Knoxville: University of Tennessee Press, 1999.

Inikori, Joseph E. *Africans and Industrial Revolution in England: A Study of International Trade and Economic Development*. Cambridge: Cambridge University Press, 2002.

Inikori, Joseph E., and Stanley L. Engerman, eds. *The Atlantic Slave Trade: Effects on Economies, Societies, and Peoples in Africa, the Americas, and Europe*. Durham, NC: Duke University Press, 1992.

Johnson, Walter. *Soul by Soul: Life Inside the Antebellum Slave Market*. Cambridge, MA: Harvard University Press, 2000.

Jordan, Winthrop. *White over Black: American Attitudes toward the Negro, 1550–1812*. Chapel Hill: University of North Carolina Press, 1968.

Klein, Herbert S. *The Atlantic Slave Trade*. Cambridge: Cambridge University Press, 1999.

———. *The Middle Passage: Comparative Studies in the Atlantic Slave Trade*. Princeton, NJ: Princeton University Press, 1978.

Klein, Herbert S., Stanley L. Engerman, Robin Haines, and Ralph Shlomowitz. "Transoceanic Mortality: The Slave Trade in Comparative Perspective." *William and Mary Quarterly* 58, 1 (2001): 93–117.

Law, Robin. *Ouidah: The Social History of a West African Slaving Port, 1727–1892*. Athens: Ohio University Press, 2005.

———. "Slave Raiders and Middlemen, Monopolists and Free-Traders: The Supply of Slaves for the Atlantic Trade in Dahomey, c. 1715–1850." *Journal of African History* 30, 1 (1989): 45–68.

———. "Trade and Politics behind the Slave Coast: The Lagoon Traffic and the Rise of Lagos, 1500–1800." *Journal of African History* 24, 3 (1983): 321–348.

Law, Robin, and Paul E. Lovejoy. *The Biography of Mahommah Gardo Baquaqua: His Passage from Slavery to Freedom in Africa and America*. Princeton, NJ: Markus Wiener, 2001.

Lovejoy, Paul E. *Transformations in Slavery: A History of Slavery in Africa*. Cambridge: Cambridge University Press, 1993.

Manning, Patrick. *Slavery and African Life: Occidental, Oriental, and African Slave Trades*. African Studies Series, ed. J. M. Lonsdale. Cambridge: Cambridge University Press, 2000.

Mannix, Daniel Pratt, with Malcolm Cowley. *Black Cargoes: A History of the Atlantic Slave Trade, 1518–1865*. New York: Viking, 1962.

Miller, Joseph C. *Way of Death: Merchant Capitalism and the Angolan Slave Trade*. Madison: University of Wisconsin Press, 1988.

Mintz, Sidney W., and Richard Price. *The Birth of African-American Culture: An Anthropological Perspective*. Boston: Beacon Press, 1992.

Morgan, Kenneth. "Slave Sales in Colonial Charleston." *English Historical Review* 113 (1998): 905–927.

Morgan, Philip D. *Slave Counterpoint: Black Culture in the Eighteenth-Century Chesapeake and Lowcountry*. Chapel Hill: University of North Carolina Press, 1998.

Moses, William J. *Liberian Dreams: Back-to-Africa Narratives from the 1850s*. University Park: Pennsylvania State University Press, 1998.

Mouser, Bruce L. *A Slaving Voyage to Africa and Jamaica: The Log of the Sandown, 1793–1794*. Bloomington: Indiana University Press, 2002.

Northrup, David, ed. *The Atlantic Slave Trade*. Boston: Houghton Mifflin, 2002.

———. "The Compatibility of the Slave and Palm Oil Trades in the Bight of Biafra." *Journal of African History* 17, 3 (1976): 353–364.

Nwokeji, G. Ugo. "African Conceptions of Gender and the Slave Traffic." *William and Mary Quarterly* 58, 1 (2001): 47–66.

Ott, Thomas O. *The Haitian Revolution, 1789–1804.* Knoxville: University of Tennessee Press, 1973.

Palmer, Colin A. *Human Cargoes: The British Slave Trade to Spanish America, 1700–1739.* Urbana: University of Illinois Press, 1981.

Patterson, Orlando. *Slavery and Social Death.* Cambridge, MA: Harvard University Press, 1982.

Perbi, Akosua Adoma. *A History of Indigenous Slavery in Ghana: From the Fifteenth to the Nineteenth Centuries.* Accra, Ghana: Sub-Saharan Publishers, 2004.

Pierce, Yolanda. *Hell without Fires: Slavery, Christianity, and the Antebellum Spiritual Narrative.* Gainesville: University Press of Florida, 2005.

Postma, Johannes Menne. *The Dutch in the Atlantic Slave Trade, 1600–1850.* Cambridge: Cambridge University Press, 1990.

Postma, Johannes Menne, and Victor Enthoven, eds. *Riches from Atlantic Commerce: Dutch Transatlantic Trade and Shipping, 1585–1817.* Leiden: Brill, 2003.

Rawley, James A., with Stephen D. Behrendt. *The Trans-Atlantic Slave Trade: A History.* Rev. ed. Lincoln: University of Nebraska Press, 2005.

Rediker, Marcus Buford. *Villains of All Nations: Atlantic Pirates in the Golden Age.* Boston: Beacon Press, 2004.

Reynolds, Edward. *Stand the Storm: A History of the Atlantic Slave Trade.* London: Allison and Busby, 1985.

Rice, Alan. *Radical Narratives of the Black Atlantic.* New York: Continuum, 2003.

Rodney, Walter. *How Europe Underdeveloped Africa.* Washington, DC: Howard University Press, 1981.

Roese, Peter M., and Dmitri M. Bondarenko. *A Popular History of Benin: The Rise and Fall of a Mighty Forest Kingdom.* Frankfurt am Main: Peter Lang, 2003.

Scarr, Deryck. *Slaving and Slavery in the Indian Ocean.* London: Macmillan, 1998.

Schwartz, Stuart B. *Sugar Plantations in the Formation of Brazilian Society: Bahia, 1550–1835.* Cambridge: Cambridge University Press, 1985.

Shepherd, Verene A., and Hilary McD. Beckles, eds. *Caribbean Slavery in the Atlantic World: A Student Reader.* Oxford: James Curry Publishers, 2000.

Sheridan, Richard B. "The Guinea Surgeons on the Middle Passage: The Provision of Medical Services in the British Slave Trade." *International Journal of African Historical Studies* 14, 4 (1981): 601–625.

Shillington, Kevin. *History of Africa.* 2nd ed. New York: Palgrave Macmillan, 2005.

Solow, Barbara, ed. *Slavery and the Rise of the Atlantic System.* New York: Cambridge University Press, 1991.

Sparks, Randy L. *The Two Princes of Calabar: An Eighteenth-Century Atlantic Odyssey.* Cambridge, MA: Harvard University Press, 2004.

Steckel, Richard H., and Richard A. Jensen. "New Evidence on the Causes of Slave and Crew Mortality in the Atlantic Slave Trade." *Journal of Economic History* 46, 1 (1986): 57–77.

Stein, Robert. *The French Slave Trade in the Eighteenth Century: An Old Regime Business.* Madison: University of Wisconsin Press, 1979.

Sundiata, Ibrahim K. *From Slaving to Neoslavery: The Bight of Biafra and Fernanado Po in the Era of Abolition, 1827–1930.* Madison: University of Wisconsin Press, 1996.

Sweet, James H. *Recreating Africa: Culture, Kinship, and Religion in the African-Portuguese World, 1441–1770.* Chapel Hill: University of North Carolina Press, 2003.

Thomas, Hugh. *The Slave Trade: The Story of the Atlantic Slave Trade, 1440–1870.* New York: Simon and Schuster, 1997.

Thornton, John K. *Africa and Africans in the Making of the Atlantic World, 1400–1800.* 2nd ed. Cambridge: Cambridge University Press, 1998.

———. *The Kingdom of Kongo: Civil War and Transition, 1641–1718.* Madison: University of Wisconsin Press, 1983.

Van Dantzig, Albert. *Forts and Castles of Ghana.* Accra, Ghana: Sedco Publishing, 1980.

Walvin, James. *Black Ivory: A History of British Slavery.* Washington, DC: Howard University Press, 1994.

Ward, W.E.F. *The Royal Navy and the Slavers: The Suppression of the Atlantic Slave Trade.* New York: Pantheon, 1969.

Williams, Eric Eustace. *Capitalism and Slavery; with a new introduction by Colin A. Palmer.* Chapel Hill: University of North Carolina Press, 1994 (1944).

INDEX

Page numbers in **bold** indicate main entries.

ABOUT THE EDITORS AND CONTRIBUTORS

Editors

Toyin Falola is a Distinguished Teaching Professor and the Frances Higginbotham Nalle Centennial Professor in History at the University of Texas at Austin.

Amanda Warnock is a doctoral candidate in the history department at the University of Texas at Austin.

Contributors

Edmund Abaka is an associate professor of history and director of Africana studies at the University of Miami.

Gustavo Acioli Lopes is a doctoral candidate in the economic history program at São Paulo University.

Wayne Ackerson earned his doctorate from Temple University and teaches at his alma mater, Salisbury University.

Saheed Aderinto is a graduate student in the history department at the University of Texas at Austin.

Joseph Avitable is a doctoral candidate in global history at the University of Rochester.

Joseph Jusuf Bangura is an assistant professor of history and director of African studies at Kalamazoo College.

Manuel Barcia is a lecturer in Latin American studies at the University of Leeds.

Stephen R. Berry received his Ph.D. from Duke University.

Curwen Best is senior lecturer in literature and popular culture, University of the West Indies, Cave Hill Campus, Barbados.

Dmitri M. Bondarenko is the senior research fellow and chair of the department of cultural anthropology at the Russian Academy of Sciences in Moscow.

Michael Bonislawski is an assistant professor of history at Salem State College.

Emily Brownell is a graduate student in the history department at the University of Texas at Austin.

Oyeniyi Bukola Adeyemi is the Pioneer Chair in the department of history and strategic studies at Redeemer's University, Nigeria.

Tara Bynum is a graduate student at Johns Hopkins University.

Abdin Chande is an assistant professor of history at Adelphi University.

Reginald Clarke is a senior librarian at the University of the West Indies, St. Augustine Campus, Trinidad and Tobago.

Eric Covey is a doctoral student in American studies at the University of Texas at Austin.

Kelley Deetz received her B.A. in black studies and history at the College of William and Mary.

Roy Doron is a graduate student in the history department at the University of Texas at Austin.

Kwame Essien is a graduate student at the University of Texas at Austin.

Namulundah Florence received her doctorate in education administration at Fordham University.

Cécile Fromont is a graduate student in the department of the history of art and architecture at Harvard University.

Cheryl Fury teaches at the University of New Brunswick and St. Stephen's University.

Trevor Getz is an assistant professor of the history of Africa at San Francisco State University.

Sandra Ingrid Gift is senior program officer in the Quality Assurance Unit at the University of the West Indies, St. Augustine Campus, Trinidad and Tobago.

Richard Graham is a professor emeritus of history at the University of Texas at Austin.

Robert Gudmestad is an assistant professor of history at the University of Memphis.

James Hamilton is university curator and honorary reader at the University of Birmingham, England.

John Craig Hammond is an assistant professor of history at Purdue University–Calumet in Hammond, Indiana.

Lauren Whitney Hammond is a graduate student in the history department at the University of Texas at Austin.

Walter Hawthorne is an associate professor of African history at Michigan State University.

Sharon A. Roger Hepburn is associate professor of history at Radford University.

Rachel Horlings is a doctoral student at Syracuse University.

Nadine Hunt is a doctoral candidate in the department of history at York University.

Steven B. Jacobson is associated with the University of Hawaii at Manoa.

Adam Jones teaches African history and culture at the University of Leipzig, Germany.

Nicholas Jones is a doctoral student in the department of Spanish and Portuguese at New York University.

Jessica M. Kubiak is a student at the University of Pittsburgh, Bradford Campus.

Tom Lansford is the assistant dean of the College of Arts and Letters and an associate professor of political science at the University of Southern Mississippi.

Mawuena Logan is a lecturer in African and African Diaspora literatures at The University of the West Indies, Mona, Jamaica.

Michael Lombardo is a research coordinator and sports journalist.

Patrick Luck is a graduate student in the history department at Johns Hopkins University.

Carole Maccotta is a doctoral candidate in French and Francophone literatures at the University of North Carolina at Chapel Hill.

Maximiliano Mac Menz has a Ph.D. in economic history from São Paulo University.

Jane Mangan is an assistant professor of history at Davidson College in Davidson, North Carolina.

Edward D. Maris-Wolf is a graduate student at the College of William and Mary and editorial assistant at the Omohundro Institute for Early American History and Culture.

Silvia Marzagalli is a professor of early modern history at the University of Nice, France.

Matthew Mason is an assistant professor of history at Brigham Young University.

David D. Moore is the curator of nautical archaeology at the North Carolina Maritime Museum in Beaufort.

William Morgan is a doctoral candidate at the University of Texas at Austin.

Sowande' M. Mustakeem is a doctoral candidate at Michigan State University.

Timothy Neeno is a freelance writer.

Cassandra Newman recently graduated from American University with a master's degree in international peace and conflict resolution.

Linda A. Newson is a professor of geography at King's College London.

G. Ugo Nwokeji is an assistant professor in the department of African American studies at the University of California–Berkeley.

'BioDun J. Ogundayo is an assistant professor of French and comparative literature at the University of Pittsburgh, Bradford Campus.

Rasheed Olaniyi teaches in the department of history at the University of Ibadan, Nigeria.

Oyekemi Olajope Oyelakin is a doctoral student in the department of history at the University of Ibadan, Nigeria.

Adam Paddock is a graduate student at the University of Texas at Austin.

Steve Puig is a doctoral student in French at the City University of New York.

Brian W. Refford is a lecturer in British and early modern European history at DeSales University in Center Valley, Pennsylvania.

Corinne Richter is an independent scholar primarily interested in Europe and the Mediterranean in the eighteenth and nineteenth centuries.

Erika M. Robb is a graduate student in the department of anthropology at the University of Wisconsin–Madison.

Natalie Suzette Robertson is a senior scholar at the U.S. National Slavery Museum and a professor in the department of political science and history at Hampton University.

Mohammed Bashir Salau is a visiting assistant professor of history at Whitman College.

James E. Seelye, Jr. is a doctoral candidate at the University of Toledo.

Mitra Sharafi is a doctoral candidate at Princeton University and junior research fellow at Sidney Sussex College, Cambridge University.

Rebecca Shumway is an assistant professor of history at the University of Pittsburgh.

Valika Smeulders is a doctoral candidate at the Erasmus University in Rotterdam.

Tristan Stubbs is a doctoral candidate in history at Pembroke College, University of Cambridge.

Gail Swanson is an independent researcher focusing on the Florida Keys.

Kathryn Vercillo is a San Francisco–based writer and independent scholar.

Natalie Washington-Weik is a doctoral student at the University of Texas at Austin.

Terrance Weik is an assistant professor of archaeology and anthropology at the University of South Carolina.

Pedro Welch is deputy dean, Faculty of Humanities and Education, and senior lecturer in the department of history and philosophy at the University of the West Indies, Cave Hill.

Cheryl A. Wells is an assistant professor at the University of Wyoming.

Ilya T. Wick is a graduate student at the University of Wisconsin–Madison.

Leslie Wilson is a legal and policy consultant.

Carmen Lenore Wright teaches American history at the Dr. Henry A. Wise High School, Upper Marlboro, Maryland.

Michael Max P. Zeuske is a professor of history at the University of Cologne, Germany.

Greenwood Milestones in African American History

Encyclopedia of Antislavery and Abolition
Edited by Peter Hinks and John McKivigan

Encyclopedia of the Great Black Migration
Edited by Steven A. Reich

Encyclopedia of Slave Resistance and Rebellion
Edited by Junius P. Rodriguez

Encyclopedia of American Race Riots
Edited by Walter Rucker and James Nathaniel Upton

Encyclopedia of the Reconstruction Era
Edited by Richard Zuczek